# BERTRAND RUSSELL

## SELECTED WORKS COLLECTION

*The Problems of Philosophy*
*The Analysis of Mind*
*Why Men Fight*
*Free Thought and Official Propaganda*
*Political Ideals*

# Bertrand Russell

C L A S S Y
PUBLISHING

**BERTRAND RUSSELL SELECTED WORKS COLLECTION**
by Bertrand Russell

Published by Classy Publishing, 2023

www.classypublishing.com
info@classypublishing.com

ISBN: 978-93-5522-305-0

Typeset in Minion Pro
Cover Design by Classy Publishing

# CONTENTS

## THE PROBLEMS OF PHILOSOPHY

## THE ANALYSIS OF MIND

## WHY MEN FIGHT

## FREE THOUGHT AND OFFICIAL PROPAGANDA

## POLITICAL IDEALS

# THE PROBLEMS
# OF PHILOSOPHY

# CHAPTER I

## Appearance and Reality

Is there any knowledge in the world which is so certain that no reasonable man could doubt it? This question, which at first sight might not seem difficult, is really one of the most difficult that can be asked. When we have realized the obstacles in the way of a straightforward and confident answer, we shall be well launched on the study of philosophy—for philosophy is merely the attempt to answer such ultimate questions, not carelessly and dogmatically, as we do in ordinary life and even in the sciences, but critically, after exploring all that makes such questions puzzling, and after realizing all the vagueness and confusion that underlie our ordinary ideas.

In daily life, we assume as certain many things which, on a closer scrutiny, are found to be so full of apparent contradictions that only a great amount of thought enables us to know what it is that we really may believe. In the search for certainty, it is natural to begin with our present experiences, and in some sense, no doubt, knowledge is to be derived from them. But any statement as to what it is that our immediate experiences make us know is very likely to be wrong. It seems to me that I am now sitting in a chair, at a table of a certain shape, on which I see sheets of paper with writing or print. By turning my head I see out of the window buildings and clouds and the sun. I believe that the sun is about ninety-three million miles from the earth; that it is a hot globe many times bigger than the earth; that, owing to the earth's rotation, it rises every morning, and will continue to do so for an indefinite time in the future. I believe that, if any other normal person comes into my room, he will see the same chairs and tables and books and papers as I see, and that the table which I see is the same as the table which I feel pressing against my arm. All this seems to be so evident as to be hardly worth stating, except in answer to a man who doubts whether I know anything. Yet all this may be reasonably doubted, and all of it requires much careful discussion before we can be sure that we have stated it in a form that is wholly true.

To make our difficulties plain, let us concentrate attention on the table. To the eye it is oblong, brown and shiny, to the touch it is smooth and cool and hard; when I tap it, it gives out a wooden sound. Any one else who sees and feels and hears the table will agree with this description, so that it might seem as if no difficulty would arise; but as soon as we try to be more precise our troubles begin. Although I believe

2

that the table is 'really' of the same colour all over, the parts that reflect the light look much brighter than the other parts, and some parts look white because of reflected light. I know that, if I move, the parts that reflect the light will be different, so that the apparent distribution of colours on the table will change. It follows that if several people are looking at the table at the same moment, no two of them will see exactly the same distribution of colours, because no two can see it from exactly the same point of view, and any change in the point of view makes some change in the way the light is reflected.

For most practical purposes these differences are unimportant, but to the painter they are all-important: the painter has to unlearn the habit of thinking that things seem to have the colour which common sense says they 'really' have, and to learn the habit of seeing things as they appear. Here we have already the beginning of one of the distinctions that cause most trouble in philosophy—the distinction between 'appearance' and 'reality', between what things seem to be and what they are. The painter wants to know what things seem to be, the practical man and the philosopher want to know what they are; but the philosopher's wish to know this is stronger than the practical man's, and is more troubled by knowledge as to the difficulties of answering the question.

To return to the table. It is evident from what we have found, that there is no colour which pre-eminently appears to be *the* colour of the table, or even of any one particular part of the table—it appears to be of different colours from different points of view, and there is no reason for regarding some of these as more really its colour than others. And we know that even from a given point of view the colour will seem different by artificial light, or to a colour-blind man, or to a man wearing blue spectacles, while in the dark there will be no colour at all, though to touch and hearing the table will be unchanged. This colour is not something which is inherent in the table, but something depending upon the table and the spectator and the way the light falls on the table. When, in ordinary life, we speak of *the* colour of the table, we only mean the sort of colour which it will seem to have to a normal spectator from an ordinary point of view under usual conditions of light. But the other colours which appear under other conditions have just as good a right to be considered real; and therefore, to avoid favouritism, we are compelled to deny that, in itself, the table has any one particular colour.

The same thing applies to the texture. With the naked eye one can see the grain, but otherwise the table looks smooth and even. If we looked at it through a microscope, we should see roughnesses and hills and valleys, and all sorts of differences that are imperceptible to the naked eye. Which of these is the 'real' table? We are naturally tempted to say that what we see through the microscope is more real, but that in turn would be changed by a still more powerful microscope. If, then, we cannot trust what we see with the naked eye, why should we trust what we see through a microscope? Thus, again, the confidence in our senses with which we began deserts us.

The shape of the table is no better. We are all in the habit of judging as to the 'real' shapes of things, and we do this so unreflectingly that we come to think we actually see the real shapes. But, in fact, as we all have to learn if we try to draw, a given thing looks different in shape from every different point of view. If our table is 'really' rectangular, it will look, from almost all points of view, as if it had two acute angles and two obtuse angles. If opposite sides are parallel, they will look as if they converged to a point away from the spectator; if they are of equal length, they will look as if the nearer side were longer. All these things are not commonly noticed in looking at a table, because experience has taught us to construct the 'real' shape from the apparent shape, and the 'real' shape is what interests us as practical men. But the 'real' shape is not what we see; it is something inferred from what we see. And what we see is constantly changing in shape as we move about the room; so that here again the senses seem not to give us the truth about the table itself, but only about the appearance of the table.

Similar difficulties arise when we consider the sense of touch. It is true that the table always gives us a sensation of hardness, and we feel that it resists pressure. But the sensation we obtain depends upon how hard we press the table and also upon what part of the body we press with; thus the various sensations due to various pressures or various parts of the body cannot be supposed to reveal *directly* any definite property of the table, but at most to be *signs* of some property which perhaps *causes* all the sensations, but is not actually apparent in any of them. And the same applies still more obviously to the sounds which can be elicited by rapping the table.

Thus it becomes evident that the real table, if there is one, is not the same as what we immediately experience by sight or touch or hearing. The real table, if there is one, is not *immediately* known to us at all, but must be an inference from what is immediately known. Hence, two very difficult questions at once arise; namely, (1) Is there a real table at all? (2) If so, what sort of object can it be?

It will help us in considering these questions to have a few simple terms of which the meaning is definite and clear. Let us give the name of 'sense-data' to the things that are immediately known in sensation: such things as colours, sounds, smells, hardnesses, roughnesses, and so on. We shall give the name 'sensation' to the experience of being immediately aware of these things. Thus, whenever we see a colour, we have a sensation *of* the colour, but the colour itself is a sense-datum, not a sensation. The colour is that *of* which we are immediately aware, and the awareness itself is the sensation. It is plain that if we are to know anything about the table, it must be by means of the sense-data—brown colour, oblong shape, smoothness, etc.— which we associate with the table; but, for the reasons which have been given, we cannot say that the table is the sense-data, or even that the sense-data are directly properties of the table. Thus a problem arises as to the relation of the sense-data to the real table, supposing there is such a thing.

The real table, if it exists, we will call a 'physical object'. Thus we have to consider the relation of sense-data to physical objects. The collection of all physical objects is called 'matter'. Thus our two questions may be re-stated as follows: (1) Is there any such thing as matter? (2) If so, what is its nature?

The philosopher who first brought prominently forward the reasons for regarding the immediate objects of our senses as not existing independently of us was Bishop Berkeley (1685-1753). His *Three Dialogues between Hylas and Philonous, in Opposition to Sceptics and Atheists*, undertake to prove that there is no such thing as matter at all, and that the world consists of nothing but minds and their ideas. Hylas has hitherto believed in matter, but he is no match for Philonous, who mercilessly drives him into contradictions and paradoxes, and makes his own denial of matter seem, in the end, as if it were almost common sense. The arguments employed are of very different value: some are important and sound, others are confused or quibbling. But Berkeley retains the merit of having shown that the existence of matter is capable of being denied without absurdity, and that if there are any things that exist independently of us they cannot be the immediate objects of our sensations.

There are two different questions involved when we ask whether matter exists, and it is important to keep them clear. We commonly mean by 'matter' something which is opposed to 'mind', something which we think of as occupying space and as radically incapable of any sort of thought or consciousness. It is chiefly in this sense that Berkeley denies matter; that is to say, he does not deny that the sense-data which we commonly take as signs of the existence of the table are really signs of the existence of *something* independent of us, but he does deny that this something is non-mental, that it is neither mind nor ideas entertained by some mind. He admits that there must be something which continues to exist when we go out of the room or shut our eyes, and that what we call seeing the table does really give us reason for believing in something which persists even when we are not seeing it. But he thinks that this something cannot be radically different in nature from what we see, and cannot be independent of seeing altogether, though it must be independent of *our* seeing. He is thus led to regard the 'real' table as an idea in the mind of God. Such an idea has the required permanence and independence of ourselves, without being—as matter would otherwise be—something quite unknowable, in the sense that we can only infer it, and can never be directly and immediately aware of it.

Other philosophers since Berkeley have also held that, although the table does not depend for its existence upon being seen by me, it does depend upon being seen (or otherwise apprehended in sensation) by *some* mind—not necessarily the mind of God, but more often the whole collective mind of the universe. This they hold, as Berkeley does, chiefly because they think there can be nothing real—or at any rate nothing known to be real except minds and their thoughts and feelings. We might state the argument by which they support their view in some such way as this: 'Whatever can be thought of is an idea in the mind of the person thinking of it;

therefore nothing can be thought of except ideas in minds; therefore anything else is inconceivable, and what is inconceivable cannot exist.'

Such an argument, in my opinion, is fallacious; and of course those who advance it do not put it so shortly or so crudely. But whether valid or not, the argument has been very widely advanced in one form or another; and very many philosophers, perhaps a majority, have held that there is nothing real except minds and their ideas. Such philosophers are called 'idealists'. When they come to explaining matter, they either say, like Berkeley, that matter is really nothing but a collection of ideas, or they say, like Leibniz (1646-1716), that what appears as matter is really a collection of more or less rudimentary minds.

But these philosophers, though they deny matter as opposed to mind, nevertheless, in another sense, admit matter. It will be remembered that we asked two questions; namely, (1) Is there a real table at all? (2) If so, what sort of object can it be? Now both Berkeley and Leibniz admit that there is a real table, but Berkeley says it is certain ideas in the mind of God, and Leibniz says it is a colony of souls. Thus both of them answer our first question in the affirmative, and only diverge from the views of ordinary mortals in their answer to our second question. In fact, almost all philosophers seem to be agreed that there is a real table: they almost all agree that, however much our sense-data—colour, shape, smoothness, etc.—may depend upon us, yet their occurrence is a sign of something existing independently of us, something differing, perhaps, completely from our sense-data, and yet to be regarded as causing those sense-data whenever we are in a suitable relation to the real table.

Now obviously this point in which the philosophers are agreed—the view that there *is* a real table, whatever its nature may be—is vitally important, and it will be worth while to consider what reasons there are for accepting this view before we go on to the further question as to the nature of the real table. Our next chapter, therefore, will be concerned with the reasons for supposing that there is a real table at all.

Before we go farther it will be well to consider for a moment what it is that we have discovered so far. It has appeared that, if we take any common object of the sort that is supposed to be known by the senses, what the senses *immediately* tell us is not the truth about the object as it is apart from us, but only the truth about certain sense-data which, so far as we can see, depend upon the relations between us and the object. Thus what we directly see and feel is merely 'appearance', which we believe to be a sign of some 'reality' behind. But if the reality is not what appears, have we any means of knowing whether there is any reality at all? And if so, have we any means of finding out what it is like?

Such questions are bewildering, and it is difficult to know that even the strangest hypotheses may not be true. Thus our familiar table, which has roused but the slightest thoughts in us hitherto, has become a problem full of surprising possibilities. The one thing we know about it is that it is not what it seems. Beyond this modest result, so far, we have the most complete liberty of conjecture. Leibniz tells us it is a community of souls: Berkeley tells us it is an idea in the mind of God; sober science, scarcely less wonderful, tells us it is a vast collection of electric charges in violent motion.

Among these surprising possibilities, doubt suggests that perhaps there is no table at all. Philosophy, if it cannot *answer* so many questions as we could wish, has at least the power of *asking* questions which increase the interest of the world, and show the strangeness and wonder lying just below the surface even in the commonest things of daily life.

# CHAPTER II

## The Existence of Matter

In this chapter we have to ask ourselves whether, in any sense at all, there is such a thing as matter. Is there a table which has a certain intrinsic nature, and continues to exist when I am not looking, or is the table merely a product of my imagination, a dream-table in a very prolonged dream? This question is of the greatest importance. For if we cannot be sure of the independent existence of objects, we cannot be sure of the independent existence of other people's bodies, and therefore still less of other people's minds, since we have no grounds for believing in their minds except such as are derived from observing their bodies. Thus if we cannot be sure of the independent existence of objects, we shall be left alone in a desert—it may be that the whole outer world is nothing but a dream, and that we alone exist. This is an uncomfortable possibility; but although it cannot be strictly proved to be false, there is not the slightest reason to suppose that it is true. In this chapter we have to see why this is the case.

Before we embark upon doubtful matters, let us try to find some more or less fixed point from which to start. Although we are doubting the physical existence of the table, we are not doubting the existence of the sense-data which made us think there was a table; we are not doubting that, while we look, a certain colour and shape appear to us, and while we press, a certain sensation of hardness is experienced by us. All this, which is psychological, we are not calling in question. In fact, whatever else may be doubtful, some at least of our immediate experiences seem absolutely certain.

Descartes (1596-1650), the founder of modern philosophy, invented a method which may still be used with profit—the method of systematic doubt. He determined that he would believe nothing which he did not see quite clearly and distinctly to be true. Whatever he could bring himself to doubt, he would doubt, until he saw reason for not doubting it. By applying this method he gradually became convinced that the only existence of which he could be *quite* certain was his own. He imagined a deceitful demon, who presented unreal things to his senses in a perpetual phantasmagoria; it might be very improbable that such a demon existed, but still it was possible, and therefore doubt concerning things perceived by the senses was possible.

But doubt concerning his own existence was not possible, for if he did not exist, no demon could deceive him. If he doubted, he must exist; if he had any experiences whatever, he must exist. Thus his own existence was an absolute certainty to him. 'I think, therefore I am,' he said (*Cogito, ergo sum*); and on the basis of this certainty he set to work to build up again the world of knowledge which his doubt had laid in ruins. By inventing the method of doubt, and by showing that subjective things are the most certain, Descartes performed a great service to philosophy, and one which makes him still useful to all students of the subject.

But some care is needed in using Descartes' argument. 'I think, therefore I am' says rather more than is strictly certain. It might seem as though we were quite sure of being the same person to-day as we were yesterday, and this is no doubt true in some sense. But the real Self is as hard to arrive at as the real table, and does not seem to have that absolute, convincing certainty that belongs to particular experiences. When I look at my table and see a certain brown colour, what is quite certain at once is not '*I* am seeing a brown colour', but rather, 'a brown colour is being seen'. This of course involves something (or somebody) which (or who) sees the brown colour; but it does not of itself involve that more or less permanent person whom we call 'I'. So far as immediate certainty goes, it might be that the something which sees the brown colour is quite momentary, and not the same as the something which has some different experience the next moment.

Thus it is our particular thoughts and feelings that have primitive certainty. And this applies to dreams and hallucinations as well as to normal perceptions: when we dream or see a ghost, we certainly do have the sensations we think we have, but for various reasons it is held that no physical object corresponds to these sensations. Thus the certainty of our knowledge of our own experiences does not have to be limited in any way to allow for exceptional cases. Here, therefore, we have, for what it is worth, a solid basis from which to begin our pursuit of knowledge.

The problem we have to consider is this: Granted that we are certain of our own sense-data, have we any reason for regarding them as signs of the existence of something else, which we can call the physical object? When we have enumerated all the sense-data which we should naturally regard as connected with the table, have we said all there is to say about the table, or is there still something else—something not a sense-datum, something which persists when we go out of the room? Common sense unhesitatingly answers that there is. What can be bought and sold and pushed about and have a cloth laid on it, and so on, cannot be a *mere* collection of sense-data. If the cloth completely hides the table, we shall derive no sense-data from the table, and therefore, if the table were merely sense-data, it would have ceased to exist, and the cloth would be suspended in empty air, resting, by a miracle, in the place where the table formerly was. This seems plainly absurd; but whoever wishes to become a philosopher must learn not to be frightened by absurdities.

One great reason why it is felt that we must secure a physical object in addition to the sense-data, is that we want the same object for different people. When ten people are sitting round a dinner-table, it seems preposterous to maintain that they are not seeing the same tablecloth, the same knives and forks and spoons and glasses. But the sense-data are private to each separate person; what is immediately present to the sight of one is not immediately present to the sight of another: they all see things from slightly different points of view, and therefore see them slightly differently. Thus, if there are to be public neutral objects, which can be in some sense known to many different people, there must be something over and above the private and particular sense-data which appear to various people. What reason, then, have we for believing that there are such public neutral objects?

The first answer that naturally occurs to one is that, although different people may see the table slightly differently, still they all see more or less similar things when they look at the table, and the variations in what they see follow the laws of perspective and reflection of light, so that it is easy to arrive at a permanent object underlying all the different people's sense-data. I bought my table from the former occupant of my room; I could not buy *his* sense-data, which died when he went away, but I could and did buy the confident expectation of more or less similar sense-data. Thus it is the fact that different people have similar sense-data, and that one person in a given place at different times has similar sense-data, which makes us suppose that over and above the sense-data there is a permanent public object which underlies or causes the sense-data of various people at various times.

Now in so far as the above considerations depend upon supposing that there are other people besides ourselves, they beg the very question at issue. Other people are represented to me by certain sense-data, such as the sight of them or the sound of their voices, and if I had no reason to believe that there were physical objects independent of my sense-data, I should have no reason to believe that other people exist except as part of my dream. Thus, when we are trying to show that there must be objects independent of our own sense-data, we cannot appeal to the testimony of other people, since this testimony itself consists of sense-data, and does not reveal other people's experiences unless our own sense-data are signs of things existing independently of us. We must therefore, if possible, find, in our own purely private experiences, characteristics which show, or tend to show, that there are in the world things other than ourselves and our private experiences.

In one sense it must be admitted that we can never prove the existence of things other than ourselves and our experiences. No logical absurdity results from the hypothesis that the world consists of myself and my thoughts and feelings and sensations, and that everything else is mere fancy. In dreams a very complicated world may seem to be present, and yet on waking we find it was a delusion; that is to say, we find that the sense-data in the dream do not appear to have corresponded with such physical objects as we should naturally infer from our sense-data. (It is true that, when the physical world is assumed, it is possible to find physical causes for the sense-data in dreams: a door banging, for instance, may cause us to dream of a naval engagement. But although, in this case, there is a physical cause for the sense-data, there is not a physical object corresponding to the sense-data in the way in which an actual naval battle would correspond.) There is no logical impossibility in the supposition that the whole of life is a dream, in which we ourselves create all the objects that come before us. But although this is not logically impossible, there is no reason whatever to suppose that it is true; and it is, in fact, a less simple hypothesis, viewed as a means of accounting for the facts of our own life, than the common-sense hypothesis that there really are objects independent of us, whose action on us causes our sensations.

The way in which simplicity comes in from supposing that there really are physical objects is easily seen. If the cat appears at one moment in one part of the room, and at another in another part, it is natural to suppose that it has moved from the one to the other, passing over a series of intermediate positions. But if it is merely a set of sense-data, it cannot have ever been in any place where I did not see it; thus we shall have to suppose that it did not exist at all while I was not looking, but suddenly sprang into being in a new place. If the cat exists whether I see it or not, we can understand from our own experience how it gets hungry between one meal and the next; but if it does not exist when I am not seeing it, it seems odd that appetite should grow during non-existence as fast as during existence. And if the cat consists only of sense-data, it cannot be hungry, since no hunger but my own can be a sense-datum to me. Thus the behaviour of the sense-data which represent the cat to me, though it seems quite natural when regarded as an expression of hunger, becomes utterly inexplicable when regarded as mere movements and changes of patches of colour, which are as incapable of hunger as a triangle is of playing football.

But the difficulty in the case of the cat is nothing compared to the difficulty in the case of human beings. When human beings speak—that is, when we hear certain noises which we associate with ideas, and simultaneously see certain motions of lips and expressions of face—it is very difficult to suppose that what we hear is not the expression of a thought, as we know it would be if we emitted the same sounds. Of course similar things happen in dreams, where we are mistaken as to the existence of other people. But dreams are more or less suggested by what we call waking life, and are capable of being more or less accounted for on scientific principles if we assume that there really is a physical world. Thus every principle of simplicity urges us to adopt the natural view, that there really are objects other than ourselves and our sense-data which have an existence not dependent upon our perceiving them.

Of course it is not by argument that we originally come by our belief in an independent external world. We find this belief ready in ourselves as soon as we begin to reflect: it is what may be called an *instinctive* belief. We should never have been led to question this belief but for the fact that, at any rate in the case of sight, it seems as if the sense-datum itself were instinctively believed to be the independent object, whereas argument shows that the object cannot be identical with the sense-datum. This discovery, however—which is not at all paradoxical in the case of taste and smell and sound, and only slightly so in the case of touch—leaves undiminished our instinctive belief that there *are* objects *corresponding* to our sense-data. Since this belief does not lead to any difficulties, but on the contrary tends to simplify and systematize our account of our experiences, there seems no good reason for rejecting it. We may therefore admit—though with a slight doubt derived from dreams—that the external world does really exist, and is not wholly dependent for its existence upon our continuing to perceive it.

The argument which has led us to this conclusion is doubtless less strong than we could wish, but it is typical of many philosophical arguments, and it is therefore worth while to consider briefly its general character and validity. All knowledge, we find, must be built up upon our instinctive beliefs, and if these are rejected, nothing is left. But among our instinctive beliefs some are much stronger than others, while many have, by habit and association, become entangled with other beliefs, not really instinctive, but falsely supposed to be part of what is believed instinctively.

Philosophy should show us the hierarchy of our instinctive beliefs, beginning with those we hold most strongly, and presenting each as much isolated and as free from irrelevant additions as possible. It should take care to show that, in the form in which they are finally set forth, our instinctive beliefs do not clash, but form a harmonious system. There can never be any reason for rejecting one instinctive belief except that it clashes with others; thus, if they are found to harmonize, the whole system becomes worthy of acceptance.

It is of course *possible* that all or any of our beliefs may be mistaken, and therefore all ought to be held with at least some slight element of doubt. But we cannot have *reason* to reject a belief except on the ground of some other belief. Hence, by organizing our instinctive beliefs and their consequences, by considering which among them is most possible, if necessary, to modify or abandon, we can arrive, on the basis of accepting as our sole data what we instinctively believe, at an orderly systematic organization of our knowledge, in which, though the *possibility* of error remains, its likelihood is diminished by the interrelation of the parts and by the critical scrutiny which has preceded acquiescence.

This function, at least, philosophy can perform. Most philosophers, rightly or wrongly, believe that philosophy can do much more than this—that it can give us knowledge, not otherwise attainable, concerning the universe as a whole, and concerning the nature of ultimate reality. Whether this be the case or not, the more modest function we have spoken of can certainly be performed by philosophy, and certainly suffices, for those who have once begun to doubt the adequacy of common sense, to justify the arduous and difficult labours that philosophical problems involve.

# CHAPTER III

## The Nature of Matter

In the preceding chapter we agreed, though without being able to find demonstrative reasons, that it is rational to believe that our sense-data—for example, those which we regard as associated with my table—are really signs of the existence of something independent of us and our perceptions. That is to say, over and above the sensations of colour, hardness, noise, and so on, which make up the appearance of the table to me, I assume that there is something else, of which these things are appearances. The colour ceases to exist if I shut my eyes, the sensation of hardness ceases to exist if I remove my arm from contact with the table, the sound ceases to exist if I cease to rap the table with my knuckles. But I do not believe that when all these things cease the table ceases. On the contrary, I believe that it is because the table exists continuously that all these sense-data will reappear when I open my eyes, replace my arm, and begin again to rap with my knuckles. The question we have to consider in this chapter is: What is the nature of this real table, which persists independently of my perception of it?

To this question physical science gives an answer, somewhat incomplete it is true, and in part still very hypothetical, but yet deserving of respect so far as it goes. Physical science, more or less unconsciously, has drifted into the view that all natural phenomena ought to be reduced to motions. Light and heat and sound are all due to wave-motions, which travel from the body emitting them to the person who sees light or feels heat or hears sound. That which has the wave-motion is either aether or 'gross matter', but in either case is what the philosopher would call matter. The only properties which science assigns to it are position in space, and the power of motion according to the laws of motion. Science does not deny that it *may* have other properties; but if so, such other properties are not useful to the man of science, and in no way assist him in explaining the phenomena.

It is sometimes said that 'light *is* a form of wave-motion', but this is misleading, for the light which we immediately see, which we know directly by means of our senses, is *not* a form of wave-motion, but something quite different—something which we all know if we are not blind, though we cannot describe it so as to convey our knowledge to a man who is blind. A wave-motion, on the contrary, could quite well be described to a blind man, since he can acquire a knowledge of space by the sense of touch; and he can experience a wave-motion by a sea voyage almost as well as we can. But this, which a blind man can understand, is not what we mean by *light*: we mean by *light* just that which a blind man can never understand, and which we can never describe to him.

Now this something, which all of us who are not blind know, is not, according to science, really to be found in the outer world: it is something caused by the action of certain waves upon the eyes and nerves and brain of the person who sees the light. When it is said that light *is* waves, what is really meant is that waves are the physical cause of our sensations of light. But light itself, the thing which seeing people experience and blind people do not, is not supposed by science to form any part of the world that is independent of us and our senses. And very similar remarks would apply to other kinds of sensations.

It is not only colours and sounds and so on that are absent from the scientific world of matter, but also *space* as we get it through sight or touch. It is essential to science that its matter should be in *a* space, but the space in which it is cannot be exactly the space we see or feel. To begin with, space as we see it is not the same as space as we get it by the sense of touch; it is only by experience in infancy that we learn how to touch things we see, or how to get a sight of things which we feel touching us. But the space of science is neutral as between touch and sight; thus it cannot be either the space of touch or the space of sight.

Again, different people see the same object as of different shapes, according to their point of view. A circular coin, for example, though we should always *judge* it to be circular, will *look* oval unless we are straight in front of it. When we judge that it *is* circular, we are judging that it has a real shape which is not its apparent shape, but belongs to it intrinsically apart from its appearance. But this real shape, which is what concerns science, must be in a real space, not the same as anybody's *apparent* space. The real space is public, the apparent space is private to the percipient. In different people's *private* spaces the same object seems to have different shapes; thus the real space, in which it has its real shape, must be different from the private spaces. The space of science, therefore, though *connected* with the spaces we see and feel, is not identical with them, and the manner of its connexion requires investigation.

We agreed provisionally that physical objects cannot be quite like our sense-data, but may be regarded as *causing* our sensations. These physical objects are in the space of science, which we may call 'physical' space. It is important to notice that, if our sensations are to be caused by physical objects, there must be a physical space containing these objects and our sense-organs and nerves and brain. We get a sensation of touch from an object when we are in contact with it; that is to say, when some part of our body occupies a place in physical space quite close to the space occupied by the object. We see an object (roughly speaking) when no opaque body is between the object and our eyes in physical space. Similarly, we only hear or smell or taste an object when we are sufficiently near to it, or when it touches the tongue, or has some suitable position in physical space relatively to our body. We cannot begin to state what different sensations we shall derive from a given object under different circumstances unless we regard the object and our body as both in one physical space, for it is mainly the relative positions of the object and our body that determine what sensations we shall derive from the object.

Now our sense-data are situated in our private spaces, either the space of sight or the space of touch or such vaguer spaces as other senses may give us. If, as science and common sense assume, there is one public all-embracing physical space in which physical objects are, the relative positions of physical objects in physical space must more or less correspond to the relative positions of sense-data in our private spaces. There is no difficulty in supposing this to be the case. If we see on a road one house nearer to us than another, our other senses will bear out the view that it is nearer; for example, it will be reached sooner if we walk along the road. Other people will agree that the house which looks nearer to us is nearer; the ordnance map will take the same view; and thus everything points to a spatial relation between the houses corresponding to the relation between the sense-data which we see when we look at the houses. Thus we may assume that there is a physical space in which physical objects have spatial relations corresponding to those which the corresponding sense-data have in our private spaces. It is this physical space which is dealt with in geometry and assumed in physics and astronomy.

Assuming that there is physical space, and that it does thus correspond to private spaces, what can we know about it? We can know *only* what is required in order to secure the correspondence. That is to say, we can know nothing of what it is like in itself, but we can know the sort of arrangement of physical objects which results from their spatial relations. We can know, for example, that the earth and moon and sun are in one straight line during an eclipse, though we cannot know what a physical straight line is in itself, as we know the look of a straight line in our visual space. Thus we come to know much more about the *relations* of distances in physical space than about the distances themselves; we may know that one distance is greater than another, or that it is along the same straight line as the other, but we cannot have that immediate acquaintance with physical distances that we have with distances in our private spaces, or with colours or sounds or other sense-data. We can know all those things about physical space which a man born blind might know through other people about the space of sight; but the kind of things which a man born blind could never know about the space of sight we also cannot know about physical space. We can know the properties of the relations required to preserve the correspondence with sense-data, but we cannot know the nature of the terms between which the relations hold.

With regard to time, our *feeling* of duration or of the lapse of time is notoriously an unsafe guide as to the time that has elapsed by the clock. Times when we are bored or suffering pain pass slowly, times when we are agreeably occupied pass quickly, and times when we are sleeping pass almost as if they did not exist. Thus, in so far as time is constituted by duration, there is the same necessity for distinguishing a public and a private time as there was in the case of space. But in so far as time consists in an *order* of before and after, there is no need to make such a distinction; the time-order which events seem to have is, so far as we can see, the same as the time-order which they do have. At any rate no reason can be given for supposing that the two orders are not the same. The same is usually true of space: if a regiment of men are marching along a road, the shape of the regiment will look different from different points of view, but the men will appear arranged in the same order from all points of view. Hence we regard the order as true also in physical space, whereas the shape is only supposed to correspond to the physical space so far as is required for the preservation of the order.

In saying that the time-order which events seem to have is the same as the time-order which they really have, it is necessary to guard against a possible misunderstanding. It must not be supposed that the various states of different physical objects have the same time-order as the sense-data which constitute the perceptions of those objects. Considered as physical objects, the thunder and lightning are simultaneous; that is to say, the lightning is simultaneous with the disturbance of the air in the place where the disturbance begins, namely, where the lightning is. But the sense-datum which we call hearing the thunder does not take place until the disturbance of the air has travelled as far as to where we are. Similarly, it takes about eight minutes for the sun's light to reach us; thus, when we see the sun we are seeing the sun of eight minutes ago. So far as our sense-data afford evidence as to the physical sun they afford evidence as to the physical sun of eight minutes ago; if the physical sun had ceased to exist within the last eight minutes, that would make no difference to the sense-data which we call 'seeing the sun'. This affords a fresh illustration of the necessity of distinguishing between sense-data and physical objects.

What we have found as regards space is much the same as what we find in relation to the correspondence of the sense-data with their physical counterparts. If one object looks blue and another red, we may reasonably presume that there is some corresponding difference between the physical objects; if two objects both look blue, we may presume a corresponding similarity. But we cannot hope to be acquainted directly with the quality in the physical object which makes it look blue or red. Science tells us that this quality is a certain sort of wave-motion, and this sounds familiar, because we think of wave-motions in the space we see. But the wave-motions must really be in physical space, with which we have no direct acquaintance; thus the real wave-motions have not that familiarity which we might have supposed them to have. And what holds for colours is closely similar to what holds for other sense-data. Thus we find that, although the *relations* of physical objects have all sorts of knowable properties, derived from their correspondence with the relations of sense-data, the physical objects themselves remain unknown in their intrinsic nature, so far at least as can be discovered by means of the senses. The question remains whether there is any other method of discovering the intrinsic nature of physical objects.

The most natural, though not ultimately the most defensible, hypothesis to adopt in the first instance, at any rate as regards visual sense-data, would be that, though physical objects cannot, for the reasons we have been considering, be *exactly* like sense-data, yet they may be more or less like. According to this view, physical objects will, for example, really have colours, and we might, by good luck, see an object as of the colour it really is. The colour which an object seems to have at any given moment will in general be very similar, though not quite the same, from many different points of view; we might thus suppose the 'real' colour to be a sort of medium colour, intermediate between the various shades which appear from the different points of view.

Such a theory is perhaps not capable of being definitely refuted, but it can be shown to be groundless. To begin with, it is plain that the colour we see depends only upon the nature of the light-waves that strike the eye, and is therefore modified by the medium intervening between us and the object, as well as by the manner in which light is reflected from the object in the direction of the eye. The intervening air alters colours unless it is perfectly clear, and any strong reflection will alter them completely. Thus the colour we see is a result of the ray as it reaches the eye, and not simply a property of the object from which the ray comes. Hence, also, provided certain waves reach the eye, we shall see a certain colour, whether the object from which the waves start has any colour or not. Thus it is quite gratuitous to suppose that physical objects have colours, and therefore there is no justification for making such a supposition. Exactly similar arguments will apply to other sense-data.

It remains to ask whether there are any general philosophical arguments enabling us to say that, if matter is real, it must be of such and such a nature. As explained above, very many philosophers, perhaps most, have held that whatever is real must be in some sense mental, or at any rate that whatever we can know anything about must be in some sense mental. Such philosophers are called 'idealists'. Idealists tell us that what appears as matter is really something mental; namely, either (as Leibniz held) more or less rudimentary minds, or (as Berkeley contended) ideas in the minds which, as we should commonly say, 'perceive' the matter. Thus idealists deny the existence of matter as something intrinsically different from mind, though they do not deny that our sense-data are signs of something which exists independently of our private sensations. In the following chapter we shall consider briefly the reasons—in my opinion fallacious—which idealists advance in favour of their theory.

# CHAPTER IV

## Idealism

The word 'idealism' is used by different philosophers in somewhat different senses. We shall understand by it the doctrine that whatever exists, or at any rate whatever can be known to exist, must be in some sense mental. This doctrine, which is very widely held among philosophers, has several forms, and is advocated on several different grounds. The doctrine is so widely held, and so interesting in itself, that even the briefest survey of philosophy must give some account of it.

Those who are unaccustomed to philosophical speculation may be inclined to dismiss such a doctrine as obviously absurd. There is no doubt that common sense regards tables and chairs and the sun and moon and material objects generally as something radically different from minds and the contents of minds, and as having an existence which might continue if minds ceased. We think of matter as having existed long before there were any minds, and it is hard to think of it as a mere product of mental activity. But whether true or false, idealism is not to be dismissed as obviously absurd.

We have seen that, even if physical objects do have an independent existence, they must differ very widely from sense-data, and can only have a *correspondence* with sense-data, in the same sort of way in which a catalogue has a correspondence with the things catalogued. Hence common sense leaves us completely in the dark as to the true intrinsic nature of physical objects, and if there were good reason to regard them as mental, we could not legitimately reject this opinion merely because it strikes us as strange. The truth about physical objects *must* be strange. It may be unattainable, but if any philosopher believes that he has attained it, the fact that what he offers as the truth is strange ought not to be made a ground of objection to his opinion.

The grounds on which idealism is advocated are generally grounds derived from the theory of knowledge, that is to say, from a discussion of the conditions which things must satisfy in order that we may be able to know them. The first serious attempt to establish idealism on such grounds was that of Bishop Berkeley. He proved first, by arguments which were largely valid, that our sense-data cannot be supposed to have an existence independent of us, but must be, in part at least, 'in' the mind, in the sense that their existence would not continue if there were no seeing or hearing or touching or smelling or tasting. So far, his contention was almost certainly valid, even if some of his arguments were not so. But he went on to argue that sense-data were the only things of whose existence our perceptions could assure us; and that to be known is to be 'in' a mind, and therefore to be mental. Hence he concluded that nothing can ever be known except what is in some mind, and that whatever is known without being in my mind must be in some other mind.

In order to understand his argument, it is necessary to understand his use of the word 'idea'. He gives the name 'idea' to anything which is *immediately* known, as, for example, sense-data are known. Thus a particular colour which we see is an idea; so is a voice which we hear, and so on. But the term is not wholly confined to sense-data. There will also be things remembered or imagined, for with such things also we have immediate acquaintance at the moment of remembering or imagining. All such immediate data he calls 'ideas'.

He then proceeds to consider common objects, such as a tree, for instance. He shows that all we know immediately when we 'perceive' the tree consists of ideas in his sense of the word, and he argues that there is not the slightest ground for supposing that there is anything real about the tree except what is perceived. Its being, he says, consists in being perceived: in the Latin of the schoolmen its 'esse' is 'percipi'. He fully admits that the tree must continue to exist even when we shut our eyes or when no human being is near it. But this continued existence, he says, is due to the fact that God continues to perceive it; the 'real' tree, which corresponds to what we called the physical object, consists of ideas in the mind of God, ideas more or less like those we have when we see the tree, but differing in the fact that they are permanent in God's mind so long as the tree continues to exist. All our perceptions, according to him, consist in a partial participation in God's perceptions, and it is because of this participation that different people see more or less the same tree. Thus apart from minds and their ideas there is nothing in the world, nor is it possible that anything else should ever be known, since whatever is known is necessarily an idea.

There are in this argument a good many fallacies which have been important in the history of philosophy, and which it will be as well to bring to light. In the first place, there is a confusion engendered by the use of the word 'idea'. We think of an idea as essentially something in somebody's mind, and thus when we are told that a tree consists entirely of ideas, it is natural to suppose that, if so, the tree must be entirely in minds. But the notion of being 'in' the mind is ambiguous. We speak of bearing a person in mind, not meaning that the person is in our minds, but that a thought of him is in our minds. When a man says that some business he had to arrange went clean out of his mind, he does not mean to imply that the business itself was ever in his mind, but only that a thought of the business was formerly in his mind, but afterwards ceased to be in his mind. And so when Berkeley says that the tree must be in our minds if we can know it, all that he really has a right to say is that a thought of the tree must be in our minds. To argue that the tree itself must be in our minds is like arguing that a person whom we bear in mind is himself in our minds. This confusion may seem too gross to have been really committed by any competent philosopher, but various attendant circumstances rendered it possible. In order to see how it was possible, we must go more deeply into the question as to the nature of ideas.

Before taking up the general question of the nature of ideas, we must disentangle two entirely separate questions which arise concerning sense-data and physical objects. We saw that, for various reasons of detail, Berkeley was right in treating the sense-data which constitute our perception of the tree as more or less subjective, in the sense that they depend upon us as much as upon the tree, and would not exist if the tree were not being perceived. But this is an entirely different point from the one by which Berkeley seeks to prove that whatever can be immediately known must be in a mind. For this purpose arguments of detail as to the dependence of sense-data upon us are useless. It is necessary to prove, generally, that by being known, things are shown to be mental. This is what Berkeley believes himself to have done. It is this question, and not our previous question as to the difference between sense-data and the physical object, that must now concern us.

Taking the word 'idea' in Berkeley's sense, there are two quite distinct things to be considered whenever an idea is before the mind. There is on the one hand the thing of which we are aware—say the colour of my table—and on the other hand the actual awareness itself, the mental act of apprehending the thing. The mental act is undoubtedly mental, but is there any reason to suppose that the thing apprehended is in any sense mental? Our previous arguments concerning the colour did not prove it to be mental; they only proved that its existence depends upon the relation of our sense organs to the physical object—in our case, the table. That is to say, they proved that a certain colour will exist, in a certain light, if a normal eye is placed at a certain point relatively to the table. They did not prove that the colour is in the mind of the percipient.

Berkeley's view, that obviously the colour must be in the mind, seems to depend for its plausibility upon confusing the thing apprehended with the act of apprehension. Either of these might be called an 'idea'; probably either would have been called an idea by Berkeley. The act is undoubtedly in the mind; hence, when we are thinking of the act, we readily assent to the view that ideas must be in the mind. Then, forgetting that this was only true when ideas were taken as acts of apprehension, we transfer the proposition that 'ideas are in the mind' to ideas in the other sense, i.e. to the things apprehended by our acts of apprehension. Thus, by an unconscious equivocation, we arrive at the conclusion that whatever we can apprehend must be in our minds. This seems to be the true analysis of Berkeley's argument, and the ultimate fallacy upon which it rests.

This question of the distinction between act and object in our apprehending of things is vitally important, since our whole power of acquiring knowledge is bound up with it. The faculty of being acquainted with things other than itself is the main characteristic of a mind. Acquaintance with objects essentially consists in a relation between the mind and something other than the mind; it is this that constitutes the mind's power of knowing things. If we say that the things known must be in the mind, we are either unduly limiting the mind's power of knowing, or we are uttering a mere tautology. We are uttering a mere tautology if we mean by '*in the mind*' the same as by '*before* the mind', i.e. if we mean merely being apprehended by the mind. But if we mean this, we shall have to admit that what, *in this sense*, is in the mind, may nevertheless be not mental. Thus when we realize the nature of knowledge, Berkeley's argument is seen to be wrong in substance as well as in form, and his grounds for supposing that 'ideas'—i.e. the objects apprehended—must be mental, are found to have no validity whatever. Hence his grounds in favour of idealism may be dismissed. It remains to see whether there are any other grounds.

It is often said, as though it were a self-evident truism, that we cannot know that anything exists which we do not know. It is inferred that whatever can in any way be relevant to our experience must be at least capable of being known by us; whence it follows that if matter were essentially something with which we could not become acquainted, matter would be something which we could not know to exist, and which could have for us no importance whatever. It is generally also implied, for reasons which remain obscure, that what can have no importance for us cannot be real, and that therefore matter, if it is not composed of minds or of mental ideas, is impossible and a mere chimaera.

To go into this argument fully at our present stage would be impossible, since it raises points requiring a considerable preliminary discussion; but certain reasons for rejecting the argument may be noticed at once. To begin at the end: there is no reason why what cannot have any *practical* importance for us should not be real. It is true that, if *theoretical* importance is included, everything real is of *some* importance to us, since, as persons desirous of knowing the truth about the universe, we have some interest in everything that the universe contains. But if this sort of interest is included, it is not the case that matter has no importance for us, provided it exists even if we cannot know that it exists. We can, obviously, suspect that it may exist, and wonder whether it does; hence it is connected with our desire for knowledge, and has the importance of either satisfying or thwarting this desire.

Again, it is by no means a truism, and is in fact false, that we cannot know that anything exists which we do not know. The word 'know' is here used in two different senses. (1) In its first use it is applicable to the sort of knowledge which is opposed to error, the sense in which what we know is *true*, the sense which applies to our beliefs and convictions, i.e. to what are called *judgements*. In this sense of the word we know *that* something is the case. This sort of knowledge may be described as knowledge of *truths*. (2) In the second use of the word 'know' above, the word applies to our knowledge of *things*, which we may call *acquaintance*. This is the sense in which

21

we know sense-data. (The distinction involved is roughly that between *savoir* and *connaître* in French, or between *wissen* and *kennen* in German.)

Thus the statement which seemed like a truism becomes, when re-stated, the following: 'We can never truly judge that something with which we are not acquainted exists.' This is by no means a truism, but on the contrary a palpable falsehood. I have not the honour to be acquainted with the Emperor of China, but I truly judge that he exists. It may be said, of course, that I judge this because of other people's acquaintance with him. This, however, would be an irrelevant retort, since, if the principle were true, I could not know that any one else is acquainted with him. But further: there is no reason why I should not know of the existence of something with which nobody is acquainted. This point is important, and demands elucidation.

If I am acquainted with a thing which exists, my acquaintance gives me the knowledge that it exists. But it is not true that, conversely, whenever I can know that a thing of a certain sort exists, I or some one else must be acquainted with the thing. What happens, in cases where I have true judgement without acquaintance, is that the thing is known to me by *description*, and that, in virtue of some general principle, the existence of a thing answering to this description can be inferred from the existence of something with which I am acquainted. In order to understand this point fully, it will be well first to deal with the difference between knowledge by acquaintance and knowledge by description, and then to consider what knowledge of general principles, if any, has the same kind of certainty as our knowledge of the existence of our own experiences. These subjects will be dealt with in the following chapters.

# CHAPTER V

## Knowledge by Acquaintance and Knowledge by Description

In the preceding chapter we saw that there are two sorts of knowledge: knowledge of things, and knowledge of truths. In this chapter we shall be concerned exclusively with knowledge of things, of which in turn we shall have to distinguish two kinds. Knowledge of things, when it is of the kind we call knowledge by *acquaintance*, is essentially simpler than any knowledge of truths, and logically independent of knowledge of truths, though it would be rash to assume that human beings ever, in fact, have acquaintance with things without at the same time knowing some truth about them. Knowledge of things by *description*, on the contrary, always involves, as we shall find in the course of the present chapter, some knowledge of truths as its source and ground. But first of all we must make clear what we mean by 'acquaintance' and what we mean by 'description'.

We shall say that we have *acquaintance* with anything of which we are directly aware, without the intermediary of any process of inference or any knowledge of truths. Thus in the presence of my table I am acquainted with the sense-data that make up the appearance of my table—its colour, shape, hardness, smoothness, etc.; all these are things of which I am immediately conscious when I am seeing and touching my table. The particular shade of colour that I am seeing may have many things said about it—I may say that it is brown, that it is rather dark, and so on. But such statements, though they make me know truths about the colour, do not make me know the colour itself any better than I did before so far as concerns knowledge of the colour itself, as opposed to knowledge of truths about it, I know the colour perfectly and completely when I see it, and no further knowledge of it itself is even theoretically possible. Thus the sense-data which make up the appearance of my table are things with which I have acquaintance, things immediately known to me just as they are.

My knowledge of the table as a physical object, on the contrary, is not direct knowledge. Such as it is, it is obtained through acquaintance with the sense-data that make up the appearance of the table. We have seen that it is possible, without absurdity, to doubt whether there is a table at all, whereas it is not possible to doubt the sense-data. My knowledge of the table is of the kind which we shall call 'knowledge by description'. The table is 'the physical object which causes such-and-such sense-data'. This describes the table by means of the sense-data. In order to know anything at all about the table, we must know truths connecting it with things with which we have acquaintance: we must know that 'such-and-such sense-data are caused by a physical object'. There is no state of mind in which we are directly aware of the table; all our knowledge of the table is really knowledge of truths, and the actual thing which is the table is not, strictly speaking, known to us at all. We know a description, and we know that there is just one object to which this description applies, though the object itself is not directly known to us. In such a case, we say that our knowledge of the object is knowledge by description.

All our knowledge, both knowledge of things and knowledge of truths, rests upon acquaintance as its foundation. It is therefore important to consider what kinds of things there are with which we have acquaintance.

Sense-data, as we have already seen, are among the things with which we are acquainted; in fact, they supply the most obvious and striking example of knowledge by acquaintance. But if they were the sole example, our knowledge would be very much more restricted than it is. We should only know what is now present to our senses: we could not know anything about the past—not even that there was a past—nor could we know any truths about our sense-data, for all knowledge of truths, as we shall show, demands acquaintance with things which are of an essentially different character from sense-data, the things which are sometimes called 'abstract ideas', but which we shall call 'universals'. We have therefore to consider acquaintance with other things besides sense-data if we are to obtain any tolerably adequate analysis of our knowledge.

The first extension beyond sense-data to be considered is acquaintance by *memory*. It is obvious that we often remember what we have seen or heard or had otherwise present to our senses, and that in such cases we are still immediately aware of what we remember, in spite of the fact that it appears as past and not as present. This immediate knowledge by memory is the source of all our knowledge concerning the past: without it, there could be no knowledge of the past by inference, since we should never know that there was anything past to be inferred.

The next extension to be considered is acquaintance by *introspection*. We are not only aware of things, but we are often aware of being aware of them. When I see the sun, I am often aware of my seeing the sun; thus 'my seeing the sun' is an object with which I have acquaintance. When I desire food, I may be aware of my desire for food; thus 'my desiring food' is an object with which I am acquainted. Similarly we may be aware of our feeling pleasure or pain, and generally of the events which happen in our minds. This kind of acquaintance, which may be called self-consciousness, is the source of all our knowledge of mental things. It is obvious that it is only what goes on in our own minds that can be thus known immediately. What goes on in the minds of others is known to us through our perception of their bodies, that is, through the sense-data in us which are associated with their bodies. But for our acquaintance with the contents of our own minds, we should be unable to imagine the minds of others, and therefore we could never arrive at the knowledge that they have minds. It seems natural to suppose that self-consciousness is one of the things that distinguish men from animals: animals, we may suppose, though they have acquaintance with sense-data, never become aware of this acquaintance. I do not mean that they *doubt* whether they exist, but that they have never become conscious of the fact that they have sensations and feelings, nor therefore of the fact that they, the subjects of their sensations and feelings, exist.

We have spoken of acquaintance with the contents of our minds as *self-consciousness*, but it is not, of course, consciousness of our *self*: it is consciousness of particular thoughts and feelings. The question whether we are also acquainted with our bare selves, as opposed to particular thoughts and feelings, is a very difficult one, upon which it would be rash to speak positively. When we try to look into ourselves we always seem to come upon some particular thought or feeling, and not upon the 'I' which has the thought or feeling. Nevertheless there are some reasons for thinking that we are acquainted with the 'I', though the acquaintance is hard to disentangle from other things. To make clear what sort of reason there is, let us consider for a moment what our acquaintance with particular thoughts really involves.

When I am acquainted with 'my seeing the sun', it seems plain that I am acquainted with two different things in relation to each other. On the one hand there is the sense-datum which represents the sun to me, on the other hand there is that which sees this sense-datum. All acquaintance, such as my acquaintance with the sense-datum which represents the sun, seems obviously a relation between the person acquainted and the object with which the person is acquainted. When a case of acquaintance is one with which I can be acquainted (as I am acquainted with my acquaintance with the sense-datum representing the sun), it is plain that the person acquainted is myself. Thus, when I am acquainted with my seeing the sun, the whole fact with which I am acquainted is 'Self-acquainted-with-sense-datum'.

Further, we know the truth 'I am acquainted with this sense-datum'. It is hard to see how we could know this truth, or even understand what is meant by it, unless we were acquainted with something which we call 'I'. It does not seem necessary to suppose that we are acquainted with a more or less permanent person, the same to-day as yesterday, but it does seem as though we must be acquainted with that thing, whatever its nature, which sees the sun and has acquaintance with sense-data. Thus, in some sense it would seem we must be acquainted with our Selves as opposed to our particular experiences. But the question is difficult, and complicated arguments can be adduced on either side. Hence, although acquaintance with ourselves seems *probably* to occur, it is not wise to assert that it undoubtedly does occur.

We may therefore sum up as follows what has been said concerning acquaintance with things that exist. We have acquaintance in sensation with the data of the outer senses, and in introspection with the data of what may be called the inner sense—thoughts, feelings, desires, etc.; we have acquaintance in memory with things which have been data either of the outer senses or of the inner sense. Further, it is probable, though not certain, that we have acquaintance with Self, as that which is aware of things or has desires towards things.

In addition to our acquaintance with particular existing things, we also have acquaintance with what we shall call *universals*, that is to say, general ideas, such as *whiteness, diversity, brotherhood*, and so on. Every complete sentence must contain at least one word which stands for a universal, since all verbs have a meaning which is universal. We shall return to universals later on, in Chapter IX; for the present, it is only necessary to guard against the supposition that whatever we can be acquainted with must be something particular and existent. Awareness of universals is called *conceiving*, and a universal of which we are aware is called a *concept*.

It will be seen that among the objects with which we are acquainted are not included physical objects (as opposed to sense-data), nor other people's minds. These things are known to us by what I call 'knowledge by description', which we must now consider.

By a 'description' I mean any phrase of the form 'a so-and-so' or 'the so-and-so'. A phrase of the form 'a so-and-so' I shall call an 'ambiguous' description; a phrase of the form 'the so-and-so' (in the singular) I shall call a 'definite' description. Thus 'a man' is an ambiguous description, and 'the man with the iron mask' is a definite description. There are various problems connected with ambiguous descriptions, but I pass them by, since they do not directly concern the matter we are discussing, which is the nature of our knowledge concerning objects in cases where we know that there is an object answering to a definite description, though we are not acquainted with any such object. This is a matter which is concerned exclusively with definite descriptions. I shall therefore, in the sequel, speak simply of 'descriptions' when I mean 'definite descriptions'. Thus a description will mean any phrase of the form 'the so-and-so' in the singular.

We shall say that an object is 'known by description' when we know that it is 'the so-and-so', i.e. when we know that there is one object, and no more, having a certain property; and it will generally be implied that we do not have knowledge of the same object by acquaintance. We know that the man with the iron mask existed, and many propositions are known about him; but we do not know who he was. We know that the candidate who gets the most votes will be elected, and in this case we are very likely also acquainted (in the only sense in which one can be acquainted with some one else) with the man who is, in fact, the candidate who will get most votes; but we do not know which of the candidates he is, i.e. we do not know any proposition of the form 'A is the candidate who will get most votes' where A is one of the candidates by name. We shall say that we have 'merely descriptive knowledge' of the so-and-so when, although we know that the so-and-so exists, and although we may possibly be acquainted with the object which is, in fact, the so-and-so, yet we do not know any proposition 'a is the so-and-so', where a is something with which we are acquainted.

When we say 'the so-and-so exists', we mean that there is just one object which is the so-and-so. The proposition 'a is the so-and-so' means that a has the property so-and-so, and nothing else has. 'Mr. A. is the Unionist candidate for this constituency' means 'Mr. A. is a Unionist candidate for this constituency, and no one else is'. 'The Unionist candidate for this constituency exists' means 'some one is a Unionist candidate for this constituency, and no one else is'. Thus, when we are acquainted with an object which is the so-and-so, we know that the so-and-so exists; but we may know that the so-and-so exists when we are not acquainted with any object which we know to be the so-and-so, and even when we are not acquainted with any object which, in fact, is the so-and-so.

Common words, even proper names, are usually really descriptions. That is to say, the thought in the mind of a person using a proper name correctly can generally only be expressed explicitly if we replace the proper name by a description. Moreover, the description required to express the thought will vary for different people, or for the same person at different times. The only thing constant (so long as the name is rightly used) is the object to which the name applies. But so long as this remains constant, the particular description involved usually makes no difference to the truth or falsehood of the proposition in which the name appears.

Let us take some illustrations. Suppose some statement made about Bismarck. Assuming that there is such a thing as direct acquaintance with oneself, Bismarck himself might have used his name directly to designate the particular person with whom he was acquainted. In this case, if he made a judgement about himself, he himself might be a constituent of the judgement. Here the proper name has the direct use which it always wishes to have, as simply standing for a certain object, and not for a description of the object. But if a person who knew Bismarck made a judgement about him, the case is different. What this person was acquainted with were certain sense-data which he connected (rightly, we will suppose) with Bismarck's body. His body, as a physical object, and still more his mind, were only known as the body and the mind connected with these sense-data. That is, they were known by description. It is, of course, very much a matter af chance which characteristics of a man's appearance will come into a friend's mind when he thinks of him; thus the description actually in the friend's mind is accidental. The essential point is that he knows that the various descriptions all apply to the same entity, in spite of not being acquainted with the entity in question.

When we, who did not know Bismarck, make a judgement about him, the description in our minds will probably be some more or less vague mass of historical knowledge—far more, in most cases, than is required to identify him. But, for the sake of illustration, let us assume that we think of him as 'the first Chancellor of the German Empire'. Here all the words are abstract except 'German'. The word 'German' will, again, have different meanings for different people. To some it will recall travels in

Germany, to some the look of Germany on the map, and so on. But if we are to obtain a description which we know to be applicable, we shall be compelled, at some point, to bring in a reference to a particular with which we are acquainted. Such reference is involved in any mention of past, present, and future (as opposed to definite dates), or of here and there, or of what others have told us. Thus it would seem that, in some way or other, a description known to be applicable to a particular must involve some reference to a particular with which we are acquainted, if our knowledge about the thing described is not to be merely what follows *logically* from the description. For example, 'the most long-lived of men' is a description involving only universals, which must apply to some man, but we can make no judgements concerning this man which involve knowledge about him beyond what the description gives. If, however, we say, 'The first Chancellor of the German Empire was an astute diplomatist', we can only be assured of the truth of our judgement in virtue of something with which we are acquainted—usually a testimony heard or read. Apart from the information we convey to others, apart from the fact about the actual Bismarck, which gives importance to our judgement, the thought we really have contains the one or more particulars involved, and otherwise consists wholly of concepts.

All names of places—London, England, Europe, the Earth, the Solar System—similarly involve, when used, descriptions which start from some one or more particulars with which we are acquainted. I suspect that even the Universe, as considered by metaphysics, involves such a connexion with particulars. In logic, on the contrary, where we are concerned not merely with what does exist, but with whatever might or could exist or be, no reference to actual particulars is involved.

It would seem that, when we make a statement about something only known by description, we often *intend* to make our statement, not in the form involving the description, but about the actual thing described. That is to say, when we say anything about Bismarck, we should like, if we could, to make the judgement which Bismarck alone can make, namely, the judgement of which he himself is a constituent. In this we are necessarily defeated, since the actual Bismarck is unknown to us. But we know that there is an object B, called Bismarck, and that B was an astute diplomatist. We can thus *describe* the proposition we should like to affirm, namely, 'B was an astute diplomatist', where B is the object which was Bismarck. If we are describing Bismarck as 'the first Chancellor of the German Empire', the proposition we should like to affirm may be described as 'the proposition asserting, concerning the actual object which was the first Chancellor of the German Empire, that this object was an astute diplomatist'. What enables us to communicate in spite of the varying descriptions we employ is that we know there is a true proposition concerning the actual Bismarck, and that however we may vary the description (so long as the description is correct) the proposition described is still the same. This proposition, which is described and is known to be true, is what interests us; but we are not acquainted with the proposition itself, and do not know it, though we know it is true.

It will be seen that there are various stages in the removal from acquaintance with particulars: there is Bismarck to people who knew him; Bismarck to those who only know of him through history; the man with the iron mask; the longest-lived of men. These are progressively further removed from acquaintance with particulars; the first comes as near to acquaintance as is possible in regard to another person; in the second, we shall still be said to know 'who Bismarck was'; in the third, we do not know who was the man with the iron mask, though we can know many propositions about him which are not logically deducible from the fact that he wore an iron mask; in the fourth, finally, we know nothing beyond what is logically deducible from the definition of the man. There is a similar hierarchy in the region of universals. Many universals, like many particulars, are only known to us by description. But here, as in the case of particulars, knowledge concerning what is known by description is ultimately reducible to knowledge concerning what is known by acquaintance.

The fundamental principle in the analysis of propositions containing descriptions is this: *Every proposition which we can understand must be composed wholly of constituents with which we are acquainted.*

We shall not at this stage attempt to answer all the objections which may be urged against this fundamental principle. For the present, we shall merely point out that, in some way or other, it must be possible to meet these objections, for it is scarcely conceivable that we can make a judgement or entertain a supposition without knowing what it is that we are judging or supposing about. We must attach *some* meaning to the words we use, if we are to speak significantly and not utter mere noise; and the meaning we attach to our words must be something with which we are acquainted. Thus when, for example, we make a statement about Julius Caesar, it is plain that Julius Caesar himself is not before our minds, since we are not acquainted with him. We have in mind some description of Julius Caesar: 'the man who was assassinated on the Ides of March', 'the founder of the Roman Empire', or, perhaps, merely 'the man whose name was *Julius Caesar*'. (In this last description, *Julius Caesar* is a noise or shape with which we are acquainted.) Thus our statement does not mean quite what it seems to mean, but means something involving, instead of Julius Caesar, some description of him which is composed wholly of particulars and universals with which we are acquainted.

The chief importance of knowledge by description is that it enables us to pass beyond the limits of our private experience. In spite of the fact that we can only know truths which are wholly composed of terms which we have experienced in acquaintance, we can yet have knowledge by description of things which we have never experienced. In view of the very narrow range of our immediate experience, this result is vital, and until it is understood, much of our knowledge must remain mysterious and therefore doubtful.

# CHAPTER VI

## On Induction

In almost all our previous discussions we have been concerned in the attempt to get clear as to our data in the way of knowledge of existence. What things are there in the universe whose existence is known to us owing to our being acquainted with them? So far, our answer has been that we are acquainted with our sense-data, and, probably, with ourselves. These we know to exist. And past sense-data which are remembered are known to have existed in the past. This knowledge supplies our data.

But if we are to be able to draw inferences from these data—if we are to know of the existence of matter, of other people, of the past before our individual memory begins, or of the future, we must know general principles of some kind by means of which such inferences can be drawn. It must be known to us that the existence of some one sort of thing, A, is a sign of the existence of some other sort of thing, B, either at the same time as A or at some earlier or later time, as, for example, thunder is a sign of the earlier existence of lightning. If this were not known to us, we could never extend our knowledge beyond the sphere of our private experience; and this sphere, as we have seen, is exceedingly limited. The question we have now to consider is whether such an extension is possible, and if so, how it is effected.

Let us take as an illustration a matter about which none of us, in fact, feel the slightest doubt. We are all convinced that the sun will rise to-morrow. Why? Is this belief a mere blind outcome of past experience, or can it be justified as a reasonable belief? It is not easy to find a test by which to judge whether a belief of this kind is reasonable or not, but we can at least ascertain what sort of general beliefs would suffice, if true, to justify the judgement that the sun will rise to-morrow, and the many other similar judgements upon which our actions are based.

It is obvious that if we are asked why we believe that the sun will rise to-morrow, we shall naturally answer 'Because it always has risen every day'. We have a firm belief that it will rise in the future, because it has risen in the past. If we are challenged as to why we believe that it will continue to rise as heretofore, we may appeal to the laws of motion: the earth, we shall say, is a freely rotating body, and such bodies do not cease to rotate unless something interferes from outside, and there is nothing outside to interfere with the earth between now and to-morrow. Of course it might be doubted whether we are quite certain that there is nothing outside to interfere, but this is not the interesting doubt. The interesting doubt is as to whether the laws of motion will remain in operation until to-morrow. If this doubt is raised, we find ourselves in the same position as when the doubt about the sunrise was first raised.

The *only* reason for believing that the laws of motion will remain in operation is that they have operated hitherto, so far as our knowledge of the past enables us to judge. It is true that we have a greater body of evidence from the past in favour of the laws of motion than we have in favour of the sunrise, because the sunrise is merely a particular case of fulfilment of the laws of motion, and there are countless other particular cases. But the real question is: Do *any* number of cases of a law being fulfilled in the past afford evidence that it will be fulfilled in the future? If not, it becomes plain that we have no ground whatever for expecting the sun to rise to-morrow, or for expecting the bread we shall eat at our next meal not to poison us, or for any of the other scarcely conscious expectations that control our daily lives. It is to be observed that all such expectations are only *probable*; thus we have not to seek for a proof that they *must* be fulfilled, but only for some reason in favour of the view that they are *likely* to be fulfilled.

Now in dealing with this question we must, to begin with, make an important distinction, without which we should soon become involved in hopeless confusions. Experience has shown us that, hitherto, the frequent repetition of some uniform succession or coexistence has been a *cause* of our expecting the same succession or coexistence on the next occasion. Food that has a certain appearance generally has a certain taste, and it is a severe shock to our expectations when the familiar appearance is found to be associated with an unusual taste. Things which we see become associated, by habit, with certain tactile sensations which we expect if we touch them; one of the horrors of a ghost (in many ghost-stories) is that it fails to give us any sensations of touch. Uneducated people who go abroad for the first time are so surprised as to be incredulous when they find their native language not understood.

And this kind of association is not confined to men; in animals also it is very strong. A horse which has been often driven along a certain road resists the attempt to drive him in a different direction. Domestic animals expect food when they see the person who usually feeds them. We know that all these rather crude expectations of uniformity are liable to be misleading. The man who has fed the chicken every day throughout its life at last wrings its neck instead, showing that more refined views as to the uniformity of nature would have been useful to the chicken.

But in spite of the misleadingness of such expectations, they nevertheless exist. The mere fact that something has happened a certain number of times causes animals and men to expect that it will happen again. Thus our instincts certainly cause us to believe that the sun will rise to-morrow, but we may be in no better a position than the chicken which unexpectedly has its neck wrung. We have therefore to distinguish the fact that past uniformities *cause* expectations as to the future, from the question whether there is any reasonable ground for giving weight to such expectations after the question of their validity has been raised.

The problem we have to discuss is whether there is any reason for believing in what is called 'the uniformity of nature'. The belief in the uniformity of nature is the belief that everything that has happened or will happen is an instance of some general law to which there are no exceptions. The crude expectations which we have been considering are all subject to exceptions, and therefore liable to disappoint those who entertain them. But science habitually assumes, at least as a working hypothesis, that general rules which have exceptions can be replaced by general rules which have no exceptions. 'Unsupported bodies in air fall' is a general rule to which balloons and aeroplanes are exceptions. But the laws of motion and the law of gravitation, which account for the fact that most bodies fall, also account for the fact that balloons and aeroplanes can rise; thus the laws of motion and the law of gravitation are not subject to these exceptions.

The belief that the sun will rise to-morrow might be falsified if the earth came suddenly into contact with a large body which destroyed its rotation; but the laws of motion and the law of gravitation would not be infringed by such an event. The business of science is to find uniformities, such as the laws of motion and the law of gravitation, to which, so far as our experience extends, there are no exceptions. In this search science has been remarkably successful, and it may be conceded that such uniformities have held hitherto. This brings us back to the question: Have we any reason, assuming that they have always held in the past, to suppose that they will hold in the future?

It has been argued that we have reason to know that the future will resemble the past, because what was the future has constantly become the past, and has always been found to resemble the past, so that we really have experience of the future, namely of times which were formerly future, which we may call past futures. But such an argument really begs the very question at issue. We have experience of past futures, but not of future futures, and the question is: Will future futures resemble past futures? This question is not to be answered by an argument which starts from past futures alone. We have therefore still to seek for some principle which shall enable us to know that the future will follow the same laws as the past.

The reference to the future in this question is not essential. The same question arises when we apply the laws that work in our experience to past things of which we have no experience—as, for example, in geology, or in theories as to the origin of the Solar System. The question we really have to ask is: 'When two things have been found to be often associated, and no instance is known of the one occurring without the other, does the occurrence of one of the two, in a fresh instance, give any good ground for expecting the other?' On our answer to this question must depend the validity of the whole of our expectations as to the future, the whole of the results obtained by induction, and in fact practically all the beliefs upon which our daily life is based.

It must be conceded, to begin with, that the fact that two things have been found often together and never apart does not, by itself, suffice to *prove* demonstratively that they will be found together in the next case we examine. The most we can hope is that the oftener things are found together, the more probable it becomes that they will be found together another time, and that, if they have been found together often enough, the probability will amount *almost* to certainty. It can never quite reach certainty, because we know that in spite of frequent repetitions there sometimes is a failure at the last, as in the case of the chicken whose neck is wrung. Thus probability is all we ought to seek.

It might be urged, as against the view we are advocating, that we know all natural phenomena to be subject to the reign of law, and that sometimes, on the basis of observation, we can see that only one law can possibly fit the facts of the case. Now to this view there are two answers. The first is that, even if *some* law which has no exceptions applies to our case, we can never, in practice, be sure that we have discovered that law and not one to which there are exceptions. The second is that the reign of law would seem to be itself only probable, and that our belief that it will hold in the future, or in unexamined cases in the past, is itself based upon the very principle we are examining.

The principle we are examining may be called the *principle of induction*, and its two parts may be stated as follows:

(a)  When a thing of a certain sort A has been found to be associated with a thing of a certain other sort B, and has never been found dissociated from a thing of the sort B, the greater the number of cases in which A and B have been associated, the greater is the probability that they will be associated in a fresh case in which one of them is known to be present;

(b)  Under the same circumstances, a sufficient number of cases of association will make the probability of a fresh association nearly a certainty, and will make it approach certainty without limit.

As just stated, the principle applies only to the verification of our expectation in a single fresh instance. But we want also to know that there is a probability in favour of the general law that things of the sort A are *always* associated with things of the sort B, provided a sufficient number of cases of association are known, and no cases of failure of association are known. The probability of the general law is obviously less than the probability of the particular case, since if the general law is true, the particular case must also be true, whereas the particular case may be true without the general law being true. Nevertheless the probability of the general law is increased by repetitions, just as the probability of the particular case is. We may therefore repeat the two parts of our principle as regards the general law, thus:

(a)  The greater the number of cases in which a thing of the sort A has been found associated with a thing of the sort B, the more probable it is (if no cases of failure of association are known) that A is always associated with B;

b) Under the same circumstances, a sufficient number of cases of the association of A with B will make it nearly certain that A is always associated with B, and will make this general law approach certainty without limit.

It should be noted that probability is always relative to certain data. In our case, the data are merely the known cases of coexistence of A and B. There may be other data, which *might* be taken into account, which would gravely alter the probability. For example, a man who had seen a great many white swans might argue, by our principle, that on the data it was *probable* that all swans were white, and this might be a perfectly sound argument. The argument is not disproved by the fact that some swans are black, because a thing may very well happen in spite of the fact that some data render it improbable. In the case of the swans, a man might know that colour is a very variable characteristic in many species of animals, and that, therefore, an induction as to colour is peculiarly liable to error. But this knowledge would be a fresh datum, by no means proving that the probability relatively to our previous data had been wrongly estimated. The fact, therefore, that things often fail to fulfil our expectations is no evidence that our expectations will not *probably* be fulfilled in a given case or a given class of cases. Thus our inductive principle is at any rate not capable of being *disproved* by an appeal to experience.

The inductive principle, however, is equally incapable of being *proved* by an appeal to experience. Experience might conceivably confirm the inductive principle as regards the cases that have been already examined; but as regards unexamined cases, it is the inductive principle alone that can justify any inference from what has been examined to what has not been examined. All arguments which, on the basis of experience, argue as to the future or the unexperienced parts of the past or present, assume the inductive principle; hence we can never use experience to prove the inductive principle without begging the question. Thus we must either accept the inductive principle on the ground of its intrinsic evidence, or forgo all justification of our expectations about the future. If the principle is unsound, we have no reason to expect the sun to rise to-morrow, to expect bread to be more nourishing than a stone, or to expect that if we throw ourselves off the roof we shall fall. When we see what looks like our best friend approaching us, we shall have no reason to suppose that his body is not inhabited by the mind of our worst enemy or of some total stranger. All our conduct is based upon associations which have worked in the past, and which we therefore regard as likely to work in the future; and this likelihood is dependent for its validity upon the inductive principle.

The general principles of science, such as the belief in the reign of law, and the belief that every event must have a cause, are as completely dependent upon the inductive principle as are the beliefs of daily life All such general principles are believed because mankind have found innumerable instances of their truth and no instances of their falsehood. But this affords no evidence for their truth in the future, unless the inductive principle is assumed.

Thus all knowledge which, on a basis of experience tells us something about what is not experienced, is based upon a belief which experience can neither confirm nor confute, yet which, at least in its more concrete applications, appears to be as firmly rooted in us as many of the facts of experience. The existence and justification of such beliefs—for the inductive principle, as we shall see, is not the only example—raises some of the most difficult and most debated problems of philosophy. We will, in the next chapter, consider briefly what may be said to account for such knowledge, and what is its scope and its degree of certainty.

# CHAPTER VII

## On our Knowledge of General Principles

We saw in the preceding chapter that the principle of induction, while necessary to the validity of all arguments based on experience, is itself not capable of being proved by experience, and yet is unhesitatingly believed by every one, at least in all its concrete applications. In these characteristics the principle of induction does not stand alone. There are a number of other principles which cannot be proved or disproved by experience, but are used in arguments which start from what is experienced.

Some of these principles have even greater evidence than the principle of induction, and the knowledge of them has the same degree of certainty as the knowledge of the existence of sense-data. They constitute the means of drawing inferences from what is given in sensation; and if what we infer is to be true, it is just as necessary that our principles of inference should be true as it is that our data should be true. The principles of inference are apt to be overlooked because of their very obviousness—the assumption involved is assented to without our realizing that it is an assumption. But it is very important to realize the use of principles of inference, if a correct theory of knowledge is to be obtained; for our knowledge of them raises interesting and difficult questions.

In all our knowledge of general principles, what actually happens is that first of all we realize some particular application of the principle, and then we realize that the particularity is irrelevant, and that there is a generality which may equally truly be affirmed. This is of course familiar in such matters as teaching arithmetic: 'two and two are four' is first learnt in the case of some particular pair of couples, and then in some other particular case, and so on, until at last it becomes possible to see that it is true of any pair of couples. The same thing happens with logical principles. Suppose two men are discussing what day of the month it is. One of them says, 'At least you will admit that *if* yesterday was the 15th to-day must be the 16th.' 'Yes', says the other, 'I admit that.' 'And you know', the first continues, 'that yesterday was the 15th, because you dined with Jones, and your diary will tell you that was on the 15th.' 'Yes', says the second; 'therefore to-day *is* the 16th.'

Now such an argument is not hard to follow; and if it is granted that its premisses are true in fact, no one will deny that the conclusion must also be true. But it depends for its truth upon an instance of a general logical principle. The logical principle is as follows: 'Suppose it known that *if* this is true, then that is true. Suppose it also known that this *is* true, then it follows that that is true.' When it is the case that if this is true, that is true, we shall say that this 'implies' that, and that that 'follows from' this. Thus our principle states that if this implies that, and this is true, then that is true. In other words, 'anything implied by a true proposition is true', or 'whatever follows from a true proposition is true'.

This principle is really involved—at least, concrete instances of it are involved—in all demonstrations. Whenever one thing which we believe is used to prove something else, which we consequently believe, this principle is relevant. If any one asks: 'Why should I accept the results of valid arguments based on true premises?' we can only answer by appealing to our principle. In fact, the truth of the principle is impossible to doubt, and its obviousness is so great that at first sight it seems almost trivial. Such principles, however, are not trivial to the philosopher, for they show that we may have indubitable knowledge which is in no way derived from objects of sense.

The above principle is merely one of a certain number of self-evident logical principles. Some at least of these principles must be granted before any argument or proof becomes possible. When some of them have been granted, others can be proved, though these others, so long as they are simple, are just as obvious as the principles taken for granted. For no very good reason, three of these principles have been singled out by tradition under the name of 'Laws of Thought'.

They are as follows:

(1) *The law of identity*: 'Whatever is, is.'
(2) *The law of contradiction*: 'Nothing can both be and not be.'
(3) *The law of excluded middle*: 'Everything must either be or not be.'

These three laws are samples of self-evident logical principles, but are not really more fundamental or more self-evident than various other similar principles: for instance, the one we considered just now, which states that what follows from a true premiss is true. The name 'laws of thought' is also misleading, for what is important is not the fact that we think in accordance with these laws, but the fact that things behave in accordance with them; in other words, the fact that when we think in accordance with them we think *truly*. But this is a large question, to which we must return at a later stage.

In addition to the logical principles which enable us to prove from a given premiss that something is *certainly* true, there are other logical principles which enable us to prove, from a given premiss, that there is a greater or less probability that something is true. An example of such principles—perhaps the most important example is the inductive principle, which we considered in the preceding chapter.

One of the great historic controversies in philosophy is the controversy between the two schools called respectively 'empiricists' and 'rationalists'. The empiricists— who are best represented by the British philosophers, Locke, Berkeley, and Hume—

maintained that all our knowledge is derived from experience; the rationalists—who are represented by the Continental philosophers of the seventeenth century, especially Descartes and Leibniz—maintained that, in addition to what we know by experience, there are certain 'innate ideas' and 'innate principles', which we know independently of experience. It has now become possible to decide with some confidence as to the truth or falsehood of these opposing schools. It must be admitted, for the reasons already stated, that logical principles are known to us, and cannot be themselves proved by experience, since all proof presupposes them. In this, therefore, which was the most important point of the controversy, the rationalists were in the right.

On the other hand, even that part of our knowledge which is *logically* independent of experience (in the sense that experience cannot prove it) is yet elicited and caused by experience. It is on occasion of particular experiences that we become aware of the general laws which their connexions exemplify. It would certainly be absurd to suppose that there are innate principles in the sense that babies are born with a knowledge of everything which men know and which cannot be deduced from what is experienced. For this reason, the word 'innate' would not now be employed to describe our knowledge of logical principles. The phrase '*a priori*' is less objectionable, and is more usual in modern writers. Thus, while admitting that all knowledge is elicited and caused by experience, we shall nevertheless hold that some knowledge is *a priori*, in the sense that the experience which makes us think of it does not suffice to prove it, but merely so directs our attention that we see its truth without requiring any proof from experience.

There is another point of great importance, in which the empiricists were in the right as against the rationalists. Nothing can be known to *exist* except by the help of experience. That is to say, if we wish to prove that something of which we have no direct experience exists, we must have among our premises the existence of one or more things of which we have direct experience. Our belief that the Emperor of China exists, for example, rests upon testimony, and testimony consists, in the last analysis, of sense-data seen or heard in reading or being spoken to. Rationalists believed that, from general consideration as to what must be, they could deduce the existence of this or that in the actual world. In this belief they seem to have been mistaken. All the knowledge that we can acquire *a priori* concerning existence seems to be hypothetical: it tells us that if one thing exists, another must exist, or, more generally, that if one proposition is true, another must be true. This is exemplified by the principles we have already dealt with, such as '*if* this is true, and this implies that, then that is true', or '*if* this and that have been repeatedly found connected, they will probably be connected in the next instance in which one of them is found'. Thus the scope and power of *a priori* principles is strictly limited. All knowledge that something exists must be in part dependent on experience. When anything is known immediately, its existence is known by experience alone; when anything is proved to exist, without being known immediately, both experience and *a priori* principles must be required in the proof. Knowledge is called *empirical* when it rests wholly or partly upon experience. Thus all knowledge which asserts existence is empirical, and the only *a priori* knowledge concerning existence is hypothetical, giving connexions among things that exist or may exist, but not giving actual existence.

*A priori* knowledge is not all of the logical kind we have been hitherto considering. Perhaps the most important example of non-logical *a priori* knowledge is knowledge as to ethical value. I am not speaking of judgements as to what is useful or as to what is virtuous, for such judgements do require empirical premisses; I am speaking of judgements as to the intrinsic desirability of things. If something is useful, it must be useful because it secures some end; the end must, if we have gone far enough, be valuable on its own account, and not merely because it is useful for some further end. Thus all judgements as to what is useful depend upon judgements as to what has value on its own account.

We judge, for example, that happiness is more desirable than misery, knowledge than ignorance, goodwill than hatred, and so on. Such judgements must, in part at least, be immediate and *a priori*. Like our previous *a priori* judgements, they may be elicited by experience, and indeed they must be; for it seems not possible to judge whether anything is intrinsically valuable unless we have experienced something of the same kind. But it is fairly obvious that they cannot be proved by experience; for the fact that a thing exists or does not exist cannot prove either that it is good that it should exist or that it is bad. The pursuit of this subject belongs to ethics, where the impossibility of deducing what ought to be from what is has to be established. In the present connexion, it is only important to realize that knowledge as to what is intrinsically of value is *a priori* in the same sense in which logic is *a priori*, namely in the sense that the truth of such knowledge can be neither proved nor disproved by experience.

All pure mathematics is *a priori*, like logic. This was strenuously denied by the empirical philosophers, who maintained that experience was as much the source of our knowledge of arithmetic as of our knowledge of geography. They maintained that by the repeated experience of seeing two things and two other things, and finding that altogether they made four things, we were led by induction to the conclusion that two things and two other things would *always* make four things altogether. If, however, this were the source of our knowledge that two and two are four, we should proceed differently, in persuading ourselves of its truth, from the way in which we do actually proceed. In fact, a certain number of instances are needed to make us think of two abstractly, rather than of two coins or two books or two people, or two of any other specified kind. But as soon as we are able to divest our thoughts of irrelevant particularity, we become able to see the general principle that two and two are four; any one instance is seen to be *typical*, and the examination of other instances becomes unnecessary.[1]

---

[1] Cf. A. N. Whitehead, *Introduction to Mathematics* (Home University Library).

The same thing is exemplified in geometry. If we want to prove some property of *all* triangles, we draw some one triangle and reason about it; but we can avoid making use of any property which it does not share with all other triangles, and thus, from our particular case, we obtain a general result. We do not, in fact, feel our certainty that two and two are four increased by fresh instances, because, as soon as we have seen the truth of this proposition, our certainty becomes so great as to be incapable of growing greater. Moreover, we feel some quality of necessity about the proposition 'two and two are four', which is absent from even the best attested empirical generalizations. Such generalizations always remain mere facts: we feel that there might be a world in which they were false, though in the actual world they happen to be true. In any possible world, on the contrary, we feel that two and two would be four: this is not a mere fact, but a necessity to which everything actual and possible must conform.

The case may be made clearer by considering a genuinely-empirical generalization, such as 'All men are mortal.' It is plain that we believe this proposition, in the first place, because there is no known instance of men living beyond a certain age, and in the second place because there seem to be physiological grounds for thinking that an organism such as a man's body must sooner or later wear out. Neglecting the second ground, and considering merely our experience of men's mortality, it is plain that we should not be content with one quite clearly understood instance of a man dying, whereas, in the case of 'two and two are four', one instance does suffice, when carefully considered, to persuade us that the same must happen in any other instance. Also we can be forced to admit, on reflection, that there may be some doubt, however slight, as to whether *all* men are mortal. This may be made plain by the attempt to imagine two different worlds, in one of which there are men who are not mortal, while in the other two and two make five. When Swift invites us to consider the race of Struldbugs who never die, we are able to acquiesce in imagination. But a world where two and two make five seems quite on a different level. We feel that such a world, if there were one, would upset the whole fabric of our knowledge and reduce us to utter doubt.

The fact is that, in simple mathematical judgements such as 'two and two are four', and also in many judgements of logic, we can know the general proposition without inferring it from instances, although some instance is usually necessary to make clear to us what the general proposition means. This is why there is real utility in the process of *deduction*, which goes from the general to the general, or from the general to the particular, as well as in the process of *induction*, which goes from the particular to the particular, or from the particular to the general. It is an old debate among philosophers whether deduction ever gives *new* knowledge. We can now see that in certain cases, at least, it does do so. If we already know that two and two always make four, and we know that Brown and Jones are two, and so are Robinson and Smith, we can deduce that Brown and Jones and Robinson and Smith are four. This is new knowledge, not contained in our premises, because the general proposition, 'two and two are four', never told us there were such people as Brown and Jones and Robinson and Smith, and the particular premises do not tell us that there were four of them, whereas the particular proposition deduced does tell us both these things.

But the newness of the knowledge is much less certain if we take the stock instance of deduction that is always given in books on logic, namely, 'All men are mortal; Socrates is a man, therefore Socrates is mortal.' In this case, what we really know beyond reasonable doubt is that certain men, A, B, C, were mortal, since, in fact, they have died. If Socrates is one of these men, it is foolish to go the roundabout way through 'all men are mortal' to arrive at the conclusion that *probably* Socrates is mortal. If Socrates is not one of the men on whom our induction is based, we shall still do better to argue straight from our A, B, C, to Socrates, than to go round by the general proposition, 'all men are mortal'. For the probability that Socrates is mortal is greater, on our data, than the probability that all men are mortal. (This is obvious, because if all men are mortal, so is Socrates; but if Socrates is mortal, it does not follow that all men are mortal.) Hence we shall reach the conclusion that Socrates is mortal with a greater approach to certainty if we make our argument purely inductive than if we go by way of 'all men are mortal' and then use deduction.

This illustrates the difference between general propositions known *a priori* such as 'two and two are four', and empirical generalizations such as 'all men are mortal'. In regard to the former, deduction is the right mode of argument, whereas in regard to the latter, induction is always theoretically preferable, and warrants a greater confidence in the truth of our conclusion, because all empirical generalizations are more uncertain than the instances of them.

We have now seen that there are propositions known *a priori*, and that among them are the propositions of logic and pure mathematics, as well as the fundamental propositions of ethics. The question which must next occupy us is this: How is it possible that there should be such knowledge? And more particularly, how can there be knowledge of general propositions in cases where we have not examined all the instances, and indeed never can examine them all, because their number is infinite? These questions, which were first brought prominently forward by the German philosopher Kant (1724-1804), are very difficult, and historically very important.

# CHAPTER VIII

## How *A Priori* Knowledge Is Possible

Immanuel Kant is generally regarded as the greatest of the modern philosophers. Though he lived through the Seven Years War and the French Revolution, he never interrupted his teaching of philosophy at Königsberg in East Prussia. His most distinctive contribution was the invention of what he called the 'critical' philosophy, which, assuming as a datum that there is knowledge of various kinds, inquired how such knowledge comes to be possible, and deduced, from the answer to this inquiry, many metaphysical results as to the nature of the world. Whether these results were valid may well be doubted. But Kant undoubtedly deserves credit for two things: first, for having perceived that we have *a priori* knowledge which is not purely 'analytic', i.e. such that the opposite would be self-contradictory, and secondly, for having made evident the philosophical importance of the theory of knowledge.

Before the time of Kant, it was generally held that whatever knowledge was *a priori* must be 'analytic'. What this word means will be best illustrated by examples. If I say, 'A bald man is a man', 'A plane figure is a figure', 'A bad poet is a poet', I make a purely analytic judgement: the subject spoken about is given as having at least two properties, of which one is singled out to be asserted of it. Such propositions as the above are trivial, and would never be enunciated in real life except by an orator preparing the way for a piece of sophistry. They are called 'analytic' because the predicate is obtained by merely analysing the subject. Before the time of Kant it was thought that all judgements of which we could be certain *a priori* were of this kind: that in all of them there was a predicate which was only part of the subject of which it was asserted. If this were so, we should be involved in a definite contradiction if we attempted to deny anything that could be known *a priori*. 'A bald man is not bald' would assert and deny baldness of the same man, and would therefore contradict itself. Thus according to the philosophers before Kant, the law of contradiction, which asserts that nothing can at the same time have and not have a certain property, sufficed to establish the truth of all *a priori* knowledge.

Hume (1711-76), who preceded Kant, accepting the usual view as to what makes knowledge *a priori*, discovered that, in many cases which had previously been supposed analytic, and notably in the case of cause and effect, the connexion was really synthetic. Before Hume, rationalists at least had supposed that the effect could be logically deduced from the cause, if only we had sufficient knowledge. Hume argued—correctly, as would now be generally admitted—that this could not be done. Hence he inferred the far more doubtful proposition that nothing could be known *a priori* about the connexion of cause and effect. Kant, who had been educated in the rationalist tradition, was much perturbed by Hume's scepticism, and endeavoured to find an answer to it. He perceived that not only the connexion of cause and effect, but all the propositions of arithmetic and geometry, are 'synthetic', i.e. not analytic: in all these propositions, no analysis of the subject will reveal the predicate. His stock instance was the proposition $7 + 5 = 12$. He pointed out, quite truly, that 7 and 5 have to be put together to give 12: the idea of 12 is not contained in them, nor even in the idea of adding them together. Thus he was led to the conclusion that all pure mathematics, though *a priori*, is synthetic; and this conclusion raised a new problem of which he endeavoured to find the solution.

The question which Kant put at the beginning of his philosophy, namely 'How is pure mathematics possible?' is an interesting and difficult one, to which every philosophy which is not purely sceptical must find some answer. The answer of the pure empiricists, that our mathematical knowledge is derived by induction from particular instances, we have already seen to be inadequate, for two reasons: first, that the validity of the inductive principle itself cannot be proved by induction; secondly, that the general propositions of mathematics, such as 'two and two always make four', can obviously be known with certainty by consideration of a single instance, and gain nothing by enumeration of other cases in which they have been found to be true. Thus our knowledge of the general propositions of mathematics (and the same applies to logic) must be accounted for otherwise than our (merely probable) knowledge of empirical generalizations such as 'all men are mortal'.

The problem arises through the fact that such knowledge is general, whereas all experience is particular. It seems strange that we should apparently be able to know some truths in advance about particular things of which we have as yet no experience; but it cannot easily be doubted that logic and arithmetic will apply to such things. We do not know who will be the inhabitants of London a hundred years hence; but we know that any two of them and any other two of them will make four of them. This apparent power of anticipating facts about things of which we have no experience is certainly surprising. Kant's solution of the problem, though not valid in my opinion, is interesting. It is, however, very difficult, and is differently understood by different philosophers. We can, therefore, only give the merest outline of it, and even that will be thought misleading by many exponents of Kant's system.

What Kant maintained was that in all our experience there are two elements to be distinguished, the one due to the object (i.e. to what we have called the 'physical object'), the other due to our own nature. We saw, in discussing matter and sense-data, that the physical object is different from the associated sense-data, and that the sense-data are to be regarded as resulting from an interaction between the physical object and ourselves. So far, we are in agreement with Kant. But what is distinctive of Kant is the way in which he apportions the shares of ourselves and the physical object respectively. He considers that the crude material given in sensation—the colour, hardness, etc.—is due to the object, and that what we supply is the arrangement in space and time, and all the relations between sense-data which result from comparison or from considering one as the cause of the other or in any other way. His chief reason in favour of this view is that we seem to have *a priori* knowledge as to space and time and causality and comparison, but not as to the actual crude material of sensation. We can be sure, he says, that anything we shall ever experience must show the characteristics affirmed of it in our *a priori* knowledge, because these characteristics are due to our own nature, and therefore nothing can ever come into our experience without acquiring these characteristics.

The physical object, which he calls the 'thing in itself',[2] he regards as essentially unknowable; what can be known is the object as we have it in experience, which he calls the 'phenomenon'. The phenomenon, being a joint product of us and the thing in itself, is sure to have those characteristics which are due to us, and is therefore sure to conform to our *a priori* knowledge. Hence this knowledge, though true of all actual and possible experience, must not be supposed to apply outside experience. Thus in spite of the existence of *a priori* knowledge, we cannot know anything about the thing in itself or about what is not an actual or possible object of experience. In this way he tries to reconcile and harmonize the contentions of the rationalists with the arguments of the empiricists.

Apart from minor grounds on which Kant's philosophy may be criticized, there is one main objection which seems fatal to any attempt to deal with the problem of *a priori* knowledge by his method. The thing to be accounted for is our certainty that the facts must always conform to logic and arithmetic. To say that logic and arithmetic are contributed by us does not account for this. Our nature is as much a fact of the existing world as anything, and there can be no certainty that it will remain constant. It might happen, if Kant is right, that to-morrow our nature would so change as to make two and two become five. This possibility seems never to have occurred to him, yet it is one which utterly destroys the certainty and universality which he is anxious to vindicate for arithmetical propositions. It is true that this possibility, formally, is inconsistent with the Kantian view that time itself is a form imposed by the subject upon phenomena, so that our real Self is not in time and has no to-morrow. But he will still have to suppose that the time-order of phenomena is determined by characteristics of what is behind phenomena, and this suffices for the substance of our argument.

---

[2] Kant's 'thing in itself' is identical in *definition* with the physical object, namely, it is the cause of sensations. In the properties deduced from the definition it is not identical, since Kant held (in spite of some inconsistency as regards cause) that we can know that none of the categories are applicable to the 'thing in itself'.

Reflection, moreover, seems to make it clear that, if there is any truth in our arithmetical beliefs, they must apply to things equally whether we think of them or not. Two physical objects and two other physical objects must make four physical objects, even if physical objects cannot be experienced. To assert this is certainly within the scope of what we mean when we state that two and two are four. Its truth is just as indubitable as the truth of the assertion that two phenomena and two other phenomena make four phenomena. Thus Kant's solution unduly limits the scope of *a priori* propositions, in addition to failing in the attempt at explaining their certainty.

Apart from the special doctrines advocated by Kant, it is very common among philosophers to regard what is *a priori* as in some sense mental, as concerned rather with the way we must think than with any fact of the outer world. We noted in the preceding chapter the three principles commonly called 'laws of thought'. The view which led to their being so named is a natural one, but there are strong reasons for thinking that it is erroneous. Let us take as an illustration the law of contradiction. This is commonly stated in the form 'Nothing can both be and not be', which is intended to express the fact that nothing can at once have and not have a given quality. Thus, for example, if a tree is a beech it cannot also be not a beech; if my table is rectangular it cannot also be not rectangular, and so on.

Now what makes it natural to call this principle a law of *thought* is that it is by thought rather than by outward observation that we persuade ourselves of its necessary truth. When we have seen that a tree is a beech, we do not need to look again in order to ascertain whether it is also not a beech; thought alone makes us know that this is impossible. But the conclusion that the law of contradiction is a law of *thought* is nevertheless erroneous. What we believe, when we believe the law of contradiction, is not that the mind is so made that it must believe the law of contradiction. *This* belief is a subsequent result of psychological reflection, which presupposes the belief in the law of contradiction. The belief in the law of contradiction is a belief about things, not only about thoughts. It is not, e.g., the belief that if we *think* a certain tree is a beech, we cannot at the same time *think* that it is not a beech; it is the belief that if the tree *is* a beech, it cannot at the same time *be* not a beech. Thus the law of contradiction is about things, and not merely about thoughts; and although belief in the law of contradiction is a thought, the law of contradiction itself is not a thought, but a fact concerning the things in the world. If this, which we believe when we believe the law of contradiction, were not true of the things in the world, the fact that we were compelled to *think* it true would not save the law of contradiction from being false; and this shows that the law is not a law of *thought*.

A similar argument applies to any other *a priori* judgement. When we judge that two and two are four, we are not making a judgement about our thoughts, but about all actual or possible couples. The fact that our minds are so constituted as to believe that two and two are four, though it is true, is emphatically not what we assert when we assert that two and two are four. And no fact about the constitution of our minds could make it *true* that two and two are four. Thus our *a priori* knowledge, if it is not erroneous, is not merely knowledge about the constitution of our minds, but is applicable to whatever the world may contain, both what is mental and what is non-mental.

The fact seems to be that all our *a priori* knowledge is concerned with entities which do not, properly speaking, *exist*, either in the mental or in the physical world. These entities are such as can be named by parts of speech which are not substantives; they are such entities as qualities and relations. Suppose, for instance, that I am in my room. I exist, and my room exists; but does 'in' exist? Yet obviously the word 'in' has a meaning; it denotes a relation which holds between me and my room. This relation is something, although we cannot say that it exists *in the same sense* in which I and my room exist. The relation 'in' is something which we can think about and understand, for, if we could not understand it, we could not understand the sentence 'I am in my room'. Many philosophers, following Kant, have maintained that relations are the work of the mind, that things in themselves have no relations, but that the mind brings them together in one act of thought and thus produces the relations which it judges them to have.

This view, however, seems open to objections similar to those which we urged before against Kant. It seems plain that it is not thought which produces the truth of the proposition 'I am in my room'. It may be true that an earwig is in my room, even if neither I nor the earwig nor any one else is aware of this truth; for this truth concerns only the earwig and the room, and does not depend upon anything else. Thus relations, as we shall see more fully in the next chapter, must be placed in a world which is neither mental nor physical. This world is of great importance to philosophy, and in particular to the problems of *a priori* knowledge. In the next chapter we shall proceed to develop its nature and its bearing upon the questions with which we have been dealing.

# CHAPTER IX

## The World of Universals

At the end of the preceding chapter we saw that such entities as relations appear to have a being which is in some way different from that of physical objects, and also different from that of minds and from that of sense-data. In the present chapter we have to consider what is the nature of this kind of being, and also what objects there are that have this kind of being. We will begin with the latter question.

The problem with which we are now concerned is a very old one, since it was brought into philosophy by Plato. Plato's 'theory of ideas' is an attempt to solve this very problem, and in my opinion it is one of the most successful attempts hitherto made. The theory to be advocated in what follows is largely Plato's, with merely such modifications as time has shown to be necessary.

The way the problem arose for Plato was more or less as follows. Let us consider, say, such a notion as *justice*. If we ask ourselves what justice is, it is natural to proceed by considering this, that, and the other just act, with a view to discovering what they have in common. They must all, in some sense, partake of a common nature, which will be found in whatever is just and in nothing else. This common nature, in virtue of which they are all just, will be justice itself, the pure essence the admixture of which with facts of ordinary life produces the multiplicity of just acts. Similarly with any other word which may be applicable to common facts, such as 'whiteness' for example. The word will be applicable to a number of particular things because they all participate in a common nature or essence. This pure essence is what Plato calls an 'idea' or 'form'. (It must not be supposed that 'ideas', in his sense, exist in minds, though they may be apprehended by minds.) The 'idea' *justice* is not identical with anything that is just: it is something other than particular things, which particular things partake of. Not being particular, it cannot itself exist in the world of sense. Moreover it is not fleeting or changeable like the things of sense: it is eternally itself, immutable and indestructible.

Thus Plato is led to a supra-sensible world, more real than the common world of sense, the unchangeable world of ideas, which alone gives to the world of sense whatever pale reflection of reality may belong to it. The truly real world, for Plato, is the world of ideas; for whatever we may attempt to say about things in the world of sense, we can only succeed in saying that they participate in such and such ideas, which, therefore, constitute all their character. Hence it is easy to pass on into a mysticism.

47

We may hope, in a mystic illumination, to see the ideas as we see objects of sense; and we may imagine that the ideas exist in heaven. These mystical developments are very natural, but the basis of the theory is in logic, and it is as based in logic that we have to consider it.

The word 'idea' has acquired, in the course of time, many associations which are quite misleading when applied to Plato's 'ideas'. We shall therefore use the word 'universal' instead of the word 'idea', to describe what Plato meant. The essence of the sort of entity that Plato meant is that it is opposed to the particular things that are given in sensation. We speak of whatever is given in sensation, or is of the same nature as things given in sensation, as a *particular*; by opposition to this, a *universal* will be anything which may be shared by many particulars, and has those characteristics which, as we saw, distinguish justice and whiteness from just acts and white things.

When we examine common words, we find that, broadly speaking, proper names stand for particulars, while other substantives, adjectives, prepositions, and verbs stand for universals. Pronouns stand for particulars, but are ambiguous: it is only by the context or the circumstances that we know what particulars they stand for. The word 'now' stands for a particular, namely the present moment; but like pronouns, it stands for an ambiguous particular, because the present is always changing.

It will be seen that no sentence can be made up without at least one word which denotes a universal. The nearest approach would be some such statement as 'I like this'. But even here the word 'like' denotes a universal, for I may like other things, and other people may like things. Thus all truths involve universals, and all knowledge of truths involves acquaintance with universals.

Seeing that nearly all the words to be found in the dictionary stand for universals, it is strange that hardly anybody except students of philosophy ever realizes that there are such entities as universals. We do not naturally dwell upon those words in a sentence which do not stand for particulars; and if we are forced to dwell upon a word which stands for a universal, we naturally think of it as standing for some one of the particulars that come under the universal. When, for example, we hear the sentence, 'Charles I's head was cut off', we may naturally enough think of Charles I, of Charles I's head, and of the operation of cutting off *his* head, which are all particulars; but we do not naturally dwell upon what is meant by the word 'head' or the word 'cut', which is a universal: We feel such words to be incomplete and insubstantial; they seem to demand a context before anything can be done with them. Hence we succeed in avoiding all notice of universals as such, until the study of philosophy forces them upon our attention.

Even among philosophers, we may say, broadly, that only those universals which are named by adjectives or substantives have been much or often recognized, while those named by verbs and prepositions have been usually overlooked. This omission has had a very great effect upon philosophy; it is hardly too much to say that most metaphysics, since Spinoza, has been largely determined by it. The way this has occurred is, in outline, as follows: Speaking generally, adjectives and common nouns express qualities or properties of single things, whereas prepositions and verbs tend to express relations between two or more things. Thus the neglect of prepositions and verbs led to the belief that every proposition can be regarded as attributing a property to a single thing, rather than as expressing a relation between two or more things. Hence it was supposed that, ultimately, there can be no such entities as relations between things. Hence either there can be only one thing in the universe, or, if there are many things, they cannot possibly interact in any way, since any interaction would be a relation, and relations are impossible.

The first of these views, advocated by Spinoza and held in our own day by Bradley and many other philosophers, is called *monism*; the second, advocated by Leibniz but not very common nowadays, is called *monadism*, because each of the isolated things is called a *monad*. Both these opposing philosophies, interesting as they are, result, in my opinion, from an undue attention to one sort of universals, namely the sort represented by adjectives and substantives rather than by verbs and prepositions.

As a matter of fact, if any one were anxious to deny altogether that there are such things as universals, we should find that we cannot strictly prove that there are such entities as *qualities*, i.e. the universals represented by adjectives and substantives, whereas we can prove that there must be *relations*, i.e. the sort of universals generally represented by verbs and prepositions. Let us take in illustration the universal *whiteness*. If we believe that there is such a universal, we shall say that things are white because they have the quality of whiteness. This view, however, was strenuously denied by Berkeley and Hume, who have been followed in this by later empiricists. The form which their denial took was to deny that there are such things as 'abstract ideas'. When we want to think of whiteness, they said, we form an image of some particular white thing, and reason concerning this particular, taking care not to deduce anything concerning it which we cannot see to be equally true of any other white thing. As an account of our actual mental processes, this is no doubt largely true. In geometry, for example, when we wish to prove something about all triangles, we draw a particular triangle and reason about it, taking care not to use any characteristic which it does not share with other triangles. The beginner, in order to avoid error, often finds it useful to draw several triangles, as unlike each other as possible, in order to make sure that his reasoning is equally applicable to all of them. But a difficulty emerges as soon as we ask ourselves how we know that a thing is white or a triangle. If we wish to avoid the universals *whiteness* and *triangularity*, we shall choose some particular patch of white or some particular triangle, and say that anything is white or a triangle if it has the right sort of resemblance to our chosen particular. But then the resemblance required will have to be a universal. Since there are many white things, the resemblance must hold between many pairs of particular white things; and this is the characteristic of a universal. It will be useless to say that there is a different resemblance for each pair, for then we shall have to say that these resemblances resemble each other, and thus at last we shall be forced to admit resemblance as a universal. The relation of resemblance, therefore, must be a true universal. And having been forced to admit this universal, we find that it is no longer worth while to invent difficult and unplausible theories to avoid the admission of such universals as whiteness and triangularity.

Berkeley and Hume failed to perceive this refutation of their rejection of 'abstract ideas', because, like their adversaries, they only thought of *qualities*, and altogether ignored *relations* as universals. We have therefore here another respect in which the rationalists appear to have been in the right as against the empiricists, although, owing to the neglect or denial of relations, the deductions made by rationalists were, if anything, more apt to be mistaken than those made by empiricists.

Having now seen that there must be such entities as universals, the next point to be proved is that their being is not merely mental. By this is meant that whatever being belongs to them is independent of their being thought of or in any way apprehended by minds. We have already touched on this subject at the end of the preceding chapter, but we must now consider more fully what sort of being it is that belongs to universals.

Consider such a proposition as 'Edinburgh is north of London'. Here we have a relation between two places, and it seems plain that the relation subsists independently of our knowledge of it. When we come to know that Edinburgh is north of London, we come to know something which has to do only with Edinburgh and London: we do not cause the truth of the proposition by coming to know it, on the contrary we merely apprehend a fact which was there before we knew it. The part of the earth's surface where Edinburgh stands would be north of the part where London stands, even if there were no human being to know about north and south, and even if there were no minds at all in the universe. This is, of course, denied by many philosophers, either for Berkeley's reasons or for Kant's. But we have already considered these reasons, and decided that they are inadequate. We may therefore now assume it to be true that nothing mental is presupposed in the fact that Edinburgh is north of London. But this fact involves the relation 'north of', which is a universal; and it would be impossible for the whole fact to involve nothing mental if the relation 'north of', which is a constituent part of the fact, did involve anything mental. Hence we must admit that the relation, like the terms it relates, is not dependent upon thought, but belongs to the independent world which thought apprehends but does not create.

This conclusion, however, is met by the difficulty that the relation 'north of' does not seem to *exist* in the same sense in which Edinburgh and London exist. If we ask 'Where and when does this relation exist?' the answer must be 'Nowhere and nowhen'. There is no place or time where we can find the relation 'north of'. It does not exist in Edinburgh any more than in London, for it relates the two and is neutral as between them. Nor can we say that it exists at any particular time. Now everything that can be apprehended by the senses or by introspection exists at some particular time. Hence the relation 'north of' is radically different from such things. It is neither in space nor in time, neither material nor mental; yet it is something.

It is largely the very peculiar kind of being that belongs to universals which has led many people to suppose that they are really mental. We can think *of* a universal, and our thinking then exists in a perfectly ordinary sense, like any other mental act. Suppose, for example, that we are thinking of whiteness. Then *in one sense* it may be said that whiteness is 'in our mind'. We have here the same ambiguity as we noted in discussing Berkeley in Chapter IV. In the strict sense, it is not whiteness that is in our mind, but the act of thinking of whiteness. The connected ambiguity in the word 'idea', which we noted at the same time, also causes confusion here. In one sense of this word, namely the sense in which it denotes the *object* of an act of thought, whiteness is an 'idea'. Hence, if the ambiguity is not guarded against, we may come to think that whiteness is an 'idea' in the other sense, i.e. an act of thought; and thus we come to think that whiteness is mental. But in so thinking, we rob it of its essential quality of universality. One man's act of thought is necessarily a different thing from another man's; one man's act of thought at one time is necessarily a different thing from the same man's act of thought at another time. Hence, if whiteness were the thought as opposed to its object, no two different men could think of it, and no one man could think of it twice. That which many different thoughts of whiteness have in common is their *object*, and this object is different from all of them. Thus universals are not thoughts, though when known they are the objects of thoughts.

We shall find it convenient only to speak of things *existing* when they are in time, that is to say, when we can point to some time at which they exist (not excluding the possibility of their existing at all times). Thus thoughts and feelings, minds and physical objects exist. But universals do not exist in this sense; we shall say that they *subsist* or *have being*, where 'being' is opposed to 'existence' as being timeless. The world of universals, therefore, may also be described as the world of being. The world of being is unchangeable, rigid, exact, delightful to the mathematician, the logician, the builder of metaphysical systems, and all who love perfection more than life. The world of existence is fleeting, vague, without sharp boundaries, without any clear plan or arrangement, but it contains all thoughts and feelings, all the data of sense, and all physical objects, everything that can do either good or harm, everything that makes any difference to the value of life and the world. According to our temperaments, we shall prefer the contemplation of the one or of the other. The one we do not prefer will probably seem to us a pale shadow of the one we prefer, and hardly worthy to be regarded as in any sense real. But the truth is that both have the same claim on our impartial attention, both are real, and both are important to the metaphysician. Indeed no sooner have we distinguished the two worlds than it becomes necessary to consider their relations.

But first of all we must examine our knowledge of universals. This consideration will occupy us in the following chapter, where we shall find that it solves the problem of *a priori* knowledge, from which we were first led to consider universals.

51

# CHAPTER X

## On our Knowledge of Universals

In regard to one man's knowledge at a given time, universals, like particulars, may be divided into those known by acquaintance, those known only by description, and those not known either by acquaintance or by description.

Let us consider first the knowledge of universals by acquaintance. It is obvious, to begin with, that we are acquainted with such universals as white, red, black, sweet, sour, loud, hard, etc., i.e. with qualities which are exemplified in sense-data. When we see a white patch, we are acquainted, in the first instance, with the particular patch; but by seeing many white patches, we easily learn to abstract the whiteness which they all have in common, and in learning to do this we are learning to be acquainted with whiteness. A similar process will make us acquainted with any other universal of the same sort. Universals of this sort may be called 'sensible qualities'. They can be apprehended with less effort of abstraction than any others, and they seem less removed from particulars than other universals are.

We come next to relations. The easiest relations to apprehend are those which hold between the different parts of a single complex sense-datum. For example, I can see at a glance the whole of the page on which I am writing; thus the whole page is included in one sense-datum. But I perceive that some parts of the page are to the left of other parts, and some parts are above other parts. The process of abstraction in this case seems to proceed somewhat as follows: I see successively a number of sense-data in which one part is to the left of another; I perceive, as in the case of different white patches, that all these sense-data have something in common, and by abstraction I find that what they have in common is a certain relation between their parts, namely the relation which I call 'being to the left of'. In this way I become acquainted with the universal relation.

In like manner I become aware of the relation of before and after in time. Suppose I hear a chime of bells: when the last bell of the chime sounds, I can retain the whole chime before my mind, and I can perceive that the earlier bells came before the later ones. Also in memory I perceive that what I am remembering came before the present time. From either of these sources I can abstract the universal relation of before and after, just as I abstracted the universal relation 'being to the left of'. Thus time-relations, like space-relations, are among those with which we are acquainted.

Another relation with which we become acquainted in much the same way is resemblance. If I see simultaneously two shades of green, I can see that they resemble each other; if I also see a shade of red: at the same time, I can see that the two greens have more resemblance to each other than either has to the red. In this way I become acquainted with the universal *resemblance* or *similarity*.

Between universals, as between particulars, there are relations of which we may be immediately aware. We have just seen that we can perceive that the resemblance between two shades of green is greater than the resemblance between a shade of red and a shade of green. Here we are dealing with a relation, namely 'greater than', between two relations. Our knowledge of such relations, though it requires more power of abstraction than is required for perceiving the qualities of sense-data, appears to be equally immediate, and (at least in some cases) equally indubitable. Thus there is immediate knowledge concerning universals as well as concerning sense-data.

Returning now to the problem of *a priori* knowledge, which we left unsolved when we began the consideration of universals, we find ourselves in a position to deal with it in a much more satisfactory manner than was possible before. Let us revert to the proposition 'two and two are four'. It is fairly obvious, in view of what has been said, that this proposition states a relation between the universal 'two' and the universal 'four'. This suggests a proposition which we shall now endeavour to establish: namely, *All a priori knowledge deals exclusively with the relations of universals.* This proposition is of great importance, and goes a long way towards solving our previous difficulties concerning *a priori* knowledge.

The only case in which it might seem, at first sight, as if our proposition were untrue, is the case in which an *a priori* proposition states that *all* of one class of particulars belong to some other class, or (what comes to the same thing) that *all* particulars having some one property also have some other. In this case it might seem as though we were dealing with the particulars that have the property rather than with the property. The proposition 'two and two are four' is really a case in point, for this may be stated in the form 'any two and any other two are four', or 'any collection formed of two twos is a collection of four'. If we can show that such statements as this really deal only with universals, our proposition may be regarded as proved.

One way of discovering what a proposition deals with is to ask ourselves what words we must understand—in other words, what objects we must be acquainted with—in order to see what the proposition means. As soon as we see what the proposition means, even if we do not yet know whether it is true or false, it is evident that we must have acquaintance with whatever is really dealt with by the proposition. By applying this test, it appears that many propositions which might seem to be concerned with particulars are really concerned only with universals. In the special case of 'two and two are four', even when we interpret it as meaning 'any collection formed of two twos is a collection of four', it is plain that we can understand the proposition, i.e. we can see what it is that it asserts, as soon as we know what is meant by 'collection' and 'two' and 'four'. It is quite unnecessary to know all the couples in the world: if it were necessary, obviously we could never understand the proposition, since the couples are infinitely numerous and therefore cannot all be known to us. Thus although our general statement *implies* statements about particular couples, *as soon as we know that there are such particular couples*, yet it does not itself assert or imply that there are such particular couples, and thus fails to make any statement whatever about any actual particular couple. The statement made is about 'couple', the universal, and not about this or that couple.

Thus the statement 'two and two are four' deals exclusively with universals, and therefore may be known by anybody who is acquainted with the universals concerned and can perceive the relation between them which the statement asserts. It must be taken as a fact, discovered by reflecting upon our knowledge, that we have the power of sometimes perceiving such relations between universals, and therefore of sometimes knowing general *a priori* propositions such as those of arithmetic and logic. The thing that seemed mysterious, when we formerly considered such knowledge, was that it seemed to anticipate and control experience. This, however, we can now see to have been an error. *No* fact concerning anything capable of being experienced can be known independently of experience. We know *a priori* that two things and two other things together make four things, but we do *not* know *a priori* that if Brown and Jones are two, and Robinson and Smith are two, then Brown and Jones and Robinson and Smith are four. The reason is that this proposition cannot be understood at all unless we know that there are such people as Brown and Jones and Robinson and Smith, and this we can only know by experience. Hence, although our general proposition is *a priori*, all its applications to actual particulars involve experience and therefore contain an empirical element. In this way what seemed mysterious in our *a priori* knowledge is seen to have been based upon an error.

It will serve to make the point clearer if we contrast our genuine *a priori* judgement with an empirical generalization, such as 'all men are mortals'. Here as before, we can *understand* what the proposition means as soon as we understand the universals involved, namely *man* and *mortal*. It is obviously unnecessary to have an individual acquaintance with the whole human race in order to understand what our proposition means. Thus the difference between an *a priori* general proposition and an empirical generalization does not come in the *meaning* of the proposition; it comes in the nature of the *evidence* for it. In the empirical case, the evidence consists in the particular instances. We believe that all men are mortal because we know that there are innumerable instances of men dying, and no instances of their living beyond a certain age. We do not believe it because we see a connexion between the universal *man* and the universal *mortal*. It is true that if physiology can prove, assuming the general laws that govern living bodies, that no living organism can last for ever, that gives a connexion between *man* and *mortality* which would enable us to assert our proposition without appealing to the special evidence of *men* dying. But that only means that our generalization has been subsumed under a wider generalization, for which the evidence is still of the same kind, though more extensive. The progress of science is constantly producing such subsumptions, and therefore giving a constantly wider inductive basis for scientific generalizations. But although this gives a greater *degree* of certainty, it does not give a different *kind*: the ultimate ground remains inductive, i.e. derived from instances, and not an *a priori* connexion of universals such as we have in logic and arithmetic.

Two opposite points are to be observed concerning *a priori* general propositions. The first is that, if many particular instances are known, our general proposition may be arrived at in the first instance by induction, and the connexion of universals may be only subsequently perceived. For example, it is known that if we draw perpendiculars to the sides of a triangle from the opposite angles, all three perpendiculars meet in a point. It would be quite possible to be first led to this proposition by actually drawing perpendiculars in many cases, and finding that they always met in a point; this experience might lead us to look for the general proof and find it. Such cases are common in the experience of every mathematician.

The other point is more interesting, and of more philosophical importance. It is, that we may sometimes know a general proposition in cases where we do not know a single instance of it. Take such a case as the following: We know that any two numbers can be multiplied together, and will give a third called their *product*. We know that all pairs of integers the product of which is less than 100 have been actually multiplied together, and the value of the product recorded in the multiplication table. But we also know that the number of integers is infinite, and that only a finite number of pairs of integers ever have been or ever will be thought of by human beings. Hence it follows that there are pairs of integers which never have been and never will be thought of by human beings, and that all of them deal with integers the product of which is over 100. Hence we arrive at the proposition: 'All products of two integers, which never have been and never will be thought of by any human being, are over 100.' Here is a general proposition of which the truth is undeniable, and yet, from the very nature of the case, we can never give an instance; because any two numbers we may think of are excluded by the terms of the proposition.

This possibility, of knowledge of general propositions of which no instance can be given, is often denied, because it is not perceived that the knowledge of such propositions only requires a knowledge of the relations of universals, and does not require any knowledge of instances of the universals in question. Yet the knowledge of such general propositions is quite vital to a great deal of what is generally admitted to be known. For example, we saw, in our early chapters, that knowledge of physical objects, as opposed to sense-data, is only obtained by an inference, and that they are not things with which we are acquainted. Hence we can never know any proposition of the form 'this is a physical object', where 'this' is something immediately known. It follows that all our knowledge concerning physical objects is such that no actual instance can be given. We can give instances of the associated sense-data, but we cannot give instances of the actual physical objects. Hence our knowledge as to physical objects depends throughout upon this possibility of general knowledge where no instance can be given. And the same applies to our knowledge of other people's minds, or of any other class of things of which no instance is known to us by acquaintance.

We may now take a survey of the sources of our knowledge, as they have appeared in the course of our analysis. We have first to distinguish knowledge of things and knowledge of truths. In each there are two kinds, one immediate and one derivative. Our immediate knowledge of things, which we called *acquaintance*, consists of two sorts, according as the things known are particulars or universals. Among particulars, we have acquaintance with sense-data and (probably) with ourselves. Among universals, there seems to be no principle by which we can decide which can be known by acquaintance, but it is clear that among those that can be so known are sensible qualities, relations of space and time, similarity, and certain abstract logical universals. Our derivative knowledge of things, which we call knowledge by *description*, always involves both acquaintance with something and knowledge of truths. Our immediate knowledge of *truths* may be called *intuitive* knowledge, and the truths so known may be called *self-evident* truths. Among such truths are included those which merely state what is given in sense, and also certain abstract logical and arithmetical principles, and (though with less certainty) some ethical propositions. Our *derivative* knowledge of truths consists of everything that we can deduce from self-evident truths by the use of self-evident principles of deduction.

If the above account is correct, all our knowledge of truths depends upon our intuitive knowledge. It therefore becomes important to consider the nature and scope of intuitive knowledge, in much the same way as, at an earlier stage, we considered the nature and scope of knowledge by acquaintance. But knowledge of truths raises a further problem, which does not arise in regard to knowledge of things, namely the problem of *error*. Some of our beliefs turn out to be erroneous, and therefore it becomes necessary to consider how, if at all, we can distinguish knowledge from error. This problem does not arise with regard to knowledge by acquaintance, for, whatever may be the object of acquaintance, even in dreams and hallucinations, there is no error involved so long as we do not go beyond the immediate object: error can only arise when we regard the immediate object, i.e. the sense-datum, as the mark of some physical object. Thus the problems connected with knowledge of truths are more difficult than those connected with knowledge of things. As the first of the problems connected with knowledge of truths, let us examine the nature and scope of our intuitive judgements.

# CHAPTER XI

## On Intuitive Knowledge

There is a common impression that everything that we believe ought to be capable of proof, or at least of being shown to be highly probable. It is felt by many that a belief for which no reason can be given is an unreasonable belief. In the main, this view is just. Almost all our common beliefs are either inferred, or capable of being inferred, from other beliefs which may be regarded as giving the reason for them. As a rule, the reason has been forgotten, or has even never been consciously present to our minds. Few of us ever ask ourselves, for example, what reason there is to suppose the food we are just going to eat will not turn out to be poison. Yet we feel, when challenged, that a perfectly good reason could be found, even if we are not ready with it at the moment. And in this belief we are usually justified.

But let us imagine some insistent Socrates, who, whatever reason we give him, continues to demand a reason for the reason. We must sooner or later, and probably before very long, be driven to a point where we cannot find any further reason, and where it becomes almost certain that no further reason is even theoretically discoverable. Starting with the common beliefs of daily life, we can be driven back from point to point, until we come to some general principle, or some instance of a general principle, which seems luminously evident, and is not itself capable of being deduced from anything more evident. In most questions of daily life, such as whether our food is likely to be nourishing and not poisonous, we shall be driven back to the inductive principle, which we discussed in Chapter VI. But beyond that, there seems to be no further regress. The principle itself is constantly used in our reasoning, sometimes consciously, sometimes unconsciously; but there is no reasoning which, starting from some simpler self-evident principle, leads us to the principle of induction as its conclusion. And the same holds for other logical principles. Their truth is evident to us, and we employ them in constructing demonstrations; but they themselves, or at least some of them, are incapable of demonstration.

Self-evidence, however, is not confined to those among general principles which are incapable of proof. When a certain number of logical principles have been admitted, the rest can be deduced from them; but the propositions deduced are often just as self-evident as those that were assumed without proof. All arithmetic, moreover, can be deduced from the general principles of logic, yet the simple propositions of arithmetic, such as 'two and two are four', are just as self-evident as the principles of logic.

It would seem, also, though this is more disputable, that there are some self-evident ethical principles, such as 'we ought to pursue what is good'.

It should be observed that, in all cases of general principles, particular instances, dealing with familiar things, are more evident than the general principle. For example, the law of contradiction states that nothing can both have a certain property and not have it. This is evident as soon as it is understood, but it is not so evident as that a particular rose which we see cannot be both red and not red. (It is of course possible that parts of the rose may be red and parts not red, or that the rose may be of a shade of pink which we hardly know whether to call red or not; but in the former case it is plain that the rose as a whole is not red, while in the latter case the answer is theoretically definite as soon as we have decided on a precise definition of 'red'.) It is usually through particular instances that we come to be able to see the general principle. Only those who are practised in dealing with abstractions can readily grasp a general principle without the help of instances.

In addition to general principles, the other kind of self-evident truths are those immediately derived from sensation. We will call such truths 'truths of perception', and the judgements expressing them we will call 'judgements of perception'. But here a certain amount of care is required in getting at the precise nature of the truths that are self-evident. The actual sense-data are neither true nor false. A particular patch of colour which I see, for example, simply exists: it is not the sort of thing that is true or false. It is true that there is such a patch, true that it has a certain shape and degree of brightness, true that it is surrounded by certain other colours. But the patch itself, like everything else in the world of sense, is of a radically different kind from the things that are true or false, and therefore cannot properly be said to be *true*. Thus whatever self-evident truths may be obtained from our senses must be different from the sense-data from which they are obtained.

It would seem that there are two kinds of self-evident truths of perception, though perhaps in the last analysis the two kinds may coalesce. First, there is the kind which simply asserts the *existence* of the sense-datum, without in any way analysing it. We see a patch of red, and we judge 'there is such-and-such a patch of red', or more strictly 'there is that'; this is one kind of intuitive judgement of perception. The other kind arises when the object of sense is complex, and we subject it to some degree of analysis. If, for instance, we see a *round* patch of red, we may judge 'that patch of red is round'. This is again a judgement of perception, but it differs from our previous kind. In our present kind we have a single sense-datum which has both colour and shape: the colour is red and the shape is round. Our judgement analyses the datum into colour and shape, and then recombines them by stating that the red colour is round in shape. Another example of this kind of judgement is 'this is to the right of that', where 'this' and 'that' are seen simultaneously. In this kind of judgement the sense-datum contains constituents which have some relation to each other, and the judgement asserts that these constituents have this relation.

Another class of intuitive judgements, analogous to those of sense and yet quite distinct from them, are judgements of *memory*. There is some danger of confusion as to the nature of memory, owing to the fact that memory of an object is apt to be accompanied by an image of the object, and yet the image cannot be what constitutes memory. This is easily seen by merely noticing that the image is in the present, whereas what is remembered is known to be in the past. Moreover, we are certainly able to some extent to compare our image with the object remembered, so that we often know, within somewhat wide limits, how far our image is accurate; but this would be impossible, unless the object, as opposed to the image, were in some way before the mind. Thus the essence of memory is not constituted by the image, but by having immediately before the mind an object which is recognized as past. But for the fact of memory in this sense, we should not know that there ever was a past at all, nor should we be able to understand the word 'past', any more than a man born blind can understand the word 'light'. Thus there must be intuitive judgements of memory, and it is upon them, ultimately, that all our knowledge of the past depends.

The case of memory, however, raises a difficulty, for it is notoriously fallacious, and thus throws doubt on the trustworthiness of intuitive judgements in general. This difficulty is no light one. But let us first narrow its scope as far as possible. Broadly speaking, memory is trustworthy in proportion to the vividness of the experience and to its nearness in time. If the house next door was struck by lightning half a minute ago, my memory of what I saw and heard will be so reliable that it would be preposterous to doubt whether there had been a flash at all. And the same applies to less vivid experiences, so long as they are recent. I am absolutely certain that half a minute ago I was sitting in the same chair in which I am sitting now. Going backward over the day, I find things of which I am quite certain, other things of which I am almost certain, other things of which I can become certain by thought and by calling up attendant circumstances, and some things of which I am by no means certain. I am quite certain that I ate my breakfast this morning, but if I were as indifferent to my breakfast as a philosopher should be, I should be doubtful. As to the conversation at breakfast, I can recall some of it easily, some with an effort, some only with a large element of doubt, and some not at all. Thus there is a continual gradation in the degree of self-evidence of what I remember, and a corresponding gradation in the trustworthiness of my memory.

Thus the first answer to the difficulty of fallacious memory is to say that memory has degrees of self-evidence, and that these correspond to the degrees of its trustworthiness, reaching a limit of perfect self-evidence and perfect trustworthiness in our memory of events which are recent and vivid.

It would seem, however, that there are cases of very firm belief in a memory which is wholly false. It is probable that, in these cases, what is really remembered, in the sense of being immediately before the mind, is something other than what is falsely believed in, though something generally associated with it. George IV is said to have at last believed that he was at the battle of Waterloo, because he had so often said that he was. In this case, what was immediately remembered was his repeated assertion; the belief in what he was asserting (if it existed) would be produced by association with the remembered assertion, and would therefore not be a genuine case of memory. It would seem that cases of fallacious memory can probably all be dealt with in this way, i.e. they can be shown to be not cases of memory in the strict sense at all.

One important point about self-evidence is made clear by the case of memory, and that is, that self-evidence has degrees: it is not a quality which is simply present or absent, but a quality which may be more or less present, in gradations ranging from absolute certainty down to an almost imperceptible faintness. Truths of perception and some of the principles of logic have the very highest degree of self-evidence; truths of immediate memory have an almost equally high degree. The inductive principle has less self-evidence than some of the other principles of logic, such as 'what follows from a true premiss must be true'. Memories have a diminishing self-evidence as they become remoter and fainter; the truths of logic and mathematics have (broadly speaking) less self-evidence as they become more complicated. Judgements of intrinsic ethical or aesthetic value are apt to have some self-evidence, but not much.

Degrees of self-evidence are important in the theory of knowledge, since, if propositions may (as seems likely) have some degree of self-evidence without being true, it will not be necessary to abandon all connexion between self-evidence and truth, but merely to say that, where there is a conflict, the more self-evident proposition is to be retained and the less self-evident rejected.

It seems, however, highly probable that two different notions are combined in 'self-evidence' as above explained; that one of them, which corresponds to the highest degree of self-evidence, is really an infallible guarantee of truth, while the other, which corresponds to all the other degrees, does not give an infallible guarantee, but only a greater or less presumption. This, however, is only a suggestion, which we cannot as yet develop further. After we have dealt with the nature of truth, we shall return to the subject of self-evidence, in connexion with the distinction between knowledge and error.

# CHAPTER XII

## Truth and Falsehood

Our knowledge of truths, unlike our knowledge of things, has an opposite, namely *error*. So far as things are concerned, we may know them or not know them, but there is no positive state of mind which can be described as erroneous knowledge of things, so long, at any rate, as we confine ourselves to knowledge by acquaintance. Whatever we are acquainted with must be something; we may draw wrong inferences from our acquaintance, but the acquaintance itself cannot be deceptive. Thus there is no dualism as regards acquaintance. But as regards knowledge of truths, there is a dualism. We may believe what is false as well as what is true. We know that on very many subjects different people hold different and incompatible opinions: hence some beliefs must be erroneous. Since erroneous beliefs are often held just as strongly as true beliefs, it becomes a difficult question how they are to be distinguished from true beliefs. How are we to know, in a given case, that our belief is not erroneous? This is a question of the very greatest difficulty, to which no completely satisfactory answer is possible. There is, however, a preliminary question which is rather less difficult, and that is: What do we *mean* by truth and falsehood? It is this preliminary question which is to be considered in this chapter. In this chapter we are not asking how we can know whether a belief is true or false: we are asking what is meant by the question whether a belief is true or false. It is to be hoped that a clear answer to this question may help us to obtain an answer to the question what beliefs are true, but for the present we ask only 'What is truth?' and 'What is falsehood?' not 'What beliefs are true?' and 'What beliefs are false?' It is very important to keep these different questions entirely separate, since any confusion between them is sure to produce an answer which is not really applicable to either.

There are three points to observe in the attempt to discover the nature of truth, three requisites which any theory must fulfil.

(1) Our theory of truth must be such as to admit of its opposite, falsehood. A good many philosophers have failed adequately to satisfy this condition: they have constructed theories according to which all our thinking ought to have been true, and have then had the greatest difficulty in finding a place for falsehood. In this respect our theory of belief must differ from our theory of acquaintance, since in the case of acquaintance it was not necessary to take account of any opposite.

(2) It seems fairly evident that if there were no beliefs there could be no falsehood, and no truth either, in the sense in which truth is correlative to falsehood. If we imagine a world of mere matter, there would be no room for falsehood in such a world, and although it would contain what may be called 'facts', it would not contain any truths, in the sense in which truths are things of the same kind as falsehoods. In fact, truth and falsehood are properties of beliefs and statements: hence a world of mere matter, since it would contain no beliefs or statements, would also contain no truth or falsehood.

(3) But, as against what we have just said, it is to be observed that the truth or falsehood of a belief always depends upon something which lies outside the belief itself. If I believe that Charles I died on the scaffold, I believe truly, not because of any intrinsic quality of my belief, which could be discovered by merely examining the belief, but because of an historical event which happened two and a half centuries ago. If I believe that Charles I died in his bed, I believe falsely: no degree of vividness in my belief, or of care in arriving at it, prevents it from being false, again because of what happened long ago, and not because of any intrinsic property of my belief. Hence, although truth and falsehood are properties of beliefs, they are properties dependent upon the relations of the beliefs to other things, not upon any internal quality of the beliefs.

The third of the above requisites leads us to adopt the view—which has on the whole been commonest among philosophers—that truth consists in some form of correspondence between belief and fact. It is, however, by no means an easy matter to discover a form of correspondence to which there are no irrefutable objections. By this partly—and partly by the feeling that, if truth consists in a correspondence of thought with something outside thought, thought can never know when truth has been attained—many philosophers have been led to try to find some definition of truth which shall not consist in relation to something wholly outside belief. The most important attempt at a definition of this sort is the theory that truth consists in *coherence*. It is said that the mark of falsehood is failure to cohere in the body of our beliefs, and that it is the essence of a truth to form part of the completely rounded system which is The Truth.

There is, however, a great difficulty in this view, or rather two great difficulties. The first is that there is no reason to suppose that only *one* coherent body of beliefs is possible. It may be that, with sufficient imagination, a novelist might invent a past for the world that would perfectly fit on to what we know, and yet be quite different from the real past. In more scientific matters, it is certain that there are often two or more hypotheses which account for all the known facts on some subject, and although, in such cases, men of science endeavour to find facts which will rule out all the hypotheses except one, there is no reason why they should always succeed.

In philosophy, again, it seems not uncommon for two rival hypotheses to be both able to account for all the facts. Thus, for example, it is possible that life is one long dream, and that the outer world has only that degree of reality that the objects of dreams have; but although such a view does not seem inconsistent with known facts, there is no reason to prefer it to the common-sense view, according to which other people and things do really exist. Thus coherence as the definition of truth fails because there is no proof that there can be only one coherent system.

The other objection to this definition of truth is that it assumes the meaning of 'coherence' known, whereas, in fact, 'coherence' presupposes the truth of the laws of logic. Two propositions are coherent when both may be true, and are incoherent when one at least must be false. Now in order to know whether two propositions can both be true, we must know such truths as the law of contradiction. For example, the two propositions, 'this tree is a beech' and 'this tree is not a beech', are not coherent, because of the law of contradiction. But if the law of contradiction itself were subjected to the test of coherence, we should find that, if we choose to suppose it false, nothing will any longer be incoherent with anything else. Thus the laws of logic supply the skeleton or framework within which the test of coherence applies, and they themselves cannot be established by this test.

For the above two reasons, coherence cannot be accepted as giving the *meaning* of truth, though it is often a most important *test* of truth after a certain amount of truth has become known.

Hence we are driven back to *correspondence with fact* as constituting the nature of truth. It remains to define precisely what we mean by 'fact', and what is the nature of the correspondence which must subsist between belief and fact, in order that belief may be true.

In accordance with our three requisites, we have to seek a theory of truth which (1) allows truth to have an opposite, namely falsehood, (2) makes truth a property of beliefs, but (3) makes it a property wholly dependent upon the relation of the beliefs to outside things.

The necessity of allowing for falsehood makes it impossible to regard belief as a relation of the mind to a single object, which could be said to be what is believed. If belief were so regarded, we should find that, like acquaintance, it would not admit of the opposition of truth and falsehood, but would have to be always true. This may be made clear by examples. Othello believes falsely that Desdemona loves Cassio. We cannot say that this belief consists in a relation to a single object, 'Desdemona's love for Cassio', for if there were such an object, the belief would be true. There is in fact no such object, and therefore Othello cannot have any relation to such an object. Hence his belief cannot possibly consist in a relation to this object.

It might be said that his belief is a relation to a different object, namely 'that Desdemona loves Cassio'; but it is almost as difficult to suppose that there is such an object as this, when Desdemona does not love Cassio, as it was to suppose that there is 'Desdemona's love for Cassio'. Hence it will be better to seek for a theory of belief which does not make it consist in a relation of the mind to a single object.

It is common to think of relations as though they always held between two terms, but in fact this is not always the case. Some relations demand three terms, some four, and so on. Take, for instance, the relation 'between'. So long as only two terms come in, the relation 'between' is impossible: three terms are the smallest number that render it possible. York is between London and Edinburgh; but if London and Edinburgh were the only places in the world, there could be nothing which was between one place and another. Similarly *jealousy* requires three people: there can be no such relation that does not involve three at least. Such a proposition as 'A wishes B to promote C's marriage with D' involves a relation of four terms; that is to say, A and B and C and D all come in, and the relation involved cannot be expressed otherwise than in a form involving all four. Instances might be multiplied indefinitely, but enough has been said to show that there are relations which require more than two terms before they can occur.

The relation involved in *judging* or *believing* must, if falsehood is to be duly allowed for, be taken to be a relation between several terms, not between two. When Othello believes that Desdemona loves Cassio, he must not have before his mind a single object, 'Desdemona's love for Cassio', or 'that Desdemona loves Cassio ', for that would require that there should be objective falsehoods, which subsist independently of any minds; and this, though not logically refutable, is a theory to be avoided if possible. Thus it is easier to account for falsehood if we take judgement to be a relation in which the mind and the various objects concerned all occur severally; that is to say, Desdemona and loving and Cassio must all be terms in the relation which subsists when Othello believes that Desdemona loves Cassio. This relation, therefore, is a relation of four terms, since Othello also is one of the terms of the relation. When we say that it is a relation of four terms, we do not mean that Othello has a certain relation to Desdemona, and has the same relation to loving and also to Cassio. This may be true of some other relation than believing; but believing, plainly, is not a relation which Othello has to *each* of the three terms concerned, but to *all* of them together: there is only one example of the relation of believing involved, but this one example knits together four terms. Thus the actual occurrence, at the moment when Othello is entertaining his belief, is that the relation called 'believing' is knitting together into one complex whole the four terms Othello, Desdemona, loving, and Cassio. What is called belief or judgement is nothing but this relation of believing or judging, which relates a mind to several things other than itself. An *act* of belief or of judgement is the occurrence between certain terms at some particular time, of the relation of believing or judging.

We are now in a position to understand what it is that distinguishes a true judgement from a false one. For this purpose we will adopt certain definitions. In every act of judgement there is a mind which judges, and there are terms concerning which it judges. We will call the mind the *subject* in the judgement, and the remaining terms the *objects*. Thus, when Othello judges that Desdemona loves Cassio, Othello is the subject, while the objects are Desdemona and loving and Cassio. The subject and the objects together are called the *constituents* of the judgement. It will be observed that the relation of judging has what is called a 'sense' or 'direction'. We may say, metaphorically, that it puts its objects in a certain *order*, which we may indicate by means of the order of the words in the sentence. (In an inflected language, the same thing will be indicated by inflections, e.g. by the difference between nominative and accusative.) Othello's judgement that Cassio loves Desdemona differs from his judgement that Desdemona loves Cassio, in spite of the fact that it consists of the same constituents, because the relation of judging places the constituents in a different order in the two cases. Similarly, if Cassio judges that Desdemona loves Othello, the constituents of the judgement are still the same, but their order is different. This property of having a 'sense' or 'direction' is one which the relation of judging shares with all other relations. The 'sense' of relations is the ultimate source of order and series and a host of mathematical concepts; but we need not concern ourselves further with this aspect.

We spoke of the relation called 'judging' or 'believing' as knitting together into one complex whole the subject and the objects. In this respect, judging is exactly like every other relation. Whenever a relation holds between two or more terms, it unites the terms into a complex whole. If Othello loves Desdemona, there is such a complex whole as 'Othello's love for Desdemona'. The terms united by the relation may be themselves complex, or may be simple, but the whole which results from their being united must be complex. Wherever there is a relation which relates certain terms, there is a complex object formed of the union of those terms; and conversely, wherever there is a complex object, there is a relation which relates its constituents. When an act of believing occurs, there is a complex, in which 'believing' is the uniting relation, and subject and objects are arranged in a certain order by the 'sense' of the relation of believing. Among the objects, as we saw in considering 'Othello believes that Desdemona loves Cassio', one must be a relation—in this instance, the relation 'loving'. But this relation, as it occurs in the act of believing, is not the relation which creates the unity of the complex whole consisting of the subject and the objects. The relation 'loving', as it occurs in the act of believing, is one of the objects—it is a brick in the structure, not the cement. The cement is the relation 'believing'. When the belief is *true*, there is another complex unity, in which the relation which was one of the objects of the belief relates the other objects. Thus, e.g., if Othello believes *truly* that Desdemona loves Cassio, then there is a complex unity, 'Desdemona's love for Cassio', which is composed exclusively of the *objects* of the belief, in the same order as they had in the belief, with the relation which was one of the objects occurring now as the cement that binds together the other objects of the belief. On the other hand, when a belief is *false*, there is no such complex unity composed only of the objects of the belief. If Othello believes *falsely* that Desdemona loves Cassio, then there is no such complex unity as 'Desdemona's love for Cassio'.

Thus a belief is *true* when it *corresponds* to a certain associated complex, and *false* when it does not. Assuming, for the sake of definiteness, that the objects of the belief are two terms and a relation, the terms being put in a certain order by the 'sense' of the believing, then if the two terms in that order are united by the relation into a complex, the belief is true; if not, it is false. This constitutes the definition of truth and falsehood that we were in search of. Judging or believing is a certain complex unity of which a mind is a constituent; if the remaining constituents, taken in the order which they have in the belief, form a complex unity, then the belief is true; if not, it is false.

Thus although truth and falsehood are properties of beliefs, yet they are in a sense extrinsic properties, for the condition of the truth of a belief is something not involving beliefs, or (in general) any mind at all, but only the *objects* of the belief. A mind, which believes, believes truly when there is a *corresponding* complex not involving the mind, but only its objects. This correspondence ensures truth, and its absence entails falsehood. Hence we account simultaneously for the two facts that beliefs (a) depend on minds for their *existence*, (b) do not depend on minds for their *truth*.

We may restate our theory as follows: If we take such a belief as 'Othello believes that Desdemona loves Cassio', we will call Desdemona and Cassio the *object-terms*, and loving the *object-relation*. If there is a complex unity 'Desdemona's love for Cassio', consisting of the object-terms related by the object-relation in the same order as they have in the belief, then this complex unity is called the *fact corresponding to the belief*. Thus a belief is true when there is a corresponding fact, and is false when there is no corresponding fact.

It will be seen that minds do not *create* truth or falsehood. They create beliefs, but when once the beliefs are created, the mind cannot make them true or false, except in the special case where they concern future things which are within the power of the person believing, such as catching trains. What makes a belief true is a *fact*, and this fact does not (except in exceptional cases) in any way involve the mind of the person who has the belief.

Having now decided what we *mean* by truth and falsehood, we have next to consider what ways there are of knowing whether this or that belief is true or false. This consideration will occupy the next chapter.

# CHAPTER XIII

## Knowledge, Error, and Probable Opinion

The question as to what we mean by truth and falsehood, which we considered in the preceding chapter, is of much less interest than the question as to how we can know what is true and what is false. This question will occupy us in the present chapter. There can be no doubt that *some* of our beliefs are erroneous; thus we are led to inquire what certainty we can ever have that such and such a belief is not erroneous. In other words, can we ever *know* anything at all, or do we merely sometimes by good luck believe what is true? Before we can attack this question, we must, however, first decide what we mean by 'knowing', and this question is not so easy as might be supposed.

At first sight we might imagine that knowledge could be defined as 'true belief'. When what we believe is true, it might be supposed that we had achieved a knowledge of what we believe. But this would not accord with the way in which the word is commonly used. To take a very trivial instance: If a man believes that the late Prime Minister's last name began with a B, he believes what is true, since the late Prime Minister was Sir Henry Campbell Bannerman. But if he believes that Mr. Balfour was the late Prime Minister, he will still believe that the late Prime Minister's last name began with a B, yet this belief, though true, would not be thought to constitute knowledge. If a newspaper, by an intelligent anticipation, announces the result of a battle before any telegram giving the result has been received, it may by good fortune announce what afterwards turns out to be the right result, and it may produce belief in some of its less experienced readers. But in spite of the truth of their belief, they cannot be said to have knowledge. Thus it is clear that a true belief is not knowledge when it is deduced from a false belief.

In like manner, a true belief cannot be called knowledge when it is deduced by a fallacious process of reasoning, even if the premises from which it is deduced are true. If I know that all Greeks are men and that Socrates was a man, and I infer that Socrates was a Greek, I cannot be said to *know* that Socrates was a Greek, because, although my premises and my conclusion are true, the conclusion does not follow from the premises.

But are we to say that nothing is knowledge except what is validly deduced from true premises? Obviously we cannot say this. Such a definition is at once too wide and too narrow. In the first place, it is too wide, because it is not enough that our premisses should be *true*, they must also be *known*. The man who believes that Mr. Balfour was the late Prime Minister may proceed to draw valid deductions from the true premiss that the late Prime Minister's name began with a B, but he cannot be said to *know* the conclusions reached by these deductions. Thus we shall have to amend our definition by saying that knowledge is what is validly deduced from *known* premisses. This, however, is a circular definition: it assumes that we already know what is meant by 'known premisses'. It can, therefore, at best define one sort of knowledge, the sort we call derivative, as opposed to intuitive knowledge. We may say: '*Derivative* knowledge is what is validly deduced from premisses known intuitively'. In this statement there is no formal defect, but it leaves the definition of *intuitive* knowledge still to seek.

Leaving on one side, for the moment, the question of intuitive knowledge, let us consider the above suggested definition of derivative knowledge. The chief objection to it is that it unduly limits knowledge. It constantly happens that people entertain a true belief, which has grown up in them because of some piece of intuitive knowledge from which it is capable of being validly inferred, but from which it has not, as a matter of fact, been inferred by any logical process.

Take, for example, the beliefs produced by reading. If the newspapers announce the death of the King, we are fairly well justified in believing that the King is dead, since this is the sort of announcement which would not be made if it were false. And we are quite amply justified in believing that the newspaper asserts that the King is dead. But here the intuitive knowledge upon which our belief is based is knowledge of the existence of sense-data derived from looking at the print which gives the news. This knowledge scarcely rises into consciousness, except in a person who cannot read easily. A child may be aware of the shapes of the letters, and pass gradually and painfully to a realization of their meaning. But anybody accustomed to reading passes at once to what the letters mean, and is not aware, except on reflection, that he has derived this knowledge from the sense-data called seeing the printed letters. Thus although a valid inference from the-letters to their meaning is possible, and *could* be performed by the reader, it is not in fact performed, since he does not in fact perform any operation which can be called logical inference. Yet it would be absurd to say that the reader does not *know* that the newspaper announces the King's death.

We must, therefore, admit as derivative knowledge whatever is the result of intuitive knowledge even if by mere association, provided there *is* a valid logical connexion, and the person in question could become aware of this connexion by reflection. There are in fact many ways, besides logical inference, by which we pass from one belief to another: the passage from the print to its meaning illustrates these ways. These ways may be called 'psychological inference'. We shall, then, admit such psychological inference as a means of obtaining derivative knowledge, provided there is a discoverable logical inference which runs parallel to the psychological inference. This renders our definition of derivative knowledge less precise than we could wish, since the word 'discoverable' is vague: it does not tell us how much reflection may be needed in order to make the discovery. But in fact 'knowledge' is not a precise conception: it merges into 'probable opinion', as we shall see more fully in the course of the present chapter. A very precise definition, therefore, should not be sought, since any such definition must be more or less misleading.

The chief difficulty in regard to knowledge, however, does not arise over derivative knowledge, but over intuitive knowledge. So long as we are dealing with derivative knowledge, we have the test of intuitive knowledge to fall back upon. But in regard to intuitive beliefs, it is by no means easy to discover any criterion by which to distinguish some as true and others as erroneous. In this question it is scarcely possible to reach any very precise result: all our knowledge of truths is infected with some degree of doubt, and a theory which ignored this fact would be plainly wrong. Something may be done, however, to mitigate the difficulties of the question.

Our theory of truth, to begin with, supplies the possibility of distinguishing certain truths as *self-evident* in a sense which ensures infallibility. When a belief is true, we said, there is a corresponding fact, in which the several objects of the belief form a single complex. The belief is said to constitute *knowledge* of this fact, provided it fulfils those further somewhat vague conditions which we have been considering in the present chapter. But in regard to any fact, besides the knowledge constituted by belief, we may also have the kind of knowledge constituted by *perception* (taking this word in its widest possible sense). For example, if you know the hour of the sunset, you can at that hour know the fact that the sun is setting: this is knowledge of the fact by way of knowledge of *truths*; but you can also, if the weather is fine, look to the west and actually see the setting sun: you then know the same fact by the way of knowledge of *things*.

Thus in regard to any complex fact, there are, theoretically, two ways in which it may be known: (1) by means of a judgement, in which its several parts are judged to be related as they are in fact related; (2) by means of *acquaintance* with the complex fact itself, which may (in a large sense) be called perception, though it is by no means confined to objects of the senses. Now it will be observed that the second way of knowing a complex fact, the way of acquaintance, is only possible when there really is such a fact, while the first way, like all judgement, is liable to error. The second way gives us the complex whole, and is therefore only possible when its parts do actually have that relation which makes them combine to form such a complex. The first way, on the contrary, gives us the parts and the relation severally, and demands only the reality of the parts and the relation: the relation may not relate those parts in that way, and yet the judgement may occur.

It will be remembered that at the end of Chapter XI we suggested that there might be two kinds of self-evidence, one giving an absolute guarantee of truth, the other only a partial guarantee. These two kinds can now be distinguished.

We may say that a truth is self-evident, in the first and most absolute sense, when we have acquaintance with the fact which corresponds to the truth. When Othello believes that Desdemona loves Cassio, the corresponding fact, if his belief were true, would be 'Desdemona's love for Cassio'. This would be a fact with which no one could have acquaintance except Desdemona; hence in the sense of self-evidence that we are considering, the truth that Desdemona loves Cassio (if it were a truth) could only be self-evident to Desdemona. All mental facts, and all facts concerning sense-data, have this same privacy: there is only one person to whom they can be self-evident in our present sense, since there is only one person who can be acquainted with the mental things or the sense-data concerned. Thus no fact about any particular existing thing can be self-evident to more than one person. On the other hand, facts about universals do not have this privacy. Many minds may be acquainted with the same universals; hence a relation between universals may be known by acquaintance to many different people. In all cases where we know by acquaintance a complex fact consisting of certain terms in a certain relation, we say that the truth that these terms are so related has the first or absolute kind of self-evidence, and in these cases the judgement that the terms are so related *must* be true. Thus this sort of self-evidence is an absolute guarantee of truth.

But although this sort of self-evidence is an absolute guarantee of truth, it does not enable us to be *absolutely* certain, in the case of any given judgement, that the judgement in question is true. Suppose we first perceive the sun shining, which is a complex fact, and thence proceed to make the judgement 'the sun is shining'. In passing from the perception to the judgement, it is necessary to analyse the given complex fact: we have to separate out 'the sun' and 'shining' as constituents of the fact. In this process it is possible to commit an error; hence even where a *fact* has the first or absolute kind of self-evidence, a judgement believed to correspond to the fact is not absolutely infallible, because it may not really correspond to the fact. But if it does correspond (in the sense explained in the preceding chapter), then it *must* be true.

The second sort of self-evidence will be that which belongs to judgements in the first instance, and is not derived from direct perception of a fact as a single complex whole. This second kind of self-evidence will have degrees, from the very highest degree down to a bare inclination in favour of the belief. Take, for example, the case of a horse trotting away from us along a hard road. At first our certainty that we hear the hoofs is complete; gradually, if we listen intently, there comes a moment when we think perhaps it was imagination or the blind upstairs or our own heartbeats; at last we become doubtful whether there was any noise at all; then we *think* we no longer hear anything, and at last we *know* we no longer hear anything. In this process, there is a continual gradation of self-evidence, from the highest degree to the least, not in the sense-data themselves, but in the judgements based on them.

Or again: Suppose we are comparing two shades of colour, one blue and one green. We can be quite sure they are different shades of colour; but if the green colour is gradually altered to be more and more like the blue, becoming first a blue-green, then a greeny-blue, then blue, there will come a moment when we are doubtful whether we can see any difference, and then a moment when we know that we cannot see any difference. The same thing happens in tuning a musical instrument, or in any other case where there is a continuous gradation. Thus self-evidence of this sort is a matter of degree; and it seems plain that the higher degrees are more to be trusted than the lower degrees.

In derivative knowledge our ultimate premises must have some degree of self-evidence, and so must their connexion with the conclusions deduced from them. Take for example a piece of reasoning in geometry. It is not enough that the axioms from which we start should be self-evident: it is necessary also that, at each step in the reasoning, the connexion of premiss and conclusion should be self-evident. In difficult reasoning, this connexion has often only a very small degree of self-evidence; hence errors of reasoning are not improbable where the difficulty is great.

From what has been said it is evident that, both as regards intuitive knowledge and as regards derivative knowledge, if we assume that intuitive knowledge is trustworthy in proportion to the degree of its self-evidence, there will be a gradation in trustworthiness, from the existence of noteworthy sense-data and the simpler truths of logic and arithmetic, which may be taken as quite certain, down to judgements which seem only just more probable than their opposites. What we firmly believe, if it is true, is called *knowledge*, provided it is either intuitive or inferred (logically or psychologically) from intuitive knowledge from which it follows logically. What we firmly believe, if it is not true, is called *error*. What we firmly believe, if it is neither knowledge nor error, and also what we believe hesitatingly, because it is, or is derived from, something which has not the highest degree of self-evidence, may be called *probable opinion*. Thus the greater part of what would commonly pass as knowledge is more or less probable opinion.

In regard to probable opinion, we can derive great assistance from *coherence*, which we rejected as the *definition* of truth, but may often use as a *criterion*. A body of individually probable opinions, if they are mutually coherent, become more probable than any one of them would be individually. It is in this way that many scientific hypotheses acquire their probability. They fit into a coherent system of probable opinions, and thus become more probable than they would be in isolation. The same thing applies to general philosophical hypotheses. Often in a single case such hypotheses may seem highly doubtful, while yet, when we consider the order and coherence which they introduce into a mass of probable opinion, they become pretty nearly certain. This applies, in particular, to such matters as the distinction between dreams and waking life. If our dreams, night after night, were as coherent one with another as our days, we should hardly know whether to believe the dreams or the waking life. As it is, the test of coherence condemns the dreams and confirms the waking life. But this test, though it increases probability where it is successful, never gives absolute certainty, unless there is certainty already at some point in the coherent system. Thus the mere organization of probable opinion will never, by itself, transform it into indubitable knowledge.

# CHAPTER XIV

## The Limits of Philosophical Knowledge

In all that we have said hitherto concerning philosophy, we have scarcely touched on many matters that occupy a great space in the writings of most philosophers. Most philosophers—or, at any rate, very many—profess to be able to prove, by *a priori* metaphysical reasoning, such things as the fundamental dogmas of religion, the essential rationality of the universe, the illusoriness of matter, the unreality of all evil, and so on. There can be no doubt that the hope of finding reason to believe such theses as these has been the chief inspiration of many life-long students of philosophy. This hope, I believe, is vain. It would seem that knowledge concerning the universe as a whole is not to be obtained by metaphysics, and that the proposed proofs that, in virtue of the laws of logic such and such things *must* exist and such and such others cannot, are not capable of surviving a critical scrutiny. In this chapter we shall briefly consider the kind of way in which such reasoning is attempted, with a view to discovering whether we can hope that it may be valid.

The great representative, in modern times, of the kind of view which we wish to examine, was Hegel (1770-1831). Hegel's philosophy is very difficult, and commentators differ as to the true interpretation of it. According to the interpretation I shall adopt, which is that of many, if not most, of the commentators and has the merit of giving an interesting and important type of philosophy, his main thesis is that everything short of the Whole is obviously fragmentary, and obviously incapable of existing without the complement supplied by the rest of the world. Just as a comparative anatomist, from a single bone, sees what kind of animal the whole must have been, so the metaphysician, according to Hegel, sees, from any one piece of reality, what the whole of reality must be—at least in its large outlines. Every apparently separate piece of reality has, as it were, hooks which grapple it to the next piece; the next piece, in turn, has fresh hooks, and so on, until the whole universe is reconstructed. This essential incompleteness appears, according to Hegel, equally in the world of thought and in the world of things. In the world of thought, if we take any idea which is abstract or incomplete, we find, on examination, that if we forget its incompleteness, we become involved in contradictions; these contradictions turn the idea in question into its opposite, or antithesis; and in order to escape, we have to find a new, less incomplete idea, which is the synthesis of our original idea and its antithesis.

This new idea, though less incomplete than the idea we started with, will be found, nevertheless, to be still not wholly complete, but to pass into its antithesis, with which it must be combined in a new synthesis. In this way Hegel advances until he reaches the 'Absolute Idea', which, according to him, has no incompleteness, no opposite, and no need of further development. The Absolute Idea, therefore, is adequate to describe Absolute Reality; but all lower ideas only describe reality as it appears to a partial view, not as it is to one who simultaneously surveys the Whole. Thus Hegel reaches the conclusion that Absolute Reality forms one single harmonious system, not in space or time, not in any degree evil, wholly rational, and wholly spiritual. Any appearance to the contrary, in the world we know, can be proved logically—so he believes—to be entirely due to our fragmentary piecemeal view of the universe. If we saw the universe whole, as we may suppose God sees it, space and time and matter and evil and all striving and struggling would disappear, and we should see instead an eternal perfect unchanging spiritual unity.

In this conception, there is undeniably something sublime, something to which we could wish to yield assent. Nevertheless, when the arguments in support of it are carefully examined, they appear to involve much confusion and many unwarrantable assumptions. The fundamental tenet upon which the system is built up is that what is incomplete must be not self-subsistent, but must need the support of other things before it can exist. It is held that whatever has relations to things outside itself must contain some reference to those outside things in its own nature, and could not, therefore, be what it is if those outside things did not exist. A man's nature, for example, is constituted by his memories and the rest of his knowledge, by his loves and hatreds, and so on; thus, but for the objects which he knows or loves or hates, he could not be what he is. He is essentially and obviously a fragment: taken as the sum-total of reality he would be self-contradictory.

This whole point of view, however, turns upon the notion of the 'nature' of a thing, which seems to mean 'all the truths about the thing'. It is of course the case that a truth which connects one thing with another thing could not subsist if the other thing did not subsist. But a truth about a thing is not part of the thing itself, although it must, according to the above usage, be part of the 'nature' of the thing. If we mean by a thing's 'nature' all the truths about the thing, then plainly we cannot know a thing's 'nature' unless we know all the thing's relations to all the other things in the universe. But if the word 'nature' is used in this sense, we shall have to hold that the thing may be known when its 'nature' is not known, or at any rate is not known completely. There is a confusion, when this use of the word 'nature' is employed, between knowledge of things and knowledge of truths. We may have knowledge of a thing by acquaintance even if we know very few propositions about it—theoretically we need not know any propositions about it. Thus, acquaintance with a thing does not involve knowledge of its 'nature' in the above sense. And although acquaintance with a thing is involved in our knowing any one proposition about a thing, knowledge of its 'nature', in the above sense, is not involved. Hence, (1) acquaintance with a thing does not logically involve a knowledge of its relations, and (2) a knowledge of some of its relations does not involve a knowledge of all of its relations nor a knowledge of its 'nature' in the above sense. I may be acquainted, for example, with my toothache, and this knowledge may be as complete as knowledge by acquaintance ever can be, without knowing all that the dentist (who is not acquainted with it) can tell me about its cause, and without therefore knowing its 'nature' in the above sense. Thus the fact that a thing has relations does not prove that its relations are logically necessary. That is to say, from the mere fact that it is the thing it is we cannot deduce that it must have the various relations which in fact it has. This only *seems* to follow because we know it already.

It follows that we cannot prove that the universe as a whole forms a single harmonious system such as Hegel believes that it forms. And if we cannot prove this, we also cannot prove the unreality of space and time and matter and evil, for this is deduced by Hegel from the fragmentary and relational character of these things. Thus we are left to the piecemeal investigation of the world, and are unable to know the characters of those parts of the universe that are remote from our experience. This result, disappointing as it is to those whose hopes have been raised by the systems of philosophers, is in harmony with the inductive and scientific temper of our age, and is borne out by the whole examination of human knowledge which has occupied our previous chapters.

Most of the great ambitious attempts of metaphysicians have proceeded by the attempt to prove that such and such apparent features of the actual world were self-contradictory, and therefore could not be real. The whole tendency of modern thought, however, is more and more in the direction of showing that the supposed contradictions were illusory, and that very little can be proved *a priori* from considerations of what *must* be. A good illustration of this is afforded by space and time. Space and time appear to be infinite in extent, and infinitely divisible. If we travel along a straight line in either direction, it is difficult to believe that we shall finally reach a last point, beyond which there is nothing, not even empty space. Similarly, if in imagination we travel backwards or forwards in time, it is difficult to believe that we shall reach a first or last time, with not even empty time beyond it. Thus space and time appear to be infinite in extent.

Again, if we take any two points on a line, it seems evident that there must be other points between them however small the distance between them may be: every distance can be halved, and the halves can be halved again, and so on *ad infinitum*. In time, similarly, however little time may elapse between two moments, it seems evident that there will be other moments between them. Thus space and time appear to be infinitely divisible. But as against these apparent facts—infinite extent and infinite divisibility—philosophers have advanced arguments tending to show that there could be no infinite collections of things, and that therefore the number of points in space, or of instants in time, must be finite. Thus a contradiction emerged between the apparent nature of space and time and the supposed impossibility of infinite collections.

Kant, who first emphasized this contradiction, deduced the impossibility of space and time, which he declared to be merely subjective; and since his time very many philosophers have believed that space and time are mere appearance, not characteristic of the world as it really is. Now, however, owing to the labours of the mathematicians, notably Georg Cantor, it has appeared that the impossibility of infinite collections was a mistake. They are not in fact self-contradictory, but only contradictory of certain rather obstinate mental prejudices. Hence the reasons for regarding space and time as unreal have become inoperative, and one of the great sources of metaphysical constructions is dried up.

The mathematicians, however, have not been content with showing that space as it is commonly supposed to be is possible; they have shown also that many other forms of space are equally possible, so far as logic can show. Some of Euclid's axioms, which appear to common sense to be necessary, and were formerly supposed to be necessary by philosophers, are now known to derive their appearance of necessity from our mere familiarity with actual space, and not from any a priori logical foundation. By imagining worlds in which these axioms are false, the mathematicians have used logic to loosen the prejudices of common sense, and to show the possibility of spaces differing—some more, some less—from that in which we live. And some of these spaces differ so little from Euclidean space, where distances such as we can measure are concerned, that it is impossible to discover by observation whether our actual space is strictly Euclidean or of one of these other kinds. Thus the position is completely reversed. Formerly it appeared that experience left only one kind of space to logic, and logic showed this one kind to be impossible. Now, logic presents many kinds of space as possible apart from experience, and experience only partially decides between them. Thus, while our knowledge of what is has become less than it was formerly supposed to be, our knowledge of what may be is enormously increased. Instead of being shut in within narrow walls, of which every nook and cranny could be explored, we find ourselves in an open world of free possibilities, where much remains unknown because there is so much to know.

What has happened in the case of space and time has happened, to some extent, in other directions as well. The attempt to prescribe to the universe by means of a priori principles has broken down; logic, instead of being, as formerly, the bar to possibilities, has become the great liberator of the imagination, presenting innumerable alternatives which are closed to unreflective common sense, and leaving to experience the task of deciding, where decision is possible, between the many worlds which logic offers for our choice. Thus knowledge as to what exists becomes limited to what we can learn from experience—not to what we can actually experience, for, as we have seen, there is much knowledge by description concerning things of which we have no direct experience. But in all cases of knowledge by description, we need some connexion of universals, enabling us, from such and such a datum, to infer an object of a certain sort as implied by our datum. Thus in regard to physical objects, for example, the principle that sense-data are signs of physical objects is itself a connexion of universals; and it is only in virtue of this principle that experience enables us to acquire knowledge concerning physical objects. The same applies to the law of causality, or, to descend to what is less general, to such principles as the law of gravitation.

Principles such as the law of gravitation are proved, or rather are rendered highly probable, by a combination of experience with some wholly *a priori* principle, such as the principle of induction. Thus our intuitive knowledge, which is the source of all our other knowledge of truths, is of two sorts: pure empirical knowledge, which tells us of the existence and some of the properties of particular things with which we are acquainted, and pure *a priori* knowledge, which gives us connexions between universals, and enables us to draw inferences from the particular facts given in empirical knowledge. Our derivative knowledge always depends upon some pure *a priori* knowledge and usually also depends upon some pure empirical knowledge.

Philosophical knowledge, if what has been said above is true, does not differ essentially from scientific knowledge; there is no special source of wisdom which is open to philosophy but not to science, and the results obtained by philosophy are not radically different from those obtained from science. The essential characteristic of philosophy, which makes it a study distinct from science, is criticism. It examines critically the principles employed in science and in daily life; it searches out any inconsistencies there may be in these principles, and it only accepts them when, as the result of a critical inquiry, no reason for rejecting them has appeared. If, as many philosophers have believed, the principles underlying the sciences were capable, when disengaged from irrelevant detail, of giving us knowledge concerning the universe as a whole, such knowledge would have the same claim on our belief as scientific knowledge has; but our inquiry has not revealed any such knowledge, and therefore, as regards the special doctrines of the bolder metaphysicians, has had a mainly negative result. But as regards what would be commonly accepted as knowledge, our result is in the main positive: we have seldom found reason to reject such knowledge as the result of our criticism, and we have seen no reason to suppose man incapable of the kind of knowledge which he is generally believed to possess.

When, however, we speak of philosophy as a *criticism* of knowledge, it is necessary to impose a certain limitation. If we adopt the attitude of the complete sceptic, placing ourselves wholly outside all knowledge, and asking, from this outside position, to be compelled to return within the circle of knowledge, we are demanding what is impossible, and our scepticism can never be refuted. For all refutation must begin with some piece of knowledge which the disputants share; from blank doubt, no argument can begin. Hence the criticism of knowledge which philosophy employs must not be of this destructive kind, if any result is to be achieved. Against this absolute scepticism, no *logical* argument can be advanced. But it is not difficult to see that scepticism of this kind is unreasonable. Descartes' 'methodical doubt', with which modern philosophy began, is not of this kind, but is rather the kind of criticism which we are asserting to be the essence of philosophy. His 'methodical doubt' consisted in doubting whatever seemed doubtful; in pausing, with each apparent piece of knowledge, to ask himself whether, on reflection, he could feel certain that he really knew it. This is the kind of criticism which constitutes philosophy. Some knowledge, such as knowledge of the existence of our sense-data, appears quite indubitable, however calmly and thoroughly we reflect upon it. In regard to such knowledge, philosophical criticism does not require that we should abstain from belief. But there are beliefs—such, for example, as the belief that physical objects exactly resemble our sense-data—which are entertained until we begin to reflect, but are found to melt away when subjected to a close inquiry. Such beliefs philosophy will bid us reject, unless some new line of argument is found to support them. But to reject the beliefs which do not appear open to any objections, however closely we examine them, is not reasonable, and is not what philosophy advocates.

The criticism aimed at, in a word, is not that which, without reason, determines to reject, but that which considers each piece of apparent knowledge on its merits, and retains whatever still appears to be knowledge when this consideration is completed. That some risk of error remains must be admitted, since human beings are fallible. Philosophy may claim justly that it diminishes the risk of error, and that in some cases it renders the risk so small as to be practically negligible. To do more than this is not possible in a world where mistakes must occur; and more than this no prudent advocate of philosophy would claim to have performed.

# CHAPTER XV

## The Value of Philosophy

Having now come to the end of our brief and very incomplete review of the problems of philosophy, it will be well to consider, in conclusion, what is the value of philosophy and why it ought to be studied. It is the more necessary to consider this question, in view of the fact that many men, under the influence of science or of practical affairs, are inclined to doubt whether philosophy is anything better than innocent but useless trifling, hair-splitting distinctions, and controversies on matters concerning which knowledge is impossible.

This view of philosophy appears to result, partly from a wrong conception of the ends of life, partly from a wrong conception of the kind of goods which philosophy strives to achieve. Physical science, through the medium of inventions, is useful to innumerable people who are wholly ignorant of it; thus the study of physical science is to be recommended, not only, or primarily, because of the effect on the student, but rather because of the effect on mankind in general. Thus utility does not belong to philosophy. If the study of philosophy has any value at all for others than students of philosophy, it must be only indirectly, through its effects upon the lives of those who study it. It is in these effects, therefore, if anywhere, that the value of philosophy must be primarily sought.

But further, if we are not to fail in our endeavour to determine the value of philosophy, we must first free our minds from the prejudices of what are wrongly called 'practical' men. The 'practical' man, as this word is often used, is one who recognizes only material needs, who realizes that men must have food for the body, but is oblivious of the necessity of providing food for the mind. If all men were well off, if poverty and disease had been reduced to their lowest possible point, there would still remain much to be done to produce a valuable society; and even in the existing world the goods of the mind are at least as important as the goods of the body. It is exclusively among the goods of the mind that the value of philosophy is to be found; and only those who are not indifferent to these goods can be persuaded that the study of philosophy is not a waste of time.

Philosophy, like all other studies, aims primarily at knowledge. The knowledge it aims at is the kind of knowledge which gives unity and system to the body of the sciences, and the kind which results from a critical examination of the grounds of our convictions, prejudices, and beliefs. But it cannot be maintained that philosophy has had any very great measure of success in its attempts to provide definite answers to its questions. If you ask a mathematician, a mineralogist, a historian, or any other man of learning, what definite body of truths has been ascertained by his science, his answer will last as long as you are willing to listen. But if you put the same question to a philosopher, he will, if he is candid, have to confess that his study has not achieved positive results such as have been achieved by other sciences. It is true that this is partly accounted for by the fact that, as soon as definite knowledge concerning any subject becomes possible, this subject ceases to be called philosophy, and becomes a separate science. The whole study of the heavens, which now belongs to astronomy, was once included in philosophy; Newton's great work was called 'the mathematical principles of natural philosophy'. Similarly, the study of the human mind, which was a part of philosophy, has now been separated from philosophy and has become the science of psychology. Thus, to a great extent, the uncertainty of philosophy is more apparent than real: those questions which are already capable of definite answers are placed in the sciences, while those only to which, at present, no definite answer can be given, remain to form the residue which is called philosophy.

This is, however, only a part of the truth concerning the uncertainty of philosophy. There are many questions—and among them those that are of the profoundest interest to our spiritual life—which, so far as we can see, must remain insoluble to the human intellect unless its powers become of quite a different order from what they are now. Has the universe any unity of plan or purpose, or is it a fortuitous concourse of atoms? Is consciousness a permanent part of the universe, giving hope of indefinite growth in wisdom, or is it a transitory accident on a small planet on which life must ultimately become impossible? Are good and evil of importance to the universe or only to man? Such questions are asked by philosophy, and variously answered by various philosophers. But it would seem that, whether answers be otherwise discoverable or not, the answers suggested by philosophy are none of them demonstrably true. Yet, however slight may be the hope of discovering an answer, it is part of the business of philosophy to continue the consideration of such questions, to make us aware of their importance, to examine all the approaches to them, and to keep alive that speculative interest in the universe which is apt to be killed by confining ourselves to definitely ascertainable knowledge.

Many philosophers, it is true, have held that philosophy could establish the truth of certain answers to such fundamental questions. They have supposed that what is of most importance in religious beliefs could be proved by strict demonstration to be true. In order to judge of such attempts, it is necessary to take a survey of human knowledge, and to form an opinion as to its methods and its limitations. On such a subject it would be unwise to pronounce dogmatically; but if the investigations of our previous chapters have not led us astray, we shall be compelled to renounce the hope of finding philosophical proofs of religious beliefs. We cannot, therefore, include as part of the value of philosophy any definite set of answers to such questions. Hence, once more, the value of philosophy must not depend upon any supposed body of definitely ascertainable knowledge to be acquired by those who study it.

The value of philosophy is, in fact, to be sought largely in its very uncertainty. The man who has no tincture of philosophy goes through life imprisoned in the prejudices derived from common sense, from the habitual beliefs of his age or his nation, and from convictions which have grown up in his mind without the co-operation or consent of his deliberate reason. To such a man the world tends to become definite, finite, obvious; common objects rouse no questions, and unfamiliar possibilities are contemptuously rejected. As soon as we begin to philosophize, on the contrary, we find, as we saw in our opening chapters, that even the most everyday things lead to problems to which only very incomplete answers can be given. Philosophy, though unable to tell us with certainty what is the true answer to the doubts which it raises, is able to suggest many possibilities which enlarge our thoughts and free them from the tyranny of custom. Thus, while diminishing our feeling of certainty as to what things are, it greatly increases our knowledge as to what they may be; it removes the somewhat arrogant dogmatism of those who have never travelled into the region of liberating doubt, and it keeps alive our sense of wonder by showing familiar things in an unfamiliar aspect.

Apart from its utility in showing unsuspected possibilities, philosophy has a value—perhaps its chief value—through the greatness of the objects which it contemplates, and the freedom from narrow and personal aims resulting from this contemplation. The life of the instinctive man is shut up within the circle of his private interests: family and friends may be included, but the outer world is not regarded except as it may help or hinder what comes within the circle of instinctive wishes. In such a life there is something feverish and confined, in comparison with which the philosophic life is calm and free. The private world of instinctive interests is a small one, set in the midst of a great and powerful world which must, sooner or later, lay our private world in ruins. Unless we can so enlarge our interests as to include the whole outer world, we remain like a garrison in a beleaguered fortress, knowing that the enemy prevents escape and that ultimate surrender is inevitable. In such a life there is no peace, but a constant strife between the insistence of desire and the powerlessness of will. In one way or another, if our life is to be great and free, we must escape this prison and this strife.

One way of escape is by philosophic contemplation. Philosophic contemplation does not, in its widest survey, divide the universe into two hostile camps—friends and foes, helpful and hostile, good and bad—it views the whole impartially. Philosophic contemplation, when it is unalloyed, does not aim at proving that the rest of the universe is akin to man. All acquisition of knowledge is an enlargement of the Self, but this enlargement is best attained when it is not directly sought. It is obtained when the desire for knowledge is alone operative, by a study which does not wish in advance that its objects should have this or that character, but adapts the Self to the characters which it finds in its objects. This enlargement of Self is not obtained when, taking the Self as it is, we try to show that the world is so similar to this Self that knowledge of it is possible without any admission of what seems alien. The desire to prove this is a form of self-assertion and, like all self-assertion, it is an obstacle to the growth of Self which it desires, and of which the Self knows that it is capable. Self-assertion, in philosophic speculation as elsewhere, views the world as a means to its own ends; thus it makes the world of less account than Self, and the Self sets bounds to the greatness of its goods. In contemplation, on the contrary, we start from the not-Self, and through its greatness the boundaries of Self are enlarged; through the infinity of the universe the mind which contemplates it achieves some share in infinity.

For this reason greatness of soul is not fostered by those philosophies which assimilate the universe to Man. Knowledge is a form of union of Self and not-Self; like all union, it is impaired by dominion, and therefore by any attempt to force the universe into conformity with what we find in ourselves. There is a widespread philosophical tendency towards the view which tells us that Man is the measure of all things, that truth is man-made, that space and time and the world of universals are properties of the mind, and that, if there be anything not created by the mind, it is unknowable and of no account for us. This view, if our previous discussions were correct, is untrue; but in addition to being untrue, it has the effect of robbing philosophic contemplation of all that gives it value, since it fetters contemplation to Self. What it calls knowledge is not a union with the not-Self, but a set of prejudices, habits, and desires, making an impenetrable veil between us and the world beyond. The man who finds pleasure in such a theory of knowledge is like the man who never leaves the domestic circle for fear his word might not be law.

The true philosophic contemplation, on the contrary, finds its satisfaction in every enlargement of the not-Self, in everything that magnifies the objects contemplated, and thereby the subject contemplating. Everything, in contemplation, that is personal or private, everything that depends upon habit, self-interest, or desire, distorts the object, and hence impairs the union which the intellect seeks. By thus making a barrier between subject and object, such personal and private things become a prison to the intellect. The free intellect will see as God might see, without a *here* and *now*, without hopes and fears, without the trammels of customary beliefs and traditional prejudices, calmly, dispassionately, in the sole and exclusive desire of knowledge— knowledge as impersonal, as purely contemplative, as it is possible for man to attain. Hence also the free intellect will value more the abstract and universal knowledge into which the accidents of private history do not enter, than the knowledge brought by the senses, and dependent, as such knowledge must be, upon an exclusive and personal point of view and a body whose sense-organs distort as much as they reveal.

The mind which has become accustomed to the freedom and impartiality of philosophic contemplation will preserve something of the same freedom and impartiality in the world of action and emotion. It will view its purposes and desires as parts of the whole, with the absence of insistence that results from seeing them as infinitesimal fragments in a world of which all the rest is unaffected by any one man's deeds. The impartiality which, in contemplation, is the unalloyed desire for truth, is the very same quality of mind which, in action, is justice, and in emotion is that universal love which can be given to all, and not only to those who are judged useful or admirable. Thus contemplation enlarges not only the objects of our thoughts, but also the objects of our actions and our affections: it makes us citizens of the universe, not only of one walled city at war with all the rest. In this citizenship of the universe consists man's true freedom, and his liberation from the thraldom of narrow hopes and fears.

Thus, to sum up our discussion of the value of philosophy; Philosophy is to be studied, not for the sake of any definite answers to its questions, since no definite answers can, as a rule, be known to be true, but rather for the sake of the questions themselves; because these questions enlarge our conception of what is possible, enrich our intellectual imagination and diminish the dogmatic assurance which closes the mind against speculation; but above all because, through the greatness of the universe which philosophy contemplates, the mind also is rendered great, and becomes capable of that union with the universe which constitutes its highest good.

# BIBLIOGRAPHICAL NOTE

The student who wishes to acquire an elementary knowledge of philosophy will find it both easier and more profitable to read some of the works of the great philosophers than to attempt to derive an all-round view from handbooks. The following are specially recommended:

*Plato: Republic, especially Books VI and VII.*
*Descartes: Meditations.*
*Spinoza: Ethics.*
*Leibniz: The Monadology.*
*Berkeley: Three Dialogues between Hylas and Philonous.*
*Hume: Enquiry concerning Human Understanding.*
*Kant: Prolegomena to any Future Metaphysic.*

# THE ANALYSIS
# OF MIND

# LECTURE I

## Recent Criticisms of "Consciousness"

There are certain occurrences which we are in the habit of calling "mental." Among these we may take as typical BELIEVING and DESIRING. The exact definition of the word "mental" will, I hope, emerge as the lectures proceed; for the present, I shall mean by it whatever occurrences would commonly be called mental.

I wish in these lectures to analyse as fully as I can what it is that really takes place when we, e.g. believe or desire. In this first lecture I shall be concerned to refute a theory which is widely held, and which I formerly held myself: the theory that the essence of everything mental is a certain quite peculiar something called "consciousness," conceived either as a relation to objects, or as a pervading quality of psychical phenomena.

The reasons which I shall give against this theory will be mainly derived from previous authors. There are two sorts of reasons, which will divide my lecture into two parts:

(1) Direct reasons, derived from analysis and its difficulties;
(2) Indirect reasons, derived from observation of animals (comparative psychology) and of the insane and hysterical (psycho-analysis).

Few things are more firmly established in popular philosophy than the distinction between mind and matter. Those who are not professional metaphysicians are willing to confess that they do not know what mind actually is, or how matter is constituted; but they remain convinced that there is an impassable gulf between the two, and that both belong to what actually exists in the world. Philosophers, on the other hand, have maintained often that matter is a mere fiction imagined by mind, and sometimes that mind is a mere property of a certain kind of matter. Those who maintain that mind is the reality and matter an evil dream are called "idealists"—a word which has a different meaning in philosophy from that which it bears in ordinary life. Those who argue that matter is the reality and mind a mere property of protoplasm are called "materialists." They have been rare among philosophers, but common, at certain periods, among men of science. Idealists, materialists, and ordinary mortals have been in agreement on one point: that they knew sufficiently what they meant by the words "mind" and "matter" to be able to conduct their debate intelligently. Yet it was

86

just in this point, as to which they were at one, that they seem to me to have been all alike in error.

The stuff of which the world of our experience is composed is, in my belief, neither mind nor matter, but something more primitive than either. Both mind and matter seem to be composite, and the stuff of which they are compounded lies in a sense between the two, in a sense above them both, like a common ancestor. As regards matter, I have set forth my reasons for this view on former occasions,[1] and I shall not now repeat them. But the question of mind is more difficult, and it is this question that I propose to discuss in these lectures. A great deal of what I shall have to say is not original; indeed, much recent work, in various fields, has tended to show the necessity of such theories as those which I shall be advocating. Accordingly in this first lecture I shall try to give a brief description of the systems of ideas within which our investigation is to be carried on.

If there is one thing that may be said, in the popular estimation, to characterize mind, that one thing is "consciousness." We say that we are "conscious" of what we see and hear, of what we remember, and of our own thoughts and feelings. Most of us believe that tables and chairs are not "conscious." We think that when we sit in a chair, we are aware of sitting in it, but it is not aware of being sat in. It cannot for a moment be doubted that we are right in believing that there is SOME difference between us and the chair in this respect: so much may be taken as fact, and as a datum for our inquiry. But as soon as we try to say what exactly the difference is, we become involved in perplexities. Is "consciousness" ultimate and simple, something to be merely accepted and contemplated? Or is it something complex, perhaps consisting in our way of behaving in the presence of objects, or, alternatively, in the existence in us of things called "ideas," having a certain relation to objects, though different from them, and only symbolically representative of them? Such questions are not easy to answer; but until they are answered we cannot profess to know what we mean by saying that we are possessed of "consciousness."

Before considering modern theories, let us look first at consciousness from the standpoint of conventional psychology, since this embodies views which naturally occur when we begin to reflect upon the subject. For this purpose, let us as a preliminary consider different ways of being conscious.

First, there is the way of PERCEPTION. We "perceive" tables and chairs, horses and dogs, our friends, traffic passing in the street—in short, anything which we recognize through the senses. I leave on one side for the present the question whether pure sensation is to be regarded as a form of consciousness: what I am speaking of now is perception, where, according to conventional psychology, we go beyond the sensation to the "thing" which it represents. When you hear a donkey bray, you not

---

[1] *Our Knowledge of the External World* (Allen & Unwin), Chapters III and IV. Also *Mysticism and Logic*, Essays VII and VIII.

only hear a noise, but realize that it comes from a donkey. When you see a table, you not only see a coloured surface, but realize that it is hard. The addition of these elements that go beyond crude sensation is said to constitute perception. We shall have more to say about this at a later stage. For the moment, I am merely concerned to note that perception of objects is one of the most obvious examples of what is called "consciousness." We are "conscious" of anything that we perceive.

We may take next the way of MEMORY. If I set to work to recall what I did this morning, that is a form of consciousness different from perception, since it is concerned with the past. There are various problems as to how we can be conscious now of what no longer exists. These will be dealt with incidentally when we come to the analysis of memory.

From memory it is an easy step to what are called "ideas"—not in the Platonic sense, but in that of Locke, Berkeley and Hume, in which they are opposed to "impressions." You may be conscious of a friend either by seeing him or by "thinking" of him; and by "thought" you can be conscious of objects which cannot be seen, such as the human race, or physiology. "Thought" in the narrower sense is that form of consciousness which consists in "ideas" as opposed to impressions or mere memories.

We may end our preliminary catalogue with BELIEF, by which I mean that way of being conscious which may be either true or false. We say that a man is "conscious of looking a fool," by which we mean that he believes he looks a fool, and is not mistaken in this belief. This is a different form of consciousness from any of the earlier ones. It is the form which gives "knowledge" in the strict sense, and also error. It is, at least apparently, more complex than our previous forms of consciousness; though we shall find that they are not so separable from it as they might appear to be.

Besides ways of being conscious there are other things that would ordinarily be called "mental," such as desire and pleasure and pain. These raise problems of their own, which we shall reach in Lecture III. But the hardest problems are those that arise concerning ways of being "conscious." These ways, taken together, are called the "cognitive" elements in mind, and it is these that will occupy us most during the following lectures.

There is one element which SEEMS obviously in common among the different ways of being conscious, and that is, that they are all directed to OBJECTS. We are conscious "of" something. The consciousness, it seems, is one thing, and that of which we are conscious is another thing. Unless we are to acquiesce in the view that we can never be conscious of anything outside our own minds, we must say that the object of consciousness need not be mental, though the consciousness must be. (I am speaking within the circle of conventional doctrines, not expressing my own beliefs.) This direction towards an object is commonly regarded as typical of every form of cognition, and sometimes of mental life altogether. We may distinguish two different tendencies in traditional psychology. There are those who take mental phenomena naively, just as they would physical phenomena. This school of psychologists tends not to emphasize the object. On the other hand, there are those whose primary interest is in the apparent fact that we have KNOWLEDGE, that there is a world surrounding us of which we are aware. These men are interested in the mind because of its relation to the world, because knowledge, if it is a fact, is a very mysterious one. Their interest in psychology is naturally centred in the relation of consciousness to its object, a problem which, properly, belongs rather to theory of knowledge. We may take as one of the best and most typical representatives of this school the Austrian psychologist Brentano, whose "Psychology from the Empirical Standpoint,"[2] though published in 1874, is still influential and was the starting-point of a great deal of interesting work. He says (p. 115):

"Every psychical phenomenon is characterized by what the scholastics of the Middle Ages called the intentional (also the mental) inexistence of an object, and what we, although with not quite unambiguous expressions, would call relation to a content, direction towards an object (which is not here to be understood as a reality), or immanent objectivity. Each contains something in itself as an object, though not each in the same way. In presentation something is presented, in judgment something is acknowledged or rejected, in love something is loved, in hatred hated, in desire desired, and so on.

"This intentional inexistence is exclusively peculiar to psychical phenomena. No physical phenomenon shows anything similar. And so we can define psychical phenomena by saying that they are phenomena which intentionally contain an object in themselves."

The view here expressed, that relation to an object is an ultimate irreducible characteristic of mental phenomena, is one which I shall be concerned to combat. Like Brentano, I am interested in psychology, not so much for its own sake, as for the light that it may throw on the problem of knowledge. Until very lately I believed, as he did, that mental phenomena have essential reference to objects, except possibly in the case of pleasure and pain. Now I no longer believe this, even in the case of knowledge. I shall try to make my reasons for this rejection clear as we proceed. It must be evident at first glance that the analysis of knowledge is rendered more difficult by the rejection; but the apparent simplicity of Brentano's view of knowledge will be found, if I am not mistaken, incapable of maintaining itself either against an analytic scrutiny or against a host of facts in psycho-analysis and animal psychology. I do not wish to minimize the problems. I will merely observe, in mitigation of our prospective labours, that thinking, however it is to be analysed, is in itself a delightful occupation, and that there is no enemy to thinking so deadly as a false simplicity. Travelling, whether in the mental or the physical world, is a joy, and it is good to know that, in the mental world at least, there are vast countries still very imperfectly explored.

---

[2] *Psychologie vom empirischen Standpunkte,* vol. i, 1874. (The second volume was never published.)

The view expressed by Brentano has been held very generally, and developed by many writers. Among these we may take as an example his Austrian successor Meinong.[3] According to him there are three elements involved in the thought of an object. These three he calls the act, the content and the object. The act is the same in any two cases of the same kind of consciousness; for instance, if I think of Smith or think of Brown, the act of thinking, in itself, is exactly similar on both occasions. But the content of my thought, the particular event that is happening in my mind, is different when I think of Smith and when I think of Brown. The content, Meinong argues, must not be confounded with the object, since the content must exist in my mind at the moment when I have the thought, whereas the object need not do so. The object may be something past or future; it may be physical, not mental; it may be something abstract, like equality for example; it may be something imaginary, like a golden mountain; or it may even be something self-contradictory, like a round square. But in all these cases, so he contends, the content exists when the thought exists, and is what distinguishes it, as an occurrence, from other thoughts.

To make this theory concrete, let us suppose that you are thinking of St. Paul's. Then, according to Meinong, we have to distinguish three elements which are necessarily combined in constituting the one thought. First, there is the act of thinking, which would be just the same whatever you were thinking about. Then there is what makes the character of the thought as contrasted with other thoughts; this is the content. And finally there is St. Paul's, which is the object of your thought. There must be a difference between the content of a thought and what it is about, since the thought is here and now, whereas what it is about may not be; hence it is clear that the thought is not identical with St. Paul's. This seems to show that we must distinguish between content and object. But if Meinong is right, there can be no thought without an object: the connection of the two is essential. The object might exist without the thought, but not the thought without the object: the three elements of act, content and object are all required to constitute the one single occurrence called "thinking of St. Paul's."

The above analysis of a thought, though I believe it to be mistaken, is very useful as affording a schema in terms of which other theories can be stated. In the remainder of the present lecture I shall state in outline the view which I advocate, and show how various other views out of which mine has grown result from modifications of the threefold analysis into act, content and object.

The first criticism I have to make is that the ACT seems unnecessary and fictitious. The occurrence of the content of a thought constitutes the occurrence of the thought. Empirically, I cannot discover anything corresponding to the supposed act; and theoretically I cannot see that it is indispensable. We say: "*I* think so-and-

---

[3] See, e.g. his article: "Ueber Gegenstande hoherer Ordnung und deren Verhaltniss zur inneren Wahrnehmung," *Zeitschrift fur Psychologie and Physiologie der Sinnesorgane,* vol. xxi, pp. 182-272 (1899), especially pp. 185-8.

so," and this word "I" suggests that thinking is the act of a person. Meinong's "act" is the ghost of the subject, or what once was the full-blooded soul. It is supposed that thoughts cannot just come and go, but need a person to think them. Now, of course it is true that thoughts can be collected into bundles, so that one bundle is my thoughts, another is your thoughts, and a third is the thoughts of Mr. Jones. But I think the person is not an ingredient in the single thought: he is rather constituted by relations of the thoughts to each other and to the body. This is a large question, which need not, in its entirety, concern us at present. All that I am concerned with for the moment is that the grammatical forms "I think," "you think," and "Mr. Jones thinks," are misleading if regarded as indicating an analysis of a single thought. It would be better to say "it thinks in me," like "it rains here"; or better still, "there is a thought in me." This is simply on the ground that what Meinong calls the act in thinking is not empirically discoverable, or logically deducible from what we can observe.

The next point of criticism concerns the relation of content and object. The reference of thoughts to objects is not, I believe, the simple direct essential thing that Brentano and Meinong represent it as being. It seems to me to be derivative, and to consist largely in BELIEFS: beliefs that what constitutes the thought is connected with various other elements which together make up the object. You have, say, an image of St. Paul's, or merely the word "St. Paul's" in your head. You believe, however vaguely and dimly, that this is connected with what you would see if you went to St. Paul's, or what you would feel if you touched its walls; it is further connected with what other people see and feel, with services and the Dean and Chapter and Sir Christopher Wren. These things are not mere thoughts of yours, but your thought stands in a relation to them of which you are more or less aware. The awareness of this relation is a further thought, and constitutes your feeling that the original thought had an "object." But in pure imagination you can get very similar thoughts without these accompanying beliefs; and in this case your thoughts do not have objects or seem to have them. Thus in such instances you have content without object. On the other hand, in seeing or hearing it would be less misleading to say that you have object without content, since what you see or hear is actually part of the physical world, though not matter in the sense of physics. Thus the whole question of the relation of mental occurrences to objects grows very complicated, and cannot be settled by regarding reference to objects as of the essence of thoughts. All the above remarks are merely preliminary, and will be expanded later.

Speaking in popular and unphilosophical terms, we may say that the content of a thought is supposed to be something in your head when you think the thought, while the object is usually something in the outer world. It is held that knowledge of the outer world is constituted by the relation to the object, while the fact that knowledge is different from what it knows is due to the fact that knowledge comes by way of contents. We can begin to state the difference between realism and idealism in terms of this opposition of contents and objects. Speaking quite roughly and approximately, we may say that idealism tends to suppress the object, while realism tends to suppress the content. Idealism, accordingly, says that nothing can be known except thoughts, and all the reality that we know is mental; while realism maintains that we know objects directly, in sensation certainly, and perhaps also in memory and thought. Idealism does not say that nothing can be known beyond the present thought, but it maintains that the context of vague belief, which we spoke of in connection with the thought of St. Paul's, only takes you to other thoughts, never to anything radically different from thoughts. The difficulty of this view is in regard to sensation, where it seems as if we came into direct contact with the outer world. But the Berkeleian way of meeting this difficulty is so familiar that I need not enlarge upon it now. I shall return to it in a later lecture, and will only observe, for the present, that there seem to me no valid grounds for regarding what we see and hear as not part of the physical world.

Realists, on the other hand, as a rule, suppress the content, and maintain that a thought consists either of act and object alone, or of object alone. I have been in the past a realist, and I remain a realist as regards sensation, but not as regards memory or thought. I will try to explain what seem to me to be the reasons for and against various kinds of realism.

Modern idealism professes to be by no means confined to the present thought or the present thinker in regard to its knowledge; indeed, it contends that the world is so organic, so dove-tailed, that from any one portion the whole can be inferred, as the complete skeleton of an extinct animal can be inferred from one bone. But the logic by which this supposed organic nature of the world is nominally demonstrated appears to realists, as it does to me, to be faulty. They argue that, if we cannot know the physical world directly, we cannot really know any thing outside our own minds: the rest of the world may be merely our dream. This is a dreary view, and they there fore seek ways of escaping from it. Accordingly they maintain that in knowledge we are in direct contact with objects, which may be, and usually are, outside our own minds. No doubt they are prompted to this view, in the first place, by bias, namely, by the desire to think that they can know of the existence of a world outside themselves. But we have to consider, not what led them to desire the view, but whether their arguments for it are valid.

There are two different kinds of realism, according as we make a thought consist of act and object, or of object alone. Their difficulties are different, but neither seems tenable all through. Take, for the sake of definiteness, the remembering of a past event. The remembering occurs now, and is therefore necessarily not identical with the past event. So long as we retain the act, this need cause no difficulty. The act of remembering occurs now, and has on this view a certain essential relation to the past event which it remembers. There is no LOGICAL objection to this theory, but there is the objection, which we spoke of earlier, that the act seems mythical, and is not to be found by observation. If, on the other hand, we try to constitute memory without the act, we are driven to a content, since we must have something that happens NOW, as opposed to the event which happened in the past. Thus, when we reject the act, which I think we must, we are driven to a theory of memory which is more akin to idealism. These arguments, however, do not apply to sensation. It is especially sensation, I think, which is considered by those realists who retain only the object.[4] Their views, which are chiefly held in America, are in large measure derived from William James, and before going further it will be well to consider the revolutionary doctrine which he advocated. I believe this doctrine contains important new truth, and what I shall have to say will be in a considerable measure inspired by it.

William James's view was first set forth in an essay called "Does 'consciousness' exist?"[5] In this essay he explains how what used to be the soul has gradually been refined down to the "transcendental ego," which, he says, "attenuates itself to a thoroughly ghostly condition, being only a name for the fact that the 'content' of experience IS KNOWN. It loses personal form and activity—these passing over to the content—and becomes a bare Bewusstheit or Bewusstsein uberhaupt, of which in its own right absolutely nothing can be said. I believe (he continues) that 'consciousness,' when once it has evaporated to this estate of pure diaphaneity, is on the point of disappearing altogether. It is the name of a nonentity, and has no right to a place among first principles. Those who still cling to it are clinging to a mere echo, the faint rumour left behind by the disappearing 'soul' upon the air of philosophy"(p. 2).

He explains that this is no sudden change in his opinions. "For twenty years past," he says, "I have mistrusted 'consciousness' as an entity; for seven or eight years past I have suggested its non-existence to my students, and tried to give them its pragmatic equivalent in realities of experience. It seems to me that the hour is ripe for it to be openly and universally discarded"(p. 3).

His next concern is to explain away the air of paradox, for James was never wilfully paradoxical. "Undeniably," he says, "'thoughts' do exist." "I mean only to deny that the word stands for an entity, but to insist most emphatically that it does stand for a function. There is, I mean, no aboriginal stuff or quality of being, contrasted with that of which material objects are made, out of which our thoughts of them are made; but there is a function in experience which thoughts perform, and for the performance of which this quality of being is invoked. That function is KNOWING"(pp. 3-4).

James's view is that the raw material out of which the world is built up is not of two sorts, one matter and the other mind, but that it is arranged in different patterns by its inter-relations, and that some arrangements may be called mental, while others may be called physical.

"My thesis is," he says, "that if we start with the supposition that there is only one primal stuff or material in the world, a stuff of which everything is composed, and if

---

[4] This is explicitly the case with Mach's *Analysis of Sensations,* a book of fundamental importance in the present connection. (Translation of fifth German edition, Open Court Co., 1914. First German edition, 1886.)

[5] *Journal of Philosophy, Psychology and Scientific Methods,* vol. i, 1904. Reprinted in *Essays in Radical Empiricism* (Longmans, Green & Co., 1912), pp. 1-38, to which references in what follows refer.

we call that stuff 'pure experience,' then knowing can easily be explained as a particular sort of relation towards one another into which portions of pure experience may enter. The relation itself is a part of pure experience; one of its 'terms' becomes the subject or bearer of the knowledge, the knower, the other becomes the object known"(p. 4).

After mentioning the duality of subject and object, which is supposed to constitute consciousness, he proceeds in italics: "EXPERIENCE, I BELIEVE, HAS NO SUCH INNER DUPLICITY; AND THE SEPARATION OF IT INTO CONSCIOUSNESS AND CONTENT COMES, NOT BY WAY OF SUBTRACTION, BUT BY WAY OF ADDITION"(p. 9).

He illustrates his meaning by the analogy of paint as it appears in a paint-shop and as it appears in a picture: in the one case it is just "saleable matter," while in the other it "performs a spiritual function. Just so, I maintain (he continues), does a given undivided portion of experience, taken in one context of associates, play the part of a knower, of a state of mind, of 'consciousness'; while in a different context the same undivided bit of experience plays the part of a thing known, of an objective 'content.' In a word, in one group it figures as a thought, in another group as a thing"(pp. 9-10).

He does not believe in the supposed immediate certainty of thought. "Let the case be what it may in others," he says, "I am as confident as I am of anything that, in myself, the stream of thinking (which I recognize emphatically as a phenomenon) is only a careless name for what, when scrutinized, reveals itself to consist chiefly of the stream of my breathing. The 'I think' which Kant said must be able to accompany all my objects, is the 'I breathe' which actually does accompany them"(pp. 36-37).

The same view of "consciousness" is set forth in the succeeding essay, "A World of Pure Experience" (ib., pp. 39-91). The use of the phrase "pure experience" in both essays points to a lingering influence of idealism. "Experience," like "consciousness," must be a product, not part of the primary stuff of the world. It must be possible, if James is right in his main contentions, that roughly the same stuff, differently arranged, would not give rise to anything that could be called "experience." This word has been dropped by the American realists, among whom we may mention specially Professor R. B. Perry of Harvard and Mr. Edwin B. Holt. The interests of this school are in general philosophy and the philosophy of the sciences, rather than in psychology; they have derived a strong impulsion from James, but have more interest than he had in logic and mathematics and the abstract part of philosophy. They speak of "neutral" entities as the stuff out of which both mind and matter are constructed. Thus Holt says: "If the terms and propositions of logic must be substantialized, they are all strictly of one substance, for which perhaps the least dangerous name is neutral-stuff. The relation of neutral-stuff to matter and mind we shall have presently to consider at considerable length."[6]

My own belief—for which the reasons will appear in subsequent lectures—is that James is right in rejecting consciousness as an entity, and that the American

---

[6] *The Concept of Consciousness* (Geo. Allen & Co., 1914), p. 52.

realists are partly right, though not wholly, in considering that both mind and matter are composed of a neutral-stuff which, in isolation, is neither mental nor material. I should admit this view as regards sensations: what is heard or seen belongs equally to psychology and to physics. But I should say that images belong only to the mental world, while those occurrences (if any) which do not form part of any "experience" belong only to the physical world. There are, it seems to me, prima facie different kinds of causal laws, one belonging to physics and the other to psychology. The law of gravitation, for example, is a physical law, while the law of association is a psychological law. Sensations are subject to both kinds of laws, and are therefore truly "neutral" in Holt's sense. But entities subject only to physical laws, or only to psychological laws, are not neutral, and may be called respectively purely material and purely mental. Even those, however, which are purely mental will not have that intrinsic reference to objects which Brentano assigns to them and which constitutes the essence of "consciousness" as ordinarily understood. But it is now time to pass on to other modern tendencies, also hostile to "consciousness."

There is a psychological school called "Behaviourists," of whom the protagonist is Professor John B. Watson,[7] formerly of the Johns Hopkins University. To them also, on the whole, belongs Professor John Dewey, who, with James and Dr. Schiller, was one of the three founders of pragmatism. The view of the "behaviourists" is that nothing can be known except by external observation. They deny altogether that there is a separate source of knowledge called "introspection," by which we can know things about ourselves which we could never observe in others. They do not by any means deny that all sorts of things MAY go on in our minds: they only say that such things, if they occur, are not susceptible of scientific observation, and do not therefore concern psychology as a science. Psychology as a science, they say, is only concerned with BEHAVIOUR, i.e. with what we DO; this alone, they contend, can be accurately observed. Whether we think meanwhile, they tell us, cannot be known; in their observation of the behaviour of human beings, they have not so far found any evidence of thought. True, we talk a great deal, and imagine that in so doing we are showing that we can think; but behaviourists say that the talk they have to listen to can be explained without supposing that people think. Where you might expect a chapter on "thought processes" you come instead upon a chapter on "The Language Habit." It is humiliating to find how terribly adequate this hypothesis turns out to be.

Behaviourism has not, however, sprung from observing the folly of men. It is the wisdom of animals that has suggested the view. It has always been a common topic of popular discussion whether animals "think." On this topic people are prepared to take sides without having the vaguest idea what they mean by "thinking." Those who desired to investigate such questions were led to observe the behaviour of animals, in the hope that their behaviour would throw some light on their mental faculties. At first sight,

---

[7] See especially his *Behavior: an Introduction to Comparative Psychology,* New York, 1914.

it might seem that this is so. People say that a dog "knows" its name because it comes when it is called, and that it "remembers" its master, because it looks sad in his absence, but wags its tail and barks when he returns. That the dog behaves in this way is matter of observation, but that it "knows" or "remembers" anything is an inference, and in fact a very doubtful one. The more such inferences are examined, the more precarious they are seen to be. Hence the study of animal behaviour has been gradually led to abandon all attempt at mental interpretation. And it can hardly be doubted that, in many cases of complicated behaviour very well adapted to its ends, there can be no prevision of those ends. The first time a bird builds a nest, we can hardly suppose it knows that there will be eggs to be laid in it, or that it will sit on the eggs, or that they will hatch into young birds. It does what it does at each stage because instinct gives it an impulse to do just that, not because it foresees and desires the result of its actions.[8]

Careful observers of animals, being anxious to avoid precarious inferences, have gradually discovered more and more how to give an account of the actions of animals without assuming what we call "consciousness." It has seemed to the behaviourists that similar methods can be applied to human behaviour, without assuming anything not open to external observation. Let us give a crude illustration, too crude for the authors in question, but capable of affording a rough insight into their meaning. Suppose two children in a school, both of whom are asked "What is six times nine?" One says fifty-four, the other says fifty-six. The one, we say, "knows" what six times nine is, the other does not. But all that we can observe is a certain language-habit. The one child has acquired the habit of saying "six times nine is fifty-four"; the other has not. There is no more need of "thought" in this than there is when a horse turns into his accustomed stable; there are merely more numerous and complicated habits. There is obviously an observable fact called "knowing" such-and-such a thing; examinations are experiments for discovering such facts. But all that is observed or discovered is a certain set of habits in the use of words. The thoughts (if any) in the mind of the examinee are of no interest to the examiner; nor has the examiner any reason to suppose even the most successful examinee capable of even the smallest amount of thought.

Thus what is called "knowing," in the sense in which we can ascertain what other people "know," is a phenomenon exemplified in their physical behaviour, including spoken and written words. There is no reason—so Watson argues—to suppose that their knowledge IS anything beyond the habits shown in this behaviour: the inference that other people have something nonphysical called "mind" or "thought" is therefore unwarranted.

So far, there is nothing particularly repugnant to our prejudices in the conclusions of the behaviourists. We are all willing to admit that other people are thoughtless. But when it comes to ourselves, we feel convinced that we can actually perceive our own

---

[8] An interesting discussion of the question whether instinctive actions, when first performed, involve any prevision, however vague, will be found in Lloyd Morgan's *Instinct and Experience* (Methuen, 1912), chap. ii.

thinking. "Cogito, ergo sum" would be regarded by most people as having a true premiss. This, however, the behaviourist denies. He maintains that our knowledge of ourselves is no different in kind from our knowledge of other people. We may see MORE, because our own body is easier to observe than that of other people; but we do not see anything radically unlike what we see of others. Introspection, as a separate source of knowledge, is entirely denied by psychologists of this school. I shall discuss this question at length in a later lecture; for the present I will only observe that it is by no means simple, and that, though I believe the behaviourists somewhat overstate their case, yet there is an important element of truth in their contention, since the things which we can discover by introspection do not seem to differ in any very fundamental way from the things which we discover by external observation.

So far, we have been principally concerned with knowing. But it might well be maintained that desiring is what is really most characteristic of mind. Human beings are constantly engaged in achieving some end they feel pleasure in success and pain in failure. In a purely material world, it may be said, there would be no opposition of pleasant and unpleasant, good and bad, what is desired and what is feared. A man's acts are governed by purposes. He decides, let us suppose, to go to a certain place, whereupon he proceeds to the station, takes his ticket and enters the train. If the usual route is blocked by an accident, he goes by some other route. All that he does is determined—or so it seems—by the end he has in view, by what lies in front of him, rather than by what lies behind. With dead matter, this is not the case. A stone at the top of a hill may start rolling, but it shows no pertinacity in trying to get to the bottom. Any ledge or obstacle will stop it, and it will exhibit no signs of discontent if this happens. It is not attracted by the pleasantness of the valley, as a sheep or cow might be, but propelled by the steepness of the hill at the place where it is. In all this we have characteristic differences between the behaviour of animals and the behaviour of matter as studied by physics.

Desire, like knowledge, is, of course, in one sense an observable phenomenon. An elephant will eat a bun, but not a mutton chop; a duck will go into the water, but a hen will not. But when we think of our own desires, most people believe that we can know them by an immediate self-knowledge which does not depend upon observation of our actions. Yet if this were the case, it would be odd that people are so often mistaken as to what they desire. It is matter of common observation that "so-and-so does not know his own motives," or that "A is envious of B and malicious about him, but quite unconscious of being so." Such people are called self-deceivers, and are supposed to have had to go through some more or less elaborate process of concealing from themselves what would otherwise have been obvious. I believe that this is an entire mistake. I believe that the discovery of our own motives can only be made by the same process by which we discover other people's, namely, the process of observing our actions and inferring the desire which could prompt them. A desire is "conscious" when we have told ourselves that we have it. A hungry man may say to himself: "Oh, I do want my lunch." Then his desire is "conscious." But it only differs from an "unconscious" desire by the presence of appropriate words, which is by no means a fundamental difference.

The belief that a motive is normally conscious makes it easier to be mistaken as to our own motives than as to other people's. When some desire that we should be ashamed of is attributed to us, we notice that we have never had it consciously, in the sense of saying to ourselves, "I wish that would happen." We therefore look for some other interpretation of our actions, and regard our friends as very unjust when they refuse to be convinced by our repudiation of what we hold to be a calumny. Moral considerations greatly increase the difficulty of clear thinking in this matter. It is commonly argued that people are not to blame for unconscious motives, but only for conscious ones. In order, therefore, to be wholly virtuous it is only necessary to repeat virtuous formulas. We say: "I desire to be kind to my friends, honourable in business, philanthropic towards the poor, public-spirited in politics." So long as we refuse to allow ourselves, even in the watches of the night, to avow any contrary desires, we may be bullies at home, shady in the City, skinflints in paying wages and profiteers in dealing with the public; yet, if only conscious motives are to count in moral valuation, we shall remain model characters. This is an agreeable doctrine, and it is not surprising that men are un willing to abandon it. But moral considerations are the worst enemies of the scientific spirit and we must dismiss them from our minds if we wish to arrive at truth.

I believe—as I shall try to prove in a later lecture—that desire, like force in mechanics, is of the nature of a convenient fiction for describing shortly certain laws of behaviour. A hungry animal is restless until it finds food; then it becomes quiescent. The thing which will bring a restless condition to an end is said to be what is desired. But only experience can show what will have this sedative effect, and it is easy to make mistakes. We feel dissatisfaction, and think that such and-such a thing would remove it; but in thinking this, we are theorizing, not observing a patent fact. Our theorizing is often mistaken, and when it is mistaken there is a difference between what we think we desire and what in fact will bring satisfaction. This is such a common phenomenon that any theory of desire which fails to account for it must be wrong.

What have been called "unconscious" desires have been brought very much to the fore in recent years by psycho-analysis. Psycho-analysis, as every one knows, is primarily a method of understanding hysteria and certain forms of insanity[9]; but it has

---

[9] There is a wide field of "unconscious" phenomena which does not depend upon psycho-analytic theories. Such occurrences as automatic writing lead Dr. Morton Prince to say: "As I view this question of the subconscious, far too much weight is given to the point of awareness or not awareness of our conscious processes. As a matter of fact, we find entirely identical phenomena, that is, identical in every respect but one-that of awareness in which sometimes we are aware of these conscious phenomena and sometimes not"(p. 87 of *Subconscious Phenomena,* by various authors, Rebman). Dr. Morton Price conceives that there may be "consciousness" without "awareness." But this is a difficult view, and one which makes some definition of "consciousness" imperative. For nay part, I cannot see how to separate consciousness from awareness.

been found that there is much in the lives of ordinary men and women which bears a humiliating resemblance to the delusions of the insane. The connection of dreams, irrational beliefs and foolish actions with unconscious wishes has been brought to light, though with some exaggeration, by Freud and Jung and their followers. As regards the nature of these unconscious wishes, it seems to me—though as a layman I speak with diffidence—that many psycho-analysts are unduly narrow; no doubt the wishes they emphasize exist, but others, e.g. for honour and power, are equally operative and equally liable to concealment. This, however, does not affect the value of their general theories from the point of view of theoretic psychology, and it is from this point of view that their results are important for the analysis of mind.

What, I think, is clearly established, is that a man's actions and beliefs may be wholly dominated by a desire of which he is quite unconscious, and which he indignantly repudiates when it is suggested to him. Such a desire is generally, in morbid cases, of a sort which the patient would consider wicked; if he had to admit that he had the desire, he would loathe himself. Yet it is so strong that it must force an outlet for itself; hence it becomes necessary to entertain whole systems of false beliefs in order to hide the nature of what is desired. The resulting delusions in very many cases disappear if the hysteric or lunatic can be made to face the facts about himself. The consequence of this is that the treatment of many forms of insanity has grown more psychological and less physiological than it used to be. Instead of looking for a physical defect in the brain, those who treat delusions look for the repressed desire which has found this contorted mode of expression. For those who do not wish to plunge into the somewhat repulsive and often rather wild theories of psychoanalytic pioneers, it will be worth while to read a little book by Dr. Bernard Hart on "The Psychology of Insanity."[10] On this question of the mental as opposed to the physiological study of the causes of insanity, Dr. Hart says:

"The psychological conception [of insanity] is based on the view that mental processes can be directly studied without any reference to the accompanying changes which are presumed to take place in the brain, and that insanity may therefore be properly attacked from the standpoint of psychology"(p. 9).

This illustrates a point which I am anxious to make clear from the outset. Any attempt to classify modern views, such as I propose to advocate, from the old standpoint of materialism and idealism, is only misleading. In certain respects, the views which I shall be setting forth approximate to materialism; in certain others, they approximate to its opposite. On this question of the study of delusions, the practical effect of the modern theories, as Dr. Hart points out, is emancipation from the materialist method. On the other hand, as he also points out (pp. 38-9), imbecility and dementia still have to be considered physiologically, as caused by defects in the brain. There is no inconsistency in this If, as we maintain, mind and matter are neither of them the actual stuff of reality,

---

[10] Cambridge, 1912; 2nd edition, 1914. The following references are to the second edition.

but different convenient groupings of an underlying material, then, clearly, the question whether, in regard to a given phenomenon, we are to seek a physical or a mental cause, is merely one to be decided by trial. Metaphysicians have argued endlessly as to the interaction of mind and matter. The followers of Descartes held that mind and matter are so different as to make any action of the one on the other impossible. When I will to move my arm, they said, it is not my will that operates on my arm, but God, who, by His omnipotence, moves my arm whenever I want it moved. The modern doctrine of psychophysical parallelism is not appreciably different from this theory of the Cartesian school. Psycho-physical parallelism is the theory that mental and physical events each have causes in their own sphere, but run on side by side owing to the fact that every state of the brain coexists with a definite state of the mind, and vice versa. This view of the reciprocal causal independence of mind and matter has no basis except in metaphysical theory.[11] For us, there is no necessity to make any such assumption, which is very difficult to harmonize with obvious facts. I receive a letter inviting me to dinner: the letter is a physical fact, but my apprehension of its meaning is mental. Here we have an effect of matter on mind. In consequence of my apprehension of the meaning of the letter, I go to the right place at the right time; here we have an effect of mind on matter. I shall try to persuade you, in the course of these lectures, that matter is not so material and mind not so mental as is generally supposed. When we are speaking of matter, it will seem as if we were inclining to idealism; when we are speaking of mind, it will seem as if we were inclining to materialism. Neither is the truth. Our world is to be constructed out of what the American realists call "neutral" entities, which have neither the hardness and indestructibility of matter, nor the reference to objects which is supposed to characterize mind.

There is, it is true, one objection which might be felt, not indeed to the action of matter on mind, but to the action of mind on matter. The laws of physics, it may be urged, are apparently adequate to explain everything that happens to matter, even when it is matter in a man's brain. This, however, is only a hypothesis, not an established theory. There is no cogent empirical reason for supposing that the laws determining the motions of living bodies are exactly the same as those that apply to dead matter. Sometimes, of course, they are clearly the same. When a man falls from a precipice or slips on a piece of orange peel, his body behaves as if it were devoid of life. These are the occasions that make Bergson laugh. But when a man's bodily movements are what we call "voluntary," they are, at any rate prima facie, very different in their laws from the movements of what is devoid of life. I do not wish to say dogmatically that the difference is irreducible; I think it highly probable that it is not. I say only that the study of the behaviour of living bodies, in the present state of our knowledge, is distinct from physics. The study of gases was originally

---

[11] It would seem, however, that Dr. Hart accepts this theory as a methodological precept. See his contribution to *Subconscious Phenomena* (quoted above), especially pp. 121-2.

quite distinct from that of rigid bodies, and would never have advanced to its present state if it had not been independently pursued. Nowadays both the gas and the rigid body are manufactured out of a more primitive and universal kind of matter. In like manner, as a question of methodology, the laws of living bodies are to be studied, in the first place, without any undue haste to subordinate them to the laws of physics. Boyle's law and the rest had to be discovered before the kinetic theory of gases became possible. But in psychology we are hardly yet at the stage of Boyle's law. Meanwhile we need not be held up by the bogey of the universal rigid exactness of physics. This is, as yet, a mere hypothesis, to be tested empirically without any preconceptions. It may be true, or it may not. So far, that is all we can say.

Returning from this digression to our main topic, namely, the criticism of "consciousness," we observe that Freud and his followers, though they have demonstrated beyond dispute the immense importance of "unconscious" desires in determining our actions and beliefs, have not attempted the task of telling us what an "unconscious" desire actually is, and have thus invested their doctrine with an air of mystery and mythology which forms a large part of its popular attractiveness. They speak always as though it were more normal for a desire to be conscious, and as though a positive cause had to be assigned for its being unconscious. Thus "the unconscious" becomes a sort of underground prisoner, living in a dungeon, breaking in at long intervals upon our daylight respectability with dark groans and maledictions and strange atavistic lusts. The ordinary reader, almost inevitably, thinks of this underground person as another consciousness, prevented by what Freud calls the "censor" from making his voice heard in company, except on rare and dreadful occasions when he shouts so loud that every one hears him and there is a scandal. Most of us like the idea that we could be desperately wicked if only we let ourselves go. For this reason, the Freudian "unconscious" has been a consolation to many quiet and well-behaved persons.

I do not think the truth is quite so picturesque as this. I believe an "unconscious" desire is merely a causal law of our behaviour,[12] namely, that we remain restlessly active until a certain state of affairs is realized, when we achieve temporary equilibrium If we know beforehand what this state of affairs is, our desire is conscious; if not, unconscious. The unconscious desire is not something actually existing, but merely a tendency to a certain behaviour; it has exactly the same status as a force in dynamics. The unconscious desire is in no way mysterious; it is the natural primitive form of desire, from which the other has developed through our habit of observing and theorizing (often wrongly). It is not necessary to suppose, as Freud seems to do, that every unconscious wish was once conscious, and was then, in his terminology, "repressed" because we disapproved of it. On the contrary, we shall suppose that, although Freudian "repression" undoubtedly occurs and is important, it is not the usual reason for unconsciousness of our wishes. The usual reason is merely that

---

[12] Cf. Hart, *The Psychology of Insanity*, p. 19.

wishes are all, to begin with, unconscious, and only become known when they are actively noticed. Usually, from laziness, people do not notice, but accept the theory of human nature which they find current, and attribute to themselves whatever wishes this theory would lead them to expect. We used to be full of virtuous wishes, but since Freud our wishes have become, in the words of the Prophet Jeremiah, "deceitful above all things and desperately wicked." Both these views, in most of those who have held them, are the product of theory rather than observation, for observation requires effort, whereas repeating phrases does not.

The interpretation of unconscious wishes which I have been advocating has been set forth briefly by Professor John B. Watson in an article called "The Psychology of Wish Fulfilment," which appeared in "The Scientific Monthly" in November, 1916. Two quotations will serve to show his point of view:

"The Freudians (he says) have made more or less of a 'metaphysical entity' out of the censor. They suppose that when wishes are repressed they are repressed into the 'unconscious,' and that this mysterious censor stands at the trapdoor lying between the conscious and the unconscious. Many of us do not believe in a world of the unconscious (a few of us even have grave doubts about the usefulness of the term consciousness), hence we try to explain censorship along ordinary biological lines. We believe that one group of habits can 'down' another group of habits—or instincts. In this case our ordinary system of habits—those which we call expressive of our 'real selves'—inhibit or quench (keep inactive or partially inactive) those habits and instinctive tendencies which belong largely in the past"(p. 483).

Again, after speaking of the frustration of some impulses which is involved in acquiring the habits of a civilized adult, he continues:

"It is among these frustrated impulses that I would find the biological basis of the unfulfilled wish. Such 'wishes' need never have been 'conscious,' and NEED NEVER HAVE BEEN SUPPRESSED INTO FREUD'S REALM OF THE UNCONSCIOUS. It may be inferred from this that there is no particular reason for applying the term 'wish' to such tendencies"(p. 485).

One of the merits of the general analysis of mind which we shall be concerned with in the following lectures is that it removes the atmosphere of mystery from the phenomena brought to light by the psycho-analysts. Mystery is delightful, but unscientific, since it depends upon ignorance. Man has developed out of the animals, and there is no serious gap between him and the amoeba. Something closely analogous to knowledge and desire, as regards its effects on behaviour, exists among animals, even where what we call "consciousness" is hard to believe in; something equally analogous exists in ourselves in cases where no trace of "consciousness" can be found. It is therefore natural to suppose that, what ever may be the correct definition of "consciousness," "consciousness" is not the essence of life or mind. In the following lectures, accordingly, this term will disappear until we have dealt with words, when it will re-emerge as mainly a trivial and unimportant outcome of linguistic habits.

# LECTURE II

## Instinct and Habit

In attempting to understand the elements out of which mental phenomena are compounded, it is of the greatest importance to remember that from the protozoa to man there is nowhere a very wide gap either in structure or in behaviour. From this fact it is a highly probable inference that there is also nowhere a very wide mental gap. It is, of course, POSSIBLE that there may be, at certain stages in evolution, elements which are entirely new from the standpoint of analysis, though in their nascent form they have little influence on behaviour and no very marked correlatives in structure. But the hypothesis of continuity in mental development is clearly preferable if no psychological facts make it impossible. We shall find, if I am not mistaken, that there are no facts which refute the hypothesis of mental continuity, and that, on the other hand, this hypothesis affords a useful test of suggested theories as to the nature of mind.

The hypothesis of mental continuity throughout organic evolution may be used in two different ways. On the one hand, it may be held that we have more knowledge of our own minds than those of animals, and that we should use this knowledge to infer the existence of something similar to our own mental processes in animals and even in plants. On the other hand, it may be held that animals and plants present simpler phenomena, more easily analysed than those of human minds; on this ground it may be urged that explanations which are adequate in the case of animals ought not to be lightly rejected in the case of man. The practical effects of these two views are diametrically opposite: the first leads us to level up animal intelligence with what we believe ourselves to know about our own intelligence, while the second leads us to attempt a levelling down of our own intelligence to something not too remote from what we can observe in animals. It is therefore important to consider the relative justification of the two ways of applying the principle of continuity.

It is clear that the question turns upon another, namely, which can we know best, the psychology of animals or that of human beings? If we can know most about animals, we shall use this knowledge as a basis for inference about human beings; if we can know most about human beings, we shall adopt the opposite procedure. And the question whether we can know most about the psychology of human beings or about that of animals turns upon yet another, namely: Is introspection or external observation the surer method in psychology? This is a question which I propose to discuss at length in Lecture VI; I shall therefore content myself now with a statement of the conclusions to be arrived at.

We know a great many things concerning ourselves which we cannot know nearly so directly concerning animals or even other people. We know when we have a toothache, what we are thinking of, what dreams we have when we are asleep, and a host of other occurrences which we only know about others when they tell us of them, or otherwise make them inferable by their behaviour. Thus, so far as knowledge of detached facts is concerned, the advantage is on the side of self-knowledge as against external observation.

But when we come to the analysis and scientific understanding of the facts, the advantages on the side of self-knowledge become far less clear. We know, for example, that we have desires and beliefs, but we do not know what constitutes a desire or a belief. The phenomena are so familiar that it is difficult to realize how little we really know about them. We see in animals, and to a lesser extent in plants, behaviour more or less similar to that which, in us, is prompted by desires and beliefs, and we find that, as we descend in the scale of evolution, behaviour becomes simpler, more easily reducible to rule, more scientifically analysable and predictable. And just because we are not misled by familiarity we find it easier to be cautious in interpreting behaviour when we are dealing with phenomena remote from those of our own minds: Moreover, introspection, as psychoanalysis has demonstrated, is extraordinarily fallible even in cases where we feel a high degree of certainty. The net result seems to be that, though self-knowledge has a definite and important contribution to make to psychology, it is exceedingly misleading unless it is constantly checked and controlled by the test of external observation, and by the theories which such observation suggests when applied to animal behaviour. On the whole, therefore, there is probably more to be learnt about human psychology from animals than about animal psychology from human beings; but this conclusion is one of degree, and must not be pressed beyond a point.

It is only bodily phenomena that can be directly observed in animals, or even, strictly speaking, in other human beings. We can observe such things as their movements, their physiological processes, and the sounds they emit. Such things as desires and beliefs, which seem obvious to introspection, are not visible directly to external observation. Accordingly, if we begin our study of psychology by external observation, we must not begin by assuming such things as desires and beliefs, but only such things as external observation can reveal, which will be characteristics of the movements and physiological processes of animals. Some animals, for example, always run away from light and hide themselves in dark places. If you pick up a mossy stone which is lightly embedded in the earth, you will see a number of small animals scuttling away from the unwonted daylight and seeking again the darkness of which you have deprived them. Such animals are sensitive to light, in the sense that their movements are affected by it; but it would be rash to infer that they have sensations in any way analogous to our sensations of sight. Such inferences, which go beyond the observable facts, are to be avoided with the utmost care.

It is customary to divide human movements into three classes, voluntary, reflex and mechanical. We may illustrate the distinction by a quotation from William James ("Psychology," i, 12):

"If I hear the conductor calling 'all aboard' as I enter the depot, my heart first stops, then palpitates, and my legs respond to the air-waves falling on my tympanum by quickening their movements. If I stumble as I run, the sensation of falling provokes a movement of the hands towards the direction of the fall, the effect of which is to shield the body from too sudden a shock. If a cinder enter my eye, its lids close forcibly and a copious flow of tears tends to wash it out.

"These three responses to a sensational stimulus differ, however, in many respects. The closure of the eye and the lachrymation are quite involuntary, and so is the disturbance of the heart. Such involuntary responses we know as 'reflex' acts. The motion of the arms to break the shock of falling may also be called reflex, since it occurs too quickly to be deliberately intended. Whether it be instinctive or whether it result from the pedestrian education of childhood may be doubtful; it is, at any rate, less automatic than the previous acts, for a man might by conscious effort learn to perform it more skilfully, or even to suppress it altogether. Actions of this kind, with which instinct and volition enter upon equal terms, have been called 'semi-reflex.' The act of running towards the train, on the other hand, has no instinctive element about it. It is purely the result of education, and is preceded by a consciousness of the purpose to be attained and a distinct mandate of the will. It is a 'voluntary act.' Thus the animal's reflex and voluntary performances shade into each other gradually, being connected by acts which may often occur automatically, but may also be modified by conscious intelligence.

"An outside observer, unable to perceive the accompanying consciousness, might be wholly at a loss to discriminate between the automatic acts and those which volition escorted. But if the criterion of mind's existence be the choice of the proper means for the attainment of a supposed end, all the acts alike seem to be inspired by intelligence, for APPROPRIATENESS characterizes them all alike."

There is one movement, among those that James mentions at first, which is not subsequently classified, namely, the stumbling. This is the kind of movement which may be called "mechanical"; it is evidently of a different kind from either reflex or voluntary movements, and more akin to the movements of dead matter. We may define a movement of an animal's body as "mechanical" when it proceeds as if only dead matter were involved. For example, if you fall over a cliff, you move under the influence of gravitation, and your centre of gravity describes just as correct a parabola as if you were already dead. Mechanical movements have not the characteristic of appropriateness, unless by accident, as when a drunken man falls into a waterbutt and is sobered. But reflex and voluntary movements are not ALWAYS appropriate, unless in some very recondite sense. A moth flying into a lamp is not acting sensibly; no more is a man who is in such a hurry to get his ticket that he cannot remember the name of his destination. Appropriateness is a complicated and merely approximate idea, and for the present we shall do well to dismiss it from our thoughts.

As James states, there is no difference, from the point of view of the outside observer, between voluntary and reflex movements. The physiologist can discover that both depend upon the nervous system, and he may find that the movements which we call voluntary depend upon higher centres in the brain than those that are reflex. But he cannot discover anything as to the presence or absence of "will" or "consciousness," for these things can only be seen from within, if at all. For the present, we wish to place ourselves resolutely in the position of outside observers; we will therefore ignore the distinction between voluntary and reflex movements. We will call the two together "vital" movements. We may then distinguish "vital" from mechanical movements by the fact that vital movements depend for their causation upon the special properties of the nervous system, while mechanical movements depend only upon the properties which animal bodies share with matter in general.

There is need for some care if the distinction between mechanical and vital movements is to be made precise. It is quite likely that, if we knew more about animal bodies, we could deduce all their movements from the laws of chemistry and physics. It is already fairly easy to see how chemistry reduces to physics, i.e. how the differences between different chemical elements can be accounted for by differences of physical structure, the constituents of the structure being electrons which are exactly alike in all kinds of matter. We only know in part how to reduce physiology to chemistry, but we know enough to make it likely that the reduction is possible. If we suppose it effected, what would become of the difference between vital and mechanical movements?

Some analogies will make the difference clear. A shock to a mass of dynamite produces quite different effects from an equal shock to a mass of steel: in the one case there is a vast explosion, while in the other case there is hardly any noticeable disturbance. Similarly, you may sometimes find on a mountain-side a large rock poised so delicately that a touch will set it crashing down into the valley, while the rocks all round are so firm that only a considerable force can dislodge them What is analogous in these two cases is the existence of a great store of energy in unstable equilibrium ready to burst into violent motion by the addition of a very slight disturbance. Similarly, it requires only a very slight expenditure of energy to send a post-card with the words "All is discovered; fly!" but the effect in generating kinetic energy is said to be amazing. A human body, like a mass of dynamite, contains a store of energy in unstable equilibrium, ready to be directed in this direction or that by a disturbance which is physically very small, such as a spoken word. In all such cases the reduction of behaviour to physical laws can only be effected by entering into great minuteness;

so long as we confine ourselves to the observation of comparatively large masses, the way in which the equilibrium will be upset cannot be determined. Physicists distinguish between macroscopic and microscopic equations: the former determine the visible movements of bodies of ordinary size, the latter the minute occurrences in the smallest parts. It is only the microscopic equations that are supposed to be the same for all sorts of matter. The macroscopic equations result from a process of averaging out, and may be different in different cases. So, in our instance, the laws of macroscopic phenomena are different for mechanical and vital movements, though the laws of microscopic phenomena may be the same.

We may say, speaking somewhat roughly, that a stimulus applied to the nervous system, like a spark to dynamite, is able to take advantage of the stored energy in unstable equilibrium, and thus to produce movements out of proportion to the proximate cause. Movements produced in this way are vital movements, while mechanical movements are those in which the stored energy of a living body is not involved. Similarly dynamite may be exploded, thereby displaying its characteristic properties, or may (with due precautions) be carted about like any other mineral. The explosion is analogous to vital movements, the carting about to mechanical movements.

Mechanical movements are of no interest to the psychologist, and it has only been necessary to define them in order to be able to exclude them. When a psychologist studies behaviour, it is only vital movements that concern him. We shall, therefore, proceed to ignore mechanical movements, and study only the properties of the remainder.

The next point is to distinguish between movements that are instinctive and movements that are acquired by experience. This distinction also is to some extent one of degree. Professor Lloyd Morgan gives the following definition of "instinctive behaviour":

"That which is, on its first occurrence, independent of prior experience; which tends to the well-being of the individual and the preservation of the race; which is similarly performed by all members of the same more or less restricted group of animals; and which may be subject to subsequent modification under the guidance of experience."[13]

This definition is framed for the purposes of biology, and is in some respects unsuited to the needs of psychology. Though perhaps unavoidable, allusion to "the same more or less restricted group of animals" makes it impossible to judge what is instinctive in the behaviour of an isolated individual. Moreover, "the well-being of the individual and the preservation of the race" is only a usual characteristic, not a universal one, of the sort of movements that, from our point of view, are to be called instinctive; instances of harmful instincts will be given shortly. The essential point of

---

[13] *Instinct and Experience* (Methuen, 1912) p. 5.

the definition, from our point of view, is that an instinctive movement is in dependent of prior experience.

We may say that an "instinctive" movement is a vital movement performed by an animal the first time that it finds itself in a novel situation; or, more correctly, one which it would perform if the situation were novel.[14] The instincts of an animal are different at different periods of its growth, and this fact may cause changes of behaviour which are not due to learning. The maturing and seasonal fluctuation of the sex-instinct affords a good illustration. When the sex-instinct first matures, the behaviour of an animal in the presence of a mate is different from its previous behaviour in similar circumstances, but is not learnt, since it is just the same if the animal has never previously been in the presence of a mate.

On the other hand, a movement is "learnt," or embodies a "habit," if it is due to previous experience of similar situations, and is not what it would be if the animal had had no such experience.

There are various complications which blur the sharpness of this distinction in practice. To begin with, many instincts mature gradually, and while they are immature an animal may act in a fumbling manner which is very difficult to distinguish from learning. James ("Psychology," ii, 407) maintains that children walk by instinct, and that the awkwardness of their first attempts is only due to the fact that the instinct has not yet ripened. He hopes that "some scientific widower, left alone with his offspring at the critical moment, may ere long test this suggestion on the living subject." However this may be, he quotes evidence to show that "birds do not LEARN to fly," but fly by instinct when they reach the appropriate age (ib., p. 406). In the second place, instinct often gives only a rough outline of the sort of thing to do, in which case learning is necessary in order to acquire certainty and precision in action. In the third place, even in the clearest cases of acquired habit, such as speaking, some instinct is required to set in motion the process of learning. In the case of speaking, the chief instinct involved is commonly supposed to be that of imitation, but this may be questioned. (See Thorndike's "Animal Intelligence," p. 253 ff.)

In spite of these qualifications, the broad distinction between instinct and habit is undeniable. To take extreme cases, every animal at birth can take food by instinct, before it has had opportunity to learn; on the other hand, no one can ride a bicycle by instinct, though, after learning, the necessary movements become just as automatic as if they were instinctive.

The process of learning, which consists in the acquisition of habits, has been much studied in various animals.[15] For example: you put a hungry animal, say a cat, in a cage which has a door that can be opened by lifting a latch; outside the cage you

---

[14] Though this can only be decided by comparison with other members of the species, and thus exposes us to the need of comparison which we thought an objection to Professor Lloyd Morgan's definition.

[15] The scientific study of this subject may almost be said to begin with Thorndike's *Animal Intelligence* (Macmillan, 1911).

put food. The cat at first dashes all round the cage, making frantic efforts to force a way out. At last, by accident, the latch is lifted and the cat pounces on the food. Next day you repeat the experiment, and you find that the cat gets out much more quickly than the first time, although it still makes some random movements. The third day it gets out still more quickly, and before long it goes straight to the latch and lifts it at once. Or you make a model of the Hampton Court maze, and put a rat in the middle, assaulted by the smell of food on the outside. The rat starts running down the passages, and is constantly stopped by blind alleys, but at last, by persistent attempts, it gets out. You repeat this experiment day after day; you measure the time taken by the rat in reaching the food; you find that the time rapidly diminishes, and that after a while the rat ceases to make any wrong turnings. It is by essentially similar processes that we learn speaking, writing, mathematics, or the government of an empire.

Professor Watson ("Behavior," pp. 262-3) has an ingenious theory as to the way in which habit arises out of random movements. I think there is a reason why his theory cannot be regarded as alone sufficient, but it seems not unlikely that it is partly correct. Suppose, for the sake of simplicity, that there are just ten random movements which may be made by the animal—say, ten paths down which it may go—and that only one of these leads to food, or whatever else represents success in the case in question. Then the successful movement always occurs during the animal's attempts, whereas each of the others, on the average, occurs in only half the attempts. Thus the tendency to repeat a previous performance (which is easily explicable without the intervention of "consciousness") leads to a greater emphasis on the successful movement than on any other, and in time causes it alone to be performed. The objection to this view, if taken as the sole explanation, is that on improvement ought to set in till after the SECOND trial, whereas experiment shows that already at the second attempt the animal does better than the first time. Something further is, therefore, required to account for the genesis of habit from random movements; but I see no reason to suppose that what is further required involves "consciousness."

Mr. Thorndike (op. cit., p. 244) formulates two "provisional laws of acquired behaviour or learning," as follows:

"The Law of Effect is that: Of several responses made to the same situation, those which are accompanied or closely followed by satisfaction to the animal will, other things being equal, be more firmly connected with the situation, so that, when it recurs, they will be more likely to recur; those which are accompanied or closely followed by discomfort to the animal will, other things being equal, have their connections with that situation weakened, so that, when it recurs, they will be less likely to occur. The greater the satisfaction or discomfort, the greater the strengthening or weakening of the bond.

"The Law of Exercise is that: Any response to a situation will, other things being equal, be more strongly connected with the situation in proportion to the number of times it has been connected with that situation and to the average vigour and duration of the connections."

With the explanation to be presently given of the meaning of "satisfaction" and "discomfort," there seems every reason to accept these two laws.

What is true of animals, as regards instinct and habit, is equally true of men. But the higher we rise in the evolutionary scale, broadly speaking, the greater becomes the power of learning, and the fewer are the occasions when pure instinct is exhibited unmodified in adult life. This applies with great force to man, so much so that some have thought instinct less important in the life of man than in that of animals. This, however, would be a mistake. Learning is only possible when instinct supplies the driving-force. The animals in cages, which gradually learn to get out, perform random movements at first, which are purely instinctive. But for these random movements, they would never acquire the experience which afterwards enables them to produce the right movement. (This is partly questioned by Hobhouse[16]—wrongly, I think.) Similarly, children learning to talk make all sorts of sounds, until one day the right sound comes by accident. It is clear that the original making of random sounds, without which speech would never be learnt, is instinctive. I think we may say the same of all the habits and aptitudes that we acquire in all of them there has been present throughout some instinctive activity, prompting at first rather inefficient movements, but supplying the driving force while more and more effective methods are being acquired. A cat which is hungry smells fish, and goes to the larder. This is a thoroughly efficient method when there is fish in the larder, and it is often successfully practised by children. But in later life it is found that merely going to the larder does not cause fish to be there; after a series of random movements it is found that this result is to be caused by going to the City in the morning and coming back in the evening. No one would have guessed a priori that this movement of a middle-aged man's body would cause fish to come out of the sea into his larder, but experience shows that it does, and the middle-aged man therefore continues to go to the City, just as the cat in the cage continues to lift the latch when it has once found it. Of course, in actual fact, human learning is rendered easier, though psychologically more complex, through language; but at bottom language does not alter the essential character of learning, or of the part played by instinct in promoting learning. Language, however, is a subject upon which I do not wish to speak until a later lecture.

The popular conception of instinct errs by imagining it to be infallible and preternaturally wise, as well as incapable of modification. This is a complete delusion. Instinct, as a rule, is very rough and ready, able to achieve its result under ordinary circumstances, but easily misled by anything unusual. Chicks follow their mother by instinct, but when they are quite young they will follow with equal readiness any moving object remotely resembling their mother, or even a human being (James,

---

[16] *Mind in Evolution* (Macmillan, 1915), pp. 236-237.

"Psychology," ii, 396). Bergson, quoting Fabre, has made play with the supposed extraordinary accuracy of the solitary wasp Ammophila, which lays its eggs in a caterpillar. On this subject I will quote from Drever's "Instinct in Man," p. 92:

"According to Fabre's observations, which Bergson accepts, the Ammophila stings its prey EXACTLY and UNERRINGLY in EACH of the nervous centres. The result is that the caterpillar is paralyzed, but not immediately killed, the advantage of this being that the larva cannot be injured by any movement of the caterpillar, upon which the egg is deposited, and is provided with fresh meat when the time comes.

"Now Dr. and Mrs. Peckham have shown that the sting of the wasp is NOT UNERRING, as Fabre alleges, that the number of stings is NOT CONSTANT, that sometimes the caterpillar is NOT PARALYZED, and sometimes it is KILLED OUTRIGHT, and that THE DIFFERENT CIRCUMSTANCES DO NOT APPARENTLY MAKE ANY DIFFERENCE TO THE LARVA, which is not injured by slight movements of the caterpillar, nor by consuming food decomposed rather than fresh caterpillar."

This illustrates how love of the marvellous may mislead even so careful an observer as Fabre and so eminent a philosopher as Bergson.

In the same chapter of Dr. Drever's book there are some interesting examples of the mistakes made by instinct. I will quote one as a sample:

"The larva of the Lomechusa beetle eats the young of the ants, in whose nest it is reared. Nevertheless, the ants tend the Lomechusa larvae with the same care they bestow on their own young. Not only so, but they apparently discover that the methods of feeding, which suit their own larvae, would prove fatal to the guests, and accordingly they change their whole system of nursing" (loc. cit., p. 106).

Semon ("Die Mneme," pp. 207-9) gives a good illustration of an instinct growing wiser through experience. He relates how hunters attract stags by imitating the sounds of other members of their species, male or female, but find that the older a stag becomes the more difficult it is to deceive him, and the more accurate the imitation has to be. The literature of instinct is vast, and illustrations might be multiplied indefinitely. The main points as regards instinct, which need to be emphasized as against the popular conceptions of it, are:

(1) That instinct requires no prevision of the biological end which it serves;

(2) That instinct is only adapted to achieve this end in the usual circumstances of the animal in question, and has no more precision than is necessary for success AS A RULE;

(3) That processes initiated by instinct often come to be performed better after experience;

(4) That instinct supplies the impulses to experimental movements which are required for the process of learning;

(5) That instincts in their nascent stages are easily modifiable, and capable of being attached to various sorts of objects.

All the above characteristics of instinct can be established by purely external observation, except the fact that instinct does not require prevision. This, though not strictly capable of being PROVED by observation, is irresistibly suggested by the most obvious phenomena. Who can believe, for example, that a new-born baby is aware of the necessity of food for preserving life? Or that insects, in laying eggs, are concerned for the preservation of their species? The essence of instinct, one might say, is that it provides a mechanism for acting without foresight in a manner which is usually advantageous biologically. It is partly for this reason that it is so important to understand the fundamental position of instinct in prompting both animal and human behaviour.

# LECTURE III

## Desire and Feeling

Desire is a subject upon which, if I am not mistaken, true views can only be arrived at by an almost complete reversal of the ordinary unreflecting opinion. It is natural to regard desire as in its essence an attitude towards something which is imagined, not actual; this something is called the END or OBJECT of the desire, and is said to be the PURPOSE of any action resulting from the desire. We think of the content of the desire as being just like the content of a belief, while the attitude taken up towards the content is different. According to this theory, when we say: "I hope it will rain," or "I expect it will rain," we express, in the first case, a desire, and in the second, a belief, with an identical content, namely, the image of rain. It would be easy to say that, just as belief is one kind of feeling in relation to this content, so desire is another kind. According to this view, what comes first in desire is something imagined, with a specific feeling related to it, namely, that specific feeling which we call "desiring" it. The discomfort associated with unsatisfied desire, and the actions which aim at satisfying desire, are, in this view, both of them effects of the desire. I think it is fair to say that this is a view against which common sense would not rebel; nevertheless, I believe it to be radically mistaken. It cannot be refuted logically, but various facts can be adduced which make it gradually less simple and plausible, until at last it turns out to be easier to abandon it wholly and look at the matter in a totally different way.

The first set of facts to be adduced against the common sense view of desire are those studied by psycho-analysis. In all human beings, but most markedly in those suffering from hysteria and certain forms of insanity, we find what are called "unconscious" desires, which are commonly regarded as showing self-deception. Most psycho-analysts pay little attention to the analysis of desire, being interested in discovering by observation what it is that people desire, rather than in discovering what actually constitutes desire. I think the strangeness of what they report would be greatly diminished if it were expressed in the language of a behaviourist theory of desire, rather than in the language of every-day beliefs. The general description of the sort of phenomena that bear on our present question is as follows: A person states that his desires are so-and-so, and that it is these desires that inspire his actions; but the outside observer perceives that his actions are such as to realize quite different ends from those which he avows, and that these different ends are such as he might

113

be expected to desire. Generally they are less virtuous than his professed desires, and are therefore less agreeable to profess than these are. It is accordingly supposed that they really exist as desires for ends, but in a subconscious part of the mind, which the patient refuses to admit into consciousness for fear of having to think ill of himself. There are no doubt many cases to which such a supposition is applicable without obvious artificiality. But the deeper the Freudians delve into the underground regions of instinct, the further they travel from anything resembling conscious desire, and the less possible it becomes to believe that only positive self-deception conceals from us that we really wish for things which are abhorrent to our explicit life.

In the cases in question we have a conflict between the outside observer and the patient's consciousness. The whole tendency of psycho-analysis is to trust the outside observer rather than the testimony of introspection. I believe this tendency to be entirely right, but to demand a re-statement of what constitutes desire, exhibiting it as a causal law of our actions, not as something actually existing in our minds.

But let us first get a clearer statement of the essential characteristic of the phenomena.

A person, we find, states that he desires a certain end A, and that he is acting with a view to achieving it. We observe, however, that his actions are such as are likely to achieve a quite different end B, and that B is the sort of end that often seems to be aimed at by animals and savages, though civilized people are supposed to have discarded it. We sometimes find also a whole set of false beliefs, of such a kind as to persuade the patient that his actions are really a means to A, when in fact they are a means to B. For example, we have an impulse to inflict pain upon those whom we hate; we therefore believe that they are wicked, and that punishment will reform them. This belief enables us to act upon the impulse to inflict pain, while believing that we are acting upon the desire to lead sinners to repentance. It is for this reason that the criminal law has been in all ages more severe than it would have been if the impulse to ameliorate the criminal had been what really inspired it. It seems simple to explain such a state of affairs as due to "self-deception," but this explanation is often mythical. Most people, in thinking about punishment, have had no more need to hide their vindictive impulses from themselves than they have had to hide the exponential theorem. Our impulses are not patent to a casual observation, but are only to be discovered by a scientific study of our actions, in the course of which we must regard ourselves as objectively as we should the motions of the planets or the chemical reactions of a new element.

The study of animals reinforces this conclusion, and is in many ways the best preparation for the analysis of desire. In animals we are not troubled by the disturbing influence of ethical considerations. In dealing with human beings, we are perpetually distracted by being told that such-and-such a view is gloomy or cynical or pessimistic: ages of human conceit have built up such a vast myth as to our wisdom and virtue that any intrusion of the mere scientific desire to know the facts is instantly resented by those who cling to comfortable illusions. But no one cares whether animals are virtuous or not, and no one is under the delusion that they are rational. Moreover, we do not expect them to be so "conscious," and are prepared to admit that their instincts prompt useful actions without any prevision of the ends which they achieve. For all these reasons, there is much in the analysis of mind which is more easily discovered by the study of animals than by the observation of human beings.

We all think that, by watching the behaviour of animals, we can discover more or less what they desire. If this is the case—and I fully agree that it is—desire must be capable of being exhibited in actions, for it is only the actions of animals that we can observe. They MAY have minds in which all sorts of things take place, but we can know nothing about their minds except by means of inferences from their actions; and the more such inferences are examined, the more dubious they appear. It would seem, therefore, that actions alone must be the test of the desires of animals. From this it is an easy step to the conclusion that an animal's desire is nothing but a characteristic of a certain series of actions, namely, those which would be commonly regarded as inspired by the desire in question. And when it has been shown that this view affords a satisfactory account of animal desires, it is not difficult to see that the same explanation is applicable to the desires of human beings.

We judge easily from the behaviour of an animal of a familiar kind whether it is hungry or thirsty, or pleased or displeased, or inquisitive or terrified. The verification of our judgment, so far as verification is possible, must be derived from the immediately succeeding actions of the animal. Most people would say that they infer first something about the animal's state of mind—whether it is hungry or thirsty and so on—and thence derive their expectations as to its subsequent conduct. But this detour through the animal's supposed mind is wholly unnecessary. We can say simply: The animal's behaviour during the last minute has had those characteristics which distinguish what is called "hunger," and it is likely that its actions during the next minute will be similar in this respect, unless it finds food, or is interrupted by a stronger impulse, such as fear. An animal which is hungry is restless, it goes to the places where food is often to be found, it sniffs with its nose or peers with its eyes or otherwise increases the sensitiveness of its sense-organs; as soon as it is near enough to food for its sense-organs to be affected, it goes to it with all speed and proceeds to eat; after which, if the quantity of food has been sufficient, its whole demeanour changes it may very likely lie down and go to sleep. These things and others like them are observable phenomena distinguishing a hungry animal from one which is not hungry. The characteristic mark by which we recognize a series of actions which display hunger is not the animal's mental state, which we cannot observe, but something in its bodily behaviour; it is this observable trait in the bodily behaviour that I am proposing to call "hunger," not some possibly mythical and certainly unknowable ingredient of the animal's mind.

115

Generalizing what occurs in the case of hunger, we may say that what we call a desire in an animal is always displayed in a cycle of actions having certain fairly well marked characteristics. There is first a state of activity, consisting, with qualifications to be mentioned presently, of movements likely to have a certain result; these movements, unless interrupted, continue until the result is achieved, after which there is usually a period of comparative quiescence. A cycle of actions of this sort has marks by which it is broadly distinguished from the motions of dead matter. The most notable of these marks are—(1) the appropriateness of the actions for the realization of a certain result; (2) the continuance of action until that result has been achieved. Neither of these can be pressed beyond a point. Either may be (a) to some extent present in dead matter, and (b) to a considerable extent absent in animals, while vegetable are intermediate, and display only a much fainter form of the behaviour which leads us to attribute desire to animals. (a) One might say rivers "desire" the sea water, roughly speaking, remains in restless motion until it reaches either the sea or a place from which it cannot issue without going uphill, and therefore we might say that this is what it wishes while it is flowing. We do not say so, because we can account for the behaviour of water by the laws of physics; and if we knew more about animals, we might equally cease to attribute desires to them, since we might find physical and chemical reactions sufficient to account for their behaviour. (b) Many of the movements of animals do not exhibit the characteristics of the cycles which seem to embody desire. There are first of all the movements which are "mechanical," such as slipping and falling, where ordinary physical forces operate upon the animal's body almost as if it were dead matter. An animal which falls over a cliff may make a number of desperate struggles while it is in the air, but its centre of gravity will move exactly as it would if the animal were dead. In this case, if the animal is killed at the end of the fall, we have, at first sight, just the characteristics of a cycle of actions embodying desire, namely, restless movement until the ground is reached, and then quiescence. Nevertheless, we feel no temptation to say that the animal desired what occurred, partly because of the obviously mechanical nature of the whole occurrence, partly because, when an animal survives a fall, it tends not to repeat the experience.

There may be other reasons also, but of them I do not wish to speak yet. Besides mechanical movements, there are interrupted movements, as when a bird, on its way to eat your best peas, is frightened away by the boy whom you are employing for that purpose. If interruptions are frequent and completion of cycles rare, the characteristics by which cycles are observed may become so blurred as to be almost unrecognizable. The result of these various considerations is that the differences between animals and dead matter, when we confine ourselves to external unscientific observation of integral behaviour, are a matter of degree and not very precise. It is for this reason that it has always been possible for fanciful people to maintain that even stocks and stones have some vague kind of soul. The evidence that animals have souls is so very shaky that, if it is assumed to be conclusive, one might just as well go a step further and extend the argument by analogy to all matter. Nevertheless, in spite of vagueness and doubtful cases, the existence of cycles in the behaviour of animals is a broad characteristic by which they are prima facie distinguished from ordinary matter; and I think it is this characteristic which leads us to attribute desires to animals, since it makes their behaviour resemble what we do when (as we say) we are acting from desire.

I shall adopt the following definitions for describing the behaviour of animals:

A "behaviour-cycle" is a series of voluntary or reflex movements of an animal, tending to cause a certain result, and continuing until that result is caused, unless they are interrupted by death, accident, or some new behaviour-cycle. (Here "accident" may be defined as the intervention of purely physical laws causing mechanical movements.)

The "purpose" of a behaviour-cycle is the result which brings it to an end, normally by a condition of temporary quiescence-provided there is no interruption.

An animal is said to "desire" the purpose of a behaviour cycle while the behaviour-cycle is in progress.

I believe these definitions to be adequate also to human purposes and desires, but for the present I am only occupied with animals and with what can be learnt by external observation. I am very anxious that no ideas should be attached to the words "purpose" and "desire" beyond those involved in the above definitions.

We have not so far considered what is the nature of the initial stimulus to a behaviour-cycle. Yet it is here that the usual view of desire seems on the strongest ground. The hungry animal goes on making movements until it gets food; it seems natural, therefore, to suppose that the idea of food is present throughout the process, and that the thought of the end to be achieved sets the whole process in motion. Such a view, however, is obviously untenable in many cases, especially where instinct is concerned. Take, for example, reproduction and the rearing of the young. Birds mate, build a nest, lay eggs in it, sit on the eggs, feed the young birds, and care for them until they are fully grown. It is totally impossible to suppose that this series of actions, which constitutes one behaviour-cycle, is inspired by any prevision of the end, at any rate the first time it is performed.[17] We must suppose that the stimulus to the performance of each act is an impulsion from behind, not an attraction from the future. The bird does what it does, at each stage, because it has an impulse to that particular action, not because it perceives that the whole cycle of actions will contribute to the preservation of the species. The same considerations apply to other instincts. A hungry animal feels restless, and is led by instinctive impulses to perform the movements which give it nourishment; but the act of seeking food is not sufficient evidence from which to conclude that the animal has the thought of food in its "mind."

---

[17] For evidence as to birds' nests, cf. Semon, *Die Mneme*, pp. 209, 210.

Coming now to human beings, and to what we know about our own actions, it seems clear that what, with us, sets a behaviour-cycle in motion is some sensation of the sort which we call disagreeable. Take the case of hunger: we have first an uncomfortable feeling inside, producing a disinclination to sit still, a sensitiveness to savoury smells, and an attraction towards any food that there may be in our neighbourhood. At any moment during this process we may become aware that we are hungry, in the sense of saying to ourselves, "I am hungry"; but we may have been acting with reference to food for some time before this moment. While we are talking or reading, we may eat in complete unconsciousness; but we perform the actions of eating just as we should if we were conscious, and they cease when our hunger is appeased. What we call "consciousness" seems to be a mere spectator of the process; even when it issues orders, they are usually, like those of a wise parent, just such as would have been obeyed even if they had not been given. This view may seem at first exaggerated, but the more our so-called volitions and their causes are examined, the more it is forced upon us. The part played by words in all this is complicated, and a potent source of confusions; I shall return to it later. For the present, I am still concerned with primitive desire, as it exists in man, but in the form in which man shows his affinity to his animal ancestors.

Conscious desire is made up partly of what is essential to desire, partly of beliefs as to what we want. It is important to be clear as to the part which does not consist of beliefs.

The primitive non-cognitive element in desire seems to be a push, not a pull, an impulsion away from the actual, rather than an attraction towards the ideal. Certain sensations and other mental occurrences have a property which we call discomfort; these cause such bodily movements as are likely to lead to their cessation. When the discomfort ceases, or even when it appreciably diminishes, we have sensations possessing a property which we call PLEASURE. Pleasurable sensations either stimulate no action at all, or at most stimulate such action as is likely to prolong them. I shall return shortly to the consideration of what discomfort and pleasure are in themselves; for the present, it is their connection with action and desire that concerns us. Abandoning momentarily the standpoint of behaviourism, we may presume that hungry animals experience sensations involving discomfort, and stimulating such movements as seem likely to bring them to the food which is outside the cages. When they have reached the food and eaten it, their discomfort ceases and their sensations become pleasurable. It SEEMS, mistakenly, as if the animals had had this situation in mind throughout, when in fact they have been continually pushed by discomfort. And when an animal is reflective, like some men, it comes to think that it had the final situation in mind throughout; sometimes it comes to know what situation will bring satisfaction, so that in fact the discomfort does bring the thought of what will allay it. Nevertheless the sensation involving discomfort remains the prime mover.

This brings us to the question of the nature of discomfort and pleasure. Since Kant it has been customary to recognize three great divisions of mental phenomena, which are typified by knowledge, desire and feeling, where "feeling" is used to mean pleasure and discomfort. Of course, "knowledge" is too definite a word: the states of mind concerned are grouped together as "cognitive," and are to embrace not only beliefs, but perceptions, doubts, and the understanding of concepts. "Desire," also, is narrower than what is intended: for example, WILL is to be included in this category, and in fact every thing that involves any kind of striving, or "conation" as it is technically called. I do not myself believe that there is any value in this threefold division of the contents of mind. I believe that sensations (including images) supply all the "stuff" of the mind, and that everything else can be analysed into groups of sensations related in various ways, or characteristics of sensations or of groups of sensations. As regards belief, I shall give grounds for this view in later lectures. As regards desires, I have given some grounds in this lecture. For the present, it is pleasure and discomfort that concern us. There are broadly three theories that might be held in regard to them. We may regard them as separate existing items in those who experience them, or we may regard them as intrinsic qualities of sensations and other mental occurrences, or we may regard them as mere names for the causal characteristics of the occurrences which are uncomfortable or pleasant. The first of these theories, namely, that which regards discomfort and pleasure as actual contents in those who experience them, has, I think, nothing conclusive to be said in its favour.[18] It is suggested chiefly by an ambiguity in the word "pain," which has misled many people, including Berkeley, whom it supplied with one of his arguments for subjective idealism. We may use "pain" as the opposite of "pleasure," and "painful" as the opposite of "pleasant," or we may use "pain" to mean a certain sort of sensation, on a level with the sensations of heat and cold and touch. The latter use of the word has prevailed in psychological literature, and it is now no longer used as the opposite of "pleasure." Dr. H. Head, in a recent publication, has stated this distinction as follows:[19]

"It is necessary at the outset to distinguish clearly between 'discomfort' and 'pain.' Pain is a distinct sensory quality equivalent to heat and cold, and its intensity can be roughly graded according to the force expended in stimulation. Discomfort, on the other hand, is that feeling-tone which is directly opposed to pleasure. It may accompany sensations not in themselves essentially painful; as for instance that produced by tickling the sole of the foot. The reaction produced by repeated pricking contains both these elements; for it evokes that sensory quality known as pain,

---

[18] Various arguments in its favour are advanced by A. Wohlgemuth, "On the feelings and their neural correlate, with an examination of the nature of pain," *British Journal of Psychology*, viii, 4. (1917). But as these arguments are largely a *reductio ad absurdum* of other theories, among which that which I am advocating is not included, I cannot regard them as establishing their contention.

[19] "Sensation and the Cerebral Cortex," *Brain*, vol. xli, part ii (September, 1918), p. 90. Cf. also Wohlgemuth, loc. cit. pp. 437, 450.

accompanied by a disagreeable feeling-tone, which we have called discomfort. On the other hand, excessive pressure, except when applied directly over some nerve-trunk, tends to excite more discomfort than pain."

The confusion between discomfort and pain has made people regard discomfort as a more substantial thing than it is, and this in turn has reacted upon the view taken of pleasure, since discomfort and pleasure are evidently on a level in this respect. As soon as discomfort is clearly distinguished from the sensation of pain, it becomes more natural to regard discomfort and pleasure as properties of mental occurrences than to regard them as separate mental occurrences on their own account. I shall therefore dismiss the view that they are separate mental occurrences, and regard them as properties of such experiences as would be called respectively uncomfortable and pleasant.

It remains to be examined whether they are actual qualities of such occurrences, or are merely differences as to causal properties. I do not myself see any way of deciding this question; either view seems equally capable of accounting for the facts. If this is true, it is safer to avoid the assumption that there are such intrinsic qualities of mental occurrences as are in question, and to assume only the causal differences which are undeniable. Without condemning the intrinsic theory, we can define discomfort and pleasure as consisting in causal properties, and say only what will hold on either of the two theories. Following this course, we shall say:

"Discomfort" is a property of a sensation or other mental occurrence, consisting in the fact that the occurrence in question stimulates voluntary or reflex movements tending to produce some more or less definite change involving the cessation of the occurrence.

"Pleasure" is a property of a sensation or other mental occurrence, consisting in the fact that the occurrence in question either does not stimulate any voluntary or reflex movement, or, if it does, stimulates only such as tend to prolong the occurrence in question.[20]

"Conscious" desire, which we have now to consider, consists of desire in the sense hitherto discussed, together with a true belief as to its "purpose," i.e. as to the state of affairs that will bring quiescence with cessation of the discomfort. If our theory of desire is correct, a belief as to its purpose may very well be erroneous, since only experience can show what causes a discomfort to cease. When the experience needed is common and simple, as in the case of hunger, a mistake is not very probable. But in other cases—e.g. erotic desire in those who have had little or no experience of its satisfaction—mistakes are to be expected, and do in fact very often occur. The practice of inhibiting impulses, which is to a great extent necessary to civilized life, makes mistakes easier, by preventing experience of the actions to which a desire would otherwise lead, and by often causing the inhibited impulses themselves to

---

[20] Cf. Thorndike, op. cit., p. 243.

be unnoticed or quickly forgotten. The perfectly natural mistakes which thus arise constitute a large proportion of what is, mistakenly in part, called self-deception, and attributed by Freud to the "censor."

But there is a further point which needs emphasizing, namely, that a belief that something is desired has often a tendency to cause the very desire that is believed in. It is this fact that makes the effect of "consciousness" on desire so complicated.

When we believe that we desire a certain state of affairs, that often tends to cause a real desire for it. This is due partly to the influence of words upon our emotions, in rhetoric for example, and partly to the general fact that discomfort normally belongs to the belief that we desire such-and-such a thing that we do not possess. Thus what was originally a false opinion as to the object of a desire acquires a certain truth: the false opinion generates a secondary subsidiary desire, which nevertheless becomes real. Let us take an illustration. Suppose you have been jilted in a way which wounds your vanity. Your natural impulsive desire will be of the sort expressed in Donne's poem:

When by thy scorn, O Murderess, I am dead,

in which he explains how he will haunt the poor lady as a ghost, and prevent her from enjoying a moment's peace. But two things stand in the way of your expressing yourself so naturally: on the one hand, your vanity, which will not acknowledge how hard you are hit; on the other hand, your conviction that you are a civilized and humane person, who could not possibly indulge so crude a desire as revenge. You will therefore experience a restlessness which will at first seem quite aimless, but will finally resolve itself in a conscious desire to change your profession, or go round the world, or conceal your identity and live in Putney, like Arnold Bennett's hero. Although the prime cause of this desire is a false judgment as to your previous unconscious desire, yet the new conscious desire has its own derivative genuineness, and may influence your actions to the extent of sending you round the world. The initial mistake, however, will have effects of two kinds. First, in uncontrolled moments, under the influence of sleepiness or drink or delirium, you will say things calculated to injure the faithless deceiver. Secondly, you will find travel disappointing, and the East less fascinating than you had hoped—unless, some day, you hear that the wicked one has in turn been jilted. If this happens, you will believe that you feel sincere sympathy, but you will suddenly be much more delighted than before with the beauties of tropical islands or the wonders of Chinese art. A secondary desire, derived from a false judgment as to a primary desire, has its own power of influencing action, and is therefore a real desire according to our definition. But it has not the same power as a primary desire of bringing thorough satisfaction when it is realized; so long as the primary desire remains unsatisfied, restlessness continues in spite of the secondary desire's success. Hence arises a belief in the vanity of human wishes: the vain wishes are those that are secondary, but mistaken beliefs prevent us from realizing that they are secondary.

What may, with some propriety, be called self-deception arises through the operation of desires for beliefs. We desire many things which it is not in our power to achieve: that we should be universally popular and admired, that our work should be the wonder of the age, and that the universe should be so ordered as to bring ultimate happiness to all, though not to our enemies until they have repented and been purified by suffering. Such desires are too large to be achieved through our own efforts. But it is found that a considerable portion of the satisfaction which these things would bring us if they were realized is to be achieved by the much easier operation of believing that they are or will be realized. This desire for beliefs, as opposed to desire for the actual facts, is a particular case of secondary desire, and, like all secondary desire its satisfaction does not lead to a complete cessation of the initial discomfort. Nevertheless, desire for beliefs, as opposed to desire for facts, is exceedingly potent both individually and socially. According to the form of belief desired, it is called vanity, optimism, or religion. Those who have sufficient power usually imprison or put to death any one who tries to shake their faith in their own excellence or in that of the universe; it is for this reason that seditious libel and blasphemy have always been, and still are, criminal offences.

It is very largely through desires for beliefs that the primitive nature of desire has become so hidden, and that the part played by consciousness has been so confusing and so exaggerated.

We may now summarize our analysis of desire and feeling.

A mental occurrence of any kind—sensation, image, belief, or emotion—may be a cause of a series of actions, continuing, unless interrupted, until some more or less definite state of affairs is realized. Such a series of actions we call a "behaviour-cycle." The degree of definiteness may vary greatly: hunger requires only food in general, whereas the sight of a particular piece of food raises a desire which requires the eating of that piece of food. The property of causing such a cycle of occurrences is called "discomfort"; the property of the mental occurrences in which the cycle ends is called "pleasure." The actions constituting the cycle must not be purely mechanical, i.e. they must be bodily movements in whose causation the special properties of nervous tissue are involved. The cycle ends in a condition of quiescence, or of such action as tends only to preserve the status quo. The state of affairs in which this condition of quiescence is achieved is called the "purpose" of the cycle, and the initial mental occurrence involving discomfort is called a "desire" for the state of affairs that brings quiescence. A desire is called "conscious" when it is accompanied by a true belief as to the state of affairs that will bring quiescence; otherwise it is called "unconscious." All primitive desire is unconscious, and in human beings beliefs as to the purposes of desires are often mistaken. These mistaken beliefs generate secondary desires, which cause various interesting complications in the psychology of human desire, without fundamentally altering the character which it shares with animal desire.

# LECTURE IV

## Influence of Past History on Present Occurrences in Living Organisms

In this lecture we shall be concerned with a very general characteristic which broadly, though not absolutely, distinguishes the behaviour of living organisms from that of dead matter. The characteristic in question is this:

The response of an organism to a given stimulus is very often dependent upon the past history of the organism, and not merely upon the stimulus and the HITHERTO DISCOVERABLE present state of the organism.

This characteristic is embodied in the saying "a burnt child fears the fire." The burn may have left no visible traces, yet it modifies the reaction of the child in the presence of fire. It is customary to assume that, in such cases, the past operates by modifying the structure of the brain, not directly. I have no wish to suggest that this hypothesis is false; I wish only to point out that it is a hypothesis. At the end of the present lecture I shall examine the grounds in its favour. If we confine ourselves to facts which have been actually observed, we must say that past occurrences, in addition to the present stimulus and the present ascertainable condition of the organism, enter into the causation of the response.

The characteristic is not wholly confined to living organisms. For example, magnetized steel looks just like steel which has not been magnetized, but its behaviour is in some ways different. In the case of dead matter, however, such phenomena are less frequent and important than in the case of living organisms, and it is far less difficult to invent satisfactory hypotheses as to the microscopic changes of structure which mediate between the past occurrence and the present changed response. In the case of living organisms, practically everything that is distinctive both of their physical and of their mental behaviour is bound up with this persistent influence of the past. Further, speaking broadly, the change in response is usually of a kind that is biologically advantageous to the organism.

Following a suggestion derived from Semon ("Die Mneme," Leipzig, 1904; 2nd edition, 1908, English translation, Allen & Unwin, 1921; "Die mnemischen Empfindungen," Leipzig, 1909), we will give the name of "mnemic phenomena" to those responses of an organism which, so far as hitherto observed facts are concerned,

123

can only be brought under causal laws by including past occurrences in the history of the organism as part of the causes of the present response. I do not mean merely—what would always be the case—that past occurrences are part of a CHAIN of causes leading to the present event. I mean that, in attempting to state the PROXIMATE cause of the present event, some past event or events must be included, unless we take refuge in hypothetical modifications of brain structure. For example: you smell peat-smoke, and you recall some occasion when you smelt it before. The cause of your recollection, so far as hitherto observable phenomena are concerned, consists both of the peat smoke (present stimulus) and of the former occasion (past experience). The same stimulus will not produce the same recollection in another man who did not share your former experience, although the former experience left no OBSERVABLE traces in the structure of the brain. According to the maxim "same cause, same effect," we cannot therefore regard the peat-smoke alone as the cause of your recollection, since it does not have the same effect in other cases. The cause of your recollection must be both the peat-smoke and the past occurrence. Accordingly your recollection is an instance of what we are calling "mnemic phenomena."

Before going further, it will be well to give illustrations of different classes of mnemic phenomena.

(a) ACQUIRED HABITS.—In Lecture II we saw how animals can learn by experience how to get out of cages or mazes, or perform other actions which are useful to them but not provided for by their instincts alone. A cat which is put into a cage of which it has had experience behaves differently from the way in which it behaved at first. We can easily invent hypotheses, which are quite likely to be true, as to connections in the brain caused by past experience, and themselves causing the different response. But the observable fact is that the stimulus of being in the cage produces differing results with repetition, and that the ascertainable cause of the cat's behaviour is not merely the cage and its own ascertainable organization, but also its past history in regard to the cage. From our present point of view, the matter is independent of the question whether the cat's behaviour is due to some mental fact called "knowledge," or displays a merely bodily habit. Our habitual knowledge is not always in our minds, but is called up by the appropriate stimuli. If we are asked "What is the capital of France?" we answer "Paris," because of past experience; the past experience is as essential as the present question in the causation of our response. Thus all our habitual knowledge consists of acquired habits, and comes under the head of mnemic phenomena.

(b) IMAGES.—I shall have much to say about images in a later lecture; for the present I am merely concerned with them in so far as they are "copies" of past sensations. When you hear New York spoken of, some image probably comes into your mind, either of the place itself (if you have been there), or of some picture of it (if you have not). The image is due to your past experience, as well as to the present stimulus of the words "New York." Similarly, the images you have in dreams are all dependent upon your past experience, as well as upon the present stimulus to dreaming. It is generally believed that all images, in their simpler parts, are copies of sensations; if so, their mnemic character is evident. This is important, not only on its own account, but also because, as we shall see later, images play an essential part in what is called "thinking."

(c) ASSOCIATION.—The broad fact of association, on the mental side, is that when we experience something which we have experienced before, it tends to call up the context of the former experience. The smell of peat-smoke recalling a former scene is an instance which we discussed a moment ago. This is obviously a mnemic phenomenon. There is also a more purely physical association, which is indistinguishable from physical habit. This is the kind studied by Mr. Thorndike in animals, where a certain stimulus is associated with a certain act. This is the sort which is taught to soldiers in drilling, for example. In such a case there need not be anything mental, but merely a habit of the body. There is no essential distinction between association and habit, and the observations which we made concerning habit as a mnemic phenomenon are equally applicable to association.

(d) NON-SENSATIONAL ELEMENTS IN PERCEPTION.—When we perceive any object of a familiar kind, much of what appears subjectively to be immediately given is really derived from past experience. When we see an object, say a penny, we seem to be aware of its "real" shape we have the impression of something circular, not of something elliptical. In learning to draw, it is necessary to acquire the art of representing things according to the sensation, not according to the perception. And the visual appearance is filled out with feeling of what the object would be like to touch, and so on. This filling out and supplying of the "real" shape and so on consists of the most usual correlates of the sensational core in our perception. It may happen that, in the particular case, the real correlates are unusual; for example, if what we are seeing is a carpet made to look like tiles. If so, the non-sensational part of our perception will be illusory, i.e. it will supply qualities which the object in question does not in fact have. But as a rule objects do have the qualities added by perception, which is to be expected, since experience of what is usual is the cause of the addition. If our experience had been different, we should not fill out sensation in the same way, except in so far as the filling out is instinctive, not acquired. It would seem that, in man, all that makes up space perception, including the correlation of sight and touch and so on, is almost entirely acquired. In that case there is a large mnemic element in all the common perceptions by means of which we handle common objects. And, to take another kind of instance, imagine what our astonishment would be if we were to hear a cat bark or a dog mew. This emotion would be dependent upon past experience, and would therefore be a mnemic phenomenon according to the definition.

(e) MEMORY AS KNOWLEDGE.—The kind of memory of which I am now speaking is definite knowledge of some past event in one's own experience. From time to time we remember things that have happened to us, because something in the present reminds us of them. Exactly the same present fact would not call up the same memory if our past experience had been different. Thus our remembering is caused by—

(1) The present stimulus,
(2) The past occurrence.

It is therefore a mnemic phenomenon according to our definition. A definition of "mnemic phenomena" which did not include memory would, of course, be a bad one. The point of the definition is not that it includes memory, but that it includes it as one of a class of phenomena which embrace all that is characteristic in the subject matter of psychology.

(f) EXPERIENCE.—The word "experience" is often used very vaguely. James, as we saw, uses it to cover the whole primal stuff of the world, but this usage seems objection able, since, in a purely physical world, things would happen without there being any experience. It is only mnemic phenomena that embody experience. We may say that an animal "experiences" an occurrence when this occurrence modifies the animal's subsequent behaviour, i.e. when it is the mnemic portion of the cause of future occurrences in the animal's life. The burnt child that fears the fire has "experienced" the fire, whereas a stick that has been thrown on and taken off again has not "experienced" anything, since it offers no more resistance than before to being thrown on. The essence of "experience" is the modification of behaviour produced by what is experienced. We might, in fact, define one chain of experience, or one biography, as a series of occurrences linked by mnemic causation. I think it is this characteristic, more than any other, that distinguishes sciences dealing with living organisms from physics.

The best writer on mnemic phenomena known to me is Richard Semon, the fundamental part of whose theory I shall endeavour to summarize before going further:

When an organism, either animal or plant, is subjected to a stimulus, producing in it some state of excitement, the removal of the stimulus allows it to return to a condition of equilibrium. But the new state of equilibrium is different from the old, as may be seen by the changed capacity for reaction. The state of equilibrium before the stimulus may be called the "primary indifference-state"; that after the cessation of the stimulus, the "secondary indifference-state." We define the "engraphic effect" of a stimulus as the effect in making a difference between the primary and secondary indifference-states, and this difference itself we define as the "engram" due to the stimulus. "Mnemic phenomena" are defined as those due to engrams; in animals, they are specially associated with the nervous system, but not exclusively, even in man.

When two stimuli occur together, one of them, occurring afterwards, may call out the reaction for the other also. We call this an "ekphoric influence," and stimuli having this character are called "ekphoric stimuli." In such a case we call the engrams of the two stimuli "associated." All simultaneously generated engrams are associated; there is also association of successively aroused engrams, though this is reducible to simultaneous association. In fact, it is not an isolated stimulus that leaves an engram, but the totality of the stimuli at any moment; consequently any portion of this totality tends, if it recurs, to arouse the whole reaction which was aroused before. Semon holds that engrams can be inherited, and that an animal's innate habits may be due to the experience of its ancestors; on this subject he refers to Samuel Butler.

Semon formulates two "mnemic principles." The first, or "Law of Engraphy," is as follows: "All simultaneous excitements in an organism form a connected simultaneous excitement-complex, which as such works engraphically, i.e. leaves behind a connected engram-complex, which in so far forms a whole" ("Die mnemischen Empfindungen," p. 146). The second mnemic principle, or "Law of Ekphory," is as follows: "The partial return of the energetic situation which formerly worked engraphically operates ekphorically on a simultaneous engram-complex" (ib., p. 173). These two laws together represent in part a hypothesis (the engram), and in part an observable fact. The observable fact is that, when a certain complex of stimuli has originally caused a certain complex of reactions, the recurrence of part of the stimuli tends to cause the recurrence of the whole of the reactions.

Semon's applications of his fundamental ideas in various directions are interesting and ingenious. Some of them will concern us later, but for the present it is the fundamental character of mnemic phenomena that is in question.

Concerning the nature of an engram, Semon confesses that at present it is impossible to say more than that it must consist in some material alteration in the body of the organism ("Die mnemischen Empfindungen," p. 376). It is, in fact, hypothetical, invoked for theoretical uses, and not an outcome of direct observation. No doubt physiology, especially the disturbances of memory through lesions in the brain, affords grounds for this hypothesis; nevertheless it does remain a hypothesis, the validity of which will be discussed at the end of this lecture.

I am inclined to think that, in the present state of physiology, the introduction of the engram does not serve to simplify the account of mnemic phenomena. We can, I think, formulate the known laws of such phenomena in terms, wholly, of observable facts, by recognizing provisionally what we may call "mnemic causation." By this I mean that kind of causation of which I spoke at the beginning of this lecture, that kind, namely, in which the proximate cause consists not merely of a present event, but of this together with a past event. I do not wish to urge that this form of causation is ultimate, but that, in the present state of our knowledge, it affords a simplification, and enables us to state laws of behaviour in less hypothetical terms than we should otherwise have to employ.

The clearest instance of what I mean is recollection of a past event. What we observe is that certain present stimuli lead us to recollect certain occurrences, but that at times when we are not recollecting them, there is nothing discoverable in our minds that could be called memory of them. Memories, as mental facts, arise from time to time, but do not, so far as we can see, exist in any shape while they are "latent." In fact, when we say that they are "latent," we mean merely that they will exist under certain circumstances. If, then, there is to be some standing difference between the person who can remember a certain fact and the person who cannot, that standing difference must be, not in anything mental, but in the brain. It is quite probable that there is such a difference in the brain, but its nature is unknown and it remains hypothetical. Everything that has, so far, been made matter of observation as regards this question can be put together in the statement: When a certain complex of sensations has occurred to a man, the recurrence of part of the complex tends to arouse the recollection of the whole. In like manner, we can collect all mnemic phenomena in living organisms under a single law, which contains what is hitherto verifiable in Semon's two laws. This single law is:

IF A COMPLEX STIMULUS A HAS CAUSED A COMPLEX REACTION B IN AN ORGANISM, THE OCCURRENCE OF A PART OF A ON A FUTURE OCCASION TENDS TO CAUSE THE WHOLE REACTION B.

This law would need to be supplemented by some account of the influence of frequency, and so on; but it seems to contain the essential characteristic of mnemic phenomena, without admixture of anything hypothetical.

Whenever the effect resulting from a stimulus to an organism differs according to the past history of the organism, without our being able actually to detect any relevant difference in its present structure, we will speak of "mnemic causation," provided we can discover laws embodying the influence of the past. In ordinary physical causation, as it appears to common sense, we have approximate uniformities of sequence, such as "lightning is followed by thunder," "drunkenness is followed by headache," and so on. None of these sequences are theoretically invariable, since something may intervene to disturb them. In order to obtain invariable physical laws, we have to proceed to differential equations, showing the direction of change at each moment, not the integral change after a finite interval, however short. But for the purposes of daily life many sequences are to all in tents and purposes invariable. With the behaviour of human beings, however, this is by no means the case. If you say to an Englishman, "You have a smut on your nose," he will proceed to remove it, but there will be no such effect if you say the same thing to a Frenchman who knows no English. The effect of words upon the hearer is a mnemic phenomena, since it depends upon the past experience which gave him understanding of the words. If there are to be purely psychological causal laws, taking no account of the brain and the rest of the body, they will have to be of the form, not "X now causes Y now," but—

"A, B, C,... in the past, together with X now, cause Y now." For it cannot be successfully maintained that our understanding of a word, for example, is an actual existent content of the mind at times when we are not thinking of the word. It is merely what may be called a "disposition," i.e. it is capable of being aroused whenever

128

we hear the word or happen to think of it. A "disposition" is not something actual, but merely the mnemic portion of a mnemic causal law.

In such a law as "A, B, C,... in the past, together with X now, cause Y now," we will call A, B, C,... the mnemic cause, X the occasion or stimulus, and Y the reaction. All cases in which experience influences behaviour are instances of mnemic causation.

Believers in psycho-physical parallelism hold that psychology can theoretically be freed entirely from all dependence on physiology or physics. That is to say, they believe that every psychical event has a psychical cause and a physical concomitant. If there is to be parallelism, it is easy to prove by mathematical logic that the causation in physical and psychical matters must be of the same sort, and it is impossible that mnemic causation should exist in psychology but not in physics. But if psychology is to be independent of physiology, and if physiology can be reduced to physics, it would seem that mnemic causation is essential in psychology. Otherwise we shall be compelled to believe that all our knowledge, all our store of images and memories, all our mental habits, are at all times existing in some latent mental form, and are not merely aroused by the stimuli which lead to their display. This is a very difficult hypothesis. It seems to me that if, as a matter of method rather than metaphysics, we desire to obtain as much independence for psychology as is practically feasible, we shall do better to accept mnemic causation in psychology protem, and therefore reject parallelism, since there is no good ground for admitting mnemic causation in physics.

It is perhaps worth while to observe that mnemic causation is what led Bergson to deny that there is causation at all in the psychical sphere. He points out, very truly, that the same stimulus, repeated, does not have the same consequences, and he argues that this is contrary to the maxim, "same cause, same effect." It is only necessary, however, to take account of past occurrences and include them with the cause, in order to re-establish the maxim, and the possibility of psychological causal laws. The metaphysical conception of a cause lingers in our manner of viewing causal laws: we want to be able to FEEL a connection between cause and effect, and to be able to imagine the cause as "operating." This makes us unwilling to regard causal laws as MERELY observed uniformities of sequence; yet that is all that science has to offer. To ask why such-and-such a kind of sequence occurs is either to ask a meaningless question, or to demand some more general kind of sequence which includes the one in question. The widest empirical laws of sequence known at any time can only be "explained" in the sense of being subsumed by later discoveries under wider laws; but these wider laws, until they in turn are subsumed, will remain brute facts, resting solely upon observation, not upon some supposed inherent rationality.

There is therefore no a priori objection to a causal law in which part of the cause has ceased to exist. To argue against such a law on the ground that what is past cannot operate now, is to introduce the old metaphysical notion of cause, for which science can find no place. The only reason that could be validly alleged against mnemic causation would be that, in fact, all the phenomena can be explained without it. They are explained without it by Semon's "engram," or by any theory which regards the results of experience as embodied in modifications of the brain and nerves. But they are not explained, unless with extreme artificiality, by any theory which regards the latent effects of experience as psychical rather than physical. Those who desire to make psychology as far as possible independent of physiology would do well, it seems to me, if they adopted mnemic causation. For my part, however, I have no such desire, and I shall therefore endeavour to state the grounds which occur to me in favour of some such view as that of the "engram."

One of the first points to be urged is that mnemic phenomena are just as much to be found in physiology as in psychology. They are even to be found in plants, as Sir Francis Darwin pointed out (cf. Semon, "Die Mneme," 2nd edition, p. 28 n.). Habit is a characteristic of the body at least as much as of the mind. We should, therefore, be compelled to allow the intrusion of mnemic causation, if admitted at all, into non-psychological regions, which ought, one feels, to be subject only to causation of the ordinary physical sort. The fact is that a great deal of what, at first sight, distinguishes psychology from physics is found, on examination, to be common to psychology and physiology; this whole question of the influence of experience is a case in point. Now it is possible, of course, to take the view advocated by Professor J. S. Haldane, who contends that physiology is not theoretically reducible to physics and chemistry.[21] But the weight of opinion among physiologists appears to be against him on this point; and we ought certainly to require very strong evidence before admitting any such breach of continuity as between living and dead matter. The argument from the existence of mnemic phenomena in physiology must therefore be allowed a certain weight against the hypothesis that mnemic causation is ultimate.

The argument from the connection of brain-lesions with loss of memory is not so strong as it looks, though it has also, some weight. What we know is that memory, and mnemic phenomena generally, can be disturbed or destroyed by changes in the brain. This certainly proves that the brain plays an essential part in the causation of memory, but does not prove that a certain state of the brain is, by itself, a sufficient condition for the existence of memory. Yet it is this last that has to be proved. The theory of the engram, or any similar theory, has to maintain that, given a body and brain in a suitable state, a man will have a certain memory, without the need of any further conditions. What is known, however, is only that he will not have memories if his body and brain are not in a suitable state. That is to say, the appropriate state of body and brain is proved to be necessary for memory, but not to be sufficient. So far, therefore, as our definite knowledge goes, memory may require for its causation a past occurrence as well as a certain present state of the brain.

---

[21] See his *The New Physiology and Other Addresses*, Griffin, 1919, also the symposium, "Are Physical, Biological and Psychological Categories Irreducible?" in *Life and Finite Individuality*, edited for the Aristotelian Society, with an Introduction. By H. Wildon Carr, Williams & Norgate, 1918.

In order to prove conclusively that mnemic phenomena arise whenever certain physiological conditions are fulfilled, we ought to be able actually to see differences between the brain of a man who speaks English and that of a man who speaks French, between the brain of a man who has seen New York and can recall it, and that of a man who has never seen that city. It may be that the time will come when this will be possible, but at present we are very far removed from it. At present, there is, so far as I am aware, no good evidence that every difference between the knowledge possessed by A and that possessed by B is paralleled by some difference in their brains. We may believe that this is the case, but if we do, our belief is based upon analogies and general scientific maxims, not upon any foundation of detailed observation. I am myself inclined, as a working hypothesis, to adopt the belief in question, and to hold that past experience only affects present behaviour through modifications of physiological structure. But the evidence seems not quite conclusive, so that I do not think we ought to forget the other hypothesis, or to reject entirely the possibility that mnemic causation may be the ultimate explanation of mnemic phenomena. I say this, not because I think it LIKELY that mnemic causation is ultimate, but merely because I think it POSSIBLE, and because it often turns out important to the progress of science to remember hypotheses which have previously seemed improbable.

# LECTURE V

## Psychological and Physical Causal Laws

The traditional conception of cause and effect is one which modern science shows to be fundamentally erroneous, and requiring to be replaced by a quite different notion, that of LAWS OF CHANGE. In the traditional conception, a particular event A caused a particular event B, and by this it was implied that, given any event B, some earlier event A could be discovered which had a relation to it, such that—

(1)  Whenever A occurred, it was followed by B;
(2)  In this sequence, there was something "necessary," not a mere de facto occurrence of A first and then B.

The second point is illustrated by the old discussion as to whether it can be said that day causes night, on the ground that day is always followed by night. The orthodox answer was that day could not be called the cause of night, because it would not be followed by night if the earth's rotation were to cease, or rather to grow so slow that one complete rotation would take a year. A cause, it was held, must be such that under no conceivable circumstances could it fail to be followed by its effect.

As a matter of fact, such sequences as were sought by believers in the traditional form of causation have not so far been found in nature. Everything in nature is apparently in a state of continuous change,[22] so that what we call one "event" turns out to be really a process. If this event is to cause another event, the two will have to be contiguous in time; for if there is any interval between them, something may happen during that interval to prevent the expected effect. Cause and effect, therefore, will have to be temporally contiguous processes. It is difficult to believe, at any rate where physical laws are concerned, that the earlier part of the process which is the cause can make any difference to the effect, so long as the later part of the process which is the cause remains unchanged. Suppose, for example, that a man dies of arsenic poisoning, we say that his taking arsenic was the cause of death. But clearly the process by which he acquired the arsenic is irrelevant: everything that happened

---

[22] The theory of quanta suggests that the continuity is only apparent. If so, we shall be able theoretically to reach events which are not processes. But in what is directly observable there is still apparent continuity, which justifies the above remarks for the prevent.

before he swallowed it may be ignored, since it cannot alter the effect except in so far as it alters his condition at the moment of taking the dose. But we may go further: swallowing arsenic is not really the proximate cause of death, since a man might be shot through the head immediately after taking the dose, and then it would not be of arsenic that he would die. The arsenic produces certain physiological changes, which take a finite time before they end in death. The earlier parts of these changes can be ruled out in the same way as we can rule out the process by which the arsenic was acquired. Proceeding in this way, we can shorten the process which we are calling the cause more and more. Similarly we shall have to shorten the effect. It may happen that immediately after the man's death his body is blown to pieces by a bomb. We cannot say what will happen after the man's death, through merely knowing that he has died as the result of arsenic poisoning. Thus, if we are to take the cause as one event and the effect as another, both must be shortened indefinitely. The result is that we merely have, as the embodiment of our causal law, a certain direction of change at each moment. Hence we are brought to differential equations as embodying causal laws. A physical law does not say "A will be followed by B," but tells us what acceleration a particle will have under given circumstances, i.e. it tells us how the particle's motion is changing at each moment, not where the particle will be at some future moment.

Laws embodied in differential equations may possibly be exact, but cannot be known to be so. All that we can know empirically is approximate and liable to exceptions; the exact laws that are assumed in physics are known to be somewhere near the truth, but are not known to be true just as they stand. The laws that we actually know empirically have the form of the traditional causal laws, except that they are not to be regarded as universal or necessary. "Taking arsenic is followed by death" is a good empirical generalization; it may have exceptions, but they will be rare. As against the professedly exact laws of physics, such empirical generalizations have the advantage that they deal with observable phenomena. We cannot observe infinitesimals, whether in time or space; we do not even know whether time and space are infinitely divisible. Therefore rough empirical generalizations have a definite place in science, in spite of not being exact of universal. They are the data for more exact laws, and the grounds for believing that they are USUALLY true are stronger than the grounds for believing that the more exact laws are ALWAYS true.

Science starts, therefore, from generalizations of the form, "A is usually followed by B." This is the nearest approach that can be made to a causal law of the traditional sort. It may happen in any particular instance that A is ALWAYS followed by B, but we cannot know this, since we cannot foresee all the perfectly possible circumstances that might make the sequence fail, or know that none of them will actually occur. If, however, we know of a very large number of cases in which A is followed by B, and few or none in which the sequence fails, we shall in PRACTICE be justified in saying "A causes B," provided we do not attach to the notion of cause any of the metaphysical superstitions that have gathered about the word.

There is another point, besides lack of universality and necessity, which it is important to realize as regards causes in the above sense, and that is the lack of uniqueness. It is generally assumed that, given any event, there is some one phenomenon which is THE cause of the event in question. This seems to be a mere mistake. Cause, in the only sense in which it can be practically applied, means "nearly invariable antecedent." We cannot in practice obtain an antecedent which is QUITE invariable, for this would require us to take account of the whole universe, since something not taken account of may prevent the expected effect. We cannot distinguish, among nearly invariable antecedents, one as THE cause, and the others as merely its concomitants: the attempt to do this depends upon a notion of cause which is derived from will, and will (as we shall see later) is not at all the sort of thing that it is generally supposed to be, nor is there any reason to think that in the physical world there is anything even remotely analogous to what will is supposed to be. If we could find one antecedent, and only one, that was QUITE invariable, we could call that one THE cause without introducing any notion derived from mistaken ideas about will. But in fact we cannot find any antecedent that we know to be quite invariable, and we can find many that are nearly so. For example, men leave a factory for dinner when the hooter sounds at twelve o'clock. You may say the hooter is THE cause of their leaving. But innumerable other hooters in other factories, which also always sound at twelve o'clock, have just as good a right to be called the cause. Thus every event has many nearly invariable antecedents, and therefore many antecedents which may be called its cause.

The laws of traditional physics, in the form in which they deal with movements of matter or electricity, have an apparent simplicity which somewhat conceals the empirical character of what they assert. A piece of matter, as it is known empirically, is not a single existing thing, but a system of existing things. When several people simultaneously see the same table, they all see something different; therefore "the" table, which they are supposed all to see, must be either a hypothesis or a construction. "The" table is to be neutral as between different observers: it does not favour the aspect seen by one man at the expense of that seen by another. It was natural, though to my mind mistaken, to regard the "real" table as the common cause of all the appearances which the table presents (as we say) to different observers. But why should we suppose that there is some one common cause of all these appearances? As we have just seen, the notion of "cause" is not so reliable as to allow us to infer the existence of something that, by its very nature, can never be observed.

Instead of looking for an impartial source, we can secure neutrality by the equal representation of all parties. Instead of supposing that there is some unknown cause, the "real" table, behind the different sensations of those who are said to be looking at the table, we may take the whole set of these sensations (together possibly with certain other particulars) as actually BEING the table. That is to say, the table which is neutral as between different observers (actual and possible) is the set of all those particulars which would naturally be called "aspects" of the table from different points of view. (This is a first approximation, modified later.)

It may be said: If there is no single existent which is the source of all these "aspects," how are they collected together? The answer is simple: Just as they would be if there were such a single existent. The supposed "real" table underlying its appearances is, in any case, not itself perceived, but inferred, and the question whether such-and-such a particular is an "aspect" of this table is only to be settled by the connection of the particular in question with the one or more particulars by which the table is defined. That is to say, even if we assume a "real" table, the particulars which are its aspects have to be collected together by their relations to each other, not to it, since it is merely inferred from them. We have only, therefore, to notice how they are collected together, and we can then keep the collection without assuming any "real" table as distinct from the collection. When different people see what they call the same table, they see things which are not exactly the same, owing to difference of point of view, but which are sufficiently alike to be described in the same words, so long as no great accuracy or minuteness is sought. These closely similar particulars are collected together by their similarity primarily and, more correctly, by the fact that they are related to each other approximately according to the laws of perspective and of reflection and diffraction of light. I suggest, as a first approximation, that these particulars, together with such correlated others as are unperceived, jointly ARE the table; and that a similar definition applies to all physical objects.[23]

In order to eliminate the reference to our perceptions, which introduces an irrelevant psychological suggestion, I will take a different illustration, namely, stellar photography. A photographic plate exposed on a clear night reproduces the appearance of the portion of the sky concerned, with more or fewer stars according to the power of the telescope that is being used. Each separate star which is photographed produces its separate effect on the plate, just as it would upon ourselves if we were looking at the sky. If we assume, as science normally does, the continuity of physical processes, we are forced to conclude that, at the place where the plate is, and at all places between it and a star which it photographs, SOMETHING is happening which is specially connected with that star. In the days when the aether was less in doubt, we should have said that what was happening was a certain kind of transverse vibration in the aether. But it is not necessary or desirable to be so explicit: all that we need say is that SOMETHING happens which is specially connected with the star in question. It must be something specially connected with that star, since that star produces its own special effect upon the plate. Whatever it is must be the end of a process which starts from the star and radiates outwards, partly on general grounds of continuity, partly to account for the fact that light is transmitted with a certain definite velocity. We thus arrive at the conclusion that, if a certain star is visible at a certain place, or

---

[23] See *Our Knowledge of the External World* (Allen & Unwin), chaps. iii and iv.

could be photographed by a sufficiently sensitive plate at that place, something is happening there which is specially connected with that star. Therefore in every place at all times a vast multitude of things must be happening, namely, at least one for every physical object which can be seen or photographed from that place. We can classify such happenings on either of two principles:

(1) We can collect together all the happenings in one place, as is done by photography so far as light is concerned;
(2) We can collect together all the happenings, in different places, which are connected in the way that common sense regards as being due to their emanating from one object.

Thus, to return to the stars, we can collect together either—

(1) All the appearances of different stars in a given place, or,
(2) All the appearances of a given star in different places.

But when I speak of "appearances," I do so only for brevity: I do not mean anything that must "appear" to somebody, but only that happening, whatever it may be, which is connected, at the place in question, with a given physical object— according to the old orthodox theory, it would be a transverse vibration in the aether. Like the different appearances of the table to a number of simultaneous observers, the different particulars that belong to one physical object are to be collected together by continuity and inherent laws of correlation, not by their supposed causal connection with an unknown assumed existent called a piece of matter, which would be a mere unnecessary metaphysical thing in itself. A piece of matter, according to the definition that I propose, is, as a first approximation,[24] the collection of all those correlated particulars which would normally be regarded as its appearances or effects in different places. Some further elaborations are desirable, but we can ignore them for the present. I shall return to them at the end of this lecture.

According to the view that I am suggesting, a physical object or piece of matter is the collection of all those correlated particulars which would be regarded by common sense as its effects or appearances in different places. On the other hand, all the happenings in a given place represent what common sense would regard as the appearances of a number of different objects as viewed from that place. All the happenings in one place may be regarded as the view of the world from that place. I shall call the view of the world from a given place a "perspective." A photograph represents a perspective. On the other hand, if photographs of the stars were taken in all points throughout space, and in all such photographs a certain star, say Sirius, were picked out whenever it appeared, all the different appearances of Sirius, taken together, would represent Sirius. For the understanding of the difference between

---

[24] The exact definition of a piece of matter as a construction will be given later.

psychology and physics it is vital to understand these two ways of classifying particulars, namely:

(1) According to the place where they occur;
(2) According to the system of correlated particulars in different places to which they belong, such system being defined as a physical object.

Given a system of particulars which is a physical object, I shall define that one of the system which is in a given place (if any) as the "appearance of that object in that place."

When the appearance of an object in a given place changes, it is found that one or other of two things occurs. The two possibilities may be illustrated by an example. You are in a room with a man, whom you see: you may cease to see him either by shutting your eyes or by his going out of the room. In the first case, his appearance to other people remains unchanged; in the second, his appearance changes from all places. In the first case, you say that it is not he who has changed, but your eyes; in the second, you say that he has changed. Generalizing, we distinguish—

(1) Cases in which only certain appearances of the object change, while others, and especially appearances from places very near to the object, do not change;
(2) Cases where all, or almost all, the appearances of the object undergo a connected change.

In the first case, the change is attributed to the medium between the object and the place; in the second, it is attributed to the object itself.[25]

It is the frequency of the latter kind of change, and the comparatively simple nature of the laws governing the simultaneous alterations of appearances in such cases, that have made it possible to treat a physical object as one thing, and to overlook the fact that it is a system of particulars. When a number of people at a theatre watch an actor, the changes in their several perspectives are so similar and so closely correlated that all are popularly regarded as identical with each other and with the changes of the actor himself. So long as all the changes in the appearances of a body are thus correlated there is no pressing prima facie need to break up the system of appearances, or to realize that the body in question is not really one thing but a set of correlated particulars. It is especially and primarily such changes that physics deals with, i.e. it deals primarily with processes in which the unity of a physical object need not be broken up because all its appearances change simultaneously according to the same law—or, if not all, at any rate all from places sufficiently near to the object, with in creasing accuracy as we approach the object.

---

[25] The application of this distinction to motion raises complications due to relativity, but we may ignore these for our present purposes.

The changes in appearances of an object which are due to changes in the intervening medium will not affect, or will affect only very slightly, the appearances from places close to the object. If the appearances from sufficiently neighbouring places are either wholly un changed, or changed to a diminishing extent which has zero for its limit, it is usually found that the changes can be accounted for by changes in objects which are between the object in question and the places from which its appearance has changed appreciably. Thus physics is able to reduce the laws of most changes with which it deals to changes in physical objects, and to state most of its fundamental laws in terms of matter. It is only in those cases in which the unity of the system of appearances constituting a piece of matter has to be broken up, that the statement of what is happening cannot be made exclusively in terms of matter. The whole of psychology, we shall find, is included among such cases; hence their importance for our purposes.

We can now begin to understand one of the fundamental differences between physics and psychology. Physics treats as a unit the whole system of appearances of a piece of matter, whereas psychology is interested in certain of these appearances themselves. Confining ourselves for the moment to the psychology of perceptions, we observe that perceptions are certain of the appearances of physical objects. From the point of view that we have been hitherto adopting, we might define them as the appearances of objects at places from which sense-organs and the suitable parts of the nervous system form part of the intervening medium. Just as a photographic plate receives a different impression of a cluster of stars when a telescope is part of the intervening medium, so a brain receives a different impression when an eye and an optic nerve are part of the intervening medium. An impression due to this sort of intervening medium is called a perception, and is interesting to psychology on its own account, not merely as one of the set of correlated particulars which is the physical object of which (as we say) we are having a perception.

We spoke earlier of two ways of classifying particulars. One way collects together the appearances commonly regarded as a given object from different places; this is, broadly speaking, the way of physics, leading to the construction of physical objects as sets of such appearances. The other way collects together the appearances of different objects from a given place, the result being what we call a perspective. In the particular case where the place concerned is a human brain, the perspective belonging to the place consists of all the perceptions of a certain man at a given time. Thus classification by perspectives is relevant to psychology, and is essential in defining what we mean by one mind.

I do not wish to suggest that the way in which I have been defining perceptions is the only possible way, or even the best way. It is the way that arose naturally out of our present topic. But when we approach psychology from a more introspective standpoint, we have to distinguish sensations and perceptions, if possible, from other mental occurrences, if any. We have also to consider the psychological effects of sensations, as opposed to their physical causes and correlates. These problems are quite distinct from those with which we have been concerned in the present lecture, and I shall not deal with them until a later stage.

It is clear that psychology is concerned essentially with actual particulars, not merely with systems of particulars. In this it differs from physics, which, broadly speaking, is concerned with the cases in which all the particulars which make up one physical object can be treated as a single causal unit, or rather the particulars which are sufficiently near to the object of which they are appearances can be so treated. The laws which physics seeks can, broadly speaking, be stated by treating such systems of particulars as causal units. The laws which psychology seeks cannot be so stated, since the particulars themselves are what interests the psychologist. This is one of the fundamental differences between physics and psychology; and to make it clear has been the main purpose of this lecture.

I will conclude with an attempt to give a more precise definition of a piece of matter. The appearances of a piece of matter from different places change partly according to intrinsic laws (the laws of perspective, in the case of visual shape), partly according to the nature of the intervening medium—fog, blue spectacles, telescopes, microscopes, sense-organs, etc. As we approach nearer to the object, the effect of the intervening medium grows less. In a generalized sense, all the intrinsic laws of change of appearance may be called "laws of perspective." Given any appearance of an object, we can construct hypothetically a certain system of appearances to which the appearance in question would belong if the laws of perspective alone were concerned. If we construct this hypothetical system for each appearance of the object in turn, the system corresponding to a given appearance x will be independent of any distortion due to the medium beyond x, and will only embody such distortion as is due to the medium between x and the object. Thus, as the appearance by which our hypothetical system is defined is moved nearer and nearer to the object, the hypothetical system of appearances defined by its means embodies less and less of the effect of the medium. The different sets of appearances resulting from moving x nearer and nearer to the object will approach to a limiting set, and this limiting set will be that system of appearances which the object would present if the laws of perspective alone were operative and the medium exercised no distorting effect. This limiting set of appearances may be defined, for purposes of physics, as the piece of matter concerned.

# LECTURE VI

## Introspection

One of the main purposes of these lectures is to give grounds for the belief that the distinction between mind and matter is not so fundamental as is commonly supposed. In the preceding lecture I dealt in outline with the physical side of this problem. I attempted to show that what we call a material object is not itself a substance, but is a system of particulars analogous in their nature to sensations, and in fact often including actual sensations among their number. In this way the stuff of which physical objects are composed is brought into relation with the stuff of which part, at least, of our mental life is composed.

There is, however, a converse task which is equally necessary for our thesis, and that is, to show that the stuff of our mental life is devoid of many qualities which it is commonly supposed to have, and is not possessed of any attributes which make it incapable of forming part of the world of matter. In the present lecture I shall begin the arguments for this view.

Corresponding to the supposed duality of matter and mind, there are, in orthodox psychology, two ways of knowing what exists. One of these, the way of sensation and external perception, is supposed to furnish data for our knowledge of matter, the other, called "introspection," is supposed to furnish data for knowledge of our mental processes. To common sense, this distinction seems clear and easy. When you see a friend coming along the street, you acquire knowledge of an external, physical fact; when you realize that you are glad to meet him, you acquire knowledge of a mental fact. Your dreams and memories and thoughts, of which you are often conscious, are mental facts, and the process by which you become aware of them SEEMS to be different from sensation. Kant calls it the "inner sense"; sometimes it is spoken of as "consciousness of self"; but its commonest name in modern English psychology is "introspection." It is this supposed method of acquiring knowledge of our mental processes that I wish to analyse and examine in this lecture.

I will state at the outset the view which I shall aim at establishing. I believe that the stuff of our mental life, as opposed to its relations and structure, consists wholly of sensations and images. Sensations are connected with matter in the way that I tried to explain in Lecture V, i.e. each is a member of a system which is a certain physical object. Images, though they USUALLY have certain characteristics, especially

140

lack of vividness, that distinguish them from sensations, are not INVARIABLY so distinguished, and cannot therefore be defined by these characteristics. Images, as opposed to sensations, can only be defined by their different causation: they are caused by association with a sensation, not by a stimulus external to the nervous system—or perhaps one should say external to the brain, where the higher animals are concerned. The occurrence of a sensation or image does not in itself constitute knowledge but any sensation or image may come to be known if the conditions are suitable. When a sensation—like the hearing of a clap of thunder—is normally correlated with closely similar sensations in our neighbours, we regard it as giving knowledge of the external world, since we regard the whole set of similar sensations as due to a common external cause. But images and bodily sensations are not so correlated. Bodily sensations can be brought into a correlation by physiology, and thus take their place ultimately among sources of knowledge of the physical world. But images cannot be made to fit in with the simultaneous sensations and images of others. Apart from their hypothetical causes in the brain, they have a causal connection with physical objects, through the fact that they are copies of past sensations; but the physical objects with which they are thus connected are in the past, not in the present. These images remain private in a sense in which sensations are not. A sensation SEEMS to give us knowledge of a present physical object, while an image does not, except when it amounts to a hallucination, and in this case the seeming is deceptive. Thus the whole context of the two occurrences is different. But in themselves they do not differ profoundly, and there is no reason to invoke two different ways of knowing for the one and for the other. Consequently introspection as a separate kind of knowledge disappears.

The criticism of introspection has been in the main the work of American psychologists. I will begin by summarizing an article which seems to me to afford a good specimen of their arguments, namely, "The Case against Introspection," by Knight Dunlap ("Psychological Review," vol xix, No. 5, pp. 404-413, September, 1912). After a few historical quotations, he comes to two modern defenders of introspection, Stout and James. He quotes from Stout such statements as the following: "Psychical states as such become objects only when we attend to them in an introspective way. Otherwise they are not themselves objects, but only constituents of the process by which objects are recognized" ("Manual," 2nd edition, p. 134. The word "recognized" in Dunlap's quotation should be "cognized.") "The object itself can never be identified with the present modification of the individual's consciousness by which it is cognized" (ib. p. 60). This is to be true even when we are thinking about modifications of our own consciousness; such modifications are to be always at least partially distinct from the conscious experience in which we think of them.

At this point I wish to interrupt the account of Knight Dunlap's article in order to make some observations on my own account with reference to the above quotations from Stout. In the first place, the conception of "psychical states" seems to me one

141

which demands analysis of a somewhat destructive character. This analysis I shall give in later lectures as regards cognition; I have already given it as regards desire. In the second place, the conception of "objects" depends upon a certain view as to cognition which I believe to be wholly mistaken, namely, the view which I discussed in my first lecture in connection with Brentano. In this view a single cognitive occurrence contains both content and object, the content being essentially mental, while the object is physical except in introspection and abstract thought. I have already criticized this view, and will not dwell upon it now, beyond saying that "the process by which objects are cognized" appears to be a very slippery phrase. When we "see a table," as common sense would say, the table as a physical object is not the "object" (in the psychological sense) of our perception. Our perception is made up of sensations, images and beliefs, but the supposed "object" is something inferential, externally related, not logically bound up with what is occurring in us. This question of the nature of the object also affects the view we take of self-consciousness. Obviously, a "conscious experience" is different from a physical object; therefore it is natural to assume that a thought or perception whose object is a conscious experience must be different from a thought or perception whose object is a physical object. But if the relation to the object is inferential and external, as I maintain, the difference between two thoughts may bear very little relation to the difference between their objects. And to speak of "the present modification of the individual's consciousness by which an object is cognized" is to suggest that the cognition of objects is a far more direct process, far more intimately bound up with the objects, than I believe it to be. All these points will be amplified when we come to the analysis of knowledge, but it is necessary briefly to state them now in order to suggest the atmosphere in which our analysis of "introspection" is to be carried on.

Another point in which Stout's remarks seem to me to suggest what I regard as mistakes is his use of "consciousness." There is a view which is prevalent among psychologists, to the effect that one can speak of "a conscious experience" in a curious dual sense, meaning, on the one hand, an experience which is conscious of something, and, on the other hand, an experience which has some intrinsic nature characteristic of what is called "consciousness." That is to say, a "conscious experience" is characterized on the one hand by relation to its object and on the other hand by being composed of a certain peculiar stuff, the stuff of "consciousness." And in many authors there is yet a third confusion: a "conscious experience," in this third sense, is an experience of which we are conscious. All these, it seems to me, need to be clearly separated. To say that one occurrence is "conscious" of another is, to my mind, to assert an external and rather remote relation between them. I might illustrate it by the relation of uncle and nephew a man becomes an uncle through no effort of his own, merely through an occurrence elsewhere. Similarly, when you are said to be "conscious" of a table, the question whether this is really the case cannot be decided by examining only your state of mind: it is necessary also to ascertain whether your sensation is having those correlates which past experience causes you to assume, or whether the table happens, in this case, to be a mirage. And, as I explained in my first lecture, I do not believe that there is any "stuff" of consciousness, so that there is no intrinsic character by which a "conscious" experience could be distinguished from any other.

After these preliminaries, we can return to Knight Dunlap's article. His criticism of Stout turns on the difficulty of giving any empirical meaning to such notions as the "mind" or the "subject"; he quotes from Stout the sentence: "The most important drawback is that the mind, in watching its own workings, must necessarily have its attention divided between two objects," and he concludes: "Without question, Stout is bringing in here illicitly the concept of a single observer, and his introspection does not provide for the observation of this observer; for the process observed and the observer are distinct" (p. 407). The objections to any theory which brings in the single observer were considered in Lecture I, and were acknowledged to be cogent. In so far, therefore, as Stout's theory of introspection rests upon this assumption, we are compelled to reject it. But it is perfectly possible to believe in introspection without supposing that there is a single observer.

William James's theory of introspection, which Dunlap next examines, does not assume a single observer. It changed after the publication of his "Psychology," in consequence of his abandoning the dualism of thought and things. Dunlap summarizes his theory as follows:

"The essential points in James's scheme of consciousness are SUBJECT, OBJECT, and a KNOWING of the object by the subject. The difference between James's scheme and other schemes involving the same terms is that James considers subject and object to be the same thing, but at different times In order to satisfy this requirement James supposes a realm of existence which he at first called 'states of consciousness' or 'thoughts,' and later, 'pure experience,' the latter term including both the 'thoughts' and the 'knowing.' This scheme, with all its magnificent artificiality, James held on to until the end, simply dropping the term consciousness and the dualism between the thought and an external reality"(p. 409).

He adds: "All that James's system really amounts to is the acknowledgment that a succession of things are known, and that they are known by something. This is all any one can claim, except for the fact that the things are known together, and that the knower for the different items is one and the same" (ib.).

In this statement, to my mind, Dunlap concedes far more than James did in his later theory. I see no reason to suppose that "the knower for different items is one and the same," and I am convinced that this proposition could not possibly be ascertained except by introspection of the sort that Dunlap rejects. The first of these points must wait until we come to the analysis of belief: the second must be considered now. Dunlap's view is that there is a dualism of subject and object, but that the subject can never become object, and therefore there is no awareness of an awareness. He says in discussing the view that introspection reveals the occurrence of knowledge: "There can be no denial of the existence of the thing (knowing) which is alleged to be known or observed in this sort of 'introspection.' The allegation that the knowing is observed is that which may be denied. Knowing there certainly is; known, the knowing certainly is not"(p. 410). And again: "I am never aware of an awareness" (ib.). And on the next page: "It may sound paradoxical to say that one cannot observe the process (or relation) of observation, and yet may be certain that there is such a process: but there is really no inconsistency in the saying. How do I know that there is awareness? By being aware of something. There is no meaning in the term 'awareness' which is not expressed in the statement 'I am aware of a colour (or what-not).'"

But the paradox cannot be so lightly disposed of. The statement "I am aware of a colour" is assumed by Knight Dunlap to be known to be true, but he does not explain how it comes to be known. The argument against him is not conclusive, since he may be able to show some valid way of inferring our awareness. But he does not suggest any such way. There is nothing odd in the hypothesis of beings which are aware of objects, but not of their own awareness; it is, indeed, highly probable that young children and the higher animals are such beings. But such beings cannot make the statement "I am aware of a colour," which WE can make. We have, therefore, some knowledge which they lack. It is necessary to Knight Dunlap's position to maintain that this additional knowledge is purely inferential, but he makes no attempt to show how the inference is possible. It may, of course, be possible, but I cannot see how. To my mind the fact (which he admits) that we know there is awareness, is ALL BUT decisive against his theory, and in favour of the view that we can be aware of an awareness.

Dunlap asserts (to return to James) that the real ground for James's original belief in introspection was his belief in two sorts of objects, namely, thoughts and things. He suggests that it was a mere inconsistency on James's part to adhere to introspection after abandoning the dualism of thoughts and things. I do not wholly agree with this view, but it is difficult to disentangle the difference as to introspection from the difference as to the nature of knowing. Dunlap suggests (p. 411) that what is called introspection really consists of awareness of "images," visceral sensations, and so on. This view, in essence, seems to me sound. But then I hold that knowing itself consists of such constituents suitably related, and that in being aware of them we are sometimes being aware of instances of knowing. For this reason, much as I agree with his view as to what are the objects of which there is awareness, I cannot wholly agree with his conclusion as to the impossibility of introspection.

The behaviourists have challenged introspection even more vigorously than Knight Dunlap, and have gone so far as to deny the existence of images. But I think that they have confused various things which are very commonly confused, and that it is necessary to make several distinctions before we can arrive at what is true and what false in the criticism of introspection.

I wish to distinguish three distinct questions, any one of which may be meant when we ask whether introspection is a source of knowledge. The three questions are as follows:

(1) Can we observe anything about ourselves which we cannot observe about other people, or is everything we can observe PUBLIC, in the sense that another could also observe it if suitably placed?

(2) Does everything that we can observe obey the laws of physics and form part of the physical world, or can we observe certain things that lie outside physics?

(3) Can we observe anything which differs in its intrinsic nature from the constituents of the physical world, or is everything that we can observe composed of elements intrinsically similar to the constituents of what is called matter?

Any one of these three questions may be used to define introspection. I should favour introspection in the sense of the first question, i.e. I think that some of the things we observe cannot, even theoretically, be observed by any one else. The second question, tentatively and for the present, I should answer in favour of introspection; I think that images, in the actual condition of science, cannot be brought under the causal laws of physics, though perhaps ultimately they may be. The third question I should answer adversely to introspection I think that observation shows us nothing that is not composed of sensations and images, and that images differ from sensations in their causal laws, not intrinsically. I shall deal with the three questions successively.

(1) PUBLICITY OR PRIVACY OF WHAT IS OBSERVED. Confining ourselves, for the moment, to sensations, we find that there are different degrees of publicity attaching to different sorts of sensations. If you feel a toothache when the other people in the room do not, you are in no way surprised; but if you hear a clap of thunder when they do not, you begin to be alarmed as to your mental condition. Sight and hearing are the most public of the senses; smell only a trifle less so; touch, again, a trifle less, since two people can only touch the same spot successively, not simultaneously. Taste has a sort of semi-publicity, since people seem to experience similar taste-sensations when they eat similar foods; but the publicity is incomplete, since two people cannot eat actually the same piece of food.

But when we pass on to bodily sensations—headache, toothache, hunger, thirst, the feeling of fatigue, and so on—we get quite away from publicity, into a region where other people can tell us what they feel, but we cannot directly observe their feeling. As a natural result of this state of affairs, it has come to be thought that the public senses give us knowledge of the outer world, while the private senses only give us knowledge as to our own bodies. As regards privacy, all images, of whatever sort, belong with the sensations which only give knowledge of our own bodies, i.e. each is only observable by one observer. This is the reason why images of sight and hearing

145

are more obviously different from sensations of sight and hearing than images of bodily sensations are from bodily sensations; and that is why the argument in favour of images is more conclusive in such cases as sight and hearing than in such cases as inner speech.

The whole distinction of privacy and publicity, however, so long as we confine ourselves to sensations, is one of degree, not of kind. No two people, there is good empirical reason to think, ever have exactly similar sensations related to the same physical object at the same moment; on the other hand, even the most private sensation has correlations which would theoretically enable another observer to infer it.

That no sensation is ever completely public, results from differences of point of view. Two people looking at the same table do not get the same sensation, because of perspective and the way the light falls. They get only correlated sensations. Two people listening to the same sound do not hear exactly the same thing, because one is nearer to the source of the sound than the other, one has better hearing than the other, and so on. Thus publicity in sensations consists, not in having PRECISELY similar sensations, but in having more or less similar sensations correlated according to ascertainable laws. The sensations which strike us as public are those where the correlated sensations are very similar and the correlations are very easy to discover. But even the most private sensations have correlations with things that others can observe. The dentist does not observe your ache, but he can see the cavity which causes it, and could guess that you are suffering even if you did not tell him. This fact, however, cannot be used, as Watson would apparently wish, to extrude from science observations which are private to one observer, since it is by means of many such observations that correlations are established, e.g. between toothaches and cavities. Privacy, therefore does not by itself make a datum unamenable to scientific treatment. On this point, the argument against introspection must be rejected.

(2) DOES EVERYTHING OBSERVABLE OBEY THE LAWS OF PHYSICS? We come now to the second ground of objection to introspection, namely, that its data do not obey the laws of physics. This, though less emphasized, is, I think, an objection which is really more strongly felt than the objection of privacy. And we obtain a definition of introspection more in harmony with usage if we define it as observation of data not subject to physical laws than if we define it by means of privacy. No one would regard a man as introspective because he was conscious of having a stomach ache. Opponents of introspection do not mean to deny the obvious fact that we can observe bodily sensations which others cannot observe. For example, Knight Dunlap contends that images are really muscular contractions,[26] and evidently regards our awareness of muscular contractions as not coming under the head of introspection. I think it will be found that the essential characteristic of introspective data, in the

---

[26] *Psychological Review*, 1916, "Thought-Content and Feeling," p. 59. See also ib., 1912, "The Nature of Perceived Relations," where he says: "'Introspection,' divested of its mythological suggestion of the observing of consciousness, is really the observation of bodily sensations (sensibles) and feelings (feelables)"(p. 427 n.).

sense which now concerns us, has to do with LOCALIZATION: either they are not localized at all, or they are localized, like visual images, in a place already physically occupied by something which would be inconsistent with them if they were regarded as part of the physical world. If you have a visual image of your friend sitting in a chair which in fact is empty, you cannot locate the image in your body, because it is visual, nor (as a physical phenomenon) in the chair, because the chair, as a physical object, is empty. Thus it seems to follow that the physical world does not include all that we are aware of, and that images, which are introspective data, have to be regarded, for the present, as not obeying the laws of physics; this is, I think, one of the chief reasons why an attempt is made to reject them. I shall try to show in Lecture VIII that the purely empirical reasons for accepting images are overwhelming. But we cannot be nearly so certain that they will not ultimately be brought under the laws of physics. Even if this should happen, however, they would still be distinguishable from sensations by their proximate causal laws, as gases remain distinguishable from solids.

(3) CAN WE OBSERVE ANYTHING INTRINSICALLY DIFFERENT FROM SENSATIONS? We come now to our third question concerning introspection. It is commonly thought that by looking within we can observe all sorts of things that are radically different from the constituents of the physical world, e.g. thoughts, beliefs, desires, pleasures, pains and emotions. The difference between mind and matter is increased partly by emphasizing these supposed introspective data, partly by the supposition that matter is composed of atoms or electrons or whatever units physics may at the moment prefer. As against this latter supposition, I contend that the ultimate constituents of matter are not atoms or electrons, but sensations, and other things similar to sensations as regards extent and duration. As against the view that introspection reveals a mental world radically different from sensations, I propose to argue that thoughts, beliefs, desires, pleasures, pains and emotions are all built up out of sensations and images alone, and that there is reason to think that images do not differ from sensations in their intrinsic character. We thus effect a mutual rapprochement of mind and matter, and reduce the ultimate data of introspection (in our second sense) to images alone. On this third view of the meaning of introspection, therefore, our decision is wholly against it.

There remain two points to be considered concerning introspection. The first is as to how far it is trustworthy; the second is as to whether, even granting that it reveals no radically different STUFF from that revealed by what might be called external perception, it may not reveal different RELATIONS, and thus acquire almost as much importance as is traditionally assigned to it.

To begin with the trustworthiness of introspection. It is common among certain schools to regard the knowledge of our own mental processes as incomparably more certain than our knowledge of the "external" world; this view is to be found in the British philosophy which descends from Hume, and is present, somewhat veiled, in Kant and his followers. There seems no reason whatever to accept this view. Our spontaneous, unsophisticated beliefs, whether as to ourselves or as to the outer world, are always extremely rash and very liable to error. The acquisition of caution is equally necessary and equally difficult in both directions. Not only are we often un aware of entertaining a belief or desire which exists in us; we are often actually mistaken. The fallibility of introspection as regards what we desire is made evident by psycho-analysis; its fallibility as to what we know is easily demonstrated. An autobiography, when confronted by a careful editor with documentary evidence, is usually found to be full of obviously inadvertent errors. Any of us confronted by a forgotten letter written some years ago will be astonished to find how much more foolish our opinions were than we had remembered them as being. And as to the analysis of our mental operations—believing, desiring, willing, or what not—introspection unaided gives very little help: it is necessary to construct hypotheses and test them by their consequences, just as we do in physical science. Introspection, therefore, though it is one among our sources of knowledge, is not, in isolation, in any degree more trustworthy than "external" perception.

I come now to our second question: Does introspection give us materials for the knowledge of relations other than those arrived at by reflecting upon external perception? It might be contended that the essence of what is "mental" consists of relations, such as knowing for example, and that our knowledge concerning these essentially mental relations is entirely derived from introspection. If "knowing" were an unanalysable relation, this view would be incontrovertible, since clearly no such relation forms part of the subject matter of physics. But it would seem that "knowing" is really various relations, all of them complex. Therefore, until they have been analysed, our present question must remain unanswered I shall return to it at the end of the present course of lectures.

# LECTURE VII

## The Definition of Perception

In Lecture V we found reason to think that the ultimate constituents[27] of the world do not have the characteristics of either mind or matter as ordinarily understood: they are not solid persistent objects moving through space, nor are they fragments of "consciousness." But we found two ways of grouping particulars, one into "things" or "pieces of matter," the other into series of "perspectives," each series being what may be called a "biography." Before we can define either sensations or images, it is necessary to consider this twofold classification in somewhat greater detail, and to derive from it a definition of perception. It should be said that, in so far as the classification assumes the whole world of physics (including its unperceived portions), it contains hypothetical elements. But we will not linger on the grounds for admitting these, which belong to the philosophy of physics rather than of psychology.

The physical classification of particulars collects together all those that are aspects of one "thing." Given any one particular, it is found often (we do not say always) that there are a number of other particulars differing from this one in gradually increasing degrees. Those (or some of those) that differ from it only very slightly will be found to differ approximately according to certain laws which may be called, in a generalized sense, the laws of "perspective"; they include the ordinary laws of perspective as a special case. This approximation grows more and more nearly exact as the difference grows less; in technical language, the laws of perspective account for the differences to the first order of small quantities, and other laws are only required to account for second-order differences. That is to say, as the difference diminishes, the part of the difference which is not according to the laws of perspective diminishes much more rapidly, and bears to the total difference a ratio which tends towards zero as both are made smaller and smaller. By this means we can theoretically collect together a number of particulars which may be defined as the "aspects" or "appearances" of one thing at one time. If the laws of perspective were sufficiently known, the connection between different aspects would be expressed in differential equations.

---

[27] When I speak of "ultimate constituents," I do not mean necessarily such as are theoretically incapable of analysis, but only such as, at present, we can see no means of analysing. I speak of such constituents as "particulars," or as *relative* particulars" when I wish to emphasize the fact that they may be themselves complex.

149

This gives us, so far, only those particulars which constitute one thing at one time. This set of particulars may be called a "momentary thing." To define that series of "momentary things" that constitute the successive states of one thing is a problem involving the laws of dynamics. These give the laws governing the changes of aspects from one time to a slightly later time, with the same sort of differential approximation to exactness as we obtained for spatially neighbouring aspects through the laws of perspective. Thus a momentary thing is a set of particulars, while a thing (which may be identified with the whole history of the thing) is a series of such sets of particulars. The particulars in one set are collected together by the laws of perspective; the successive sets are collected together by the laws of dynamics. This is the view of the world which is appropriate to traditional physics.

The definition of a "momentary thing" involves problems concerning time, since the particulars constituting a momentary thing will not be all simultaneous, but will travel outward from the thing with the velocity of light (in case the thing is in vacuo). There are complications connected with relativity, but for our present purpose they are not vital, and I shall ignore them.

Instead of first collecting together all the particulars constituting a momentary thing, and then forming the series of successive sets, we might have first collected together a series of successive aspects related by the laws of dynamics, and then have formed the set of such series related by the laws of perspective. To illustrate by the case of an actor on the stage: our first plan was to collect together all the aspects which he presents to different spectators at one time, and then to form the series of such sets. Our second plan is first to collect together all the aspects which he presents successively to a given spectator, and then to do the same thing for the other spectators, thus forming a set of series instead of a series of sets. The first plan tells us what he does; the second the impressions he produces. This second way of classifying particulars is one which obviously has more relevance to psychology than the other. It is partly by this second method of classification that we obtain definitions of one "experience" or "biography" or "person." This method of classification is also essential to the definition of sensations and images, as I shall endeavour to prove later on. But we must first amplify the definition of perspectives and biographies.

In our illustration of the actor, we spoke, for the moment, as though each spectator's mind were wholly occupied by the one actor. If this were the case, it might be possible to define the biography of one spectator as a series of successive aspects of the actor related according to the laws of dynamics. But in fact this is not the case. We are at all times during our waking life receiving a variety of impressions, which are aspects of a variety of things. We have to consider what binds together two simultaneous sensations in one person, or, more generally, any two occurrences which forte part of one experience. We might say, adhering to the standpoint of physics, that two aspects of different things belong to the same perspective when they are in the same place. But this would not really help us, since a "place" has not yet been defined. Can we define what is meant by saying that two aspects are "in the same place," without introducing anything beyond the laws of perspective and dynamics?

I do not feel sure whether it is possible to frame such a definition or not; accordingly I shall not assume that it is possible, but shall seek other characteristics by which a perspective or biography may be defined.

When (for example) we see one man and hear another speaking at the same time, what we see and what we hear have a relation which we can perceive, which makes the two together form, in some sense, one experience. It is when this relation exists that two occurrences become associated. Semon's "engram" is formed by all that we experience at one time. He speaks of two parts of this total as having the relation of "Nebeneinander" (M. 118; M.E. 33 ff.), which is reminiscent of Herbart's "Zusammen." I think the relation may be called simply "simultaneity." It might be said that at any moment all sorts of things that are not part of my experience are happening in the world, and that therefore the relation we are seeking to define cannot be merely simultaneity. This, however, would be an error—the sort of error that the theory of relativity avoids. There is not one universal time, except by an elaborate construction; there are only local times, each of which may be taken to be the time within one biography. Accordingly, if I am (say) hearing a sound, the only occurrences that are, in any simple sense, simultaneous with my sensation are events in my private world, i.e. in my biography. We may therefore define the "perspective" to which the sensation in question belongs as the set of particulars that are simultaneous with this sensation. And similarly we may define the "biography" to which the sensation belongs as the set of particulars that are earlier or later than, or simultaneous with, the given sensation. Moreover, the very same definitions can be applied to particulars which are not sensations. They are actually required for the theory of relativity, if we are to give a philosophical explanation of what is meant by "local time" in that theory The relations of simultaneity and succession are known to us in our own experience; they may be analysable, but that does not affect their suitability for defining perspectives and biographies. Such time-relations as can be constructed between events in different biographies are of a different kind: they are not experienced, and are merely logical, being designed to afford convenient ways of stating the correlations between different biographies.

It is not only by time-relations that the parts of one biography are collected together in the case of living beings. In this case there are the mnemic phenomena which constitute the unity of one "experience," and transform mere occurrences into "experiences." I have already dwelt upon the importance of mnemic phenomena for psychology, and shall not enlarge upon them now, beyond observing that they are what transforms a biography (in our technical sense) into a life. It is they that give the continuity of a "person" or a "mind." But there is no reason to suppose that mnemic phenomena are associated with biographies except in the case of animals and plants.

151

Our two-fold classification of particulars gives rise to the dualism of body and biography in regard to everything in the universe, and not only in regard to living things. This arises as follows. Every particular of the sort considered by physics is a member of two groups:

(1) The group of particulars constituting the other aspects of the same physical object;

(2) The group of particulars that have direct time-relations to the given particular.

Each of these is associated with a place. When I look at a star, my sensation is:

(1) A member of the group of particulars which is the star, and which is associated with the place where the star is;

(2) A member of the group of particulars which is my biography, and which is associated with the place where I am.[28]

The result is that every particular of the kind relevant to physics is associated with TWO places; e.g. my sensation of the star is associated with the place where I am and with the place where the star is. This dualism has nothing to do with any "mind" that I may be supposed to possess; it exists in exactly the same sense if I am replaced by a photographic plate. We may call the two places the active and passive places respectively.[29] Thus in the case of a perception or photograph of a star, the active place is the place where the star is, while the passive place is the place where the percipient or photographic plate is.

We can thus, without departing from physics, collect together all the particulars actively at a given place, or all the particulars passively at a given place. In our own case, the one group is our body (or our brain), while the other is our mind, in so far as it consists of perceptions. In the case of the photographic plate, the first group is the plate as dealt with by physics, the second the aspect of the heavens which it photographs. (For the sake of schematic simplicity, I am ignoring various complications connected with time, which require some tedious but perfectly feasible elaborations.) Thus what may be called subjectivity in the point of view is not a distinctive peculiarity of mind: it is present just as much in the photographic plate. And the photographic plate has its biography as well as its "matter." But this biography is an affair of physics, and has none of the peculiar characteristics by which "mental" phenomena are distinguished, with the sole exception of subjectivity.

Adhering, for the moment, to the standpoint of physics, we may define a "perception" of an object as the appearance of the object from a place where there

---

[28] I have explained elsewhere the manner in which space is constructed on this theory, and in which the position of a perspective is brought into relation with the position of a physical object (*Our Knowledge of the External World*, Lecture III, pp. 90, 91).

[29] I use these as mere names; I do not want to introduce any notion of "activity."

is a brain (or, in lower animals, some suitable nervous structure), with sense-organs and nerves forming part of the intervening medium. Such appearances of objects are distinguished from appearances in other places by certain peculiarities, namely:

(1) They give rise to mnemic phenomena;
(2) They are themselves affected by mnemic phenomena.

That is to say, they may be remembered and associated or influence our habits, or give rise to images, etc., and they are themselves different from what they would have been if our past experience had been different—for example, the effect of a spoken sentence upon the hearer depends upon whether the hearer knows the language or not, which is a question of past experience. It is these two characteristics, both connected with mnemic phenomena, that distinguish perceptions from the appearances of objects in places where there is no living being.

Theoretically, though often not practically, we can, in our perception of an object, separate the part which is due to past experience from the part which proceeds without mnemic influences out of the character of the object. We may define as "sensation" that part which proceeds in this way, while the remainder, which is a mnemic phenomenon, will have to be added to the sensation to make up what is called the "perception." According to this definition, the sensation is a theoretical core in the actual experience; the actual experience is the perception. It is obvious that there are grave difficulties in carrying out these definitions, but we will not linger over them. We have to pass, as soon as we can, from the physical standpoint, which we have been hitherto adopting, to the standpoint of psychology, in which we make more use of introspection in the first of the three senses discussed in the preceding lecture.

But before making the transition, there are two points which must be made clear. First: Everything outside my own personal biography is outside my experience; therefore if anything can be known by me outside my biography, it can only be known in one of two ways:

(1) By inference from things within my biography, or
(2) By some a priori principle independent of experience.

I do not myself believe that anything approaching certainty is to be attained by either of these methods, and therefore whatever lies outside my personal biography must be regarded, theoretically, as hypothesis. The theoretical argument for adopting the hypothesis is that it simplifies the statement of the laws according to which events happen in our experience. But there is no very good ground for supposing that a simple law is more likely to be true than a complicated law, though there is good ground for assuming a simple law in scientific practice, as a working hypothesis, if it explains the facts as well as another which is less simple. Belief in the existence of things outside my own biography exists antecedently to evidence, and can only be destroyed, if at all, by a long course of philosophic doubt. For purposes of science, it is justified practically by the simplification which it introduces into the laws of physics. But from the standpoint of theoretical logic it must be regarded as a prejudice, not as a well-grounded theory. With this proviso, I propose to continue yielding to the prejudice.

The second point concerns the relating of our point of view to that which regards sensations as caused by stimuli external to the nervous system (or at least to the brain), and distinguishes images as "centrally excited," i.e. due to causes in the brain which cannot be traced back to anything affecting the sense-organs. It is clear that, if our analysis of physical objects has been valid, this way of defining sensations needs reinterpretation. It is also clear that we must be able to find such a new interpretation if our theory is to be admissible.

To make the matter clear, we will take the simplest possible illustration. Consider a certain star, and suppose for the moment that its size is negligible. That is to say, we will regard it as, for practical purposes, a luminous point. Let us further suppose that it exists only for a very brief time, say a second. Then, according to physics, what happens is that a spherical wave of light travels outward from the star through space, just as, when you drop a stone into a stagnant pond, ripples travel outward from the place where the stone hit the water. The wave of light travels with a certain very nearly constant velocity, roughly 300,000 kilometres per second. This velocity may be ascertained by sending a flash of light to a mirror, and observing how long it takes before the reflected flash reaches you, just as the velocity of sound may be ascertained by means of an echo.

What it is that happens when a wave of light reaches a given place we cannot tell, except in the sole case when the place in question is a brain connected with an eye which is turned in the right direction. In this one very special case we know what happens: we have the sensation called "seeing the star." In all other cases, though we know (more or less hypothetically) some of the correlations and abstract properties of the appearance of the star, we do not know the appearance itself. Now you may, for the sake of illustration, compare the different appearances of the star to the conjugation of a Greek verb, except that the number of its parts is really infinite, and not only apparently so to the despairing schoolboy. In vacuo, the parts are regular, and can be derived from the (imaginary) root according to the laws of grammar, i.e. of perspective. The star being situated in empty space, it may be defined, for purposes of physics, as consisting of all those appearances which it presents in vacuo, together with those which, according to the laws of perspective, it would present elsewhere if its appearances elsewhere were regular. This is merely the adaptation of the definition of matter which I gave in an earlier lecture. The appearance of a star at a certain place, if it is regular, does not require any cause or explanation beyond the existence of the star. Every regular appearance is an actual member of the system which is the star, and its causation is entirely internal to that system. We may express this by saying that a regular appearance is due to the star alone, and is actually part of the star, in the sense in which a man is part of the human race.

But presently the light of the star reaches our atmosphere. It begins to be refracted, and dimmed by mist, and its velocity is slightly diminished. At last it reaches a human eye, where a complicated process takes place, ending in a sensation which gives us our grounds for believing in all that has gone before. Now, the irregular appearances of the star are not, strictly speaking, members of the system which is the star, according to our definition of matter. The irregular appearances, however, are not merely irregular: they proceed according to laws which can be stated in terms of the matter through which the light has passed on its way. The sources of an irregular appearance are therefore twofold:

(1) The object which is appearing irregularly;
(2) The intervening medium.

It should be observed that, while the conception of a regular appearance is perfectly precise, the conception of an irregular appearance is one capable of any degree of vagueness. When the distorting influence of the medium is sufficiently great, the resulting particular can no longer be regarded as an appearance of an object, but must be treated on its own account. This happens especially when the particular in question cannot be traced back to one object, but is a blend of two or more. This case is normal in perception: we see as one what the microscope or telescope reveals to be many different objects. The notion of perception is therefore not a precise one: we perceive things more or less, but always with a very considerable amount of vagueness and confusion.

In considering irregular appearances, there are certain very natural mistakes which must be avoided. In order that a particular may count as an irregular appearance of a certain object, it is not necessary that it should bear any resemblance to the regular appearances as regard its intrinsic qualities. All that is necessary is that it should be derivable from the regular appearances by the laws which express the distorting influence of the medium. When it is so derivable, the particular in question may be regarded as caused by the regular appearances, and therefore by the object itself, together with the modifications resulting from the medium. In other cases, the particular in question may, in the same sense, be regarded as caused by several objects together with the medium; in this case, it may be called a confused appearance of several objects. If it happens to be in a brain, it may be called a confused perception of these objects. All actual perception is confused to a greater or less extent.

We can now interpret in terms of our theory the distinction between those mental occurrences which are said to have an external stimulus, and those which are said to be "centrally excited," i.e. to have no stimulus external to the brain. When a mental occurrence can be regarded as an appearance of an object external to the brain, however irregular, or even as a confused appearance of several such objects, then we may regard it as having for its stimulus the object or objects in question, or their appearances at the sense-organ concerned. When, on the other hand, a mental occurrence has not sufficient connection with objects external to the brain to be regarded as an appearance of such objects, then its physical causation (if any) will have to be sought in the brain. In the former case it can be called a perception; in the latter it cannot be so called. But the distinction is one of degree, not of kind. Until this is realized, no satisfactory theory of perception, sensation, or imagination is possible.

# LECTURE VIII

## Sensations and Images

The dualism of mind and matter, if we have been right so far, cannot be allowed as metaphysically valid. Nevertheless, we seem to find a certain dualism, perhaps not ultimate, within the world as we observe it. The dualism is not primarily as to the stuff of the world, but as to causal laws. On this subject we may again quote William James. He points out that when, as we say, we merely "imagine" things, there are no such effects as would ensue if the things were what we call "real." He takes the case of imagining a fire.

"I make for myself an experience of blazing fire; I place it near my body; but it does not warm me in the least. I lay a stick upon it and the stick either burns or remains green, as I please. I call up water, and pour it on the fire, and absolutely no difference ensues. I account for all such facts by calling this whole train of experiences unreal, a mental train. Mental fire is what won't burn real sticks; mental water is what won't necessarily (though of course it may) put out even a mental fire.... With 'real' objects, on the contrary, consequences always accrue; and thus the real experiences get sifted from the mental ones, the things from our thoughts of them, fanciful or true, and precipitated together as the stable part of the whole experience—chaos, under the name of the physical world."[30]

In this passage James speaks, by mere inadvertence, as though the phenomena which he is describing as "mental" had NO effects. This is, of course, not the case: they have their effects, just as much as physical phenomena do, but their effects follow different laws. For example, dreams, as Freud has shown, are just as much subject to laws as are the motions of the planets. But the laws are different: in a dream you may be transported from one place to another in a moment, or one person may turn into another under your eyes. Such differences compel you to distinguish the world of dreams from the physical world.

If the two sorts of causal laws could be sharply distinguished, we could call an occurrence "physical" when it obeys causal laws appropriate to the physical world, and "mental" when it obeys causal laws appropriate to the mental world. Since the mental world and the physical world interact, there would be a boundary between

---

[30] *Essays in Radical Empiricism*, pp. 32-3.

the two: there would be events which would have physical causes and mental effects, while there would be others which would have mental causes and physical effects. Those that have physical causes and mental effects we should define as "sensations." Those that have mental causes and physical effects might perhaps be identified with what we call voluntary movements; but they do not concern us at present.

These definitions would have all the precision that could be desired if the distinction between physical and psychological causation were clear and sharp. As a matter of fact, however, this distinction is, as yet, by no means sharp. It is possible that, with fuller knowledge, it will be found to be no more ultimate than the distinction between the laws of gases and the laws of rigid bodies. It also suffers from the fact that an event may be an effect of several causes according to several causal laws we cannot, in general, point to anything unique as THE cause of such-and-such an event. And finally it is by no means certain that the peculiar causal laws which govern mental events are not really physiological. The law of habit, which is one of the most distinctive, may be fully explicable in terms of the peculiarities of nervous tissue, and these peculiarities, in turn, may be explicable by the laws of physics. It seems, therefore, that we are driven to a different kind of definition. It is for this reason that it was necessary to develop the definition of perception. With this definition, we can define a sensation as the non-mnemic elements in a perception.

When, following our definition, we try to decide what elements in our experience are of the nature of sensations, we find more difficulty than might have been expected. Prima facie, everything is sensation that comes to us through the senses: the sights we see, the sounds we hear, the smells we smell, and so on; also such things as headache or the feeling of muscular strain. But in actual fact so much interpretation, so much of habitual correlation, is mixed with all such experiences, that the core of pure sensation is only to be extracted by careful investigation. To take a simple illustration: if you go to the theatre in your own country, you seem to hear equally well in the stalls or the dress circle; in either case you think you miss nothing. But if you go in a foreign country where you have a fair knowledge of the language, you will seem to have grown partially deaf, and you will find it necessary to be much nearer the stage than you would need to be in your own country. The reason is that, in hearing our own language spoken, we quickly and unconsciously fill out what we really hear with inferences to what the man must be saying, and we never realize that we have not heard the words we have merely inferred. In a foreign language, these inferences are more difficult, and we are more dependent upon actual sensation. If we found ourselves in a foreign world, where tables looked like cushions and cushions like tables, we should similarly discover how much of what we think we see is really inference. Every fairly familiar sensation is to us a sign of the things that usually go with it, and many of these things will seem to form part of the sensation. I remember in the early days of motor-cars being with a friend when a tyre burst with a loud report. He thought it was a pistol, and supported his opinion by maintaining that he had seen the flash. But of course there had been no flash. Nowadays no one sees a flash when a tyre bursts.

In order, therefore, to arrive at what really is sensation in an occurrence which, at first sight, seems to contain nothing else, we have to pare away all that is due to habit or expectation or interpretation. This is a matter for the psychologist, and by no means an easy matter. For our purposes, it is not important to determine what exactly is the sensational core in any case; it is only important to notice that there certainly is a sensational core, since habit, expectation and interpretation are diversely aroused on diverse occasions, and the diversity is clearly due to differences in what is presented to the senses. When you open your newspaper in the morning, the actual sensations of seeing the print form a very minute part of what goes on in you, but they are the starting-point of all the rest, and it is through them that the newspaper is a means of information or mis-information. Thus, although it may be difficult to determine what exactly is sensation in any given experience, it is clear that there is sensation, unless, like Leibniz, we deny all action of the outer world upon us.

Sensations are obviously the source of our knowledge of the world, including our own body. It might seem natural to regard a sensation as itself a cognition, and until lately I did so regard it. When, say, I see a person I know coming towards me in the street, it SEEMS as though the mere seeing were knowledge. It is of course undeniable that knowledge comes THROUGH the seeing, but I think it is a mistake to regard the mere seeing itself as knowledge. If we are so to regard it, we must distinguish the seeing from what is seen: we must say that, when we see a patch of colour of a certain shape, the patch of colour is one thing and our seeing of it is another. This view, however, demands the admission of the subject, or act, in the sense discussed in our first lecture. If there is a subject, it can have a relation to the patch of colour, namely, the sort of relation which we might call awareness. In that case the sensation, as a mental event, will consist of awareness of the colour, while the colour itself will remain wholly physical, and may be called the sense-datum, to distinguish it from the sensation. The subject, however, appears to be a logical fiction, like mathematical points and instants. It is introduced, not because observation reveals it, but because it is linguistically convenient and apparently demanded by grammar. Nominal entities of this sort may or may not exist, but there is no good ground for assuming that they do. The functions that they appear to perform can always be performed by classes or series or other logical constructions, consisting of less dubious entities. If we are to avoid a perfectly gratuitous assumption, we must dispense with the subject as one of the actual ingredients of the world. But when we do this, the possibility of distinguishing the sensation from the sense-datum vanishes; at least I see no way of preserving the distinction. Accordingly the sensation that we have when we see a patch of colour simply is that patch of colour, an actual constituent of the physical world, and part of what physics is concerned with. A patch of colour is certainly not knowledge, and therefore we cannot say that pure sensation is cognitive. Through its psychological effects, it is the cause of cognitions, partly by being itself a sign of things that are correlated with it, as e.g. sensations of sight and touch are correlated, and partly by giving rise to images and memories after the sensation is faded. But in itself the pure sensation is not cognitive.

In the first lecture we considered the view of Brentano, that "we may define psychical phenomena by saying that they are phenomena which intentionally contain an object." We saw reasons to reject this view in general; we are now concerned to show that it must be rejected in the particular case of sensations. The kind of argument which formerly made me accept Brentano's view in this case was exceedingly simple. When I see a patch of colour, it seemed to me that the colour is not psychical, but physical, while my seeing is not physical, but psychical. Hence I concluded that the colour is something other than my seeing of the colour. This argument, to me historically, was directed against idealism: the emphatic part of it was the assertion that the colour is physical, not psychical. I shall not trouble you now with the grounds for holding as against Berkeley that the patch of colour is physical; I have set them forth before, and I see no reason to modify them. But it does not follow that the patch of colour is not also psychical, unless we assume that the physical and the psychical cannot overlap, which I no longer consider a valid assumption. If we admit—as I think we should—that the patch of colour may be both physical and psychical, the reason for distinguishing the sense-datum from the sensation disappears, and we may say that the patch of colour and our sensation in seeing it are identical.

This is the view of William James, Professor Dewey, and the American realists. Perceptions, says Professor Dewey, are not per se cases of knowledge, but simply natural events with no more knowledge status than (say) a shower. "Let them [the realists] try the experiment of conceiving perceptions as pure natural events, not cases of awareness or apprehension, and they will be surprised to see how little they miss."[31] I think he is right in this, except in supposing that the realists will be surprised. Many of them already hold the view he is advocating, and others are very sympathetic to it. At any rate, it is the view which I shall adopt in these lectures.

The stuff of the world, so far as we have experience of it, consists, on the view that I am advocating, of innumerable transient particulars such as occur in seeing, hearing, etc., together with images more or less resembling these, of which I shall speak shortly. If physics is true, there are, besides the particulars that we experience, others, probably equally (or almost equally) transient, which make up that part of the material world that does not come into the sort of contact with a living body that is required to turn it into a sensation. But this topic belongs to the philosophy of physics, and need not concern us in our present inquiry.

Sensations are what is common to the mental and physical worlds; they may be defined as the intersection of mind and matter. This is by no means a new view; it

---

[31] Dewey, *Essays in Experimental Logic*, pp. 253, 262.

is advocated, not only by the American authors I have mentioned, but by Mach in his Analysis of Sensations, which was published in 1886. The essence of sensation, according to the view I am advocating, is its independence of past experience. It is a core in our actual experiences, never existing in isolation except possibly in very young infants. It is not itself knowledge, but it supplies the data for our knowledge of the physical world, including our own bodies.

There are some who believe that our mental life is built up out of sensations alone. This may be true; but in any case I think the only ingredients required in addition to sensations are images. What images are, and how they are to be defined, we have now to inquire.

The distinction between images and sensations might seem at first sight by no means difficult. When we shut our eyes and call up pictures of familiar scenes, we usually have no difficulty, so long as we remain awake, in discriminating between what we are imagining and what is really seen. If we imagine some piece of music that we know, we can go through it in our mind from beginning to end without any discoverable tendency to suppose that we are really hearing it. But although such cases are so clear that no confusion seems possible, there are many others that are far more difficult, and the definition of images is by no means an easy problem.

To begin with: we do not always know whether what we are experiencing is a sensation or an image. The things we see in dreams when our eyes are shut must count as images, yet while we are dreaming they seem like sensations. Hallucinations often begin as persistent images, and only gradually acquire that influence over belief that makes the patient regard them as sensations. When we are listening for a faint sound—the striking of a distant clock, or a horse's hoofs on the road—we think we hear it many times before we really do, because expectation brings us the image, and we mistake it for sensation. The distinction between images and sensations is, therefore, by no means always obvious to inspection.[32]

We may consider three different ways in which it has been sought to distinguish images from sensations, namely:

(1) By the less degree of vividness in images;
(2) By our absence of belief in their "physical reality";
(3) By the fact that their causes and effects are different from those of sensations.

I believe the third of these to be the only universally applicable criterion. The other two are applicable in very many cases, but cannot be used for purposes of definition because they are liable to exceptions. Nevertheless, they both deserve to be carefully considered.

(1) Hume, who gives the names "impressions" and "ideas" to what may, for present purposes, be identified with our "sensations" and "images," speaks of impressions

---

[32] On the distinction between images and sensation, cf. Semon, *Die mnemischen Empfindungen*, pp. 19-20.

as "those perceptions which enter with most force and violence" while he defines ideas as "the faint images of these (i.e. of impressions) in thinking and reasoning." His immediately following observations, however, show the inadequacy of his criteria of "force" and "faintness." He says:

"I believe it will not be very necessary to employ many words in explaining this distinction. Every one of himself will readily perceive the difference betwixt feeling and thinking. The common degrees of these are easily distinguished, though it is not impossible but in particular instances they may very nearly approach to each other. Thus in sleep, in a fever, in madness, or in any very violent emotions of soul, our ideas may approach to our impressions; as, on the other hand, it sometimes happens, that our impressions are so faint and low that we cannot distinguish them from our ideas. But notwithstanding this near resemblance in a few instances, they are in general so very different, that no one can make a scruple to rank them under distinct heads, and assign to each a peculiar name to mark the difference" ("Treatise of Human Nature," Part I, Section I).

I think Hume is right in holding that they should be ranked under distinct heads, with a peculiar name for each. But by his own confession in the above passage, his criterion for distinguishing them is not always adequate. A definition is not sound if it only applies in cases where the difference is glaring: the essential purpose of a definition is to provide a mark which is applicable even in marginal cases—except, of course, when we are dealing with a conception, like, e.g. baldness, which is one of degree and has no sharp boundaries. But so far we have seen no reason to think that the difference between sensations and images is only one of degree.

Professor Stout, in his "Manual of Psychology," after discussing various ways of distinguishing sensations and images, arrives at a view which is a modification of Hume's. He says (I quote from the second edition):

"Our conclusion is that at bottom the distinction between image and percept, as respectively faint and vivid states, is based on a difference of quality. The percept has an aggressiveness which does not belong to the image. It strikes the mind with varying degrees of force or liveliness according to the varying intensity of the stimulus. This degree of force or liveliness is part of what we ordinarily mean by the intensity of a sensation. But this constituent of the intensity of sensations is absent in mental imagery"(p. 419).

This view allows for the fact that sensations may reach any degree of faintness—e.g. in the case of a just visible star or a just audible sound—without becoming images, and that therefore mere faintness cannot be the characteristic mark of images. After explaining the sudden shock of a flash of lightning or a steam-whistle, Stout says that "no mere image ever does strike the mind in this manner"(p. 417). But I believe that this criterion fails in very much the same instances as those in which Hume's criterion fails in its original form. Macbeth speaks of—

that suggestion
Whose horrid image doth unfix my hair
And make my seated heart knock at my ribs
Against the use of nature.

The whistle of a steam-engine could hardly have a stronger effect than this. A very intense emotion will often bring with it—especially where some future action or some undecided issue is involved—powerful compelling images which may determine the whole course of life, sweeping aside all contrary solicitations to the will by their capacity for exclusively possessing the mind. And in all cases where images, originally recognized as such, gradually pass into hallucinations, there must be just that "force or liveliness" which is supposed to be always absent from images. The cases of dreams and fever-delirium are as hard to adjust to Professor Stout's modified criterion as to Hume's. I conclude therefore that the test of liveliness, however applicable in ordinary instances, cannot be used to define the differences between sensations and images.

(2) We might attempt to distinguish images from sensations by our absence of belief in the "physical reality" of images. When we are aware that what we are experiencing is an image, we do not give it the kind of belief that we should give to a sensation: we do not think that it has the same power of producing knowledge of the "external world." Images are "imaginary"; in SOME sense they are "unreal." But this difference is hard to analyse or state correctly. What we call the "unreality" of images requires interpretation it cannot mean what would be expressed by saying "there's no such thing." Images are just as truly part of the actual world as sensations are. All that we really mean by calling an image "unreal" is that it does not have the concomitants which it would have if it were a sensation. When we call up a visual image of a chair, we do not attempt to sit in it, because we know that, like Macbeth's dagger, it is not "sensible to feeling as to sight"—i.e. it does not have the correlations with tactile sensations which it would have if it were a visual sensation and not merely a visual image. But this means that the so-called "unreality" of images consists merely in their not obeying the laws of physics, and thus brings us back to the causal distinction between images and sensations.

This view is confirmed by the fact that we only feel images to be "unreal" when we already know them to be images. Images cannot be defined by the FEELING of unreality, because when we falsely believe an image to be a sensation, as in the case of dreams, it FEELS just as real as if it were a sensation. Our feeling of unreality results from our having already realized that we are dealing with an image, and cannot therefore be the definition of what we mean by an image. As soon as an image begins to deceive us as to its status, it also deceives us as to its correlations, which are what we mean by its "reality."

(3) This brings us to the third mode of distinguishing images from sensations, namely, by their causes and effects. I believe this to be the only valid ground of distinction. James, in the passage about the mental fire which won't burn real sticks,

distinguishes images by their effects, but I think the more reliable distinction is by their causes. Professor Stout (loc. cit., p. 127) says: "One characteristic mark of what we agree in calling sensation is its mode of production. It is caused by what we call a STIMULUS. A stimulus is always some condition external to the nervous system itself and operating upon it." I think that this is the correct view, and that the distinction between images and sensations can only be made by taking account of their causation. Sensations come through sense-organs, while images do not. We cannot have visual sensations in the dark, or with our eyes shut, but we can very well have visual images under these circumstances. Accordingly images have been defined as "centrally excited sensations," i.e. sensations which have their physiological cause in the brain only, not also in the sense-organs and the nerves that run from the sense-organs to the brain. I think the phrase "centrally excited sensations" assumes more than is necessary, since it takes it for granted that an image must have a proximate physiological cause. This is probably true, but it is an hypothesis, and for our purposes an unnecessary one. It would seem to fit better with what we can immediately observe if we were to say that an image is occasioned, through association, by a sensation or another image, in other words that it has a mnemic cause—which does not prevent it from also having a physical cause. And I think it will be found that the causation of an image always proceeds according to mnemic laws, i.e. that it is governed by habit and past experience. If you listen to a man playing the pianola without looking at him, you will have images of his hands on the keys as if he were playing the piano; if you suddenly look at him while you are absorbed in the music, you will experience a shock of surprise when you notice that his hands are not touching the notes. Your image of his hands is due to the many times that you have heard similar sounds and at the same time seen the player's hands on the piano. When habit and past experience play this part, we are in the region of mnemic as opposed to ordinary physical causation. And I think that, if we could regard as ultimately valid the difference between physical and mnemic causation, we could distinguish images from sensations as having mnemic causes, though they may also have physical causes. Sensations, on the other hand, will only have physical causes.

However this may be, the practically effective distinction between sensations and images is that in the causation of sensations, but not of images, the stimulation of nerves carrying an effect into the brain, usually from the surface of the body, plays an essential part. And this accounts for the fact that images and sensations cannot always be distinguished by their intrinsic nature.

Images also differ from sensations as regards their effects. Sensations, as a rule, have both physical and mental effects. As you watch the train you meant to catch leaving the station, there are both the successive positions of the train (physical effects) and the successive waves of fury and disappointment (mental effects). Images, on the contrary, though they MAY produce bodily movements, do so according to mnemic laws, not according to the laws of physics. All their effects, of whatever nature, follow mnemic laws. But this difference is less suitable for definition than the difference as to causes.

Professor Watson, as a logical carrying-out of his behaviourist theory, denies altogether that there are any observable phenomena such as images are supposed to be. He replaces them all by faint sensations, and especially by pronunciation of words sotto voce. When we "think" of a table (say), as opposed to seeing it, what happens, according to him, is usually that we are making small movements of the throat and tongue such as would lead to our uttering the word "table" if they were more pronounced. I shall consider his view again in connection with words; for the present I am only concerned to combat his denial of images. This denial is set forth both in his book on "Behavior" and in an article called "Image and Affection in Behavior" in the "Journal of Philosophy, Psychology and Scientific Methods," vol. x (July, 1913). It seems to me that in this matter he has been betrayed into denying plain facts in the interests of a theory, namely, the supposed impossibility of introspection. I dealt with the theory in Lecture VI; for the present I wish to reinforce the view that the facts are undeniable.

Images are of various sorts, according to the nature of the sensations which they copy. Images of bodily movements, such as we have when we imagine moving an arm or, on a smaller scale, pronouncing a word, might possibly be explained away on Professor Watson's lines, as really consisting in small incipient movements such as, if magnified and prolonged, would be the movements we are said to be imagining. Whether this is the case or not might even be decided experimentally. If there were a delicate instrument for recording small movements in the mouth and throat, we might place such an instrument in a person's mouth and then tell him to recite a poem to himself, as far as possible only in imagination. I should not be at all surprised if it were found that actual small movements take place while he is "mentally" saying over the verses. The point is important, because what is called "thought" consists mainly (though I think not wholly) of inner speech. If Professor Watson is right as regards inner speech, this whole region is transferred from imagination to sensation. But since the question is capable of experimental decision, it would be gratuitous rashness to offer an opinion while that decision is lacking.

But visual and auditory images are much more difficult to deal with in this way, because they lack the connection with physical events in the outer world which belongs to visual and auditory sensations. Suppose, for example, that I am sitting in my room, in which there is an empty arm-chair. I shut my eyes, and call up a visual image of a friend sitting in the arm-chair. If I thrust my image into the world of physics, it contradicts all the usual physical laws. My friend reached the chair without coming in at the door in the usual way; subsequent inquiry will show that he was somewhere else at the moment. If regarded as a sensation, my image has all the marks of the supernatural. My image, therefore, is regarded as an event in me, not as having that position in the orderly happenings of the public world that belongs to sensations. By saying that it is an event in me, we leave it possible that it may be PHYSIOLOGICALLY caused: its privacy may be only due to its connection with my body. But in any case it is not a public event, like an actual person walking in at the door and sitting down in my chair. And it cannot, like inner speech, be regarded as a SMALL sensation, since it occupies just as large an area in my visual field as the actual sensation would do.

Professor Watson says: "I should throw out imagery altogether and attempt to show that all natural thought goes on in terms of sensori-motor processes in the larynx." This view seems to me flatly to contradict experience. If you try to persuade any uneducated person that she cannot call up a visual picture of a friend sitting in a chair, but can only use words describing what such an occurrence would be like, she will conclude that you are mad. (This statement is based upon experiment.) Galton, as every one knows, investigated visual imagery, and found that education tends to kill it: the Fellows of the Royal Society turned out to have much less of it than their wives. I see no reason to doubt his conclusion that the habit of abstract pursuits makes learned men much inferior to the average in power of visualizing, and much more exclusively occupied with words in their "thinking." And Professor Watson is a very learned man.

I shall henceforth assume that the existence of images is admitted, and that they are to be distinguished from sensations by their causes, as well as, in a lesser degree, by their effects. In their intrinsic nature, though they often differ from sensations by being more dim or vague or faint, yet they do not always or universally differ from sensations in any way that can be used for defining them. Their privacy need form no bar to the scientific study of them, any more than the privacy of bodily sensations does. Bodily sensations are admitted by even the most severe critics of introspection, although, like images, they can only be observed by one observer. It must be admitted, however, that the laws of the appearance and disappearance of images are little known and difficult to discover, because we are not assisted, as in the case of sensations, by our knowledge of the physical world.

There remains one very important point concerning images, which will occupy us much hereafter, and that is, their resemblance to previous sensations. They are said to be "copies" of sensations, always as regards the simple qualities that enter into them, though not always as regards the manner in which these are put together. It is generally believed that we cannot imagine a shade of colour that we have never seen, or a sound that we have never heard. On this subject Hume is the classic. He says, in the definitions already quoted:

"Those perceptions, which enter with most force and violence, we may name IMPRESSIONS; and under this name I comprehend all our sensations, passions and emotions, as they make their first appearance in the soul. By IDEAS I mean the faint images of these in thinking and reasoning."

He next explains the difference between simple and complex ideas, and explains that a complex idea may occur without any similar complex impression. But as regards simple ideas, he states that "every simple idea has a simple impression, which resembles it, and every simple impression a correspondent idea." He goes on to enunciate the general principle "that all our simple ideas in their first appearance are derived from simple impressions, which are correspondent to them, and which they exactly represent" ("Treatise of Human Nature," Part I, Section I).

It is this fact, that images resemble antecedent sensations, which enables us to call them images "of" this or that. For the understanding of memory, and of knowledge generally, the recognizable resemblance of images and sensations is of fundamental importance.

There are difficulties in establishing Hume's principles, and doubts as to whether it is exactly true. Indeed, he himself signalized an exception immediately after stating his maxim. Nevertheless, it is impossible to doubt that in the main simple images are copies of similar simple sensations which have occurred earlier, and that the same is true of complex images in all cases of memory as opposed to mere imagination. Our power of acting with reference to what is sensibly absent is largely due to this characteristic of images, although, as education advances, images tend to be more and more replaced by words. We shall have much to say in the next two lectures on the subject of images as copies of sensations. What has been said now is merely by way of reminder that this is their most notable characteristic.

I am by no means confident that the distinction between images and sensations is ultimately valid, and I should be glad to be convinced that images can be reduced to sensations of a peculiar kind. I think it is clear, however, that, at any rate in the case of auditory and visual images, they do differ from ordinary auditory and visual sensations, and therefore form a recognizable class of occurrences, even if it should prove that they can be regarded as a sub-class of sensations. This is all that is necessary to validate the use of images to be made in the sequel.

# LECTURE IX

## Memory

Memory, which we are to consider to-day, introduces us to knowledge in one of its forms. The analysis of knowledge will occupy us until the end of the thirteenth lecture, and is the most difficult part of our whole enterprise.

I do not myself believe that the analysis of knowledge can be effected entirely by means of purely external observation, such as behaviourists employ. I shall discuss this question in later lectures. In the present lecture I shall attempt the analysis of memory-knowledge, both as an introduction to the problem of knowledge in general, and because memory, in some form, is presupposed in almost all other knowledge. Sensation, we decided, is not a form of knowledge. It might, however, have been expected that we should begin our discussion of knowledge with PERCEPTION, i.e. with that integral experience of things in the environment, out of which sensation is extracted by psychological analysis. What is called perception differs from sensation by the fact that the sensational ingredients bring up habitual associates—images and expectations of their usual correlates—all of which are subjectively indistinguishable from the sensation. The FACT of past experience is essential in producing this filling-out of sensation, but not the RECOLLECTION of past experience. The non-sensational elements in perception can be wholly explained as the result of habit, produced by frequent correlations. Perception, according to our definition in Lecture VII, is no more a form of knowledge than sensation is, except in so far as it involves expectations. The purely psychological problems which it raises are not very difficult, though they have sometimes been rendered artificially obscure by unwillingness to admit the fallibility of the non-sensational elements of perception. On the other hand, memory raises many difficult and very important problems, which it is necessary to consider at the first possible moment.

One reason for treating memory at this early stage is that it seems to be involved in the fact that images are recognized as "copies" of past sensible experience. In the preceding lecture I alluded to Hume's principle "that all our simple ideas in their first appearance are derived from simple impressions, which are correspondent to them, and which they exactly represent." Whether or not this principle is liable to exceptions, everyone would agree that is has a broad measure of truth, though the word "exactly" might seem an overstatement, and it might seem more correct

168

to say that ideas APPROXIMATELY represent impressions. Such modifications of Hume's principle, however, do not affect the problem which I wish to present for your consideration, namely: Why do we believe that images are, sometimes or always, approximately or exactly, copies of sensations? What sort of evidence is there? And what sort of evidence is logically possible? The difficulty of this question arises through the fact that the sensation which an image is supposed to copy is in the past when the image exists, and can therefore only be known by memory, while, on the other hand, memory of past sensations seems only possible by means of present images. How, then, are we to find any way of comparing the present image and the past sensation? The problem is just as acute if we say that images differ from their prototypes as if we say that they resemble them; it is the very possibility of comparison that is hard to understand.[33] We think we can know that they are alike or different, but we cannot bring them together in one experience and compare them. To deal with this problem, we must have a theory of memory. In this way the whole status of images as "copies" is bound up with the analysis of memory.

In investigating memory beliefs, there are certain points which must be borne in mind. In the first place, everything constituting a memory-belief is happening now, not in that past time to which the belief is said to refer. It is not logically necessary to the existence of a memory-belief that the event remembered should have occurred, or even that the past should have existed at all. There is no logical impossibility in the hypothesis that the world sprang into being five minutes ago, exactly as it then was, with a population that "remembered" a wholly unreal past. There is no logically necessary connection between events at different times; therefore nothing that is happening now or will happen in the future can disprove the hypothesis that the world began five minutes ago. Hence the occurrences which are CALLED knowledge of the past are logically independent of the past; they are wholly analysable into present contents, which might, theoretically, be just what they are even if no past had existed.

I am not suggesting that the non-existence of the past should be entertained as a serious hypothesis. Like all sceptical hypotheses, it is logically tenable, but uninteresting. All that I am doing is to use its logical tenability as a help in the analysis of what occurs when we remember.

In the second place, images without beliefs are insufficient to constitute memory; and habits are still more insufficient. The behaviourist, who attempts to make psychology a record of behaviour, has to trust his memory in making the record. "Habit" is a concept involving the occurrence of similar events at different times; if the behaviourist feels confident that there is such a phenomenon as habit, that can only be because he trusts his memory, when it assures him that there have been

---

[33] How, for example, can we obtain such knowledge as the following: "If we look at, say, a red nose and perceive it, and after a little while *ekphore*, its memory-image, we note immediately how unlike, in its likeness, this memory-image is to the original perception" (A. Wohlgemuth, "On the Feelings and their Neural Correlate with an Examination of the Nature of Pain," *Journal of Psychology*, vol. viii, part iv, June, 1917).

other times. And the same applies to images. If we are to know as it is supposed we do—that images are "copies," accurate or inaccurate, of past events, something more than the mere occurrence of images must go to constitute this knowledge. For their mere occurrence, by itself, would not suggest any connection with anything that had happened before.

Can we constitute memory out of images together with suitable beliefs? We may take it that memory-images, when they occur in true memory, are (a) known to be copies, (b) sometimes known to be imperfect copies (cf. footnote on previous page). How is it possible to know that a memory-image is an imperfect copy, without having a more accurate copy by which to replace it? This would SEEM to suggest that we have a way of knowing the past which is independent of images, by means of which we can criticize image-memories. But I do not think such an inference is warranted.

What results, formally, from our knowledge of the past through images of which we recognize the inaccuracy, is that such images must have two characteristics by which we can arrange them in two series, of which one corresponds to the more or less remote period in the past to which they refer, and the other to our greater or less confidence in their accuracy. We will take the second of these points first.

Our confidence or lack of confidence in the accuracy of a memory-image must, in fundamental cases, be based upon a characteristic of the image itself, since we cannot evoke the past bodily and compare it with the present image. It might be suggested that vagueness is the required characteristic, but I do not think this is the case. We sometimes have images that are by no means peculiarly vague, which yet we do not trust—for example, under the influence of fatigue we may see a friend's face vividly and clearly, but horribly distorted. In such a case we distrust our image in spite of its being unusually clear. I think the characteristic by which we distinguish the images we trust is the feeling of FAMILIARITY that accompanies them. Some images, like some sensations, feel very familiar, while others feel strange. Familiarity is a feeling capable of degrees. In an image of a well-known face, for example, some parts may feel more familiar than others; when this happens, we have more belief in the accuracy of the familiar parts than in that of the unfamiliar parts. I think it is by this means that we become critical of images, not by some imageless memory with which we compare them. I shall return to the consideration of familiarity shortly.

I come now to the other characteristic which memory-images must have in order to account for our knowledge of the past. They must have some characteristic which makes us regard them as referring to more or less remote portions of the past. That is to say if we suppose that A is the event remembered, B the remembering, and t the interval of time between A and B, there must be some characteristic of B which is capable of degrees, and which, in accurately dated memories, varies as t varies. It may increase as t increases, or diminish as t increases. The question which of these occurs is not of any importance for the theoretic serviceability of the characteristic in question.

In actual fact, there are doubtless various factors that concur in giving us the feeling of greater or less remoteness in some remembered event. There may be a specific feeling which could be called the feeling of "pastness," especially where immediate memory is concerned. But apart from this, there are other marks. One of these is context. A recent memory has, usually, more context than a more distant one. When a remembered event has a remembered context, this may occur in two ways, either (a) by successive images in the same order as their prototypes, or (b) by remembering a whole process simultaneously, in the same way in which a present process may be apprehended, through akoluthic sensations which, by fading, acquire the mark of just-pastness in an increasing degree as they fade, and are thus placed in a series while all sensibly present. It will be context in this second sense, more specially, that will give us a sense of the nearness or remoteness of a remembered event.

There is, of course, a difference between knowing the temporal relation of a remembered event to the present, and knowing the time-order of two remembered events. Very often our knowledge of the temporal relation of a remembered event to the present is inferred from its temporal relations to other remembered events. It would seem that only rather recent events can be placed at all accurately by means of feelings giving their temporal relation to the present, but it is clear that such feelings must play an essential part in the process of dating remembered events.

We may say, then, that images are regarded by us as more or less accurate copies of past occurrences because they come to us with two sorts of feelings: (1) Those that may be called feelings of familiarity; (2) those that may be collected together as feelings giving a sense of pastness. The first lead us to trust our memories, the second to assign places to them in the time-order.

We have now to analyse the memory-belief, as opposed to the characteristics of images which lead us to base memory-beliefs upon them.

If we had retained the "subject" or "act" in knowledge, the whole problem of memory would have been comparatively simple. We could then have said that remembering is a direct relation between the present act or subject and the past occurrence remembered: the act of remembering is present, though its object is past. But the rejection of the subject renders some more complicated theory necessary. Remembering has to be a present occurrence in some way resembling, or related to, what is remembered. And it is difficult to find any ground, except a pragmatic one, for supposing that memory is not sheer delusion, if, as seems to be the case, there is not, apart from memory, any way of ascertaining that there really was a past occurrence having the required relation to our present remembering. What, if we followed Meinong's terminology, we should call the "object" in memory, i.e. the past event which we are said to be remembering, is unpleasantly remote from the "content," i.e. the present mental occurrence in remembering. There is an awkward gulf between the two, which raises difficulties for the theory of knowledge. But we must not falsify

171

observation to avoid theoretical difficulties. For the present, therefore, let us forget these problems, and try to discover what actually occurs in memory.

Some points may be taken as fixed, and such as any theory of memory must arrive at. In this case, as in most others, what may be taken as certain in advance is rather vague. The study of any topic is like the continued observation of an object which is approaching us along a road: what is certain to begin with is the quite vague knowledge that there is SOME object on the road. If you attempt to be less vague, and to assert that the object is an elephant, or a man, or a mad dog, you run a risk of error; but the purpose of continued observation is to enable you to arrive at such more precise knowledge. In like manner, in the study of memory, the certainties with which you begin are very vague, and the more precise propositions at which you try to arrive are less certain than the hazy data from which you set out. Nevertheless, in spite of the risk of error, precision is the goal at which we must aim.

The first of our vague but indubitable data is that there is knowledge of the past. We do not yet know with any precision what we mean by "knowledge," and we must admit that in any given instance our memory may be at fault. Nevertheless, whatever a sceptic might urge in theory, we cannot practically doubt that we got up this morning, that we did various things yesterday, that a great war has been taking place, and so on. How far our knowledge of the past is due to memory, and how far to other sources, is of course a matter to be investigated, but there can be no doubt that memory forms an indispensable part of our knowledge of the past.

The second datum is that we certainly have more capacity for knowing the past than for knowing the future. We know some things about the future, for example what eclipses there will be; but this knowledge is a matter of elaborate calculation and inference, whereas some of our knowledge of the past comes to us without effort, in the same sort of immediate way in which we acquire knowledge of occurrences in our present environment. We might provisionally, though perhaps not quite correctly, define "memory" as that way of knowing about the past which has no analogue in our knowledge of the future; such a definition would at least serve to mark the problem with which we are concerned, though some expectations may deserve to rank with memory as regards immediacy.

A third point, perhaps not quite so certain as our previous two, is that the truth of memory cannot be wholly practical, as pragmatists wish all truth to be. It seems clear that some of the things I remember are trivial and without any visible importance for the future, but that my memory is true (or false) in virtue of a past event, not in virtue of any future consequences of my belief. The definition of truth as the correspondence between beliefs and facts seems peculiarly evident in the case of memory, as against not only the pragmatist definition but also the idealist definition by means of coherence. These considerations, however, are taking us away from psychology, to which we must now return.

It is important not to confuse the two forms of memory which Bergson distinguishes in the second chapter of his "Matter and Memory," namely the sort that consists of habit, and the sort that consists of independent recollection. He gives the instance of learning a lesson by heart: when I know it by heart I am said to "remember" it, but this merely means that I have acquired certain habits; on the other hand, my recollection of (say) the second time I read the lesson while I was learning it is the recollection of a unique event, which occurred only once. The recollection of a unique event cannot, so Bergson contends, be wholly constituted by habit, and is in fact something radically different from the memory which is habit. The recollection alone is true memory. This distinction is vital to the understanding of memory. But it is not so easy to carry out in practice as it is to draw in theory. Habit is a very intrusive feature of our mental life, and is often present where at first sight it seems not to be. There is, for example, a habit of remembering a unique event. When we have once described the event, the words we have used easily become habitual. We may even have used words to describe it to ourselves while it was happening; in that case, the habit of these words may fulfil the function of Bergson's true memory, while in reality it is nothing but habit-memory. A gramophone, by the help of suitable records, might relate to us the incidents of its past; and people are not so different from gramophones as they like to believe.

In spite, however, of a difficulty in distinguishing the two forms of memory in practice, there can be no doubt that both forms exist. I can set to work now to remember things I never remembered before, such as what I had to eat for breakfast this morning, and it can hardly be wholly habit that enables me to do this. It is this sort of occurrence that constitutes the essence of memory Until we have analysed what happens in such a case as this, we have not succeeded in understanding memory.

The sort of memory with which we are here concerned is the sort which is a form of knowledge. Whether knowledge itself is reducible to habit is a question to which I shall return in a later lecture; for the present I am only anxious to point out that, whatever the true analysis of knowledge may be, knowledge of past occurrences is not proved by behaviour which is due to past experience. The fact that a man can recite a poem does not show that he remembers any previous occasion on which he has recited or read it. Similarly, the performances of animals in getting out of cages or mazes to which they are accustomed do not prove that they remember having been in the same situation before. Arguments in favour of (for example) memory in plants are only arguments in favour of habit-memory, not of knowledge-memory. Samuel Butler's arguments in favour of the view that an animal remembers something of the lives of its ancestors[34] are, when examined, only arguments in favour of habit-memory. Semon's two books, mentioned in an earlier lecture, do not touch knowledge-memory at all closely. They give laws according to which images of past occurrences come into

---

[34] See his *Life and Habit* and *Unconscious Memory*.

our minds, but do not discuss our belief that these images refer to past occurrences, which is what constitutes knowledge-memory. It is this that is of interest to theory of knowledge. I shall speak of it as "true" memory, to distinguish it from mere habit acquired through past experience. Before considering true memory, it will be well to consider two things which are on the way towards memory, namely the feeling of familiarity and recognition.

We often feel that something in our sensible environment is familiar, without having any definite recollection of previous occasions on which we have seen it. We have this feeling normally in places where we have often been before—at home, or in well-known streets. Most people and animals find it essential to their happiness to spend a good deal of their time in familiar surroundings, which are especially comforting when any danger threatens. The feeling of familiarity has all sorts of degrees, down to the stage where we dimly feel that we have seen a person before. It is by no means always reliable; almost everybody has at some time experienced the well-known illusion that all that is happening now happened before at some time. There are occasions when familiarity does not attach itself to any definite object, when there is merely a vague feeling that SOMETHING is familiar. This is illustrated by Turgenev's "Smoke," where the hero is long puzzled by a haunting sense that something in his present is recalling something in his past, and at last traces it to the smell of heliotrope. Whenever the sense of familiarity occurs without a definite object, it leads us to search the environment until we are satisfied that we have found the appropriate object, which leads us to the judgment: "THIS is familiar." I think we may regard familiarity as a definite feeling, capable of existing without an object, but normally standing in a specific relation to some feature of the environment, the relation being that which we express in words by saying that the feature in question is familiar. The judgment that what is familiar has been experienced before is a product of reflection, and is no part of the feeling of familiarity, such as a horse may be supposed to have when he returns to his stable. Thus no knowledge as to the past is to be derived from the feeling of familiarity alone.

A further stage is RECOGNITION. This may be taken in two senses, the first when a thing not merely feels familiar, but we know it is such-and-such. We recognize our friend Jones, we know cats and dogs when we see them, and so on. Here we have a definite influence of past experience, but not necessarily any actual knowledge of the past. When we see a cat, we know it is a cat because of previous cats we have seen, but we do not, as a rule, recollect at the moment any particular occasion when we have seen a cat. Recognition in this sense does not necessarily involve more than a habit of association: the kind of object we are seeing at the moment is associated with the word "cat," or with an auditory image of purring, or whatever other characteristic we may happen to recognize in the cat of the moment. We are, of course, in fact able to judge, when we recognize an object, that we have seen it before, but this judgment is something over and above recognition in this first sense, and may very probably be impossible to animals that nevertheless have the experience of recognition in this first sense of the word.

There is, however, another sense of the word, in which we mean by recognition, not knowing the name of a thing or some other property of it, but knowing that we have seen it before In this sense recognition does involve knowledge about the Fast. This knowledge is memory in one sense, though in another it is not. It does not involve a definite memory of a definite past event, but only the knowledge that something happening now is similar to something that happened before. It differs from the sense of familiarity by being cognitive; it is a belief or judgment, which the sense of familiarity is not. I do not wish to undertake the analysis of belief at present, since it will be the subject of the twelfth lecture; for the present I merely wish to emphasize the fact that recognition, in our second sense, consists in a belief, which we may express approximately in the words: "This has existed before."

There are, however, several points in which such an account of recognition is inadequate. To begin with, it might seem at first sight more correct to define recognition as "I have seen this before" than as "this has existed before." We recognize a thing (it may be urged) as having been in our experience before, whatever that may mean; we do not recognize it as merely having been in the world before. I am not sure that there is anything substantial in this point. The definition of "my experience" is difficult; broadly speaking, it is everything that is connected with what I am experiencing now by certain links, of which the various forms of memory are among the most important. Thus, if I recognize a thing, the occasion of its previous existence in virtue of which I recognize it forms part of "my experience" by DEFINITION: recognition will be one of the marks by which my experience is singled out from the rest of the world. Of course, the words "this has existed before" are a very inadequate translation of what actually happens when we form a judgment of recognition, but that is unavoidable: words are framed to express a level of thought which is by no means primitive, and are quite incapable of expressing such an elementary occurrence as recognition. I shall return to what is virtually the same question in connection with true memory, which raises exactly similar problems.

A second point is that, when we recognize something, it was not in fact the very same thing, but only something similar, that we experienced on a former occasion. Suppose the object in question is a friend's face. A person's face is always changing, and is not exactly the same on any two occasions. Common sense treats it as one face with varying expressions; but the varying expressions actually exist, each at its proper time, while the one face is merely a logical construction. We regard two objects as the same, for common-sense purposes, when the reaction they call for is practically the same. Two visual appearances, to both of which it is appropriate to say: "Hullo, Jones!" are treated as appearances of one identical object, namely Jones. The name "Jones" is applicable to both, and it is only reflection that shows us that many diverse particulars are collected together to form the meaning of the name

"Jones." What we see on any one occasion is not the whole series of particulars that make up Jones, but only one of them (or a few in quick succession). On another occasion we see another member of the series, but it is sufficiently similar to count as the same from the standpoint of common sense. Accordingly, when we judge "I have seen THIS before," we judge falsely if "this" is taken as applying to the actual constituent of the world that we are seeing at the moment. The word "this" must be interpreted vaguely so as to include anything sufficiently like what we are seeing at the moment. Here, again, we shall find a similar point as regards true memory; and in connection with true memory we will consider the point again. It is sometimes suggested, by those who favour behaviourist views, that recognition consists in behaving in the same way when a stimulus is repeated as we behaved on the first occasion when it occurred. This seems to be the exact opposite of the truth. The essence of recognition is in the DIFFERENCE between a repeated stimulus and a new one. On the first occasion there is no recognition; on the second occasion there is. In fact, recognition is another instance of the peculiarity of causal laws in psychology, namely, that the causal unit is not a single event, but two or more events Habit is the great instance of this, but recognition is another. A stimulus occurring once has a certain effect; occurring twice, it has the further effect of recognition. Thus the phenomenon of recognition has as its cause the two occasions when the stimulus has occurred; either alone is insufficient. This complexity of causes in psychology might be connected with Bergson's arguments against repetition in the mental world. It does not prove that there are no causal laws in psychology, as Bergson suggests; but it does prove that the causal laws of psychology are Prima facie very different from those of physics. On the possibility of explaining away the difference as due to the peculiarities of nervous tissue I have spoken before, but this possibility must not be forgotten if we are tempted to draw unwarranted metaphysical deductions.

True memory, which we must now endeavour to understand, consists of knowledge of past events, but not of all such knowledge. Some knowledge of past events, for example what we learn through reading history, is on a par with the knowledge we can acquire concerning the future: it is obtained by inference, not (so to speak) spontaneously. There is a similar distinction in our knowledge of the present: some of it is obtained through the senses, some in more indirect ways. I know that there are at this moment a number of people in the streets of New York, but I do not know this in the immediate way in which I know of the people whom I see by looking out of my window. It is not easy to state precisely wherein the difference between these two sorts of knowledge consists, but it is easy to feel the difference. For the moment, I shall not stop to analyse it, but shall content myself with saying that, in this respect, memory resembles the knowledge derived from the senses. It is immediate, not inferred, not abstract; it differs from perception mainly by being referred to the past.

In regard to memory, as throughout the analysis of knowledge, there are two very distinct problems, namely (1) as to the nature of the present occurrence in knowing; (2) as to the relation of this occurrence to what is known. When we remember, the knowing is now, while what is known is in the past. Our two questions are, in the case of memory:

(1)  What is the present occurrence when we remember?

(2)  What is the relation of this present occurrence to the past event which is remembered?

Of these two questions, only the first concerns the psychologist; the second belongs to theory of knowledge. At the same time, if we accept the vague datum with which we began, to the effect that, in some sense, there is knowledge of the past, we shall have to find, if we can, such an account of the present occurrence in remembering as will make it not impossible for remembering to give us knowledge of the past. For the present, however, we shall do well to forget the problems concerning theory of knowledge, and concentrate upon the purely psychological problem of memory.

Between memory-image and sensation there is an intermediate experience concerning the immediate past. For example, a sound that we have just heard is present to us in a way which differs both from the sensation while we are hearing the sound and from the memory-image of something heard days or weeks ago. James states that it is this way of apprehending the immediate past that is "the ORIGINAL of our experience of pastness, from whence we get the meaning of the term"("Psychology," i, p. 604). Everyone knows the experience of noticing (say) that the clock HAS BEEN striking, when we did not notice it while it was striking. And when we hear a remark spoken, we are conscious of the earlier words while the later ones are being uttered, and this retention feels different from recollection of something definitely past. A sensation fades gradually, passing by continuous gradations to the status of an image. This retention of the immediate past in a condition intermediate between sensation and image may be called "immediate memory." Everything belonging to it is included with sensation in what is called the "specious present." The specious present includes elements at all stages on the journey from sensation to image. It is this fact that enables us to apprehend such things as movements, or the order of the words in a spoken sentence. Succession can occur within the specious present, of which we can distinguish some parts as earlier and others as later. It is to be supposed that the earliest parts are those that have faded most from their original force, while the latest parts are those that retain their full sensational character. At the beginning of a stimulus we have a sensation; then a gradual transition; and at the end an image. Sensations while they are fading are called "akoluthic" sensations.[35]

---

[35] See Semon, *Die mnemischen Empfindungen*, chap. vi.

When the process of fading is completed (which happens very quickly), we arrive at the image, which is capable of being revived on subsequent occasions with very little change. True memory, as opposed to "immediate memory," applies only to events sufficiently distant to have come to an end of the period of fading. Such events, if they are represented by anything present, can only be represented by images, not by those intermediate stages, between sensations and images, which occur during the period of fading.

Immediate memory is important both because it provides experience of succession, and because it bridges the gulf between sensations and the images which are their copies. But it is now time to resume the consideration of true memory.

Suppose you ask me what I ate for breakfast this morning. Suppose, further, that I have not thought about my breakfast in the meantime, and that I did not, while I was eating it, put into words what it consisted of. In this case my recollection will be true memory, not habit-memory. The process of remembering will consist of calling up images of my breakfast, which will come to me with a feeling of belief such as distinguishes memory-images from mere imagination-images. Or sometimes words may come without the intermediary of images; but in this case equally the feeling of belief is essential.

Let us omit from our consideration, for the present, the memories in which words replace images. These are always, I think, really habit-memories, the memories that use images being the typical true memories.

Memory-images and imagination-images do not differ in their intrinsic qualities, so far as we can discover. They differ by the fact that the images that constitute memories, unlike those that constitute imagination, are accompanied by a feeling of belief which may be expressed in the words "this happened." The mere occurrence of images, without this feeling of belief, constitutes imagination; it is the element of belief that is the distinctive thing in memory.[36]

There are, if I am not mistaken, at least three different kinds of belief-feeling, which we may call respectively memory, expectation and bare assent. In what I call bare assent, there is no time-element in the feeling of belief, though there may be in the content of what is believed. If I believe that Caesar landed in Britain in B.C. 55, the time-determination lies, not in the feeling of belief, but in what is believed. I do not remember the occurrence, but have the same feeling towards it as towards the announcement of an eclipse next year. But when I have seen a flash of lightning and am waiting for the thunder, I have a belief-feeling analogous to memory, except that it refers to the future: I have an image of thunder, combined with a feeling which may be expressed in the words: "this will happen." So, in memory, the pastness lies, not in the content of what is believed, but in the nature of the belief-feeling. I might have just the same images and expect their realization; I might entertain them without any belief,

---

[36] For belief of a specific kind, cf. Dorothy Wrinch "On the Nature of Memory," *Mind*, January, 1920.

as in reading a novel; or I might entertain them together with a time-determination, and give bare assent, as in reading history. I shall return to this subject in a later lecture, when we come to the analysis of belief. For the present, I wish to make it clear that a certain special kind of belief is the distinctive characteristic of memory.

The problem as to whether memory can be explained as habit or association requires to be considered afresh in connection with the causes of our remembering something. Let us take again the case of my being asked what I had for breakfast this morning. In this case the question leads to my setting to work to recollect. It is a little strange that the question should instruct me as to what it is that I am to recall. This has to do with understanding words, which will be the topic of the next lecture; but something must be said about it now. Our understanding of the words "breakfast this morning" is a habit, in spite of the fact that on each fresh day they point to a different occasion. "This morning" does not, whenever it is used, mean the same thing, as "John" or "St. Paul's" does; it means a different period of time on each different day. It follows that the habit which constitutes our understanding of the words "this morning" is not the habit of associating the words with a fixed object, but the habit of associating them with something having a fixed time-relation to our present. This morning has, to-day, the same time-relation to my present that yesterday morning had yesterday. In order to understand the phrase "this morning" it is necessary that we should have a way of feeling time-intervals, and that this feeling should give what is constant in the meaning of the words "this morning." This appreciation of time-intervals is, however, obviously a product of memory, not a presupposition of it. It will be better, therefore, if we wish to analyse the causation of memory by something not presupposing memory, to take some other instance than that of a question about "this morning."

Let us take the case of coming into a familiar room where something has been changed—say a new picture hung on the wall. We may at first have only a sense that SOMETHING is unfamiliar, but presently we shall remember, and say "that picture was not on the wall before." In order to make the case definite, we will suppose that we were only in the room on one former occasion. In this case it seems fairly clear what happens. The other objects in the room are associated, through the former occasion, with a blank space of wall where now there is a picture. They call up an image of a blank wall, which clashes with perception of the picture. The image is associated with the belief-feeling which we found to be distinctive of memory, since it can neither be abolished nor harmonized with perception. If the room had remained unchanged, we might have had only the feeling of familiarity without the definite remembering; it is the change that drives us from the present to memory of the past.

We may generalize this instance so as to cover the causes of many memories. Some present feature of the environment is associated, through past experiences, with something now absent; this absent something comes before us as an image, and is contrasted with present sensation. In cases of this sort, habit (or association)

179

explains why the present feature of the environment brings up the memory-image, but it does not explain the memory-belief. Perhaps a more complete analysis could explain the memory-belief also on lines of association and habit, but the causes of beliefs are obscure, and we cannot investigate them yet. For the present we must content ourselves with the fact that the memory-image can be explained by habit. As regards the memory-belief, we must, at least provisionally, accept Bergson's view that it cannot be brought under the head of habit, at any rate when it first occurs, i.e. when we remember something we never remembered before.

We must now consider somewhat more closely the content of a memory-belief. The memory-belief confers upon the memory-image something which we may call "meaning;" it makes us feel that the image points to an object which existed in the past. In order to deal with this topic we must consider the verbal expression of the memory-belief. We might be tempted to put the memory-belief into the words: "Something like this image occurred." But such words would be very far from an accurate translation of the simplest kind of memory-belief. "Something like this image" is a very complicated conception. In the simplest kind of memory we are not aware of the difference between an image and the sensation which it copies, which may be called its "prototype." When the image is before us, we judge rather "this occurred." The image is not distinguished from the object which existed in the past: the word "this" covers both, and enables us to have a memory-belief which does not introduce the complicated notion "something like this."

It might be objected that, if we judge "this occurred" when in fact "this" is a present image, we judge falsely, and the memory-belief, so interpreted, becomes deceptive. This, however, would be a mistake, produced by attempting to give to words a precision which they do not possess when used by unsophisticated people. It is true that the image is not absolutely identical with its prototype, and if the word "this" meant the image to the exclusion of everything else, the judgment "this occurred" would be false. But identity is a precise conception, and no word, in ordinary speech, stands for anything precise. Ordinary speech does not distinguish between identity and close similarity. A word always applies, not only to one particular, but to a group of associated particulars, which are not recognized as multiple in common thought or speech. Thus primitive memory, when it judges that "this occurred," is vague, but not false.

Vague identity, which is really close similarity, has been a source of many of the confusions by which philosophy has lived. Of a vague subject, such as a "this," which is both an image and its prototype, contradictory predicates are true simultaneously: this existed and does not exist, since it is a thing remembered, but also this exists and did not exist, since it is a present image. Hence Bergson's interpenetration of the present by the past, Hegelian continuity and identity-in-diversity, and a host of other notions which are thought to be profound because they are obscure and confused. The contradictions resulting from confounding image and prototype in memory force us to precision. But when we become precise, our remembering becomes different from that of ordinary life, and if we forget this we shall go wrong in the analysis of ordinary memory.

Vagueness and accuracy are important notions, which it is very necessary to understand. Both are a matter of degree. All thinking is vague to some extent, and complete accuracy is a theoretical ideal not practically attainable. To understand what is meant by accuracy, it will be well to consider first instruments of measurement, such as a balance or a thermometer. These are said to be accurate when they give different results for very slightly different stimuli.[37] A clinical thermometer is accurate when it enables us to detect very slight differences in the temperature of the blood. We may say generally that an instrument is accurate in proportion as it reacts differently to very slightly different stimuli. When a small difference of stimulus produces a great difference of reaction, the instrument is accurate; in the contrary case it is not.

Exactly the same thing applies in defining accuracy of thought or perception. A musician will respond differently to very minute differences in playing which would be quite imperceptible to the ordinary mortal. A negro can see the difference between one negro and another one is his friend, another his enemy. But to us such different responses are impossible: we can merely apply the word "negro" indiscriminately. Accuracy of response in regard to any particular kind of stimulus is improved by practice. Understanding a language is a case in point. Few Frenchmen can hear any difference between the sounds "hall" and "hole," which produce quite different impressions upon us. The two statements "the hall is full of water" and "the hole is full of water" call for different responses, and a hearing which cannot distinguish between them is inaccurate or vague in this respect.

Precision and vagueness in thought, as in perception, depend upon the degree of difference between responses to more or less similar stimuli. In the case of thought, the response does not follow immediately upon the sensational stimulus, but that makes no difference as regards our present question. Thus to revert to memory: A memory is "vague" when it is appropriate to many different occurrences: for instance, "I met a man" is vague, since any man would verify it. A memory is "precise" when the occurrences that would verify it are narrowly circumscribed: for instance, "I met Jones" is precise as compared to "I met a man." A memory is "accurate" when it is both precise and true, i.e. in the above instance, if it was Jones I met. It is precise even if it is false, provided some very definite occurrence would have been required to make it true.

It follows from what has been said that a vague thought has more likelihood of being true than a precise one. To try and hit an object with a vague thought is like trying to hit the bull's eye with a lump of putty: when the putty reaches the target, it

---

[37] This is a necessary but not a sufficient condition. The subject of accuracy and vagueness will be considered again in Lecture XIII.

flattens out all over it, and probably covers the bull's eye along with the rest. To try and hit an object with a precise thought is like trying to hit the bull's eye with a bullet. The advantage of the precise thought is that it distinguishes between the bull's eye and the rest of the target. For example, if the whole target is represented by the fungus family and the bull's eye by mushrooms, a vague thought which can only hit the target as a whole is not much use from a culinary point of view. And when I merely remember that I met a man, my memory may be very inadequate to my practical requirements, since it may make a great difference whether I met Brown or Jones. The memory "I met Jones" is relatively precise. It is accurate if I met Jones, inaccurate if I met Brown, but precise in either case as against the mere recollection that I met a man.

The distinction between accuracy and precision is however, not fundamental. We may omit precision from out thoughts and confine ourselves to the distinction between accuracy and vagueness. We may then set up the following definitions:

An instrument is "reliable" with respect to a given set of stimuli when to stimuli which are not relevantly different it gives always responses which are not relevantly different.

An instrument is a "measure" of a set of stimuli which are serially ordered when its responses, in all cases where they are relevantly different, are arranged in a series in the same order.

The "degree of accuracy" of an instrument which is a reliable measurer is the ratio of the difference of response to the difference of stimulus in cases where the difference of stimulus is small.[38] That is to say, if a small difference of stimulus produces a great difference of response, the instrument is very accurate; in the contrary case, very inaccurate.

A mental response is called "vague" in proportion to its lack of accuracy, or rather precision.

These definitions will be found useful, not only in the case of memory, but in almost all questions concerned with knowledge.

It should be observed that vague beliefs, so far from being necessarily false, have a better chance of truth than precise ones, though their truth is less valuable than that of precise beliefs, since they do not distinguish between occurrences which may differ in important ways.

The whole of the above discussion of vagueness and accuracy was occasioned by the attempt to interpret the word "this" when we judge in verbal memory that "this occurred." The word "this," in such a judgment, is a vague word, equally applicable to the present memory-image and to the past occurrence which is its prototype. A vague word is not to be identified with a general word, though in practice the distinction may often be blurred. A word is general when it is understood to be applicable to a number of different objects in virtue of some common property. A word is vague

---

[38] Strictly speaking, the limit of this, i.e. the derivative of the response with respect to the stimulus.

when it is in fact applicable to a number of different objects because, in virtue of some common property, they have not appeared, to the person using the word, to be distinct. I emphatically do not mean that he has judged them to be identical, but merely that he has made the same response to them all and has not judged them to be different. We may compare a vague word to a jelly and a general word to a heap of shot. Vague words precede judgments of identity and difference; both general and particular words are subsequent to such judgments. The word "this" in the primitive memory-belief is a vague word, not a general word; it covers both the image and its prototype because the two are not distinguished.[39]

But we have not yet finished our analysis of the memory-belief. The tense in the belief that "this occurred" is provided by the nature of the belief-feeling involved in memory; the word "this," as we have seen, has a vagueness which we have tried to describe. But we must still ask what we mean by "occurred." The image is, in one sense, occurring now; and therefore we must find some other sense in which the past event occurred but the image does not occur.

There are two distinct questions to be asked: (1) What causes us to say that a thing occurs? (2) What are we feeling when we say this? As to the first question, in the crude use of the word, which is what concerns us, memory-images would not be said to occur; they would not be noticed in themselves, but merely used as signs of the past event. Images are "merely imaginary"; they have not, in crude thought, the sort of reality that belongs to outside bodies. Roughly speaking, "real" things would be those that can cause sensations, those that have correlations of the sort that constitute physical objects. A thing is said to be "real" or to "occur" when it fits into a context of such correlations. The prototype of our memory-image did fit into a physical context, while our memory-image does not. This causes us to feel that the prototype was "real," while the image is "imaginary."

But the answer to our second question, namely as to what we are feeling when we say a thing "occurs" or is "real," must be somewhat different. We do not, unless we are unusually reflective, think about the presence or absence of correlations: we merely have different feelings which, intellectualized, may be represented as expectations of the presence or absence of correlations. A thing which "feels real" inspires us with hopes or fears, expectations or curiosities, which are wholly absent when a thing "feels imaginary." The feeling of reality is a feeling akin to respect: it belongs PRIMARILY to whatever can do things to us without our voluntary co-operation. This feeling of reality, related to the memory-image, and referred to the past by the specific kind of

---

[39] On the vague and the general cf. Ribot: *Evolution of General Ideas*, Open Court Co., 1899, p. 32: "The sole permissible formula is this: Intelligence progresses from the indefinite to the definite. If 'indefinite' is taken as synonymous with general, it may be said that the particular does not appear at the outset, but neither does the general in any exact sense: the vague would be more appropriate. In other words, no sooner has the intellect progressed beyond the moment of perception and of its immediate reproduction in memory, than the generic image makes its appearance, i.e. a state intermediate between the particular and the general, participating in the nature of the one and of the other—a confused simplification."

belief-feeling that is characteristic of memory, seems to be what constitutes the act of remembering in its pure form.

We may now summarize our analysis of pure memory.

Memory demands (a) an image, (b) a belief in past existence. The belief may be expressed in the words "this existed."

The belief, like every other, may be analysed into (1) the believing, (2) what is believed. The believing is a specific feeling or sensation or complex of sensations, different from expectation or bare assent in a way that makes the belief refer to the past; the reference to the past lies in the belief-feeling, not in the content believed. There is a relation between the belief-feeling and the content, making the belief-feeling refer to the content, and expressed by saying that the content is what is believed.

The content believed may or may not be expressed in words. Let us take first the case when it is not. In that case, if we are merely remembering that something of which we now have an image occurred, the content consists of (a) the image, (b) the feeling, analogous to respect, which we translate by saying that something is "real" as opposed to "imaginary," (c) a relation between the image and the feeling of reality, of the sort expressed when we say that the feeling refers to the image. This content does not contain in itself any time-determination.

The time-determination lies in the nature of the belief feeling, which is that called "remembering" or (better) "recollecting." It is only subsequent reflection upon this reference to the past that makes us realize the distinction between the image and the event recollected. When we have made this distinction, we can say that the image "means" the past event.

The content expressed in words is best represented by the words "the existence of this," since these words do not involve tense, which belongs to the belief-feeling, not to the content. Here "this" is a vague term, covering the memory-image and anything very like it, including its prototype. "Existence" expresses the feeling of a "reality" aroused primarily by whatever can have effects upon us without our voluntary co-operation. The word "of" in the phrase "the existence of this" represents the relation which subsists between the feeling of reality and the "this."

This analysis of memory is probably extremely faulty, but I do not know how to improve it.

NOTE.-When I speak of a FEELING of belief, I use the word "feeling" in a popular sense, to cover a sensation or an image or a complex of sensations or images or both; I use this word because I do not wish to commit myself to any special analysis of the belief-feeling.

# LECTURE X

## Words and Meaning

The problem with which we shall be concerned in this lecture is the problem of determining what is the relation called "meaning." The word "Napoleon," we say, "means" a certain person. In saying this, we are asserting a relation between the word "Napoleon" and the person so designated. It is this relation that we must now investigate.

Let us first consider what sort of object a word is when considered simply as a physical thing, apart from its meaning. To begin with, there are many instances of a word, namely all the different occasions when it is employed. Thus a word is not something unique and particular, but a set of occurrences. If we confine ourselves to spoken words, a word has two aspects, according as we regard it from the point of view of the speaker or from that of the hearer. From the point of view of the speaker, a single instance of the use of a word consists of a certain set of movements in the throat and mouth, combined with breath. From the point of view of the hearer, a single instance of the use of a word consists of a certain series of sounds, each being approximately represented by a single letter in writing, though in practice a letter may represent several sounds, or several letters may represent one sound. The connection between the spoken word and the word as it reaches the hearer is causal. Let us confine ourselves to the spoken word, which is the more important for the analysis of what is called "thought." Then we may say that a single instance of the spoken word consists of a series of movements, and the word consists of a whole set of such series, each member of the set being very similar to each other member. That is to say, any two instances of the word "Napoleon" are very similar, and each instance consists of a series of movements in the mouth.

A single word, accordingly, is by no means simple it is a class of similar series of movements (confining ourselves still to the spoken word). The degree of similarity required cannot be precisely defined: a man may pronounce the word "Napoleon" so badly that it can hardly be determined whether he has really pronounced it or not. The instances of a word shade off into other movements by imperceptible degrees. And exactly analogous observations apply to words heard or written or read. But in what has been said so far we have not even broached the question of the DEFINITION of a word, since "meaning" is clearly what distinguishes a word from other sets of similar movements, and "meaning" remains to be defined.

It is natural to think of the meaning of a word as something conventional. This, however, is only true with great limitations. A new word can be added to an existing language by a mere convention, as is done, for instance, with new scientific terms. But the basis of a language is not conventional, either from the point of view of the individual or from that of the community. A child learning to speak is learning habits and associations which are just as much determined by the environment as the habit of expecting dogs to bark and cocks to crow. The community that speaks a language has learnt it, and modified it by processes almost all of which are not deliberate, but the results of causes operating according to more or less ascertainable laws. If we trace any Indo-European language back far enough, we arrive hypothetically (at any rate according to some authorities) at the stage when language consisted only of the roots out of which subsequent words have grown. How these roots acquired their meanings is not known, but a conventional origin is clearly just as mythical as the social contract by which Hobbes and Rousseau supposed civil government to have been established. We can hardly suppose a parliament of hitherto speechless elders meeting together and agreeing to call a cow a cow and a wolf a wolf. The association of words with their meanings must have grown up by some natural process, though at present the nature of the process is unknown.

Spoken and written words are, of course, not the only way of conveying meaning. A large part of one of Wundt's two vast volumes on language in his "Volkerpsychologie" is concerned with gesture-language. Ants appear to be able to communicate a certain amount of information by means of their antennae. Probably writing itself, which we now regard as merely a way of representing speech, was originally an independent language, as it has remained to this day in China. Writing seems to have consisted originally of pictures, which gradually became conventionalized, coming in time to represent syllables, and finally letters on the telephone principle of "T for Tommy." But it would seem that writing nowhere began as an attempt to represent speech it began as a direct pictorial representation of what was to be expressed. The essence of language lies, not in the use of this or that special means of communication, but in the employment of fixed associations (however these may have originated) in order that something now sensible—a spoken word, a picture, a gesture, or what not—may call up the "idea" of something else. Whenever this is done, what is now sensible may be called a "sign" or "symbol," and that of which it is intended to call up the "idea" may be called its "meaning." This is a rough outline of what constitutes "meaning." But we must fill in the outline in various ways. And, since we are concerned with what is called "thought," we must pay more attention than we otherwise should do to the private as opposed to the social use of language. Language profoundly affects our thoughts, and it is this aspect of language that is of most importance to us in our present inquiry. We are almost more concerned with the internal speech that is never uttered than we are with the things said out loud to other people.

When we ask what constitutes meaning, we are not asking what is the meaning of this or that particular word. The word "Napoleon" means a certain individual; but we are asking, not who is the individual meant, but what is the relation of the word to the individual which makes the one mean the other. But just as it is useful to realize the nature of a word as part of the physical world, so it is useful to realize the sort of thing that a word may mean. When we are clear both as to what a word is in its physical aspect, and as to what sort of thing it can mean, we are in a better position to discover the relation of the two which is meaning.

The things that words mean differ more than words do. There are different sorts of words, distinguished by the grammarians; and there are logical distinctions, which are connected to some extent, though not so closely as was formerly supposed, with the grammatical distinctions of parts of speech. It is easy, however, to be misled by grammar, particularly if all the languages we know belong to one family. In some languages, according to some authorities, the distinction of parts of speech does not exist; in many languages it is widely different from that to which we are accustomed in the Indo-European languages. These facts have to be borne in mind if we are to avoid giving metaphysical importance to mere accidents of our own speech.

In considering what words mean, it is natural to start with proper names, and we will again take "Napoleon" as our instance. We commonly imagine, when we use a proper name, that we mean one definite entity, the particular individual who was called "Napoleon." But what we know as a person is not simple. There MAY be a single simple ego which was Napoleon, and remained strictly identical from his birth to his death. There is no way of proving that this cannot be the case, but there is also not the slightest reason to suppose that it is the case. Napoleon as he was empirically known consisted of a series of gradually changing appearances: first a squalling baby, then a boy, then a slim and beautiful youth, then a fat and slothful person very magnificently dressed This series of appearances, and various occurrences having certain kinds of causal connections with them, constitute Napoleon as empirically known, and therefore are Napoleon in so far as he forms part of the experienced world. Napoleon is a complicated series of occurrences, bound together by causal laws, not, like instances of a word, by similarities. For although a person changes gradually, and presents similar appearances on two nearly contemporaneous occasions, it is not these similarities that constitute the person, as appears from the "Comedy of Errors" for example.

Thus in the case of a proper name, while the word is a set of similar series of movements, what it means is a series of occurrences bound together by causal laws of that special kind that makes the occurrences taken together constitute what we call one person, or one animal or thing, in case the name applies to an animal or thing instead of to a person. Neither the word nor what it names is one of the ultimate indivisible constituents of the world. In language there is no direct way of designating one of the ultimate brief existents that go to make up the collections we call things

187

or persons. If we want to speak of such existents—which hardly happens except in philosophy—we have to do it by means of some elaborate phrase, such as "the visual sensation which occupied the centre of my field of vision at noon on January 1, 1919." Such ultimate simples I call "particulars." Particulars MIGHT have proper names, and no doubt would have if language had been invented by scientifically trained observers for purposes of philosophy and logic. But as language was invented for practical ends, particulars have remained one and all without a name.

We are not, in practice, much concerned with the actual particulars that come into our experience in sensation; we are concerned rather with whole systems to which the particulars belong and of which they are signs. What we see makes us say "Hullo, there's Jones," and the fact that what we see is a sign of Jones (which is the case because it is one of the particulars that make up Jones) is more interesting to us than the actual particular itself. Hence we give the name "Jones" to the whole set of particulars, but do not trouble to give separate names to the separate particulars that make up the set.

Passing on from proper names, we come next to general names, such as "man," "cat," "triangle." A word such as "man" means a whole class of such collections of particulars as have proper names. The several members of the class are assembled together in virtue of some similarity or common property. All men resemble each other in certain important respects; hence we want a word which shall be equally applicable to all of them. We only give proper names to the individuals of a species when they differ inter se in practically important respects. In other cases we do not do this. A poker, for instance, is just a poker; we do not call one "John" and another "Peter."

There is a large class of words, such as "eating," "walking," "speaking," which mean a set of similar occurrences. Two instances of walking have the same name because they resemble each other, whereas two instances of Jones have the same name because they are causally connected. In practice, however, it is difficult to make any precise distinction between a word such as "walking" and a general name such as "man." One instance of walking cannot be concentrated into an instant: it is a process in time, in which there is a causal connection between the earlier and later parts, as between the earlier and later parts of Jones. Thus an instance of walking differs from an instance of man solely by the fact that it has a shorter life. There is a notion that an instance of walking, as compared with Jones, is unsubstantial, but this seems to be a mistake. We think that Jones walks, and that there could not be any walking unless there were somebody like Jones to perform the walking. But it is equally true that there could be no Jones unless there were something like walking for him to do. The notion that actions are performed by an agent is liable to the same kind of criticism as the notion that thinking needs a subject or ego, which we rejected in Lecture I. To say that it is Jones who is walking is merely to say that the walking in question is part of the whole series of occurrences which is Jones. There is no LOGICAL impossibility in walking occurring as an isolated phenomenon, not forming part of any such series as we call a "person."

We may therefore class with "eating," "walking," "speaking" words such as "rain," "sunrise," "lightning," which do not denote what would commonly be called actions. These words illustrate, incidentally, how little we can trust to the grammatical distinction of parts of speech, since the substantive "rain" and the verb "to rain" denote precisely the same class of meteorological occurrences. The distinction between the class of objects denoted by such a word and the class of objects denoted by a general name such as "man," "vegetable," or "planet," is that the sort of object which is an instance of (say) "lightning" is much simpler than (say) an individual man. (I am speaking of lightning as a sensible phenomenon, not as it is described in physics.) The distinction is one of degree, not of kind. But there is, from the point of view of ordinary thought, a great difference between a process which, like a flash of lightning, can be wholly comprised within one specious present and a process which, like the life of a man, has to be pieced together by observation and memory and the apprehension of causal connections. We may say broadly, therefore, that a word of the kind we have been discussing denotes a set of similar occurrences, each (as a rule) much more brief and less complex than a person or thing. Words themselves, as we have seen, are sets of similar occurrences of this kind. Thus there is more logical affinity between a word and what it means in the case of words of our present sort than in any other case.

There is no very great difference between such words as we have just been considering and words denoting qualities, such as "white" or "round." The chief difference is that words of this latter sort do not denote processes, however brief, but static features of the world. Snow falls, and is white; the falling is a process, the whiteness is not. Whether there is a universal, called "whiteness," or whether white things are to be defined as those having a certain kind of similarity to a standard thing, say freshly fallen snow, is a question which need not concern us, and which I believe to be strictly insoluble. For our purposes, we may take the word "white" as denoting a certain set of similar particulars or collections of particulars, the similarity being in respect of a static quality, not of a process.

From the logical point of view, a very important class of words are those that express relations, such as "in," "above," "before," "greater," and so on. The meaning of one of these words differs very fundamentally from the meaning of one of any of our previous classes, being more abstract and logically simpler than any of them. If our business were logic, we should have to spend much time on these words. But as it is psychology that concerns us, we will merely note their special character and pass on, since the logical classification of words is not our main business.

We will consider next the question what is implied by saying that a person "understands" a word, in the sense in which one understands a word in one's own language, but not in a language of which one is ignorant. We may say that a person understands a word when (a) suitable circumstances make him use it, (b) the hearing of it causes suitable behaviour in him. We may call these two active and passive understanding respectively. Dogs often have passive understanding of some words, but not active understanding, since they cannot use words.

It is not necessary, in order that a man should "understand" a word, that he should "know what it means," in the sense of being able to say "this word means so-and-so." Understanding words does not consist in knowing their dictionary definitions, or in being able to specify the objects to which they are appropriate. Such understanding as this may belong to lexicographers and students, but not to ordinary mortals in ordinary life. Understanding language is more like understanding cricket[40]: it is a matter of habits, acquired in oneself and rightly presumed in others. To say that a word has a meaning is not to say that those who use the word correctly have ever thought out what the meaning is: the use of the word comes first, and the meaning is to be distilled out of it by observation and analysis. Moreover, the meaning of a word is not absolutely definite: there is always a greater or less degree of vagueness. The meaning is an area, like a target: it may have a bull's eye, but the outlying parts of the target are still more or less within the meaning, in a gradually diminishing degree as we travel further from the bull's eye. As language grows more precise, there is less and less of the target outside the bull's eye, and the bull's eye itself grows smaller and smaller; but the bull's eye never shrinks to a point, and there is always a doubtful region, however small, surrounding it.[41]

A word is used "correctly" when the average hearer will be affected by it in the way intended. This is a psychological, not a literary, definition of "correctness." The literary definition would substitute, for the average hearer, a person of high education living a long time ago; the purpose of this definition is to make it difficult to speak or write correctly.

The relation of a word to its meaning is of the nature of a causal law governing our use of the word and our actions when we hear it used. There is no more reason why a person who uses a word correctly should be able to tell what it means than there is why a planet which is moving correctly should know Kepler's laws.

To illustrate what is meant by "understanding" words and sentences, let us take instances of various situations.

Suppose you are walking in London with an absent-minded friend, and while crossing a street you say, "Look out, there's a motor coming." He will glance round and jump aside without the need of any "mental" intermediary. There need be no "ideas," but only a stiffening of the muscles, followed quickly by action. He "understands"

---

[40] This point of view, extended to the analysis of "thought" is urged with great force by J. B. Watson, both in his *Behavior,* and in *Psychology from the Standpoint of a Behaviorist* (Lippincott. 1919), chap. ix.

[41] On the understanding of words, a very admirable little book is Ribot's *Evolution of General Ideas,* Open Court Co., 1899. Ribot says (p. 131): "We learn to understand a concept as we learn to walk, dance, fence or play a musical instrument: it is a habit, i.e. an organized memory. General terms cover an organized, latent knowledge which is the hidden capital without which we should be in a state of bankruptcy, manipulating false money or paper of no value. General ideas are habits in the intellectual order."

the words, because he does the right thing. Such "understanding" may be taken to belong to the nerves and brain, being habits which they have acquired while the language was being learnt. Thus understanding in this sense may be reduced to mere physiological causal laws.

If you say the same thing to a Frenchman with a slight knowledge of English he will go through some inner speech which may be represented by "Que dit-il? Ah, oui, une automobile!" After this, the rest follows as with the Englishman. Watson would contend that the inner speech must be incipiently pronounced; we should argue that it MIGHT be merely imaged. But this point is not important in the present connection.

If you say the same thing to a child who does not yet know the word "motor," but does know the other words you are using, you produce a feeling of anxiety and doubt you will have to point and say, "There, that's a motor." After that the child will roughly understand the word "motor," though he may include trains and steam-rollers If this is the first time the child has heard the word "motor," he may for a long time continue to recall this scene when he hears the word.

So far we have found four ways of understanding words:

(1) On suitable occasions you use the word properly.
(2) When you hear it you act appropriately.
(3) You associate the word with another word (say in a different language) which has the appropriate effect on behaviour.
(4) When the word is being first learnt, you may associate it with an object, which is what it "means," or a representative of various objects that it "means."

In the fourth case, the word acquires, through association, some of the same causal efficacy as the object. The word "motor" can make you leap aside, just as the motor can, but it cannot break your bones. The effects which a word can share with its object are those which proceed according to laws other than the general laws of physics, i.e. those which, according to our terminology, involve vital movements as opposed to merely mechanical movements. The effects of a word that we understand are always mnemic phenomena in the sense explained in Lecture IV, in so far as they are identical with, or similar to, the effects which the object itself might have.

So far, all the uses of words that we have considered can be accounted for on the lines of behaviourism.

But so far we have only considered what may be called the "demonstrative" use of language, to point out some feature in the present environment. This is only one of the ways in which language may be used. There are also its narrative and imaginative uses, as in history and novels. Let us take as an instance the telling of some remembered event.

We spoke a moment ago of a child who hears the word "motor" for the first time when crossing a street along which a motor-car is approaching. On a later occasion, we will suppose, the child remembers the incident and relates it to someone else. In this case, both the active and passive understanding of words is different from what it is when words are used demonstratively. The child is not seeing a motor, but only remembering one; the hearer does not look round in expectation of seeing a motor coming, but "understands" that a motor came at some earlier time. The whole of this occurrence is much more difficult to account for on behaviourist lines. It is clear that, in so far as the child is genuinely remembering, he has a picture of the past occurrence, and his words are chosen so as to describe the picture; and in so far as the hearer is genuinely apprehending what is said, the hearer is acquiring a picture more or less like that of the child. It is true that this process may be telescoped through the operation of the word-habit. The child may not genuinely remember the incident, but only have the habit of the appropriate words, as in the case of a poem which we know by heart, though we cannot remember learning it. And the hearer also may only pay attention to the words, and not call up any corresponding picture. But it is, nevertheless, the possibility of a memory-image in the child and an imagination-image in the hearer that makes the essence of the narrative "meaning" of the words. In so far as this is absent, the words are mere counters, capable of meaning, but not at the moment possessing it.

Yet this might perhaps be regarded as something of an overstatement. The words alone, without the use of images, may cause appropriate emotions and appropriate behaviour. The words have been used in an environment which produced certain emotions; by a telescoped process, the words alone are now capable of producing similar emotions. On these lines it might be sought to show that images are unnecessary. I do not believe, however, that we could account on these lines for the entirely different response produced by a narrative and by a description of present facts. Images, as contrasted with sensations, are the response expected during a narrative; it is understood that present action is not called for. Thus it seems that we must maintain our distinction words used demonstratively describe and are intended to lead to sensations, while the same words used in narrative describe and are only intended to lead to images.

We have thus, in addition to our four previous ways in which words can mean, two new ways, namely the way of memory and the way of imagination. That is to say:

(5) Words may be used to describe or recall a memory-image: to describe it when it already exists, or to recall it when the words exist as a habit and are known to be descriptive of some past experience.

(6) Words may be used to describe or create an imagination-image: to describe it, for example, in the case of a poet or novelist, or to create it in the ordinary case for giving information-though, in the latter case, it is intended that the imagination-image, when created, shall be accompanied by belief that something of the sort occurred.

These two ways of using words, including their occurrence in inner speech, may be spoken of together as the use of words in "thinking." If we are right, the use of words in thinking depends, at least in its origin, upon images, and cannot be fully dealt with on behaviourist lines. And this is really the most essential function of words, namely that, originally through their connection with images, they bring us into touch with what is remote in time or space. When they operate without the medium of images, this seems to be a telescoped process. Thus the problem of the meaning of words is brought into connection with the problem of the meaning of images.

To understand the function that words perform in what is called "thinking," we must understand both the causes and the effects of their occurrence. The causes of the occurrence of words require somewhat different treatment according as the object designated by the word is sensibly present or absent. When the object is present, it may itself be taken as the cause of the word, through association. But when it is absent there is more difficulty in obtaining a behaviourist theory of the occurrence of the word. The language-habit consists not merely in the use of words demonstratively, but also in their use to express narrative or desire. Professor Watson, in his account of the acquisition of the language-habit, pays very little attention to the use of words in narrative and desire. He says ("Behavior," pp. 329-330):

"The stimulus (object) to which the child often responds, a box, e.g. by movements such as opening and closing and putting objects into it, may serve to illustrate our argument. The nurse, observing that the child reacts with his hands, feet, etc., to the box, begins to say 'box' when the child is handed the box, 'open box' when the child opens it, 'close box' when he closes it, and 'put doll in box' when that act is executed. This is repeated over and over again. In the process of time it comes about that without any other stimulus than that of the box which originally called out the bodily habits, he begins to say 'box' when he sees it, 'open box' when he opens it, etc. The visible box now becomes a stimulus capable of releasing either the bodily habits or the word-habit, i.e. development has brought about two things: (1) a series of functional connections among arcs which run from visual receptor to muscles of throat, and (2) a series of already earlier connected arcs which run from the same receptor to the bodily muscles.... The object meets the child's vision. He runs to it and tries to reach it and says 'box.'... Finally the word is uttered without the movement of going towards the box being executed.... Habits are formed of going to the box when the arms are full of toys. The child has been taught to deposit them there. When his arms are laden with toys and no box is there, the word-habit arises and he calls 'box'; it is handed to him, and he opens it and deposits the toys therein. This roughly marks what we would call the genesis of a true language-habit."(pp. 329-330).[42]

We need not linger over what is said in the above passage as to the use of the word "box" in the presence of the box. But as to its use in the absence of the box, there

---

[42] Just the same account of language is given in Professor Watson's more recent book (reference above).

is only one brief sentence, namely: "When his arms are laden with toys and no box is there, the word-habit arises and he calls 'box.'" This is inadequate as it stands, since the habit has been to use the word when the box is present, and we have to explain its extension to cases in which the box is absent.

Having admitted images, we may say that the word "box," in the absence of the box, is caused by an image of the box. This may or may not be true—in fact, it is true in some cases but not in others. Even, however, if it were true in all cases, it would only slightly shift our problem: we should now have to ask what causes an image of the box to arise. We might be inclined to say that desire for the box is the cause. But when this view is investigated, it is found that it compels us to suppose that the box can be desired without the child's having either an image of the box or the word "box." This will require a theory of desire which may be, and I think is, in the main true, but which removes desire from among things that actually occur, and makes it merely a convenient fiction, like force in mechanics.[43] With such a view, desire is no longer a true cause, but merely a short way of describing certain processes.

In order to explain the occurrence of either the word or the image in the absence of the box, we have to assume that there is something, either in the environment or in our own sensations, which has frequently occurred at about the same time as the word "box." One of the laws which distinguish psychology (or nerve-physiology?) from physics is the law that, when two things have frequently existed in close temporal contiguity, either comes in time to cause the other.[44] This is the basis both of habit and of association. Thus, in our case, the arms full of toys have frequently been followed quickly by the box, and the box in turn by the word "box." The box itself is subject to physical laws, and does not tend to be caused by the arms full of toys, however often it may in the past have followed them—always provided that, in the case in question, its physical position is such that voluntary movements cannot lead to it. But the word "box" and the image of the box are subject to the law of habit; hence it is possible for either to be caused by the arms full of toys. And we may lay it down generally that, whenever we use a word, either aloud or in inner speech, there is some sensation or image (either of which may be itself a word) which has frequently occurred at about the same time as the word, and now, through habit, causes the word. It follows that the law of habit is adequate to account for the use of words in the absence of their objects; moreover, it would be adequate even without introducing images. Although, therefore, images seem undeniable, we cannot derive an additional argument in their favour from the use of words, which could, theoretically, be explained without introducing images.

When we understand a word, there is a reciprocal association between it and the images of what it "means." Images may cause us to use words which mean them, and

---

[43] See Lecture III, above.

[44] For a more exact statement of this law, with the limitations suggested by experiment, see A. Wohlgemuth, "On Memory and the Direction of Associations," *British Journal of Psychology*, vol. v, part iv (March, 1913).

these words, heard or read, may in turn cause the appropriate images. Thus speech is a means of producing in our hearers the images which are in us. Also, by a telescoped process, words come in time to produce directly the effects which would have been produced by the images with which they were associated. The general law of telescoped processes is that, if A causes B and B causes C, it will happen in time that A will cause C directly, without the intermediary of B. This is a characteristic of psychological and neural causation. In virtue of this law, the effects of images upon our actions come to be produced by words, even when the words do not call up appropriate images. The more familiar we are with words, the more our "thinking" goes on in words instead of images. We may, for example, be able to describe a person's appearance correctly without having at any time had any image of him, provided, when we saw him, we thought of words which fitted him; the words alone may remain with us as a habit, and enable us to speak as if we could recall a visual image of the man. In this and other ways the understanding of a word often comes to be quite free from imagery; but in first learning the use of language it would seem that imagery always plays a very important part.

Images as well as words may be said to have "meaning"; indeed, the meaning of images seems more primitive than the meaning of words. What we call (say) an image of St. Paul's may be said to "mean" St. Paul's. But it is not at all easy to say exactly what constitutes the meaning of an image. A memory-image of a particular occurrence, when accompanied by a memory-belief, may be said to mean the occurrence of which it is an image. But most actual images do not have this degree of definiteness. If we call up an image of a dog, we are very likely to have a vague image, which is not representative of some one special dog, but of dogs in general. When we call up an image of a friend's face, we are not likely to reproduce the expression he had on some one particular occasion, but rather a compromise expression derived from many occasions. And there is hardly any limit to the vagueness of which images are capable. In such cases, the meaning of the image, if defined by relation to the prototype, is vague: there is not one definite prototype, but a number, none of which is copied exactly.[45]

There is, however, another way of approaching the meaning of images, namely through their causal efficacy. What is called an image "of" some definite object, say St. Paul's, has some of the effects which the object would have. This applies especially to the effects that depend upon association. The emotional effects, also, are often similar: images may stimulate desire almost as strongly as do the objects they represent. And conversely desire may cause images[46]: a hungry man will have images of food, and so on. In all these ways the causal laws concerning images are connected with the causal laws concerning the objects which the images "mean." An image may thus come to

---

[45] Cf. Semon, *Mnemische Empfindungen*, chap. xvi, especially pp. 301-308.

[46] This phrase is in need of interpretation, as appears from the analysis of desire. But the reader can easily supply the interpretation for himself.

fulfil the function of a general idea. The vague image of a dog, which we spoke of a moment ago, will have effects which are only connected with dogs in general, not the more special effects which would be produced by some dogs but not by others. Berkeley and Hume, in their attack on general ideas, do not allow for the vagueness of images: they assume that every image has the definiteness that a physical object would have This is not the case, and a vague image may well have a meaning which is general.

In order to define the "meaning" of an image, we have to take account both of its resemblance to one or more prototypes, and of its causal efficacy. If there were such a thing as a pure imagination-image, without any prototype whatever, it would be destitute of meaning. But according to Hume's principle, the simple elements in an image, at least, are derived from prototypes-except possibly in very rare exceptional cases. Often, in such instances as our image of a friend's face or of a nondescript dog, an image is not derived from one prototype, but from many; when this happens, the image is vague, and blurs the features in which the various prototypes differ. To arrive at the meaning of the image in such a case, we observe that there are certain respects, notably associations, in which the effects of images resemble those of their prototypes. If we find, in a given case, that our vague image, say, of a nondescript dog, has those associative effects which all dogs would have, but not those belonging to any special dog or kind of dog, we may say that our image means "dog" in general. If it has all the associations appropriate to spaniels but no others, we shall say it means "spaniel"; while if it has all the associations appropriate to one particular dog, it will mean that dog, however vague it may be as a picture. The meaning of an image, according to this analysis, is constituted by a combination of likeness and associations. It is not a sharp or definite conception, and in many cases it will be impossible to decide with any certainty what an image means. I think this lies in the nature of things, and not in defective analysis.

We may give somewhat more precision to the above account of the meaning of images, and extend it to meaning in general. We find sometimes that, IN MNEMIC CAUSATION, an image or word, as stimulus, has the same effect (or very nearly the same effect) as would belong to some object, say, a certain dog. In that case we say that the image or word means that object. In other cases the mnemic effects are not all those of one object, but only those shared by objects of a certain kind, e.g. by all dogs. In this case the meaning of the image or word is general: it means the whole kind. Generality and particularity are a matter of degree. If two particulars differ sufficiently little, their mnemic effects will be the same; therefore no image or word can mean the one as opposed to the other; this sets a bound to the particularity of meaning. On the other hand, the mnemic effects of a number of sufficiently dissimilar objects will have nothing discoverable in common; hence a word which aims at complete generality, such as "entity" for example, will have to be devoid of mnemic effects, and therefore of meaning. In practice, this is not the case: such words have VERBAL associations, the learning of which constitutes the study of metaphysics.

The meaning of a word, unlike that of an image, is wholly constituted by mnemic causal laws, and not in any degree by likeness (except in exceptional cases). The word "dog" bears no resemblance to a dog, but its effects, like those of an image of a dog, resemble the effects of an actual dog in certain respects. It is much easier to say definitely what a word means than what an image means, since words, however they originated, have been framed in later times for the purpose of having meaning, and men have been engaged for ages in giving increased precision to the meanings of words. But although it is easier to say what a word means than what an image means, the relation which constitutes meaning is much the same in both cases. A word, like an image, has the same associations as its meaning has. In addition to other associations, it is associated with images of its meaning, so that the word tends to call up the image and the image tends to call up the word., But this association is not essential to the intelligent use of words. If a word has the right associations with other objects, we shall be able to use it correctly, and understand its use by others, even if it evokes no image. The theoretical understanding of words involves only the power of associating them correctly with other words; the practical understanding involves associations with other bodily movements.

The use of words is, of course, primarily social, for the purpose of suggesting to others ideas which we entertain or at least wish them to entertain. But the aspect of words that specially concerns us is their power of promoting our own thought. Almost all higher intellectual activity is a matter of words, to the nearly total exclusion of everything else. The advantages of words for purposes of thought are so great that I should never end if I were to enumerate them. But a few of them deserve to be mentioned.

In the first place, there is no difficulty in producing a word, whereas an image cannot always be brought into existence at will, and when it comes it often contains much irrelevant detail. In the second place, much of our thinking is concerned with abstract matters which do not readily lend themselves to imagery, and are apt to be falsely conceived if we insist upon finding images that may be supposed to represent them. The word is always concrete and sensible, however abstract its meaning may be, and thus by the help of words we are able to dwell on abstractions in a way which would otherwise be impossible. In the third place, two instances of the same word are so similar that neither has associations not capable of being shared by the other. Two instances of the word "dog" are much more alike than (say) a pug and a great dane; hence the word "dog" makes it much easier to think about dogs in general. When a number of objects have a common property which is important but not obvious, the invention of a name for the common property helps us to remember it and to think of the whole set of objects that possess it. But it is unnecessary to prolong the catalogue of the uses of language in thought.

At the same time, it is possible to conduct rudimentary thought by means of images, and it is important, sometimes, to check purely verbal thought by reference to what it means. In philosophy especially the tyranny of traditional words is dangerous, and we have to be on our guard against assuming that grammar is the key to metaphysics, or that the structure of a sentence corresponds at all accurately with the structure of the fact that it asserts. Sayce maintained that all European philosophy since Aristotle has been dominated by the fact that the philosophers spoke Indo-European languages, and therefore supposed the world, like the sentences they were used to, necessarily divisible into subjects and predicates. When we come to the consideration of truth and falsehood, we shall see how necessary it is to avoid assuming too close a parallelism between facts and the sentences which assert them. Against such errors, the only safeguard is to be able, once in a way, to discard words for a moment and contemplate facts more directly through images. Most serious advances in philosophic thought result from some such comparatively direct contemplation of facts. But the outcome has to be expressed in words if it is to be communicable. Those who have a relatively direct vision of facts are often incapable of translating their vision into words, while those who possess the words have usually lost the vision. It is partly for this reason that the highest philosophical capacity is so rare: it requires a combination of vision with abstract words which is hard to achieve, and too quickly lost in the few who have for a moment achieved it.

# LECTURE XI

## General Ideas and Thought

It is said to be one of the merits of the human mind that it is capable of framing abstract ideas, and of conducting nonsensational thought. In this it is supposed to differ from the mind of animals. From Plato onward the "idea" has played a great part in the systems of idealizing philosophers. The "idea" has been, in their hands, always something noble and abstract, the apprehension and use of which by man confers upon him a quite special dignity.

The thing we have to consider to-day is this: seeing that there certainly are words of which the meaning is abstract, and seeing that we can use these words intelligently, what must be assumed or inferred, or what can be discovered by observation, in the way of mental content to account for the intelligent use of abstract words?

Taken as a problem in logic, the answer is, of course, that absolutely nothing in the way of abstract mental content is inferable from the mere fact that we can use intelligently words of which the meaning is abstract. It is clear that a sufficiently ingenious person could manufacture a machine moved by olfactory stimuli which, whenever a dog appeared in its neighbourhood, would say, "There is a dog," and when a cat appeared would throw stones at it. The act of saying "There is a dog," and the act of throwing stones, would in such a case be equally mechanical. Correct speech does not of itself afford any better evidence of mental content than the performance of any other set of biologically useful movements, such as those of flight or combat. All that is inferable from language is that two instances of a universal, even when they differ very greatly, may cause the utterance of two instances of the same word which only differ very slightly. As we saw in the preceding lecture, the word "dog" is useful, partly, because two instances of this word are much more similar than (say) a pug and a great dane. The use of words is thus a method of substituting for two particulars which differ widely, in spite of being instances of the same universal, two other particulars which differ very little, and which are also instances of a universal, namely the name of the previous universal. Thus, so far as logic is concerned, we are entirely free to adopt any theory as to general ideas which empirical observation may recommend.

Berkeley and Hume made a vigorous onslaught on "abstract ideas." They meant by an idea approximately what we should call an image. Locke having maintained that he could form an idea of triangle in general, without deciding what sort of triangle it was to be, Berkeley contended that this was impossible. He says:

"Whether others, have this wonderful faculty of abstracting their ideas, they best can tell: for myself, I dare be confident I have it not. I find, indeed, I have indeed a faculty of imagining, or representing to myself, the ideas of those particular things I have perceived, and of variously compounding and dividing them. I can imagine a man with two heads, or the upper parts of a man joined to the body of a horse. I can consider the hand, the eye, the nose, each by itself abstracted or separated from the rest of the body. But, then, whatever hand or eye I imagine, it must have some particular shape and colour. Likewise the idea of a man that I frame to myself must be either of a white, or a black, or a tawny, a straight, or a crooked, a tall, or a low, or a middle-sized man. I cannot by any effort of thought conceive the abstract idea above described. And it is equally impossible for me to form the abstract idea of motion distinct from the body moving, and which is neither swift nor slow, curvilinear nor rectilinear; and the like may be said of all other abstract general ideas whatsoever. To be plain, I own myself able to abstract in one sense, as when I consider some particular parts of qualities separated from others, with which, though they are united in some object, yet it is possible they may really exist without them. But I deny that I can abstract from one another, or conceive separately, those qualities which it is impossible should exist so separated; or that I can frame a general notion, by abstracting from particulars in the manner aforesaid—which last are the two proper acceptations of ABSTRACTION. And there is ground to think most men will acknowledge themselves to be in my case. The generality of men which are simple and illiterate never pretend to ABSTRACT NOTIONS. It is said they are difficult and not to be attained without pains and study; we may therefore reasonably conclude that, if such there be, they are confined only to the learned.

"I proceed to examine what can be alleged in defence of the doctrine of abstraction, and try if I can discover what it is that inclines the men of speculation to embrace an opinion so remote from common sense as that seems to be. There has been a late excellent and deservedly esteemed philosopher who, no doubt, has given it very much countenance, by seeming to think the having abstract general ideas is what puts the widest difference in point of understanding betwixt man and beast. 'The having of general ideas,' saith he, 'is that which puts a perfect distinction betwixt man and brutes, and is an excellency which the faculties of brutes do by no means attain unto. For, it is evident we observe no footsteps in them of making use of general signs for universal ideas; from which we have reason to imagine that they have not the faculty of abstracting, or making general ideas, since they have no use of words or any other general signs.' And a little after: 'Therefore, I think, we may suppose that it is in this that the species of brutes are discriminated from men, and it is that proper difference wherein they are wholly separated, and which at last widens to so wide a distance. For, if they have any ideas at all, and are not bare machines (as some would have them), we cannot deny them to have some reason. It seems as evident to me that they do, some of them, in certain instances reason as that they have sense; but it is only in particular ideas, just as they receive them from their senses. They are the best of them tied up within those narrow bounds, and have not (as I think) the faculty to enlarge them by any kind of abstraction.* ("Essay on Human Understanding," Bk. II, chap. xi, paragraphs 10 and 11.) I readily agree with this learned author, that the faculties of brutes can by no means attain to abstraction. But, then, if this be made the distinguishing property of that sort of animals, I fear a great many of those that pass for men must be reckoned into their number. The reason that is here assigned why we have no grounds to think brutes have abstract general ideas is, that we observe in them no use of words or any other general signs; which is built on this supposition-that the making use of words implies the having general ideas. From which it follows that men who use language are able to abstract or generalize their ideas. That this is the sense and arguing of the author will further appear by his answering the question he in another place puts: 'Since all things that exist are only particulars, how come we by general terms?' His answer is: 'Words become general by being made the signs of general ideas.' ("Essay on Human Understanding," Bk. III, chap. III, paragraph 6.) But it seems that a word becomes general by being made the sign, not of an abstract general idea, but of several particular ideas, any one of which it indifferently suggests to the mind. For example, when it is said 'the change of motion is proportional to the impressed force,' or that 'whatever has extension is divisible,' these propositions are to be understood of motion and extension in general; and nevertheless it will not follow that they suggest to my thoughts an idea of motion without a body moved, or any determinate direction and velocity, or that I must conceive an abstract general idea of extension, which is neither line, surface, nor solid, neither great nor small, black, white, nor red, nor of any other determinate colour. It is only implied that whatever particular motion I consider, whether it be swift or slow, perpendicular, horizontal, or oblique, or in whatever object, the axiom concerning it holds equally true. As does the other of every particular extension, it matters not whether line, surface, or solid, whether of this or that magnitude or figure.

"By observing how ideas become general, we may the better judge how words are made so. And here it is to be noted that I do not deny absolutely there are general ideas, but only that there are any ABSTRACT general ideas; for, in the passages we have quoted wherein there is mention of general ideas, it is always supposed that they are formed by abstraction, after the manner set forth in sections 8 and 9. Now, if we will annex a meaning to our words, and speak only of what we can conceive, I believe we shall acknowledge that an idea which, considered in itself, is particular, becomes general by being made to represent or stand for all other particular ideas of the same sort. To make this plain by an example, suppose a geometrician is demonstrating the method of cutting a line in two equal parts. He draws, for instance, a black line of an inch in length: this, which in itself is a particular line, is nevertheless with regard to its signification general, since, as it is there used, it represents all particular lines whatsoever; so that what is demonstrated of it is demonstrated of all lines, or, in other words, of a line in general. And, as THAT PARTICULAR LINE becomes general by being made a sign, so the NAME 'line,' which taken absolutely is particular, by being a sign is made general. And as the former owes its generality not to its being the sign of an abstract or general line, but of all particular right lines that may possibly exist, so the latter must be thought to derive its generality from the same cause, namely, the various particular lines which it indifferently denotes."[47]

Berkeley's view in the above passage, which is essentially the same as Hume's, does not wholly agree with modern psychology, although it comes nearer to agreement than does the view of those who believe that there are in the mind single contents which can be called abstract ideas. The way in which Berkeley's view is inadequate is chiefly in the fact that images are as a rule not of one definite prototype, but of a number of related similar prototypes. On this subject Semon has written well. In "Die Mneme," pp. 217 ff., discussing the effect of repeated similar stimuli in producing and modifying our images, he says: "We choose a case of mnemic excitement whose existence we can perceive for ourselves by introspection, and seek to ekphore the bodily picture of our nearest relation in his absence, and have thus a pure mnemic excitement before us. At first it may seem to us that a determinate quite concrete picture becomes manifest in us, but just when we are concerned with a person with whom we are in constant contact, we shall find that the ekphored picture has something so to speak generalized. It is something like those American photographs which seek to display what is general about a type by combining a great number of photographs of different heads over each other on one plate. In our opinion, the generalizations happen by the homophonic working of different pictures of the same face which we have come across in the most different conditions and situations, once pale, once reddened, once cheerful, once earnest, once in this light, and once in that. As soon as we do not let the whole series of repetitions resound in us uniformly, but give our attention to one particular moment out of the many... this particular mnemic stimulus at once overbalances its simultaneously roused predecessors and successors, and we perceive the face in question with concrete definiteness in that particular situation." A little later he says: "The result is—at least in man, but probably also in the higher animals—the development of a sort of PHYSIOLOGICAL abstraction. Mnemic homophony gives us, without the addition of other processes of thought, a picture of our friend X which is in a certain sense abstract, not the concrete in any one situation, but X cut loose from any particular point of time. If the circle of ekphored engrams is drawn even more widely, abstract pictures of a higher order appear: for instance, a white man or a negro. In my opinion, the first form of abstract concepts in general is based upon such abstract pictures. The physiological abstraction which takes place in

---

[47] Introduction to *A Treatise concerning the Principles of Human Knowledge*, paragraphs 10, 11, and 12.

the above described manner is a predecessor of purely logical abstraction. It is by no means a monopoly of the human race, but shows itself in various ways also among the more highly organized animals." The same subject is treated in more detail in Chapter xvi of "Die mnemischen Empfindungen," but what is said there adds nothing vital to what is contained in the above quotations.

It is necessary, however, to distinguish between the vague and the general. So long as we are content with Semon's composite image, we MAY get no farther than the vague. The question whether this image takes us to the general or not depends, I think, upon the question whether, in addition to the generalized image, we have also particular images of some of the instances out of which it is compounded. Suppose, for example, that on a number of occasions you had seen one negro, and that you did not know whether this one was the same or different on the different occasions. Suppose that in the end you had an abstract memory-image of the different appearances presented by the negro on different occasions, but no memory-image of any one of the single appearances. In that case your image would be vague. If, on the other hand, you have, in addition to the generalized image, particular images of the several appearances, sufficiently clear to be recognized as different, and as instances of the generalized picture, you will then not feel the generalized picture to be adequate to any one particular appearance, and you will be able to make it function as a general idea rather than a vague idea. If this view is correct, no new general content needs to be added to the generalized image. What needs to be added is particular images compared and contrasted with the generalized image. So far as I can judge by introspection, this does occur in practice. Take for example Semon's instance of a friend's face. Unless we make some special effort of recollection, the face is likely to come before us with an average expression, very blurred and vague, but we can at will recall how our friend looked on some special occasion when he was pleased or angry or unhappy, and this enables us to realize the generalized character of the vague image.

There is, however, another way of distinguishing between the vague, the particular and the general, and this is not by their content, but by the reaction which they produce. A word, for example, may be said to be vague when it is applicable to a number of different individuals, but to each as individuals; the name Smith, for example, is vague: it is always meant to apply to one man, but there are many men to each of whom it applies.[48] The word "man," on the other hand, is general. We say, "This is Smith," but we do not say "This is man," but "This is a man." Thus we may say that a word embodies a vague idea when its effects are appropriate to an individual, but are the same for various similar individuals, while a word embodies a general idea when its effects are different from those appropriate to individuals. In what

---

[48] "Smith" would only be a quite satisfactory representation of vague words if we failed to discriminate between different people called Smith.

this difference consists it is, however, not easy to say. I am inclined to think that it consists merely in the knowledge that no one individual is represented, so that what distinguishes a general idea from a vague idea is merely the presence of a certain accompanying belief. If this view is correct, a general idea differs from a vague one in a way analogous to that in which a memory-image differs from an imagination-image. There also we found that the difference consists merely of the fact that a memory-image is accompanied by a belief, in this case as to the past.

It should also be said that our images even of quite particular occurrences have always a greater or a less degree of vagueness. That is to say, the occurrence might have varied within certain limits without causing our image to vary recognizably. To arrive at the general it is necessary that we should be able to contrast it with a number of relatively precise images or words for particular occurrences; so long as all our images and words are vague, we cannot arrive at the contrast by which the general is defined. This is the justification for the view which I quoted on p. 184 from Ribot (op. cit., p. 32), viz. that intelligence progresses from the indefinite to the definite, and that the vague appears earlier than either the particular or the general.

I think the view which I have been advocating, to the effect that a general idea is distinguished from a vague one by the presence of a judgment, is also that intended by Ribot when he says (op. cit., p. 92): "The generic image is never, the concept is always, a judgment. We know that for logicians (formerly at any rate) the concept is the simple and primitive element; next comes the judgment, uniting two or several concepts; then ratiocination, combining two or several judgments. For the psychologists, on the contrary, affirmation is the fundamental act; the concept is the result of judgment (explicit or implicit), of similarities with exclusion of differences."

A great deal of work professing to be experimental has been done in recent years on the psychology of thought. A good summary of such work up to the year agog is contained in Titchener's "Lectures on the Experimental Psychology of the Thought Processes" (1909). Three articles in the "Archiv fur die gesammte Psychologie" by Watt,[49] Messer[50] and Buhler[51] contain a great deal of the material amassed by the methods which Titchener calls experimental.

For my part I am unable to attach as much importance to this work as many psychologists do. The method employed appears to me hardly to fulfil the conditions of scientific experiment. Broadly speaking, what is done is, that a set of questions are asked of various people, their answers are recorded, and likewise their own accounts, based upon introspection, of the processes of thought which led them to give those answers. Much too much reliance seems to me to be placed upon the correctness of their introspection. On introspection as a method I have spoken earlier (Lecture VI).

---

[49] Henry J. Watt, *Experimentelle Beitrage zu einer Theorie des Denkens*, vol. iv (1905) pp. 289-436.

[50] August Messer, *Experimentell-psychologische Untersuchu gen uber das Denken*, vol. iii (1906), pp. 1-224.

[51] Karl Buhler, *Uber Gedanken*, vol. ix (1907), pp. 297-365.

I am not prepared, like Professor Watson, to reject it wholly, but I do consider that it is exceedingly fallible and quite peculiarly liable to falsification in accordance with preconceived theory. It is like depending upon the report of a shortsighted person as to whom he sees coming along the road at a moment when he is firmly convinced that Jones is sure to come. If everybody were shortsighted and obsessed with beliefs as to what was going to be visible, we might have to make the best of such testimony, but we should need to correct its errors by taking care to collect the simultaneous evidence of people with the most divergent expectations. There is no evidence that this was done in the experiments in question, nor indeed that the influence of theory in falsifying the introspection was at all adequately recognized. I feel convinced that if Professor Watson had been one of the subjects of the questionnaires, he would have given answers totally different from those recorded in the articles in question. Titchener quotes an opinion of Wundt on these investigations, which appears to me thoroughly justified. "These experiments," he says, "are not experiments at all in the sense of a scientific methodology; they are counterfeit experiments, that seem methodical simply because they are ordinarily performed in a psychological laboratory, and involve the co-operation of two persons, who purport to be experimenter and observer. In reality, they are as unmethodical as possible; they possess none of the special features by which we distinguish the introspections of experimental psychology from the casual introspections of everyday life."[52] Titchener, of course, dissents from this opinion, but I cannot see that his reasons for dissent are adequate. My doubts are only increased by the fact that Buhler at any rate used trained psychologists as his subjects. A trained psychologist is, of course, supposed to have acquired the habit of observation, but he is at least equally likely to have acquired a habit of seeing what his theories require. We may take Buhler's "Uber Gedanken" to illustrate the kind of results arrived at by such methods. Buhler says (p. 303): "We ask ourselves the general question: 'WHAT DO WE EXPERIENCE WHEN WE THINK?' Then we do not at all attempt a preliminary determination of the concept 'thought,' but choose for analysis only such processes as everyone would describe as processes of thought." The most important thing in thinking, he says, is "awareness that..." (Bewusstheit dass), which he calls a thought. It is, he says, thoughts in this sense that are essential to thinking. Thinking, he maintains, does not need language or sensuous presentations. "I assert rather that in principle every object can be thought (meant) distinctly, without any help from sensuous presentation (Anschauungshilfen). Every individual shade of blue colour on the picture that hangs in my room I can think with complete distinctness unsensuously (unanschaulich), provided it is possible that the object should be given to me in another manner than by the help of sensations. How that is possible we shall see later." What he calls a thought (Gedanke) cannot be reduced, according to him, to other psychic occurrences. He maintains that thoughts consist

---

[52] Titchener, op. cit., p. 79.

for the most part of known rules (p. 342). It is clearly essential to the interest of this theory that the thought or rule alluded to by Buhler should not need to be expressed in words, for if it is expressed in words it is immediately capable of being dealt with on the lines with which the behaviourists have familiarized us. It is clear also that the supposed absence of words rests solely upon the introspective testimony of the persons experimented upon. I cannot think that there is sufficient certainty of their reliability in this negative observation to make us accept a difficult and revolutionary view of thought, merely because they have failed to observe the presence of words or their equivalent in their thinking. I think it far more likely, especially in view of the fact that the persons concerned were highly educated, that we are concerned with telescoped processes, in which habit has caused a great many intermediate terms to be elided or to be passed over so quickly as to escape observation.

I am inclined to think that similar remarks apply to the general idea of "imageless thinking," concerning which there has been much controversy. The advocates of imageless thinking are not contending merely that there can be thinking which is purely verbal; they are contending that there can be thinking which proceeds neither in words nor in images. My own feeling is that they have rashly assumed the presence of thinking in cases where habit has rendered thinking unnecessary. When Thorndike experimented with animals in cages, he found that the associations established were between a sensory stimulus and a bodily movement (not the idea of it), without the need of supposing any non-physiological intermediary (op. cit., p. 100 ff.). The same thing, it seems to me, applies to ourselves. A certain sensory situation produces in us a certain bodily movement. Sometimes this movement consists in uttering words. Prejudice leads us to suppose that between the sensory stimulus and the utterance of the words a process of thought must have intervened, but there seems no good reason for such a supposition. Any habitual action, such as eating or dressing, may be performed on the appropriate occasion, without any need of thought, and the same seems to be true of a painfully large proportion of our talk. What applies to uttered speech applies of course equally to the internal speech which is not uttered. I remain, therefore, entirely unconvinced that there is any such phenomenon as thinking which consists neither of images nor of words, or that "ideas" have to be added to sensations and images as part of the material out of which mental phenomena are built.

The question of the nature of our consciousness of the universal is much affected by our view as to the general nature of the relation of consciousness to its object. If we adopt the view of Brentano, according to which all mental content has essential reference to an object, it is then natural to suppose that there is some peculiar kind of mental content of which the object is a universal, as oppose to a particular. According to this view, a particular cat can be PERceived or imagined, while the universal "cat" is CONceived. But this whole manner of viewing our dealings with universals has to be abandoned when the relation of a mental occurrence to its "object" is regarded as merely indirect and causal, which is the view that we have adopted. The mental content is, of course, always particular, and the question as to what it "means" (in case it means anything) is one which cannot be settled by merely examining the intrinsic character of the mental content, but only by knowing its causal connections in the case of the person concerned. To say that a certain thought "means" a universal as opposed to either a vague or a particular, is to say something exceedingly complex. A horse will behave in a certain manner whenever he smells a bear, even if the smell is derived from a bearskin. That is to say, any environment containing an instance of the universal "smell of a bear" produces closely similar behaviour in the horse, but we do not say that the horse is conscious of this universal. There is equally little reason to regard a man as conscious of the same universal, because under the same circumstances he can react by saying, "I smell a bear." This reaction, like that of the horse, is merely closely similar on different occasions where the environment affords instances of the same universal. Words of which the logical meaning is universal can therefore be employed correctly, without anything that could be called consciousness of universals. Such consciousness in the only sense in which it can be said to exist is a matter of reflective judgment consisting in the observation of similarities and differences. A universal never appears before the mind as a single object in the sort of way in which something perceived appears. I THINK a logical argument could be produced to show that universals are part of the structure of the world, but they are an inferred part, not a part of our data. What exists in us consists of various factors, some open to external observation, others only visible to introspection. The factors open to external observation are primarily habits, having the peculiarity that very similar reactions are produced by stimuli which are in many respects very different from each other. Of this the reaction of the horse to the smell of the bear is an instance, and so is the reaction of the man who says "bear" under the same circumstances. The verbal reaction is, of course, the most important from the point of view of what may be called knowledge of universals. A man who can always use the word "dog" when he sees a dog may be said, in a certain sense, to know the meaning of the word "dog," and IN THAT SENSE to have knowledge of the universal "dog." But there is, of course, a further stage reached by the logician in which he not merely reacts with the word "dog," but sets to work to discover what it is in the environment that causes in him this almost identical reaction on different occasions. This further stage consists in knowledge of similarities and differences: similarities which are necessary to the applicability of the word "dog," and differences which are compatible with it. Our knowledge of these similarities and differences is never exhaustive, and therefore our knowledge of the meaning of a universal is never complete.

In addition to external observable habits (including the habit of words), there is also the generic image produced by the superposition, or, in Semon's phrase, homophony, of a number of similar perceptions. This image is vague so long as the multiplicity of its prototypes is not recognized, but becomes universal when it exists alongside of the more specific images of its instances, and is knowingly contrasted with them. In this case we find again, as we found when we were discussing words in general in the preceding lecture, that images are not logically necessary in order to account for observable behaviour, i.e. in this case intelligent speech. Intelligent speech could exist as a motor habit, without any accompaniment of images, and this conclusion applies to words of which the meaning is universal, just as much as to words of which the meaning is relatively particular. If this conclusion is valid, it follows that behaviourist psychology, which eschews introspective data, is capable of being an independent science, and of accounting for all that part of the behaviour of other people which is commonly regarded as evidence that they think. It must be admitted that this conclusion considerably weakens the reliance which can be placed upon introspective data. They must be accepted simply on account of the fact that we seem to perceive them, not on account of their supposed necessity for explaining the data of external observation.

This, at any rate, is the conclusion to which we are forced, so long as, with the behaviourists, we accept common-sense views of the physical world. But if, as I have urged, the physical world itself, as known, is infected through and through with subjectivity, if, as the theory of relativity suggests, the physical universe contains the diversity of points of view which we have been accustomed to regard as distinctively psychological, then we are brought back by this different road to the necessity for trusting observations which are in an important sense private. And it is the privacy of introspective data which causes much of the behaviourists' objection to them.

This is an example of the difficulty of constructing an adequate philosophy of any one science without taking account of other sciences. The behaviourist philosophy of psychology, though in many respects admirable from the point of view of method, appears to me to fail in the last analysis because it is based upon an inadequate philosophy of physics. In spite, therefore, of the fact that the evidence for images, whether generic or particular, is merely introspective, I cannot admit that images should be rejected, or that we should minimize their function in our knowledge of what is remote in time or space.

# LECTURE XII

## Belief

Belief, which is our subject to-day, is the central problem in the analysis of mind. Believing seems the most "mental" thing we do, the thing most remote from what is done by mere matter. The whole intellectual life consists of beliefs, and of the passage from one belief to another by what is called "reasoning." Beliefs give knowledge and error; they are the vehicles of truth and falsehood. Psychology, theory of knowledge and metaphysics revolve about belief, and on the view we take of belief our philosophical outlook largely depends.

Before embarking upon the detailed analysis of belief, we shall do well to note certain requisites which any theory must fulfil.

(1) Just as words are characterized by meaning, so beliefs are characterized by truth or falsehood. And just as meaning consists in relation to the object meant, so truth and falsehood consist in relation to something that lies outside the belief. You may believe that such-and-such a horse will win the Derby. The time comes, and your horse wins or does not win; according to the outcome, your belief was true or false. You may believe that six times nine is fifty-six; in this case also there is a fact which makes your belief false. You may believe that America was discovered in 1492, or that it was discovered in 1066. In the one case your belief is true, in the other false; in either case its truth or falsehood depends upon the actions of Columbus, not upon anything present or under your control. What makes a belief true or false I call a "fact." The particular fact that makes a given belief true or false I call its "objective,"[53] and the relation of the belief to its objective I call the "reference" or the "objective reference" of the belief. Thus, if I believe that Columbus crossed the Atlantic in 1492, the "objective" of my belief is Columbus's actual voyage, and the "reference" of my belief is the relation between my belief and the voyage—that relation, namely, in virtue of which the voyage makes my belief true (or, in another case, false). "Reference" of beliefs differs from "meaning" of words in various ways, but especially in the fact that it is of two kinds, "true" reference and "false" reference. The truth or falsehood of a belief does not depend upon anything intrinsic to the belief, but upon the nature of its relation to its objective. The intrinsic nature of belief can be treated without reference

---

[53] This terminology is suggested by Meinong, but is not exactly the same as his.

to what makes it true or false. In the remainder of the present lecture I shall ignore truth and falsehood, which will be the subject of Lecture XIII. It is the intrinsic nature of belief that will concern us to-day.

(2) We must distinguish between believing and what is believed. I may believe that Columbus crossed the Atlantic, that all Cretans are liars, that two and two are four, or that nine times six is fifty-six; in all these cases the believing is just the same, and only the contents believed are different. I may remember my breakfast this morning, my lecture last week, or my first sight of New York. In all these cases the feeling of memory-belief is just the same, and only what is remembered differs. Exactly similar remarks apply to expectations. Bare assent, memory and expectation are forms of belief; all three are different from what is believed, and each has a constant character which is independent of what is believed.

In Lecture I we criticized the analysis of a presentation into act, content and object. But our analysis of belief contains three very similar elements, namely the believing, what is believed and the objective. The objections to the act (in the case of presentations) are not valid against the believing in the case of beliefs, because the believing is an actual experienced feeling, not something postulated, like the act. But it is necessary first to complete our preliminary requisites, and then to examine the content of a belief. After that, we shall be in a position to return to the question as to what constitutes believing.

(3) What is believed, and the believing, must both consist of present occurrences in the believer, no matter what may be the objective of the belief. Suppose I believe, for example, "that Caesar crossed the Rubicon." The objective of my belief is an event which happened long ago, which I never saw and do not remember. This event itself is not in my mind when I believe that it happened. It is not correct to say that I am believing the actual event; what I am believing is something now in my mind, something related to the event (in a way which we shall investigate in Lecture XIII), but obviously not to be confounded with the event, since the event is not occurring now but the believing is. What a man is believing at a given moment is wholly determinate if we know the contents of his mind at that moment; but Caesar's crossing of the Rubicon was an historical physical event, which is distinct from the present contents of every present mind. What is believed, however true it may be, is not the actual fact that makes the belief true, but a present event related to the fact. This present event, which is what is believed, I shall call the "content" of the belief. We have already had occasion to notice the distinction between content and objective in the case of memory-beliefs, where the content is "this occurred" and the objective is the past event.

(4) Between content and objective there is sometimes a very wide gulf, for example in the case of "Caesar crossed the Rubicon." This gulf may, when it is first perceived, give us a feeling that we cannot really "know" anything about the outer world. All we can "know," it may be said, is what is now in our thoughts. If Caesar

and the Rubicon cannot be bodily in our thoughts, it might seem as though we must remain cut off from knowledge of them. I shall not now deal at length with this feeling, since it is necessary first to define "knowing," which cannot be done yet. But I will say, as a preliminary answer, that the feeling assumes an ideal of knowing which I believe to be quite mistaken. It assumes, if it is thought out, something like the mystic unity of knower and known. These two are often said to be combined into a unity by the fact of cognition; hence when this unity is plainly absent, it may seem as if there were no genuine cognition. For my part, I think such theories and feelings wholly mistaken: I believe knowing to be a very external and complicated relation, incapable of exact definition, dependent upon causal laws, and involving no more unity than there is between a signpost and the town to which it points. I shall return to this question on a later occasion; for the moment these provisional remarks must suffice.

(5) The objective reference of a belief is connected with the fact that all or some of the constituents of its content have meaning. If I say "Caesar conquered Gaul," a person who knows the meaning of the three words composing my statement knows as much as can be known about the nature of the objective which would make my statement true. It is clear that the objective reference of a belief is, in general, in some way derivative from the meanings of the words or images that occur in its content. There are, however, certain complications which must be borne in mind. In the first place, it might be contended that a memory-image acquires meaning only through the memory-belief, which would seem, at least in the case of memory, to make belief more primitive than the meaning of images. In the second place, it is a very singular thing that meaning, which is single, should generate objective reference, which is dual, namely true and false. This is one of the facts which any theory of belief must explain if it is to be satisfactory.

It is now time to leave these preliminary requisites, and attempt the analysis of the contents of beliefs.

The first thing to notice about what is believed, i.e. about the content of a belief, is that it is always complex: We believe that a certain thing has a certain property, or a certain relation to something else, or that it occurred or will occur (in the sense discussed at the end of Lecture IX); or we may believe that all the members of a certain class have a certain property, or that a certain property sometimes occurs among the members of a class; or we may believe that if one thing happens, another will happen (for example, "if it rains I shall bring my umbrella"), or we may believe that something does not happen, or did not or will not happen (for example, "it won't rain"); or that one of two things must happen (for example, "either you withdraw your accusation, or I shall bring a libel action"). The catalogue of the sorts of things we may believe is infinite, but all of them are complex.

Language sometimes conceals the complexity of a belief. We say that a person believes in God, and it might seem as if God formed the whole content of the belief. But what is really believed is that God exists, which is very far from being simple.

Similarly, when a person has a memory-image with a memory-belief, the belief is "this occurred," in the sense explained in Lecture IX; and "this occurred" is not simple. In like manner all cases where the content of a belief seems simple at first sight will be found, on examination, to confirm the view that the content is always complex.

The content of a belief involves not merely a plurality of constituents, but definite relations between them; it is not determinate when its constituents alone are given. For example, "Plato preceded Aristotle" and "Aristotle preceded Plato" are both contents which may be believed, but, although they consist of exactly the same constituents, they are different, and even incompatible.

The content of a belief may consist of words only, or of images only, or of a mixture of the two, or of either or both together with one or more sensations. It must contain at least one constituent which is a word or an image, and it may or may not contain one or more sensations as constituents. Some examples will make these various possibilities clear.

We may take first recognition, in either of the forms "this is of such-and-such a kind" or "this has occurred before." In either case, present sensation is a constituent. For example, you hear a noise, and you say to yourself "tram." Here the noise and the word "tram" are both constituents of your belief; there is also a relation between them, expressed by "is" in the proposition "that is a tram." As soon as your act of recognition is completed by the occurrence of the word "tram," your actions are affected: you hurry if you want the tram, or cease to hurry if you want a bus. In this case the content of your belief is a sensation (the noise) and a word ("tram") related in a way which may be called predication.

The same noise may bring into your mind the visual image of a tram, instead of the word "tram." In this case your belief consists of a sensation and an image suitable related. Beliefs of this class are what are called "judgments of perception." As we saw in Lecture VIII, the images associated with a sensation often come with such spontaneity and force that the unsophisticated do not distinguish them from the sensation; it is only the psychologist or the skilled observer who is aware of the large mnemic element that is added to sensation to make perception. It may be objected that what is added consists merely of images without belief. This is no doubt sometimes the case, but is certainly sometimes not the case. That belief always occurs in perception as opposed to sensation it is not necessary for us to maintain; it is enough for our purposes to note that it sometimes occurs, and that when it does, the content of our belief consists of a sensation and an image suitably related.

In a PURE memory-belief only images occur. But a mixture of words and images is very common in memory. You have an image of the past occurrence, and you say to yourself: "Yes, that's how it was." Here the image and the words together make up the content of the belief. And when the remembering of an incident has become a habit, it may be purely verbal, and the memory-belief may consist of words alone.

The more complicated forms of belief tend to consist only of words. Often images of various kinds accompany them, but they are apt to be irrelevant, and to form no part of what is actually believed. For example, in thinking of the Solar System, you are likely to have vague images of pictures you have seen of the earth surrounded by clouds, Saturn and his rings, the sun during an eclipse, and so on; but none of these form part of your belief that the planets revolve round the sun in elliptical orbits. The only images that form an actual part of such beliefs are, as a rule, images of words. And images of words, for the reasons considered in Lecture VIII, cannot be distinguished with any certainty from sensations, when, as is often, if not usually, the case, they are kinaesthetic images of pronouncing the words.

It is impossible for a belief to consist of sensations alone, except when, as in the case of words, the sensations have associations which make them signs possessed of meaning. The reason is that objective reference is of the essence of belief, and objective reference is derived from meaning. When I speak of a belief consisting partly of sensations and partly of words, I do not mean to deny that the words, when they are not mere images, are sensational, but that they occur as signs, not (so to speak) in their own right. To revert to the noise of the tram, when you hear it and say "tram," the noise and the word are both sensations (if you actually pronounce the word), but the noise is part of the fact which makes your belief true, whereas the word is not part of this fact. It is the MEANING of the word "tram," not the actual word, that forms part of the fact which is the objective of your belief. Thus the word occurs in the belief as a symbol, in virtue of its meaning, whereas the noise enters into both the belief and its objective. It is this that distinguishes the occurrence of words as symbols from the occurrence of sensations in their own right: the objective contains the sensations that occur in their own right, but contains only the meanings of the words that occur as symbols.

For the sake of simplicity, we may ignore the cases in which sensations in their own right form part of the content of a belief, and confine ourselves to images and words. We may also omit the cases in which both images and words occur in the content of a belief. Thus we become confined to two cases: (a) when the content consists wholly of images, (b) when it consists wholly of words. The case of mixed images and words has no special importance, and its omission will do no harm.

Let us take in illustration a case of memory. Suppose you are thinking of some familiar room. You may call up an image of it, and in your image the window may be to the left of the door. Without any intrusion of words, you may believe in the correctness of your image. You then have a belief, consisting wholly of images, which becomes, when put into words, "the window is to the left of the door." You may yourself use these words and proceed to believe them. You thus pass from an image-content to the corresponding word-content. The content is different in the two cases, but its objective reference is the same. This shows the relation of image-beliefs to word-beliefs in a very simple case. In more elaborate cases the relation becomes much less simple.

It may be said that even in this very simple case the objective reference of the word-content is not quite the same as that of the image-content, that images have a wealth of concrete features which are lost when words are substituted, that the window in the image is not a mere window in the abstract, but a window of a certain shape and size, not merely to the left of the door, but a certain distance to the left, and so on. In reply, it may be admitted at once that there is, as a rule, a certain amount of truth in the objection. But two points may be urged to minimize its force. First, images do not, as a rule, have that wealth of concrete detail that would make it IMPOSSIBLE to express them fully in words. They are vague and fragmentary: a finite number of words, though perhaps a large number, would exhaust at least their SIGNIFICANT features. For—and this is our second point—images enter into the content of a belief through the fact that they are capable of meaning, and their meaning does not, as a rule, have as much complexity as they have: some of their characteristics are usually devoid of meaning. Thus it may well be possible to extract in words all that has meaning in an image-content; in that case the word-content and the image-content will have exactly the same objective reference.

The content of a belief, when expressed in words, is the same thing (or very nearly the same thing) as what in logic is called a "proposition." A proposition is a series of words (or sometimes a single word) expressing the kind of thing that can be asserted or denied. "That all men are mortal," "that Columbus discovered America," "that Charles I died in his bed," "that all philosophers are wise," are propositions. Not any series of words is a proposition, but only such series of words as have "meaning," or, in our phraseology, "objective reference." Given the meanings of separate words, and the rules of syntax, the meaning of a proposition is determinate. This is the reason why we can understand a sentence we never heard before. You probably never heard before the proposition "that the inhabitants of the Andaman Islands habitually eat stewed hippopotamus for dinner," but there is no difficulty in understanding the proposition. The question of the relation between the meaning of a sentence and the meanings of the separate words is difficult, and I shall not pursue it now; I brought it up solely as being illustrative of the nature of propositions.

We may extend the term "proposition" so as to cover the image-contents of beliefs consisting of images. Thus, in the case of remembering a room in which the window is to the left of the door, when we believe the image-content the proposition will consist of the image of the window on the left together with the image of the door on the right. We will distinguish propositions of this kind as "image-propositions" and propositions in words as "word-propositions." We may identify propositions in general with the contents of actual and possible beliefs, and we may say that it is propositions that are true or false. In logic we are concerned with propositions rather than beliefs, since logic is not interested in what people do in fact believe, but only in the conditions which determine the truth or falsehood of possible beliefs. Whenever possible, except when actual beliefs are in question, it is generally a simplification to deal with propositions.

It would seem that image-propositions are more primitive than word-propositions, and may well ante-date language. There is no reason why memory-images, accompanied by that very simple belief-feeling which we decided to be the essence of memory, should not have occurred before language arose; indeed, it would be rash to assert positively that memory of this sort does not occur among the higher animals. Our more elementary beliefs, notably those that are added to sensation to make perception, often remain at the level of images. For example, most of the visual objects in our neighbourhood rouse tactile images: we have a different feeling in looking at a sofa from what we have in looking at a block of marble, and the difference consists chiefly in different stimulation of our tactile imagination. It may be said that the tactile images are merely present, without any accompanying belief; but I think this view, though sometimes correct, derives its plausibility as a general proposition from our thinking of explicit conscious belief only. Most of our beliefs, like most of our wishes, are "unconscious," in the sense that we have never told ourselves that we have them. Such beliefs display themselves when the expectations that they arouse fail in any way. For example, if someone puts tea (without milk) into a glass, and you drink it under the impression that it is going to be beer; or if you walk on what appears to be a tiled floor, and it turns out to be a soft carpet made to look like tiles. The shock of surprise on an occasion of this kind makes us aware of the expectations that habitually enter into our perceptions; and such expectations must be classed as beliefs, in spite of the fact that we do not normally take note of them or put them into words. I remember once watching a cock pigeon running over and over again to the edge of a looking-glass to try to wreak vengeance on the particularly obnoxious bird whom he expected to find there, judging by what he saw in the glass. He must have experienced each time the sort of surprise on finding nothing, which is calculated to lead in time to the adoption of Berkeley's theory that objects of sense are only in the mind. His expectation, though not expressed in words, deserved, I think, to be called a belief.

I come now to the question what constitutes believing, as opposed to the content believed.

To begin with, there are various different attitudes that may be taken towards the same content. Let us suppose, for the sake of argument, that you have a visual image of your breakfast-table. You may expect it while you are dressing in the morning; remember it as you go to your work; feel doubt as to its correctness when questioned as to your powers of visualizing; merely entertain the image, without connecting it with anything external, when you are going to sleep; desire it if you are hungry, or feel aversion for it if you are ill. Suppose, for the sake of definiteness, that the content is "an egg for breakfast." Then you have the following attitudes "I expect there will be an egg for breakfast"; "I remember there was an egg for breakfast"; "Was there an egg for breakfast?" "An egg for breakfast: well, what of it?" "I hope there will be an egg for breakfast"; "I am afraid there will be an egg for breakfast and it is sure to be bad." I do not suggest that this is a list of all possible attitudes on the subject; I say only that they are different attitudes, all concerned with the one content "an egg for breakfast."

These attitudes are not all equally ultimate. Those that involve desire and aversion have occupied us in Lecture III. For the present, we are only concerned with such as are cognitive. In speaking of memory, we distinguished three kinds of belief directed towards the same content, namely memory, expectation and bare assent without any time-determination in the belief-feeling. But before developing this view, we must examine two other theories which might be held concerning belief, and which, in some ways, would be more in harmony with a behaviourist outlook than the theory I wish to advocate.

(1) The first theory to be examined is the view that the differentia of belief consists in its causal efficacy I do not wish to make any author responsible for this theory: I wish merely to develop it hypothetically so that we may judge of its tenability.

We defined the meaning of an image or word by causal efficacy, namely by associations: an image or word acquires meaning, we said, through having the same associations as what it means.

We propose hypothetically to define "belief" by a different kind of causal efficacy, namely efficacy in causing voluntary movements. (Voluntary movements are defined as those vital movements which are distinguished from reflex movements as involving the higher nervous centres. I do not like to distinguish them by means of such notions as "consciousness" or "will," because I do not think these notions, in any definable sense, are always applicable. Moreover, the purpose of the theory we are examining is to be, as far as possible, physiological and behaviourist, and this purpose is not achieved if we introduce such a conception as "consciousness" or "will." Nevertheless, it is necessary for our purpose to find some way of distinguishing between voluntary and reflex movements, since the results would be too paradoxical, if we were to say that reflex movements also involve beliefs.) According to this definition, a content is said to be "believed" when it causes us to move. The images aroused are the same if you say to me, "Suppose there were an escaped tiger coming along the street," and if you say to me, "There is an escaped tiger coming along the street." But my actions will be very different in the two cases: in the first, I shall remain calm; in the second, it is possible that I may not. It is suggested, by the theory we are considering, that this difference of effects constitutes what is meant by saying that in the second case I believe the proposition suggested, while in the first case I do not. According to this view, images or words are "believed" when they cause bodily movements.

I do not think this theory is adequate, but I think it is suggestive of truth, and not so easily refutable as it might appear to be at first sight.

It might be objected to the theory that many things which we certainly believe do not call for any bodily movements. I believe that Great Britain is an island, that whales are mammals, that Charles I was executed, and so on; and at first sight it seems obvious that such beliefs, as a rule, do not call for any action on my part. But when we investigate the matter more closely, it becomes more doubtful. To begin with, we must distinguish belief as a mere DISPOSITION from actual active belief. We speak as if we always believed that Charles I was executed, but that only means that we are always ready to believe it when the subject comes up. The phenomenon we are concerned to analyse is the active belief, not the permanent disposition. Now, what are the occasions when, we actively believe that Charles I was executed? Primarily: examinations, when we perform the bodily movement of writing it down; conversation, when we assert it to display our historical erudition; and political discourses, when we are engaged in showing what Soviet government leads to. In all these cases bodily movements (writing or speaking) result from our belief.

But there remains the belief which merely occurs in "thinking." One may set to work to recall some piece of history one has been reading, and what one recalls is believed, although it probably does not cause any bodily movement whatever. It is true that what we believe always MAY influence action. Suppose I am invited to become King of Georgia: I find the prospect attractive, and go to Cook's to buy a third-class ticket to my new realm. At the last moment I remember Charles I and all the other monarchs who have come to a bad end; I change my mind, and walk out without completing the transaction. But such incidents are rare, and cannot constitute the whole of my belief that Charles I was executed. The conclusion seems to be that, although a belief always MAY influence action if it becomes relevant to a practical issue, it often exists actively (not as a mere disposition) without producing any voluntary movement whatever. If this is true, we cannot define belief by the effect on voluntary movements.

There is another, more theoretical, ground for rejecting the view we are examining. It is clear that a proposition can be either believed or merely considered, and that the content is the same in both cases. We can expect an egg for breakfast, or merely entertain the supposition that there may be an egg for breakfast. A moment ago I considered the possibility of being invited to become King of Georgia, but I do not believe that this will happen. Now, it seems clear that, since believing and considering have different effects if one produces bodily movements while the other does not, there must be some intrinsic difference between believing and considering[54]; for if they were precisely similar, their effects also would be precisely similar. We have seen that the difference between believing a given proposition and merely considering it does not lie in the content; therefore there must be, in one case or in both, something additional to the content which distinguishes the occurrence of a belief from the occurrence of a mere consideration of the same content. So far as the theoretical argument goes, this additional element may exist only in belief, or only in consideration, or there may be one sort of additional element in the case of belief,

---

[54] Cf. Brentano, *Psychologie vom empirischen Standpunkte*, p. 268 (criticizing Bain, *The Emotions and the Will*).

and another in the case of consideration. This brings us to the second view which we have to examine.

(1) The theory which we have now to consider regards belief as belonging to every idea which is entertained, except in so far as some positive counteracting force interferes. In this view belief is not a positive phenomenon, though doubt and disbelief are so. What we call belief, according to this hypothesis, involves only the appropriate content, which will have the effects characteristic of belief unless something else operating simultaneously inhibits them. James (Psychology, vol. ii, p. 288) quotes with approval, though inaccurately, a passage from Spinoza embodying this view:

"Let us conceive a boy imagining to himself a horse, and taking note of nothing else. As this imagination involves the existence of the horse, AND THE BOY HAS NO PERCEPTION WHICH ANNULS ITS EXISTENCE [James's italics], he will necessarily contemplate the horse as present, nor will he be able to doubt of its existence, however little certain of it he may be. I deny that a man in so far as he imagines [percipit] affirms nothing. For what is it to imagine a winged horse but to affirm that the horse [that horse, namely] has wings? For if the mind had nothing before it but the winged horse, it would contemplate the same as present, would have no cause to doubt of its existence, nor any power of dissenting from its existence, unless the imagination of the winged horse were joined to an idea which contradicted [tollit] its existence" ("Ethics," vol. ii, p. 49, Scholium).

To this doctrine James entirely assents, adding in italics:

*"Any object which remains uncontradicted is ipso facto believed and posited as absolute reality."*

If this view is correct, it follows (though James does not draw the inference) that there is no need of any specific feeling called "belief," and that the mere existence of images yields all that is required. The state of mind in which we merely consider a proposition, without believing or disbelieving it, will then appear as a sophisticated product, the result of some rival force adding to the image-proposition a positive feeling which may be called suspense or non-belief—a feeling which may be compared to that of a man about to run a race waiting for the signal. Such a man, though not moving, is in a very different condition from that of a man quietly at rest And so the man who is considering a proposition without believing it will be in a state of tension, restraining the natural tendency to act upon the proposition which he would display if nothing interfered. In this view belief primarily consists merely in the existence of the appropriate images without any counteracting forces.

There is a great deal to be said in favour of this view, and I have some hesitation in regarding it as inadequate. It fits admirably with the phenomena of dreams and hallucinatory images, and it is recommended by the way in which it accords with mental development. Doubt, suspense of judgment and disbelief all seem later and more complex than a wholly unreflecting assent. Belief as a positive phenomenon, if it exists, may be regarded, in this view, as a product of doubt, a decision after debate, an acceptance, not merely of THIS, but of THIS-RATHER-THAN-THAT. It is not difficult to suppose that a dog has images (possible olfactory) of his absent master, or of the rabbit that he dreams of hunting. But it is very difficult to suppose that he can entertain mere imagination-images to which no assent is given.

I think it must be conceded that a mere image, without the addition of any positive feeling that could be called "belief," is apt to have a certain dynamic power, and in this sense an uncombated image has the force of a belief. But although this may be true, it accounts only for some of the simplest phenomena in the region of belief. It will not, for example, explain memory. Nor can it explain beliefs which do not issue in any proximate action, such as those of mathematics. I conclude, therefore, that there must be belief-feelings of the same order as those of doubt or disbelief, although phenomena closely analogous to those of belief can be produced by mere uncontradicted images.

(3) I come now to the view of belief which I wish to advocate. It seems to me that there are at least three kinds of belief, namely memory, expectation and bare assent. Each of these I regard as constituted by a certain feeling or complex of sensations, attached to the content believed. We may illustrate by an example. Suppose I am believing, by means of images, not words, that it will rain. We have here two interrelated elements, namely the content and the expectation. The content consists of images of (say) the visual appearance of rain, the feeling of wetness, the patter of drops, interrelated, roughly, as the sensations would be if it were raining. Thus the content is a complex fact composed of images. Exactly the same content may enter into the memory "it was raining" or the assent "rain occurs." The difference of these cases from each other and from expectation does not lie in the content. The difference lies in the nature of the belief-feeling. I, personally, do not profess to be able to analyse the sensations constituting respectively memory, expectation and assent; but I am not prepared to say that they cannot be analysed. There may be other belief-feelings, for example in disjunction and implication; also a disbelief-feeling.

It is not enough that the content and the belief-feeling should coexist: it is necessary that there should be a specific relation between them, of the sort expressed by saying that the content is what is believed. If this were not obvious, it could be made plain by an argument. If the mere co-existence of the content and the belief-feeling sufficed, whenever we were having (say) a memory-feeling we should be remembering any proposition which came into our minds at the same time. But this is not the case, since we may simultaneously remember one proposition and merely consider another.

We may sum up our analysis, in the case of bare assent to a proposition not expressed in words, as follows: (a) We have a proposition, consisting of interrelated images, and possibly partly of sensations; (b) we have the feeling of assent, which is presumably a complex sensation demanding analysis; (c) we have a relation, actually subsisting, between the assent and the proposition, such as is expressed by saying that the proposition in question is what is assented to. For other forms of belief-feeling or of content, we have only to make the necessary substitutions in this analysis.

If we are right in our analysis of belief, the use of words in expressing beliefs is apt to be misleading. There is no way of distinguishing, in words, between a memory and an assent to a proposition about the past: "I ate my breakfast" and "Caesar conquered Gaul" have the same verbal form, though (assuming that I remember my breakfast) they express occurrences which are psychologically very different. In the one case, what happens is that I remember the content "eating my breakfast"; in the other case, I assent to the content "Caesar's conquest of Gaul occurred." In the latter case, but not in the former, the pastness is part of the content believed. Exactly similar remarks apply to the difference between expectation, such as we have when waiting for the thunder after a flash of lightning, and assent to a proposition about the future, such as we have in all the usual cases of inferential knowledge as to what will occur. I think this difficulty in the verbal expression of the temporal aspects of beliefs is one among the causes which have hampered philosophy in the consideration of time.

The view of belief which I have been advocating contains little that is novel except the distinction of kinds of belief-feeling—such as memory and expectation. Thus James says: "Everyone knows the difference between imagining a thing and believing in its existence, between supposing a proposition and acquiescing in its truth...IN ITS INNER NATURE, BELIEF, OR THE SENSE OF REALITY, IS A SORT OF FEELING MORE ALLIED TO THE EMOTIONS THAN TO ANYTHING ELSE" ("Psychology," vol. ii, p. 283. James's italics). He proceeds to point out that drunkenness, and, still more, nitrous-oxide intoxication, will heighten the sense of belief: in the latter case, he says, a man's very soul may sweat with conviction, and he be all the time utterly unable to say what he is convinced of. It would seem that, in such cases, the feeling of belief exists unattached, without its usual relation to a content believed, just as the feeling of familiarity may sometimes occur without being related to any definite familiar object. The feeling of belief, when it occurs in this separated heightened form, generally leads us to look for a content to which to attach it. Much of what passes for revelation or mystic insight probably comes in this way: the belief-feeling, in abnormal strength, attaches itself, more or less accidentally, to some content which we happen to think of at the appropriate moment. But this is only a speculation, upon which I do not wish to lay too much stress.

# LECTURE XIII

## Truth and Falsehood

The definition of truth and falsehood, which is our topic to-day, lies strictly outside our general subject, namely the analysis of mind. From the psychological standpoint, there may be different kinds of belief, and different degrees of certainty, but there cannot be any purely psychological means of distinguishing between true and false beliefs. A belief is rendered true or false by relation to a fact, which may lie outside the experience of the person entertaining the belief. Truth and falsehood, except in the case of beliefs about our own minds, depend upon the relations of mental occurrences to outside things, and thus take us beyond the analysis of mental occurrences as they are in themselves. Nevertheless, we can hardly avoid the consideration of truth and falsehood. We wish to believe that our beliefs, sometimes at least, yield KNOWLEDGE, and a belief does not yield knowledge unless it is true. The question whether our minds are instruments of knowledge, and, if so, in what sense, is so vital that any suggested analysis of mind must be examined in relation to this question. To ignore this question would be like describing a chronometer without regard to its accuracy as a time-keeper, or a thermometer without mentioning the fact that it measures temperature.

Many difficult questions arise in connection with knowledge. It is difficult to define knowledge, difficult to decide whether we have any knowledge, and difficult, even if it is conceded that we sometimes have knowledge to discover whether we can ever know that we have knowledge in this or that particular case. I shall divide the discussion into four parts:

I. We may regard knowledge, from a behaviourist standpoint, as exhibited in a certain kind of response to the environment. This response must have some characteristics which it shares with those of scientific instruments, but must also have others that are peculiar to knowledge. We shall find that this point of view is important, but not exhaustive of the nature of knowledge.

II. We may hold that the beliefs that constitute knowledge are distinguished from such as are erroneous or uncertain by properties which are intrinsic either to single beliefs or to systems of beliefs, being in either case discoverable without reference to outside fact. Views of this kind have been widely held among philosophers, but we shall find no reason to accept them.

221

III. We believe that some beliefs are true, and some false. This raises the problem of VERIFIABILITY: are there any circumstances which can justifiably give us an unusual degree of certainty that such and such a belief is true? It is obvious that there are circumstances which in fact cause a certainty of this sort, and we wish to learn what we can from examining these circumstances.

IV. Finally, there is the formal problem of defining truth and falsehood, and deriving the objective reference of a proposition from the meanings of its component words.

We will consider these four problems in succession.

I. We may regard a human being as an instrument, which makes various responses to various stimuli. If we observe these responses from outside, we shall regard them as showing knowledge when they display two characteristics, ACCURACY and APPROPRIATENESS. These two are quite distinct, and even sometimes incompatible. If I am being pursued by a tiger, accuracy is furthered by turning round to look at him, but appropriateness by running away without making any search for further knowledge of the beast. I shall return to the question of appropriateness later; for the present it is accuracy that I wish to consider.

When we are viewing a man from the outside, it is not his beliefs, but his bodily movements, that we can observe. His knowledge must be inferred from his bodily movements, and especially from what he says and writes. For the present we may ignore beliefs, and regard a man's knowledge as actually consisting in what he says and does. That is to say, we will construct, as far as possible, a purely behaviouristic account of truth and falsehood.

If you ask a boy "What is twice two?" and the boy says "four," you take that as prima facie evidence that the boy knows what twice two is. But if you go on to ask what is twice three, twice four, twice five, and so on, and the boy always answers "four," you come to the conclusion that he knows nothing about it. Exactly similar remarks apply to scientific instruments. I know a certain weather-cock which has the pessimistic habit of always pointing to the north-east. If you were to see it first on a cold March day, you would think it an excellent weather-cock; but with the first warm day of spring your confidence would be shaken. The boy and the weather-cock have the same defect: they do not vary their response when the stimulus is varied. A good instrument, or a person with much knowledge, will give different responses to stimuli which differ in relevant ways. This is the first point in defining accuracy of response.

We will now assume another boy, who also, when you first question him, asserts that twice two is four. But with this boy, instead of asking him different questions, you make a practice of asking him the same question every day at breakfast. You find that he says five, or six, or seven, or any other number at random, and you conclude that he also does not know what twice two is, though by good luck he answered right the first time. This boy is like a weather-cock which, instead of being stuck fast, is always going round and round, changing without any change of wind. This boy and weather-cock have the opposite defect to that of the previous pair: they give different responses to stimuli which do not differ in any relevant way.

In connection with vagueness in memory, we already had occasion to consider the definition of accuracy. Omitting some of the niceties of our previous discussion, we may say that an instrument is ACCURATE when it avoids the defects of the two boys and weather-cocks, that is to say, when—

(a)  It gives different responses to stimuli which differ in relevant ways;
(b)  It gives the same response to stimuli which do not differ in relevant ways.

What are relevant ways depends upon the nature and purpose of the instrument. In the case of a weather-cock, the direction of the wind is relevant, but not its strength; in the case of the boy, the meaning of the words of your question is relevant, but not the loudness of your voice, or whether you are his father or his schoolmaster If, however, you were a boy of his own age, that would be relevant, and the appropriate response would be different.

It is clear that knowledge is displayed by accuracy of response to certain kinds of stimuli, e.g. examinations. Can we say, conversely, that it consists wholly of such accuracy of response? I do not think we can; but we can go a certain distance in this direction. For this purpose we must define more carefully the kind of accuracy and the kind of response that may be expected where there is knowledge.

From our present point of view, it is difficult to exclude perception from knowledge; at any rate, knowledge is displayed by actions based upon perception. A bird flying among trees avoids bumping into their branches; its avoidance is a response to visual sensations. This response has the characteristic of accuracy, in the main, and leads us to say that the bird "knows," by sight, what objects are in its neighbourhood. For a behaviourist, this must certainly count as knowledge, however it may be viewed by analytic psychology. In this case, what is known, roughly, is the stimulus; but in more advanced knowledge the stimulus and what is known become different. For example, you look in your calendar and find that Easter will be early next year. Here the stimulus is the calendar, whereas the response concerns the future. Even this can be paralleled among instruments: the behaviour of the barometer has a present stimulus but foretells the future, so that the barometer might be said, in a sense, to know the future. However that may be, the point I am emphasizing as regards knowledge is that what is known may be quite different from the stimulus, and no part of the cause of the knowledge-response. It is only in sense-knowledge that the stimulus and what is known are, with qualifications, identifiable. In knowledge of the future, it is obvious that they are totally distinct, since otherwise the response would precede the stimulus. In abstract knowledge also they are distinct, since abstract facts have no date. In knowledge of the past there are complications, which we must briefly examine.

Every form of memory will be, from our present point of view, in one sense a delayed response. But this phrase does not quite clearly express what is meant. If you light a fuse and connect it with a heap of dynamite, the explosion of the dynamite may be spoken of, in a sense, as a delayed response to your lighting of the fuse. But that only means that it is a somewhat late portion of a continuous process of which the earlier parts have less emotional interest. This is not the case with habit. A display of habit has two sorts of causes: (a) the past occurrences which generated the habit, (b) the present occurrence which brings it into play. When you drop a weight on your toe, and say what you do say, the habit has been caused by imitation of your undesirable associates, whereas it is brought into play by the dropping of the weight. The great bulk of our knowledge is a habit in this sense: whenever I am asked when I was born, I reply correctly by mere habit. It would hardly be correct to say that getting born was the stimulus, and that my reply is a delayed response But in cases of memory this way of speaking would have an element of truth. In an habitual memory, the event remembered was clearly an essential part of the stimulus to the formation of the habit. The present stimulus which brings the habit into play produces a different response from that which it would produce if the habit did not exist. Therefore the habit enters into the causation of the response, and so do, at one remove, the causes of the habit. It follows that an event remembered is an essential part of the causes of our remembering.

In spite, however, of the fact that what is known is SOMETIMES an indispensable part of the cause of the knowledge, this circumstance is, I think, irrelevant to the general question with which we are concerned, namely What sort of response to what sort of stimulus can be regarded as displaying knowledge? There is one characteristic which the response must have, namely, it must consist of voluntary movements. The need of this characteristic is connected with the characteristic of APPROPRIATENESS, which I do not wish to consider as yet. For the present I wish only to obtain a clearer idea of the sort of ACCURACY that a knowledge-response must have. It is clear from many instances that accuracy, in other cases, may be purely mechanical. The most complete form of accuracy consists in giving correct answers to questions, an achievement in which calculating machines far surpass human beings. In asking a question of a calculating machine, you must use its language: you must not address it in English, any more than you would address an Englishman in Chinese. But if you address it in the language it understands, it will tell you what is 34521 times 19987, without a moment's hesitation or a hint of inaccuracy. We do not say the machine KNOWS the answer, because it has no purpose of its own in giving the answer: it does not wish to impress you with its cleverness, or feel proud of being such a good machine. But as far as mere accuracy goes, the machine leaves nothing to be desired.

Accuracy of response is a perfectly clear notion in the case of answers to questions, but in other cases it is much more obscure. We may say generally that an object whether animate or inanimate, is "sensitive" to a certain feature of the environment if it behaves differently according to the presence or absence of that feature. Thus iron is sensitive to anything magnetic. But sensitiveness does not constitute knowledge, and knowledge of a fact which is not sensible is not sensitiveness to that fact, as we have seen in distinguishing the fact known from the stimulus. As soon as we pass beyond the simple case of question and answer, the definition of knowledge by means of behaviour demands the consideration of purpose. A carrier pigeon flies home, and so we say it "knows" the way. But if it merely flew to some place at random, we should not say that it "knew" the way to that place, any more than a stone rolling down hill knows the way to the valley.

On the features which distinguish knowledge from accuracy of response in general, not much can be said from a behaviourist point of view without referring to purpose. But the necessity of SOMETHING besides accuracy of response may be brought out by the following consideration: Suppose two persons, of whom one believed whatever the other disbelieved, and disbelieved whatever the other believed. So far as accuracy and sensitiveness of response alone are concerned, there would be nothing to choose between these two persons. A thermometer which went down for warm weather and up for cold might be just as accurate as the usual kind; and a person who always believes falsely is just as sensitive an instrument as a person who always believes truly. The observable and practical difference between them would be that the one who always believed falsely would quickly come to a bad end. This illustrates once more that accuracy of response to stimulus does not alone show knowledge, but must be reinforced by appropriateness, i.e. suitability for realizing one's purpose. This applies even in the apparently simple case of answering questions: if the purpose of the answers is to deceive, their falsehood, not their truth, will be evidence of knowledge. The proportion of the combination of appropriateness with accuracy in the definition of knowledge is difficult; it seems that both enter in, but that appropriateness is only required as regards the general type of response, not as regards each individual instance.

II. I have so far assumed as unquestionable the view that the truth or falsehood of a belief consists in a relation to a certain fact, namely the objective of the belief. This view has, however, been often questioned. Philosophers have sought some intrinsic criterion by which true and false beliefs could be distinguished.[55] I am afraid their chief reason for this search has been the wish to feel more certainty than seems otherwise possible as to what is true and what is false. If we could discover the

---

[55] The view that such a criterion exists is generally held by those whose views are in any degree derived from Hegel. It may be illustrated by the following passage from Lossky, *The Intuitive Basis of Knowledge* (Macmillan, 1919), p. 268: "Strictly speaking, a false judgment is not a judgment at all. The predicate does not follow from the subject S alone, but from the subject plus a certain addition C, *which in no sense belongs to the content of the judgment*. What takes place may be a process of association of ideas, of imagining, or the like, but is not a process of judging. An experienced psychologist will be able by careful observation to detect that in this process there is wanting just the specific element of the objective dependence of the predicate upon the subject which is characteristic of a judgment. It must be admitted, however, that an exceptional power of observation is needed in order to distinguish, by means of introspection, mere combination of ideas from judgments."

truth of a belief by examining its intrinsic characteristics, or those of some collection of beliefs of which it forms part, the pursuit of truth, it is thought, would be a less arduous business than it otherwise appears to be. But the attempts which have been made in this direction are not encouraging. I will take two criteria which have been suggested, namely, (1) self-evidence, (2) mutual coherence. If we can show that these are inadequate, we may feel fairly certain that no intrinsic criterion hitherto suggested will suffice to distinguish true from false beliefs.

(1) Self-evidence.—Some of our beliefs seem to be peculiarly indubitable. One might instance the belief that two and two are four, that two things cannot be in the same place at the same time, nor one thing in two places, or that a particular buttercup that we are seeing is yellow. The suggestion we are to examine is that such: beliefs have some recognizable quality which secures their truth, and the truth of whatever is deduced from them according to self-evident principles of inference. This theory is set forth, for example, by Meinong in his book, "Ueber die Erfahrungsgrundlagen unseres Wissens."

If this theory is to be logically tenable, self-evidence must not consist merely in the fact that we believe a proposition. We believe that our beliefs are sometimes erroneous, and we wish to be able to select a certain class of beliefs which are never erroneous. If we are to do this, it must be by some mark which belongs only to certain beliefs, not to all; and among those to which it belongs there must be none that are mutually inconsistent. If, for example, two propositions p and q were self-evident, and it were also self-evident that p and q could not both be true, that would condemn self-evidence as a guarantee of truth. Again, self-evidence must not be the same thing as the absence of doubt or the presence of complete certainty. If we are completely certain of a proposition, we do not seek a ground to support our belief. If self-evidence is alleged as a ground of belief, that implies that doubt has crept in, and that our self-evident proposition has not wholly resisted the assaults of scepticism. To say that any given person believes some things so firmly that he cannot be made to doubt them is no doubt true. Such beliefs he will be willing to use as premises in reasoning, and to him personally they will seem to have as much evidence as any belief can need. But among the propositions which one man finds indubitable there will be some that another man finds it quite possible to doubt. It used to seem self-evident that there could not be men at the Antipodes, because they would fall off, or at best grow giddy from standing on their heads. But New Zealanders find the falsehood of this proposition self-evident. Therefore, if self-evidence is a guarantee of truth, our ancestors must have been mistaken in thinking their beliefs about the Antipodes self-evident. Meinong meets this difficulty by saying that some beliefs are falsely thought to be self-evident, but in the case of others it is self-evident that they are self-evident, and these are wholly reliable. Even this, however, does not remove the practical risk of error, since we may mistakenly believe it self-evident that a certain belief is self-evident. To remove all risk of error, we shall need an endless series of more and more complicated self-evident beliefs, which cannot possibly be realized in practice. It would seem, therefore, that self-evidence is useless as a practical criterion for insuring truth.

The same result follows from examining instances. If we take the four instances mentioned at the beginning of this discussion, we shall find that three of them are logical, while the fourth is a judgment of perception. The proposition that two and two are four follows by purely logical deduction from definitions: that means that its truth results, not from the properties of objects, but from the meanings of symbols. Now symbols, in mathematics, mean what we choose; thus the feeling of self-evidence, in this case, seems explicable by the fact that the whole matter is within our control. I do not wish to assert that this is the whole truth about mathematical propositions, for the question is complicated, and I do not know what the whole truth is. But I do wish to suggest that the feeling of self-evidence in mathematical propositions has to do with the fact that they are concerned with the meanings of symbols, not with properties of the world such as external observation might reveal.

Similar considerations apply to the impossibility of a thing being in two places at once, or of two things being in one place at the same time. These impossibilities result logically, if I am not mistaken, from the definitions of one thing and one place. That is to say, they are not laws of physics, but only part of the intellectual apparatus which we have manufactured for manipulating physics. Their self-evidence, if this is so, lies merely in the fact that they represent our decision as to the use of words, not a property of physical objects.

Judgments of perception, such as "this buttercup is yellow," are in a quite different position from judgments of logic, and their self-evidence must have a different explanation. In order to arrive at the nucleus of such a judgment, we will eliminate, as far as possible, the use of words which take us beyond the present fact, such as "buttercup" and "yellow." The simplest kind of judgment underlying the perception that a buttercup is yellow would seem to be the perception of similarity in two colours seen simultaneously. Suppose we are seeing two buttercups, and we perceive that their colours are similar. This similarity is a physical fact, not a matter of symbols or words; and it certainly seems to be indubitable in a way that many judgments are not.

The first thing to observe, in regard to such judgments, is that as they stand they are vague. The word "similar" is a vague word, since there are degrees of similarity, and no one can say where similarity ends and dissimilarity begins. It is unlikely that our two buttercups have EXACTLY the same colour, and if we judged that they had we should have passed altogether outside the region of self-evidence. To make our proposition more precise, let us suppose that we are also seeing a red rose at the same time. Then we may judge that the colours of the buttercups are more similar to each other than to the colour of the rose. This judgment seems more complicated, but has certainly gained in precision. Even now, however, it falls short of complete precision, since similarity is not prima facie measurable, and it would require much discussion to decide what we mean by greater or less similarity. To this process of the pursuit of precision there is strictly no limit.

The next thing to observe (although I do not personally doubt that most of our judgments of perception are true) is that it is very difficult to define any class of such judgments which can be known, by its intrinsic quality, to be always exempt from error. Most of our judgments of perception involve correlations, as when we judge that a certain noise is that of a passing cart. Such judgments are all obviously liable to error, since there is no correlation of which we have a right to be certain that it is invariable. Other judgments of perception are derived from recognition, as when we say "this is a buttercup," or even merely "this is yellow." All such judgments entail some risk of error, though sometimes perhaps a very small one; some flowers that look like buttercups are marigolds, and colours that some would call yellow others might call orange. Our subjective certainty is usually a result of habit, and may lead us astray in circumstances which are unusual in ways of which we are unaware.

For such reasons, no form of self-evidence seems to afford an absolute criterion of truth. Nevertheless, it is perhaps true that judgments having a high degree of subjective certainty are more apt to be true than other judgments. But if this be the case, it is a result to be demonstrated, not a premiss from which to start in defining truth and falsehood. As an initial guarantee, therefore, neither self-evidence nor subjective certainty can be accepted as adequate.

(2) Coherence.—Coherence as the definition of truth is advocated by idealists, particularly by those who in the main follow Hegel. It is set forth ably in Mr. Joachim's book, "The Nature of Truth" (Oxford, 1906). According to this view, any set of propositions other than the whole of truth can be condemned on purely logical grounds, as internally inconsistent; a single proposition, if it is what we should ordinarily call false, contradicts itself irremediably, while if it is what we should ordinarily call true, it has implications which compel us to admit other propositions, which in turn lead to others, and so on, until we find ourselves committed to the whole of truth. One might illustrate by a very simple example: if I say "so-and-so is a married man," that is not a self-subsistent proposition. We cannot logically conceive of a universe in which this proposition constituted the whole of truth. There must be also someone who is a married woman, and who is married to the particular man in question. The view we are considering regards everything that can be said about any one object as relative in the same sort of way as "so-and-so is a married man." But everything, according to this view, is relative, not to one or two other things, but to all other things, so that from one bit of truth the whole can be inferred.

The fundamental objection to this view is logical, and consists in a criticism of its doctrine as to relations. I shall omit this line of argument, which I have developed elsewhere.[56] For the moment I will content myself with saying that the powers of logic seem to me very much less than this theory supposes. If it were taken seriously, its advocates ought to profess that any one truth is logically inferable from any other, and that, for example, the fact that Caesar conquered Gaul, if adequately considered, would enable us to discover what the weather will be to-morrow. No such claim is put forward in practice, and the necessity of empirical observation is not denied; but according to the theory it ought to be.

Another objection is that no endeavour is made to show that we cannot form a consistent whole composed partly or wholly of false propositions, as in a novel. Leibniz's conception of many possible worlds seems to accord much better with modern logic and with the practical empiricism which is now universal. The attempt to deduce the world by pure thought is attractive, and in former times was largely supposed capable of success. But nowadays most men admit that beliefs must be tested by observation, and not merely by the fact that they harmonize with other beliefs. A consistent fairy-tale is a different thing from truth, however elaborate it may be. But to pursue this topic would lead us into difficult technicalities; I shall therefore assume, without further argument, that coherence is not sufficient as a definition of truth.

III. Many difficult problems arise as regards the verifiability of beliefs. We believe various things, and while we believe them we think we know them. But it sometimes turns out that we were mistaken, or at any rate we come to think we were. We must be mistaken either in our previous opinion or in our subsequent recantation; therefore our beliefs are not all correct, and there are cases of belief which are not cases of knowledge. The question of verifiability is in essence this: can we discover any set of beliefs which are never mistaken or any test which, when applicable, will always enable us to discriminate between true and false beliefs? Put thus broadly and abstractly, the answer must be negative. There is no way hitherto discovered of wholly eliminating the risk of error, and no infallible criterion. If we believe we have found a criterion, this belief itself may be mistaken; we should be begging the question if we tried to test the criterion by applying the criterion to itself.

But although the notion of an absolute criterion is chimerical, there may be relative criteria, which increase the probability of truth. Common sense and science hold that there are. Let us see what they have to say.

One of the plainest cases of verification, perhaps ultimately the only case, consists in the happening of something expected. You go to the station believing that there will be a train at a certain time; you find the train, you get into it, and it starts at the expected time This constitutes verification, and is a perfectly definite experience. It is, in a sense, the converse of memory instead of having first sensations and then images accompanied by belief, we have first images accompanied by belief and

---

[56] In the article on "The Monistic Theory of Truth" in *Philosophical Essays* (Longmans, 1910), reprinted from the "Proceedings of the Aristotelian Society," 1906-7.

then sensations. Apart from differences as to the time-order and the accompanying feelings, the relation between image and sensation is closely similar in the two cases of memory and expectation; it is a relation of similarity, with difference as to causal efficacy—broadly, the image has the psychological but not the physical effects that the sensation would have. When an image accompanied by an expectation-belief is thus succeeded by a sensation which is the "meaning" of the image, we say that the expectation-belief has been verified. The experience of verification in this sense is exceedingly familiar; it happens every time that accustomed activities have results that are not surprising, in eating and walking and talking and all our daily pursuits.

But although the experience in question is common, it is not wholly easy to give a theoretical account of it. How do we know that the sensation resembles the previous image? Does the image persist in presence of the sensation, so that we can compare the two? And even if SOME image does persist, how do we know that it is the previous image unchanged? It does not seem as if this line of inquiry offered much hope of a successful issue. It is better, I think, to take a more external and causal view of the relation of expectation to expected occurrence. If the occurrence, when it comes, gives us the feeling of expectedness, and if the expectation, beforehand, enabled us to act in a way which proves appropriate to the occurrence, that must be held to constitute the maximum of verification. We have first an expectation, then a sensation with the feeling of expectedness related to memory of the expectation. This whole experience, when it occurs, may be defined as verification, and as constituting the truth of the expectation. Appropriate action, during the period of expectation, may be regarded as additional verification, but is not essential. The whole process may be illustrated by looking up a familiar quotation, finding it in the expected words, and in the expected part of the book. In this case we can strengthen the verification by writing down beforehand the words which we expect to find.

I think all verification is ultimately of the above sort. We verify a scientific hypothesis indirectly, by deducing consequences as to the future, which subsequent experience confirms. If somebody were to doubt whether Caesar had crossed the Rubicon, verification could only be obtained from the future. We could proceed to display manuscripts to our historical sceptic, in which it was said that Caesar had behaved in this way. We could advance arguments, verifiable by future experience, to prove the antiquity of the manuscript from its texture, colour, etc. We could find inscriptions agreeing with the historian on other points, and tending to show his general accuracy. The causal laws which our arguments would assume could be verified by the future occurrence of events inferred by means of them. The existence and persistence of causal laws, it is true, must be regarded as a fortunate accident, and how long it will continue we cannot tell. Meanwhile verification remains often practically possible. And since it is sometimes possible, we can gradually discover what kinds of beliefs tend to be verified by experience, and what kinds tend to be falsified; to the former kinds we give an increased degree of assent, to the latter kinds a diminished degree. The process is not absolute or infallible, but it has been found capable of sifting beliefs and building up science. It affords no theoretical refutation of the sceptic, whose position must remain logically unassailable; but if complete scepticism is rejected, it gives the practical method by which the system of our beliefs grows gradually towards the unattainable ideal of impeccable knowledge.

IV. I come now to the purely formal definition of the truth or falsehood of a belief. For this definition it is necessary first of all to consider the derivation of the objective reference of a proposition from the meanings of its component words or images.

Just as a word has meaning, so a proposition has an objective reference. The objective reference of a proposition is a function (in the mathematical sense) of the meanings of its component words. But the objective reference differs from the meaning of a word through the duality of truth and falsehood. You may believe the proposition "to-day is Tuesday" both when, in fact, to-day is Tuesday, and when to-day is not Tuesday. If to-day is not Tuesday, this fact is the objective of your belief that to-day is Tuesday. But obviously the relation of your belief to the fact is different in this case from what it is in the case when to-day is Tuesday. We may say, metaphorically, that when to-day is Tuesday, your belief that it is Tuesday points TOWARDS the fact, whereas when to-day not Tuesday your belief points AWAY FROM the fact. Thus the objective reference of a belief is not determined by the fact alone, but by the direction of the belief towards or away from the fact.[57] If, on a Tuesday, one man believes that it is Tuesday while another believes that it is not Tuesday, their beliefs have the same objective, namely the fact that it is Tuesday but the true belief points towards the fact while the false one points away from it. Thus, in order to define the reference of a proposition we have to take account not only of the objective, but also of the direction of pointing, towards the objective in the case of a true proposition and away from it in the case of a false one.

This mode of stating the nature of the objective reference of a proposition is necessitated by the circumstance that there are true and false propositions, but not true and false facts. If to-day is Tuesday, there is not a false objective "to-day is not Tuesday," which could be the objective of the false belief "to-day is not Tuesday." This is the reason why two beliefs which are each other's contradictories have the same objective. There is, however, a practical inconvenience, namely that we cannot determine the objective reference of a proposition, according to this definition, unless we know whether the proposition is true or false. To avoid this inconvenience, it is better to adopt a slightly different phraseology, and say: The "meaning" of the proposition "to-day is Tuesday" consists in pointing to the fact "to-day is Tuesday" if that is a fact, or away from the fact "to-day is not Tuesday" if that is a fact. The "meaning" of the proposition "to-day is not Tuesday" will be exactly the opposite. By

---

[57] I owe this way of looking at the matter to my friend Ludwig Wittgenstein.

this hypothetical form we are able to speak of the meaning of a proposition without knowing whether it is true or false. According to this definition, we know the meaning of a proposition when we know what would make it true and what would make it false, even if we do not know whether it is in fact true or false.

The meaning of a proposition is derivative from the meanings of its constituent words. Propositions occur in pairs, distinguished (in simple cases) by the absence or presence of the word "not." Two such propositions have the same objective, but opposite meanings: when one is true, the other is false, and when one is false, the other is true.

The purely formal definition of truth and falsehood offers little difficulty. What is required is a formal expression of the fact that a proposition is true when it points towards its objective, and false when it points away from it, In very simple cases we can give a very simple account of this: we can say that true propositions actually resemble their objectives in a way in which false propositions do not. But for this purpose it is necessary to revert to image-propositions instead of word-propositions. Let us take again the illustration of a memory-image of a familiar room, and let us suppose that in the image the window is to the left of the door. If in fact the window is to the left of the door, there is a correspondence between the image and the objective; there is the same relation between the window and the door as between the images of them. The image-memory consists of the image of the window to the left of the image of the door. When this is true, the very same relation relates the terms of the objective (namely the window and the door) as relates the images which mean them. In this case the correspondence which constitutes truth is very simple.

In the case we have just been considering the objective consists of two parts with a certain relation (that of left-to-right), and the proposition consists of images of these parts with the very same relation. The same proposition, if it were false, would have a less simple formal relation to its objective. If the image-proposition consists of an image of the window to the left of an image of the door, while in fact the window is not to the left of the door, the proposition does not result from the objective by the mere substitution of images for their prototypes. Thus in this unusually simple case we can say that a true proposition "corresponds" to its objective in a formal sense in which a false proposition does not. Perhaps it may be possible to modify this notion of formal correspondence in such a way as to be more widely applicable, but if so, the modifications required will be by no means slight. The reasons for this must now be considered.

To begin with, the simple type of correspondence we have been exhibiting can hardly occur when words are substituted for images, because, in word-propositions, relations are usually expressed by words, which are not themselves relations. Take such a proposition as "Socrates precedes Plato." Here the word "precedes" is just as solid as the words "Socrates" and "Plato"; it MEANS a relation, but is not a relation. Thus the objective which makes our proposition true consists of TWO terms with a relation between them, whereas our proposition consists of THREE terms with a relation of order between them. Of course, it would be perfectly possible, theoretically, to indicate a few chosen relations, not by words, but by relations between the other words. "Socrates-Plato" might be used to mean "Socrates precedes Plato"; "Plato-Socrates" might be used to mean "Plato was born before Socrates and died after him"; and so on. But the possibilities of such a method would be very limited. For aught I know, there may be languages that use it, but they are not among the languages with which I am acquainted. And in any case, in view of the multiplicity of relations that we wish to express, no language could advance far without words for relations. But as soon as we have words for relations, word-propositions have necessarily more terms than the facts to which they refer, and cannot therefore correspond so simply with their objectives as some image-propositions can.

The consideration of negative propositions and negative facts introduces further complications. An image-proposition is necessarily positive: we can image the window to the left of the door, or to the right of the door, but we can form no image of the bare negative "the window not to the left of the door." We can DISBELIEVE the image-proposition expressed by "the window to the left of the door," and our disbelief will be true if the window is not to the left of the door. But we can form no image of the fact that the window is not to the left of the door. Attempts have often been made to deny such negative facts, but, for reasons which I have given elsewhere,[58] I believe these attempts to be mistaken, and I shall assume that there are negative facts.

Word-propositions, like image-propositions, are always positive facts. The fact that Socrates precedes Plato is symbolized in English by the fact that the word "precedes" occurs between the words "Socrates" and "Plato." But we cannot symbolize the fact that Plato does not precede Socrates by not putting the word "precedes" between "Plato" and "Socrates." A negative fact is not sensible, and language, being intended for communication, has to be sensible. Therefore we symbolize the fact that Plato does not precede Socrates by putting the words "does not precede" between "Plato" and "Socrates." We thus obtain a series of words which is just as positive a fact as the series "Socrates precedes Plato." The propositions asserting negative facts are themselves positive facts; they are merely different positive facts from those asserting positive facts.

We have thus, as regards the opposition of positive and negative, three different sorts of duality, according as we are dealing with facts, image-propositions, or word-propositions. We have, namely:

(1) Positive and negative facts;
(2) Image-propositions, which may be believed or disbelieved, but do not allow any duality of content corresponding to positive and negative facts;
(3) Word-propositions, which are always positive facts, but are of two kinds: one verified by a positive objective, the other by a negative objective.

---

[58] *Monist*, January, 1919, p. 42 ff.

Owing to these complications, the simplest type of correspondence is impossible when either negative facts or negative propositions are involved.

Even when we confine ourselves to relations between two terms which are both imaged, it may be impossible to form an image-proposition in which the relation of the terms is represented by the same relation of the images. Suppose we say "Caesar was 2,000 years before Foch," we express a certain temporal relation between Caesar and Foch; but we cannot allow 2,000 years to elapse between our image of Caesar and our image of Foch. This is perhaps not a fair example, since "2,000 years before" is not a direct relation. But take a case where the relation is direct, say, "the sun is brighter than the moon." We can form visual images of sunshine and moonshine, and it may happen that our image of the sunshine is the brighter of the two, but this is by no means either necessary or sufficient. The act of comparison, implied in our judgment, is something more than the mere coexistence of two images, one of which is in fact brighter than the other. It would take us too far from our main topic if we were to go into the question what actually occurs when we make this judgment. Enough has been said to show that the correspondence between the belief and its objective is more complicated in this case than in that of the window to the left of the door, and this was all that had to be proved.

In spite of these complications, the general nature of the formal correspondence which makes truth is clear from our instances. In the case of the simpler kind of propositions, namely those that I call "atomic" propositions, where there is only one word expressing a relation, the objective which would verify our proposition, assuming that the word "not" is absent, is obtained by replacing each word by what it means, the word meaning a relation being replaced by this relation among the meanings of the other words. For example, if the proposition is "Socrates precedes Plato," the objective which verifies it results from replacing the word "Socrates" by Socrates, the word "Plato" by Plato, and the word "precedes" by the relation of preceding between Socrates and Plato. If the result of this process is a fact, the proposition is true; if not, it is false. When our proposition is "Socrates does not precede Plato," the conditions of truth and falsehood are exactly reversed. More complicated propositions can be dealt with on the same lines. In fact, the purely formal question, which has occupied us in this last section, offers no very formidable difficulties.

I do not believe that the above formal theory is untrue, but I do believe that it is inadequate. It does not, for example, throw any light upon our preference for true beliefs rather than false ones. This preference is only explicable by taking account of the causal efficacy of beliefs, and of the greater appropriateness of the responses resulting from true beliefs. But appropriateness depends upon purpose, and purpose thus becomes a vital part of theory of knowledge.

# LECTURE XIV

## Emotions and Will

On the two subjects of the present lecture I have nothing original to say, and I am treating them only in order to complete the discussion of my main thesis, namely that all psychic phenomena are built up out of sensations and images alone.

Emotions are traditionally regarded by psychologists as a separate class of mental occurrences: I am, of course, not concerned to deny the obvious fact that they have characteristics which make a special investigation of them necessary. What I am concerned with is the analysis of emotions. It is clear that an emotion is essentially complex, and we have to inquire whether it ever contains any non-physiological material not reducible to sensations and images and their relations.

Although what specially concerns us is the analysis of emotions, we shall find that the more important topic is the physiological causation of emotions. This is a subject upon which much valuable and exceedingly interesting work has been done, whereas the bare analysis of emotions has proved somewhat barren. In view of the fact that we have defined perceptions, sensations, and images by their physiological causation, it is evident that our problem of the analysis of the emotions is bound up with the problem of their physiological causation.

Modern views on the causation of emotions begin with what is called the James-Lange theory. James states this view in the following terms ("Psychology," vol. ii, p. 449):

"Our natural way of thinking about these coarser emotions, grief, fear, rage, love, is that the mental perception of some fact excites the mental affection called the emotion, and that this latter state of mind gives rise to the bodily expression. My theory, on the contrary, is that THE BODILY CHANGES FOLLOW DIRECTLY THE PERCEPTION OF THE EXCITING FACT, AND THAT OUR FEELING OF THE SAME CHANGES AS THEY OCCUR *IS* THE EMOTION (James's italics). Common sense says: we lose our fortune, are sorry and weep; we meet a bear, are frightened and run; we are insulted by a rival, are angry and strike. The hypothesis here to be defended says that this order of sequence is incorrect, that the one mental state is not immediately induced by the other, that the bodily manifestations must first be interposed between, and that the more rational statement is that we feel sorry because we cry, angry because we strike, afraid because we tremble, and not that we cry, strike, or tremble, because we are sorry, angry, or fearful, as the case may be. Without the bodily states following on the perception, the latter would be purely cognitive in form, pale, colourless, destitute of emotional warmth."

Round this hypothesis a very voluminous literature has grown up. The history of its victory over earlier criticism, and its difficulties with the modern experimental work of Sherrington and Cannon, is well told by James R. Angell in an article called "A Reconsideration of James's Theory of Emotion in the Light of Recent Criticisms."[59] In this article Angell defends James's theory and to me—though I speak with diffidence on a question as to which I have little competence—it appears that his defence is on the whole successful.

Sherrington, by experiments on dogs, showed that many of the usual marks of emotion were present in their behaviour even when, by severing the spinal cord in the lower cervical region, the viscera were cut off from all communication with the brain, except that existing through certain cranial nerves. He mentions the various signs which "contributed to indicate the existence of an emotion as lively as the animal had ever shown us before the spinal operation had been made."* He infers that the physiological condition of the viscera cannot be the cause of the emotion displayed under such circumstances, and concludes: "We are forced back toward the likelihood that the visceral expression of emotion is SECONDARY to the cerebral action occurring with the psychical state.... We may with James accept visceral and organic sensations and the memories and associations of them as contributory to primitive emotion, but we must regard them as re-enforcing rather than as initiating the psychosis."[60]

Angell suggests that the display of emotion in such cases may be due to past experience, generating habits which would require only the stimulation of cerebral reflex arcs. Rage and some forms of fear, however, may, he thinks, gain expression without the brain. Rage and fear have been especially studied by Cannon, whose work is of the greatest importance. His results are given in his book, "Bodily Changes in Pain, Hunger, Fear and Rage" (D. Appleton and Co., 1916).

The most interesting part of Cannon's book consists in the investigation of the effects produced by secretion of adrenin. Adrenin is a substance secreted into the blood by the adrenal glands. These are among the ductless glands, the functions of which, both in physiology and in connection with the emotions, have only come to be known during recent years. Cannon found that pain, fear and rage occurred in circumstances which affected the supply of adrenin, and that an artificial injection of adrenin could, for example, produce all the symptoms of fear. He studied the effects of adrenin on various parts of the body; he found that it causes the pupils to dilate, hairs to stand erect, blood vessels to be constricted, and so on. These effects were

---

[59] *Psychological Review*, 1916.
[60] Quoted by Angell, loc. cit.

still produced if the parts in question were removed from the body and kept alive artificially.[61]

Cannon's chief argument against James is, if I understand him rightly, that similar affections of the viscera may accompany dissimilar emotions, especially fear and rage. Various different emotions make us cry, and therefore it cannot be true to say, as James does, that we "feel sorry because we cry," since sometimes we cry when we feel glad. This argument, however, is by no means conclusive against James, because it cannot be shown that there are no visceral differences for different emotions, and indeed it is unlikely that this is the case.

As Angell says (loc. cit.): "Fear and joy may both cause cardiac palpitation, but in one case we find high tonus of the skeletal muscles, in the other case relaxation and the general sense of weakness."

Angell's conclusion, after discussing the experiments of Sherrington and Cannon, is: "I would therefore submit that, so far as concerns the critical suggestions by these two psychologists, James's essential contentions are not materially affected." If it were necessary for me to take sides on this question, I should agree with this conclusion; but I think my thesis as to the analysis of emotion can be maintained without coming to a probably premature conclusion upon the doubtful parts of the physiological problem.

According to our definitions, if James is right, an emotion may be regarded as involving a confused perception of the viscera concerned in its causation, while if Cannon and Sherrington are right, an emotion involves a confused perception of its external stimulus. This follows from what was said in Lecture VII. We there defined a perception as an appearance, however irregular, of one or more objects external to the brain. And in order to be an appearance of one or more objects, it is only necessary that the occurrence in question should be connected with them by a continuous chain, and should vary when they are varied sufficiently. Thus the question whether a mental occurrence can be called a perception turns upon the question whether anything can be inferred from it as to its causes outside the brain: if such inference is possible, the occurrence in question will come within our definition of a perception. And in that case, according to the definition in Lecture VIII, its non-mnemic elements will be sensations. Accordingly, whether emotions are caused by changes in the viscera or by sensible objects, they contain elements which are sensations according to our definition.

An emotion in its entirety is, of course, something much more complex than a perception. An emotion is essentially a process, and it will be only what one may call a cross-section of the emotion that will be a perception, of a bodily condition according to James, or (in certain cases) of an external object according to his opponents. An emotion in its entirety contains dynamic elements, such as motor impulses, desires,

---

[61] Cannon's work is not unconnected with that of Mosso, who maintains, as the result of much experimental work, that "the seat of the emotions lies in the sympathetic nervous system." An account of the work of both these men will be found in Goddard's *Psychology of the Normal and Sub-normal* (Kegan Paul, 1919), chap. vii and Appendix.

pleasures and pains. Desires and pleasures and pains, according to the theory adopted in Lecture III, are characteristics of processes, not separate ingredients. An emotion—rage, for example—will be a certain kind of process, consisting of perceptions and (in general) bodily movements. The desires and pleasures and pains involved are properties of this process, not separate items in the stuff of which the emotion is composed. The dynamic elements in an emotion, if we are right in our analysis, contain, from our point of view, no ingredients beyond those contained in the processes considered in Lecture III. The ingredients of an emotion are only sensations and images and bodily movements succeeding each other according to a certain pattern. With this conclusion we may leave the emotions and pass to the consideration of the will.

The first thing to be defined when we are dealing with Will is a VOLUNTARY MOVEMENT. We have already defined vital movements, and we have maintained that, from a behaviourist standpoint, it is impossible to distinguish which among such movements are reflex and which voluntary. Nevertheless, there certainly is a distinction. When we decide in the morning that it is time to get up, our consequent movement is voluntary. The beating of the heart, on the other hand, is involuntary: we can neither cause it nor prevent it by any decision of our own, except indirectly, as e.g. by drugs. Breathing is intermediate between the two: we normally breathe without the help of the will, but we can alter or stop our breathing if we choose.

James ("Psychology," chap. xxvi) maintains that the only distinctive characteristic of a voluntary act is that it involves an idea of the movement to be performed, made up of memory-images of the kinaesthetic sensations which we had when the same movement occurred on some former occasion. He points out that, on this view, no movement can be made voluntarily unless it has previously occurred involuntarily.[62]

I see no reason to doubt the correctness of this view. We shall say, then, that movements which are accompanied by kinaesthetic sensations tend to be caused by the images of those sensations, and when so caused are called VOLUNTARY.

Volition, in the emphatic sense, involves something more than voluntary movement. The sort of case I am thinking of is decision after deliberation. Voluntary movements are a part of this, but not the whole. There is, in addition to them, a judgment: "This is what I shall do"; there is also a sensation of tension during doubt, followed by a different sensation at the moment of deciding. I see no reason whatever to suppose that there is any specifically new ingredient; sensations and images, with their relations and causal laws, yield all that seems to be wanted for the analysis of the will, together with the fact that kinaesthetic images tend to cause the movements with which they are connected. Conflict of desires is of course essential in the causation of the emphatic kind of will: there will be for a time kinaesthetic images of incompatible movements, followed by the exclusive image of the movement which is said to be willed. Thus will seems to add no new irreducible ingredient to the analysis of the mind.

---

[62] *Psychology*, Vol. ii, pp. 492-3.

# LECTURE XV

## Characteristics of Mental Phenomena

At the end of our journey it is time to return to the question from which we set out, namely: What is it that characterizes mind as opposed to matter? Or, to state the same question in other terms: How is psychology to be distinguished from physics? The answer provisionally suggested at the outset of our inquiry was that psychology and physics are distinguished by the nature of their causal laws, not by their subject matter. At the same time we held that there is a certain subject matter, namely images, to which only psychological causal laws are applicable; this subject matter, therefore, we assigned exclusively to psychology. But we found no way of defining images except through their causation; in their intrinsic character they appeared to have no universal mark by which they could be distinguished from sensations.

In this last lecture I propose to pass in review various suggested methods of distinguishing mind from matter. I shall then briefly sketch the nature of that fundamental science which I believe to be the true metaphysic, in which mind and matter alike are seen to be constructed out of a neutral stuff, whose causal laws have no such duality as that of psychology, but form the basis upon which both physics and psychology are built.

In search for the definition of "mental phenomena," let us begin with "consciousness," which is often thought to be the essence of mind. In the first lecture I gave various arguments against the view that consciousness is fundamental, but I did not attempt to say what consciousness is. We must find a definition of it, if we are to feel secure in deciding that it is not fundamental. It is for the sake of the proof that it is not fundamental that we must now endeavour to decide what it is.

"Consciousness," by those who regard it as fundamental, is taken to be a character diffused throughout our mental life, distinct from sensations and images, memories, beliefs and desires, but present in all of them.[63] Dr. Henry Head, in an article which I quoted in Lecture III, distinguishing sensations from purely physiological occurrences, says: "Sensation, in the strict sense of the term, demands the existence of consciousness." This statement, at first sight, is one to which we feel inclined to assent, but I believe we are mistaken if we do so. Sensation is the sort of thing of which

---

[63] Cf. Lecture VI.

we MAY be conscious, but not a thing of which we MUST be conscious. We have been led, in the course of our inquiry, to admit unconscious beliefs and unconscious desires. There is, so far as I can see, no class of mental or other occurrences of which we are always conscious whenever they happen.

The first thing to notice is that consciousness must be of something. In view of this, I should define "consciousness" in terms of that relation of an image of a word to an object which we defined, in Lecture XI, as "meaning." When a sensation is followed by an image which is a "copy" of it, I think it may be said that the existence of the image constitutes consciousness of the sensation, provided it is accompanied by that sort of belief which, when we reflect upon it, makes us feel that the image is a "sign" of something other than itself. This is the sort of belief which, in the case of memory, we expressed in the words "this occurred"; or which, in the case of a judgment of perception, makes us believe in qualities correlated with present sensations, as e.g., tactile and visual qualities are correlated. The addition of some element of belief seems required, since mere imagination does not involve consciousness of anything, and there can be no consciousness which is not of something. If images alone constituted consciousness of their prototypes, such imagination-images as in fact have prototypes would involve consciousness of them; since this is not the case, an element of belief must be added to the images in defining consciousness. The belief must be of that sort that constitutes objective reference, past or present. An image, together with a belief of this sort concerning it, constitutes, according to our definition, consciousness of the prototype of the image.

But when we pass from consciousness of sensations to consciousness of objects of perception, certain further points arise which demand an addition to our definition. A judgment of perception, we may say, consists of a core of sensation, together with associated images, with belief in the present existence of an object to which sensation and images are referred in a way which is difficult to analyse. Perhaps we might say that the belief is not fundamentally in any PRESENT existence, but is of the nature of an expectation: for example, when we see an object, we expect certain sensations to result if we proceed to touch it. Perception, then, will consist of a present sensation together with expectations of future sensations. (This, of course, is a reflective analysis, not an account of the way perception appears to unchecked introspection.) But all such expectations are liable to be erroneous, since they are based upon correlations which are usual but not invariable. Any such correlation may mislead us in a particular case, for example, if we try to touch a reflection in a looking-glass under the impression that it is "real." Since memory is fallible, a similar difficulty arises as regards consciousness of past objects. It would seem odd to say that we can be "conscious" of a thing which does not or did not exist. The only way to avoid this awkwardness is to add to our definition the proviso that the beliefs involved in consciousness must be TRUE.

In the second place, the question arises as to whether we can be conscious of images. If we apply our definition to this case, it seems to demand images of images.

In order, for example, to be conscious of an image of a cat, we shall require, according to the letter of the definition, an image which is a copy of our image of the cat, and has this image for its prototype. Now, it hardly seems probable, as a matter of observation, that there are images of images, as opposed to images of sensations. We may meet this difficulty in two ways, either by boldly denying consciousness of images, or by finding a sense in which, by means of a different accompanying belief, an image, instead of meaning its prototype, can mean another image of the same prototype.

The first alternative, which denies consciousness of images, has already been discussed when we were dealing with Introspection in Lecture VI. We then decided that there must be, in some sense, consciousness of images. We are therefore left with the second suggested way of dealing with knowledge of images. According to this second hypothesis, there may be two images of the same prototype, such that one of them means the other, instead of meaning the prototype. It will be remembered that we defined meaning by association a word or image means an object, we said, when it has the same associations as the object. But this definition must not be interpreted too absolutely: a word or image will not have ALL the same associations as the object which it means. The word "cat" may be associated with the word "mat," but it would not happen except by accident that a cat would be associated with a mat. And in like manner an image may have certain associations which its prototype will not have, e.g. an association with the word "image." When these associations are active, an image means an image, instead of meaning its prototype. If I have had images of a given prototype many times, I can mean one of these, as opposed to the rest, by recollecting the time and place or any other distinctive association of that one occasion. This happens, for example, when a place recalls to us some thought we previously had in that place, so that we remember a thought as opposed to the occurrence to which it referred. Thus we may say that we think of an image A when we have a similar image B associated with recollections of circumstances connected with A, but not with its prototype or with other images of the same prototype. In this way we become aware of images without the need of any new store of mental contents, merely by the help of new associations. This theory, so far as I can see, solves the problems of introspective knowledge, without requiring heroic measures such as those proposed by Knight Dunlap, whose views we discussed in Lecture VI.

According to what we have been saying, sensation itself is not an instance of consciousness, though the immediate memory by which it is apt to be succeeded is so. A sensation which is remembered becomes an object of consciousness as soon as it begins to be remembered, which will normally be almost immediately after its occurrence (if at all); but while it exists it is not an object of consciousness. If, however, it is part of a perception, say of some familiar person, we may say that the person perceived is an object of consciousness. For in this case the sensation is a SIGN of the perceived object in much the same way in which a memory-image is a sign of a remembered object. The essential practical function of "consciousness" and "thought" is that they enable us to act with reference to what is distant in time or space, even though it is not at present stimulating our senses. This reference to absent objects is possible through association and habit. Actual sensations, in themselves, are not cases of consciousness, because they do not bring in this reference to what is absent. But their connection with consciousness is very close, both through immediate memory, and through the correlations which turn sensations into perceptions.

Enough has, I hope, been said to show that consciousness is far too complex and accidental to be taken as the fundamental characteristic of mind. We have seen that belief and images both enter into it. Belief itself, as we saw in an earlier lecture, is complex. Therefore, if any definition of mind is suggested by our analysis of consciousness, images are what would naturally suggest themselves. But since we found that images can only be defined causally, we cannot deal with this suggestion, except in connection with the difference between physical and psychological causal laws.

I come next to those characteristics of mental phenomena which arise out of mnemic causation. The possibility of action with reference to what is not sensibly present is one of the things that might be held to characterize mind. Let us take first a very elementary example. Suppose you are in a familiar room at night, and suddenly the light goes out. You will be able to find your way to the door without much difficulty by means of the picture of the room which you have in your mind. In this case visual images serve, somewhat imperfectly it is true, the purpose which visual sensations would otherwise serve. The stimulus to the production of visual images is the desire to get out of the room, which, according to what we found in Lecture III, consists essentially of present sensations and motor impulses caused by them. Again, words heard or read enable you to act with reference to the matters about which they give information; here, again, a present sensible stimulus, in virtue of habits formed in the past, enables you to act in a manner appropriate to an object which is not sensibly present. The whole essence of the practical efficiency of "thought" consists in sensitiveness to signs: the sensible presence of A, which is a sign of the present or future existence of B, enables us to act in a manner appropriate to B. Of this, words are the supreme example, since their effects as signs are prodigious, while their intrinsic interest as sensible occurrences on their own account is usually very slight. The operation of signs may or may not be accompanied by consciousness. If a sensible stimulus A calls up an image of B, and we then act with reference to B, we have what may be called consciousness of B. But habit may enable us to act in a manner appropriate to B as soon as A appears, without ever having an image of B. In that case, although A operates as a sign, it operates without the help of consciousness. Broadly speaking, a very familiar sign tends to operate directly in this manner, and the intervention of consciousness marks an imperfectly established habit.

The power of acquiring experience, which characterizes men and animals, is an example of the general law that, in mnemic causation, the causal unit is not one event at one time, but two or more events at two or more times.& A burnt child fears the fire, that is to say, the neighbourhood of fire has a different effect upon a child which has had the sensations of burning than upon one which has not. More correctly, the observed effect, when a child which has been burnt is put near a fire, has for its cause, not merely the neighbourhood of the fire, but this together with the previous burning. The general formula, when an animal has acquired experience through some event A, is that, when B occurs at some future time, the animal to which A has happened acts differently from an animal which A has not happened. Thus A and B together, not either separately, must be regarded as the cause of the animal's behaviour, unless we take account of the effect which A has had in altering the animal's nervous tissue, which is a matter not patent to external observation except under very special circumstances. With this possibility, we are brought back to causal laws, and to the suggestion that many things which seem essentially mental are really neural. Perhaps it is the nerves that acquire experience rather than the mind. If so, the possibility of acquiring experience cannot be used to define mind.[64]

Very similar considerations apply to memory, if taken as the essence of mind. A recollection is aroused by something which is happening now, but is different from the effect which the present occurrence would have produced if the recollected event had not occurred. This may be accounted for by the physical effect of the past event on the brain, making it a different instrument from that which would have resulted from a different experience. The causal peculiarities of memory may, therefore, have a physiological explanation. With every special class of mental phenomena this possibility meets us afresh. If psychology is to be a separate science at all, we must seek a wider ground for its separateness than any that we have been considering hitherto.

We have found that "consciousness" is too narrow to characterize mental phenomena, and that mnemic causation is too wide. I come now to a characteristic which, though difficult to define, comes much nearer to what we require, namely subjectivity.

Subjectivity, as a characteristic of mental phenomena, was considered in Lecture VII, in connection with the definition of perception. We there decided that those particulars which constitute the physical world can be collected into sets in two ways, one of which makes a bundle of all those particulars that are appearances of a given thing from different places, while the other makes a bundle of all those particulars which are appearances of different things from a given place. A bundle of this latter sort, at a given time, is called a "perspective"; taken throughout a period of time, it is called a "biography." Subjectivity is the characteristic of perspectives and biographies, the characteristic of giving the view of the world from a certain place. We saw in Lecture VII that this characteristic involves none of the other characteristics that are

---

[64] Cf. Lecture IV.

commonly associated with mental phenomena, such as consciousness, experience and memory. We found in fact that it is exhibited by a photographic plate, and, strictly speaking, by any particular taken in conjunction with those which have the same "passive" place in the sense defined in Lecture VII. The particulars forming one perspective are connected together primarily by simultaneity; those forming one biography, primarily by the existence of direct time-relations between them. To these are to be added relations derivable from the laws of perspective. In all this we are clearly not in the region of psychology, as commonly understood; yet we are also hardly in the region of physics. And the definition of perspectives and biographies, though it does not yet yield anything that would be commonly called "mental," is presupposed in mental phenomena, for example in mnemic causation: the causal unit in mnemic causation, which gives rise to Semon's engram, is the whole of one perspective—not of any perspective, but of a perspective in a place where there is nervous tissue, or at any rate living tissue of some sort. Perception also, as we saw, can only be defined in terms of perspectives. Thus the conception of subjectivity, i.e. of the "passive" place of a particular, though not alone sufficient to define mind, is clearly an essential element in the definition.

I have maintained throughout these lectures that the data of psychology do not differ in, their intrinsic character from the data of physics. I have maintained that sensations are data for psychology and physics equally, while images, which may be in some sense exclusively psychological data, can only be distinguished from sensations by their correlations, not by what they are in themselves. It is now necessary, however, to examine the notion of a "datum," and to obtain, if possible, a definition of this notion.

The notion of "data" is familiar throughout science, and is usually treated by men of science as though it were perfectly clear. Psychologists, on the other hand, find great difficulty in the conception. "Data" are naturally defined in terms of theory of knowledge: they are those propositions of which the truth is known without demonstration, so that they may be used as premises in proving other propositions. Further, when a proposition which is a datum asserts the existence of something, we say that the something is a datum, as well as the proposition asserting its existence. Thus those objects of whose existence we become certain through perception are said to be data.

There is some difficulty in connecting this epistemological definition of "data" with our psychological analysis of knowledge; but until such a connection has been effected, we have no right to use the conception "data."

It is clear, in the first place, that there can be no datum apart from a belief. A sensation which merely comes and goes is not a datum; it only becomes a datum when it is remembered. Similarly, in perception, we do not have a datum unless we have a JUDGMENT of perception. In the sense in which objects (as opposed to propositions) are data, it would seem natural to say that those objects of which we are conscious are data. But consciousness, as we have seen, is a complex notion, involving beliefs, as well as mnemic phenomena such as are required for perception and memory. It follows that no datum is theoretically indubitable, since no belief is infallible; it follows also that every datum has a greater or less degree of vagueness, since there is always some vagueness in memory and the meaning of images.

Data are not those things of which our consciousness is earliest in time. At every period of life, after we have become capable of thought, some of our beliefs are obtained by inference, while others are not. A belief may pass from either of these classes into the other, and may therefore become, or cease to be, a belief giving a datum. When, in what follows, I speak of data, I do not mean the things of which we feel sure before scientific study begins, but the things which, when a science is well advanced, appear as affording grounds for other parts of the science, without themselves being believed on any ground except observation. I assume, that is to say, a trained observer, with an analytic attention, knowing the sort of thing to look for, and the sort of thing that will be important. What he observes is, at the stage of science which he has reached, a datum for his science. It is just as sophisticated and elaborate as the theories which he bases upon it, since only trained habits and much practice enable a man to make the kind of observation that will be scientifically illuminating. Nevertheless, when once it has been observed, belief in it is not based on inference and reasoning, but merely upon its having been seen. In this way its logical status differs from that of the theories which are proved by its means.

In any science other than psychology the datum is primarily a perception, in which only the sensational core is ultimately and theoretically a datum, though some such accretions as turn the sensation into a perception are practically unavoidable. But if we postulate an ideal observer, he will be able to isolate the sensation, and treat this alone as datum. There is, therefore, an important sense in which we may say that, if we analyse as much as we ought, our data, outside psychology, consist of sensations, which include within themselves certain spatial and temporal relations.

Applying this remark to physiology, we see that the nerves and brain as physical objects are not truly data; they are to be replaced, in the ideal structure of science, by the sensations through which the physiologist is said to perceive them. The passage from these sensations to nerves and brain as physical objects belongs really to the initial stage in the theory of physics, and ought to be placed in the reasoned part, not in the part supposed to be observed. To say we see the nerves is like saying we hear the nightingale; both are convenient but inaccurate expressions. We hear a sound which we believe to be causally connected with the nightingale, and we see a sight which we believe to be causally connected with a nerve. But in each case it is only the sensation that ought, in strictness, to be called a datum. Now, sensations are certainly among the data of psychology. Therefore all the data of the physical sciences are also psychological data. It remains to inquire whether all the data of psychology are also data of physical science, and especially of physiology.

If we have been right in our analysis of mind, the ultimate data of psychology are only sensations and images and their relations. Beliefs, desires, volitions, and so on, appeared to us to be complex phenomena consisting of sensations and images variously interrelated. Thus (apart from certain relations) the occurrences which seem most distinctively mental, and furthest removed from physics, are, like physical objects, constructed or inferred, not part of the original stock of data in the perfected science. From both ends, therefore, the difference between physical and psychological data is diminished. Is there ultimately no difference, or do images remain as irreducibly and exclusively psychological? In view of the causal definition of the difference between images and sensations, this brings us to a new question, namely: Are the causal laws of psychology different from those of any other science, or are they really physiological?

Certain ambiguities must be removed before this question can be adequately discussed.

First, there is the distinction between rough approximate laws and such as appear to be precise and general. I shall return to the former presently; it is the latter that I wish to discuss now.

Matter, as defined at the end of Lecture V, is a logical fiction, invented because it gives a convenient way of stating causal laws. Except in cases of perfect regularity in appearances (of which we can have no experience), the actual appearances of a piece of matter are not members of that ideal system of regular appearances which is defined as being the matter in question. But the matter is, after all, inferred from its appearances, which are used to VERIFY physical laws. Thus, in so far as physics is an empirical and verifiable science, it must assume or prove that the inference from appearances to matter is, in general, legitimate, and it must be able to tell us, more or less, what appearances to expect. It is through this question of verifiability and empirical applicability to experience that we are led to a theory of matter such as I advocate. From the consideration of this question it results that physics, in so far as it is an empirical science, not a logical phantasy, is concerned with particulars of just the same sort as those which psychology considers under the name of sensations. The causal laws of physics, so interpreted, differ from those of psychology only by the fact that they connect a particular with other appearances in the same piece of matter, rather than with other appearances in the same perspective. That is to say, they group together particulars having the same "active" place, while psychology groups together those having the same "passive" place. Some particulars, such as images, have no "active" place, and therefore belong exclusively to psychology.

We can now understand the distinction between physics and psychology. The nerves and brain are matter: our visual sensations when we look at them may be, and I think are, members of the system constituting irregular appearances of this matter, but are not the whole of the system. Psychology is concerned, inter alia, with our sensations when we see a piece of matter, as opposed to the matter which we see.

Assuming, as we must, that our sensations have physical causes, their causal laws are nevertheless radically different from the laws of physics, since the consideration of a single sensation requires the breaking up of the group of which it is a member. When a sensation is used to verify physics, it is used merely as a sign of a certain material phenomenon, i.e. of a group of particulars of which it is a member. But when it is studied by psychology, it is taken away from that group and put into quite a different context, where it causes images or voluntary movements. It is primarily this different grouping that is characteristic of psychology as opposed to all the physical sciences, including physiology; a secondary difference is that images, which belong to psychology, are not easily to be included among the aspects which constitute a physical thing or piece of matter.

There remains, however, an important question, namely: Are mental events causally dependent upon physical events in a sense in which the converse dependence does not hold? Before we can discuss the answer to this question, we must first be clear as to what our question means.

When, given A, it is possible to infer B, but given B, it is not possible to infer A, we say that B is dependent upon A in a sense in which A is not dependent upon B. Stated in logical terms, this amounts to saying that, when we know a many-one relation of A to B, B is dependent upon A in respect of this relation. If the relation is a causal law, we say that B is causally dependent upon A. The illustration that chiefly concerns us is the system of appearances of a physical object. We can, broadly speaking, infer distant appearances from near ones, but not vice versa. All men look alike when they are a mile away, hence when we see a man a mile off we cannot tell what he will look like when he is only a yard away. But when we see him a yard away, we can tell what he will look like a mile away. Thus the nearer view gives us more valuable information, and the distant view is causally dependent upon it in a sense in which it is not causally dependent upon the distant view.

It is this greater causal potency of the near appearance that leads physics to state its causal laws in terms of that system of regular appearances to which the nearest appearances increasingly approximate, and that makes it value information derived from the microscope or telescope. It is clear that our sensations, considered as irregular appearances of physical objects, share the causal dependence belonging to comparatively distant appearances; therefore in our sensational life we are in causal dependence upon physical laws.

This, however, is not the most important or interesting part of our question. It is the causation of images that is the vital problem. We have seen that they are subject to mnenic causation, and that mnenic causation may be reducible to ordinary physical causation in nervous tissue. This is the question upon which our attitude must turn towards what may be called materialism. One sense of materialism is the view that all mental phenomena are causally dependent upon physical phenomena in the above-defined sense of causal dependence. Whether this is the case or not, I do not profess to know. The question seems to me the same as the question whether mnemic causation is ultimate, which we considered without deciding in Lecture IV. But I think the bulk of the evidence points to the materialistic answer as the more probable.

In considering the causal laws of psychology, the distinction between rough generalizations and exact laws is important. There are many rough generalizations in psychology, not only of the sort by which we govern our ordinary behaviour to each other, but also of a more nearly scientific kind. Habit and association belong among such laws. I will give an illustration of the kind of law that can be obtained. Suppose a person has frequently experienced A and B in close temporal contiguity, an association will be established, so that A, or an image of A, tends to cause an image of B. The question arises: will the association work in either direction, or only from the one which has occurred earlier to the one which has occurred later? In an article by Mr. Wohlgemuth, called "The Direction of Associations" ("British Journal of Psychology," vol. v, part iv, March, 1913), it is claimed to be proved by experiment that, in so far as motor memory (i.e. memory of movements) is concerned, association works only from earlier to later, while in visual and auditory memory this is not the case, but the later of two neighbouring experiences may recall the earlier as well as the earlier the later. It is suggested that motor memory is physiological, while visual and auditory memory are more truly psychological. But that is not the point which concerns us in the illustration. The point which concerns us is that a law of association, established by purely psychological observation, is a purely psychological law, and may serve as a sample of what is possible in the way of discovering such laws. It is, however, still no more than a rough generalization, a statistical average. It cannot tell us what will result from a given cause on a given occasion. It is a law of tendency, not a precise and invariable law such as those of physics aim at being.

If we wish to pass from the law of habit, stated as a tendency or average, to something more precise and invariable, we seem driven to the nervous system. We can more or less guess how an occurrence produces a change in the brain, and how its repetition gradually produces something analogous to the channel of a river, along which currents flow more easily than in neighbouring paths. We can perceive that in this way, if we had more knowledge, the tendency to habit through repetition might be replaced by a precise account of the effect of each occurrence in bringing about a modification of the sort from which habit would ultimately result. It is such considerations that make students of psychophysiology materialistic in their methods, whatever they may be in their metaphysics. There are, of course, exceptions, such as Professor J. S. Haldane,[65] who maintains that it is theoretically impossible to obtain physiological explanations of psychical phenomena, or physical explanations of physiological phenomena. But I think the bulk of expert opinion, in practice, is on the other side.

---

[65] See his book, *The New Physiology and Other Addresses* (Charles Griffin & Co., 1919).

The question whether it is possible to obtain precise causal laws in which the causes are psychological, not material, is one of detailed investigation. I have done what I could to make clear the nature of the question, but I do not believe that it is possible as yet to answer it with any confidence. It seems to be by no means an insoluble question, and we may hope that science will be able to produce sufficient grounds for regarding one answer as much more probable than the other. But for the moment I do not see how we can come to a decision.

I think, however, on grounds of the theory of matter explained in Lectures V and VII, that an ultimate scientific account of what goes on in the world, if it were ascertainable, would resemble psychology rather than physics in what we found to be the decisive difference between them. I think, that is to say, that such an account would not be content to speak, even formally, as though matter, which is a logical fiction, were the ultimate reality. I think that, if our scientific knowledge were adequate to the task, which it neither is nor is likely to become, it would exhibit the laws of correlation of the particulars constituting a momentary condition of a material unit, and would state the causal laws[66] of the world in terms of these particulars, not in terms of matter. Causal laws so stated would, I believe, be applicable to psychology and physics equally; the science in which they were stated would succeed in achieving what metaphysics has vainly attempted, namely a unified account of what really happens, wholly true even if not the whole of truth, and free from all convenient fictions or unwarrantable assumptions of metaphysical entities. A causal law applicable to particulars would count as a law of physics if it could be stated in terms of those fictitious systems of regular appearances which are matter; if this were not the case, it would count as a law of psychology if one of the particulars were a sensation or an image, i.e. were subject to mnemic causation. I believe that the realization of the complexity of a material unit, and its analysis into constituents analogous to sensations, is of the utmost importance to philosophy, and vital for any understanding of the relations between mind and matter, between our perceptions and the world which they perceive. It is in this direction, I am convinced, that we must look for the solution of many ancient perplexities.

It is probable that the whole science of mental occurrences, especially where its initial definitions are concerned, could be simplified by the development of the fundamental unifying science in which the causal laws of particulars are sought, rather than the causal laws of those systems of particulars that constitute the material units of physics. This fundamental science would cause physics to become derivative, in the sort of way in which theories of the constitution of the atom make chemistry derivative from physics; it would also cause psychology to appear less singular and isolated among sciences. If we are right in this, it is a wrong philosophy of matter

---

[66] In a perfected science, causal laws will take the form of differential equations—or of finite-difference equations, if the theory of quanta should prove correct.

which has caused many of the difficulties in the philosophy of mind—difficulties which a right philosophy of matter would cause to disappear.

The conclusions at which we have arrived may be summed up as follows:

I.   Physics and psychology are not distinguished by their material. Mind and matter alike are logical constructions; the particulars out of which they are constructed, or from which they are inferred, have various relations, some of which are studied by physics, others by psychology. Broadly speaking, physics group particulars by their active places, psychology by their passive places.

II.  The two most essential characteristics of the causal laws which would naturally be called psychological are SUBJECTIVITY and MNEMIC CAUSATION; these are not unconnected, since the causal unit in mnemic causation is the group of particulars having a given passive place at a given time, and it is by this manner of grouping that subjectivity is defined.

III. Habit, memory and thought are all developments of mnemic causation. It is probable, though not certain, that mnemic causation is derivative from ordinary physical causation in nervous (and other) tissue.

IV.  Consciousness is a complex and far from universal characteristic of mental phenomena.

V.   Mind is a matter of degree, chiefly exemplified in number and complexity of habits.

VI.  All our data, both in physics and psychology, are subject to psychological causal laws; but physical causal laws, at least in traditional physics, can only be stated in terms of matter, which is both inferred and constructed, never a datum. In this respect psychology is nearer to what actually exists.

# WHY MEN FIGHT

# I

## The Principle of Growth

To all who are capable of new impressions and fresh thought, some modification of former beliefs and hopes has been brought by the war. What the modification has been has depended, in each case, upon character and circumstance; but in one form or another it has been almost universal. To me, the chief thing to be learnt through the war has been a certain view of the springs of human action, what they are, and what we may legitimately hope that they will become. This view, if it is true, seems to afford a basis for political philosophy more capable of standing erect in a time of crisis than the philosophy of traditional Liberalism has shown itself to be. The following lectures, though only one of them will deal with war, all are inspired by a view of the springs of action which has been suggested by the war. And all of them are informed by the hope of seeing such political institutions established in Europe as shall make men averse to war—a hope which I firmly believe to be realizable, though not without a great and fundamental reconstruction of economic and social life.

To one who stands outside the cycle of beliefs and passions which make the war seem necessary, an isolation, an almost unbearable separation from the general activity, becomes unavoidable. At the very moment when the universal disaster raises compassion in the highest degree, compassion itself compels aloofness from the impulse to self-destruction which has swept over Europe. The helpless longing to save men from the ruin towards which they are hastening makes it necessary to oppose the stream, to incur hostility, to be thought unfeeling, to lose for the moment the power of winning belief. It is impossible to prevent others from feeling hostile, but it is possible to avoid any reciprocal hostility on one's own part, by imaginative understanding and the sympathy which grows out of it. And without understanding and sympathy it is impossible to find a cure for the evil from which the world is suffering.

There are two views of the war neither of which seems to me adequate. The usual view in this country is that it is due to the wickedness of the Germans; the view of most pacifists is that it is due to the diplomatic tangle and to the ambitions of Governments. I think both these views fail to realize the extent to which war grows out of ordinary human nature. Germans, and also the men who compose Governments, are on the whole average human beings, actuated by the same passions that actuate others, not differing much from the rest of the world except in their circumstances. War is accepted by men who are neither Germans nor diplomatists with a readiness, an acquiescence in untrue and inadequate reasons, which would not be possible if any deep repugnance to war were widespread in other nations or classes. The untrue things which men believe, and the true things which they disbelieve, are an index to their impulses—not necessarily to individual impulses in each case (since beliefs are contagious), but to the general impulses of the community. We all believe many things which we have no good ground for believing, because, subconsciously, our nature craves certain kinds of action which these beliefs would render reasonable if they were true. Unfounded beliefs are the homage which impulse pays to reason; and thus it is with the beliefs which, opposite but similar, make men here and in Germany believe it their duty to prosecute the war.

The first thought which naturally occurs to one who accepts this view is that it would be well if men were more under the dominion of reason. War, to those who see that it must necessarily do untold harm to all the combatants, seems a mere madness, a collective insanity in which all that has been known in time of peace is forgotten. If impulses were more controlled, if thought were less dominated by passion, men would guard their minds against the approaches of war fever, and disputes would be adjusted amicably. This is true, but it is not by itself sufficient. It is only those in whom the desire to think truly is itself a passion who will find this desire adequate to control the passions of war. Only passion can control passion, and only a contrary impulse or desire can check impulse. Reason, as it is preached by traditional moralists, is too negative, too little living, to make a good life. It is not by reason alone that wars can be prevented, but by a positive life of impulses and passions antagonistic to those that lead to war. It is the life of impulse that needs to be changed, not only the life of conscious thought.

All human activity springs from two sources: impulse and desire. The part played by desire has always been sufficiently recognized. When men find themselves not fully contented, and not able instantly to procure what will cause content, imagination brings before their minds the thought of things which they believe would make them happy. All desire involves an interval of time between the consciousness of a need and the opportunity for satisfying it. The acts inspired by desire may be in themselves painful, the time before satisfaction can be achieved may be very long, the object desired may be something outside our own lives, and even after our own death. Will, as a directing force, consists mainly in following desires for more or less distant objects, in spite of the painfulness of the acts involved and the solicitations of incompatible but more immediate desires and impulses. All this is familiar, and political philosophy hitherto has been almost entirely based upon desire as the source of human actions.

But desire governs no more than a part of human activity, and that not the most important but only the more conscious, explicit, and civilized part.

In all the more instinctive part of our nature we are dominated by impulses to certain kinds of activity, not by desires for certain ends. Children run and shout, not because of any good which they expect to realize, but because of a direct impulse to running and shouting. Dogs bay the moon, not because they consider that it is to their advantage to do so, but because they feel an impulse to bark. It is not any purpose, but merely an impulse, that prompts such actions as eating, drinking, love-making, quarreling, boasting. Those who believe that man is a rational animal will say that people boast in order that others may have a good opinion of them; but most of us can recall occasions when we have boasted in spite of knowing that we should be despised for it. Instinctive acts normally achieve some result which is agreeable to the natural man, but they are not performed from desire for this result. They are performed from direct impulse, and the impulse is often strong even in cases in which the normal desirable result cannot follow. Grown men like to imagine themselves more rational than children and dogs, and unconsciously conceal from themselves how great a part impulse plays in their lives. This unconscious concealment always follows a certain general plan. When an impulse is not indulged in the moment in which it arises, there grows up a desire for the expected consequences of indulging the impulse. If some of the consequences which are reasonably to be expected are clearly disagreeable, a conflict between foresight and impulse arises. If the impulse is weak, foresight may conquer; this is what is called acting on reason. If the impulse is strong, either foresight will be falsified, and the disagreeable consequences will be forgotten, or, in men of a heroic mold, the consequences may be recklessly accepted. When Macbeth realizes that he is doomed to defeat, he does not shrink from the fight; he exclaims:—

> Lay on, Macduff,
> And damned be him that first cries, Hold, enough!

But such strength and recklessness of impulse is rare. Most men, when their impulse is strong, succeed in persuading themselves, usually by a subconscious selectiveness of attention, that agreeable consequences will follow from the indulgence of their impulse. Whole philosophies, whole systems of ethical valuation, spring up in this way: they are the embodiment of a kind of thought which is subservient to impulse, which aims at providing a quasi-rational ground for the indulgence of impulse. The only thought which is genuine is that which springs out of the intellectual impulse of curiosity, leading to the desire to know and understand. But most of what passes for thought is inspired by some non-intellectual impulse, and is merely a means of persuading ourselves that we shall not be disappointed or do harm if we indulge this impulse.[1]

When an impulse is restrained, we feel discomfort or even violent pain. We may indulge the impulse in order to escape from this pain, and our action is then one

---

[1] On this subject compare Bernard Hart's "Psychology of Insanity" (Cambridge University Press, 1914), chap. v, especially pp. 62–5.

which has a purpose. But the pain only exists because of the impulse, and the impulse itself is directed to an act, not to escaping from the pain of restraining the impulse. The impulse itself remains without a purpose, and the purpose of escaping from pain only arises when the impulse has been momentarily restrained.

Impulse is at the basis of our activity, much more than desire. Desire has its place, but not so large a place as it seemed to have. Impulses bring with them a whole train of subservient fictitious desires: they make men feel that they desire the results which will follow from indulging the impulses, and that they are acting for the sake of these results, when in fact their action has no motive outside itself. A man may write a book or paint a picture under the belief that he desires the praise which it will bring him; but as soon as it is finished, if his creative impulse is not exhausted, what he has done grows uninteresting to him, and he begins a new piece of work. What applies to artistic creation applies equally to all that is most vital in our lives: direct impulse is what moves us, and the desires which we think we have are a mere garment for the impulse.

Desire, as opposed to impulse, has, it is true, a large and increasing share in the regulation of men's lives. Impulse is erratic and anarchical, not easily fitted into a well-regulated system; it may be tolerated in children and artists, but it is not thought proper to men who hope to be taken seriously. Almost all paid work is done from desire, not from impulse: the work itself is more or less irksome, but the payment for it is desired. The serious activities that fill a man's working hours are, except in a few fortunate individuals, governed mainly by purposes, not by impulses towards those activities. In this hardly any one sees an evil, because the place of impulse in a satisfactory existence is not recognized.

An impulse, to one who does not share it actually or imaginatively, will always seem to be mad. All impulse is essentially blind, in the sense that it does not spring from any prevision of consequences. The man who does not share the impulse will form a different estimate as to what the consequences will be, and as to whether those that must ensue are desirable. This difference of opinion will seem to be ethical or intellectual, whereas its real basis is a difference of impulse. No genuine agreement will be reached, in such a case, so long as the difference of impulse persists. In all men who have any vigorous life, there are strong impulses such as may seem utterly unreasonable to others. Blind impulses sometimes lead to destruction and death, but at other times they lead to the best things the world contains. Blind impulse is the source of war, but it is also the source of science, and art, and love. It is not the weakening of impulse that is to be desired, but the direction of impulse towards life and growth rather than towards death and decay.

The complete control of impulse by will, which is sometimes preached by moralists, and often enforced by economic necessity, is not really desirable. A life governed by purposes and desires, to the exclusion of impulse, is a tiring life; it exhausts vitality, and leaves a man, in the end, indifferent to the very purposes which he has been trying to achieve. When a whole nation lives in this way, the whole nation tends to become feeble, without enough grasp to recognize and overcome the obstacles to its desires. Industrialism and organization are constantly forcing civilized nations to live more and more by purpose rather than impulse. In the long run such a mode of existence, if it does not dry up the springs of life, produces new impulses, not of the kind which the will has been in the habit of controlling or of which thought is conscious. These new impulses are apt to be worse in their effects than those that have been checked. Excessive discipline, especially when it is imposed from without, often issues in impulses of cruelty and destruction; this is one reason why militarism has a bad effect on national character. Either lack of vitality, or impulses which are oppressive and against life, will almost always result if the spontaneous impulses are not able to find an outlet. A man's impulses are not fixed from the beginning by his native disposition: within certain wide limits, they are profoundly modified by his circumstances and his way of life. The nature of these modifications ought to be studied, and the results of such study ought to be taken account of in judging the good or harm that is done by political and social institutions.

The war has grown, in the main, out of the life of impulse, not out of reason or desire. There is an impulse of aggression, and an impulse of resistance to aggression. Either may, on occasion, be in accordance with reason, but both are operative in many cases in which they are quite contrary to reason. Each impulse produces a whole harvest of attendant beliefs. The beliefs appropriate to the impulse of aggression may be seen in Bernhardi, or in the early Mohammedan conquerors, or, in full perfection, in the Book of Joshua. There is first of all a conviction of the superior excellence of one's own group, a certainty that they are in some sense the chosen people. This justifies the feeling that only the good and evil of one's own group is of real importance, and that the rest of the world is to be regarded merely as material for the triumph or salvation of the higher race. In modern politics this attitude is embodied in imperialism. Europe as a whole has this attitude towards Asia and Africa, and many Germans have this attitude towards the rest of Europe.

Correlative to the impulse of aggression is the impulse of resistance to aggression. This impulse is exemplified in the attitude of the Israelites to the Philistines or of medieval Europe to the Mohammedans. The beliefs which it produces are beliefs in the peculiar wickedness of those whose aggression is feared, and in the immense value of national customs which they might suppress if they were victorious. When the war broke out, all the reactionaries in England and France began to speak of the danger to democracy, although until that moment they had opposed democracy with all their strength. They were not insincere in so speaking: the impulse of resistance to Germany made them value whatever was endangered by the German attack. They loved democracy because they hated Germany; but they thought they hated Germany because they loved democracy.

The correlative impulses of aggression and resistance to aggression have both been operative in all the countries engaged in the war. Those who have not been dominated by one or other of these impulses may be roughly divided into three classes. There are, first, men whose national sentiment is antagonistic to the State to which they are subject. This class includes some Irish, Poles, Finns, Jews, and other members of oppressed nations. From our point of view, these men may be omitted from our consideration, since they have the same impulsive nature as those who fight, and differ merely in external circumstances.

The second class of men who have not been part of the force supporting the war have been those whose impulsive nature is more or less atrophied. Opponents of pacifism suppose that all pacifists belong to this class, except when they are in German pay. It is thought that pacifists are bloodless, men without passions, men who can look on and reason with cold detachment while their brothers are giving their lives for their country. Among those who are merely passively pacifist, and do no more than abstain from actively taking part in the war, there may be a certain proportion of whom this is true. I think the supporters of war would be right in decrying such men. In spite of all the destruction which is wrought by the impulses that lead to war, there is more hope for a nation which has these impulses than for a nation in which all impulse is dead. Impulse is the expression of life, and while it exists there is hope of its turning towards life instead of towards death; but lack of impulse is death, and out of death no new life will come.

The active pacifists, however, are not of this class: they are not men without impulsive force but men in whom some impulse to which war is hostile is strong enough to overcome the impulses that lead to war. It is not the act of a passionless man to throw himself athwart the whole movement of the national life, to urge an outwardly hopeless cause, to incur obloquy and to resist the contagion of collective emotion. The impulse to avoid the hostility of public opinion is one of the strongest in human nature, and can only be overcome by an unusual force of direct and uncalculating impulse; it is not cold reason alone that can prompt such an act.

Impulses may be divided into those that make for life and those that make for death. The impulses embodied in the war are among those that make for death. Any one of the impulses that make for life, if it is strong enough, will lead a man to stand out against the war. Some of these impulses are only strong in highly civilized men; some are part of common humanity. The impulses towards art and science are among the more civilized of those that make for life. Many artists have remained wholly untouched by the passions of the war, not from feebleness of feeling, but because the creative instinct, the pursuit of a vision, makes them critical of the assaults of national passion, and not responsive to the myth in which the impulse of pugnacity clothes itself. And the few men in whom the scientific impulse is dominant have noticed the rival myths of warring groups, and have been led through understanding to neutrality.

257

But it is not out of such refined impulses that a popular force can be generated which shall be sufficient to transform the world.

There are three forces on the side of life which require no exceptional mental endowment, which are not very rare at present, and might be very common under better social institutions. They are love, the instinct of constructiveness, and the joy of life. All three are checked and enfeebled at present by the conditions under which men live—not only the less outwardly fortunate, but also the majority of the well-to-do. Our institutions rest upon injustice and authority: it is only by closing our hearts against sympathy and our minds against truth that we can endure the oppressions and unfairnesses by which we profit. The conventional conception of what constitutes success leads most men to live a life in which their most vital impulses are sacrificed, and the joy of life is lost in listless weariness. Our economic system compels almost all men to carry out the purposes of others rather than their own, making them feel impotent in action and only able to secure a certain modicum of passive pleasure. All these things destroy the vigor of the community, the expansive affections of individuals, and the power of viewing the world generously. All these things are unnecessary and can be ended by wisdom and courage. If they were ended, the impulsive life of men would become wholly different, and the human race might travel towards a new happiness and a new vigor. To urge this hope is the purpose of these lectures.

The impulses and desires of men and women, in so far as they are of real importance in their lives, are not detached one from another, but proceed from a central principle of growth, an instinctive urgency leading them in a certain direction, as trees seek the light. So long as this instinctive movement is not thwarted, whatever misfortunes may occur are not fundamental disasters, and do not produce those distortions which result from interference with natural growth. This intimate center in each human being is what imagination must apprehend if we are to understand him intuitively. It differs from man to man, and determines for each man the type of excellence of which he is capable. The utmost that social institutions can do for a man is to make his own growth free and vigorous: they cannot force him to grow according to the pattern of another man. There are in men some impulses and desires—for example, those towards drugs—which do not grow out of the central principle; such impulses, when they become strong enough to be harmful, have to be checked by self-discipline. Other impulses, though they may grow out of the central principle in the individual, may be injurious to the growth of others, and they need to be checked in the interest of others. But in the main, the impulses which are injurious to others tend to result from thwarted growth, and to be least in those who have been unimpeded in their instinctive development.

Men, like trees, require for their growth the right soil and a sufficient freedom from oppression. These can be helped or hindered by political institutions. But the soil and the freedom required for a man's growth are immeasurably more difficult to discover and to obtain than the soil and the freedom required for the growth of a tree. And the full growth which may be hoped for cannot be defined or demonstrated; it is subtle and complex, it can only be felt by a delicate intuition and dimly apprehended by imagination and respect. It depends not only or chiefly upon the physical environment, but upon beliefs and affections, upon opportunities for action, and upon the whole life of the community. The more developed and civilized the type of man the more elaborate are the conditions of his growth, and the more dependent they become upon the general state of the society in which he lives. A man's needs and desires are not confined to his own life. If his mind is comprehensive and his imagination vivid, the failures of the community to which he belongs are his failures, and its successes are his successes: according as his community succeeds or fails, his own growth is nourished or impeded.

In the modern world, the principle of growth in most men and women is hampered by institutions inherited from a simpler age. By the progress of thought and knowledge, and by the increase in command over the forces of the physical world, new possibilities of growth have come into existence, and have given rise to new claims which must be satisfied if those who make them are not to be thwarted. There is less acquiescence in limitations which are no longer unavoidable, and less possibility of a good life while those limitations remain. Institutions which give much greater opportunities to some classes than to others are no longer recognized as just by the less fortunate, though the more fortunate still defend them vehemently. Hence arises a universal strife, in which tradition and authority are arrayed against liberty and justice. Our professed morality, being traditional, loses its hold upon those who are in revolt. Coöperation between the defenders of the old and the champions of the new has become almost impossible. An intimate disunion has entered into almost all the relations of life in continually increasing measure. In the fight for freedom, men and women become increasingly unable to break down the walls of the Ego and achieve the growth which comes from a real and vital union.

All our institutions have their historic basis in Authority. The unquestioned authority of the Oriental despot found its religious expression in the omnipotent Creator, whose glory was the sole end of man, and against whom man had no rights. This authority descended to the Emperor and Pope, to the kings of the Middle Ages, to the nobles in the feudal hierarchy, and even to every husband and father in his dealings with his wife and children. The Church was the direct embodiment of the Divine authority, the State and the law were constituted by the authority of the King, private property in land grew out of the authority of conquering barons, and the family was governed by the authority of the pater-familias.

The institutions of the Middle Ages permitted only a fortunate few to develop freely: the vast majority of mankind existed to minister to the few. But so long as authority was genuinely respected and acknowledged even by its least fortunate subjects, medieval society remained organic and not fundamentally hostile to life, since outward submission was compatible with inward freedom because it was voluntary. The institutions of Western Christendom embodied a theory which was really believed, as no theory by which our present institutions can be defended is now believed.

The medieval theory of life broke down through its failure to satisfy men's demands for justice and liberty. Under the stress of oppression, when rulers exceeded their theoretical powers, the victims were forced to realize that they themselves also had rights, and need not live merely to increase the glory of the few. Gradually it came to be seen that if men have power, they are likely to abuse it, and that authority in practice means tyranny. Because the claim to justice was resisted by the holders of power, men became more and more separate units, each fighting for his own rights, not a genuine community bound together by an organic common purpose. This absence of a common purpose has become a source of unhappiness. One of the reasons which led many men to welcome the outbreak of the present war was that it made each nation again a whole community with a single purpose. It did this by destroying, for the present, the beginnings of a single purpose in the civilized world as a whole; but these beginnings were as yet so feeble that few were much affected by their destruction. Men rejoiced in the new sense of unity with their compatriots more than they minded the increased separation from their enemies.

The hardening and separation of the individual in the course of the fight for freedom has been inevitable, and is not likely ever to be wholly undone. What is necessary, if an organic society is to grow up, is that our institutions should be so fundamentally changed as to embody that new respect for the individual and his rights which modern feeling demands. The medieval Empire and Church swept away the individual. There were heretics, but they were massacred relentlessly, without any of the qualms aroused by later persecutions. And they, like their persecutors, were persuaded that there ought to be one universal Church: they differed only as to what its creed should be. Among a few men of art and letters, the Renaissance undermined the medieval theory, without, however, replacing it by anything but skepticism and confusion. The first serious breach in this medieval theory was caused by Luther's assertion of the right of private judgment and the fallibility of General Councils. Out of this assertion grew inevitably, with time, the belief that a man's religion could not be determined for him by authority, but must be left to the free choice of each individual. It was in matters of religion that the battle for liberty began, and it is in matters of religion that it has come nearest to a complete victory.[2]

The development through extreme individualism to strife, and thence, one hopes, to a new reintegration, is to be seen in almost every department of life. Claims are advanced in the name of justice, and resisted in the name of tradition and prescriptive

---

[2] This was written before Christianity had become punishable by hard labor, penal servitude, or even death, under the Military Service Act (No. 2). [Note added in 1916.]

right. Each side honestly believes that it deserves to triumph, because two theories of society exist side by side in our thought, and men choose, unconsciously, the theory which fits their case. Because the battle is long and arduous all general theory is gradually forgotten; in the end, nothing remains but self-assertion, and when the oppressed win freedom they are as oppressive as their former masters.

This is seen most crudely in the case of what is called nationalism. Nationalism, in theory, is the doctrine that men, by their sympathies and traditions, form natural groups, called "nations," each of which ought to be united under one central Government. In the main this doctrine may be conceded. But in practice the doctrine takes a more personal form. "I belong," the oppressed nationalist argues, "by sympathy and tradition to nation A, but I am subject to a government which is in the hands of nation B. This is an injustice, not only because of the general principle of nationalism, but because nation A is generous, progressive, and civilized, while nation B is oppressive, retrograde, and barbarous. Because this is so, nation A deserves to prosper, while nation B deserves to be abased." The inhabitants of nation B are naturally deaf to the claims of abstract justice, when they are accompanied by personal hostility and contempt. Presently, however, in the course of war, nation A acquires its freedom. The energy and pride which have achieved freedom generates a momentum which leads on, almost infallibly, to the attempt at foreign conquest, or to the refusal of liberty to some smaller nation. "What? You say that nation C, which forms part of our State, has the same rights against us as we had against nation A? But that is absurd. Nation C is swinish and turbulent, incapable of good government, needing a strong hand if it is not to be a menace and a disturbance to all its neighbors." So the English used to speak of the Irish, so the Germans and Russians speak of the Poles, so the Galician Poles speak of the Ruthenes, so the Austrians used to speak of the Magyars, so the Magyars speak of the South Slav sympathizers with Serbia, so the Serbs speak of the Macedonian Bulgars. In this way nationalism, unobjectionable in theory, leads by a natural movement to oppression and wars of conquest. No sooner was France free from the English, in the fifteenth century, than it embarked upon the conquest of Italy; no sooner was Spain freed from the Moors than it entered into more than a century of conflict with France for the supremacy in Europe. The case of Germany is very interesting in this respect. At the beginning of the eighteenth century German culture was French: French was the language of the Courts, the language in which Leibnitz wrote his philosophy, the universal language of polite letters and learning. National consciousness hardly existed. Then a series of great men created a self-respect in Germany by their achievements in poetry, music, philosophy, and science. But politically German nationalism was only created by Napoleon's oppression and the uprising of 1813. After centuries during which every disturbance of the peace of Europe began with a French or Swedish or Russian invasion of Germany, the Germans discovered that by sufficient effort and union they could keep foreign armies off their territory. But the effort required had been too great to cease when its purely defensive purpose had been achieved by the defeat of Napoleon. Now, a hundred years later, they are still engaged in the same movement, which has become one of aggression and conquest. Whether we are now seeing the end of the movement it is not yet possible to guess.

If men had any strong sense of a community of nations, nationalism would serve to define the boundaries of the various nations. But because men only feel community within their own nation, nothing but force is able to make them respect the rights of other nations, even when they are asserting exactly similar rights on their own behalf.

Analogous development is to be expected, with the course of time, in the conflict between capital and labor which has existed since the growth of the industrial system, and in the conflict between men and women, which is still in its infancy.

What is wanted, in these various conflicts, is some principle, genuinely believed, which will have justice for its outcome. The tug of war of mutual self-assertion can only result in justice through an accidental equality of force. It is no use to attempt any bolstering up of institutions based on authority, since all such institutions involve injustice, and injustice once realized cannot be perpetuated without fundamental damage both to those who uphold it and to those who resist it. The damage consists in the hardening of the walls of the Ego, making them a prison instead of a window. Unimpeded growth in the individual depends upon many contacts with other people, which must be of the nature of free coöperation, not of enforced service. While the belief in authority was alive, free coöperation was compatible with inequality and subjection, but now equality and mutual freedom are necessary. All institutions, if they are not to hamper individual growth, must be based as far as possible upon voluntary combination, rather than the force of the law or the traditional authority of the holders of power. None of our institutions can survive the application of this principle without great and fundamental changes; but these changes are imperatively necessary if the world is to be withheld from dissolving into hard separate units each at war with all the others.

The two chief sources of good relations between individuals are instinctive liking and a common purpose. Of these two, a common purpose might seem more important politically, but, in fact, it is often the outcome, not the cause, of instinctive liking, or of a common instinctive aversion. Biological groups, from the family to the nation, are constituted by a greater or less degree of instinctive liking, and build their common purposes on this foundation.

Instinctive liking is the feeling which makes us take pleasure in another person's company, find an exhilaration in his presence, wish to talk with him, work with him, play with him. The extreme form of it is being in love, but its fainter forms, and even the very faintest, have political importance. The presence of a person who is instinctively disliked tends to make any other person more likable. An anti-Semite will love any fellow-Christian when a Jew is present. In China, or the wilds of Africa, any white man would be welcomed with joy. A common aversion is one of the most frequent causes of mild instinctive liking.

Men differ enormously in the frequency and intensity of their instinctive likings, and the same man will differ greatly at different times. One may take Carlyle and Walt Whitman as opposite poles in this respect. To Carlyle, at any rate in later life, most men and women were repulsive; they inspired an instinctive aversion which made him find pleasure in imagining them under the guillotine or perishing in battle. This led him to belittle most men, finding satisfaction only in those who had been notably destructive of human life—Frederick the Great, Dr. Francia, and Governor Eyre. It led him to love war and violence, and to despise the weak and the oppressed—for example, the "thirty thousand distressed needlewomen," on whom he was never weary of venting his scorn. His morals and his politics, in later life, were inspired through and through by repugnance to almost the whole human race.

Walt Whitman, on the contrary, had a warm, expansive feeling towards the vast majority of men and women. His queer catalogues seemed to him interesting because each item came before his imagination as an object of delight. The sort of joy which most people feel only in those who are exceptionally beautiful or splendid Walt Whitman felt in almost everybody. Out of this universal liking grew optimism, a belief in democracy, and a conviction that it is easy for men to live together in peace and amity. His philosophy and politics, like Carlyle's, were based upon his instinctive attitude towards ordinary men and women.

There is no objective reason to be given to show that one of these attitudes is essentially more rational than the other. If a man finds people repulsive, no argument can prove to him that they are not so. But both his own desires and other people's are much more likely to find satisfaction if he resembles Walt Whitman than if he resembles Carlyle. A world of Walt Whitmans would be happier and more capable of realizing its purposes than a world of Carlyles. For this reason, we shall desire, if we can, to increase the amount of instinctive liking in the world and diminish the amount of instinctive aversion. This is perhaps the most important of all the effects by which political institutions ought to be judged.

The other source of good relations between individuals is a common purpose, especially where that purpose cannot be achieved without knowing its cause. Economic organizations, such as unions and political parties are constituted almost wholly by a common purpose; whatever instinctive liking may come to be associated with them is the result of the common purpose, not its cause. Economic organizations, such as railway companies, subsist for a purpose, but this purpose need only actually exist in those who direct the organization: the ordinary wage-earner need have no purpose beyond earning his wages. This is a defect in economic organizations, and ought to be remedied. One of the objects of syndicalism is to remedy this defect.

Marriage is (or should be) based on instinctive liking, but as soon as there are children, or the wish for children, it acquires the additional strength of a common purpose. It is this chiefly which distinguishes it from an irregular connection not intended to lead to children. Often, in fact, the common purpose survives, and remains a strong tie, after the instinctive liking has faded.

A nation, when it is real and not artificial, is founded upon a faint degree of instinctive liking for compatriots and a common instinctive aversion from foreigners. When an Englishman returns to Dover or Folkestone after being on the Continent, he feels something friendly in the familiar ways: the casual porters, the shouting paper boys, the women serving bad tea, all warm his heart, and seem more "natural," more what human beings ought to be, than the foreigners with their strange habits of behavior. He is ready to believe that all English people are good souls, while many foreigners are full of designing wickedness. It is such feelings that make it easy to organize a nation into a governmental unit. And when that has happened, a common purpose is added, as in marriage. Foreigners would like to invade our country and lay it waste, to kill us in battle, to humble our pride. Those who coöperate with us in preventing this disaster are our friends, and their coöperation intensifies our instinctive liking. But common purposes do not constitute the whole source of our love of country: allies, even of long standing, do not call out the same feelings as are called out by our compatriots. Instinctive liking, resulting largely from similar habits and customs, is an essential element in patriotism, and, indeed, the foundation upon which the whole feeling rests.

If men's natural growth is to be promoted and not hindered by the environment, if as many as possible of their desires and needs are to be satisfied, political institutions must, as far as possible, embody common purposes and foster instinctive liking. These two objects are interconnected, for nothing is so destructive of instinctive liking as thwarted purposes and unsatisfied needs, and nothing facilitates coöperation for common purposes so much as instinctive liking. When a man's growth is unimpeded, his self-respect remains intact, and he is not inclined to regard others as his enemies. But when, for whatever reason, his growth is impeded, or he is compelled to grow into some twisted and unnatural shape, his instinct presents the environment as his enemy, and he becomes filled with hatred. The joy of life abandons him, and malevolence takes the place of friendliness. The malevolence of hunchbacks and cripples is proverbial; and a similar malevolence is to be found in those who have been crippled in less obvious ways. Real freedom, if it could be brought about, would go a long way towards destroying hatred.

There is a not uncommon belief that what is instinctive in us cannot be changed, but must be simply accepted and made the best of. This is by no means the case. No doubt we have a certain native disposition, different in different people, which coöperates with outside circumstances in producing a certain character. But even the instinctive part of our character is very malleable. It may be changed by beliefs, by material circumstances, by social circumstances, and by institutions. A Dutchman has probably much the same native disposition as a German, but his instincts in adult life are very different owing to the absence of militarism and of the pride of a Great Power. It is obvious that the instincts of celibates become profoundly different from those of other men and women. Almost any instinct is capable of many different forms according to the nature of the outlets which it finds. The same instinct which leads to artistic or intellectual creativeness may, under other circumstances, lead to love of war. The fact that an activity or belief is an outcome of instinct is therefore no reason for regarding it as unalterable.

This applies to people's instinctive likes and dislikes as well as to their other instincts. It is natural to men, as to other animals, to like some of their species and dislike others; but the proportion of like and dislike depends on circumstances, often on quite trivial circumstances. Most of Carlyle's misanthropy is attributable to dyspepsia; probably a suitable medical regimen would have given him a completely different outlook on the world. The defect of punishment, as a means of dealing with impulses which the community wishes to discourage, is that it does nothing to prevent the existence of the impulses, but merely endeavors to check their indulgence by an appeal to self-interest. This method, since it does not eradicate the impulses, probably only drives them to find other outlets even when it is successful in its immediate object; and if the impulses are strong, mere self-interest is not likely to curb them effectually, since it is not a very powerful motive except with unusually reasonable and rather passionless people. It is thought to be a stronger motive than it is, because our moods make us deceive ourselves as to our interest, and lead us to believe that it is consistent with the actions to which we are prompted by desire or impulse.

Thus the commonplace that human nature cannot be changed is untrue. We all know that our own characters and those of our acquaintance are greatly affected by circumstances; and what is true of individuals is true also of nations. The root causes of changes in average human nature are generally either purely material changes—for instance, of climate—or changes in the degree of man's control over the material world. We may ignore the purely material changes, since these do not much concern the politician. But the changes due to man's increased control over the material world, by inventions and science, are of profound present importance. Through the industrial revolution, they have radically altered the daily lives of men; and by creating huge economic organizations, they have altered the whole structure of society. The general beliefs of men, which are, in the main, a product of instinct and circumstance, have become very different from what they were in the eighteenth century. But our institutions are not yet suited either to the instincts developed by our new circumstances, or to our real beliefs. Institutions have a life of their own, and often outlast the circumstances which made them a fit garment for instinct. This applies, in varying degrees, to almost all the institutions which we have inherited from the past: the State, private property, the patriarchal family, the Churches, armies and navies. All of these have become in some degree oppressive, in some measures hostile to life.

In any serious attempt at political reconstruction, it is necessary to realize what are the vital needs of ordinary men and women. It is customary, in political thought, to assume that the only needs with which politics is concerned are economic needs. This view is quite inadequate to account for such an event as the present war, since any economic motives that may be assigned for it are to a great extent mythical, and its true causes must be sought for outside the economic sphere. Needs which are normally satisfied without conscious effort remain unrecognized, and this results in a working theory of human needs which is far too simple. Owing chiefly to industrialism, many needs which were formerly satisfied without effort now remain unsatisfied in most men and women. But the old unduly simple theory of human needs survives, making men overlook the source of the new lack of satisfaction, and invent quite false theories as to why they are dissatisfied. Socialism as a panacea seems to me to be mistaken in this way, since it is too ready to suppose that better economic conditions will of themselves make men happy. It is not only more material goods that men need, but more freedom, more self-direction, more outlet for creativeness, more opportunity for the joy of life, more voluntary coöperation, and less involuntary subservience to purposes not their own. All these things the institutions of the future must help to produce, if our increase of knowledge and power over Nature is to bear its full fruit in bringing about a good life.

# II

# The State

Under the influence of socialism, most liberal thought in recent years has been in favor of increasing the power of the State, but more or less hostile to the power of private property. On the other hand, syndicalism has been hostile both to the State and to private property. I believe that syndicalism is more nearly right than socialism in this respect, that both private property and the State, which are the two most powerful institutions of the modern world, have become harmful to life through excess of power, and that both are hastening the loss of vitality from which the civilized world increasingly suffers. The two institutions are closely connected, but for the present I wish to consider only the State. I shall try to show how great, how unnecessary, how harmful, many of its powers are, and how enormously they might be diminished without loss of what is useful in its activity. But I shall admit that in certain directions its functions ought to be extended rather than curtailed.

Some of the functions of the State, such as the Post Office and elementary education, might be performed by private agencies, and are only undertaken by the State from motives of convenience. But other matters, such as the law, the police, the Army, and the Navy, belong more essentially to the State: so long as there is a State at all it is difficult to imagine these matters in private hands. The distinction between socialism and individualism turns on the nonessential functions of the State, which the socialist wishes to extend and the individualist to restrict. It is the essential functions, which are admitted by individualists and socialists alike, that I wish to criticize, since the others do not appear to me in themselves objectionable.

The essence of the State is that it is the repository of the collective force of its citizens. This force takes two forms, one internal and one external. The internal form is the law and the police; the external form is the power of waging war, as embodied in the Army and Navy. The State is constituted by the combination of all the inhabitants in a certain area using their united force in accordance with the commands of a Government. In a civilized State force is only employed against its own citizens in accordance with rules previously laid down, which constitute the criminal law. But the employment of force against foreigners is not regulated by any code of rules, and proceeds, with few exceptions, according to some real or fancied national interest.

There can be no doubt that force employed according to law is less pernicious than force employed capriciously. If international law could acquire sufficient hold on men's allegiance to regulate the relations of States, a very great advance on our present condition would have been made. The primitive anarchy which precedes law is worse than law. But I believe there is a possibility of a stage to some extent above law, where the advantages now secured by the law are secured without loss of freedom, and without the disadvantages which the law and the police render inevitable. Probably some repository of force in the background will remain necessary, but the actual employment of force may become very rare, and the degree of force required very small. The anarchy which precedes law gives freedom only to the strong; the condition to be aimed at will give freedom as nearly as possible to every one. It will do this, not by preventing altogether the existence of organized force, but by limiting the occasions for its employment to the greatest possible extent.

The power of the State is only limited internally by the fear of rebellion and externally by the fear of defeat in war. Subject to these restrictions, it is absolute. In practice, it can seize men's property through taxation, determine the law of marriage and inheritance, punish the expression of opinions which it dislikes, put men to death for wishing the region they inhabit to belong to a different State, and order all able-bodied males to risk their lives in battle whenever it considers war desirable. On many matters disagreement with the purposes and opinions of the State is criminal. Probably the freest States in the world, before the war, were America and England; yet in America no immigrant may land until he has professed disbelief in anarchism and polygamy, while in England men were sent to prison in recent years for expressing disagreement with the Christian religion[3] or agreement with the teaching of Christ.[4] In time of war, all criticism of the external policy of the State is criminal. Certain objects having appeared desirable to the majority, or to the effective holders of power, those who do not consider these objects desirable are exposed to pains and penalties not unlike those suffered by heretics in the past. The extent of the tyranny thus exercised is concealed by its very success: few men consider it worth while to incur a persecution which is almost certain to be thorough and effective.

Universal military service is perhaps the extreme example of the power of the State, and the supreme illustration of the difference between its attitude to its own citizens and its attitude to the citizens of other States. The State punishes, with impartial rigor, both those who kill their compatriots and those who refuse to kill foreigners. On the whole, the latter is considered the graver crime. The phenomenon of war is familiar, and men fail to realize its strangeness; to those who stand inside the cycle of instincts which lead to war it all seems natural and reasonable. But to those who stand outside the strangeness of it grows with familiarity. It is amazing that the vast majority of men should tolerate a system which compels them to submit to

---

[3] The blasphemy prosecutions.

[4] The syndicalist prosecutions. [The punishment of conscientious objectors must now be added, 1916.]

all the horrors of the battlefield at any moment when their Government commands them to do so. A French artist, indifferent to politics, attentive only to his painting, suddenly finds himself called upon to shoot Germans, who, his friends assure him, are a disgrace to the human race. A German musician, equally unknowing, is called upon to shoot the perfidious Frenchman. Why cannot the two men declare a mutual neutrality? Why not leave war to those who like it and bring it on? Yet if the two men declared a mutual neutrality they would be shot by their compatriots. To avoid this fate they try to shoot each other. If the world loses the artist, not the musician, Germany rejoices; if the world loses the musician, not the artist, France rejoices. No one remembers the loss to civilization, which is equal whichever is killed.

This is the politics of Bedlam. If the artist and the musician had been allowed to stand aside from the war, nothing but unmitigated good to mankind would have resulted. The power of the State, which makes this impossible, is a wholly evil thing, quite as evil as the power of the Church which in former days put men to death for unorthodox thought. Yet if, even in time of peace, an international league were founded to consist of Frenchmen and Germans in equal numbers, all pledged not to take part in war, the French State and the German State would persecute it with equal ferocity. Blind obedience, unlimited willingness to kill and die are exacted of the modern citizens of a democracy as much as of the Janizaries of medieval sultans or the secret agents of Oriental despots.[5]

The power of the State may be brought to bear, as it often is in England, through public opinion rather than through the laws. By oratory and the influence of the Press, public opinion is largely created by the State, and a tyrannous public opinion is as great an enemy to liberty as tyrannous laws. If the young man who will not fight finds that he is dismissed from his employment, insulted in the streets, cold-shouldered by his friends, and thrown over with scorn by any woman who may formerly have liked him, he will feel the penalty quite as hard to bear as a death sentence.[6] A free

---

[5] In a democratic country it is the majority who must after all rule, and the minority will be obliged to submit with the best grace possible (*Westminster Gazette* on Conscription, December 29, 1915).

[6] Some very strong remarks on the conduct of the "white feather" women were made by Mr. Reginald Kemp, the Deputy Coroner for West Middlesex, at an inquest at Ealing on Saturday on Richard Charles Roberts, aged thirty-four, a taxicab driver, of Shepherd's Bush, who committed suicide in consequence of worry caused by his rejection from the Army and the taunts of women and other amateur recruiters.

It was stated that he tried to join the Army in October, but was rejected on account of a weak heart. That alone, said his widow, had depressed him, and he had been worried because he thought he would lose his license owing to the state of his heart. He had also been troubled by the dangerous illness of a child.

A soldier relative said that the deceased's life had been made "a perfect misery" by women who taunted him and called him a coward because he did not join the Army. A few days ago two women in Maida Vale insulted him "something shocking."

The Coroner, speaking with some warmth, said the conduct of such women was abominable. It was scandalous that women who knew nothing of individual circumstances should be allowed to go about making unbearable the lives of men who had tried to do their duty. It was a pity they had nothing better to do. Here was a man who perhaps had been driven to death by a pack of silly women. He hoped something would soon be done to put a stop to such conduct (*Daily News*, July 26, 1915).

community requires not only legal freedom, but a tolerant public opinion, an absence of that instinctive inquisition into our neighbors' affairs which, under the guise of upholding a high moral standard, enables good people to indulge unconsciously a disposition to cruelty and persecution. Thinking ill of others is not in itself a good reason for thinking well of ourselves. But so long as this is not recognized, and so long as the State can manufacture public opinion, except in the rare cases where it is revolutionary, public opinion must be reckoned as a definite part of the power of the State.

The power of the State outside its own borders is in the main derived from war or the threat of war. Some power is derived from the ability to persuade its citizens to lend money or not to lend it, but this is unimportant in comparison with the power derived from armies and navies. The external activity of the State—with exceptions so rare as to be negligible—is selfish. Sometimes selfishness is mitigated by the need of retaining the goodwill of other States, but this only modifies the methods employed, not the ends pursued. The ends pursued, apart from mere defense against other States, are, on the one hand, opportunities for successful exploitation of weak or uncivilized countries, on the other hand, power and prestige, which are considered more glorious and less material than money. In pursuit of these objects, no State hesitates to put to death innumerable foreigners whose happiness is not compatible with exploitation or subjection, or to devastate territories into which it is thought necessary to strike terror. Apart from the present war, such acts have been performed within the last twenty years by many minor States and by all the Great Powers[7] except Austria; and in the case of Austria only the opportunity, not the will, was lacking.

Why do men acquiesce in the power of the State? There are many reasons, some traditional, some very present and pressing.

The traditional reason for obedience to the State is personal loyalty to the sovereign. European States grew up under the feudal system, and were originally the several territories owned by feudal chiefs. But this source of obedience has decayed, and probably now counts for little except in Japan, and to a lesser extent in Russia.

Tribal feeling, which always underlay loyalty to the sovereign, has remained as strong as it ever was, and is now the chief support for the power of the State. Almost every man finds it essential to his happiness to feel himself a member of a group, animated by common friendships and enmities and banded together for defense and attack. But such groups are of two kinds: there are those which are essentially enlargements of the family, and there are those which are based upon a conscious common purpose. Nations belong to the first kind, Churches to the second. At times when men are profoundly swayed by creeds national divisions tend to break down, as they did in the wars of religion after the Reformation. At such times a common

---

[7] By England in South Africa, America in the Philippines, France in Morocco, Italy in Tripoli, Germany in Southwest Africa, Russia in Persia and Manchuria, Japan in Manchuria.

creed is a stronger bond than a common nationality. To a much slighter extent, the same thing has occurred in the modern world with the rise of socialism. Men who disbelieve in private property, and feel the capitalist the real enemy, have a bond which transcends national divisions. It has not been found strong enough to resist the passions aroused by the present war, but it has made them less bitter among socialists than among others, and has kept alive the hope of a European community to be reconstructed when the war is over. In the main, however, the universal disbelief in creeds has left tribal feeling triumphant, and has made nationalism stronger than at any previous period of the world's history. A few sincere Christians, a few sincere socialists, have found in their creed a force capable of resisting the assaults of national passion, but they have been too few to influence the course of events or even to cause serious anxiety to the Governments.

It is chiefly tribal feeling that generates the unity of a national State, but it is not only tribal feeling that generates its strength. Its strength results principally from two fears, neither of which is unreasonable: the fear of crime and anarchy within, and the fear of aggression from without.

The internal orderliness of a civilized community is a great achievement, chiefly brought about by the increased authority of the State. It would be inconvenient if peaceable citizens were constantly in imminent risk of being robbed and murdered. Civilized life would become almost impossible if adventurous people could organize private armies for purposes of plunder. These conditions existed in the Middle Ages, and have not passed away without a great struggle. It is thought by many—especially by the rich, who derive the greatest advantage from law and order—that any diminution in the power of the State might bring back a condition of universal anarchy. They regard strikes as portents of dissolution. They are terrified by such organizations as the Confédération Générale du Travail and the International Workers of the World. They remember the French Revolution, and feel a not unnatural desire to keep their heads on their shoulders. They dread particularly any political theory which seems to excuse private crimes, such as sabotage and political assassination. Against these dangers they see no protection except the maintenance of the authority of the State, and the belief that all resistance to the State is wicked.

Fear of the danger within is enhanced by fear of the danger without. Every State is exposed at all times to the risk of foreign invasion. No means has hitherto been devised for minimizing this risk except the increase of armaments. But the armaments which are nominally intended to repel invasion may also be used to invade. And so the means adopted to diminish the external fear have the effect of increasing it, and of enormously enhancing the destructiveness of war when it does break out. In this way a reign of terror becomes universal, and the State acquires everywhere something of the character of the Comité du Salut Public.

The tribal feeling out of which the State develops is natural, and the fear by which the State is strengthened is reasonable under present circumstances. And in addition

271

to these two, there is a third source of strength in a national State, namely patriotism in its religious aspect.

Patriotism is a very complex feeling, built up out of primitive instincts and highly intellectual convictions. There is love of home and family and friends, making us peculiarly anxious to preserve our own country from invasion. There is the mild instinctive liking for compatriots as against foreigners. There is pride, which is bound up with the success of the community to which we feel that we belong. There is a belief, suggested by pride but reinforced by history, that one's own nation represents a great tradition and stands for ideals that are important to the human race. But besides all these, there is another element, at once nobler and more open to attack, an element of worship, of willing sacrifice, of joyful merging of the individual life in the life of the nation. This religious element in patriotism is essential to the strength of the State, since it enlists the best that is in most men on the side of national sacrifice.

The religious element in patriotism is reinforced by education, especially by a knowledge of the history and literature of one's own country, provided it is not accompanied by much knowledge of the history and literature of other countries. In every civilized country all instruction of the young emphasizes the merits of their own nation and the faults of other nations. It comes to be universally believed that one's own nation, because of its superiority, deserves support in a quarrel, however the quarrel may have originated. This belief is so genuine and deep that it makes men endure patiently, almost gladly, the losses and hardships and sufferings entailed by war. Like all sincerely believed religions, it gives an outlook on life, based upon instinct but sublimating it, causing a devotion to an end greater than any personal end, but containing many personal ends as it were in solution.

Patriotism as a religion is unsatisfactory because of its lack of universality. The good at which it aims is a good for one's own nation only, not for all mankind. The desires which it inspires in an Englishman are not the same as the desires which it inspires in a German. A world full of patriots may be a world full of strife. The more intensely a nation believes in its patriotism, the more fanatically indifferent it will become to the damage suffered by other nations. When once men have learnt to subordinate their own good to the good of a larger whole, there can be no valid reason for stopping short of the human race. It is the admixture of national pride that makes it so easy in practice for men's impulses towards sacrifice to stop short at the frontiers of their own country. It is this admixture that poisons patriotism, and makes it inferior, as a religion, to beliefs which aim at the salvation of all mankind. We cannot avoid having more love for our own country than for other countries, and there is no reason why we should wish to avoid it, any more than we should wish to love all individual men and women equally. But any adequate religion will lead us to temper inequality of affection by love of justice, and to universalize our aims by realizing the common needs of man. This change was effected by Christianity in Judaism, and must be effected in any merely national religion before it can be purged of evil.

In practice, patriotism has many other enemies to contend with. Cosmopolitanism cannot fail to grow as men acquire more knowledge of foreign countries by education and travel. There is also a kind of individualism which is continually increasing, a realization that every man ought to be as nearly free as possible to choose his own ends, not compelled by a geographical accident to pursue ends forced upon him by the community. Socialism, syndicalism, and anti-capitalist movements generally, are against patriotism in their tendency, since they make men aware that the present State is largely concerned in defending the privileges of the rich, and that many of the conflicts between States have their origin in the financial interests of a few plutocrats. This kind of opposition is perhaps temporary, a mere incident in the struggle of labor to acquire power. Australia, where labor feels its triumph secure, is full of patriotism and militarism, based upon determination to prevent foreign labor from sharing the benefits of a privileged position. It is not unlikely that England might develop a similar nationalism if it became a socialist State. But it is probable that such nationalism would be purely defensive. Schemes of foreign aggression, entailing great loss of life and wealth in the nation which adopts them, would hardly be initiated except by those whose instincts of dominion have been sharpened through the power derived from private property and the institutions of the capitalist State.

The evil wrought in the modern world by the excessive power of the State is very great, and very little recognized.

The chief harm wrought by the State is promotion of efficiency in war. If all States increase their strength, the balance of power is unchanged, and no one State has a better chance of victory than before. And when the means of offense exist, even though their original purpose may have been defensive, the temptation to use them is likely, sooner or later, to prove overwhelming. In this way the very measures which promoted security within the borders of the State promote insecurity elsewhere. It is of the essence of the State to suppress violence within and to facilitate it without. The State makes an entirely artificial division of mankind and of our duties toward them: towards one group we are bound by the law, towards the other only by the prudence of highwaymen. The State is rendered evil by its exclusions, and by the fact that, whenever it embarks upon aggressive war, it becomes a combination of men for murder and robbery. The present system is irrational, since external and internal anarchy must be both right or both wrong. It is supported because, so long as others adopt it, it is thought the only road to safety, and because it secures the pleasures of triumph and dominion, which cannot be obtained in a good community. If these pleasures were no longer sought, or no longer possible to obtain, the problem of securing safety from invasion would not be difficult.

Apart from war, the modern great State is harmful from its vastness and the resulting sense of individual helplessness. The citizen who is out of sympathy with the aims of the State, unless he is a man of very rare gifts, cannot hope to persuade the State to adopt purposes which seem to him better. Even in a democracy, all questions except a very few are decided by a small number of officials and eminent men; and even the few questions which are left to the popular vote are decided by a diffused mass-psychology, not by individual initiative. This is especially noticeable in a country like the United States, where, in spite of democracy, most men have a sense of almost complete impotence in regard to all large issues. In so vast a country the popular will is like one of the forces of Nature, and seems nearly as much outside the control of any one man. This state of things leads, not only in America but in all large States, to something of the weariness and discouragement that we associate with the Roman Empire. Modern States, as opposed to the small city States of ancient Greece or medieval Italy, leave little room for initiative, and fail to develop in most men any sense of ability to control their political destinies. The few men who achieve power in such States are men of abnormal ambition and thirst for dominion, combined with skill in cajolery and subtlety in negotiation. All the rest are dwarfed by knowledge of their own impotence.

A curious survival from the old monarchical idea of the State is the belief that there is some peculiar wickedness in a wish to secede on the part of any section of the population. If Ireland or Poland desires independence, it is thought obvious that this desire must be strenuously resisted, and any attempt to secure it is condemned as "high treason." The only instance to the contrary that I can remember is the separation of Norway and Sweden, which was commended but not imitated. In other cases, nothing but defeat in war has induced States to part with territory: although this attitude is taken for granted, it is not one which would be adopted if the State had better ends in view. The reason for its adoption is that the chief end of almost all great States is power, especially power in war. And power in war is often increased by the inclusion of unwilling citizens. If the well-being of the citizens were the end in view, the question whether a certain area should be included, or should form a separate State, would be left freely to the decision of that area. If this principle were adopted, one of the main reasons for war would be obviated, and one of the most tyrannical elements in the State would be removed.

The principal source of the harm done by the State is the fact that power is its chief end. This is not the case in America, because America is safe against aggression;[8] but in all other great nations the chief aim of the State is to possess the greatest possible amount of external force. To this end, the liberty of the citizens is curtailed, and anti-militarist propaganda is severely punished. This attitude is rooted in pride and fear: pride, which refuses to be conciliatory, and fear, which dreads the results of foreign pride conflicting with our own pride. It seems something of a historical accident that these two passions, which by no means exhaust the political passions of the ordinary man, should so completely determine the external policy of the State. Without pride, there would be no occasion for fear: fear on the part of one nation

---

[8] This was written in 1915.

is due to the supposed pride of another nation. Pride of dominion, unwillingness to decide disputes otherwise than by force or the threat of force, is a habit of mind greatly encouraged by the possession of power. Those who have long been in the habit of exercising power become autocratic and quarrelsome, incapable of regarding an equal otherwise than as a rival. It is notorious that head masters' conferences are more liable to violent disagreements than most similar bodies: each head master tries to treat the others as he treats his own boys; they resent such treatment, and he resents their resentment. Men who have the habit of authority are peculiarly unfit for friendly negotiation; but the official relations of States are mainly in the hands of men with a great deal of authority in their own country. This is, of course, more particularly the case where there is a monarch who actually governs. If is less true where there is a governing oligarchy, and still less true where there is some approach to real democracy. But it is true to a considerable extent in all countries, because Prime Ministers and Foreign Secretaries are necessarily men in authority. The first step towards remedying this state of things is a genuine interest in foreign affairs on the part of the ordinary citizen, and an insistence that national pride shall not be allowed to jeopardize his other interests. During war, when he is roused, he is willing to sacrifice everything to pride; but in quiet times he will be far more ready than men in authority to realize that foreign affairs, like private concerns, ought to be settled amicably according to principles, not brutally by force or the threat of force.

The effect of personal bias in the men who actually compose the Government may be seen very clearly in labor disputes. French syndicalists affirm that the State is simply a product of capitalism, a part of the weapons which capital employs in its conflict with labor. Even in democratic States there is much to bear out this view. In strikes it is common to order out the soldiers to coerce the strikers; although the employers are much fewer, and much easier to coerce, the soldiers are never employed against them. When labor troubles paralyze the industry of a country, it is the men who are thought to be unpatriotic, not the masters, though clearly the responsibility belongs to both sides. The chief reason for this attitude on the part of Governments is that the men composing them belong, by their success if not by their origin, to the same class as the great employers of labor. Their bias and their associates combine to make them view strikes and lockouts from the standpoint of the rich. In a democracy public opinion and the need of conciliating political supporters partially correct these plutocratic influences, but the correction is always only partial. And the same influences which warp the views of Governments on labor questions also warp their views on foreign affairs, with the added disadvantage that the ordinary citizen has much fewer means of arriving at an independent judgment.

The excessive power of the State, partly through internal oppression, but principally through war and the fear of war, is one of the chief causes of misery in the modern world, and one of the main reasons for the discouragement which prevents men from growing to their full mental stature. Some means of curing this excessive power must be found if men are not to be organized into despair, as they were in the Roman Empire.

The State has one purpose which is on the whole good, namely, the substitution of law for force in the relations of men. But this purpose can only be fully achieved by a world-State, without which international relations cannot be made subject to law. And although law is better than force, law is still not the best way of settling disputes. Law is too static, too much on the side of what is decaying, too little on the side of what is growing. So long as law is in theory supreme, it will have to be tempered, from time to time, by internal revolution and external war. These can only be prevented by perpetual readiness to alter the law in accordance with the present balance of forces. If this is not done, the motives for appealing to force will sooner or later become irresistible. A world-State or federation of States, if it is to be successful, will have to decide questions, not by the legal maxims which would be applied by the Hague tribunal, but as far as possible in the same sense in which they would be decided by war. The function of authority should be to render the appeal to force unnecessary, not to give decisions contrary to those which would be reached by force.

This view may be thought by some to be immoral. It may be said that the object of civilization should be to secure justice, not to give the victory to the strong. But when this antithesis is allowed to pass, it is forgotten that love of justice may itself set force in motion. A Legislature which wishes to decide an issue in the same way as it would be decided if there were an appeal to force will necessarily take account of justice, provided justice is so flagrantly on one side that disinterested parties are willing to take up the quarrel. If a strong man assaults a weak man in the streets of London, the balance of force is on the side of the weak man, because, even if the police did not appear, casual passers-by would step in to defend him. It is sheer cant to speak of a contest of might against right, and at the same time to hope for a victory of the right. If the contest is really between might and right, that *means* that right will be beaten. What is obscurely intended, when this phrase is used, is that the stronger side is only rendered stronger by men's sense of right. But men's sense of right is very subjective, and is only one factor in deciding the preponderance of force. What is desirable in a Legislature is, not that it should decide by its personal sense of right, but that it should decide in a way which is felt to make an appeal to force unnecessary.

Having considered what the State ought not to do, I come now to what it ought to do.

Apart from war and the preservation of internal order, there are certain more positive functions which the State performs, and certain others which it ought to perform.

We may lay down two principles as regards these positive functions.

First: there are matters in which the welfare of the whole community depends upon the practically universal attainment of a certain minimum; in such cases the State has the right to insist upon this minimum being attained.

Secondly: there are ways in which, by insisting upon the maintenance of law, the State, if it does nothing further, renders possible various forms of injustice which would otherwise be prevented by the anger of their victims. Such injustices ought, as far as possible, to be prevented by the State.

The most obvious example of a matter where the general welfare depends upon a universal minimum is sanitation and the prevention of infectious diseases. A single case of plague, if it is neglected, may cause disaster to a whole community. No one can reasonably maintain, on general grounds of liberty, that a man suffering from plague ought to be left free to spread infection far and wide. Exactly similar considerations apply to drainage, notification of fevers, and kindred matters. The interference with liberty remains an evil, but in some cases it is clearly a smaller evil than the spread of disease which liberty would produce. The stamping out of malaria and yellow fever by destroying mosquitoes is perhaps the most striking example of the good which can be done in this way. But when the good is small or doubtful, and the interference with liberty is great, it becomes better to endure a certain amount of preventable disease rather than suffer a scientific tyranny.

Compulsory education comes under the same head as sanitation. The existence of ignorant masses in a population is a danger to the community; when a considerable percentage are illiterate, the whole machinery of government has to take account of the fact. Democracy in its modern form would be quite impossible in a nation where many men cannot read. But in this case there is not the same need of absolute universality as in the case of sanitary measures. The gipsies, whose mode of life has been rendered almost impossible by the education authorities, might well have been allowed to remain a picturesque exception. But apart from such rather unimportant exceptions, the argument for compulsory education is irresistible.

What the State does for the care of children at present is less than what ought to be done, not more. Children are not capable of looking after their own interests, and parental responsibility is in many ways inadequate. It is clear that the State alone can insist upon the children being provided with the minimum of knowledge and health which, for the time being, satisfies the conscience of the community.

The encouragement of scientific research is another matter which comes rightly within the powers of the State, because the benefits of discoveries accrue to the community, while the investigations are expensive and never individually certain of achieving any result. In this matter, Great Britain lags behind all other civilized countries.

The second kind of powers which the State ought to possess are those that aim at diminishing economic injustice. It is this kind that has been emphasized by socialists. The law creates or facilitates monopolies, and monopolies are able to exact a toll from the community. The most glaring example is the private ownership of land. Railways are at present controlled by the State, since rates are fixed by law; and it is clear that if they were uncontrolled, they would acquire a dangerous degree of power.[9] Such considerations, if they stood alone, would justify complete socialism. But I think justice, by itself, is, like law, too static to be made a supreme political principle: it does not, when it has been achieved, contain any seeds of new life or any impetus to development. For this reason, when we wish to remedy an injustice, it is important to consider whether, in so doing, we shall be destroying the incentive to some form of vigorous action which is on the whole useful to the community. No such form of action, so far as I can see, is associated with private ownership of land or of any other source of economic rent; if this is the case, it follows that the State ought to be the primary recipient of rent.

If all these powers are allowed to the State, what becomes of the attempt to rescue individual liberty from its tyranny?

This is part of the general problem which confronts all those who still care for the ideals which inspired liberalism, namely the problem of combining liberty and personal initiative with organization. Politics and economics are more and more dominated by vast organizations, in face of which the individual is in danger of becoming powerless. The State is the greatest of these organizations, and the most serious menace to liberty. And yet it seems that many of its functions must be extended rather than curtailed.

There is one way by which organization and liberty can be combined, and that is, by securing power for voluntary organizations, consisting of men who have chosen to belong to them because they embody some purpose which all their members consider important, not a purpose imposed by accident or outside force. The State, being geographical, cannot be a wholly voluntary association, but for that very reason there is need of a strong public opinion to restrain it from a tyrannical use of its powers. This public opinion, in most matters, can only be secured by combinations of those who have certain interests or desires in common.

The positive purposes of the State, over and above the preservation of order, ought as far as possible to be carried out, not by the State itself, but by independent organizations, which should be left completely free so long as they satisfied the State that they were not falling below a necessary minimum. This occurs to a certain limited extent at present in regard to elementary education. The universities, also, may be regarded as acting for the State in the matter of higher education and research, except that in their case no minimum of achievement is exacted. In the economic sphere, the State ought to exercise control, but ought to leave initiative to others. There is every reason to multiply opportunities of initiative, and to give the greatest possible share of initiative to each individual, for if this is not done there will be a general sense of impotence and discouragement. There ought to be a constant endeavor to leave the more positive aspects of government in the hands of voluntary organizations,

---

[9] This would be as true under a syndicalist régime as it is at present.

the purpose of the State being merely to exact efficiency and to secure an amicable settlement of disputes, whether within or without its own borders. And with this ought to be combined the greatest possible toleration of exceptions and the least possible insistence upon uniform system.

A good deal may be achieved through local government by trades as well as by areas. This is the most original idea in syndicalism, and it is valuable as a check upon the tyranny which the community may be tempted to exercise over certain classes of its members. All strong organizations which embody a sectional public opinion, such as trade unions, coöperative societies, professions, and universities, are to be welcomed as safeguards of liberty and opportunities for initiative. And there is need of a strong public opinion in favor of liberty itself. The old battles for freedom of thought and freedom of speech, which it was thought had been definitively won, will have to be fought all over again, since most men are only willing to accord freedom to opinions which happen to be popular. Institutions cannot preserve liberty unless men realize that liberty is precious and are willing to exert themselves to keep it alive.

There is a traditional objection to every *imperium in imperio*, but this is only the jealousy of the tyrant. In actual fact, the modern State contains many organizations which it cannot defeat, except perhaps on rare occasions when public opinion is roused against them. Mr. Lloyd George's long fight with the medical profession over the Insurance Act was full of Homeric fluctuations of fortune. The Welsh miners recently routed the whole power of the State, backed by an excited nation. As for the financiers, no Government would dream of a conflict with them. When all other classes are exhorted to patriotism, they are allowed their 4½ per cent. and an increase of interest on their consols. It is well understood on all sides that an appeal to *their* patriotism would show gross ignorance of the world. It is against the traditions of the State to extort their money by threatening to withdraw police protection. This is not due to the difficulty of such a measure, but only to the fact that great wealth wins genuine admiration from us all, and we cannot bear to think of a very rich man being treated with disrespect.

The existence of strong organizations within the State, such as trade unions, is not undesirable except from the point of view of the official who wishes to wield unlimited power, or of the rival organizations, such as federations of employers, which would prefer a disorganized adversary. In view of the vastness of the State, most men can find little political outlet for initiative except in subordinate organizations formed for specific purposes. Without an outlet for political initiative, men lose their social vigor and their interest in public affairs: they become a prey to corrupt wire-pullers, or to sensation-mongers who have the art of capturing a tired and vagrant attention. The cure for this is to increase rather than diminish the powers of voluntary organizations, to give every man a sphere of political activity small enough for his interest and his capacity, and to confine the functions of the State, as far as possible, to the maintenance of peace among rival interests. The essential merit of the State is that it prevents the internal use of force by private persons. Its essential demerits are, that it promotes the external use of force, and that, by its great size, it makes each individual feel impotent even in a democracy. I shall return in a later lecture to the question of preventing war. The prevention of the sense of individual impotence cannot be achieved by a return to the small City State, which would be as reactionary as a return to the days before machinery. It must be achieved by a method which is in the direction of present tendencies. Such a method would be the increasing devolution of positive political initiative to bodies formed voluntarily for specific purposes, leaving the State rather in the position of a federal authority or a court of arbitration. The State will then confine itself to insisting upon *some* settlement of rival interests: its only principle in deciding what is the right settlement will be an attempt to find the measure most acceptable, on the whole, to all the parties concerned. This is the direction in which democratic States naturally tend, except in so far as they are turned aside by war or the fear of war. So long as war remains a daily imminent danger, the State will remain a Moloch, sacrificing sometimes the life of the individual, and always his unfettered development, to the barren struggle for mastery in the competition with other States. In internal as in external affairs, the worst enemy of freedom is war.

# III

# War as an Institution

In spite of the fact that most nations at most times, are at peace, war is one of the permanent institutions of all free communities, just as Parliament is one of our permanent institutions in spite of the fact that it is not always sitting. It is war as a permanent institution that I wish to consider: why men tolerate it; why they ought not to tolerate it; what hope there is of their coming not to tolerate it; and how they could abolish it if they wished to do so.

War is a conflict between two groups, each of which attempts to kill and maim as many as possible of the other group in order to achieve some object which it desires. The object is generally either power or wealth. It is a pleasure to exercise authority over other men, and it is a pleasure to live on the produce of other men's labor. The victor in war can enjoy more of these delights than the vanquished. But war, like all other natural activities, is not so much prompted by the end which it has in view as by an impulse to the activity itself. Very often men desire an end, not on its own account, but because their nature demands the actions which will lead to the end. And so it is in this case: the ends to be achieved by war appear in prospect far more important than they will appear when they are realized, because war itself is a fulfilment of one side of our nature. If men's actions sprang from desires for what would in fact bring happiness, the purely rational arguments against war would have long ago put an end to it. What makes war difficult to suppress is that it springs from an impulse, rather than from a calculation of the advantages to be derived from war.

War differs from the employment of force by the police through the fact that the actions of the police are ordered by a neutral authority, whereas in war it is the parties to the dispute themselves who set force in motion. This distinction is not absolute, since the State is not always wholly neutral in internal disturbances. When strikers are shot down, the State is taking the side of the rich. When opinions adverse to the existing State are punished, the State is obviously one of the parties to the dispute. And from the suppression of individual opinion up to civil war all gradations are possible. But broadly speaking, force employed according to laws previously laid down by the community as a whole may be distinguished from force employed by one community against another on occasions of which the one community is the sole judge. I have dwelt upon this difference because I do not think the use of force by the police can be wholly eliminated, and I think a similar use of force in international affairs is the best hope of permanent peace. At present, international affairs are regulated by the principle that a nation must not intervene unless its interests are involved: diplomatic usage forbids intervention for the mere maintenance of international law. America may protest when American citizens are drowned by German submarines, but must not protest when no American citizens are involved. The case would be analogous in internal affairs if the police would only interfere with murder when it happened that a policeman had been killed. So long as this principle prevails in the relations of States, the power of neutrals cannot be effectively employed to prevent war.

In every civilized country two forces coöperate to produce war. In ordinary times some men—usually a small proportion of the population—are bellicose: they predict war, and obviously are not unhappy in the prospect. So long as war is not imminent, the bulk of the population pay little attention to these men, and do not actively either support or oppose them. But when war begins to seem very near, a war fever seizes hold of people, and those who were already bellicose find themselves enthusiastically supported by all but an insignificant minority. The impulses which inspire war fever are rather different from those which make some men bellicose in ordinary times. Only educated men are likely to be warlike at ordinary times, since they alone are vividly aware of other countries or of the part which their own nation might play in the affairs of the world. But it is only their knowledge, not their nature, that distinguishes them from their more ignorant compatriots.

To take the most obvious example, German policy, in recent years before the war, was not averse from war, and not friendly to England. It is worth while to try to understand the state of mind from which this policy sprang.

The men who direct German policy are, to begin with, patriotic to an extent which is almost unknown in France and England. The interests of Germany appear to them unquestionably the only interests they need take into account. What injury may, in pursuing those interests, be done to other nations, what destruction may be brought upon populations and cities, what irreparable damage may result to civilization, it is not for them to consider. If they can confer what they regard as benefits upon Germany, everything else is of no account.

The second noteworthy point about German policy is that its conception of national welfare is mainly competitive. It is not the *intrinsic* wealth of Germany, whether materially or mentally, that the rulers of Germany consider important: it is the *comparative* wealth in the competition with other civilized countries. For this reason the destruction of good things abroad appears to them almost as desirable as the creation of good things in Germany. In most parts of the world the French are regarded as the most civilized of nations: their art and their literature and their way of life have an attraction for foreigners which those of Germany do not have. The English have developed political liberty, and the art of maintaining an Empire with a minimum of coercion, in a way for which Germany, hitherto, has shown no aptitude. These are grounds for envy, and envy wishes to destroy what is good in other countries. German militarists, quite rightly, judged that what was best in France and England would probably be destroyed by a great war, even if France and England were not in the end defeated in the actual fighting. I have seen a list of young French writers killed on the battlefield; probably the German authorities have also seen it, and have reflected with joy that another year of such losses will destroy French literature for a generation—perhaps, through loss of tradition, for ever. Every outburst against liberty in our more bellicose newspapers, every incitement to persecution of defenseless Germans, every mark of growing ferocity in our attitude, must be read with delight by German patriots, as proving their success in robbing us of our best, and in forcing us to imitate whatever is worst in Prussia.

But what the rulers of Germany have envied us most was power and wealth—the power derived from command of the seas and the straits, the wealth derived from a century of industrial supremacy. In both these respects they feel that their deserts are higher than ours. They have devoted far more thought and skill to military and industrial organization. Their average of intelligence and knowledge is far superior; their capacity for pursuing an attainable end, unitedly and with forethought, is infinitely greater. Yet we, merely (as they think) because we had a start in the race, have achieved a vastly larger Empire than they have, and an enormously greater control of capital. All this is unbearable; yet nothing but a great war can alter it.

Besides all these feelings, there is in many Germans, especially in those who know us best, a hot hatred of us on account of our pride. Farinata degli Uberti surveyed Hell "*come avesse lo Inferno in gran dispitto.*" Just so, by German accounts, English officer prisoners look round them among their captors—holding aloof, as though the enemy were noxious, unclean creatures, toads or slugs or centipedes, which a man does not touch willingly, and shakes off with loathing if he is forced to touch them for a moment. It is easy to imagine how the devils hated Farinata, and inflicted greater pains upon him than upon his neighbors, hoping to win recognition by some slight wincing on his part, driven to frenzy by his continuing to behave as if they did not exist. In just the same way the Germans are maddened by our spiritual immobility. At bottom we have regarded the Germans as one regards flies on a hot day: they are a nuisance, one has to brush them off, but it would not occur to one to be turned aside by them. Now that the initial certainty of victory has faded, we begin to be affected inwardly by the Germans. In time, if we continue to fail in our military enterprises, we shall realize that they are human beings, not just a tiresome circumstance. Then perhaps we shall hate them with a hatred which they will have no reason to resent. And from such a hatred it will be only a short journey to a genuine *rapprochement*.

The problem which must be solved, if the future of the world is to be less terrible than its present, is the problem of preventing nations from getting into the moods of England and Germany at the outbreak of the war. These two nations as they were at that moment might be taken as almost mythical representatives of pride and envy—

cold pride and hot envy. Germany declaimed passionately: "You, England, swollen and decrepit, you overshadow my whole growth—your rotting branches keep the sun from shining upon me and the rain from nourishing me. Your spreading foliage must be lopped, your symmetrical beauty must be destroyed, that I too may have freedom to grow, that my young vigor may no longer be impeded by your decaying mass." England, bored and aloof, unconscious of the claims of outside forces, attempted absent-mindedly to sweep away the upstart disturber of meditation; but the upstart was not swept away, and remains so far with every prospect of making good his claim. The claim and the resistance to it are alike folly. Germany had no good ground for envy; we had no good ground for resisting whatever in Germany's demands was compatible with our continued existence. Is there any method of averting such reciprocal folly in the future?

I think if either the English or the Germans were capable of thinking in terms of individual welfare rather than national pride, they would have seen that, at every moment during the war the wisest course would have been to conclude peace at once, on the best terms that could have been obtained. This course, I am convinced, would have been the wisest for each separate nation, as well as for civilization in general. The utmost evil that the enemy could inflict through an unfavorable peace would be a trifle compared to the evil which all the nations inflict upon themselves by continuing to fight. What blinds us to this obvious fact is pride, the pride which makes the acknowledgment of defeat intolerable, and clothes itself in the garb of reason by suggesting all kinds of evils which are supposed to result from admitting defeat. But the only real evil of defeat is humiliation, and humiliation is subjective; we shall not feel humiliated if we become persuaded that it was a mistake to engage in the war, and that it is better to pursue other tasks not dependent upon world-dominion. If either the English or the Germans could admit this inwardly, any peace which did not destroy national independence could be accepted without real loss in the self-respect which is essential to a good life.

The mood in which Germany embarked upon the war was abominable, but it was a mood fostered by the habitual mood of England. We have prided ourselves upon our territory and our wealth; we have been ready at all times to defend by force of arms what we have conquered in India and Africa. If we had realized the futility of empire, and had shown a willingness to yield colonies to Germany without waiting for the threat of force, we might have been in a position to persuade the Germans that their ambitions were foolish, and that the respect of the world was not to be won by an imperialist policy. But by our resistance we showed that we shared their standards. We, being in possession, became enamored of the *status quo*. The Germans were willing to make war to upset the *status quo*; we were willing to make war to prevent its being upset in Germany's favor. So convinced were we of the sacredness of the *status quo* that we never realized how advantageous it was to us, or how, by insisting upon it, we shared the responsibility for the war. In a world where nations grow and decay, where forces change and populations become cramped, it is not possible or desirable to maintain the *status quo* for ever. If peace is to be preserved, nations must learn to accept unfavorable alterations of the map without feeling that they must first be defeated in war, or that in yielding they incur a humiliation.

It is the insistence of legalists and friends of peace upon the maintenance of the *status quo* that has driven Germany into militarism. Germany had as good a right to an Empire as any other Great Power, but could only acquire an Empire through war. Love of peace has been too much associated with a static conception of international relations. In economic disputes we all know that whatever is vigorous in the wage-earning classes is opposed to "industrial peace," because the existing distribution of wealth is felt to be unfair. Those who enjoy a privileged position endeavor to bolster up their claims by appealing to the desire for peace, and decrying those who promote strife between the classes. It never occurs to them that by opposing changes without considering whether they are just, the capitalists share the responsibility for the class war. And in exactly the same way England shares the responsibility for Germany's war. If actual war is ever to cease there will have to be political methods of achieving the results which now can only be achieved by successful fighting, and nations will have voluntarily to admit adverse claims which appear just in the judgment of neutrals.

It is only by some such admission, embodying itself in a Parliament of the nations with full power to alter the distribution of territory, that militarism can be permanently overcome. It may be that the present war will bring, in the Western nations, a change of mood and outlook sufficient to make such an institution possible. It may be that more wars and more destruction will be necessary before the majority of civilized men rebel against the brutality and futile destruction of modern war. But unless our standards of civilization and our powers of constructive thought are to be permanently lowered, I cannot doubt that, sooner or later, reason will conquer the blind impulses which now lead nations into war. And if a large majority of the Great Powers had a firm determination that peace should be preserved, there would be no difficulty in devising diplomatic machinery for the settlement of disputes, and in establishing educational systems which would implant in the minds of the young an ineradicable horror of the slaughter which they are now taught to admire.

Besides the conscious and deliberate forces leading to war, there are the inarticulate feelings of common men, which, in most civilized countries, are always ready to burst into war fever at the bidding of statesmen. If peace is to be secure, the readiness to catch war fever must be somehow diminished. Whoever wishes to succeed in this must first understand what war fever is and why it arises.

The men who have an important influence in the world, whether for good or evil, are dominated as a rule by a threefold desire: they desire, first, an activity which calls fully into play the faculties in which they feel that they excel; secondly, the sense of successfully overcoming resistance; thirdly, the respect of others on account of their success. The third of these desires is sometimes absent: some men who have been great have been without the "last infirmity," and have been content with their own sense of success, or merely with the joy of difficult effort. But as a rule all three are present. Some men's talents are specialized, so that their choice of activities is circumscribed by the nature of their faculties; other men have, in youth, such a wide range of possible aptitudes that their choice is chiefly determined by the varying degrees of respect which public opinion gives to different kinds of success.

The same desires, usually in a less marked degree, exist in men who have no exceptional talents. But such men cannot achieve anything very difficult by their individual efforts; for them, as units, it is impossible to acquire the sense of greatness or the triumph of strong resistance overcome. Their separate lives are unadventurous and dull. In the morning they go to the office or the plow, in the evening they return tired and silent, to the sober monotony of wife and children. Believing that security is the supreme good, they have insured against sickness and death, and have found an employment where they have little fear of dismissal and no hope of any great rise. But security, once achieved, brings a Nemesis of ennui. Adventure, imagination, risk, also have their claims; but how can these claims be satisfied by the ordinary wage-earner? Even if it were possible to satisfy them, the claims of wife and children have priority and must not be neglected.

To this victim of order and good organization the realization comes, in some moment of sudden crisis, that he belongs to a nation, that his nation may take risks, may engage in difficult enterprises, enjoy the hot passion of doubtful combat, stimulate adventure and imagination by military expeditions to Mount Sinai and the Garden of Eden. What his nation does, in some sense, he does; what his nation suffers, he suffers. The long years of private caution are avenged by a wild plunge into public madness. All the horrid duties of thrift and order and care which he has learnt to fulfil in private are thought not to apply to public affairs: it is patriotic and noble to be reckless for the nation, though it would be wicked to be reckless for oneself. The old primitive passions, which civilization has denied, surge up all the stronger for repression. In a moment imagination and instinct travel back through the centuries, and the wild man of the woods emerges from the mental prison in which he has been confined. This is the deeper part of the psychology of the war fever.

But besides the irrational and instinctive element in the war fever, there is always also, if only as a liberator of primitive impulse, a certain amount of quasi-rational calculation and what is euphemistically called "thought." The war fever very seldom seizes a nation unless it believes that it will be victorious. Undoubtedly, under the influence of excitement, men over-estimate their chances of success; but there is some proportion between what is hoped and what a rational man would expect. Holland, though quite as humane as England, had no impulse to go to war on behalf of Belgium, because the likelihood of disaster was so obviously overwhelming. The London populace, if they had known how the war was going to develop, would not have rejoiced as they did on that August Bank Holiday long ago. A nation which has had a recent experience of war, and has come to know that a war is almost always more painful than it is expected to be at the outset, becomes much less liable to war fever until a new generation grows up. The element of rationality in war fever is recognized by Governments and journalists who desire war, as may be seen by their invariably minimizing the perils of a war which they wish to provoke. At the beginning of the South African War Sir William Butler was dismissed, apparently for suggesting that sixty thousand men and three months might not suffice to subdue the Boer Republics. And when the war proved long and difficult, the nation turned against those who had made it. We may assume, I think, without attributing too great a share to reason in human affairs, that a nation would not suffer from war fever in a case where every sane man could see that defeat was very probable.

The importance of this lies in the fact that it would make aggressive war very unlikely if its chances of success were very small. If the peace-loving nations were sufficiently strong to be obviously capable of defeating the nations which were willing to wage aggressive war, the peace-loving nations might form an alliance and agree to fight jointly against any nation which refused to submit its claims to an International Council. Before the present war we might have reasonably hoped to secure the peace of the world in some such way; but the military strength of Germany has shown that such a scheme has no great chance of success at present. Perhaps at some not far distant date it may be made more feasible by developments of policy in America.

The economic and political forces which make for war could be easily curbed if the will to peace existed strongly in all civilized nations. But so long as the populations are liable to war fever, all work for peace must be precarious; and if war fever could not be aroused, political and economic forces would be powerless to produce any long or very destructive war. The fundamental problem for the pacifist is to prevent the impulse towards war which seizes whole communities from time to time. And this can only be done by far-reaching changes in education, in the economic structure of society, and in the moral code by which public opinion controls the lives of men and women.[10]

A great many of the impulses which now lead nations to go to war are in themselves essential to any vigorous or progressive life. Without imagination and love of adventure a society soon becomes stagnant and begins to decay. Conflict, provided it is not destructive and brutal, is necessary in order to stimulate men's activities, and to secure the victory of what is living over what is dead or merely traditional. The wish for the triumph of one's cause, the sense of solidarity with large bodies of men, are not things which a wise man will wish to destroy. It is only the outcome in death and destruction and hatred that is evil. The problem is, to keep these impulses, without making war the outlet for them.

---

[10] These changes, which are to be desired on their own account, not only in order to prevent war, will be discussed in later lectures.

All Utopias that have hitherto been constructed are intolerably dull. Any man with any force in him would rather live in this world, with all its ghastly horrors, than in Plato's Republic or among Swift's Houyhnhnms. The men who make Utopias proceed upon a radically false assumption as to what constitutes a good life. They conceive that it is possible to imagine a certain state of society and a certain way of life which should be once for all recognized as good, and should then continue for ever and ever. They do not realize that much the greater part of a man's happiness depends upon activity, and only a very small remnant consists in passive enjoyment. Even the pleasures which do consist in enjoyment are only satisfactory, to most men, when they come in the intervals of activity. Social reformers, like inventors of Utopias, are apt to forget this very obvious fact of human nature. They aim rather at securing more leisure, and more opportunity for enjoying it, than at making work itself more satisfactory, more consonant with impulse, and a better outlet for creativeness and the desire to employ one's faculties. Work, in the modern world, is, to almost all who depend on earnings, mere work, not an embodiment of the desire for activity. Probably this is to a considerable extent inevitable. But in so far as it can be prevented something will be done to give a peaceful outlet to some of the impulses which lead to war.

It would, of course, be easy to bring about peace if there were no vigor in the world. The Roman Empire was pacific and unproductive; the Athens of Pericles was the most productive and almost the most warlike community known to history. The only form of production in which our own age excels is science, and in science Germany, the most warlike of Great Powers, is supreme. It is useless to multiply examples; but it is plain that the very same vital energy which produces all that is best also produces war and the love of war. This is the basis of the opposition to pacifism felt by many men whose aims and activities are by no means brutal. Pacifism, in practice, too often expresses merely lack of force, not the refusal to use force in thwarting others. Pacifism, if it is to be both victorious and beneficent, must find an outlet, compatible with humane feeling, for the vigor which now leads nations into war and destruction.

This problem was considered by William James in an admirable address on "The Moral Equivalent of War," delivered to a congress of pacifists during the Spanish-American War of 1898. His statement of the problem could not be bettered; and so far as I know, he is the only writer who has faced the problem adequately. But his solution is not adequate; perhaps no adequate solution is possible. The problem, however, is one of degree: every additional peaceful outlet for men's energies diminishes the force which urges nations towards war, and makes war less frequent and less fierce. And as a question of degree, it is capable of more or less partial solutions.[11]

---

[11] What is said on this subject in the present lecture is only preliminary, since the subsequent lectures all deal with some aspect of the same problem.

Every vigorous man needs some kind of contest, some sense of resistance overcome, in order to feel that he is exercising his faculties. Under the influence of economics, a theory has grown up that what men desire is wealth; this theory has tended to verify itself, because people's actions are more often determined by what they think they desire than by what they really desire. The less active members of a community often do in fact desire wealth, since it enables them to gratify a taste for passive enjoyment, and to secure respect without exertion. But the energetic men who make great fortunes seldom desire the actual money: they desire the sense of power through a contest, and the joy of successful activity. For this reason, those who are the most ruthless in making money are often the most willing to give it away; there are many notorious examples of this among American millionaires. The only element of truth in the economic theory that these men are actuated by desire for money is this: owing to the fact that money is what is *believed* to be desirable, the making of money is recognized as the test of success. What is desired is visible and indubitable success; but this can only be achieved by being one of the few who reach a goal which many men would wish to reach. For this reason, public opinion has a great influence in directing the activities of vigorous men. In America a millionaire is more respected than a great artist; this leads men who might become either the one or the other to choose to become millionaires. In Renaissance Italy great artists were more respected than millionaires, and the result was the opposite of what it is in America.

Some pacifists and all militarists deprecate social and political conflicts. In this the militarists are in the right, from their point of view; but the pacifists seem to me mistaken. Conflicts of party politics, conflicts between capital and labor, and generally all those conflicts of principle which do not involve war, serve many useful purposes, and do very little harm. They increase men's interest in public affairs, they afford a comparatively innocent outlet for the love of contest, and they help to alter laws and institutions, when changing conditions or greater knowledge create the wish for an alteration. Everything that intensifies political life tends to bring about a peaceful interest of the same kind as the interest which leads to desire for war. And in a democratic community political questions give every voter a sense of initiative and power and responsibility which relieves his life of something of its narrow unadventurousness. The object of the pacifist should be to give men more and more political control over their own lives, and in particular to introduce democracy into the management of industry, as the syndicalists advise.

The problem for the reflective pacifist is two-fold: how to keep his own country at peace, and how to preserve the peace of the world. It is impossible that the peace of the world should be preserved while nations are liable to the mood in which Germany entered upon the war—unless, indeed, one nation were so obviously stronger than all others combined as to make war unnecessary for that one and hopeless for all the others. As this war has dragged on its weary length, many people must have asked themselves whether national independence is worth the price that has to be paid for it. Would it not perhaps be better to secure universal peace by the supremacy of one Power? "To secure peace by a world federation"—so a submissive pacifist may argue—"would require some faint glimmerings of reason in rulers and peoples, and is therefore out of the question; but to secure it by allowing Germany to dictate terms to Europe would be easy, in view of Germany's amazing military success. Since there is no other way of ending war"—so our advocate of peace at any price would contend— "let us adopt this way, which happens at the moment to be open to us." It is worth while to consider this view more attentively than is commonly considered.

There is one great historic example of a long peace secured in this way; I mean the Roman Empire. We in England boast of the *Pax Britannica* which we have imposed, in this way, upon the warring races and religions in India. If we are right in boasting of this, if we have in fact conferred a benefit upon India by enforced peace, the Germans would be right in boasting if they could impose a *Pax Germanica* upon Europe. Before the war, men might have said that India and Europe are not analogous, because India is less civilized than Europe; but now, I hope, no one would have the effrontery to maintain anything so preposterous. Repeatedly in modern history there has been a chance of achieving European unity by the hegemony of a single State; but always England, in obedience to the doctrine of the Balance of Power, has prevented this consummation, and preserved what our statesmen have called the "liberties of Europe." It is this task upon which we are now engaged. But I do not think our statesmen, or any others among us, have made much effort to consider whether the task is worth what it costs.

In one case we were clearly wrong: in our resistance to revolutionary France. If revolutionary France could have conquered the Continent and Great Britain, the world would now be happier, more civilized, and more free, as well as more peaceful. But revolutionary France was a quite exceptional case, because its early conquests were made in the name of liberty, against tyrants, not against peoples; and everywhere the French armies were welcomed as liberators by all except rulers and bigots. In the case of Philip II we were as clearly right as we were wrong in 1793. But in both cases our action is not to be judged by some abstract diplomatic conception of the "liberties of Europe," but by the ideals of the Power seeking hegemony, and by the probable effect upon the welfare of ordinary men and women throughout Europe.

"Hegemony" is a very vague word, and everything turns upon the degree of interference with liberty which it involves. There is a degree of interference with liberty which is fatal to many forms of national life; for example, Italy in the seventeenth and eighteenth centuries was crushed by the supremacy of Spain and Austria. If the Germans were actually to annex French provinces, as they did in 1871, they would probably inflict a serious injury upon those provinces, and make them less fruitful for civilization in general. For such reasons national liberty is a matter of real importance, and a Europe actually governed by Germany would probably be very dead and unproductive. But if "hegemony" merely means increased weight in diplomatic questions, more coaling stations and possessions in Africa, more power of securing advantageous commercial treaties, then it can hardly be supposed that it would do any vital damage to other nations; certainly it would not do so much damage as the present war is doing. I cannot doubt that, before the war, a hegemony of this kind would have abundantly satisfied the Germans. But the effect of the war, so far, has been to increase immeasurably all the dangers which it was intended to avert. We have now only the choice between certain exhaustion of Europe in fighting Germany and possible damage to the national life of France by German tyranny. Stated in terms of civilization and human welfare, not in terms of national prestige, that is now in fact the issue.

Assuming that war is not ended by one State conquering all the others, the only way in which it can be permanently ended is by a world-federation. So long as there are many sovereign States, each with its own Army, there can be no security that there will not be war. There will have to be in the world only one Army and one Navy before there will be any reason to think that wars have ceased. This means that, so far as the military functions of the State are concerned, there will be only one State, which will be world-wide.

The civil functions of the State—legislative, administrative, and judicial—have no very essential connection with the military functions, and there is no reason why both kinds of functions should normally be exercised by the same State. There is, in fact, every reason why the civil State and the military State should be different. The greater modern States are already too large for most civil purposes, but for military purposes they are not large enough, since they are not world-wide. This difference as to the desirable area for the two kinds of State introduces a certain perplexity and hesitation, when it is not realized that the two functions have little necessary connection: one set of considerations points towards small States, the other towards continually larger States. Of course, if there were an international Army and Navy, there would have to be some international authority to set them in motion. But this authority need never concern itself with any of the internal affairs of national States: it need only declare the rules which should regulate their relations, and pronounce judicially when those rules have been so infringed as to call for the intervention of the international force. How easily the limit of the authority could be fixed may be seen by many actual examples.

The civil and military State are often different in practice, for many purposes. The South American Republics are sovereign for all purposes except their relations with Europe, in regard to which they are subject to the United States: in dealings with Europe, the Army and Navy of the United States are their Army and Navy. Our self-governing Dominions depend for their defense, not upon their own forces but upon our Navy. Most Governments, nowadays, do not aim at formal annexation of a country which they wish to incorporate, but only at a protectorate—that is, civil autonomy subject to military control. Such autonomy is, of course, in practice incomplete, because it does not enable the "protected" country to adopt measures which are vetoed by the Power in military control. But it may be very nearly complete, as in the case of our self-governing Dominions. At the other extreme, it may become a mere farce, as in Egypt. In the case of an alliance, there is complete autonomy of the separate allied countries, together with what is practically a combination of their military forces into one single force.

The great advantage of a large military State is that it increases the area over which internal war is not possible except by revolution. If England and Canada have a disagreement, it is taken as a matter of course that a settlement shall be arrived at by discussion, not by force. Still more is this the case if Manchester and Liverpool have a quarrel, in spite of the fact that each is autonomous for many local purposes. No one would have thought it reasonable that Liverpool should go to war to prevent the construction of the Manchester Ship Canal, although almost any two Great Powers would have gone to war over an issue of the same relative importance. England and Russia would probably have gone to war over Persia if they had not been allies; as it is, they arrived by diplomacy at much the same iniquitous result as they would otherwise have reached by fighting. Australia and Japan would probably fight if they were both completely independent; but both depend for their liberties upon the British Navy, and therefore they have to adjust their differences peaceably.

The chief disadvantage of a large military State is that, when external war occurs, the area affected is greater. The quadruple Entente forms, for the present, one military State; the result is that, because of a dispute between Austria and Serbia, Belgium is devastated and Australians are killed in the Dardanelles. Another disadvantage is that it facilitates oppression. A large military State is practically omnipotent against a small State, and can impose its will, as England and Russia did in Persia and as Austria-Hungary has been doing in Serbia. It is impossible to make sure of avoiding oppression by any purely mechanical guarantees; only a liberal and humane spirit can afford a real protection. It has been perfectly possible for England to oppress Ireland, in spite of democracy and the presence of Irish Members at Westminster. Nor has the presence of Poles in the Reichstag prevented the oppression of Prussian Poland. But democracy and representative government undoubtedly make oppression less probable: they afford a means by which those who might be oppressed can cause their wishes and grievances to be publicly known, they render it certain that only a minority can be oppressed, and then only if the majority are nearly unanimous in wishing to oppress them. Also the practice of oppression affords much more pleasure to the governing classes, who actually carry it out, than to the mass of the population. For this reason the mass of the population, where it has power, is likely to be less tyrannical than an oligarchy or a bureaucracy.

In order to prevent war and at the same time preserve liberty it is necessary that there should be only one military State in the world, and that when disputes between different countries arise, it should act according to the decision of a central authority.

This is what would naturally result from a federation of the world, if such a thing ever came about. But the prospect is remote, and it is worth while to consider why it is so remote.

The unity of a nation is produced by similar habits, instinctive liking, a common history, and a common pride. The unity of a nation is partly due to intrinsic affinities between its citizens, but partly also to the pressure and contrast of the outside world: if a nation were isolated, it would not have the same cohesion or the same fervor of patriotism. When we come to alliances of nations, it is seldom anything except outside pressure that produces solidarity. England and America, to some extent, are drawn together by the same causes which often make national unity: a (more or less) common language, similar political institutions, similar aims in international politics. But England, France, and Russia were drawn together solely by fear of Germany; if Germany had been annihilated by a natural cataclysm, they would at once have begun to hate one another, as they did before Germany was strong. For this reason, the possibility of coöperation in the present alliance against Germany affords no ground whatever for hoping that all the nations of the world might coöperate permanently in a peaceful alliance. The present motive for cohesion, namely a common fear, would be gone, and could not be replaced by any other motive unless men's thoughts and purposes were very different from what they are now.

The ultimate fact from which war results is not economic or political, and does not rest upon any mechanical difficulty of inventing means for the peaceful settlement of international disputes. The ultimate fact from which war results is the fact that a large proportion of mankind have an impulse to conflict rather than harmony, and can only be brought to coöperate with others in resisting or attacking a common enemy. This is the case in private life as well as in the relations of States. Most men, when they feel themselves sufficiently strong, set to work to make themselves feared rather than loved; the wish to gain the good opinion of others is confined, as a rule, to those who have not acquired secure power. The impulse to quarreling and self-assertion, the pleasure of getting one's own way in spite of opposition, is native to most men. It is this impulse, rather than any motive of calculated self-interest, which produces war, and causes the difficulty of bringing about a World-State. And this impulse is not confined to one nation; it exists, in varying degrees, in all the vigorous nations of the world.

But although this impulse is strong, there is no reason why it should be allowed to lead to war. It was exactly the same impulse which led to duelling; yet now civilized men conduct their private quarrels without bloodshed. If political contest within a World-State were substituted for war, imagination would soon accustom itself to the new situation, as it has accustomed itself to absence of duelling. Through the influence of institutions and habits, without any fundamental change in human nature, men would learn to look back upon war as we look upon the burning of heretics or upon human sacrifice to heathen deities. If I were to buy a revolver costing several pounds, in order to shoot my friend with a view to stealing sixpence out of his pocket, I should be thought neither very wise nor very virtuous. But if I can get sixty-five million accomplices to join me in this criminal absurdity, I become one of a great and glorious nation, nobly sacrificing the cost of my revolver, perhaps even my life, in order to secure the sixpence for the honor of my country. Historians, who are almost invariably sycophants, will praise me and my accomplices if we are successful, and say that we are worthy successors of the heroes who overthrew the might of Imperial Rome. But if my opponents are victorious, if their sixpences are defended at the cost of many pounds each and the lives of a large proportion of the population, then historians will call me a brigand (as I am), and praise the spirit and self-sacrifice of those who resisted me.

War is surrounded with glamour, by tradition, by Homer and the Old Testament, by early education, by elaborate myths as to the importance of the issues involved, by the heroism and self-sacrifice, which these myths call out. Jephthah sacrificing his daughter is a heroic figure, but he would have let her live if he had not been deceived by a myth. Mothers sending their sons to the battlefield are heroic, but they are as much deceived as Jephthah. And, in both cases alike, the heroism which issues in cruelty would be dispelled if there were not some strain of barbarism in the imaginative outlook from which myths spring. A God who can be pleased by the sacrifice of an innocent girl could only be worshiped by men to whom the thought of receiving such a sacrifice is not wholly abhorrent. A nation which believes that its welfare can only be secured by suffering and inflicting hundreds of thousands of equally horrible sacrifices, is a nation which has no very spiritual conception of what constitutes national welfare. It would be better a hundredfold to forgo material comfort, power, pomp, and outward glory than to kill and be killed, to hate and be hated, to throw away in a mad moment of fury the bright heritage of the ages. We have learnt gradually to free our God from the savagery with which the primitive Israelites and the Fathers endowed Him: few of us now believe that it is His pleasure to torture most of the human race in an eternity of hell-fire. But we have not yet learnt to free our national ideals from the ancient taint. Devotion to the nation is perhaps the deepest and most widespread religion of the present age. Like the ancient religions, it demands its persecutions, its holocausts, its lurid heroic cruelties; like them, it is noble, primitive, brutal, and mad. Now, as in the past, religion, lagging behind private consciences through the weight of tradition, steels the hearts of men against mercy and their minds against truth. If the world is to be saved, men must learn to be noble without being cruel, to be filled with faith and yet open to truth, to be inspired by great purposes without hating those who try to thwart them. But before this can happen, men must first face the terrible realization that the gods before whom they have bowed down were false gods and the sacrifices they have made were vain.

# IV

# Property

Among the many gloomy novelists of the realistic school, perhaps the most full of gloom is Gissing. In common with all his characters, he lives under the weight of a great oppression: the power of the fearful and yet adored idol of Money. One of his typical stories is "Eve's Ransom," where the heroine, with various discreditable subterfuges, throws over the poor man whom she loves in order to marry the rich man whose income she loves still better. The poor man, finding that the rich man's income has given her a fuller life and a better character than the poor man's love could have given her, decides that she has done quite right, and that he deserves to be punished for his lack of money. In this story, as in his other books, Gissing has set forth, quite accurately, the actual dominion of money, and the impersonal worship which it exacts from the great majority of civilized mankind.

Gissing's facts are undeniable, and yet his attitude produces a revolt in any reader who has vital passions and masterful desires. His worship of money is bound up with his consciousness of inward defeat. And in the modern world generally, it is the decay of life which has promoted the religion of material goods; and the religion of material goods, in its turn, has hastened the decay of life on which it thrives. The man who worships money has ceased to hope for happiness through his own efforts or in his own activities: he looks upon happiness as a passive enjoyment of pleasures derived from the outside world. The artist or the lover does not worship money in his moments of ardor, because his desires are specific, and directed towards objects which only he can create. And conversely, the worshiper of money can never achieve greatness as an artist or a lover.

Love of money has been denounced by moralists since the world began. I do not wish to add another to the moral denunciations, of which the efficacy in the past has not been encouraging. I wish to show how the worship of money is both an effect and a cause of diminishing vitality, and how our institutions might be changed so as to make the worship of money grow less and the general vitality grow more. It is not the desire for money as a means to definite ends that is in question. A struggling artist may desire money in order to have leisure for his art, but this desire is finite, and can be satisfied fully by a very modest sum. It is the *worship* of money that I wish to consider: the belief that all values may be measured in terms of money, and that

295

money is the ultimate test of success in life. This belief is held in fact, if not in words, by multitudes of men and women, and yet it is not in harmony with human nature, since it ignores vital needs and the instinctive tendency towards some specific kind of growth. It makes men treat as unimportant those of their desires which run counter to the acquisition of money, and yet such desires are, as a rule, more important to well-being than any increase of income. It leads men to mutilate their own natures from a mistaken theory of what constitutes success, and to give admiration to enterprises which add nothing to human welfare. It promotes a dead uniformity of character and purpose, a diminution in the joy of life, and a stress and strain which leaves whole communities weary, discouraged, and disillusioned.

America, the pioneer of Western progress, is thought by many to display the worship of money in its most perfect form. A well-to-do American, who already has more than enough money to satisfy all reasonable requirements, almost always continues to work at his office with an assiduity which would only be pardonable if starvation were the alternative.

But England, except among a small minority, is almost as much given over to the worship of money as America. Love of money in England takes, as a rule, the form of snobbishly desiring to maintain a certain social status, rather than of striving after an indefinite increase of income. Men postpone marriage until they have an income enabling them to have as many rooms and servants in their house as they feel that their dignity requires. This makes it necessary for them while they are young to keep a watch upon their affections, lest they should be led into an imprudence: they acquire a cautious habit of mind, and a fear of "giving themselves away," which makes a free and vigorous life impossible. In acting as they do they imagine that they are being virtuous, since they would feel it a hardship for a woman to be asked to descend to a lower social status than that of her parents, and a degradation to themselves to marry a woman whose social status was not equal to their own. The things of nature are not valued in comparison with money. It is not thought a hardship for a woman to have to accept, as her only experience of love, the prudent and limited attentions of a man whose capacity for emotion has been lost during years of wise restraint or sordid relations with women whom he did not respect. The woman herself does not know that it is a hardship; for she, too, has been taught prudence for fear of a descent in the social scale, and from early youth she has had it instilled into her that strong feeling does not become a young woman. So the two unite to slip through life in ignorance of all that is worth knowing. Their ancestors were not restrained from passion by the fear of hell-fire, but they are restrained effectually by a worse fear, the fear of coming down in the world.

The same motives which lead men to marry late also lead them to limit their families. Professional men wish to send their sons to a public school, though the education they will obtain is no better than at a grammar school, and the companions with whom they will associate are more vicious. But snobdom has decided that public schools are best, and from its verdict there is no appeal. What makes them the best is that they are the most expensive. And the same social struggle, in varying forms, runs through all classes except the very highest and the very lowest. For this purpose men and women make great moral efforts, and show amazing powers of self-control; but all their efforts and all their self-control, being not used for any creative end, serve merely to dry up the well-spring of life within them, to make them feeble, listless, and trivial. It is not in such a soil that the passion which produces genius can be nourished. Men's souls have exchanged the wilderness for the drawing-room: they have become cramped and petty and deformed, like Chinese women's feet. Even the horrors of war have hardly awakened them from the smug somnambulism of respectability. And it is chiefly the worship of money that has brought about this deathlike slumber of all that makes men great.

In France the worship of money takes the form of thrift. It is not easy to make a fortune in France, but an inherited competence is very common, and where it exists the main purpose of life is to hand it on undiminished, if not increased. The French *rentier* is one of the great forces in international politics: it is he through whom France has been strengthened in diplomacy and weakened in war, by increasing the supply of French capital and diminishing the supply of French men. The necessity of providing a *dot* for daughters, and the subdivision of property by the law of inheritance, have made the family more powerful, as an institution, than in any other civilized country. In order that the family may prosper, it is kept small, and the individual members are often sacrificed to it. The desire for family continuity makes men timid and unadventurous: it is only in the organized proletariat that the daring spirit survives which made the Revolution and led the world in political thought and practice. Through the influence of money, the strength of the family has become a weakness to the nation by making the population remain stationary and even tend to decline. The same love of safety is beginning to produce the same effects elsewhere; but in this, as in many better things, France has led the way.

In Germany the worship of money is more recent than in France, England, and America; indeed, it hardly existed until after the Franco-Prussian War. But it has been adopted now with the same intensity and whole-heartedness which have always marked German beliefs. It is characteristic that, as in France the worship of money is associated with the family, so in Germany it is associated with the State. Liszt, in deliberate revolt against the English economists, taught his compatriots to think of economics in national terms, and the German who develops a business is felt, by others as well as by himself, to be performing a service to the State. Germans believe that England's greatness is due to industrialism and Empire, and that our success in these is due to an intense nationalism. The apparent internationalism of our Free Trade policy they regard as mere hypocrisy. They have set themselves to imitate what they believe we really are, with only the hypocrisy omitted. It must be admitted that their success has been amazing. But in the process they have destroyed almost all that made Germany of value to the world, and they have not adopted whatever of good there may have been among us, since that was all swept aside in the wholesale condemnation of "hypocrisy." And in adopting our worst faults, they have made them far worse by a system, a thoroughness, and a unanimity of which we are happily incapable. Germany's religion is of great importance to the world, since Germans have a power of real belief, and have the energy to acquire the virtues and vices which their creed demands. For the sake of the world, as well as for the sake of Germany, we must hope that they will soon abandon the worship of wealth which they have unfortunately learnt from us.

Worship of money is no new thing, but it is a more harmful thing than it used to be, for several reasons. Industrialism has made work more wearisome and intense, less capable of affording pleasure and interest by the way to the man who has undertaken it for the sake of money. The power of limiting families has opened a new field for the operation of thrift. The general increase in education and self-discipline has made men more capable of pursuing a purpose consistently in spite of temptations, and when the purpose is against life it becomes more destructive with every increase of tenacity in those who adopt it. The greater productivity resulting from industrialism has enabled us to devote more labor and capital to armies and navies for the protection of our wealth from envious neighbors, and for the exploitation of inferior races, which are ruthlessly wasted by the capitalist régime. Through the fear of losing money, forethought and anxiety eat away men's power of happiness, and the dread of misfortune becomes a greater misfortune than the one which is dreaded. The happiest men and women, as we can all testify from our own experience, are those who are indifferent to money because they have some positive purpose which shuts it out. And yet all our political thought, whether imperialist, radical, or socialist, continues to occupy itself almost exclusively with men's economic desires, as though they alone had real importance.

In judging of an industrial system, whether the one under which we live or one proposed by reformers, there are four main tests which may be applied. We may consider whether the system secures (1) the maximum of production, or (2) justice in distribution, or (3) a tolerable existence for producers, or (4) the greatest possible freedom and stimulus to vitality and progress. We may say, broadly, that the present system aims only at the first of these objects, while socialism aims at the second and third. Some defenders of the present system contend that technical progress is better promoted by private enterprise than it would be if industry were in the hands of the State; to this extent they recognize the fourth of the objects we have enumerated. But they recognize it only on the side of the goods and the capitalist, not on the side of the wage-earner. I believe that the fourth is much the most important of the objects to be aimed at, that the present system is fatal to it, and that orthodox socialism might well prove equally fatal.

One of the least questioned assumptions of the capitalist system is, that production ought to be increased in amount by every possible means: by new kinds of machinery, by employment of women and boys, by making hours of labor as long as is compatible with efficiency. Central African natives, accustomed to living on raw fruits of the earth and defeating Manchester by dispensing with clothes, are compelled to work by a hut tax which they can only pay by taking employment under European capitalists. It is admitted that they are perfectly happy while they remain free from European influences, and that industrialism brings upon them, not only the unwonted misery of confinement, but also death from diseases to which white men have become partially immune. It is admitted that the best negro workers are the "raw natives," fresh from the bush, uncontaminated by previous experience of wage-earning. Nevertheless, no one effectively contends that they ought to be preserved from the deterioration which we bring, since no one effectively doubts that it is good to increase the world's production at no matter what cost.

The belief in the importance of production has a fanatical irrationality and ruthlessness. So long as something is produced, what it is that is produced seems to be thought a matter of no account. Our whole economic system encourages this view, since fear of unemployment makes any kind of work a boon to wage-earners. The mania for increasing production has turned men's thoughts away from much more important problems, and has prevented the world from getting the benefits it might have got out of the increased productivity of labor.

When we are fed and clothed and housed, further material goods are needed only for ostentation.[12] With modern methods, a certain proportion of the population, without working long hours, could do all the work that is really necessary in the way of producing commodities. The time which is now spent in producing luxuries could be spent partly in enjoyment and country holidays, partly in better education, partly in work that is not manual or subserving manual work. We could, if we wished, have far more science and art, more diffused knowledge and mental cultivation, more leisure for wage-earners, and more capacity for intelligent pleasures. At present not only wages, but almost all earned incomes, can only be obtained by working much longer hours than men ought to work. A man who earns £800 a year by hard work could not, as a rule, earn £400 a year by half as much work. Often he could not earn anything if he were not willing to work practically all day and every day. Because of the excessive belief in the value of production, it is thought right and proper for men to work long hours, and the good that might result from shorter hours is not realized. And all the cruelties of the industrial system, not only in Europe but even more in the tropics, arouse only an occasional feeble protest from a few philanthropists. This is because, owing to the distortion produced by our present economic methods, men's conscious desires, in such matters, cover only a very small part, and that not the most important part, of the real needs affected by industrial work. If this is to be remedied,

---

[12] Except by that small minority who are capable of artistic enjoyment.

it can only be by a different economic system, in which the relation of activity to needs will be less concealed and more direct.

The purpose of maximizing production will not be achieved in the long run if our present industrial system continues. Our present system is wasteful of human material, partly through damage to the health and efficiency of industrial workers, especially when women and children are employed, partly through the fact that the best workers tend to have small families and that the more civilized races are in danger of gradual extinction. Every great city is a center of race-deterioration. For the case of London this has been argued with a wealth of statistical detail by Sir H. Llewelyn Smith;[13] and it cannot easily be doubted that it is equally true in other cases. The same is true of material resources: the minerals, the virgin forests, and the newly developed wheatfields of the world are being exhausted with a reckless prodigality which entails almost a certainty of hardship for future generations.

Socialists see the remedy in State ownership of land and capital, combined with a more just system of distribution. It cannot be denied that our present system of distribution is indefensible from every point of view, including the point of view of justice. Our system of distribution is regulated by law, and is capable of being changed in many respects which familiarity makes us regard as natural and inevitable. We may distinguish four chief sources of recognized legal rights to private property: (1) a man's right to what he has made himself; (2) the right to interest on capital which has been lent; (3) the ownership of land; (4) inheritance. These form a crescendo of respectability: capital is more respectable than labor, land is more respectable than capital, and any form of wealth is more respectable when it is inherited than when it has been acquired by our own exertions.

A man's right to the produce of his own labor has never, in fact, had more than a very limited recognition from the law. The early socialists, especially the English forerunners of Marx, used to insist upon this right as the basis of a just system of distribution, but in the complication of modern industrial processes it is impossible to say what a man has produced. What proportion of the goods carried by a railway should belong to the goods porters concerned in their journey? When a surgeon saves a man's life by an operation, what proportion of the commodities which the man subsequently produces can the surgeon justly claim? Such problems are insoluble. And there is no special justice, even if they were soluble, in allowing to each man what he himself produces. Some men are stronger, healthier, cleverer, than others, but there is no reason for increasing these natural injustices by the artificial injustices of the law. The principle recommends itself partly as a way of abolishing the very rich, partly as a way of stimulating people to work hard. But the first of these objects can be better obtained in other ways, and the second ceases to be obviously desirable as soon as we cease to worship money.

---

[13] Booth's "Life and Labour of the People," vol. iii.

Interest arises naturally in any community in which private property is unrestricted and theft is punished, because some of the most economical processes of production are slow, and those who have the skill to perform them may not have the means of living while they are being completed. But the power of lending money gives such great wealth and influence to private capitalists that unless strictly controlled it is not compatible with any real freedom for the rest of the population. Its effects at present, both in the industrial world and in international politics, are so bad that it seems imperatively necessary to devise some means of curbing its power.

Private property in land has no justification except historically through power of the sword. In the beginning of feudal times, certain men had enough military strength to be able to force those whom they disliked not to live in a certain area. Those whom they chose to leave on the land became their serfs, and were forced to work for them in return for the gracious permission to stay. In order to establish law in place of private force, it was necessary, in the main, to leave undisturbed the rights which had been acquired by the sword. The land became the property of those who had conquered it, and the serfs were allowed to give rent instead of service. There is no justification for private property in land, except the historical necessity to conciliate turbulent robbers who would not otherwise have obeyed the law. This necessity arose in Europe many centuries ago, but in Africa the whole process is often quite recent. It is by this process, slightly disguised, that the Kimberley diamond mines and the Rand gold mines were acquired in spite of prior native rights. It is a singular example of human inertia that men should have continued until now to endure the tyranny and extortion which a small minority are able to inflict by their possession of the land. No good to the community, of any sort or kind, results from the private ownership of land. If men were reasonable, they would decree that it should cease to-morrow, with no compensation beyond a moderate life income to the present holders.

The mere abolition of rent would not remove injustice, since it would confer a capricious advantage upon the occupiers of the best sites and the most fertile land. It is necessary that there should be rent, but it should be paid to the State or to some body which performs public services; or, if the total rental were more than is required for such purposes, it might be paid into a common fund and divided equally among the population. Such a method would be just, and would not only help to relieve poverty, but would prevent wasteful employment of land and the tyranny of local magnates. Much that appears as the power of capital is really the power of the landowner—for example, the power of railway companies and mine-owners. The evil and injustice of the present system are glaring, but men's patience of preventable evils to which they are accustomed is so great that it is impossible to guess when they will put an end to this strange absurdity.

Inheritance, which is the source of the greater part of the unearned income in the world, is regarded by most men as a natural right. Sometimes, as in England, the right is inherent in the owner of property, who may dispose of it in any way that seems good to him. Sometimes, as in France, his right is limited by the right of his family to inherit at least a portion of what he has to leave. But neither the right to dispose of property by will nor the right of children to inherit from parents has any basis outside the instincts of possession and family pride.

There may be reasons for allowing a man whose work is exceptionally fruitful—for instance, an inventor—to enjoy a larger income than is enjoyed by the average citizen, but there can be no good reason for allowing this privilege to descend to his children and grandchildren and so on for ever. The effect is to produce an idle and exceptionally fortunate class, who are influential through their money, and opposed to reform for fear it should be directed against themselves. Their whole habit of thought becomes timid, since they dread being forced to acknowledge that their position is indefensible; yet snobbery and the wish to secure their favor leads almost the whole middle-class to ape their manners and adopt their opinions. In this way they become a poison infecting the outlook of almost all educated people.

It is sometimes said that without the incentive of inheritance men would not work so well. The great captains of industry, we are assured, are actuated by the desire to found a family, and would not devote their lives to unremitting toil without the hope of gratifying this desire. I do not believe that any large proportion of really useful work is done from this motive. Ordinary work is done for the sake of a living, and the very best work is done for the interest of the work itself. Even the captains of industry, who are thought (perhaps by themselves as well as by others) to be aiming at founding a family, are probably more actuated by love of power and by the adventurous pleasure of great enterprises. And if there were some slight diminution in the amount of work done, it would be well worth while in order to get rid of the idle rich, with the oppression, feebleness, and corruption which they inevitably introduce.

The present system of distribution is not based upon any principle. Starting from a system imposed by conquest, the arrangements made by the conquerors for their own benefit were stereotyped by the law, and have never been fundamentally reconstructed. On what principles ought the reconstruction to be based?

Socialism, which is the most widely advocated scheme of reconstruction, aims chiefly at *justice*: the present inequalities of wealth are unjust, and socialism would abolish them. It is not essential to socialism that all men should have the same income, but it is essential that inequalities should be justified, in each case, by inequality of need or of service performed. There can be no disputing that the present system is grossly unjust, and that almost all that is unjust in it is harmful. But I do not think justice alone is a sufficient principle upon which to base an economic reconstruction. Justice would be secured if all were equally unhappy, as well as if all were equally happy. Justice, by itself, when once realized, contains no source of new life. The old type of Marxian revolutionary socialist never dwelt, in imagination, upon the life of communities after the establishment of the millennium. He imagined that, like the Prince and Princess in a fairy story, they would live happily ever after. But that is not a condition possible to human nature. Desire, activity, purpose, are essential to a tolerable life, and a millennium, though it may be a joy in prospect, would be intolerable if it were actually achieved.

The more modern socialists, it is true, have lost most of the religious fervor which characterized the pioneers, and view socialism as a tendency rather than a definite goal. But they still retain the view that what is of most political importance to a man is his income, and that the principal aim of a democratic politician ought to be to increase the wages of labor. I believe this involves too passive a conception of what constitutes happiness. It is true that, in the industrial world, large sections of the population are too poor to have any possibility of a good life; but it is not true that a good life will come of itself with a diminution of poverty. Very few of the well-to-do classes have a good life at present, and perhaps socialism would only substitute the evils which now afflict the more prosperous in place of the evils resulting from destitution.

In the existing labor movement, although it is one of the most vital sources of change, there are certain tendencies against which reformers ought to be on their guard. The labor movement is in essence a movement in favor of justice, based upon the belief that the sacrifice of the many to the few is not necessary now, whatever may have been the case in the past. When labor was less productive and education was less widespread, an aristocratic civilization may have been the only one possible: it may have been necessary that the many should contribute to the life of the few, if the few were to transmit and increase the world's possessions in art and thought and civilized existence. But this necessity is past or rapidly passing, and there is no longer any valid objection to the claims of justice. The labor movement is morally irresistible, and is not now seriously opposed except by prejudice and simple self-assertion. All living thought is on its side; what is against it is traditional and dead. But although it itself is living, it is not by any means certain that it will make for life.

Labor is led by current political thought in certain directions which would become repressive and dangerous if they were to remain strong after labor had triumphed. The aspirations of the labor movement are, on the whole, opposed by the great majority of the educated classes, who feel a menace, not only or chiefly to their personal comfort, but to the civilized life in which they have their part, which they profoundly believe to be important to the world. Owing to the opposition of the educated classes, labor, when it is revolutionary and vigorous, tends to despise all that the educated classes represent. When it is more respectful, as its leaders tend to be in England, the subtle and almost unconscious influence of educated men is apt to sap revolutionary ardor, producing doubt and uncertainty instead of the swift, simple assurance by which victory might have been won. The very sympathy which the best men in the well-to-do classes extend to labor, their very readiness to admit the justice of its claims, may have the effect of softening the opposition of labor leaders to the status quo, and of opening their minds to the suggestion that no fundamental change is possible. Since these influences affect leaders much more than the rank and file, they tend to produce in the rank and file a distrust of leaders, and a desire to seek out new leaders who will be less ready to concede the claims of the more fortunate classes. The result may be in the end a labor movement as hostile to the life of the mind as some terrified property-owners believe it to be at present.

The claims of justice, narrowly interpreted, may reinforce this tendency. It may be thought unjust that some men should have larger incomes or shorter hours of work than other men. But efficiency in mental work, including the work of education, certainly requires more comfort and longer periods of rest than are required for efficiency in physical work, if only because mental work is not physiologically wholesome. If this is not recognized, the life of the mind may suffer through short-sightedness even more than through deliberate hostility.

Education suffers at present, and may long continue to suffer, through the desire of parents that their children should earn money as soon as possible. Every one knows that the half-time system, for example, is bad; but the power of organized labor keeps it in existence. It is clear that the cure for this evil, as for those that are concerned with the population question, is to relieve parents of the expense of their children's education, and at the same time to take away their right to appropriate their children's earnings.

The way to prevent any dangerous opposition of labor to the life of the mind is not to oppose the labor movement, which is too strong to be opposed with justice. The right way is, to show by actual practice that thought is useful to labor, that without thought its positive aims cannot be achieved, and that there are men in the world of thought who are willing to devote their energies to helping labor in its struggle. Such men, if they are wise and sincere, can prevent labor from becoming destructive of what is living in the intellectual world.

Another danger in the aims of organized labor is the danger of conservatism as to methods of production. Improvements of machinery or organization bring great advantages to employers, but involve temporary and sometimes permanent loss to the wage-earners. For this reason, and also from mere instinctive dislike of any change of habits, strong labor organizations are often obstacles to technical progress. The ultimate basis of all social progress must be increased technical efficiency, a greater result from a given amount of labor. If labor were to offer an effective opposition to this kind of progress, it would in the long run paralyze all other progress. The way to overcome the opposition of labor is not by hostility or moral homilies, but by giving to labor the direct interest in economical processes which now belongs to the employers. Here, as elsewhere, the unprogressive part of a movement which is essentially progressive is to be eliminated, not by decrying the whole movement but by giving it a wider sweep, making it more progressive, and leading it to demand an even greater change in the structure of society than any that it had contemplated in its inception.

The most important purpose that political institutions can achieve is to keep alive in individuals creativeness, vigor, vitality, and the joy of life. These things existed, for example, in Elizabethan England in a way in which they do not exist now. They stimulated adventure, poetry, music, fine architecture, and set going the whole movement out of which England's greatness has sprung in every direction in which England has been great. These things coexisted with injustice, but outweighed it, and made a national life more admirable than any that is likely to exist under socialism.

What is wanted in order to keep men full of vitality is opportunity, not security. Security is merely a refuge from fear; opportunity is the source of hope. The chief test of an economic system is not whether it makes men prosperous, or whether it secures distributive justice (though these are both very desirable), but whether it leaves men's instinctive growth unimpeded. To achieve this purpose, there are two main conditions which it should fulfil: it should not cramp men's private affections, and it should give the greatest possible outlet to the impulse of creation. There is in most men, until it becomes atrophied by disuse, an instinct of constructiveness, a wish to make something. The men who achieve most are, as a rule, those in whom this instinct is strongest: such men become artists, men of science, statesmen, empire-builders, or captains of industry, according to the accidents of temperament and opportunity. The most beneficent and the most harmful careers are inspired by this impulse. Without it, the world would sink to the level of Tibet: it would subsist, as it is always prone to do, on the wisdom of its ancestors, and each generation would sink more deeply into a lifeless traditionalism.

But it is not only the remarkable men who have the instinct of constructiveness, though it is they who have it most strongly. It is almost universal in boys, and in men it usually survives in a greater or less degree, according to the greater or less outlet which it is able to find. Work inspired by this instinct is satisfying, even when it is irksome and difficult, because every effort is as natural as the effort of a dog pursuing a hare. The chief defect of the present capitalistic system is that work done for wages very seldom affords any outlet for the creative impulse. The man who works for wages has no choice as to what he shall make: the whole creativeness of the processes concentrate in the employer who orders the work to be done. For this reason the work becomes a merely external means to a certain result, the earning of wages. Employers grow indignant about the trade union rules for limitation of output, but they have no right to be indignant, since they do not permit the men whom they employ to have any share in the purpose for which the work is undertaken. And so the process of production, which should form one instinctive cycle, becomes divided into separate purposes, which can no longer provide any satisfaction of instinct for those who do the work.

This result is due to our industrial system, but it would not be avoided by socialism. In a socialist community, the State would be the employer, and the individual workman would have almost as little control over his work as he has at present. Such control as he could exercise would be indirect, through political channels, and would be too slight and roundabout to afford any appreciable satisfaction. It is to be feared that instead of an increase of self-direction, there would only be an increase of mutual interference.

The total abolition of private capitalistic enterprise, which is demanded by Marxian socialism, seems scarcely necessary. Most men who construct sweeping systems of reform, like most of those who defend the *status quo*, do not allow enough for the importance of exceptions and the undesirability of rigid system. Provided the sphere of capitalism is restricted, and a large proportion of the population are rescued from its dominion, there is no reason to wish it wholly abolished. As a competitor and a rival, it might serve a useful purpose in preventing more democratic enterprises from sinking into sloth and technical conservatism. But it is of the very highest importance that capitalism should become the exception rather than the rule, and that the bulk of the world's industry should be conducted on a more democratic system.

Much of what is to be said against militarism in the State is also to be said against capitalism in the economic sphere. Economic organizations, in the pursuit of efficiency, grow larger and larger, and there is no possibility of reversing this process. The causes of their growth are technical, and large organizations must be accepted as an essential part of civilized society. But there is no reason why their government should be centralized and monarchical. The present economic system, by robbing most men of initiative, is one of the causes of the universal weariness which devitalizes urban and industrial populations, making them perpetually seek excitement, and leading them to welcome even the outbreak of war as a relief from the dreary monotony of their daily lives.

If the vigor of the nation is to be preserved, if we are to retain any capacity for new ideas, if we are not to sink into a Chinese condition of stereotyped immobility, the monarchical organization of industry must be swept away. All large businesses must become democratic and federal in their government. The whole wage-earning system is an abomination, not only because of the social injustice which it causes and perpetuates, but also because it separates the man who does the work from the purpose for which the work is done. The whole of the controlling purpose is concentrated in the capitalist; the purpose of the wage-earner is not the produce, but the wages. The purpose of the capitalist is to secure the maximum of work for the minimum of wages; the purpose of the wage-earner is to secure the maximum of wages for the minimum of work. A system involving this essential conflict of interests cannot be expected to work smoothly or successfully, or to produce a community with any pride in efficiency.

Two movements exist, one already well advanced, the other in its infancy, which seem capable, between them, of effecting most of what is needed. The two movements I mean are the coöperative movement and syndicalism. The coöperative movement is capable of replacing the wage system over a very wide field, but it is not easy to see how it could be applied to such things as railways. It is just in these cases that the principles of syndicalism are most easily applicable.

If organization is not to crush individuality, membership of an organization ought to be voluntary, not compulsory, and ought always to carry with it a voice in the management. This is not the case with economic organizations, which give no opportunity for the pride and pleasure that men find in an activity of their own choice, provided it is not utterly monotonous.

It must be admitted, however, that much of the mechanical work which is necessary in industry is probably not capable of being made interesting in itself. But it will seem less tedious than it does at present if those who do it have a voice in the management of their industry. And men who desire leisure for other occupations might be given the opportunity of doing uninteresting work during a few hours of the day for a low wage; this would give an opening to all who wished for some activity not immediately profitable to themselves. When everything that is possible has been done to make work interesting, the residue will have to be made endurable, as almost all work is at present, by the inducement of rewards outside the hours of labor. But if these rewards are to be satisfactory, it is essential that the uninteresting work should not necessarily absorb a man's whole energies, and that opportunities should exist for more or less continuous activities during the remaining hours. Such a system might be an immeasurable boon to artists, men of letters, and others who produce for their own satisfaction works which the public does not value soon enough to secure a living for the producers; and apart from such rather rare cases, it might provide an opportunity for young men and women with intellectual ambitions to continue their education after they have left school, or to prepare themselves for careers which require an exceptionally long training.

The evils of the present system result from the separation between the several interests of consumer, producer, and capitalist. No one of these three has the same interests as the community or as either of the other two. The coöperative system amalgamates the interests of consumer and capitalist; syndicalism would amalgamate the interests of producer and capitalist. Neither amalgamates all three, or makes the interests of those who direct industry quite identical with those of the community. Neither, therefore, would wholly prevent industrial strife, or obviate the need of the State as arbitrator. But either would be better than the present system, and probably a mixture of both would cure most of the evils of industrialism as it exists now. It is surprising that, while men and women have struggled to achieve political democracy, so little has been done to introduce democracy in industry. I believe incalculable benefits might result from industrial democracy, either on the coöperative model or with recognition of a trade or industry as a unit for purposes of government, with some kind of Home Rule such as syndicalism aims at securing. There is no reason why all governmental units should be geographical: this system was necessary in the past because of the slowness of means of communication, but it is not necessary now. By some such system many men might come to feel again a pride in their work, and to find again that outlet for the creative impulse which is now denied to all but a fortunate few. Such a system requires the abolition of the land-owner and the restriction of the capitalist, but does not entail equality of earnings. And unlike socialism, it is not a static or final system: it is hardly more than a framework for energy and initiative. It is only by some such method, I believe, that the free growth of the individual can be reconciled with the huge technical organizations which have been rendered necessary by industrialism.

# V

## Education

No political theory is adequate unless it is applicable to children as well as to men and women. Theorists are mostly childless, or, if they have children, they are carefully screened from the disturbances which would be caused by youthful turmoil. Some of them have written books on education, but without, as a rule, having any actual children present to their minds while they wrote. Those educational theorists who have had a knowledge of children, such as the inventors of Kindergarten and the Montessori system,[14] have not always had enough realization of the ultimate goal of education to be able to deal successfully with advanced instruction. I have not the knowledge either of children or of education which would enable me to supply whatever defects there may be in the writings of others. But some questions, concerning education as a political institution, are involved in any hope of social reconstruction, and are not usually considered by writers on educational theory. It is these questions that I wish to discuss.

The power of education in forming character and opinion is very great and very generally recognized. The genuine beliefs, though not usually the professed precepts, of parents and teachers are almost unconsciously acquired by most children; and even if they depart from these beliefs in later life, something of them remains deeply implanted, ready to emerge in a time of stress or crisis. Education is, as a rule, the strongest force on the side of what exists and against fundamental change: threatened institutions, while they are still powerful, possess themselves of the educational machine, and instil a respect for their own excellence into the malleable minds of the young. Reformers retort by trying to oust their opponents from their position of vantage. The children themselves are not considered by either party; they are merely so much material, to be recruited into one army or the other. If the children themselves were considered, education would not aim at making them belong to this party or that, but at enabling them to choose intelligently between the parties; it would aim at making them able to think, not at making them think what their teachers think. Education as a political weapon could not exist if we respected the rights of children. If we respected the rights of children, we should educate them so as to give them

---

[14] As regards the education of young children, Madame Montessori's methods seem to me full of wisdom.

the knowledge and the mental habits required for forming independent opinions; but education as a political institution endeavors to form habits and to circumscribe knowledge in such a way as to make one set of opinions inevitable.

The two principles of *justice* and *liberty*, which cover a very great deal of the social reconstruction required, are not by themselves sufficient where education is concerned. Justice, in the literal sense of equal rights, is obviously not wholly possible as regards children. And as for liberty, it is, to begin with, essentially negative: it condemns all avoidable interference with freedom, without giving a positive principle of construction. But education is essentially constructive, and requires some positive conception of what constitutes a good life. And although liberty is to be respected in education as much as is compatible with instruction, and although a very great deal more liberty than is customary can be allowed without loss to instruction, yet it is clear that some departure from complete liberty is unavoidable if children are to be taught anything, except in the case of unusually intelligent children who are kept isolated from more normal companions. This is one reason for the great responsibility which rests upon teachers: the children must, necessarily, be more or less at the mercy of their elders, and cannot make themselves the guardians of their own interests. Authority in education is to some extent unavoidable, and those who educate have to find a way of exercising authority in accordance with the *spirit* of liberty.

Where authority is unavoidable, what is needed is *reverence*. A man who is to educate really well, and is to make the young grow and develop into their full stature, must be filled through and through with the spirit of reverence. It is reverence towards others that is lacking in those who advocate machine-made cast-iron systems: militarism, capitalism, Fabian scientific organization, and all the other prisons into which reformers and reactionaries try to force the human spirit. In education, with its codes of rules emanating from a Government office, its large classes and fixed curriculum and overworked teachers, its determination to produce a dead level of glib mediocrity, the lack of reverence for the child is all but universal. Reverence requires imagination and vital warmth; it requires most imagination in respect of those who have least actual achievement or power. The child is weak and superficially foolish, the teacher is strong, and in an every-day sense wiser than the child. The teacher without reverence, or the bureaucrat without reverence, easily despises the child for these outward inferiorities. He thinks it is his duty to "mold" the child: in imagination he is the potter with the clay. And so he gives to the child some unnatural shape, which hardens with age, producing strains and spiritual dissatisfactions, out of which grow cruelty and envy, and the belief that others must be compelled to undergo the same distortions.

Tho man who has reverence will not think it his duty to "mold" the young. He feels in all that lives, but especially in human beings, and most of all in children, something sacred, indefinable, unlimited, something individual and strangely precious, the growing principle of life, an embodied fragment of the dumb striving of the world. In the presence of a child he feels an unaccountable humility—a humility not easily defensible on any rational ground, and yet somehow nearer to wisdom than the easy self-confidence of many parents and teachers. The outward helplessness of the child and the appeal of dependence make him conscious of the responsibility of a trust. His imagination shows him what the child may become, for good or evil, how its impulses may be developed or thwarted, how its hopes must be dimmed and the life in it grow less living, how its trust will be bruised and its quick desires replaced by brooding will. All this gives him a longing to help the child in its own battle; he would equip and strengthen it, not for some outside end proposed by the State or by any other impersonal authority, but for the ends which the child's own spirit is obscurely seeking. The man who feels this can wield the authority of an educator without infringing the principle of liberty.

It is not in a spirit of reverence that education is conducted by States and Churches and the great institutions that are subservient to them. What is considered in education is hardly ever the boy or girl, the young man or young woman, but almost always, in some form, the maintenance of the existing order. When the individual is considered, it is almost exclusively with a view to worldly success—making money or achieving a good position. To be ordinary, and to acquire the art of getting on, is the ideal which is set before the youthful mind, except by a few rare teachers who have enough energy of belief to break through the system within which they are expected to work. Almost all education has a political motive: it aims at strengthening some group, national or religious or even social, in the competition with other groups. It is this motive, in the main, which determines the subjects taught, the knowledge offered and the knowledge withheld, and also decides what mental habits the pupils are expected to acquire. Hardly anything is done to foster the inward growth of mind and spirit; in fact, those who have had most education are very often atrophied in their mental and spiritual life, devoid of impulse, and possessing only certain mechanical aptitudes which take the place of living thought.

Some of the things which education achieves at present must continue to be achieved by education in any civilized country. All children must continue to be taught how to read and write, and some must continue to acquire the knowledge needed for such professions as medicine or law or engineering. The higher education required for the sciences and the arts is necessary for those to whom it is suited. Except in history and religion and kindred matters, the actual instruction is only inadequate, not positively harmful. The instruction might be given in a more liberal spirit, with more attempt to show its ultimate uses; and of course much of it is traditional and dead. But in the main it is necessary, and would have to form a part of any educational system.

It is in history and religion and other controversial subjects that the actual instruction is positively harmful. These subjects touch the interests by which schools are maintained; and the interests maintain the schools in order that certain views on these subjects may be instilled. History, in every country, is so taught as to magnify that country: children learn to believe that their own country has always been in the right and almost always victorious, that it has produced almost all the great men, and that it is in all respects superior to all other countries. Since these beliefs are flattering, they are easily absorbed, and hardly ever dislodged from instinct by later knowledge.

To take a simple and almost trivial example: the facts about the battle of Waterloo are known in great detail and with minute accuracy; but the facts as taught in elementary schools will be widely different in England, France, and Germany. The ordinary English boy imagines that the Prussians played hardly any part; the ordinary German boy imagines that Wellington was practically defeated when the day was retrieved by Blücher's gallantry. If the facts were taught accurately in both countries, national pride would not be fostered to the same extent, neither nation would feel so certain of victory in the event of war, and the willingness to fight would be diminished. It is this result which has to be prevented. Every State wishes to promote national pride, and is conscious that this cannot be done by unbiased history. The defenseless children are taught by distortions and suppressions and suggestions. The false ideas as to the history of the world which are taught in the various countries are of a kind which encourages strife and serves to keep alive a bigoted nationalism. If good relations between States were desired, one of the first steps ought to be to submit all teaching of history to an international commission, which should produce neutral textbooks free from the patriotic bias which is now demanded everywhere.[15]

Exactly the same thing applies to religion. Elementary schools are practically always in the hands either of some religious body or of a State which has a certain attitude towards religion. A religious body exists through the fact that its members all have certain definite beliefs on subjects as to which the truth is not ascertainable. Schools conducted by religious bodies have to prevent the young, who are often inquiring by nature, from discovering that these definite beliefs are opposed by others which are no more unreasonable, and that many of the men best qualified to judge think that there is no good evidence in favor of any definite belief. When the State is militantly secular, as in France, State schools become as dogmatic as those that are in the hands of the Churches (I understand that the word "God" must not be mentioned in a French elementary school). The result in all these cases is the same: free inquiry is checked, and on the most important matter in the world the child is met with dogma or with stony silence.

---

[15] THE TEACHING OF PATRIOTISM. HIS MAJESTY'S APPROVAL.

The King has been graciously pleased to accept a copy of the little book containing suggestions to local education authorities and teachers in Wales as to the teaching of patriotism which has just been issued by the Welsh Department of the Board of Education in connection with the observance of the National Anniversary of St. David's Day. His Private Secretary (Lord Stamfordham), in writing to Mr. Alfred T. Davies, the Permanent Secretary of the Welsh Department, says that his Majesty is much pleased with the contents of the book, and trusts that the principles inculcated in it will bear good fruit in the lives and characters of the coming generation.—*Morning Post*, January 29, 1916.

It is not only in elementary education that these evils exist. In more advanced education they take subtler forms, and there is more attempt to conceal them, but they are still present. Eton and Oxford set a certain stamp upon a man's mind, just as a Jesuit College does. It can hardly be said that Eton and Oxford have a *conscious* purpose, but they have a purpose which is none the less strong and effective for not being formulated. In almost all who have been through them they produce a worship of "good form," which is as destructive to life and thought as the medieval Church. "Good form" is quite compatible with a superficial open-mindedness, a readiness to hear all sides, and a certain urbanity towards opponents. But it is not compatible with fundamental open-mindedness, or with any inward readiness to give weight to the other side. Its essence is the assumption that what is most important is a certain kind of behavior, a behavior which minimizes friction between equals and delicately impresses inferiors with a conviction of their own crudity. As a political weapon for preserving the privileges of the rich in a snobbish democracy it is unsurpassable. As a means of producing an agreeable social *milieu* for those who have money with no strong beliefs or unusual desires it has some merit. In every other respect it is abominable.

The evils of "good form" arise from two sources: its perfect assurance of its own rightness, and its belief that correct manners are more to be desired than intellect, or artistic creation, or vital energy, or any of the other sources of progress in the world. Perfect assurance, by itself, is enough to destroy all mental progress in those who have it. And when it is combined with contempt for the angularities and awkwardnesses that are almost invariably associated with great mental power, it becomes a source of destruction to all who come in contact with it. "Good form" is itself dead and incapable of growth; and by its attitude to those who are without it it spreads its own death to many who might otherwise have life. The harm which it has done to well-to-do Englishmen, and to men whose abilities have led the well-to-do to notice them, is incalculable.

The prevention of free inquiry is unavoidable so long as the purpose of education is to produce belief rather than thought, to compel the young to hold positive opinions on doubtful matters rather than to let them see the doubtfulness and be encouraged to independence of mind. Education ought to foster the wish for truth, not the conviction that some particular creed is the truth. But it is creeds that hold men together in fighting organizations: Churches, States, political parties. It is intensity of belief in a creed that produces efficiency in fighting: victory comes to those who feel the strongest certainty about matters on which doubt is the only rational attitude. To produce this intensity of belief and this efficiency in fighting, the child's nature is warped, and its free outlook is cramped, by cultivating inhibitions as a check to the growth of new ideas. In those whose minds are not very active the result is the omnipotence of prejudice; while the few whose thought cannot be wholly killed become cynical, intellectually hopeless, destructively critical, able to make all that is living seem foolish, unable themselves to supply the creative impulses which they destroy in others.

The success in fighting which is achieved by suppressing freedom of thought is brief and very worthless. In the long run mental vigor is as essential to success as it is to a good life. The conception of education as a form of drill, a means of producing unanimity through slavishness, is very common, and is defended chiefly on the ground that it leads to victory. Those who enjoy parallels from ancient history will point to the victory of Sparta over Athens to enforce their moral. But it is Athens that has had power over men's thoughts and imaginations, not Sparta: any one of us, if we could be born again into some past epoch, would rather be born an Athenian than a Spartan. And in the modern world so much intellect is required in practical affairs that even the external victory is more likely to be won by intelligence than by docility. Education in credulity leads by quick stages to mental decay; it is only by keeping alive the spirit of free inquiry that the indispensable minimum of progress can be achieved.

Certain mental habits are commonly instilled by those who are engaged in educating: obedience and discipline, ruthlessness in the struggle for worldly success, contempt towards opposing groups, and an unquestioning credulity, a passive acceptance of the teacher's wisdom. All these habits are against life. Instead of obedience and discipline, we ought to aim at preserving independence and impulse. Instead of ruthlessness, education should try to develop justice in thought. Instead of contempt, it ought to instil reverence, and the attempt at understanding; towards the opinions of others it ought to produce, not necessarily acquiescence, but only such opposition as is combined with imaginative apprehension and a clear realization of the grounds for opposition. Instead of credulity, the object should be to stimulate constructive doubt, the love of mental adventure, the sense of worlds to conquer by enterprise and boldness in thought. Contentment with the *status quo*, and subordination of the individual pupil to political aims, owing to the indifference to the things of the mind, are the immediate causes of these evils; but beneath these causes there is one more fundamental, the fact that education is treated as a means of acquiring power over the pupil, not as a means of nourishing his own growth. It is in this that lack of reverence shows itself; and it is only by more reverence that a fundamental reform can be effected.

Obedience and discipline are supposed to be indispensable if order is to be kept in a class, and if any instruction is to be given. To some extent this is true; but the extent is much less than it is thought to be by those who regard obedience and discipline as in themselves desirable. Obedience, the yielding of one's will to outside direction, is the counterpart of authority. Both may be necessary in certain cases. Refractory children, lunatics, and criminals may require authority, and may need to be forced to obey. But in so far as this is necessary it is a misfortune: what is to be desired is the free choice of ends with which it is not necessary to interfere. And educational reformers have shown that this is far more possible than our fathers would ever have believed.[16]

What makes obedience seem necessary in schools is the large classes and overworked teachers demanded by a false economy. Those who have no experience of teaching are incapable of imagining the expense of spirit entailed by any really living instruction. They think that teachers can reasonably be expected to work as many hours as bank clerks. Intense fatigue and irritable nerves are the result, and an absolute necessity of performing the day's task mechanically. But the task cannot be performed mechanically except by exacting obedience.

If we took education seriously, and thought it as important to keep alive the minds of children as to secure victory in war, we should conduct education quite differently: we should make sure of achieving the end, even if the expense were a hundredfold greater than it is. To many men and women a small amount of teaching is a delight, and can be done with a fresh zest and life which keeps most pupils interested without any need of discipline. The few who do not become interested might be separated from the rest, and given a different kind of instruction. A teacher ought to have only as much teaching as can be done, on most days, with actual pleasure in the work, and with an awareness of the pupil's mental needs. The result would be a relation of friendliness instead of hostility between teacher and pupil, a realization on the part of most pupils that education serves to develop their own lives and is not merely an outside imposition, interfering with play and demanding many hours of sitting still. All that is necessary to this end is a (greater expenditure of money), to secure teachers with more leisure and with a natural love of teaching.

Discipline, as it exists in schools, is very largely an evil. There is a kind of discipline which is necessary to almost all achievement, and which perhaps is not sufficiently valued by those who react against the purely external discipline of traditional methods. The desirable kind of discipline is the kind that comes from within, which consists in the power of pursuing a distant object steadily, foregoing and suffering many things on the way. This involves the subordination of impulse to will, the power of a directing action by large creative desires even at moments when they are not vividly alive. Without this, no serious ambition, good or bad, can be realized, no consistent purpose can dominate. This kind of discipline is very necessary, but can only result from strong desires for ends not immediately attainable, and can only be produced by education if education fosters such desires, which it seldom does at present. Such discipline springs from one's own will, not from outside authority. It is not this kind which is sought in most schools, and it is not this kind which seems to me an evil.

Although elementary education encourages the undesirable discipline that consists in passive obedience, and although hardly any existing education encourages

---

[16] What Madame Montessori has achieved in the way of minimizing obedience and discipline with advantage to education is almost miraculous.

the moral discipline of consistent self-direction, there is a certain kind of purely mental discipline which is produced by the traditional higher education. The kind I mean is that which enables a man to concentrate his thoughts at will upon any matter that he has occasion to consider, regardless of preoccupations or boredom or intellectual difficulty. This quality, though it has no important intrinsic excellence, greatly enhances the efficiency of the mind as an instrument. It is this that enables a lawyer to master the scientific details of a patent case which he forgets as soon as judgment has been given, or a civil servant to deal quickly with many different administrative questions in succession. It is this that enables men to forget private cares during business hours. In a complicated world it is a very necessary faculty for those whose work requires mental concentration.

Success in producing mental discipline is the chief merit of traditional higher education. I doubt whether it can be achieved except by compelling or persuading active attention to a prescribed task. It is for this reason chiefly that I do not believe methods such as Madame Montessori's applicable when the age of childhood has been passed. The essence of her method consists in giving a choice of occupations, any one of which is interesting to most children, and all of which are instructive. The child's attention is wholly spontaneous, as in play; it enjoys acquiring knowledge in this way, and does not acquire any knowledge which it does not desire. I am convinced that this is the best method of education with young children: the actual results make it almost impossible to think otherwise. But it is difficult to see how this method can lead to control of attention by the will. Many things which must be thought about are uninteresting, and even those that are interesting at first often become very wearisome before they have been considered as long as is necessary. The power of giving prolonged attention is very important, and it is hardly to be widely acquired except as a habit induced originally by outside pressure. Some few boys, it is true, have sufficiently strong intellectual desires to be willing to undergo all that is necessary by their own initiative and free will; but for all others an external inducement is required in order to make them learn any subject thoroughly. There is among educational reformers a certain fear of demanding great efforts, and in the world at large a growing unwillingness to be bored. Both these tendencies have their good sides, but both also have their dangers. The mental discipline which is jeopardized can be preserved by mere advice without external compulsion whenever a boy's intellectual interest and ambition can be sufficiently stimulated. A good teacher ought to be able to do this for any boy who is capable of much mental achievement; and for many of the others the present purely bookish education is probably not the best. In this way, so long as the importance of mental discipline is realized, it can probably be attained, whenever it is attainable, by appealing to the pupil's consciousness of his own needs. So long as teachers are not expected to succeed by this method, it is easy for them to slip into a slothful dullness, and blame their pupils when the fault is really their own.

Ruthlessness in the economic struggle will almost unavoidably be taught in schools so long as the economic structure of society remains unchanged. This must be particularly the case in middle-class schools, which depend for their numbers upon the good opinion of parents, and secure the good opinion of parents by advertising the successes of pupils. This is one of many ways in which the competitive organization of the State is harmful. Spontaneous and disinterested desire for knowledge is not at all uncommon in the young, and might be easily aroused in many in whom it remains latent. But it is remorselessly checked by teachers who think only of examinations, diplomas, and degrees. For the abler boys there is no time for thought, no time for the indulgence of intellectual taste, from the moment of first going to school until the moment of leaving the university. From first to last there is nothing but one long drudgery of examination tips and textbook facts. The most intelligent, at the end, are disgusted with learning, longing only to forget it and to escape into a life of action. Yet there, as before, the economic machine holds them prisoners, and all their spontaneous desires are bruised and thwarted.

The examination system, and the fact that instruction is treated mainly as training for a livelihood, leads the young to regard knowledge, from a purely utilitarian point of view, as the road to money, not as the gateway to wisdom. This would not matter so much if it affected only those who have no genuine intellectual interests. But unfortunately it affects most those whose intellectual interests are strongest, since it is upon them that the pressure of examinations falls with most severity. To them most, but to all in some degree, education appears as a means of acquiring superiority over others; it is infected through and through with ruthlessness and glorification of social inequality. Any free, disinterested consideration shows that, whatever inequalities might remain in a Utopia, the actual inequalities are almost all contrary to justice. But our educational system tends to conceal this from all except the failures, since those who succeed are on the way to profit by the inequalities, with every encouragement from the men who have directed their education.

Passive acceptance of the teacher's wisdom is easy to most boys and girls. It involves no effort of independent thought, and seems rational because the teacher knows more than his pupils; it is moreover the way to win the favor of the teacher unless he is a very exceptional man. Yet the habit of passive acceptance is a disastrous one in later life. It causes men to seek a leader, and to accept as a leader whoever is established in that position. It makes the power of Churches, Governments, party caucuses, and all the other organizations by which plain men are misled into supporting old systems which are harmful to the nation and to themselves. It is possible that there would not be much independence of thought even if education did everything to promote it; but there would certainly be more than there is at present. If the object were to make pupils think, rather than to make them accept certain conclusions, education would be conducted quite differently: there would be less rapidity of instruction and more discussion, more occasions when pupils were encouraged to express themselves, more attempt to make education concern itself with matters in which the pupils felt some interest.

Above all, there would be an endeavor to rouse and stimulate the love of mental adventure. The world in which we live is various and astonishing: some of the things that seem plainest grow more and more difficult the more they are considered; other things, which might have been thought quite impossible to discover, have nevertheless been laid bare by genius and industry. The powers of thought, the vast regions which it can master, the much more vast regions which it can only dimly suggest to imagination, give to those whose minds have traveled beyond the daily round an amazing richness of material, an escape from the triviality and wearisomeness of familiar routine, by which the whole of life is filled with interest, and the prison walls of the commonplace are broken down. The same love of adventure which takes men to the South Pole, the same passion for a conclusive trial of strength which leads some men to welcome war, can find in creative thought an outlet which is neither wasteful nor cruel, but increases the dignity of man by incarnating in life some of that shining splendor which the human spirit is bringing down out of the unknown. To give this joy, in a greater or less measure, to all who are capable of it, is the supreme end for which the education of the mind is to be valued.

It will be said that the joy of mental adventure must be rare, that there are few who can appreciate it, and that ordinary education can take no account of so aristocratic a good. I do not believe this. The joy of mental adventure is far commoner in the young than in grown men and women. Among children it is very common, and grows naturally out of the period of make-believe and fancy. It is rare in later life because everything is done to kill it during education. Men fear thought as they fear nothing else on earth—more than ruin, more even than death. Thought is subversive and revolutionary, destructive and terrible; thought is merciless to privilege, established institutions, and comfortable habits; thought is anarchic and lawless, indifferent to authority, careless of the well-tried wisdom of the ages. Thought looks into the pit of hell and is not afraid. It sees man, a feeble speck, surrounded by unfathomable depths of silence; yet it bears itself proudly, as unmoved as if it were lord of the universe. Thought is great and swift and free, the light of the world, and the chief glory of man.

But if thought is to become the possession of many, not the privilege of the few, we must have done with fear. It is fear that holds men back—fear lest their cherished beliefs should prove delusions, fear lest the institutions by which they live should prove harmful, fear lest they themselves should prove less worthy of respect than they have supposed themselves to be. "Should the working man think freely about property? Then what will become of us, the rich? Should young men and young women think freely about sex? Then what will become of morality? Should soldiers think freely about war? Then what will become of military discipline? Away with thought! Back into the shades of prejudice, lest property, morals, and war should be endangered! Better men should be stupid, slothful, and oppressive than that their thoughts should be free. For if their thoughts were free they might not think as we do. And at all costs this disaster must be averted." So the opponents of thought argue in the unconscious depths of their souls. And so they act in their churches, their schools, and their universities.

No institution inspired by fear can further life. Hope, not fear, is the creative principle in human affairs. All that has made man great has sprung from the attempt to secure what is good, not from the struggle to avert what was thought evil. It is because modern education is so seldom inspired by a great hope that it so seldom achieves a great result. The wish to preserve the past rather than the hope of creating the future dominates the minds of those who control the teaching of the young. Education should not aim at a passive awareness of dead facts, but at an activity directed towards the world that our efforts are to create. It should be inspired, not by a regretful hankering after the extinct beauties of Greece and the Renaissance, but by a shining vision of the society that is to be, of the triumphs that thought will achieve in the time to come, and of the ever-widening horizon of man's survey over the universe. Those who are taught in this spirit will be filled with life and hope and joy, able to bear their part in bringing to mankind a future less somber than the past, with faith in the glory that human effort can create.

# VI

# Marriage and the Population Question

The influence of the Christian religion on daily life has decayed very rapidly throughout Europe during the last hundred years. Not only has the proportion of nominal believers declined, but even among those who believe the intensity and dogmatism of belief is enormously diminished. But there is one social institution which is still profoundly affected by the Christian tradition—I mean the institution of marriage. The law and public opinion as regards marriage are dominated even now to a very great extent by the teachings of the Church, which continue to influence in this way the lives of men, women, and children in their most intimate concerns.

It is marriage as a political institution that I wish to consider, not marriage as a matter for the private morality of each individual. Marriage is regulated by law, and is regarded as a matter in which the community has a right to interfere. It is only the action of the community in regard to marriage that I am concerned to discuss: whether the present action furthers the life of the community, and if not, in what ways it ought to be changed.

There are two questions to be asked in regard to any marriage system: first, how it affects the development and character of the men and women concerned; secondly, what is its influence on the propagation and education of children. These two questions are entirely distinct, and a system may well be desirable from one of these two points of view when it is very undesirable from the other. I propose first to describe the present English law and public opinion and practice in regard to the relations of the sexes, then to consider their effects as regards children, and finally to consider how these effects, which are bad, could be obviated by a system which would also have a better influence on the character and development of men and women.

The law in England is based upon the expectation that the great majority of marriages will be lifelong. A marriage can only be dissolved if either the wife or the husband, but not both, can be proved to have committed adultery. In case the husband is the "guilty party," he must also be guilty of cruelty or desertion. Even when these conditions are fulfilled, in practice only the well-to-do can be divorced, because the expense is very great.[17] A

---

[17] There was a provision for suits *in forma pauperis*, but for various reasons this provision was nearly useless; a new and somewhat better provision has recently been made, but is still very far from satisfactory.

marriage cannot be dissolved for insanity or crime, or for cruelty, however abominable, or for desertion, or for adultery by both parties; and it cannot be dissolved for any cause whatever if both husband and wife have agreed that they wish it dissolved. In all these cases the law regards the man and woman as bound together for life. A special official, the King's Proctor, is employed to prevent divorce when there is collusion and when both parties have committed adultery.[18]

This interesting system embodies the opinions held by the Church of England some fifty years ago, and by most Nonconformists then and now. It rests upon the assumption that adultery is sin, and that when this sin has been committed by one party to the marriage, the other is entitled to revenge if he is rich. But when both have

---

[18] The following letter (*New Statesman*, December 4, 1915) illustrates the nature of his activities:—

### DIVORCE AND WAR.

*To the Editor of the "New Statesman."*

SIR,—The following episodes may be of interest to your readers. Under the new facilities for divorce offered to the London poor, a poor woman recently obtained a decree *nisi* for divorce against her husband, who had often covered her body with bruises, infected her with a dangerous disease, and committed bigamy. By this bigamous marriage the husband had ten illegitimate children. In order to prevent this decree being made absolute, the Treasury spent at least £200 of the taxes in briefing a leading counsel and an eminent junior counsel and in bringing about ten witnesses from a city a hundred miles away to prove that this woman had committed casual acts of adultery in 1895 and 1898. The net result is that this woman will probably be forced by destitution into further adultery, and that the husband will be able to treat his mistress exactly as he treated his wife, with impunity, so far as disease is concerned. In nearly every other civilized country the marriage would have been dissolved, the children could have been legitimated by subsequent marriage, and the lawyers employed by the Treasury would not have earned the large fees they did from the community for an achievement which seems to most other lawyers thoroughly anti-social in its effects. If any lawyers really feel that society is benefited by this sort of litigation, why cannot they give their services for nothing, like the lawyers who assisted the wife? If we are to practise economy in war-time, why cannot the King's Proctor be satisfied with a junior counsel only? The fact remains that many persons situated like the husband and wife in question prefer to avoid having illegitimate children, and the birth-rate accordingly suffers.

The other episode is this. A divorce was obtained by Mr. A. against Mrs. A. and Mr. B. Mr. B. was married and Mrs. B., on hearing of the divorce proceedings, obtained a decree nisi against Mr. B. Mr. B. is at any moment liable to be called to the Front, but Mrs. B. has for some months declined to make the decree *nisi* absolute, and this prevents him marrying Mrs. A., as he feels in honor bound to do. Yet the law allows any petitioner, male or female, to obtain a decree *nisi* and to refrain from making it absolute for motives which are probably discreditable. The Divorce Law Commissioners strongly condemned this state of things, and the hardship in question is immensely aggravated in war-time, just as the war has given rise to many cases of bigamy owing to the chivalrous desire of our soldiers to obtain for the *de facto* wife and family the separation allowance of the State. The legal wife is often united by similar ties to another man. I commend these facts to consideration in your columns, having regard to your frequent complaints of a falling birth-rate. The iniquity of our marriage laws is an important contributory cause to the fall in question.

Yours, etc.,<br>E. S. P. HAYNES.

*November 29th.*

committed the same sin, or when the one who has not committed it feels no righteous anger, the right to revenge does not exist. As soon as this point of view is understood, the law, which at first seems somewhat strange, is seen to be perfectly consistent. It rests, broadly speaking, upon four propositions: (1) that sexual intercourse outside marriage is sin; (2) that resentment of adultery by the "innocent" party is a righteous horror of wrong-doing; (3) that his resentment, but nothing else, may be rightly regarded as making a common life impossible; (4) that the poor have no right to fine feelings. The Church of England, under the influence of the High Church, has ceased to believe the third of these propositions, but it still believes the first and second, and does nothing actively to show that it disbelieves the fourth.

The penalty for infringing the marriage law is partly financial, but depends mainly upon public opinion. A rather small section of the public genuinely believes that sexual relations outside marriage are wicked; those who believe this are naturally kept in ignorance of the conduct of friends who feel otherwise, and are able to go through life not knowing how others live or what others think. This small section of the public regards as depraved not only actions, but opinions, which are contrary to its principles. It is able to control the professions of politicians through its influence on elections, and the votes of the House of Lords through the presence of the Bishops. By these means it governs legislation, and makes any change in the marriage law almost impossible. It is able, also, to secure in most cases that a man who openly infringes the marriage law shall be dismissed from his employment or ruined by the defection of his customers or clients. A doctor or lawyer, or a tradesman in a country town, cannot make a living, nor can a politician be in Parliament, if he is publicly known to be "immoral." Whatever a man's own conduct may be, he is not likely to defend publicly those who have been branded, lest some of the odium should fall on him. Yet so long as a man has not been branded, few men will object to him, whatever they may know privately of his behavior in these respects.

Owing to the nature of the penalty, it falls very unequally upon different professions. An actor or journalist usually escapes all punishment. An urban workingman can almost always do as he likes. A man of private means, unless he wishes to take part in public life, need not suffer at all if he has chosen his friends suitably. Women, who formerly suffered more than men, now suffer less, since there are large circles in which no social penalty is inflicted, and a very rapidly increasing number of women who do not believe the conventional code. But for the majority of men outside the working classes the penalty is still sufficiently severe to be prohibitive.

The result of this state of things is a widespread but very flimsy hypocrisy, which allows many infractions of the code, and forbids only those which must become public. A man may not live openly with a woman who is not his wife, an unmarried woman may not have a child, and neither man nor woman may get into the divorce court. Subject to these restrictions, there is in practice very great freedom. It is this practical freedom which makes the state of the law seem tolerable to those who do not accept the principles upon which it is based. What has to be sacrificed to propitiate the holders of strict views is not pleasure, but only children and a common life and truth and honesty. It cannot be supposed that this is the result desired by those who maintain the code, but equally it cannot be denied that this is the result which they do in fact achieve. Extra-matrimonial relations which do not lead to children and are accompanied by a certain amount of deceit remain unpunished, but severe penalties fall on those which are honest or lead to children.

Within marriage, the expense of children leads to continually greater limitation of families. The limitation is greatest among those who have most sense of parental responsibility and most wish to educate their children well, since it is to them that the expense of children is most severe. But although the economic motive for limiting families has hitherto probably been the strongest, it is being continually reinforced by another. Women are acquiring freedom—not merely outward and formal freedom, but inward freedom, enabling them to think and feel genuinely, not according to received maxims. To the men who have prated confidently of women's natural instincts, the result would be surprising if they were aware of it. Very large numbers of women, when they are sufficiently free to think for themselves, do not desire to have children, or at most desire one child in order not to miss the experience which a child brings. There are women who are intelligent and active-minded who resent the slavery to the body which is involved in having children. There are ambitious women, who desire a career which leaves no time for children. There are women who love pleasure and gaiety, and women who love the admiration of men; such women will at least postpone child-bearing until their youth is past. All these classes of women are rapidly becoming more numerous, and it may be safely assumed that their numbers will continue to increase for many years to come.

It is too soon to judge with any confidence as to the effects of women's freedom upon private life and upon the life of the nation. But I think it is not too soon to see that it will be profoundly different from the effect expected by the pioneers of the women's movement. Men have invented, and women in the past have often accepted, a theory that women are the guardians of the race, that their life centers in motherhood, that all their instincts and desires are directed, consciously or unconsciously, to this end. Tolstoy's Natacha illustrates this theory: she is charming, gay, liable to passion, until she is married; then she becomes merely a virtuous mother, without any mental life. This result has Tolstoy's entire approval. It must be admitted that it is very desirable from the point of view of the nation, whatever we may think of it in relation to private life. It must also be admitted that it is probably common among women who are physically vigorous and not highly civilized. But in countries like France and England it is becoming increasingly rare. More and more women find motherhood unsatisfying, not what their needs demand. And more and more there comes to be a conflict between their personal development and the future of the community. It is difficult to know what ought to be done to mitigate this conflict, but I think it is worth while to see what are likely to be its effects if it is not mitigated.

Owing to the combination of economic prudence with the increasing freedom of women, there is at present a selective birth-rate of a very singular kind.[19] In France the population is practically stationary, and in England it is rapidly becoming so; this means that some sections are dwindling while others are increasing. Unless some change occurs, the sections that are dwindling will practically become extinct, and the population will be almost wholly replenished from the sections that are now increasing.[20] The sections that are dwindling include the whole middle-class and the skilled artisans. The sections that are increasing are the very poor, the shiftless and drunken, the feeble-minded—feeble-minded women, especially, are apt to be very prolific. There is an increase in those sections of the population which still actively believe the Catholic religion, such as the Irish and the Bretons, because the Catholic religion forbids limitation of families. Within the classes that are dwindling, it is the best elements that are dwindling most rapidly. Working-class boys of exceptional ability rise, by means of scholarships, into the professional class; they naturally desire to marry into the class to which they belong by education, not into the class from which they spring; but as they have no money beyond what they earn, they cannot marry young, or afford a large family. The result is that in each generation the best elements are extracted from the working classes and artificially sterilized, at least in comparison with those who are left. In the professional classes the young women who have initiative, energy, or intelligence are as a rule not inclined to marry young, or to have more than one or two children when they do marry. Marriage has been in the past the only obvious means of livelihood for women; pressure from parents and fear of becoming an old maid combined to force many women to marry in spite of a complete absence of inclination for the duties of a wife. But now a young woman of ordinary intelligence can easily earn her own living, and can acquire freedom and experience without the permanent ties of a husband and a family of children. The result is that if she marries she marries late.

For these reasons, if an average sample of children were taken out of the population of England, and their parents were examined, it would be found that prudence, energy, intellect, and enlightenment were less common among the parents than in the population in general; while shiftlessness, feeble-mindedness, stupidity, and superstition were more common than in the population in general. It would be

---

[19] Some interesting facts were given by Mr. Sidney Webb in two letters to *The Times*, October 11 and 16, 1906; there is also a Fabian tract on the subject: "The Decline in the Birth-Rate," by Sidney Webb (No. 131). Some further information may be found in "The Declining Birth-Rate: Its National and International Significance," by A. Newsholme, M.D., M.R.C.S. (Cassell, 1911).

[20] The fall in the death-rate, and especially in the infant mortality, which has occurred concurrently with the fall in the birth-rate, has hitherto been sufficiently great to allow the population of Great Britain to go on increasing. But there are obvious limits to the fall of the death-rate, whereas the birth-rate might easily fall to a point which would make an actual diminution of numbers unavoidable.

found that those who are prudent or energetic or intelligent or enlightened actually fail to reproduce their own numbers; that is to say, they do not on the average have as many as two children each who survive infancy. On the other hand, those who have the opposite qualities have, on the average, more than two children each, and more than reproduce their own numbers.

It is impossible to estimate the effect which this will have upon the character of the population without a much greater knowledge of heredity than exists at present. But so long as children continue to live with their parents, parental example and early education must have a great influence in developing their character, even if we leave heredity entirely out of account. Whatever may be thought of genius, there can be no doubt that intelligence, whether through heredity or through education, tends to run in families, and that the decay of the families in which it is common must lower the mental standard of the population. It seems unquestionable that if our economic system and our moral standards remain unchanged, there will be, in the next two or three generations, a rapid change for the worse in the character of the population in all civilized countries, and an actual diminution of numbers in the most civilized.

The diminution of numbers, in all likelihood, will rectify itself in time through the elimination of those characteristics which at present lead to a small birth-rate. Men and women who can still believe the Catholic faith will have a biological advantage; gradually a race will grow up which will be impervious to all the assaults of reason, and will believe imperturbably that limitation of families leads to hell-fire. Women who have mental interests, who care about art or literature or politics, who desire a career or who value their liberty, will gradually grow rarer, and be more and more replaced by a placid maternal type which has no interests outside the home and no dislike of the burden of motherhood. This result, which ages of masculine domination have vainly striven to achieve, is likely to be the final outcome of women's emancipation and of their attempt to enter upon a wider sphere than that to which the jealousy of men confined them in the past.

Perhaps, if the facts could be ascertained, it would be found that something of the same kind occurred in the Roman Empire. The decay of energy and intelligence during the second, third, and fourth centuries of our era has always remained more or less mysterious. But there is reason to think that then, as now, the best elements of the population in each generation failed to reproduce themselves, and that the least vigorous were, as a rule, those to whom the continuance of the race was due. One might be tempted to suppose that civilization, when it has reached a certain height, becomes unstable, and tends to decay through some inherent weakness, some failure to adapt the life of instinct to the intense mental life of a period of high culture. But such vague theories have always something glib and superstitious which makes them worthless as scientific explanations or as guides to action. It is not by a literary formula, but by detailed and complex thought, that a true solution is to be found.

Let us first be clear as to what we desire. There is no importance in an increasing population; on the contrary, if the population of Europe were stationary, it would be much easier to promote economic reform and to avoid war. What is regrettable *at present* is not the decline of the birth-rate in itself, but the fact that the decline is greatest in the best elements of the population. There is reason, however, to fear in the future three bad results: first, an absolute decline in the numbers of English, French, and Germans; secondly, as a consequence of this decline, their subjugation by less civilized races and the extinction of their tradition; thirdly, a revival of their numbers on a much lower plane of civilization, after generations of selection of those who have neither intelligence nor foresight. If this result is to be avoided, the present unfortunate selectiveness of the birth-rate must be somehow stopped.

The problem is one which applies to the whole of Western civilization. There is no difficulty in discovering a theoretical solution, but there is great difficulty in persuading men to adopt a solution in practice, because the effects to be feared are not immediate and the subject is one upon which people are not in the habit of using their reason. If a rational solution is ever adopted, the cause will probably be international rivalry. It is obvious that if one State—say Germany—adopted a rational means of dealing with the matter, it would acquire an enormous advantage over other States unless they did likewise. After the war, it is possible that population questions will attract more attention than they did before, and it is likely that they will be studied from the point of view of international rivalry. This motive, unlike reason and humanity, is perhaps strong enough to overcome men's objections to a scientific treatment of the birth-rate.

In the past, at most periods and in most societies, the instincts of men and women led of themselves to a more than sufficient birth-rate; Malthus's statement of the population question had been true enough up to the time when he wrote. It is still true of barbarous and semi-civilized races, and of the worst elements among civilized races. But it has become false as regards the more civilized half of the population in Western Europe and America. Among them, instinct no longer suffices to keep numbers even stationary.

We may sum up the reasons for this in order of importance, as follows:—

1. The expense of children is very great if parents are conscientious.
2. An increasing number of women desire to have no children, or only one or two, in order not to be hampered in their own careers.
3. Owing to the excess of women, a large number of women remain unmarried. These women, though not debarred in practice from relations with men, are debarred by the code from having children. In this class are to be found an enormous and increasing number of women who earn their own living as typists, in shops, or otherwise. The war has opened many employments to women from which they were formerly excluded, and this change is probably only in part temporary.

If the sterilizing of the best parts of the population is to be arrested, the first and most pressing necessity is the removal of the economic motives for limiting families. The expense of children ought to be borne wholly by the community. Their food and clothing and education ought to be provided, not only to the very poor as a matter of charity, but to all classes as a matter of public interest. In addition to this, a woman who is capable of earning money, and who abandons wage-earning for motherhood, ought to receive from the State as nearly as possible what she would have received if she had not had children. The only condition attached to State maintenance of the mother and the children should be that both parents are physically and mentally sound in all ways likely to affect the children. Those who are not sound should not be debarred from having children, but should continue, as at present, to bear the expense of children themselves.

It ought to be recognized that the law is only concerned with marriage through the question of children, and should be indifferent to what is called "morality," which is based upon custom and texts of the Bible, not upon any real consideration of the needs of the community. The excess women, who at present are in every way discouraged from having children, ought no longer to be discouraged. If the State is to undertake the expense of children, it has the right, on eugenic grounds, to know who the father is, and to demand a certain stability in a union. But there is no reason to demand or expect a lifelong stability, or to exact any ground for divorce beyond mutual consent. This would make it possible for the women who must at present remain unmarried to have children if they wished it. In this way an enormous and unnecessary waste would be prevented, and a great deal of needless unhappiness would be avoided.

There is no necessity to begin such a system all at once. It might be begun tentatively with certain exceptionally desirable sections of the community. It might then be extended gradually, with the experience of its working which had been derived from the first experiment. If the birth-rate were very much increased, the eugenic conditions exacted might be made more strict.

There are of course various practical difficulties in the way of such a scheme: the opposition of the Church and the upholders of traditional morality, the fear of weakening parental responsibility, and the expense. All these, however, might be overcome. But there remains one difficulty which it seems impossible to overcome completely in England, and that is, that the whole conception is anti-democratic, since it regards some men as better than others, and would demand that the State should bestow a better education upon the children of some men than upon the children of others. This is contrary to all the principles of progressive politics in England. For this reason it can hardly be expected that any such method of dealing with the population question will ever be adopted in its entirety in this country. Something of the sort may well be done in Germany, and if so, it will assure German hegemony as no merely military victory could do. But among ourselves we can only hope to see it adopted in some partial, piecemeal fashion, and probably only after a change in the economic structure of society which will remove most of the artificial inequalities that progressive parties are rightly trying to diminish.

So far we have been considering the question of the reproduction of the race, rather than the effect of sex relations in fostering or hindering the development of men and women. From the point of view of the race, what seems needed is a complete removal of the economic burdens due to children from all parents who are not physically or mentally unfit, and as much freedom in the law as is compatible with public knowledge of paternity. Exactly the same changes seem called for when the question is considered from the point of view of the men and women concerned.

In regard to marriage, as with all the other traditional bonds between human beings, a very extraordinary change is taking place, wholly inevitable, wholly necessary as a stage in the development of a new life, but by no means wholly satisfactory until it is completed. All the traditional bonds were based on *authority*—of the king, the feudal baron, the priest, the father, the husband. All these bonds, just because they were based on authority, are dissolving or already dissolved, and the creation of other bonds to take their place is as yet very incomplete. For this reason human relations have at present an unusual triviality, and do less than they did formerly to break down the hard walls of the Ego.

The ideal of marriage in the past depended upon the authority of the husband, which was admitted as a right by the wife. The husband was free, the wife was a willing slave. In all matters which concerned husband and wife jointly, it was taken for granted that the husband's fiat should be final. The wife was expected to be faithful, while the husband, except in very religious societies, was only expected to throw a decent veil over his infidelities. Families could not be limited except by continence, and a wife had no recognized right to demand continence, however she might suffer from frequent children.

So long as the husband's right to authority was unquestioningly believed by both men and women, this system was fairly satisfactory, and afforded to both a certain instinctive fulfilment which is rarely achieved among educated people now. Only one will, the husband's, had to be taken into account, and there was no need of the difficult adjustments required when common decisions have to be reached by two equal wills. The wife's desires were not treated seriously enough to enable them to thwart the husband's needs, and the wife herself, unless she was exceptionally selfish, did not seek self-development, or see in marriage anything but an opportunity for duties. Since she did not seek or expect much happiness, she suffered less, when happiness was not attained, than a woman does now: her suffering contained no element of indignation or surprise, and did not readily turn into bitterness and sense of injury.

The saintly, self-sacrificing woman whom our ancestors praised had her place in a certain organic conception of society, the conception of the ordered hierarchy of authorities which dominated the Middle Ages. She belongs to the same order of ideas as the faithful servant, the loyal subject, and the orthodox son of the Church. This whole order of ideas has vanished from the civilized world, and it is to be hoped that it has vanished for ever, in spite of the fact that the society which it produced was vital and in some ways full of nobility. The old order has been destroyed by the new ideals of justice and liberty, beginning with religion, passing on to politics, and reaching at last the private relations of marriage and the family. When once the question has been asked, "Why should a woman submit to a man?" when once the answers derived from tradition and the Bible have ceased to satisfy, there is no longer any possibility of maintaining the old subordination. To every man who has the power of thinking impersonally and freely, it is obvious, as soon as the question is asked, that the rights of women are precisely the same as the rights of men. Whatever dangers and difficulties, whatever temporary chaos, may be incurred in the transition to equality, the claims of reason are so insistent and so clear that no opposition to them can hope to be long successful.

Mutual liberty, which is now demanded, is making the old form of marriage impossible. But a new form, which shall be an equally good vehicle for instinct, and an equal help to spiritual growth, has not yet been developed. For the present, women who are conscious of liberty as something to be preserved are also conscious of the difficulty of preserving it. The wish for mastery is an ingredient in most men's sexual passions, especially in those which are strong and serious. It survives in many men whose theories are entirely opposed to despotism. The result is a fight for liberty on the one side and for life on the other. Women feel that they must protect their individuality; men feel, often very dumbly, that the repression of instinct which is demanded of them is incompatible with vigor and initiative. The clash of these opposing moods makes all real mingling of personalities impossible; the man and woman remain hard, separate units, continually asking themselves whether anything of value to themselves is resulting from the union. The effect is that relations tend to become trivial and temporary, a pleasure rather than the satisfaction of a profound need, an excitement, not an attainment. The fundamental loneliness into which we are born remains untouched, and the hunger for inner companionship remains unappeased.

No cheap and easy solution of this trouble is possible. It is a trouble which affects most the most civilized men and women, and is an outcome of the increasing sense of individuality which springs inevitably from mental progress. I doubt if there is any radical cure except in some form of religion, so firmly and sincerely believed as to dominate even the life of instinct. The individual is not the end and aim of his own being: outside the individual, there is the community, the future of mankind, the immensity of the universe in which all our hopes and fears are a mere pin-point. A man and woman with reverence for the spirit of life in each other, with an equal sense of their own unimportance beside the whole life of man, may become comrades without interference with liberty, and may achieve the union of instinct without doing violence to the life of mind and spirit. As religion dominated the old form of marriage, so religion must dominate the new. But it must be a new religion, based upon liberty, justice, and love, not upon authority and law and hell-fire.

A bad effect upon the relations of men and women has been produced by the romantic movement, through directing attention to what ought to be an incidental good, not the purpose for which relations exist. Love is what gives intrinsic value to a marriage, and, like art and thought, it is one of the supreme things which make human life worth preserving. But though there is no good marriage without love, the best marriages have a purpose which goes beyond love. The love of two people for each other is too circumscribed, too separate from the community, to be by itself the main purpose of a good life. It is not in itself a sufficient source of activities, it is not sufficiently prospective, to make an existence in which ultimate satisfaction can be found. It brings its great moments, and then its times which are less great, which are unsatisfying because they are less great. It becomes, sooner or later, retrospective, a tomb of dead joys, not a well-spring of new life. This evil is inseparable from any purpose which is to be achieved in a single supreme emotion. The only adequate purposes are those which stretch out into the future, which can never be fully achieved, but are always growing, and infinite with the infinity of human endeavor. And it is only when love is linked to some infinite purpose of this kind that it can have the seriousness and depth of which it is capable.

For the great majority of men and women seriousness in sex relations is most likely to be achieved through children. Children are to most people rather a need than a desire: instinct is as a rule only consciously directed towards what used to lead to children. The desire for children is apt to develop in middle life, when the adventure of one's own existence is past, when the friendships of youth seem less important than they once did, when the prospect of a lonely old age begins to terrify, and the feeling of having no share in the future becomes oppressive. Then those who, while they were young, have had no sense that children would be a fulfilment of their needs, begin to regret their former contempt for the normal, and to envy acquaintances whom before they had thought humdrum. But owing to economic causes it is often impossible for the young, and especially for the best of the young, to have children without sacrificing things of vital importance to their own lives. And so youth passes, and the need is felt too late.

Needs without corresponding desires have grown increasingly common as life has grown more different from that primitive existence from which our instincts are derived, and to which, rather than to that of the present day, they are still very largely adapted. An unsatisfied need produces, in the end, as much pain and as much distortion of character as if it had been associated with a conscious desire. For this reason, as well as for the sake of the race, it is important to remove the present economic inducements to childlessness. There is no necessity whatever to urge parenthood upon those who feel disinclined to it, but there is necessity not to place obstacles in the way of those who have no such disinclination.

In speaking of the importance of preserving seriousness in the relations of men and women, I do not mean to suggest that relations which are not serious are always harmful. Traditional morality has erred by laying stress on what ought not to happen, rather than on what ought to happen. What is important is that men and women should find, sooner or later, the best relation of which their natures are capable. It is not always possible to know in advance what will be the best, or to be sure of not missing the best if everything that can be doubted is rejected. Among primitive races, a man wants a female, a woman wants a male, and there is no such differentiation as makes one a much more suitable companion than another. But with the increasing complexity of disposition that civilized life brings, it becomes more and more difficult to find the man or woman who will bring happiness, and more and more necessary to make it not too difficult to acknowledge a mistake.

The present marriage law is an inheritance from a simpler age, and is supported, in the main, by unreasoning fears and by contempt for all that is delicate and difficult in the life of the mind. Owing to the law, large numbers of men and women are condemned, so far as their ostensible relations are concerned, to the society of an utterly uncongenial companion, with all the embittering consciousness that escape is practically impossible. In these circumstances, happier relations with others are often sought, but they have to be clandestine, without a common life, and without children. Apart from the great evil of being clandestine, such relations have some almost inevitable drawbacks. They are liable to emphasize sex unduly, to be exciting and disturbing; and it is hardly possible that they should bring a real satisfaction of instinct. It is the combination of love, children, and a common life that makes the best relation between a man and a woman. The law at present confines children and a common life within the bonds of monogamy, but it cannot confine love. By forcing many to separate love from children and a common life, the law cramps their lives, prevents them from reaching the full measure of their possible development, and inflicts a wholly unnecessary torture upon those who are not content to become frivolous.

To sum up: The present state of the law, of public opinion, and of our economic system is tending to degrade the quality of the race, by making the worst half of the population the parents of more than half of the next generation. At the same time, women's claim to liberty is making the old form of marriage a hindrance to the development of both men and women. A new system is required, if the European nations are not to degenerate, and if the relations of men and women are to have the strong happiness and organic seriousness which belonged to the best marriages in the past. The new system must be based upon the fact that to produce children is a service to the State, and ought not to expose parents to heavy pecuniary penalties. It will have to recognize that neither the law nor public opinion should concern itself with the private relations of men and women, except where children are concerned. It ought to remove the inducements to make relations clandestine and childless. It ought to admit that, although lifelong monogamy is best when it is successful, the increasing complexity of our needs makes it increasingly often a failure for which divorce is the best preventive. Here, as elsewhere, liberty is the basis of political wisdom. And when liberty has been won, what remains to be desired must be left to the conscience and religion of individual men and women.

# VII

## Religion and the Churches

Almost all the changes which the world has undergone since the end of the Middle Ages are due to the discovery and diffusion of new knowledge. This was the primary cause of the Renaissance, the Reformation, and the industrial revolution. It was also, very directly, the cause of the decay of dogmatic religion. The study of classical texts and early Church history, Copernican astronomy and physics, Darwinian biology and comparative anthropology, have each in turn battered down some part of the edifice of Catholic dogma, until, for almost all thinking and instructed people, the most that seems defensible is some inner spirit, some vague hope, and some not very definite feeling of moral obligation. This result might perhaps have remained limited to the educated minority but for the fact that the Churches have almost everywhere opposed political progress with the same bitterness with which they have opposed progress in thought. Political conservatism has brought the Churches into conflict with whatever was vigorous in the working classes, and has spread free thought in wide circles which might otherwise have remained orthodox for centuries. The decay of dogmatic religion is, for good or evil, one of the most important facts in the modern world. Its effects have hardly yet begun to show themselves: what they will be it is impossible to say, but they will certainly be profound and far-reaching.

Religion is partly personal, partly social: to the Protestant primarily personal, to the Catholic primarily social. It is only when the two elements are intimately blended that religion becomes a powerful force in molding society. The Catholic Church, as it existed from the time of Constantine to the time of the Reformation, represented a blending which would have seemed incredible if it had not been actually achieved, the blending of Christ and Cæsar, of the morality of humble submission with the pride of Imperial Rome. Those who loved the one could find it in the Thebaid; those who loved the other could admire it in the pomp of metropolitan archbishops. In St. Francis and Innocent III the same two sides of the Church are still represented. But since the Reformation personal religion has been increasingly outside the Catholic Church, while the religion which has remained Catholic has been increasingly a matter of institutions and politics and historic continuity. This division has weakened the force of religion: religious bodies have not been strengthened by the enthusiasm and single-mindedness of the men in whom personal religion is strong, and these men have not found their teaching diffused and made permanent by the power of ecclesiastical institutions.

The Catholic Church achieved, during the Middle Ages, the most organic society and the most harmonious inner synthesis of instinct, mind, and spirit, that the Western world has ever known. St. Francis, Thomas Aquinas, and Dante represent its summit as regards individual development. The cathedrals, the mendicant Orders, and the triumph of the Papacy over the Empire represent its supreme political success. But the perfection which had been achieved was a narrow perfection: instinct, mind, and spirit all suffered from curtailment in order to fit into the pattern; laymen found themselves subject to the Church in ways which they resented, and the Church used its power for rapacity and oppression. The perfect synthesis was an enemy to new growth, and after the time of Dante all that was living in the world had first to fight for its right to live against the representatives of the old order. This fight is even now not ended. Only when it is quite ended, both in the external world of politics and in the internal world of men's own thoughts, will it be possible for a new organic society and a new inner synthesis to take the place which the Church held for a thousand years.

The clerical profession suffers from two causes, one of which it shares with some other professions, while the other is peculiar to itself. The cause peculiar to it is the convention that clergymen are more virtuous than other men. Any average selection of mankind, set apart and told that it excels the rest in virtue, must tend to sink below the average. This is an ancient commonplace in regard to princes and those who used to be called "the great." But it is no less true as regards those of the clergy who are not genuinely and by nature as much better than the average as they are conventionally supposed to be. The other source of harm to the clerical profession is endowments. Property which is only available for those who will support an established institution has a tendency to warp men's judgments as to the excellence of the institution. The tendency is aggravated when the property is associated with social consideration and opportunities for petty power. It is at its worst when the institution is tied by law to an ancient creed, almost impossible to change, and yet quite out of touch with the unfettered thought of the present day. All these causes combine to damage the moral force of the Church.

It is not so much that the creed of the Church is the wrong one. What is amiss is the mere existence of a creed. As soon as income, position, and power are dependent upon acceptance of no matter what creed, intellectual honesty is imperiled. Men will tell themselves that a formal assent is justified by the good which it will enable them to do. They fail to realize that, in those whose mental life has any vigor, loss of complete intellectual integrity puts an end to the power of doing good, by producing gradually in all directions an inability to see truth simply. The strictness of party discipline has introduced the same evil in politics; there, because the evil is comparatively new, it is visible to many who think it unimportant as regards the Church. But the evil is greater as regards the Church, because religion is of more importance than politics, and because it is more necessary that the exponents of religion should be wholly free from taint.

The evils we have been considering seem inseparable from the existence of a professional priesthood. If religion is not to be harmful in a world of rapid change, it must, like the Society of Friends, be carried on by men who have other occupations during the week, who do their religious work from enthusiasm, without receiving any payment. And such men, because they know the everyday world, are not likely to fall into a remote morality which no one regards as applicable to common life. Being free, they will not be bound to reach certain conclusions decided in advance, but will be able to consider moral and religious questions genuinely, without bias. Except in a quite stationary society, no religious life can be living or a real support to the spirit unless it is freed from the incubus of a professional priesthood.

It is largely for these reasons that so little of what is valuable in morals and religion comes nowadays from the men who are eminent in the religious world. It is true that among professed believers there are many who are wholly sincere, who feel still the inspiration which Christianity brought before it had been weakened by the progress of knowledge. These sincere believers are valuable to the world because they keep alive the conviction that the life of the spirit is what is of most importance to men and women. Some of them, in all the countries now at war, have had the courage to preach peace and love in the name of Christ, and have done what lay in their power to mitigate the bitterness of hatred. All praise is due to these men, and without them the world would be even worse than it is.

But it is not through even the most sincere and courageous believers in the traditional religion that a new spirit can come into the world. It is not through them that religion can be brought back to those who have lost it because their minds were active, not because their spirit was dead. Believers in the traditional religion necessarily look to the past for inspiration rather than to the future. They seek wisdom in the teaching of Christ, which, admirable as it is, remains quite inadequate for many of the social and spiritual issues of modern life. Art and intellect and all the problems of government are ignored in the Gospels. Those who, like Tolstoy, endeavor seriously to take the Gospels as a guide to life are compelled to regard the ignorant peasant as the best type of man, and to brush aside political questions by an extreme and impracticable anarchism.

If a religious view of life and the world is ever to reconquer the thoughts and feelings of free-minded men and women, much that we are accustomed to associate with religion will have to be discarded. The first and greatest change that is required is to establish a morality of initiative, not a morality of submission, a morality of hope rather than fear, of things to be done rather than of things to be left undone. It is not the whole duty of man to slip through the world so as to escape the wrath of God. The world is *our* world, and it rests with us to make it a heaven or a hell. The power is ours, and the kingdom and the glory would be ours also if we had courage and insight

335

to create them. The religious life that we must seek will not be one of occasional solemnity and superstitious prohibitions, it will not be sad or ascetic, it will concern itself little with rules of conduct. It will be inspired by a vision of what human life may be, and will be happy with the joy of creation, living in a large free world of initiative and hope. It will love mankind, not for what they are to the outward eye, but for what imagination shows that they have it in them to become. It will not readily condemn, but it will give praise to positive achievement rather than negative sinlessness, to the joy of life, the quick affection, the creative insight, by which the world may grow young and beautiful and filled with vigor.

"Religion" is a word which has many meanings and a long history. In origin, it was concerned with certain rites, inherited from a remote past, performed originally for some reason long since forgotten, and associated from time to time with various myths to account for their supposed importance. Much of this lingers still. A religious man is one who goes to church, a communicant, one who "practises," as Catholics say. How he behaves otherwise, or how he feels concerning life and man's place in the world, does not bear upon the question whether he is "religious" in this simple but historically correct sense. Many men and women are religious in this sense without having in their natures anything that deserves to be called religion in the sense in which I mean the word. The mere familiarity of the Church service has made them impervious to it; they are unconscious of all the history and human experience by which the liturgy has been enriched, and unmoved by the glibly repeated words of the Gospel, which condemn almost all the activities of those who fancy themselves disciples of Christ. This fate must overtake any habitual rite: it is impossible that it should continue to produce much effect after it has been performed so often as to grow mechanical.

The activities of men may be roughly derived from three sources, not in actual fact sharply separate one from another, but sufficiently distinguishable to deserve different names. The three sources I mean are instinct, mind, and spirit, and of these three it is the life of the spirit that makes religion.

The life of instinct includes all that man shares with the lower animals, all that is concerned with self-preservation and reproduction and the desires and impulses derivative from these. It includes vanity and love of possessions, love of family, and even much of what makes love of country. It includes all the impulses that are essentially concerned with the biological success of oneself or one's group—for among gregarious animals the life of instinct includes the group. The impulses which it includes may not in fact make for success, and may often in fact militate against it, but are nevertheless those of which success is the *raison d'être*, those which express the animal nature of man and his position among a world of competitors.

The life of the mind is the life of pursuit of knowledge, from mere childish curiosity up to the greatest efforts of thought. Curiosity exists in animals, and serves an obvious biological purpose; but it is only in men that it passes beyond the investigation of particular objects which may be edible or poisonous, friendly or hostile. Curiosity is the primary impulse out of which the whole edifice of scientific knowledge has grown. Knowledge has been found so useful that most actual acquisition of it is no longer prompted by curiosity; innumerable other motives now contribute to foster the intellectual life. Nevertheless, direct love of knowledge and dislike of error still play a very large part, especially with those who are most successful in learning. No man acquires much knowledge unless the acquisition is in itself delightful to him, apart from any consciousness of the use to which the knowledge may be put. The impulse to acquire knowledge and the activities which center round it constitute what I mean by the life of the mind. The life of the mind consists of thought which is wholly or partially impersonal, in the sense that it concerns itself with objects on their own account, and not merely on account of their bearing upon our instinctive life.

The life of the spirit centers round impersonal feeling, as the life of the mind centers round impersonal thought. In this sense, all art belongs to the life of the spirit, though its greatness is derived from its being also intimately bound up with the life of instinct. Art starts from instinct and rises into the region of the spirit; religion starts from the spirit and endeavors to dominate and inform the life of instinct. It is possible to feel the same interest in the joys and sorrows of others as in our own, to love and hate independently of all relation to ourselves, to care about the destiny of man and the development of the universe without a thought that we are personally involved. Reverence and worship, the sense of an obligation to mankind, the feeling of imperativeness and acting under orders which traditional religion has interpreted as Divine inspiration, all belong to the life of the spirit. And deeper than all these lies the sense of a mystery half revealed, of a hidden wisdom and glory, of a transfiguring vision in which common things lose their solid importance and become a thin veil behind which the ultimate truth of the world is dimly seen. It is such feelings that are the source of religion, and if they were to die most of what is best would vanish out of life.

Instinct, mind, and spirit are all essential to a full life; each has its own excellence and its own corruption. Each can attain a spurious excellence at the expense of the others; each has a tendency to encroach upon the others; but in the life which is to be sought all three will be developed in coördination, and intimately blended in a single harmonious whole. Among uncivilized men instinct is supreme, and mind and spirit hardly exist. Among educated men at the present day mind is developed, as a rule, at the expense of both instinct and spirit, producing a curious inhumanity and lifelessness, a paucity of both personal and impersonal desires, which leads to cynicism and intellectual destructiveness. Among ascetics and most of those who would be called saints, the life of the spirit has been developed at the expense of instinct and mind, producing an outlook which is impossible to those who have a healthy animal life and to those who have a love of active thought. It is not in any of these one-sided developments that we can find wisdom or a philosophy which will bring new life to the civilized world.

Among civilized men and women at the present day it is rare to find instinct, mind, and spirit in harmony. Very few have achieved a practical philosophy which gives its due place to each; as a rule, instinct is at war with either mind or spirit, and mind and spirit are at war with each other. This strife compels men and women to direct much of their energy inwards, instead of being able to expend it all in objective activities. When a man achieves a precarious inward peace by the defeat of a part of his nature, his vital force is impaired, and his growth is no longer quite healthy. If men are to remain whole, it is very necessary that they should achieve a reconciliation of instinct, mind, and spirit.

Instinct is the source of vitality, the bond that unites the life of the individual with the life of the race, the basis of all profound sense of union with others, and the means by which the collective life nourishes the life of the separate units. But instinct by itself leaves us powerless to control the forces of Nature, either in ourselves or in our physical environment, and keeps us in bondage to the same unthinking impulse by which the trees grow. Mind can liberate us from this bondage, by the power of impersonal thought, which enables us to judge critically the purely biological purposes towards which instinct more or less blindly tends. But mind, in its dealings with instinct, is *merely* critical: so far as instinct is concerned, the unchecked activity of the mind is apt to be destructive and to generate cynicism. Spirit is an antidote to the cynicism of mind: it universalizes the emotions that spring from instinct, and by universalizing them makes them impervious to mental criticism. And when thought is informed by spirit it loses its cruel, destructive quality; it no longer promotes the death of instinct, but only its purification from insistence and ruthlessness and its emancipation from the prison walls of accidental circumstance. It is instinct that gives force, mind that gives the means of directing force to desired ends, and spirit that suggests impersonal uses for force of a kind that thought cannot discredit by criticism. This is an outline of the parts that instinct, mind, and spirit would play in a harmonious life.

Instinct, mind, and spirit are each a help to the others when their development is free and unvitiated; but when corruption comes into any one of the three, not only does that one fail, but the others also become poisoned. All three must grow together. And if they are to grow to their full stature in any one man or woman, that man or woman must not be isolated, but must be one of a society where growth is not thwarted and made crooked.

The life of instinct, when it is unchecked by mind or spirit, consists of instinctive cycles, which begin with impulses to more or less definite acts, and pass on to satisfaction of needs through the consequences of these impulsive acts. Impulse and desire are not directed towards the whole cycle, but only towards its initiation: the rest is left to natural causes. We desire to eat, but we do not desire to be nourished unless we are valetudinarians. Yet without the nourishment eating is a mere momentary pleasure, not part of the general impulse to life. Men desire sexual intercourse, but they do not as a rule desire children strongly or often. Yet without the hope of children and its occasional realization, sexual intercourse remains for most people an isolated and separate pleasure, not uniting their personal life with the life of mankind, not continuous with the central purposes by which they live, and not capable of bringing that profound sense of fulfilment which comes from completion by children. Most men, unless the impulse is atrophied through disuse, feel a desire to create something, great or small according to their capacities. Some few are able to satisfy this desire: some happy men can create an Empire, a science, a poem, or a picture. The men of science, who have less difficulty than any others in finding an outlet for creativeness, are the happiest of intelligent men in the modern world, since their creative activity affords full satisfaction to mind and spirit as well as to the instinct of creation.[21] In them a beginning is to be seen of the new way of life which is to be sought; in their happiness we may perhaps find the germ of a future happiness for all mankind. The rest, with few exceptions, are thwarted in their creative impulses. They cannot build their own house or make their own garden, or direct their own labor to producing what their free choice would lead them to produce. In this way the instinct of creation, which should lead on to the life of mind and spirit, is checked and turned aside. Too often it is turned to destruction, as the only effective action which remains possible. Out of its defeat grows envy, and out of envy grows the impulse to destroy the creativeness of more fortunate men. This is one of the greatest sources of corruption in the life of instinct.

The life of instinct is important, not only on its own account, or because of the direct usefulness of the actions which it inspires, but also because, if it is unsatisfactory, the individual life becomes detached and separated from the general life of man. All really profound sense of unity with others depends upon instinct, upon coöperation or agreement in some instinctive purpose. This is most obvious in the relations of men and women and parents and children. But it is true also in wider relations. It is true of large assemblies swayed by a strong common emotion, and even of a whole nation in times of stress. It is part of what makes the value of religion as a social institution. Where this feeling is wholly absent, other human beings seem distant and aloof. Where it is actively thwarted, other human beings become objects of instinctive hostility. The aloofness or the instinctive hostility may be masked by religious love, which can be given to all men regardless of their relation to ourselves. But religious love does not bridge the gulf that parts man from man: it looks across the gulf, it views others with compassion or impersonal sympathy, but it does not live with the same life with which they live. Instinct alone can do this, but only when it is fruitful and sane and direct. To this end it is necessary that instinctive cycles should be fairly

---

[21] I should add artists but for the fact that most modern artists seem to find much greater difficulty in creation than men of science usually find.

often completed, not interrupted in the middle of their course. At present they are constantly interrupted, partly by purposes which conflict with them for economic or other reasons, partly by the pursuit of pleasure, which picks out the most agreeable part of the cycle and avoids the rest. In this way instinct is robbed of its importance and seriousness; it becomes incapable of bringing any real fulfilment, its demands grow more and more excessive, and life becomes no longer a whole with a single movement, but a series of detached moments, some of them pleasurable, most of them full of weariness and discouragement.

The life of the mind, although supremely excellent in itself, cannot bring health into the life of instinct, except when it results in a not too difficult outlet for the instinct of creation. In other cases it is, as a rule, too widely separated from instinct, too detached, too destitute of inward growth, to afford either a vehicle for instinct or a means of subtilizing and refining it. Thought is in its essence impersonal and detached, instinct is in its essence personal and tied to particular circumstances: between the two, unless both reach a high level, there is a war which is not easily appeased. This is the fundamental reason for vitalism, futurism, pragmatism, and the various other philosophies which advertise themselves as vigorous and virile. All these represent the attempt to find a mode of thought which shall not be hostile to instinct. The attempt, in itself, is deserving of praise, but the solution offered is far too facile. What is proposed amounts to a subordination of thought to instinct, a refusal to allow thought to achieve its own ideal. Thought which does not rise above what is personal is not thought in any true sense: it is merely a more or less intelligent use of instinct. It is thought and spirit that raise man above the level of the brutes. By discarding them we may lose the proper excellence of men, but cannot acquire the excellence of animals. Thought must achieve its full growth before a reconciliation with instinct is attempted.

When refined thought and unrefined instinct coexist, as they do in many intellectual men, the result is a complete disbelief in any important good to be achieved by the help of instinct. According to their disposition, some such men will as far as possible discard instinct and become ascetic, while others will accept it as a necessity, leaving it degraded and separated from all that is really important in their lives. Either of these courses prevents instinct from remaining vital, or from being a bond with others; either produces a sense of physical solitude, a gulf across which the minds and spirits of others may speak, but not their instincts. To very many men, the instinct of patriotism, when the war broke out, was the first instinct that had bridged the gulf, the first that had made them feel a really profound unity with others. This instinct, just because, in its intense form, it was new and unfamiliar, had remained uninfected by thought, not paralyzed or devitalized by doubt and cold detachment. The sense of unity which it brought is capable of being brought by the instinctive life of more normal times, if thought and spirit are not hostile to it. And so long as this sense of unity is absent, instinct and spirit cannot be in harmony, nor can the life of the community have vigor and the seeds of new growth.

The life of the mind, because of its detachment, tends to separate a man inwardly from other men, so long as it is not balanced by the life of the spirit. For this reason, mind without spirit can render instinct corrupt or atrophied, but cannot add any excellence to the life of instinct. On this ground, some men are hostile to thought. But no good purpose is served by trying to prevent the growth of thought, which has its own insistence, and if checked in the directions in which it tends naturally, will turn into other directions where it is more harmful. And thought is in itself god-like: if the opposition between thought and instinct were irreconcilable, it would be thought that ought to conquer. But the opposition is not irreconcilable: all that is necessary is that both thought and instinct should be informed by the life of the spirit.

In order that human life should have vigor, it is necessary for the instinctive impulses to be strong and direct; but in order that human life should be good, these impulses must be dominated and controlled by desires less personal and ruthless, less liable to lead to conflict than those that are inspired by instinct alone. Something impersonal and universal is needed over and above what springs out of the principle of individual growth. It is this that is given by the life of the spirit.

Patriotism affords an example of the kind of control which is needed. Patriotism is compounded out of a number of instinctive feelings and impulses: love of home, love of those whose ways and outlook resemble our own, the impulse to coöperation in a group, the sense of pride in the achievements of one's group. All these impulses and desires, like everything belonging to the life of instinct, are personal, in the sense that the feelings and actions which they inspire towards others are determined by the relation of those others to ourselves, not by what those others are intrinsically. All these impulses and desires unite to produce a love of man's own country which is more deeply implanted in the fiber of his being, and more closely united to his vital force, than any love not rooted in instinct. But if spirit does not enter in to generalize love of country, the exclusiveness of instinctive love makes it a source of hatred of other countries. What spirit can effect is to make us realize that other countries equally are worthy of love, that the vital warmth which makes us love our own country reveals to us that it deserves to be loved, and that only the poverty of our nature prevents us from loving all countries as we love our own. In this way instinctive love can be extended in imagination, and a sense of the value of all mankind can grow up, which is more living and intense than any that is possible to those whose instinctive love is weak. Mind can only show us that it is irrational to love our own country best; it can weaken patriotism, but cannot strengthen the love of all mankind. Spirit alone can do this, by extending and universalizing the love that is born of instinct. And in doing this it checks and purifies whatever is insistent or ruthless or oppressively personal in the life of instinct.

The same extension through spirit is necessary with other instinctive loves, if they are not to be enfeebled or corrupted by thought. The love of husband and wife is capable of being a very good thing, and when men and women are sufficiently primitive nothing but instinct and good fortune is needed to make it reach a certain limited perfection. But as thought begins to assert its right to criticize instinct the old simplicity becomes impossible. The love of husband and wife, as unchecked instinct leaves it, is too narrow and personal to stand against the shafts of satire, until it is enriched by the life of the spirit. The romantic view of marriage, which our fathers and mothers professed to believe, will not survive an imaginative peregrination down a street of suburban villas, each containing its couple, each couple having congratulated themselves as they first crossed the threshold, that here they could love in peace, without interruption from others, without contact with the cold outside world. The separateness and stuffiness, the fine names for cowardices and timid vanities, that are shut within the four walls of thousands upon thousands of little villas, present themselves coldly and mercilessly to those in whom mind is dominant at the expense of spirit.

Nothing is good in the life of a human being except the very best that his nature can achieve. As men advance, things which have been good cease to be good, merely because something better is possible. So it is with the life of instinct: for those whose mental life is strong, much that was really good while mind remained less developed has now become bad merely through the greater degree of truth in their outlook on the world. The instinctive man in love feels that his emotion is unique, that the lady of his heart has perfections such as no other woman ever equaled. The man who has acquired the power of impersonal thought realizes, when he is in love, that he is one of so many millions of men who are in love at this moment, that not more than one of all the millions can be right in thinking his love supreme, and that it is not likely that that one is oneself. He perceives that the state of being in love in those whose instinct is unaffected by thought or spirit, is a state of illusion, serving the ends of Nature and making a man a slave to the life of the species, not a willing minister to the impersonal ends which he sees to be good. Thought rejects this slavery; for no end that Nature may have in view will thought abdicate, or forgo its right to think truly. "Better the world should perish than that I or any other human being should believe a lie"—this is the religion of thought, in whose scorching flames the dross of the world is being burnt away. It is a good religion, and its work of destruction must be completed. But it is not all that man has need of. New growth must come after the destruction, and new growth can come only through the spirit.

Both patriotism and the love of man and woman, when they are merely instinctive, have the same defects: their exclusions, their enclosing walls, their indifference or hostility to the outside world. It is through this that thought is led to satire, that comedy has infected what men used to consider their holiest feelings. The satire and the comedy are justified, but not the death of instinct which they may produce if they remain in supreme command. They are justified, not as the last word of wisdom but as the gateway of pain through which men pass to a new life, where instinct is purified and yet nourished by the deeper desires and insight of spirit.

The man who has the life of the spirit within him views the love of man and woman, both in himself and in others, quite differently from the man who is exclusively dominated by mind. He sees, in his moments of insight, that in all human beings there is something deserving of love, something mysterious, something appealing, a cry out of the night, a groping journey, and a possible victory. When his instinct loves, he welcomes its help in seeing and feeling the value of the human being whom he loves. Instinct becomes a reinforcement to spiritual insight. What instinct tells him spiritual insight confirms, however much the mind may be aware of littlenesses, limitations, and enclosing walls that prevent the spirit from shining forth. His spirit divines in all men what his instinct shows him in the object of his love.

The love of parents for children has need of the same transformation. The purely instinctive love, unchecked by thought, uninformed by spirit, is exclusive, ruthless, and unjust. No benefit to others is felt, by the purely instinctive parent, to be worth an injury to one's own children. Honor and conventional morality place certain important practical limitations on the vicarious selfishness of parents, since a civilized community exacts a certain minimum before it will give respect. But within the limits allowed by public opinion, parental affection, when it is merely instinctive, will seek the advantage of children without regard to others. Mind can weaken the impulse to injustice, and diminish the force of instinctive love, but it cannot keep the whole force of instinctive love and turn it to more universal ends. Spirit can do this. It can leave the instinctive love of children undimmed, and extend the poignant devotion of a parent, in imagination, to the whole world. And parental love itself will prompt the parent who has the life of the spirit to give to his children the sense of justice, the readiness for service, the reverence, the will that controls self-seeking, which he feels to be a greater good than any personal success.

The life of the spirit has suffered in recent times by its association with traditional religion, by its apparent hostility to the life of the mind, and by the fact that it has seemed to center in renunciation. The life of the spirit demands readiness for renunciation when the occasion arises, but is in its essence as positive and as capable of enriching individual existence as mind and instinct are. It brings with it the joy of vision, of the mystery and profundity of the world, of the contemplation of life, and above all the joy of universal love. It liberates those who have it from the prison-house of insistent personal passion and mundane cares. It gives freedom and breadth and beauty to men's thoughts and feelings, and to all their relations with others. It brings the solution of doubts, the end of the feeling that all is vanity. It restores harmony between mind and instinct, and leads the separated unit back into his place in the life of mankind. For those who have once entered the world of thought, it is only through spirit that happiness and peace can return.

# VIII

## What We Can Do

What can we do for the world while we live?

Many men and women would wish to serve mankind, but they are perplexed and their power seems infinitesimal. Despair seizes them; those who have the strongest passion suffer most from the sense of impotence, and are most liable to spiritual ruin through lack of hope.

So long as we think only of the immediate future, it seems that what we can do is not much. It is probably impossible for us to bring the war to an end. We cannot destroy the excessive power of the State or of private property. We cannot, here and now, bring new life into education. In such matters, though we may see the evil, we cannot quickly cure it by any of the ordinary methods of politics. We must recognize that the world is ruled in a wrong spirit, and that a change of spirit will not come from one day to the next. Our expectations must not be for to-morrow, but for the time when what is thought now by a few shall have become the common thought of many. If we have courage and patience, we can think the thoughts and feel the hopes by which, sooner or later, men will be inspired, and weariness and discouragement will be turned into energy and ardor. For this reason, the first thing we have to do is to be clear in our own minds as to the kind of life we think good and the kind of change that we desire in the world.

The ultimate power of those whose thought is vital is far greater than it seems to men who suffer from the irrationality of contemporary politics. Religious toleration was once the solitary speculation of a few bold philosophers. Democracy, as a theory, arose among a handful of men in Cromwell's army; by them, after the Restoration, it was carried to America, where it came to fruition in the War of Independence. From America, Lafayette and the other Frenchmen who fought by the side of Washington brought the theory of democracy to France, where it united itself with the teaching of Rousseau and inspired the Revolution. Socialism, whatever we may think of its merits, is a great and growing power, which is transforming economic and political life; and socialism owes its origin to a very small number of isolated theorists. The movement against the subjection of women, which has become irresistible and is not far from complete triumph, began in the same way with a few impracticable idealists—Mary Wollstonecraft, Shelley, John Stuart Mill. The power of thought, in the long run, is greater than any other human power. Those who have the ability to think and the imagination to think in accordance with men's needs, are likely to achieve the good they aim at sooner or later, though probably not while they are still alive.

But those who wish to gain the world by thought must be content to lose it as a support in the present. Most men go through life without much questioning, accepting the beliefs and practices which they find current, feeling that the world will be their ally if they do not put themselves in opposition to it. New thought about the world is incompatible with this comfortable acquiescence; it requires a certain intellectual detachment, a certain solitary energy, a power of inwardly dominating the world and the outlook that the world engenders. Without some willingness to be lonely new thought cannot be achieved. And it will not be achieved to any purpose if the loneliness is accompanied by aloofness, so that the wish for union with others dies, or if intellectual detachment leads to contempt. It is because the state of mind required is subtle and difficult, because it is hard to be intellectually detached yet not aloof, that fruitful thought on human affairs is not common, and that most theorists are either conventional or sterile. The right kind of thought is rare and difficult, but it is not impotent. It is not the fear of impotence that need turn us aside from thought if we have the wish to bring new hope into the world.

In seeking a political theory which is to be useful at any given moment, what is wanted is not the invention of a Utopia, but the discovery of the best direction of movement. The direction which is good at one time may be superficially very different from that which is good at another time. Useful thought is that which indicates the right direction for the present time. But in judging what is the right direction there are two general principles which are always applicable.

1. The growth and vitality of individuals and communities is to be promoted as far as possible.
2. The growth of one individual or one community is to be as little as possible at the expense of another.

The second of these principles, as applied by an individual in his dealings with others, is the principle of *reverence*, that the life of another has the same importance which we feel in our own life. As applied impersonally in politics, it is the principle of *liberty*, or rather it includes the principle of liberty as a part. Liberty in itself is a negative principle; it tells us not to interfere, but does not give any basis for construction. It shows that many political and social institutions are bad and ought to be swept away, but it does not show what ought to be put in their place. For this reason a further principle is required, if our political theory is not to be purely destructive.

The combination of our two principles is not in practice an easy matter. Much of the vital energy of the world runs into channels which are oppressive. The Germans have shown themselves extraordinarily full of vital energy, but unfortunately in a form which seems incompatible with the vitality of their neighbors. Europe in general has more vital energy than Africa, but it has used its energy to drain Africa, through industrialism, of even such life as the negroes possessed. The vitality of southeastern Europe is being drained to supply cheap labor for the enterprise of American millionaires. The vitality of men has been in the past a hindrance to the development of women, and it is possible that in the near future women may become a similar hindrance to men. For such reasons the principle of reverence, though not in itself sufficient, is of very great importance, and is able to indicate many of the political changes that the world requires.

In order that both principles may be capable of being satisfied, what is needed is a unifying or integration, first of our individual lives, then of the life of the community and of the world, without sacrifice of individuality. The life of an individual, the life of a community, and even the life of mankind, ought to be, not a number of separate fragments but in some sense a whole. When this is the case, the growth of the individual is fostered, and is not incompatible with the growth of other individuals. In this way the two principles are brought into harmony.

What integrates an individual life is a consistent creative purpose or unconscious direction. Instinct alone will not suffice to give unity to the life of a civilized man or woman: there must be some dominant object, an ambition, a desire for scientific or artistic creation, a religious principle, or strong and lasting affections. Unity of life is very difficult for a man or woman who has suffered a certain kind of defeat, the kind by which what should have been the dominant impulse is checked and made abortive. Most professions inflict this kind of defeat upon a man at the very outset. If a man becomes a journalist, he probably has to write for a newspaper whose politics he dislikes; this kills his pride in work and his sense of independence. Most medical men find it very hard to succeed without humbug, by which whatever scientific conscience they may have had is destroyed. Politicians are obliged, not only to swallow the party program but to pretend to be saints, in order to conciliate religious supporters; hardly any man can enter Parliament without hypocrisy. In no profession is there any respect for the native pride without which a man cannot remain whole; the world ruthlessly crushes it out, because it implies independence, and men desire to enslave others more than they desire to be free themselves. Inward freedom is infinitely precious, and a society which will preserve it is immeasurably to be desired.

The principle of growth in a man is not crushed necessarily by preventing him from doing some definite thing, but it is often crushed by persuading him to do something else. The things that crush growth are those that produce a sense of impotence in the directions in which the vital impulse wishes to be effective. The worst things are those to which the will assents. Often, chiefly from failure of self-knowledge, a man's will is on a lower level than his impulse: his impulse is towards some kind of creation, while his will is towards a conventional career, with a sufficient income and the respect of his contemporaries. The stereotyped illustration is the artist who produces shoddy work to please the public. But something of the artist's definiteness of impulse exists in very many men who are not artists. Because the impulse is deep and dumb, because what is called common sense is often against it, because a young man can only follow it if he is willing to set up his own obscure feelings against the wisdom and prudent maxims of elders and friends, it happens in ninety-nine cases out of a hundred that the creative impulse, out of which a free and vigorous life might have sprung, is checked and thwarted at the very outset: the young man consents to become a tool, not an independent workman; a mere means to the fulfilment of others, not the artificer of what his own nature feels to be good. In the moment when he makes this act of consent something dies within him. He can never again become a whole man, never again have the undamaged self-respect, the upright pride, which might have kept him happy in his soul in spite of all outward troubles and difficulties—except, indeed, through conversion and a fundamental change in his way of life.

Outward prohibitions, to which the will gives no assent, are far less harmful than the subtler inducements which seduce the will. A serious disappointment in love may cause the most poignant pain, but to a vigorous man it will not do the same inward damage as is done by marrying for money. The achievement of this or that special desire is not what is essential: what is essential is the direction, the *kind* of effectiveness which is sought. When the fundamental impulse is opposed by will, it is made to feel helpless: it has no longer enough hope to be powerful as a motive. Outward compulsion does not do the same damage unless it produces the same sense of impotence; and it will not produce the same sense of impotence if the impulse is strong and courageous. Some thwarting of special desires is unavoidable even in the best imaginable community, since some men's desires, unchecked, lead to the oppression or destruction of others. In a good community Napoleon could not have been allowed the profession of his choice, but he might have found happiness as a pioneer in Western America. He could not have found happiness as a City clerk, and no tolerable organization of society would compel him to become a City clerk.

The integration of an individual life requires that it should embody whatever creative impulse a man may possess, and that his education should have been such as to elicit and fortify this impulse. The integration of a community requires that the different creative impulses of different men and women should work together towards some common life, some common purpose, not necessarily conscious, in which all the members of the community find a help to their individual fulfilment. Most of the activities that spring from vital impulses consist of two parts: one creative, which furthers one's own life and that of others with the same kind of impulse or circumstances, and one possessive, which hinders the life of some group with a different kind of impulse or circumstances. For this reason, much of what is in itself most vital may nevertheless work against life, as, for example, seventeenth-century Puritanism did in England, or as nationalism does throughout Europe at the present day. Vitality easily leads to strife or oppression, and so to loss of vitality. War, at its outset, integrates the life of a nation, but it disintegrates the life of the world, and in the long run the life of a nation too, when it is as severe as the present war.

The war has made it clear that it is impossible to produce a secure integration of the life of a single community while the relations between civilized countries are governed by aggressiveness and suspicion. For this reason any really powerful movement of reform will have to be international. A merely national movement is sure to fail through fear of danger from without. Those who desire a better world, or even a radical improvement in their own country, will have to coöperate with those who have similar desires in other countries, and to devote much of their energy to overcoming that blind hostility which the war has intensified. It is not in partial integrations, such as patriotism alone can produce, that any ultimate hope is to be found. The problem is, in national and international questions as in the individual life, to keep what is creative in vital impulses, and at the same time to turn into other channels the part which is at present destructive.

Men's impulses and desires may be divided into those that are creative and those that are possessive. Some of our activities are directed to creating what would not otherwise exist, others are directed towards acquiring or retaining what exists already. The typical creative impulse is that of the artist; the typical possessive impulse is that of property. The best life is that in which creative impulses play the largest part and possessive impulses the smallest. The best institutions are those which produce the greatest possible creativeness and the least possessiveness compatible with self-preservation. Possessiveness may be defensive or aggressive: in the criminal law it is defensive, and in criminals it is aggressive. It may perhaps be admitted that the criminal law is less abominable than the criminal, and that defensive possessiveness is unavoidable so long as aggressive possessiveness exists. But not even the most purely defensive forms of possessiveness are in themselves admirable; indeed, as soon as they are strong they become hostile to the creative impulses. "Take no thought, saying, What shall we eat? or What shall we drink, or Wherewithal shall we be clothed?" Whoever has known a strong creative impulse has known the value of this precept in its exact and literal sense: it is preoccupation with possessions, more than anything else, that prevents men from living freely and nobly. The State and Property are the great embodiments of possessiveness; it is for this reason that they are against life, and that they issue in war. Possession means taking or keeping some good thing which another is prevented from enjoying; creation means putting into the world a good thing which otherwise no one would be able to enjoy. Since the material goods of the world must be divided among the population, and since some men are by nature brigands, there must be defensive possession, which will be regulated, in a good community, by some principle of impersonal justice. But all this is only the preface to a good life or good political institutions, in which creation will altogether outweigh possession, and distributive justice will exist as an uninteresting matter of course.

The supreme principle, both in politics and in private life, should be *to promote all that is creative, and so to diminish the impulses and desires that center round possession.* The State at present is very largely an embodiment of possessive impulses: internally, it protects the rich against the poor; externally, it uses force for the exploitation of inferior races, and for competition with other States. Our whole economic system is concerned exclusively with possession; yet the production of goods is a form of creation, and except in so far as it is irredeemably mechanical and monotonous, it might afford a vehicle for creative impulses. A great deal might be achieved towards this end by forming the producers of a certain kind of commodity into an autonomous democracy, subject to State control as regards the price of their commodity but not as to the manner of its production.

Education, marriage, and religion are essentially creative, yet all three have been vitiated by the intrusion of possessive motives. Education is usually treated as a means of prolonging the *status quo* by instilling prejudices, rather than of creating free thought and a noble outlook by the example of generous feeling and the stimulus of mental adventure. In marriage, love, which is creative, is kept in chains by jealousy, which is possessive. Religion, which should set free the creative vision of the spirit, is usually more concerned to repress the life of instinct and to combat the subversiveness of thought. In all these ways the fear that grows out of precarious possession has replaced the hope inspired by creative force. The wish to plunder others is recognized, in theory, to be bad; but the fear of being plundered is little better. Yet these two motives between them dominate nine-tenths of politics and private life.

The creative impulses in different men are essentially harmonious, since what one man creates cannot be a hindrance to what another is wishing to create. It is the possessive impulses that involve conflict. Although, morally and politically, the creative and possessive impulses are opposites, yet psychologically either passes easily into the other, according to the accidents of circumstance and opportunity. The genesis of impulses and the causes which make them change ought to be studied; education and social institutions ought to be made such as to strengthen the impulses which harmonize in different men, and to weaken those that involve conflict. I have no doubt that what might be accomplished in this way is almost unlimited.

It is rather through impulse than through will that individual lives and the life of the community can derive the strength unity of a single direction. Will is of two kinds, of which one is directed outward and the other inward. The first, which is directed outward, is called into play by external obstacles, either the opposition of others or the technical difficulties of an undertaking. This kind of will is an expression of strong impulse or desire, whenever instant success is impossible; it exists in all whose life is vigorous, and only decays when their vital force is enfeebled. It is necessary to success in any difficult enterprise, and without it great achievement is very rare. But the will which is directed inward is only necessary in so far as there is an inner conflict of impulses or desires; a perfectly harmonious nature would have no occasion for inward will. Such perfect harmony is of course a scarcely realizable ideal: in all men impulses arise which are incompatible with their central purpose, and which must be checked if their life as a whole is not to be a failure. But this will happen least with those whose central impulses are strongest; and it will happen less often in a society which aims at freedom than in a society like ours, which is full of artificial incompatibilities created by antiquated institutions and a tyrannous public opinion. The power to exert inward will when the occasion arises must always be needed by those who wish their lives to embody some central purpose, but with better institutions the occasions when inward will is necessary might be made fewer and less important. This result is very much to be desired, because when will checks impulses which are only accidentally harmful, it diverts a force which might be spent on overcoming outward obstacles, and if the impulses checked are strong and serious, it actually diminishes the vital force available. A life full of inhibitions is likely not to remain a very vigorous life but to become listless and without zest. Impulse tends to die when it is constantly held in check, and if it does not die, it is apt to work underground, and issue in some form much worse than that in which it has been checked. For these reasons the necessity for using inward will ought to be avoided as much as possible, and consistency of action ought to spring rather from consistency of impulse than from control of impulse by will.

The unifying of life ought not to demand the suppression of the casual desires that make amusement and play; on the contrary, everything ought to be done to make it easy to combine the main purposes of life with all kinds of pleasure that are not in their nature harmful. Such things as habitual drunkenness, drugs, cruel sports, or pleasure in inflicting pain are essentially harmful, but most of the amusements that civilized men naturally enjoy are either not harmful at all or only accidentally harmful through some effect which might be avoided in a better society. What is needed is, not asceticism or a drab Puritanism, but capacity for strong impulses and desires directed towards large creative ends. When such impulses and desires are vigorous, they bring with them, of themselves, what is needed to make a good life.

But although amusement and adventure ought to have their share, it is impossible to create a good life if they are what is mainly desired. Subjectivism, the habit of directing thought and desire to our own states of mind rather than to something objective, inevitably makes life fragmentary and unprogressive. The man to whom amusement is the end of life tends to lose interest gradually in the things out of which he has been in the habit of obtaining amusement, since he does not value these things on their own account, but on account of the feelings which they arouse in him. When they are no longer amusing, boredom drives him to seek some new stimulus, which fails him in its turn. Amusement consists in a series of moments without any essential continuity; a purpose which unifies life is one which requires some prolonged activity, and is like building a monument rather than a child's castle in the sand.

Subjectivism has other forms beside the mere pursuit of amusement. Many men, when they are in love, are more interested in their own emotion than in the object of their love; such love does not lead to any essential union, but leaves fundamental separateness undiminished. As soon as the emotion grows less vivid the experience has served its purpose, and there seems no motive for prolonging it. In another way, the same evil of subjectivism was fostered by Protestant religion and morality, since they directed attention to sin and the state of the soul rather than to the outer world and our relations with it. None of these forms of subjectivism can prevent a man's life from being fragmentary and isolated. Only a life which springs out of dominant impulses directed to objective ends can be a satisfactory whole, or be intimately united with the lives of others.

The pursuit of pleasure and the pursuit of virtue alike suffer from subjectivism: Epicureanism and Stoicism are infected with the same taint. Marcus Aurelius, enacting good laws in order that he might be virtuous, is not an attractive figure. Subjectivism is a natural outcome of a life in which there is much more thought than action: while outer things are being remembered or desired, not actually experienced, they seem to become mere ideas. What they are in themselves becomes less interesting to us than the effects which they produce in our own minds. Such a result tends to be brought about by increasing civilization, because increasing civilization continually diminishes the need for vivid action and enhances the opportunities for thought. But thought will not have this bad result if it is active thought, directed towards achieving some purpose; it is only passive thought that leads to subjectivism. What is needed is to keep thought in intimate union with impulses and desires, making it always itself an activity with an objective purpose. Otherwise, thought and impulse become enemies, to the great detriment of both.

In order to make the lives of average men and women less fragmentary and separate, and to give greater opportunity for carrying out creative impulses, it is not enough to know the goal we wish to reach, or to proclaim the excellence of what we desire to achieve. It is necessary to understand the effect of institutions and beliefs upon the life of impulse, and to discover ways of improving this effect by a change in institutions. And when this intellectual work has been done, our thought will still remain barren unless we can bring it into relation with some powerful political force. The only powerful political force from which any help is to be expected in bringing about such changes as seem needed is Labor. The changes required are very largely such as Labor may be expected to welcome, especially during the time of hardship after the war. When the war is over, labor discontent is sure to be very prevalent throughout Europe, and to constitute a political force by means of which a great and sweeping reconstruction may be effected.

The civilized world has need of fundamental change if it is to be saved from decay—change both in its economic structure and in its philosophy of life. Those of us who feel the need of change must not sit still in dull despair: we can, if we choose, profoundly influence the future. We can discover and preach the kind of change that is required—the kind that preserves what is positive in the vital beliefs of our time, and, by eliminating what is negative and inessential, produces a synthesis to which all that is not purely reactionary can give allegiance. As soon as it has become clear what *kind* of change is required, it will be possible to work out its parts in more detail. But until the war is ended there is little use in detail, since we do not know what kind of world the war will leave. The only thing that seems indubitable is that much new thought will be required in the new world produced by the war. Traditional views will give little help. It is clear that men's most important actions are not guided by the sort of motives that are emphasized in traditional political philosophies. The impulses by which the war has been produced and sustained come out of a deeper region than that of most political argument. And the opposition to the war on the part of those few who have opposed it comes from the same deep region. A political theory, if it is to hold in times of stress, must take account of the impulses that underlie explicit thought: it must appeal to them, and it must discover how to make them fruitful rather than destructive.

Economic systems have a great influence in promoting or destroying life. Except slavery, the present industrial system is the most destructive of life that has ever existed. Machinery and large-scale production are ineradicable, and must survive in any better system which is to replace the one under which we live. Industrial federal democracy is probably the best direction for reform to take.

Philosophies of life, when they are widely believed, also have a very great influence on the vitality of a community. The most widely accepted philosophy of life at present is that what matters most to a man's happiness is his income. This philosophy, apart from other demerits, is harmful because it leads men to aim at a result rather than an activity, an enjoyment of material goods in which men are not differentiated, rather than a creative impulse which embodies each man's individuality. More refined philosophies, such as are instilled by higher education, are too apt to fix attention on the past rather than the future, and on correct behavior rather than effective action. It is not in such philosophies that men will find the energy to bear lightly the weight of tradition and of ever-accumulating knowledge.

The world has need of a philosophy, or a religion, which will promote life. But in order to promote life it is necessary to value something other than mere life. Life devoted only to life is animal without any real human value, incapable of preserving men permanently from weariness and the feeling that all is vanity. If life is to be fully human it must serve some end which seems, in some sense, outside human life, some end which is impersonal and above mankind, such as God or truth or beauty. Those who best promote life do not have life for their purpose. They aim rather at what seems like a gradual incarnation, a bringing into our human existence of something eternal, something that appears to imagination to live in a heaven remote from strife and failure and the devouring jaws of Time. Contact with this eternal world—even if it be only a world of our imagining—brings a strength and a fundamental peace which cannot be wholly destroyed by the struggles and apparent failures of our temporal life. It is this happy contemplation of what is eternal that Spinoza calls the intellectual love of God. To those who have once known it, it is the key of wisdom.

What we have to do practically is different for each one of us, according to our capacities and opportunities. But if we have the life of the spirit within us, what we must do and what we must avoid will become apparent to us.

By contact with what is eternal, by devoting our life to bringing something of the Divine into this troubled world, we can make our own lives creative even now, even in the midst of the cruelty and strife and hatred that surround us on every hand. To make the individual life creative is far harder in a community based on possession than it would be in such a community as human effort may be able to build up in the future. Those who are to begin the regeneration of the world must face loneliness, opposition, poverty, obloquy. They must be able to live by truth and love, with a rational unconquerable hope; they must be honest and wise, fearless, and guided by a consistent purpose. A body of men and women so inspired will conquer—first the difficulties and perplexities of their individual lives, then, in time, though perhaps only in a long time, the outer world. Wisdom and hope are what the world needs; and though it fights against them, it gives its respect to them in the end.

When the Goths sacked Rome, St. Augustine wrote the "City of God," putting a spiritual hope in place of the material reality that had been destroyed. Throughout the centuries that followed St. Augustine's hope lived and gave life, while Rome sank to a village of hovels. For us, too, it is necessary to create a new hope, to build up by our thought a better world than the one which is hurling itself into ruin. Because the times are bad, more is required of us than would be required in normal times. Only a supreme fire of thought and spirit can save future generations from the death that has befallen the generation which we knew and loved.

It has been my good fortune to come in contact as a teacher with young men of many different nations—young men in whom hope was alive, in whom the creative energy existed that would have realized in the world some part at least of the imagined beauty by which they lived. They have been swept into the war, some on one side, some on the other. Some are still fighting, some are maimed for life, some are dead; of those who survive it is to be feared that many will have lost the life of the spirit, that hope will have died, that energy will be spent, and that the years to come will be only a weary journey towards the grave. Of all this tragedy, not a few of those who teach seem to have no feeling: with ruthless logic, they prove that these young men have been sacrificed unavoidably for some coldly abstract end; undisturbed themselves, they lapse quickly into comfort after any momentary assault of feeling. In such men the life of the spirit is dead. If it were living, it would go out to meet the spirit in the young, with a love as poignant as the love of father or mother. It would be unaware of the bounds of self; their tragedy would be its own. Something would cry out: "No, this is not right; this is not good; this is not a holy cause, in which the brightness of youth is destroyed and dimmed. It is we, the old, who have sinned; we have sent these young men to the battlefield for our evil passions, our spiritual death, our failure to live generously out of the warmth of the heart and out of the living vision of the spirit. Let us come out of this death, for it is we who are dead, not the young men who have died through our fear of life. Their very ghosts have more life than we: they hold us up for ever to the shame and obloquy of all the ages to come. Out of their ghosts must come life, and it is we whom they must vivify."

# FREE THOUGHT
# AND
# OFFICIAL PROPAGANDA

DELIVERED AT SOUTH PLACE INSTITUTE ON MARCH 24, 1922

# Chairman's Introductory Address

I have come here to-night, partly because I want to hear Mr. Russell, and partly because of an old affection for South Place and its traditions. I myself have been for more than forty years a professional teacher; and it is as a teacher—who thirty-seven years ago was dismissed for refusing religious conformity—that I most easily approach the problem of free thought. Though systems of education professing to teach men and women how to think have been in use in Europe for, perhaps, three thousand years, we have not yet reached that degree of success which would be shown if most educated people came to much the same conclusions on the great problems of life from a study of the same evidence. Everywhere you have rebels; but ninety per cent. of French or American students of history come to French or American conclusions, and eighty-five per cent. of English students come to English conclusions; eighty per cent. of Eton boys hold Eton political opinions all their lives; ninety per cent. of the Irish Catholic population of the United States seem to hold generation after generation identical opinions on religion and politics which are not held by the vast majority of Americans. It may be said that in these cases only one kind of evidence is allowed to reach the students in each institution. But everybody reads newspapers, and talks with his neighbours, and travels, and visits museums; and most intelligent people read books and magazines. Sooner or later much of the same evidence reaches us all. I myself believe that one of the main reasons why we do not to a greater degree draw the same conclusions from that evidence is that we do not really learn the difficult art of thought. A boy at school is taught to memorize and to understand mathematical formulæ or foreign languages or scientific statements. But in weighing evidence the effort of memorizing, and even the effort of understanding, are not of the first importance. The effective process is a sort of painful and watchful expectancy. A schoolboy or a college student finds that he has an uncomfortable sense of unreality in repeating some accustomed formula, or writing an essay to enforce some accustomed line of argument. He shrinks from that feeling, as all animals shrink from discomfort. If he were taught what are the conditions of effective thought, and were encouraged to act on that lesson, he would know that it is only by resolutely fastening on such vague and painful premonitions, and forcing them to come into full consciousness and disclose their deeper causes and tendencies that he can arrive at new truth or make some old truth his own.

But who is going to tell him this secret? Every day in London thousands of clever and sympathetic boys and girls begin the day by sitting through three-quarters of an hour of the dreary "Cowper-Temple" instruction which consists, as Bishop Temple once said, of teaching at everybody's expense what nobody believes. They may be conscious or half-conscious of a feeling of unreality; but, even if they have not been taught that it is a sacred duty to "struggle against doubt," they shrink, as the cleverest of them feel that the teacher is shrinking, from any further exploration on that path.

Perhaps some day the teachers and students of the ordinary school and college subjects may learn something from those little isolated institutions where men and women try to prepare themselves for the creative arts. The young painter or sculptor or member of a group of young poets is often queerly ignorant and one-sided. But he lives in another world from that of the big conventional sixth-form boy at Harrow or St. Paul's, or the hockey-playing athlete of a girls' High School, because he has felt the pain and the exhilaration reached through pain by which alone new truth and new beauty are born into the world.

# Free Thought and Official Propaganda

Moncure Conway, in whose honour we are assembled to-day, devoted his life to two great objects: freedom of thought and freedom of the individual. In regard to both these objects, something has been gained since his time, but something also has been lost. New dangers, somewhat different in form from those of past ages, threaten both kinds of freedom, and unless a vigorous and vigilant public opinion can be aroused in defence of them, there will be much less of both a hundred years hence than there is now. My purpose in this address is to emphasize the new dangers and to consider how they can be met.

Let us begin by trying to be clear as to what we mean by "free thought." This expression has two senses. In its narrower sense it means thought which does not accept the dogmas of traditional religion. In this sense a man is a "free thinker" if he is not a Christian or a Mussulman or a Buddhist or a Shintoist or a member of any of the other bodies of men who accept some inherited orthodoxy. In Christian countries a man is called a "free thinker" if he does not decidedly believe in God, though this would not suffice to make a man a "free thinker" in a Buddhist country.

I do not wish to minimize the importance of free thought in this sense. I am myself a dissenter from all known religions, and I hope that every kind of religious belief will die out. I do not believe that, on the balance, religious belief has been a force for good. Although I am prepared to admit that in certain times and places it has had some good effects, I regard it as belonging to the infancy of human reason, and to a stage of development which we are now outgrowing.

But there is also a wider sense of "free thought," which I regard as of still greater importance. Indeed, the harm done by traditional religions seems chiefly traceable to the fact that they have prevented free thought in this wider sense. The wider sense is not so easy to define as the narrower, and it will be well to spend some little time in trying to arrive at its essence.

When we speak of anything as "free," our meaning is not definite unless we can say what it is free *from*. Whatever or whoever is "free" is not subject to some external compulsion, and to be precise we ought to say what this kind of compulsion is. Thus thought is "free" when it is free from certain kinds of outward control which are often present. Some of these kinds of control which must be absent if thought is to be "free" are obvious, but others are more subtle and elusive.

358

To begin with the most obvious. Thought is not "free" when legal penalties are incurred by the holding or not holding of certain opinions, or by giving expression to one's belief or lack of belief on certain matters. Very few countries in the world have as yet even this elementary kind of freedom. In England, under the Blasphemy Laws, it is illegal to express disbelief in the Christian religion, though in practice the law is not set in motion against the well-to-do. It is also illegal to teach what Christ taught on the subject of non-resistance. Therefore, whoever wishes to avoid becoming a criminal must profess to agree with Christ's teaching, but must avoid saying what that teaching was. In America no one can enter the country without first solemnly declaring that he disbelieves in anarchism and polygamy; and, once inside, he must also disbelieve in communism. In Japan it is illegal to express disbelief in the divinity of the Mikado. It will thus be seen that a voyage round the world is a perilous adventure. A Mohammedan, a Tolstoyan, a Bolshevik, or a Christian cannot undertake it without at some point becoming a criminal, or holding his tongue about what he considers important truths. This, of course, applies only to steerage passengers; saloon passengers are allowed to believe whatever they please, provided they avoid offensive obtrusiveness.

It is clear that the most elementary condition, if thought is to be free, is the absence of legal penalties for the expression of opinions. No great country has yet reached to this level, although most of them think they have. The opinions which are still persecuted strike the majority as so monstrous and immoral that the general principle of toleration cannot be held to apply to them. But this is exactly the same view as that which made possible the tortures of the Inquisition. There was a time when Protestantism seemed as wicked as Bolshevism seems now. Please do not infer from this remark that I am either a Protestant or a Bolshevik.

Legal penalties are, however, in the modern world, the least of the obstacles to freedom of thoughts. The two great obstacles are economic penalties and distortion of evidence. It is clear that thought is not free if the profession of certain opinions makes it impossible to earn a living. It is clear also that thought is not free if all the arguments on one side of a controversy are perpetually presented as attractively as possible, while the arguments on the other side can only be discovered by diligent search. Both these obstacles exist in every large country known to me, except China, which is the last refuge of freedom. It is these obstacles with which I shall be concerned—their present magnitude, the likelihood of their increase, and the possibility of their diminution.

We may say that thought is free when it is exposed to free competition among beliefs—i.e., when all beliefs are able to state their case, and no legal or pecuniary advantages or disadvantages attach to beliefs. This is an ideal which, for various reasons, can never be fully attained. But it is possible to approach very much nearer to it than we do at present.

Three incidents in my own life will serve to show how, in modern England, the scales are weighted in favour of Christianity. My reason for mentioning them is that many people do not at all realize the disadvantages to which avowed Agnosticism still exposes people.

The first incident belongs to a very early stage in my life. My father was a Freethinker, but died when I was only three years old. Wishing me to be brought up without superstition, he appointed two Freethinkers as my guardians. The Courts, however, set aside his will, and had me educated in the Christian faith. I am afraid the result was disappointing, but that was not the fault of the law. If he had directed that I should be educated as a Christadelphian or a Muggletonian or a Seventh-Day Adventist, the Courts would not have dreamed of objecting. A parent has a right to ordain that any imaginable superstition shall be instilled into his children after his death, but has not the right to say that they shall be kept free from superstition if possible.

The second incident occurred in the year 1910. I had at that time a desire to stand for Parliament as a Liberal, and the Whips recommended me to a certain constituency. I addressed the Liberal Association, who expressed themselves favourably, and my adoption seemed certain. But, on being questioned by a small inner caucus, I admitted that I was an Agnostic. They asked whether the fact would come out, and I said it probably would. They asked whether I should be willing to go to church occasionally, and I replied that I should not. Consequently, they selected another candidate, who was duly elected, has been in Parliament ever since, and is a member of the present Government.

The third incident occurred immediately afterwards. I was invited by Trinity College, Cambridge, to become a lecturer, but not a Fellow. The difference is not pecuniary; it is that a Fellow has a voice in the government of the College, and cannot be dispossessed during the term of his Fellowship except for grave immorality. The chief reason for not offering me a Fellowship was that the clerical party did not wish to add to the anti-clerical vote. The result was that they were able to dismiss me in 1916, when they disliked my views on the War.[1] If I had been dependent on my lectureship, I should have starved.

These three incidents illustrate different kinds of disadvantages attaching to avowed freethinking even in modern England. Any other avowed Freethinker could supply similar incidents from his personal experience, often of a far more serious character. The net result is that people who are not well-to-do dare not be frank about their religious beliefs.

It is not, of course, only or even chiefly in regard to religion that there is lack of freedom. Belief in communism or free love handicaps a man much more than Agnosticism. Not only is it a disadvantage to hold those views, but it is very much more difficult to obtain publicity for the arguments in their favour. On the other hand, in Russia the advantages and disadvantages are exactly reversed: comfort and power

---

[1] I should add that they re-appointed me later, when war passions had begun to cool.

are achieved by professing Atheism, communism, and free love, and no opportunity exists for propaganda against these opinions. The result is that in Russia one set of fanatics feels absolute certainty about one set of doubtful propositions, while in the rest of the world another set of fanatics feels equal certainty about a diametrically opposite set of equally doubtful propositions. From such a situation war, bitterness, and persecution inevitably result on both sides.

William James used to preach the "will to believe." For my part, I should wish to preach the "will to doubt." None of our beliefs are quite true; all have at least a penumbra of vagueness and error. The methods of increasing the degree of truth in our beliefs are well known; they consist in hearing all sides, trying to ascertain all the relevant facts, controlling our own bias by discussion with people who have the opposite bias, and cultivating a readiness to discard any hypothesis which has proved inadequate. These methods are practised in science, and have built up the body of scientific knowledge. Every man of science whose outlook is truly scientific is ready to admit that what passes for scientific knowledge at the moment is sure to require correction with the progress of discovery; nevertheless, it is near enough to the truth to serve for most practical purposes, though not for all. In science, where alone something approximating to genuine knowledge is to be found, men's attitude is tentative and full of doubt.

In religion and politics, on the contrary, though there is as yet nothing approaching scientific knowledge, everybody considers it *de rigueur* to have a dogmatic opinion, to be backed up by inflicting starvation, prison, and war, and to be carefully guarded from argumentative competition with any different opinion. If only men could be brought into a tentatively agnostic frame of mind about these matters, nine-tenths of the evils of the modern world would be cured. War would become impossible, because each side would realize that both sides must be in the wrong. Persecution would cease. Education would aim at expanding the mind, not at narrowing it. Men would be chosen for jobs on account of fitness to do the work, not because they flattered the irrational dogmas of those in power. Thus rational doubt alone, if it could be generated, would suffice to introduce the millennium.

We have had in recent years a brilliant example of the scientific temper of mind in the theory of relativity and its reception by the world. Einstein, a German-Swiss-Jew pacifist, was appointed to a research professorship by the German Government in the early days of the War; his predictions were verified by an English expedition which observed the eclipse of 1919, very soon after the Armistice. His theory upsets the whole theoretical framework of traditional physics; it is almost as damaging to orthodox dynamics as Darwin was to *Genesis*. Yet physicists everywhere have shown complete readiness to accept his theory as soon as it appeared that the evidence was in its favour. But none of them, least of all Einstein himself, would claim that he has said the last word. He has not built a monument of infallible dogma to stand for all time. There are difficulties he cannot solve; his doctrines will have to be modified in their turn as they have modified Newton's. This critical undogmatic receptiveness is the true attitude of science.

What would have happened if Einstein had advanced something equally new in the sphere of religion or politics? English people would have found elements of Prussianism in his theory; anti-Semites would have regarded it as a Zionist plot; nationalists in all countries would have found it tainted with lily-livered pacifism, and proclaimed it a mere dodge for escaping military service. All the old-fashioned professors would have approached Scotland Yard to get the importation of his writings prohibited. Teachers favourable to him would have been dismissed. He, meantime, would have captured the Government of some backward country, where it would have become illegal to teach anything except his doctrine, which would have grown into a mysterious dogma not understood by anybody. Ultimately the truth or falsehood of his doctrine would be decided on the battlefield, without the collection of any fresh evidence for or against it. This method is the logical outcome of William James's will to believe.

What is wanted is not the will to believe, but the wish to find out, which is its exact opposite.

If it is admitted that a condition of rational doubt would be desirable, it becomes important to inquire how it comes about that there is so much irrational certainty in the world. A great deal of this is due to the inherent irrationality and credulity of average human nature. But this seed of intellectual original sin is nourished and fostered by other agencies, among which three play the chief part—namely, education, propaganda, and economic pressure. Let us consider these in turn.

(1) *Education.*—Elementary education, in all advanced countries, is in the hands of the State. Some of the things taught are known to be false by the officials who prescribe them, and many others are known to be false, or at any rate very doubtful, by every unprejudiced person. Take, for example, the teaching of history. Each nation aims only at self-glorification in the school text-books of history. When a man writes his autobiography he is expected to show a certain modesty; but when a nation writes its autobiography there is no limit to its boasting and vainglory. When I was young, school books taught that the French were wicked and the Germans virtuous; now they teach the opposite. In neither case is there the slightest regard for truth. German school books, dealing with the battle of Waterloo, represent Wellington as all but defeated when Blücher saved the situation; English books represent Blücher as having made very little difference. The writers of both the German and the English books know that they are not telling the truth. American school books used to be violently anti-British; since the War they have become equally pro-British, without aiming at truth in either case (see *The Freeman*, Feb. 15, 1922, p. 532). Both before and since, one of the chief purposes of education in the United States has been to turn the motley collection of immigrant children into "good Americans." Apparently it has not occurred to any one that a "good American," like a "good German" or a "good

Japanese," must be, *pro tanto*, a bad human being. A "good American" is a man or woman imbued with the belief that America is the finest country on earth, and ought always to be enthusiastically supported in any quarrel. It is just possible that these propositions are true; if so, a rational man will have no quarrel with them. But if they are true, they ought to be taught everywhere, not only in America. It is a suspicious circumstance that such propositions are never believed outside the particular country which they glorify. Meanwhile the whole machinery of the State, in all the different countries, is turned on to making defenceless children believe absurd propositions the effect of which is to make them willing to die in defence of sinister interests under the impression that they are fighting for truth and right. This is only one of countless ways in which education is designed, not to give true knowledge, but to make the people pliable to the will of their masters. Without an elaborate system of deceit in the elementary schools it would be impossible to preserve the camouflage of democracy.

Before leaving the subject of education, I will take another example from America[2]—not because America is any worse than other countries, but because it is the most modern, showing the dangers that are growing rather than those that are diminishing. In the State of New York a school cannot be established without a licence from the State, even if it is to be supported wholly by private funds. A recent law decrees that a licence shall not be granted to any school "where it shall appear that the instruction proposed to be given includes the teachings of the doctrine that organized Governments shall be overthrown by force, violence, or unlawful means." As the *New Republic* points out, there is no limitation to this or that organized Government. The law therefore would have made it illegal, during the War, to teach the doctrine that the Kaiser's Government should be overthrown by force; and, since then, the support of Kolchak or Denikin against the Soviet Government would have been illegal. Such consequences, of course, were not intended, and result only from bad draughtsmanship. What was intended appears from another law passed at the same time, applying to teachers in State schools. This law provides that certificates permitting persons to teach in such schools shall be issued only to those who have "shown satisfactorily" that they are "loyal and obedient to the Government of this State and of the United States," and shall be refused to those who have advocated, no matter where or when, "a form of government other than the Government of this State or of the United States." The committee which framed these laws, as quoted by the *New Republic*, laid it down that the teacher who "does not approve of the present social system......must surrender his office," and that "no person who is not eager to combat the theories of social change should be entrusted with the task of fitting the young and old for the responsibilities of citizenship." Thus, according to the law of the State of New York, Christ and George Washington were too degraded morally to be fit for the education of the young. If Christ were to go to New York and say, "Suffer the

---

[2] See *The New Republic*, Feb. 1, 1922, p. 259 *ff.*

little children to come unto me," the President of the New York School Board would reply: "Sir, I see no evidence that you are eager to combat theories of social change. Indeed, I have heard it said that you advocate what you call the *kingdom* of heaven, whereas this country, thank God, is a republic. It is clear that the Government of your kingdom of heaven would differ materially from that of New York State, therefore no children will be allowed access to you." If he failed to make this reply, he would not be doing his duty as a functionary entrusted with the administration of the law.

The effect of such laws is very serious. Let it be granted, for the sake of argument, that the government and the social system in the State of New York are the best that have ever existed on this planet; yet even then both would presumably be capable of improvement. Any person who admits this obvious proposition is by law incapable of teaching in a State school. Thus the law decrees that the teachers shall all be either hypocrites or fools.

The growing danger exemplified by the New York law is that resulting from the monopoly of power in the hands of a single organization, whether the State or a Trust or federation of Trusts. In the case of education, the power is in the hands of the State, which can prevent the young from hearing of any doctrine which it dislikes. I believe there are still some people who think that a democratic State is scarcely distinguishable from the people. This, however, is a delusion. The State is a collection of officials, different for different purposes, drawing comfortable incomes so long as the *status quo* is preserved. The only alteration they are likely to desire in the *status quo* is an increase of bureaucracy and of the power of bureaucrats. It is, therefore, natural that they should take advantage of such opportunities as war excitement to acquire inquisitorial powers over their employees, involving the right to inflict starvation upon any subordinate who opposes them. In matters of the mind, such as education, this state of affairs is fatal. It puts an end to all possibility of progress or freedom or intellectual initiative. Yet it is the natural result of allowing the whole of elementary education to fall under the sway of a single organization.

Religious toleration, to a certain extent, has been won because people have ceased to consider religion so important as it was once thought to be. But in politics and economics, which have taken the place formerly occupied by religion, there is a growing tendency to persecution, which is not by any means confined to one party. The persecution of opinion in Russia is more severe than in any capitalist country. I met in Petrograd an eminent Russian poet, Alexander Block, who has since died as the result of privations. The Bolsheviks allowed him to teach æsthetics, but he complained that they insisted on his teaching the subject "from a Marxian point of view." He had been at a loss to discover how the theory of rhythmics was connected with Marxism, although, to avoid starvation, he had done his best to find out. Of course, it has been impossible in Russia ever since the Bolsheviks came into power to print anything critical of the dogmas upon which their regime is founded.

The examples of America and Russia illustrate the conclusion to which we seem to be driven—namely, that so long as men continue to have the present fanatical belief in the importance of politics free thought on political matters will be impossible, and there is only too much danger that the lack of freedom will spread to all other matters, as it has done in Russia. Only some degree of political scepticism can save us from this misfortune.

It must not be supposed that the officials in charge of education desire the young to become educated. On the contrary, their problem is to impart information without imparting intelligence. Education should have two objects: first, to give definite knowledge—reading and writing, languages and mathematics, and so on; secondly, to create those mental habits which will enable people to acquire knowledge and form sound judgments for themselves. The first of these we may call information, the second intelligence. The utility of information is admitted practically as well as theoretically; without a literate population a modern State is impossible. But the utility of intelligence is admitted only theoretically, not practically; it is not desired that ordinary people should think for themselves, because it is felt that people who think for themselves are awkward to manage and cause administrative difficulties. Only the guardians, in Plato's language, are to think; the rest are to obey, or to follow leaders like a herd of sheep. This doctrine, often unconsciously, has survived the introduction of political democracy, and has radically vitiated all national systems of education.

The country which has succeeded best in giving information without intelligence is the latest addition to modern civilization, Japan. Elementary education in Japan is said to be admirable from the point of view of instruction. But, in addition to instruction, it has another purpose, which is to teach worship of the Mikado—a far stronger creed now than before Japan became modernized.[3] Thus the schools have been used simultaneously to confer knowledge and to promote superstition. Since we are not tempted to Mikado-worship, we see clearly what is absurd in Japanese teaching. Our own national superstitions strike us as natural and sensible, so that we do not take such a true view of them as we do of the superstitions of Nippon. But if a travelled Japanese were to maintain the thesis that our schools teach superstitions just as inimical to intelligence as belief in the divinity of the Mikado, I suspect that he would be able to make out a very good case.

For the present I am not in search of remedies, but am only concerned with diagnosis. We are faced with the paradoxical fact that education has become one of the chief obstacles to intelligence and freedom of thought. This is due primarily to the fact that the State claims a monopoly; but that is by no means the sole cause.

(2) *Propaganda.*—Our system of education turns young people out of the schools able to read, but for the most part unable to weigh evidence or to form

---

[3] See *The Invention of a New Religion.* By Professor Chamberlain, of Tokio. Published by the Rationalist Press Association. (Now out of print.)

an independent opinion. They are then assailed, throughout the rest of their lives, by statements designed to make them believe all sorts of absurd propositions, such as that Blank's pills cure all ills, that Spitzbergen is warm and fertile, and that Germans eat corpses. The art of propaganda, as practised by modern politicians and governments, is derived from the art of advertisement. The science of psychology owes a great deal to advertisers. In former days most psychologists would probably have thought that a man could not convince many people of the excellence of his own wares by merely stating emphatically that they were excellent. Experience shows, however, that they were mistaken in this. If I were to stand up once in a public place and state that I am the most modest man alive, I should be laughed at; but if I could raise enough money to make the same statement on all the busses and on hoardings along all the principal railway lines, people would presently become convinced that I had an abnormal shrinking from publicity. If I were to go to a small shopkeeper and say: "Look at your competitor over the way, he is getting your business; don't you think it would be a good plan to leave your business and stand up in the middle of the road and try to shoot him before he shoots you?"—if I were to say this, any small shopkeeper would think me mad. But when the Government says it with emphasis and a brass band, the small shopkeepers become enthusiastic, and are quite surprised when they find afterwards that business has suffered. Propaganda, conducted by the means which advertisers have found successful, is now one of the recognized methods of government in all advanced countries, and is especially the method by which democratic opinion is created.

There are two quite different evils about propaganda as now practised. On the one hand, its appeal is generally to irrational causes of belief rather than to serious argument; on the other hand, it gives an unfair advantage to those who can obtain most publicity, whether through wealth or through power. For my part, I am inclined to think that too much fuss is sometimes made about the fact that propaganda appeals to emotion rather than reason. The line between emotion and reason is not so sharp as some people think. Moreover, a clever man could frame a sufficiently rational argument in favour of any position which has any chance of being adopted. There are always good arguments on both sides of any real issue. Definite mis-statements of fact can be legitimately objected to, but they are by no means necessary. The mere words "Pear's Soap," which affirm nothing, cause people to buy that article. If, wherever these words appear, they were replaced by the words "The Labour Party," millions of people would be led to vote for the Labour Party, although the advertisements had claimed no merit for it whatever. But if both sides in a controversy were confined by law to statements which a committee of eminent logicians considered relevant and valid, the main evil of propaganda, as at present conducted, would remain. Suppose, under such a law, two parties with an equally good case, one of whom had a million pounds to spend on propaganda, while the other had only a hundred thousand. It is obvious that the arguments in favour of the richer party would become more widely known than those in favour of the poorer party, and therefore the richer party would win. This situation is, of course, intensified when one party is the Government. In Russia the Government has an almost complete monopoly of propaganda, but that is not necessary. The advantages which it possesses over its opponents will generally be sufficient to give it the victory, unless it has an exceptionally bad case.

The objection to propaganda is not only its appeal to unreason, but still more the unfair advantage which it gives to the rich and powerful. Equality of opportunity among opinions is essential if there is to be real freedom of thought; and equality of opportunity among opinions can only be secured by elaborate laws directed to that end, which there is no reason to expect to see enacted. The cure is not to be sought primarily in such laws, but in better education and a more sceptical public opinion. For the moment, however, I am not concerned to discuss cures.

(3) *Economic pressure.*—I have already dealt with some aspects of this obstacle to freedom of thought, but I wish now to deal with it on more general lines, as a danger which is bound to increase unless very definite steps are taken to counteract it. The supreme example of economic pressure applied against freedom of thought is Soviet Russia, where, until the trade agreement, the Government could and did inflict starvation upon people whose opinions it disliked—for example, Kropotkin. But in this respect Russia is only somewhat ahead of other countries. In France, during the Dreyfus affair, any teacher would have lost his position if he had been in favour of Dreyfus at the start or against him at the end. In America at the present day I doubt if a university professor, however eminent, could get employment if he were to criticize the Standard Oil Company, because all college presidents have received or hope to receive benefactions from Mr. Rockefeller. Throughout America Socialists are marked men, and find it extremely difficult to obtain work unless they have great gifts. The tendency, which exists wherever industrialism is well developed, for trusts and monopolies to control all industry, leads to a diminution of the number of possible employers, so that it becomes easier and easier to keep secret black books by means of which any one not subservient to the great corporations can be starved. The growth of monopolies is introducing in America many of the evils associated with State Socialism as it has existed in Russia. From the standpoint of liberty, it makes no difference to a man whether his only possible employer is the State or a Trust.

In America, which is the most advanced country industrially, and to a lesser extent in other countries which are approximating to the American condition, it is necessary for the average citizen, if he wishes to make a living, to avoid incurring the hostility of certain big men. And these big men have an outlook—religious, moral, and political—with which they expect their employees to agree, at least outwardly. A man who openly dissents from Christianity, or believes in a relaxation of the marriage laws, or objects to the power of the great corporations, finds America a very uncomfortable country, unless he happens to be an eminent writer. Exactly the same kind of restraints upon freedom of thought are bound to occur in every country where economic organization has been carried to the point of practical monopoly. Therefore the safeguarding of liberty in the world which is growing up is far more difficult than it was in the nineteenth century, when free competition was still a reality. Whoever cares about the freedom of the mind must face this situation fully and frankly, realizing the inapplicability of methods which answered well enough while industrialism was in its infancy.

There are two simple principles which, if they were adopted, would solve almost all social problems. The first is that education should have for one of its aims to teach people only to believe propositions when there is some reason to think that they are true. The second is that jobs should be given solely for fitness to do the work.

To take the second point first. The habit of considering a man's religious, moral, and political opinions before appointing him to a post or giving him a job is the modern form of persecution, and it is likely to become quite as efficient as the Inquisition ever was. The old liberties can be legally retained without being of the slightest use. If, in practice, certain opinions lead a man to starve, it is poor comfort to him to know that his opinions are not punishable by law. There is a certain public feeling against starving men for not belonging to the Church of England, or for holding slightly unorthodox opinions in politics. But there is hardly any feeling against the rejection of Atheists or Mormons, extreme communists, or men who advocate free love. Such men are thought to be wicked, and it is considered only natural to refuse to employ them. People have hardly yet waked up to the fact that this refusal, in a highly industrial State, amounts to a very rigorous form of persecution.

If this danger were adequately realized, it would be possible to rouse public opinion, and to secure that a man's beliefs should not be considered in appointing him to a post. The protection of minorities is vitally important; and even the most orthodox of us may find himself in a minority some day, so that we all have an interest in restraining the tyranny of majorities. Nothing except public opinion can solve this problem. Socialism would make it somewhat more acute, since it would eliminate the opportunities that now arise through exceptional employers. Every increase in the size of industrial undertakings makes it worse, since it diminishes the number of independent employers. The battle must be fought exactly as the battle of religious toleration was fought. And as in that case, so in this, a decay in the intensity of belief is likely to prove the decisive factor. While men were convinced of the absolute truth of Catholicism or Protestantism, as the case might be, they were willing to persecute on account of them. While men are quite certain of their modern creeds, they will persecute on their behalf. Some element of doubt is essential to the practice, though not to the theory, of toleration. And this brings me to my other point, which concerns the aims of education.

If there is to be toleration in the world, one of the things taught in schools must be the habit of weighing evidence, and the practice of not giving full assent to propositions which there is no reason to believe true. For example, the art of reading the newspapers should be taught. The schoolmaster should select some incident which happened a good many years ago, and roused political passions in its day. He should then read to the school children what was said by the newspapers on one side, what was said by those on the other, and some impartial account of what really happened. He should show how, from the biased account of either side, a practised reader could infer what really happened, and he should make them understand that everything in newspapers is more or less untrue. The cynical scepticism which would result from this teaching would make the children in later life immune from those appeals to idealism by which decent people are induced to further the schemes of scoundrels.

History should be taught in the same way. Napoleon's campaigns of 1813 and 1814, for instance, might be studied in the *Moniteur*, leading up to the surprise which Parisians felt when they saw the Allies arriving under the walls of Paris after they had (according to the official bulletins) been beaten by Napoleon in every battle. In the more advanced classes, students should be encouraged to count the number of times that Lenin has been assassinated by Trotsky, in order to learn contempt for death. Finally, they should be given a school history approved by the Government, and asked to infer what a French school history would say about our wars with France. All this would be a far better training in citizenship than the trite moral maxims by which some people believe that civic duty can be inculcated.

It must, I think, be admitted that the evils of the world are due to moral defects quite as much as to lack of intelligence. But the human race has not hitherto discovered any method of eradicating moral defects; preaching and exhortation only add hypocrisy to the previous list of vices. Intelligence, on the contrary, is easily improved by methods known to every competent educator. Therefore, until some method of teaching virtue has been discovered, progress will have to be sought by improvement of intelligence rather than of morals. One of the chief obstacles to intelligence is credulity, and credulity could be enormously diminished by instruction as to the prevalent forms of mendacity. Credulity is a greater evil in the present day than it ever was before, because, owing to the growth of education, it is much easier than it used to be to spread misinformation, and, owing to democracy, the spread of misinformation is more important than in former times to the holders of power. Hence the increase in the circulation of newspapers.

If I am asked how the world is to be induced to adopt these two maxims—namely (1) that jobs should be given to people on account of their fitness to perform them; (2) that one aim of education should be to cure people of the habit of believing propositions for which there is no evidence—I can only say that it must be done by generating an enlightened public opinion. And an enlightened public opinion can only be generated by the efforts of those who desire that it should exist. I do not believe that the economic changes advocated by Socialists will, of themselves, do anything towards curing the evils we have been considering. I think that, whatever happens in politics, the trend of economic development will make the preservation of mental freedom increasingly difficult, unless public opinion insists that the employer shall control nothing in the life of the employee except his work. Freedom in education could easily be secured, if it were desired, by limiting the function of the State to inspection and payment, and confining inspection rigidly to the definite instruction. But that, as things stand, would leave education in the hands of the Churches, because, unfortunately, they are more anxious to teach their beliefs than Freethinkers are to teach their doubts. It would, however, give a free field, and would make it possible for a liberal education to be given if it were really desired. More than that ought not to be asked of the law.

My plea throughout this address has been for the spread of the scientific temper, which is an altogether different thing from the knowledge of scientific results. The scientific temper is capable of regenerating mankind and providing an issue for all our troubles. The results of science, in the form of mechanism, poison gas, and the yellow press, bid fair to lead to the total downfall of our civilization. It is a curious antithesis, which a Martian might contemplate with amused detachment. But for us it is a matter of life and death. Upon its issue depends the question whether our grandchildren are to live in a happier world, or are to exterminate each other by scientific methods, leaving perhaps to negroes and Papuans the future destinies of mankind.

# APPENDIX

## The Conway Memorial Lectureship

At a general meeting of the South Place Ethical Society, held on October 22, 1908, it was resolved, after full discussion, that an effort should be made to establish a series of lectures, to be printed and widely circulated, as a permanent Memorial to Dr. Conway.

Moncure Conway's untiring zeal for the emancipation of the human mind from the thraldom of obsolete or waning beliefs, his pleadings for sympathy with the oppressed and for a wider and profounder conception of human fraternity than the world has yet reached, claim, it is urged, an offering of gratitude more permanent than the eloquent obituary or reverential service of mourning.

The range of the lectures (of which the thirteenth is published herewith) must be regulated by the financial support accorded to the scheme; but it is hoped that sufficient funds will be eventually forthcoming for the endowment of periodical lectures by distinguished public men, to further the cause of social, political, and religious freedom, with which Dr. Conway's name must ever be associated.

The Conway Memorial Lecture Committee, although not yet in possession of the necessary capital for the permanent endowment of the Lectureship, have inaugurated and maintained the work while inviting further contributions. The funds in hand, together with those which may reasonably be expected from supporters of the Movement, will ensure the delivery of an annual lecture for some years at least.

The Committee earnestly appeal for either donations or subscriptions from year to year until the Memorial is permanently established. Contributions may be forwarded to the Hon. Treasurer.

On behalf of the Executive Committee:—

(Mrs.) C. FLETCHER SMITH and ERNEST CARR, *Hon. Secretaries.*
(Mrs.) F. M. COCKBURN, *Hon. Treasurer,* "Peradeniya," Northampton Road, Croydon.

# POLITICAL IDEALS

# CHAPTER I

## Political Ideals

In dark days, men need a clear faith and a well-grounded hope; and as the outcome of these, the calm courage which takes no account of hardships by the way. The times through which we are passing have afforded to many of us a confirmation of our faith. We see that the things we had thought evil are really evil, and we know more definitely than we ever did before the directions in which men must move if a better world is to arise on the ruins of the one which is now hurling itself into destruction. We see that men's political dealings with one another are based on wholly wrong ideals, and can only be saved by quite different ideals from continuing to be a source of suffering, devastation, and sin.

Political ideals must be based upon ideals for the individual life. The aim of politics should be to make the lives of individuals as good as possible. There is nothing for the politician to consider outside or above the various men, women, and children who compose the world. The problem of politics is to adjust the relations of human beings in such a way that each severally may have as much of good in his existence as possible. And this problem requires that we should first consider what it is that we think good in the individual life.

To begin with, we do not want all men to be alike. We do not want to lay down a pattern or type to which men of all sorts are to be made by some means or another to approximate. This is the ideal of the impatient administrator. A bad teacher will aim at imposing his opinion, and turning out a set of pupils all of whom will give the same definite answer on a doubtful point. Mr. Bernard Shaw is said to hold that *Troilus and Cressida* is the best of Shakespeare's plays. Although I disagree with this opinion, I should welcome it in a pupil as a sign of individuality; but most teachers would not tolerate such a heterodox view. Not only teachers, but all commonplace persons in authority, desire in their subordinates that kind of uniformity which makes their actions easily predictable and never inconvenient. The result is that they crush initiative and individuality when they can, and when they cannot, they quarrel with it.

It is not one ideal for all men, but a separate ideal for each separate man, that has to be realized if possible. Every man has it in his being to develop into something good or bad: there is a best possible for him, and a worst possible. His circumstances will determine whether his capacities for good are developed or crushed, and whether his bad impulses are strengthened or gradually diverted into better channels.

But although we cannot set up in any detail an ideal of character which is to be universally applicable—although we cannot say, for instance, that all men ought to be industrious, or self-sacrificing, or fond of music—there are some broad principles which can be used to guide our estimates as to what is possible or desirable.

We may distinguish two sorts of goods, and two corresponding sorts of impulses. There are goods in regard to which individual possession is possible, and there are goods in which all can share alike. The food and clothing of one man is not the food and clothing of another; if the supply is insufficient, what one man has is obtained at the expense of some other man. This applies to material goods generally, and therefore to the greater part of the present economic life of the world. On the other hand, mental and spiritual goods do not belong to one man to the exclusion of another. If one man knows a science, that does not prevent others from knowing it; on the contrary, it helps them to acquire the knowledge. If one man is a great artist or poet, that does not prevent others from painting pictures or writing poems, but helps to create the atmosphere in which such things are possible. If one man is full of good-will toward others, that does not mean that there is less good-will to be shared among the rest; the more good-will one man has, the more he is likely to create among others. In such matters there is no *possession*, because there is not a definite amount to be shared; any increase anywhere tends to produce an increase everywhere.

There are two kinds of impulses, corresponding to the two kinds of goods. There are *possessive* impulses, which aim at acquiring or retaining private goods that cannot be shared; these center in the impulse of property. And there are *creative* or constructive impulses, which aim at bringing into the world or making available for use the kind of goods in which there is no privacy and no possession.

The best life is the one in which the creative impulses play the largest part and the possessive impulses the smallest. This is no new discovery. The Gospel says: "Take no thought, saying, What shall we eat? or What shall we drink? or, Wherewithal shall we be clothed?" The thought we give to these things is taken away from matters of more importance. And what is worse, the habit of mind engendered by thinking of these things is a bad one; it leads to competition, envy, domination, cruelty, and almost all the moral evils that infest the world. In particular, it leads to the predatory use of force. Material possessions can be taken by force and enjoyed by the robber. Spiritual possessions cannot be taken in this way. You may kill an artist or a thinker, but you cannot acquire his art or his thought. You may put a man to death because he loves his fellow-men, but you will not by so doing acquire the love which made his happiness. Force is impotent in such matters; it is only as regards material goods that it is effective. For this reason the men who believe in force are the men whose thoughts and desires are preoccupied with material goods.

375

The possessive impulses, when they are strong, infect activities which ought to be purely creative. A man who has made some valuable discovery may be filled with jealousy of a rival discoverer. If one man has found a cure for cancer and another has found a cure for consumption, one of them may be delighted if the other man's discovery turns out a mistake, instead of regretting the suffering of patients which would otherwise have been avoided. In such cases, instead of desiring knowledge for its own sake, or for the sake of its usefulness, a man is desiring it as a means to reputation. Every creative impulse is shadowed by a possessive impulse; even the aspirant to saintliness may be jealous of the more successful saint. Most affection is accompanied by some tinge of jealousy, which is a possessive impulse intruding into the creative region. Worst of all, in this direction, is the sheer envy of those who have missed everything worth having in life, and who are instinctively bent on preventing others from enjoying what they have not had. There is often much of this in the attitude of the old toward the young.

There is in human beings, as in plants and animals, a certain natural impulse of growth, and this is just as true of mental as of physical development. Physical development is helped by air and nourishment and exercise, and may be hindered by the sort of treatment which made Chinese women's feet small. In just the same way mental development may be helped or hindered by outside influences. The outside influences that help are those that merely provide encouragement or mental food or opportunities for exercising mental faculties. The influences that hinder are those that interfere with growth by applying any kind of force, whether discipline or authority or fear or the tyranny of public opinion or the necessity of engaging in some totally incongenial occupation. Worst of all influences are those that thwart or twist a man's fundamental impulse, which is what shows itself as conscience in the moral sphere; such influences are likely to do a man an inward danger from which he will never recover.

Those who realize the harm that can be done to others by any use of force against them, and the worthlessness of the goods that can be acquired by force, will be very full of respect for the liberty of others; they will not try to bind them or fetter them; they will be slow to judge and swift to sympathize; they will treat every human being with a kind of tenderness, because the principle of good in him is at once fragile and infinitely precious. They will not condemn those who are unlike themselves; they will know and feel that individuality brings differences and uniformity means death. They will wish each human being to be as much a living thing and as little a mechanical product as it is possible to be; they will cherish in each one just those things which the harsh usage of a ruthless world would destroy. In one word, all their dealings with others will be inspired by a deep impulse of *reverence*.

What we shall desire for individuals is now clear: strong creative impulses, overpowering and absorbing the instinct of possession; reverence for others; respect for the fundamental creative impulse in ourselves. A certain kind of self-respect or native pride is necessary to a good life; a man must not have a sense of utter inward defeat if he is to remain whole, but must feel the courage and the hope and the will to live by the best that is in him, whatever outward or inward obstacles it may encounter. So far as it lies in a man's own power, his life will realize its best possibilities if it has three things: creative rather than possessive impulses, reverence for others, and respect for the fundamental impulse in himself.

Political and social institutions are to be judged by the good or harm that they do to individuals. Do they encourage creativeness rather than possessiveness? Do they embody or promote a spirit of reverence between human beings? Do they preserve self-respect?

In all these ways the institutions under which we live are very far indeed from what they ought to be.

Institutions, and especially economic systems, have a profound influence in molding the characters of men and women. They may encourage adventure and hope, or timidity and the pursuit of safety. They may open men's minds to great possibilities, or close them against everything but the risk of obscure misfortune. They may make a man's happiness depend upon what he adds to the general possessions of the world, or upon what he can secure for himself of the private goods in which others cannot share. Modern capitalism forces the wrong decision of these alternatives upon all who are not heroic or exceptionally fortunate.

Men's impulses are molded, partly by their native disposition, partly by opportunity and environment, especially early environment. Direct preaching can do very little to change impulses, though it can lead people to restrain the direct expression of them, often with the result that the impulses go underground and come to the surface again in some contorted form. When we have discovered what kinds of impulse we desire, we must not rest content with preaching, or with trying to produce the outward manifestation without the inner spring; we must try rather to alter institutions in the way that will, of itself, modify the life of impulse in the desired direction.

At present our institutions rest upon two things: property and power. Both of these are very unjustly distributed; both, in the actual world, are of great importance to the happiness of the individual. Both are possessive goods; yet without them many of the goods in which all might share are hard to acquire as things are now.

Without property, as things are, a man has no freedom, and no security for the necessities of a tolerable life; without power, he has no opportunity for initiative. If men are to have free play for their creative impulses, they must be liberated from sordid cares by a certain measure of security, and they must have a sufficient share of power to be able to exercise initiative as regards the course and conditions of their lives.

Few men can succeed in being creative rather than possessive in a world which is wholly built on competition, where the great majority would fall into utter destitution if they became careless as to the acquisition of material goods, where honor and power and respect are given to wealth rather than to wisdom, where the law embodies and consecrates the injustice of those who have toward those who have not. In such an environment even those whom nature has endowed with great creative gifts become infected with the poison of competition. Men combine in groups to attain more strength in the scramble for material goods, and loyalty to the group spreads a halo of quasi-idealism round the central impulse of greed. Trade-unions and the Labor party are no more exempt from this vice than other parties and other sections of society; though they are largely inspired by the hope of a radically better world. They are too often led astray by the immediate object of securing for themselves a large share of material goods. That this desire is in accordance with justice, it is impossible to deny; but something larger and more constructive is needed as a political ideal, if the victors of to-morrow are not to become the oppressors of the day after. The inspiration and outcome of a reforming movement ought to be freedom and a generous spirit, not niggling restrictions and regulations.

The present economic system concentrates initiative in the hands of a small number of very rich men. Those who are not capitalists have, almost always, very little choice as to their activities when once they have selected a trade or profession; they are not part of the power that moves the mechanism, but only a passive portion of the machinery. Despite political democracy, there is still an extraordinary degree of difference in the power of self-direction belonging to a capitalist and to a man who has to earn his living. Economic affairs touch men's lives, at most times, much more intimately than political questions. At present the man who has no capital usually has to sell himself to some large organization, such as a railway company, for example. He has no voice in its management, and no liberty in politics except what his trade-union can secure for him. If he happens to desire a form of liberty which is not thought important by his trade-union, he is powerless; he must submit or starve.

Exactly the same thing happens to professional men. Probably a majority of journalists are engaged in writing for newspapers whose politics they disagree with; only a man of wealth can own a large newspaper, and only an accident can enable the point of view or the interests of those who are not wealthy to find expression in a newspaper. A large part of the best brains of the country are in the civil service, where the condition of their employment is silence about the evils which cannot be concealed from them. A Nonconformist minister loses his livelihood if his views displease his congregation; a member of Parliament loses his seat if he is not sufficiently supple or sufficiently stupid to follow or share all the turns and twists of public opinion. In every walk of life, independence of mind is punished by failure, more and more as economic organizations grow larger and more rigid. Is it surprising that men become increasingly docile, increasingly ready to submit to dictation and to forego the right of thinking for themselves? Yet along such lines civilization can only sink into a Byzantine immobility.

Fear of destitution is not a motive out of which a free creative life can grow, yet it is the chief motive which inspires the daily work of most wage-earners. The hope of possessing more wealth and power than any man ought to have, which is the corresponding motive of the rich, is quite as bad in its effects; it compels men to close their minds against justice, and to prevent themselves from thinking honestly on social questions while in the depths of their hearts they uneasily feel that their pleasures are bought by the miseries of others. The injustices of destitution and wealth alike ought to be rendered impossible. Then a great fear would be removed from the lives of the many, and hope would have to take on a better form in the lives of the few.

But security and liberty are only the negative conditions for good political institutions. When they have been won, we need also the positive condition: encouragement of creative energy. Security alone might produce a smug and stationary society; it demands creativeness as its counterpart, in order to keep alive the adventure and interest of life, and the movement toward perpetually new and better things. There can be no final goal for human institutions; the best are those that most encourage progress toward others still better. Without effort and change, human life cannot remain good. It is not a finished Utopia that we ought to desire, but a world where imagination and hope are alive and active.

It is a sad evidence of the weariness mankind has suffered from excessive toil that his heavens have usually been places where nothing ever happened or changed. Fatigue produces the illusion that only rest is needed for happiness; but when men have rested for a time, boredom drives them to renewed activity. For this reason, a happy life must be one in which there is activity. If it is also to be a useful life, the activity ought to be as far as possible creative, not merely predatory or defensive. But creative activity requires imagination and originality, which are apt to be subversive of the *status quo*. At present, those who have power dread a disturbance of the *status quo*, lest their unjust privileges should be taken away. In combination with the instinct for conventionality,[1] which man shares with the other gregarious animals, those who profit by the existing order have established a system which punishes originality and starves imagination from the moment of first going to school down to the time of death and burial. The whole spirit in which education is conducted needs to be changed, in order that children may be encouraged to think and feel for themselves, not to acquiesce passively in the thoughts and feelings of others. It is not rewards after the event that will produce initiative, but a certain mental atmosphere. There have been times when such an atmosphere existed: the great days of Greece, and Elizabethan England, may serve as examples. But in our own day the tyranny of vast machine-like organizations, governed from above by men who know and care little for the lives of those whom they control, is killing individuality and freedom of mind, and forcing men more and more to conform to a uniform pattern.

---

[1] In England this is called "a sense of humor."

Vast organizations are an inevitable element in modern life, and it is useless to aim at their abolition, as has been done by some reformers, for instance, William Morris. It is true that they make the preservation of individuality more difficult, but what is needed is a way of combining them with the greatest possible scope for individual initiative.

One very important step toward this end would be to render democratic the government of every organization. At present, our legislative institutions are more or less democratic, except for the important fact that women are excluded. But our administration is still purely bureaucratic, and our economic organizations are monarchical or oligarchic. Every limited liability company is run by a small number of self-appointed or coöpted directors. There can be no real freedom or democracy until the men who do the work in a business also control its management.

Another measure which would do much to increase liberty would be an increase of self-government for subordinate groups, whether geographical or economic or defined by some common belief, like religious sects. A modern state is so vast and its machinery is so little understood that even when a man has a vote he does not feel himself any effective part of the force which determines its policy. Except in matters where he can act in conjunction with an exceptionally powerful group, he feels himself almost impotent, and the government remains a remote impersonal circumstance, which must be simply endured, like the weather. By a share in the control of smaller bodies, a man might regain some of that sense of personal opportunity and responsibility which belonged to the citizen of a city-state in ancient Greece or medieval Italy.

When any group of men has a strong corporate consciousness—such as belongs, for example, to a nation or a trade or a religious body—liberty demands that it should be free to decide for itself all matters which are of great importance to the outside world. This is the basis of the universal claim for national independence. But nations are by no means the only groups which ought to have self-government for their internal concerns. And nations, like other groups, ought not to have complete liberty of action in matters which are of equal concern to foreign nations. Liberty demands self-government, but not the right to interfere with others. The greatest degree of liberty is not secured by anarchy. The reconciliation of liberty with government is a difficult problem, but it is one which any political theory must face.

The essence of government is the use of force in accordance with law to secure certain ends which the holders of power consider desirable. The coercion of an individual or a group by force is always in itself more or less harmful. But if there were no government, the result would not be an absence of force in men's relations to each other; it would merely be the exercise of force by those who had strong predatory instincts, necessitating either slavery or a perpetual readiness to repel force with force on the part of those whose instincts were less violent. This is the state of affairs at present in international relations, owing to the fact that no international government exists. The results of anarchy between states should suffice to persuade us that anarchism has no solution to offer for the evils of the world.

There is probably one purpose, and only one, for which the use of force by a government is beneficent, and that is to diminish the total amount of force used m the world. It is clear, for example, that the legal prohibition of murder diminishes the total amount of violence in the world. And no one would maintain that parents should have unlimited freedom to ill-treat their children. So long as some men wish to do violence to others, there cannot be complete liberty, for either the wish to do violence must be restrained, or the victims must be left to suffer. For this reason, although individuals and societies should have the utmost freedom as regards their own affairs, they ought not to have complete freedom as regards their dealings with others. To give freedom to the strong to oppress the weak is not the way to secure the greatest possible amount of freedom in the world. This is the basis of the socialist revolt against the kind of freedom which used to be advocated by *laissez-faire* economists.

Democracy is a device—the best so far invented—for diminishing as much as possible the interference of governments with liberty. If a nation is divided into two sections which cannot both have their way, democracy theoretically insures that the majority shall have their way. But democracy is not at all an adequate device unless it is accompanied by a very great amount of devolution. Love of uniformity, or the mere pleasure of interfering, or dislike of differing tastes and temperaments, may often lead a majority to control a minority in matters which do not really concern the majority. We should none of us like to have the internal affairs of Great Britain settled by a parliament of the world, if ever such a body came into existence. Nevertheless, there are matters which such a body could settle much better than any existing instrument of government.

The theory of the legitimate use of force in human affairs, where a government exists, seems clear. Force should only be used against those who attempt to use force against others, or against those who will not respect the law in cases where a common decision is necessary and a minority are opposed to the action of the majority. These seem legitimate occasions for the use of force; and they should be legitimate occasions in international affairs, if an international government existed. The problem of the legitimate occasions for the use of force in the absence of a government is a different one, with which we are not at present concerned.

Although a government must have the power to use force, and may on occasion use it legitimately, the aim of the reformers to have such institutions as will diminish the need for actual coercion will be found to have this effect. Most of us abstain, for instance, from theft, not because it is illegal, but because we feel no desire to steal. The more men learn to live creatively rather than possessively, the less their wishes will lead them to thwart others or to attempt violent interference with their liberty. Most of the conflicts of interests, which lead individuals or organizations into disputes, are purely imaginary, and would be seen to be so if men aimed more at the goods in

381

which all can share, and less at those private possessions that are the source of strife. In proportion as men live creatively, they cease to wish to interfere with others by force. Very many matters in which, at present, common action is thought indispensable, might well be left to individual decision. It used to be thought absolutely necessary that all the inhabitants of a country should have the same religion, but we now know that there is no such necessity. In like manner it will be found, as men grow more tolerant in their instincts, that many uniformities now insisted upon are useless and even harmful.

Good political institutions would weaken the impulse toward force and domination in two ways: first, by increasing the opportunities for the creative impulses, and by shaping education so as to strengthen these impulses; secondly, by diminishing the outlets for the possessive instincts. The diffusion of power, both in the political and the economic sphere, instead of its concentration in the hands of officials and captains of industry, would greatly diminish the opportunities for acquiring the habit of command, out of which the desire for exercising tyranny is apt to spring. Autonomy, both for districts and for organizations, would leave fewer occasions when governments were called upon to make decisions as to other people's concerns. And the abolition of capitalism and the wage system would remove the chief incentive to fear and greed, those correlative passions by which all free life is choked and gagged.

Few men seem to realize how many of the evils from which we suffer are wholly unnecessary, and that they could be abolished by a united effort within a few years. If a majority in every civilized country so desired, we could, within twenty years, abolish all abject poverty, quite half the illness in the world, the whole economic slavery which binds down nine tenths of our population; we could fill the world with beauty and joy, and secure the reign of universal peace. It is only because men are apathetic that this is not achieved, only because imagination is sluggish, and what always has been is regarded as what always must be. With good-will, generosity, intelligence, these things could be brought about.

# CHAPTER II

## Capitalism and the Wage System

### I

The world is full of preventible evils which most men would be glad to see prevented.

Nevertheless, these evils persist, and nothing effective is done toward abolishing them.

This paradox produces astonishment in inexperienced reformers, and too often produces disillusionment in those who have come to know the difficulty of changing human institutions.

War is recognized as an evil by an immense majority in every civilized country; but this recognition does not prevent war.

The unjust distribution of wealth must be obviously an evil to those who are not prosperous, and they are nine tenths of the population. Nevertheless it continues unabated.

The tyranny of the holders of power is a source of needless suffering and misfortune to very large sections of mankind; but power remains in few hands, and tends, if anything, to grow more concentrated.

I wish first to study the evils of our present institutions, and the causes of the very limited success of reformers in the past, and then to suggest reasons for the hope of a more lasting and permanent success in the near future.

The war has come as a challenge to all who desire a better world. The system which cannot save mankind from such an appalling disaster is at fault somewhere, and cannot be amended in any lasting way unless the danger of great wars in the future can be made very small.

But war is only the final flower of an evil tree. Even in times of peace, most men live lives of monotonous labor, most women are condemned to a drudgery which almost kills the possibility of happiness before youth is past, most children are allowed to grow up in ignorance of all that would enlarge their thoughts or stimulate their imagination. The few who are more fortunate are rendered illiberal by their unjust privileges, and oppressive through fear of the awakening indignation of the masses. From the highest to the lowest, almost all men are absorbed in the economic struggle: the struggle to acquire what is their due or to retain what is not their due. Material possessions, in fact or in desire, dominate our outlook, usually to the exclusion of all generous and creative impulses. Possessiveness—the passion to have and to hold—is the ultimate source of war, and the foundation of all the ills from which the political world is suffering. Only by diminishing the strength of this passion and its hold upon our daily lives can new institutions bring permanent benefit to mankind.

Institutions which will diminish the sway of greed are possible, but only through a complete reconstruction of our whole economic system. Capitalism and the wage system must be abolished; they are twin monsters which are eating up the life of the world. In place of them we need a system which will hold in cheek men's predatory impulses, and will diminish the economic injustice that allows some to be rich in idleness while others are poor in spite of unremitting labor; but above all we need a system which will destroy the tyranny of the employer, by making men at the same time secure against destitution and able to find scope for individual initiative in the control of the industry by which they live. A better system can do all these things, and can be established by the democracy whenever it grows weary of enduring evils which there is no reason to endure.

We may distinguish four purposes at which an economic system may aim: first, it may aim at the greatest possible production of goods and at facilitating technical progress; second, it may aim at securing distributive justice; third, it may aim at giving security against destitution; and, fourth, it may aim at liberating creative impulses and diminishing possessive impulses.

Of these four purposes the last is the most important. Security is chiefly important as a means to it. State socialism, though it might give material security and more justice than we have at present, would probably fail to liberate creative impulses or produce a progressive society.

Our present system fails in all four purposes. It is chiefly defended on the ground that it achieves the first of the four purposes, namely, the greatest possible production of material goods, but it only does this in a very short-sighted way, by methods which are wasteful in the long run both of human material and of natural resources.

Capitalistic enterprise involves a ruthless belief in the importance of increasing material production to the utmost possible extent now and in the immediate future. In obedience to this belief, new portions of the earth's surface are continually brought under the sway of industrialism. Vast tracts of Africa become recruiting grounds for the labor required in the gold and diamond mines of the Rand, Rhodesia, and Kimberley; for this purpose, the population is demoralized, taxed, driven into revolt, and exposed to the contamination of European vice and disease. Healthy and vigorous races from Southern Europe are tempted to America, where sweating and slum life reduce their vitality if they do not actually cause their death. What damage is done to our own urban populations by the conditions under which they live, we all know. And what is true of the human riches of the world is no less true of the physical resources. The mines, forests, and wheat-fields of the world are all being exploited at a rate which must practically exhaust them at no distant date. On the side of material production, the world is living too fast; in a kind of delirium, almost all the energy of the world has rushed into the immediate production of something, no matter what, and no matter at what cost. And yet our present system is defended on the ground that it safeguards progress!

It cannot be said that our present economic system is any more successful in regard to the other three objects which ought to be aimed at. Among the many obvious evils of capitalism and the wage system, none are more glaring than that they encourage predatory instincts, that they allow economic injustice, and that they give great scope to the tyranny of the employer.

As to predatory instincts, we may say, broadly speaking, that in a state of nature there would be two ways of acquiring riches—one by production, the other by robbery. Under our existing system, although what is recognized as robbery is forbidden, there are nevertheless many ways of becoming rich without contributing anything to the wealth of the community. Ownership of land or capital, whether acquired or inherited, gives a legal right to a permanent income. Although most people have to produce in order to live, a privileged minority are able to live in luxury without producing anything at all. As these are the men who are not only the most fortunate but also the most respected, there is a general desire to enter their ranks, and a widespread unwillingness to face the fact that there is no justification whatever for incomes derived in this way. And apart from the passive enjoyment of rent or interest, the methods of acquiring wealth are very largely predatory. It is not, as a rule, by means of useful inventions, or of any other action which increases the general wealth of the community, that men amass fortunes; it is much more often by skill in exploiting or circumventing others. Nor is it only among the rich that our present régime promotes a narrowly acquisitive spirit. The constant risk of destitution compels most men to fill a great part of their time and thought with the economic struggle. There is a theory that this increases the total output of wealth by the community. But for reasons to which I shall return later, I believe this theory to be wholly mistaken.

Economic injustice is perhaps the most obvious evil of our present system. It would be utterly absurd to maintain that the men who inherit great wealth deserve better of the community than those who have to work for their living. I am not prepared to maintain that economic justice requires an exactly equal income for everybody. Some kinds of work require a larger income for efficiency than others do; but there is economic injustice as soon as a man has more than his share, unless it is because his efficiency in his work requires it, or as a reward for some definite service. But this point is so obvious that it needs no elaboration.

The modern growth of monopolies in the shape of trusts, cartels, federations of employers and so on has greatly increased the power of the capitalist to levy toll on the community. This tendency will not cease of itself, but only through definite action on the part of those who do not profit by the capitalist régime. Unfortunately the distinction between the proletariat and the capitalist is not so sharp as it was in the minds of socialist theorizers. Trade-unions have funds in various securities; friendly societies are large capitalists; and many individuals eke out their wages by invested savings. All this increases the difficulty of any clear-cut radical change in our economic system. But it does not diminish the desirability of such a change.

Such a system as that suggested by the French syndicalists, in which each trade would be self-governing and completely independent, without the control of any central authority, would not secure economic justice. Some trades are in a much stronger bargaining position than others. Coal and transport, for example, could paralyze the national life, and could levy blackmail by threatening to do so. On the other hand, such people as school teachers, for example, could rouse very little terror by the threat of a strike and would be in a very weak bargaining position. Justice can never be secured by any system of unrestrained force exercised by interested parties in their own interests. For this reason the abolition of the state, which the syndicalists seem to desire, would be a measure not compatible with economic justice.

The tyranny of the employer, which at present robs the greater part of most men's lives of all liberty and all initiative, is unavoidable so long as the employer retains the right of dismissal with consequent loss of pay. This right is supposed to be essential in order that men may have an incentive to work thoroughly. But as men grow more civilized, incentives based on hope become increasingly preferable to those that are based on fear. It would be far better that men should be rewarded for working well than that they should be punished for working badly. This system is already in operation in the civil service, where a man is only dismissed for some exceptional degree of vice or virtue, such as murder or illegal abstention from it. Sufficient pay to ensure a livelihood ought to be given to every person who is willing to work, independently of the question whether the particular work at which he is skilled is wanted at the moment or not. If it is not wanted, some new trade which is wanted ought to be taught at the public expense. Why, for example, should a hansom-cab driver be allowed to suffer on account of the introduction of taxies? He has not committed any crime, and the fact that his work is no longer wanted is due to causes entirely outside his control. Instead of being allowed to starve, he ought to be given instruction in motor driving or in whatever other trade may seem most suitable. At present, owing to the fact that all industrial changes tend to cause hardships to some section of wage-earners, there is a tendency to technical conservatism on the part of labor, a dislike of innovations, new processes, and new methods. But such changes, if they are in the permanent interest of the community, ought to be carried out without allowing them to bring unmerited loss to those sections of the community whose labor is no longer wanted in the old form. The instinctive conservatism of mankind is sure to make all processes of production change more slowly than they should. It is a pity to add to this by the avoidable conservatism which is forced upon organized labor at present through the unjust workings of a change.

It will be said that men will not work well if the fear of dismissal does not spur them on. I think it is only a small percentage of whom this would be true at present. And those of whom it would be true might easily become industrious if they were given more congenial work or a wiser training. The residue who cannot be coaxed into industry by any such methods are probably to be regarded as pathological cases, requiring medical rather than penal treatment. And against this residue must be set the very much larger number who are now ruined in health or in morale by the terrible uncertainty of their livelihood and the great irregularity of their employment. To very many, security would bring a quite new possibility of physical and moral health.

The most dangerous aspect of the tyranny of the employer is the power which it gives him of interfering with men's activities outside their working hours. A man may be dismissed because the employer dislikes his religion or his politics, or chooses to think his private life immoral. He may be dismissed because he tries to produce a spirit of independence among his fellow employees. He may fail completely to find employment merely on the ground that he is better educated than most and therefore more dangerous. Such cases actually occur at present. This evil would not be remedied, but rather intensified, under state socialism, because, where the State is the only employer, there is no refuge from its prejudices such as may now accidentally arise through the differing opinions of different men. The State would be able to enforce any system of beliefs it happened to like, and it is almost certain that it would do so. Freedom of thought would be penalized, and all independence of spirit would die out.

Any rigid system would involve this evil. It is very necessary that there should be diversity and lack of complete systematization. Minorities must be able to live and develop their opinions freely. If this is not secured, the instinct of persecution and conformity will force all men into one mold and make all vital progress impossible.

For these reasons, no one ought to be allowed to suffer destitution so long as he or she is *willing* to work. And no kind of inquiry ought to be made into opinion or private life. It is only on this basis that it is possible to build up an economic system not founded upon tyranny and terror.

## II

The power of the economic reformer is limited by the technical productivity of labor. So long as it was necessary to the bare subsistence of the human race that most men should work very long hours for a pittance, so long no civilization was possible except an aristocratic one; if there were to be men with sufficient leisure for any mental life, there had to be others who were sacrificed for the good of the few. But the time when such a system was necessary has passed away with the progress of machinery. It would be possible now, if we had a wise economic system, for all who have mental needs to find satisfaction for them. By a few hours a day of manual work, a man can produce as much as is necessary for his own subsistence; and if he is willing to forgo luxuries, that is all that the community has a right to demand of him. It ought to be open to all who so desire to do short hours of work for little pay, and devote their leisure to whatever pursuit happens to attract them. No doubt the great majority of those who chose this course would spend their time in mere amusement, as most of the rich do at present. But it could not be said, in such a society, that they were parasites upon the labor of others. And there would be a minority who would give their hours of nominal idleness to science or art or literature, or some other pursuit out of which fundamental progress may come. In all such matters, organization and system can only do harm. The one thing that can be done is to provide opportunity, without repining at the waste that results from most men failing to make good use of the opportunity.

But except in cases of unusual laziness or eccentric ambition, most men would elect to do a full day's work for a full day's pay. For these, who would form the immense majority, the important thing is that ordinary work should, as far as possible, afford interest and independence and scope for initiative. These things are more important than income, as soon as a certain minimum has been reached. They can be secured by gild socialism, by industrial self-government subject to state control as regards the relations of a trade to the rest of the community. So far as I know, they cannot be secured in any other way.

Guild socialism, as advocated by Mr. Orage and the "New Age," is associated with a polemic against "political" action, and in favor of direct economic action by trade-unions. It shares this with syndicalism, from which most of what is new in it is derived. But I see no reason for this attitude; political and economic action seem to me equally necessary, each in its own time and place. I think there is danger in the attempt to use the machinery of the present capitalist state for socialistic purposes. But there is need of political action to transform the machinery of the state, side by side with the transformation which we hope to see in economic institutions. In this country, neither transformation is likely to be brought about by a sudden revolution; we must expect each to come step by step, if at all, and I doubt if either could or should advance very far without the other.

The economic system we should ultimately wish to see would be one in which the state would be the sole recipient of economic rent, while private capitalistic enterprises should be replaced by self-governing combinations of those who actually do the work. It ought to be optional whether a man does a whole day's work for a whole day's pay, or half a day's work for half a day's pay, except in cases where such an arrangement would cause practical inconvenience. A man's pay should not cease through the accident of his work being no longer needed, but should continue so long as he is willing to work, a new trade being taught him at the public expense, if necessary. Unwillingness to work should be treated medically or educationally, when it could not be overcome by a change to some more congenial occupation.

The workers in a given industry should all be combined in one autonomous unit, and their work should not be subject to any outside control. The state should fix the price at which they produce, but should leave the industry self-governing in all other respects. In fixing prices, the state should, as far as possible, allow each industry to profit by any improvements which it might introduce into its own processes, but should endeavor to prevent undeserved loss or gain through changes in external economic conditions. In this way there would be every incentive to progress, with the least possible danger of unmerited destitution. And although large economic organizations will continue, as they are bound to do, there will be a diffusion of power which will take away the sense of individual impotence from which men and women suffer at present.

### III

Some men, though they may admit that such a system would be desirable, will argue that it is impossible to bring it about, and that therefore we must concentrate on more immediate objects.

I think it must be conceded that a political party ought to have proximate aims, measures which it hopes to carry in the next session or the next parliament, as well as a more distant goal. Marxian socialism, as it existed in Germany, seemed to me to suffer in this way: although the party was numerically powerful, it was politically weak, because it had no minor measures to demand while waiting for the revolution. And when, at last, German socialism was captured by those who desired a less impracticable policy, the modification which occurred was of exactly the wrong kind: acquiescence in bad policies, such as militarism and imperialism, rather than advocacy of partial reforms which, however inadequate, would still have been steps in the right direction.

A similar defect was inherent in the policy of French syndicalism as it existed before the war. Everything was to wait for the general strike; after adequate preparation, one day the whole proletariat would unanimously refuse to work, the property owners would acknowledge their defeat, and agree to abandon all their privileges rather than starve. This is a dramatic conception; but love of drama is a great enemy of true vision. Men cannot be trained, except under very rare circumstances, to do something suddenly which is very different from what they have been doing before. If the general strike were to succeed, the victors, despite their anarchism, would be compelled at once to form an administration, to create a new police force to prevent looting and wanton destruction, to establish a provisional government issuing dictatorial orders to the various sections of revolutionaries. Now the syndicalists are opposed in principle to all political action; they would feel that they were departing from their theory in taking the necessary practical steps, and they would be without the required training because of their previous abstention from politics. For these reasons it is likely that, even after a syndicalist revolution, actual power would fall into the hands of men who were not really syndicalists.

Another objection to a program which is to be realized suddenly at some remote date by a revolution or a general strike is that enthusiasm flags when there is nothing to do meanwhile, and no partial success to lessen the weariness of waiting. The only sort of movement which can succeed by such methods is one where the sentiment and the program are both very simple, as is the case in rebellions of oppressed nations. But the line of demarcation between capitalist and wage-earner is not sharp, like the line between Turk and Armenian, or between an Englishman and a native of India. Those who have advocated the social revolution have been mistaken in their political methods, chiefly because they have not realized how many people there are in the community whose sympathies and interests lie half on the side of capital, half on the side of labor. These people make a clear-cut revolutionary policy very difficult.

For these reasons, those who aim at an economic reconstruction which is not likely to be completed to-morrow must, if they are to have any hope of success, be able to approach their goal by degrees, through measures which are of some use in themselves, even if they should not ultimately lead to the desired end. There must be activities which train men for those that they are ultimately to carry out, and there must be possible achievements in the near future, not only a vague hope of a distant paradise.

But although I believe that all this is true, I believe no less firmly that really vital and radical reform requires some vision beyond the immediate future, some realization of what human beings might make of human life if they chose. Without some such hope, men will not have the energy and enthusiasm necessary to overcome opposition, or the steadfastness to persist when their aims are for the moment unpopular. Every man who has really sincere desire for any great amelioration in the conditions of life has first to face ridicule, then persecution, then cajolery and attempts at subtle corruption. We know from painful experience how few pass unscathed through these three ordeals. The last especially, when the reformer is shown all the kingdoms of the earth, is difficult, indeed almost impossible, except for those who have made their ultimate goal vivid to themselves by clear and definite thought.

Economic systems are concerned essentially with the production and distribution of material goods. Our present system is wasteful on the production side, and unjust on the side of distribution. It involves a life of slavery to economic forces for the great majority of the community, and for the minority a degree of power over the lives of others which no man ought to have. In a good community the production of the necessaries of existence would be a mere preliminary to the important and interesting part of life, except for those who find a pleasure in some part of the work of producing necessaries. It is not in the least necessary that economic needs should dominate man as they do at present. This is rendered necessary at present, partly by the inequalities of wealth, partly by the fact that things of real value, such as a good education, are difficult to acquire, except for the well-to-do.

Private ownership of land and capital is not defensible on grounds of justice, or on the ground that it is an economical way of producing what the community needs. But the chief objections to it are that it stunts the lives of men and women, that it enshrines a ruthless possessiveness in all the respect which is given to success, that it leads men to fill the greater part of their time and thought with the acquisition of purely material goods, and that it affords a terrible obstacle to the advancement of civilization and creative energy.

The approach to a system free from these evils need not be sudden; it is perfectly possible to proceed step by step towards economic freedom and industrial self-government. It is not true that there is any outward difficulty in creating the kind of institutions that we have been considering. If organized labor wishes to create them, nothing could stand in its way. The difficulty involved is merely the difficulty of inspiring men with hope, of giving them enough imagination to see that the evils from which they suffer are unnecessary, and enough thought to understand how the evils are to be cured. This is a difficulty which can be overcome by time and energy. But it will not be overcome if the leaders of organized labor have no breadth of outlook, no vision, no hopes beyond some slight superficial improvement within the framework of the existing system. Revolutionary action may be unnecessary, but revolutionary thought is indispensable, and, as the outcome of thought, a rational and constructive hope.

# CHAPTER III

## Pitfalls in Socialism

### I

In its early days, socialism was a revolutionary movement of which the object was the liberation of the wage-earning classes and the establishment of freedom and justice. The passage from capitalism to the new régime was to be sudden and violent: capitalists were to be expropriated without compensation, and their power was not to be replaced by any new authority.

Gradually a change came over the spirit of socialism. In France, socialists became members of the government, and made and unmade parliamentary majorities. In Germany, social democracy grew so strong that it became impossible for it to resist the temptation to barter away some of its intransigeance in return for government recognition of its claims. In England, the Fabians taught the advantage of reform as against revolution, and of conciliatory bargaining as against irreconcilable antagonism.

The method of gradual reform has many merits as compared to the method of revolution, and I have no wish to preach revolution. But gradual reform has certain dangers, to wit, the ownership or control of businesses hitherto in private hands, and by encouraging legislative interference for the benefit of various sections of the wage-earning classes. I think it is at least doubtful whether such measures do anything at all to contribute toward the ideals which inspired the early socialists and still inspire the great majority of those who advocate some form of socialism.

Let us take as an illustration such a measure as state purchase of railways. This is a typical object of state socialism, thoroughly practicable, already achieved in many countries, and clearly the sort of step that must be taken in any piecemeal approach to complete collectivism. Yet I see no reason to believe that any real advance toward democracy, freedom, or economic justice is achieved when a state takes over the railways after full compensation to the shareholders.

Economic justice demands a diminution, if not a total abolition, of the proportion of the national income which goes to the recipients of rent and interest. But when the holders of railway shares are given government stock to replace their shares, they are given the prospect of an income in perpetuity equal to what they might reasonably expect to have derived from their shares. Unless there is reason to expect a great increase in the earnings of railways, the whole operation does nothing to alter the distribution of wealth. This could only be effected if the present owners were expropriated, or paid less than the market value, or given a mere life-interest as compensation. When full value is given, economic justice is not advanced in any degree.

There is equally little advance toward freedom. The men employed on the railway have no more voice than they had before in the management of the railway, or in the wages and conditions of work. Instead of having to fight the directors, with the possibility of an appeal to the government, they now have to fight the government directly; and experience does not lead to the view that a government department has any special tenderness toward the claims of labor. If they strike, they have to contend against the whole organized power of the state, which they can only do successfully if they happen to have a strong public opinion on their side. In view of the influence which the state can always exercise on the press, public opinion is likely to be biased against them, particularly when a nominally progressive government is in power. There will no longer be the possibility of divergences between the policies of different railways. Railway men in England derived advantages for many years from the comparatively liberal policy of the North Eastern Railway, which they were able to use as an argument for a similar policy elsewhere. Such possibilities are excluded by the dead uniformity of state administration.

And there is no real advance toward democracy. The administration of the railways will be in the hands of officials whose bias and associations separate them from labor, and who will develop an autocratic temper through the habit of power. The democratic machinery by which these officials are nominally controlled is cumbrous and remote, and can only be brought into operation on first-class issues which rouse the interest of the whole nation. Even then it is very likely that the superior education of the officials and the government, combined with the advantages of their position, will enable them to mislead the public as to the issues, and alienate the general sympathy even from the most excellent cause.

I do not deny that these evils exist at present; I say only that they will not be remedied by such measures as the nationalization of railways in the present economic and political environment. A greater upheaval, and a greater change in men's habits of mind, is necessary for any really vital progress.

## II

State socialism, even in a nation which possesses the form of political democracy, is not a truly democratic system. The way in which it fails to be democratic may be made plain by an analogy from the political sphere. Every democrat recognizes that the Irish ought to have self-government for Irish affairs, and ought not to be told that they have no grievance because they share in the Parliament of the United Kingdom. It is essential to democracy that any group of citizens whose interests or desires separate them at all widely from the rest of the community should be free to decide their internal affairs for themselves. And what is true of national or local groups is equally true of economic groups, such as miners or railway men. The national machinery of general elections is by no means sufficient to secure for groups of this kind the freedom which they ought to have.

The power of officials, which is a great and growing danger in the modern state, arises from the fact that the majority of the voters, who constitute the only ultimate popular control over officials, are as a rule not interested in any one particular question, and are therefore not likely to interfere effectively against an official who is thwarting the wishes of the minority who are interested. The official is nominally subject to indirect popular control, but not to the control of those who are directly affected by his action. The bulk of the public will either never hear about the matter in dispute, or, if they do hear, will form a hasty opinion based upon inadequate information, which is far more likely to come from the side of the officials than from the section of the community which is affected by the question at issue. In an important political issue, some degree of knowledge is likely to be diffused in time; but in other matters there is little hope that this will happen.

It may be said that the power of officials is much less dangerous than the power of capitalists, because officials have no economic interests that are opposed to those of wage-earners. But this argument involves far too simple a theory of political human nature—a theory which orthodox socialism adopted from the classical political economy, and has tended to retain in spite of growing evidence of its falsity. Economic self-interest, and even economic class-interest, is by no means the only important political motive. Officials, whose salary is generally quite unaffected by their decisions on particular questions, are likely, if they are of average honesty, to decide according to their view of the public interest; but their view will none the less have a bias which will often lead them wrong. It is important to understand this bias before entrusting our destinies too unreservedly to government departments.

The first thing to observe is that, in any very large organization, and above all in a great state, officials and legislators are usually very remote from those whom they govern, and not imaginatively acquainted with the conditions of life to which their decisions will be applied. This makes them ignorant of much that they ought to know, even when they are industrious and willing to learn whatever can be taught by statistics and blue-books. The one thing they understand intimately is the office routine and the administrative rules. The result is an undue anxiety to secure a uniform system. I have heard of a French minister of education taking out his watch, and remarking, "At this moment all the children of such and such an age in France are learning so and so." This is the ideal of the administrator, an ideal utterly fatal to free growth, initiative, experiment, or any far reaching innovation. Laziness is not one of the motives recognized in textbooks on political theory, because all ordinary knowledge of human nature is considered unworthy of the dignity of these works; yet we all know that laziness is an immensely powerful motive with all but a small minority of mankind.

Unfortunately, in this case laziness is reinforced by love of power, which leads energetic officials to create the systems which lazy officials like to administer. The energetic official inevitably dislikes anything that he does not control. His official sanction must be obtained before anything can be done. Whatever he finds in existence he wishes to alter in some way, so as to have the satisfaction of feeling his power and making it felt. If he is conscientious, he will think out some perfectly uniform and rigid scheme which he believes to be the best possible, and he will then impose this scheme ruthlessly, whatever promising growths he may have to lop down for the sake of symmetry. The result inevitably has something of the deadly dullness of a new rectangular town, as compared with the beauty and richness of an ancient city which has lived and grown with the separate lives and individualities of many generations. What has grown is always more living than what has been decreed; but the energetic official will always prefer the tidiness of what he has decreed to the apparent disorder of spontaneous growth.

The mere possession of power tends to produce a love of power, which is a very dangerous motive, because the only sure proof of power consists in preventing others from doing what they wish to do. The essential theory of democracy is the diffusion of power among the whole people, so that the evils produced by one man's possession of great power shall be obviated. But the diffusion of power through democracy is only effective when the voters take an interest in the question involved. When the question does not interest them, they do not attempt to control the administration, and all actual power passes into the hands of officials.

For this reason, the true ends of democracy are not achieved by state socialism or by any system which places great power in the hands of men subject to no popular control except that which is more or less indirectly exercised through parliament.

Any fresh survey of men's political actions shows that, in those who have enough energy to be politically effective, love of power is a stronger motive than economic self-interest. Love of power actuates the great millionaires, who have far more money than they can spend, but continue to amass wealth merely in order to control more and more of the world's finance.[2] Love of power is obviously the ruling motive of many politicians. It is also the chief cause of wars, which are admittedly almost always a bad speculation from the mere point of view of wealth. For this reason, a new economic system which merely attacks economic motives and does not interfere with the concentration of power is not likely to effect any very great improvement in the world. This is one of the chief reasons for regarding state socialism with suspicion.

---

[2] Cf. J. A. Hobson, *The Evolution of Modern Capitalism.*

## III

The problem of the distribution of power is a more difficult one than the problem of the distribution of wealth. The machinery of representative government has concentrated on *ultimate* power as the only important matter, and has ignored immediate executive power. Almost nothing has been done to democratize administration. Government officials, in virtue of their income, security, and social position, are likely to be on the side of the rich, who have been their daily associates ever since the time of school and college. And whether or not they are on the side of the rich, they are not likely, for the reasons we have been considering, to be genuinely in favor of progress. What applies to government officials applies also to members of Parliament, with the sole difference that they have had to recommend themselves to a constituency. This, however, only adds hypocrisy to the other qualities of a ruling caste. Whoever has stood in the lobby of the House of Commons watching members emerge with wandering eye and hypothetical smile, until the constituent is espied, his arm taken, "my dear fellow" whispered in his ear, and his steps guided toward the inner precincts—whoever, observing this, has realized that these are the arts by which men become and remain legislators, can hardly fail to feel that democracy as it exists is not an absolutely perfect instrument of government. It is a painful fact that the ordinary voter, at any rate in England, is quite blind to insincerity. The man who does not care about any definite political measures can generally be won by corruption or flattery, open or concealed; the man who is set on securing reforms will generally prefer an ambitious windbag to a man who desires the public good without possessing a ready tongue. And the ambitious windbag, as soon as he has become a power by the enthusiasm he has aroused, will sell his influence to the governing clique, sometimes openly, sometimes by the more subtle method of intentionally failing at a crisis. This is part of the normal working of democracy as embodied in representative institutions. Yet a cure must be found if democracy is not to remain a farce.

One of the sources of evil in modern large democracies is the fact that most of the electorate have no direct or vital interest in most of the questions that arise. Should Welsh children be allowed the use of the Welsh language in schools? Should gipsies be compelled to abandon their nomadic life at the bidding of the education authorities? Should miners have an eight-hour day? Should Christian Scientists be compelled to call in doctors in case of serious illness? These are matters of passionate interest to certain sections of the community, but of very little interest to the great majority. If they are decided according to the wishes of the numerical majority, the intense desires of a minority will be overborne by the very slight and uninformed whims of the indifferent remainder. If the minority are geographically concentrated, so that they can decide elections in a certain number of constituencies, like the Welsh and the miners, they have a good chance of getting their way, by the wholly beneficent process which its enemies describe as log-rolling. But if they are scattered and politically feeble, like the gipsies and the Christian Scientists, they stand a very poor chance against the prejudices of the majority. Even when they are geographically concentrated, like the Irish, they may fail to obtain their wishes, because they arouse some hostility or some instinct of domination in the majority. Such a state of affairs is the negation of all democratic principles.

The tyranny of the majority is a very real danger. It is a mistake to suppose that the majority is necessarily right. On every new question the majority is always wrong at first. In matters where the state must act as a whole, such as tariffs, for example, decision by majorities is probably the best method that can be devised. But there are a great many questions in which there is no need of a uniform decision. Religion is recognized as one of these. Education ought to be one, provided a certain minimum standard is attained. Military service clearly ought to be one. Wherever divergent action by different groups is possible without anarchy, it ought to be permitted. In such cases it will be found by those who consider past history that, whenever any new fundamental issue arises, the majority are in the wrong, because they are guided by prejudice and habit. Progress comes through the gradual effect of a minority in converting opinion and altering custom. At one time—not so very long ago—it was considered monstrous wickedness to maintain that old women ought not to be burnt as witches. If those who held this opinion had been forcibly suppressed, we should still be steeped in medieval superstition. For such reasons, it is of the utmost importance that the majority should refrain from imposing its will as regards matters in which uniformity is not absolutely necessary.

IV

The cure for the evils and dangers which we have been considering is a very great extension of devolution and federal government. Wherever there is a national consciousness, as in Wales and Ireland, the area in which it exists ought to be allowed to decide all purely local affairs without external interference. But there are many matters which ought to be left to the management, not of local groups, but of trade groups, or of organizations embodying some set of opinions. In the East, men are subject to different laws according to the religion they profess. Something of this kind is necessary if any semblance of liberty is to exist where there is great divergence in beliefs.

Some matters are essentially geographical; for instance, gas and water, roads, tariffs, armies and navies. These must be decided by an authority representing an area. How large the area ought to be, depends upon accidents of topography and sentiment, and also upon the nature of the matter involved. Gas and water require a small area, roads a somewhat larger one, while the only satisfactory area for an army or a navy is the whole planet, since no smaller area will prevent war.

But the proper unit in most economic questions, and also in most questions that are intimately concerned with personal opinions, is not geographical at all. The internal management of railways ought not to be in the hands of the geographical state, for reasons which we have already considered. Still less ought it to be in the hands of a set of irresponsible capitalists. The only truly democratic system would be one which left the internal management of railways in the hands of the men who work on them. These men should elect the general manager, and a parliament of directors if necessary. All questions of wages, conditions of labor, running of trains, and acquisition of material, should be in the hands of a body responsible only to those actually engaged in the work of the railway.

The same arguments apply to other large trades: mining, iron and steel, cotton, and so on. British trade-unionism, it seems to me, has erred in conceiving labor and capital as both permanent forces, which were to be brought to some equality of strength by the organization of labor. This seems to me too modest an ideal. The ideal which I should wish to substitute involves the conquest of democracy and self-government in the economic sphere as in the political sphere, and the total abolition of the power now wielded by the capitalist. The man who works on a railway ought to have a voice in the government of the railway, just as much as the man who works in a state has a right to a voice in the management of his state. The concentration of business initiative in the hands of the employers is a great evil, and robs the employees of their legitimate share of interest in the larger problems of their trade.

French syndicalists were the first to advocate the system of trade autonomy as a better solution than state socialism. But in their view the trades were to be independent, almost like sovereign states at present. Such a system would not promote peace, any more than it does at present in international relations. In the affairs of any body of men, we may broadly distinguish what may be called questions of home politics from questions of foreign politics. Every group sufficiently well-marked to constitute a political entity ought to be autonomous in regard to internal matters, but not in regard to those that directly affect the outside world. If two groups are both entirely free as regards their relations to each other, there is no way of averting the danger of an open or covert appeal to force. The relations of a group of men to the outside world ought, whenever possible, to be controlled by a neutral authority. It is here that the state is necessary for adjusting the relations between different trades. The men who make some commodity should be entirely free as regards hours of labor, distribution of the total earnings of the trade, and all questions of business management. But they should not be free as regards the price of what they produce, since price is a matter concerning their relations to the rest of the community. If there were nominal freedom in regard to price, there would be a danger of a constant tug-of-war, in which those trades which were most immediately necessary to the existence of the community could always obtain an unfair advantage. Force is no more admirable in the economic sphere than in dealings between states. In order to secure the maximum of freedom with the minimum of force, the universal principle is: *Autonomy within each politically important group, and a neutral authority for deciding questions involving relations between groups.* The neutral authority should, of course, rest on a democratic basis, but should, if possible, represent a constituency wider than that of the groups concerned. In international affairs the only adequate authority would be one representing all civilized nations.

In order to prevent undue extension of the power of such authorities, it is desirable and necessary that the various autonomous groups should be very jealous of their liberties, and very ready to resist by political means any encroachments upon their independence. State socialism does not tolerate such groups, each with their own officials responsible to the group. Consequently it abandons the internal affairs of a group to the control of men not responsible to that group or specially aware of its needs. This opens the door to tyranny and to the destruction of initiative. These dangers are avoided by a system which allows any group of men to combine for any given purpose, provided it is not predatory, and to claim from the central authority such self-government as is necessary to the carrying out of the purpose. Churches of various denominations afford an instance. Their autonomy was won by centuries of warfare and persecution. It is to be hoped that a less terrible struggle will be required to achieve the same result in the economic sphere. But whatever the obstacles, I believe the importance of liberty is as great in the one case as it has been admitted to be in the other.

# CHAPTER IV

## Individual Liberty and Public Control

### I

Society cannot exist without law and order, and cannot advance except through the initiative of vigorous innovators. Yet law and order are always hostile to innovations, and innovators are almost always, to some extent, anarchists. Those whose minds are dominated by fear of a relapse towards barbarism will emphasize the importance of law and order, while those who are inspired by the hope of an advance towards civilization will usually be more conscious of the need of individual initiative. Both temperaments are necessary, and wisdom lies in allowing each to operate freely where it is beneficent. But those who are on the side of law and order, since they are reinforced by custom and the instinct for upholding the *status quo*, have no need of a reasoned defense. It is the innovators who have difficulty in being allowed to exist and work. Each generation believes that this difficulty is a thing of the past, but each generation is only tolerant of *past* innovations. Those of its own day are met with the same persecution as though the principle of toleration had never been heard of.

"In early society," says Westermarck, "customs are not only moral rules, but the only moral rules ever thought of. The savage strictly complies with the Hegelian command that no man must have a private conscience. The following statement, which refers to the Tinnevelly Shanars, may be quoted as a typical example: 'Solitary individuals amongst them rarely adopt any new opinions, or any new course of procedure. They follow the multitude to do evil, and they follow the multitude to do good. They think in herds.'"[3]

Those among ourselves who have never thought a thought or done a deed in the slightest degree different from the thoughts and deeds of our neighbors will congratulate themselves on the difference between us and the savage. But those who have ever attempted any real innovation cannot help feeling that the people they know are not so very unlike the Tinnevelly Shanars.

Under the influence of socialism, even progressive opinion, in recent years, has been hostile to individual liberty. Liberty is associated, in the minds of reformers,

---

[3] *The Origin and Development of the Moral Ideas,* 2d edition, Vol. I, p. 119.

with *laissez-faire*, the Manchester School, and the exploitation of women and children which resulted from what was euphemistically called "free competition." All these things were evil, and required state interference; in fact, there is need of an immense increase of state action in regard to cognate evils which still exist. In everything that concerns the economic life of the community, as regards both distribution and conditions of production, what is required is more public control, not less—how much more, I do not profess to know.

Another direction in which there is urgent need of the substitution of law and order for anarchy is international relations. At present, each sovereign state has complete individual freedom, subject only to the sanction of war. This individual freedom will have to be curtailed in regard to external relations if wars are ever to cease.

But when we pass outside the sphere of material possessions, we find that the arguments in favor of public control almost entirely disappear.

Religion, to begin with, is recognized as a matter in which the state ought not to interfere. Whether a man is Christian, Mahometan, or Jew is a question of no public concern, so long as he obeys the laws; and the laws ought to be such as men of all religions can obey. Yet even here there are limits. No civilized state would tolerate a religion demanding human sacrifice. The English in India put an end to suttee, in spite of a fixed principle of non-interference with native religious customs. Perhaps they were wrong to prevent suttee, yet almost every European would have done the same. We cannot *effectively* doubt that such practices ought to be stopped, however we may theorize in favor of religious liberty.

In such cases, the interference with liberty is imposed from without by a higher civilization. But the more common case, and the more interesting, is when an independent state interferes on behalf of custom against individuals who are feeling their way toward more civilized beliefs and institutions.

"In New South Wales," says Westermarck, "the first-born of every lubra used to be eaten by the tribe 'as part of a religious ceremony.' In the realm of Khai-muh, in China, according to a native account, it was customary to kill and devour the eldest son alive. Among certain tribes in British Columbia the first child is often sacrificed to the sun. The Indians of Florida, according to Le Moyne de Morgues, sacrificed the first-born son to the chief...."[4]

There are pages and pages of such instances.

There is nothing analogous to these practices among ourselves. When the first-born in Florida was told that his king and country needed him, this was a mere mistake, and with us mistakes of this kind do not occur. But it is interesting to inquire how these superstitions died out, in such cases, for example, as that of Khai-muh, where foreign compulsion is improbable. We may surmise that

---

[4] *Op cit.*, p. 459.

some parents, under the selfish influence of parental affection, were led to doubt whether the sun would really be angry if the eldest child were allowed to live. Such rationalism would be regarded as very dangerous, since it was calculated to damage the harvest. For generations the opinion would be cherished in secret by a handful of cranks, who would not be able to act upon it. At last, by concealment or flight, a few parents would save their children from the sacrifice. Such parents would be regarded as lacking all public spirit, and as willing to endanger the community for their private pleasure. But gradually it would appear that the state remained intact, and the crops were no worse than in former years. Then, by a fiction, a child would be deemed to have been sacrificed if it was solemnly dedicated to agriculture or some other work of national importance chosen by the chief. It would be many generations before the child would be allowed to choose its own occupation after it had grown old enough to know its own tastes and capacities. And during all those generations, children would be reminded that only an act of grace had allowed them to live at all, and would exist under the shadow of a purely imaginary duty to the state.

The position of those parents who first disbelieved in the utility of infant sacrifice illustrates all the difficulties which arise in connection with the adjustment of individual freedom to public control. The authorities, believing the sacrifice necessary for the good of the community, were bound to insist upon it; the parents, believing it useless, were equally bound to do everything in their power toward saving the child. How ought both parties to act in such a case?

The duty of the skeptical parent is plain: to save the child by any possible means, to preach the uselessness of the sacrifice in season and out of season, and to endure patiently whatever penalty the law may indict for evasion. But the duty of the authorities is far less clear. So long as they remain firmly persuaded that the universal sacrifice of the first-born is indispensable, they are bound to persecute those who seek to undermine this belief. But they will, if they are conscientious, very carefully examine the arguments of opponents, and be willing in advance to admit that these arguments *may* be sound. They will carefully search their own hearts to see whether hatred of children or pleasure in cruelty has anything to do with their belief. They will remember that in the past history of Khai-muh there are innumerable instances of beliefs, now known to be false, on account of which those who disagreed with the prevalent view were put to death. Finally they will reflect that, though errors which are traditional are often wide-spread, new beliefs seldom win acceptance unless they are nearer to the truth than what they replace; and they will conclude that a new belief is probably either an advance, or so unlikely to become common as to be innocuous. All these considerations will make them hesitate before they resort to punishment.

## II

The study of past times and uncivilized races makes it clear beyond question that the customary beliefs of tribes or nations are almost invariably false. It is difficult to divest ourselves completely of the customary beliefs of our own age and nation, but it is not very difficult to achieve a certain degree of doubt in regard to them. The Inquisitor who burnt men at the stake was acting with true humanity if all his beliefs were correct; but if they were in error at any point, he was inflicting a wholly unnecessary cruelty. A good working maxim in such matters is this: Do not trust customary beliefs so far as to perform actions which must be disastrous unless the beliefs in question are wholly true. The world would be utterly bad, in the opinion of the average Englishman, unless he could say "Britannia rules the waves"; in the opinion of the average German, unless he could say "Deutschland über alles." For the sake of these beliefs, they are willing to destroy European civilization. If the beliefs should happen to be false, their action is regrettable.

One fact which emerges from these considerations is that no obstacle should be placed in the way of thought and its expression, nor yet in the way of statements of fact. This was formerly common ground among liberal thinkers, though it was never quite realized in the practice of civilized countries. But it has recently become, throughout Europe, a dangerous paradox, on account of which men suffer imprisonment or starvation. For this reason it has again become worth stating. The grounds for it are so evident that I should be ashamed to repeat them if they were not universally ignored. But in the actual world it is very necessary to repeat them.

To attain complete truth is not given to mortals, but to advance toward it by successive steps is not impossible. On any matter of general interest, there is usually, in any given community at any given time, a received opinion, which is accepted as a matter of course by all who give no special thought to the matter. Any questioning of the received opinion rouses hostility, for a number of reasons.

The most important of these is the instinct of conventionality, which exists in all gregarious animals and often leads them to put to death any markedly peculiar member of the herd.

The next most important is the feeling of insecurity aroused by doubt as to the beliefs by which we are in the habit of regulating our lives. Whoever has tried to explain the philosophy of Berkeley to a plain man will have seen in its unadulterated form the anger aroused by this feeling. What the plain man derives from Berkeley's philosophy at a first hearing is an uncomfortable suspicion that nothing is solid, so that it is rash to sit on a chair or to expect the floor to sustain us. Because this suspicion is uncomfortable, it is irritating, except to those who regard the whole argument as merely nonsense. And in a more or less analogous way any questioning of what has been taken for granted destroys the feeling of standing on solid ground, and produces a condition of bewildered fear.

A third reason which makes men dislike novel opinions is that vested interests are bound up with old beliefs. The long fight of the church against science, from Giordano Bruno to Darwin, is attributable to this motive among others. The horror of socialism which existed in the remote past was entirely attributable to this cause. But it would be a mistake to assume, as is done by those who seek economic motives everywhere, that vested interests are the principal source of anger against novelties in thought. If this were the case, intellectual progress would be much more rapid than it is.

The instinct of conventionality, horror of uncertainty, and vested interests, all militate against the acceptance of a new idea. And it is even harder to think of a new idea than to get it accepted; most people might spend a lifetime in reflection without ever making a genuinely original discovery.

In view of all these obstacles, it is not likely that any society at any time will suffer from a plethora of heretical opinions. Least of all is this likely in a modern civilized society, where the conditions of life are in constant rapid change, and demand, for successful adaptation, an equally rapid change in intellectual outlook. There should be an attempt, therefore, to encourage, rather than discourage, the expression of new beliefs and the dissemination of knowledge tending to support them. But the very opposite is, in fact, the case. From childhood upward, everything is done to make the minds of men and women conventional and sterile. And if, by misadventure, some spark of imagination remains, its unfortunate possessor is considered unsound and dangerous, worthy only of contempt in time of peace and of prison or a traitor's death in time of war. Yet such men are known to have been in the past the chief benefactors of mankind, and are the very men who receive most honor as soon as they are safely dead.

The whole realm of thought and opinion is utterly unsuited to public control; it ought to be as free, and as spontaneous as is possible to those who know what others have believed. The state is justified in insisting that children shall be educated, but it is not justified in forcing their education to proceed on a uniform plan and to be directed to the production of a dead level of glib uniformity. Education, and the life of the mind generally, is a matter in which individual initiative is the chief thing needed; the function of the state should begin and end with insistence on some kind of education, and, if possible, a kind which promotes mental individualism, not a kind which happens to conform to the prejudices of government officials.

### III

Questions of practical morals raise more difficult problems than questions of mere opinion. The thugs honestly believe it their duty to commit murders, but the government does not acquiesce. The conscientious objectors honestly hold the opposite opinion, and again the government does not acquiesce. Killing is a state prerogative; it is equally criminal to do it unbidden and not to do it when bidden. The same applies to theft, unless it is on a large scale or by one who is already rich. Thugs and thieves are men who use force in their dealings with their neighbors, and we may lay it down broadly that the private use of force should be prohibited except in rare cases, however conscientious may be its motive. But this principle will not justify compelling men to use force at the bidding of the state, when they do not believe it justified by the occasion. The punishment of conscientious objectors seems clearly a violation of individual liberty within its legitimate sphere.

It is generally assumed without question that the state has a right to punish certain kinds of sexual irregularity. No one doubts that the Mormons sincerely believed polygamy to be a desirable practice, yet the United States required them to abandon its legal recognition, and probably any other Christian country would have done likewise. Nevertheless, I do not think this prohibition was wise. Polygamy is legally permitted in many parts of the world, but is not much practised except by chiefs and potentates. If, as Europeans generally believe, it is an undesirable custom, it is probable that the Mormons would have soon abandoned it, except perhaps for a few men of exceptional position. If, on the other hand, it had proved a successful experiment, the world would have acquired a piece of knowledge which it is now unable to possess. I think in all such cases the law should only intervene when there is some injury inflicted without the consent of the injured person.

It is obvious that men and women would not tolerate having their wives or husbands selected by the state, whatever eugenists might have to say in favor of such a plan. In this it seems clear that ordinary public opinion is in the right, not because people choose wisely, but because any choice of their own is better than a forced marriage. What applies to marriage ought also to apply to the choice of a trade or profession; although some men have no marked preferences, most men greatly prefer some occupations to others, and are far more likely to be useful citizens if they follow their preferences than if they are thwarted by a public authority.

The case of the man who has an intense conviction that he ought to do a certain kind of work is peculiar, and perhaps not very common; but it is important because it includes some very important individuals. Joan of Arc and Florence Nightingale defied convention in obedience to a feeling of this sort; reformers and agitators in unpopular causes, such as Mazzini, have belonged to this class; so have many men of science. In cases of this kind the individual conviction deserves the greatest respect, even if there seems no obvious justification for it. Obedience to the impulse is very unlikely to do much harm, and may well do great good. The practical difficulty is to distinguish such impulses from desires which produce similar manifestations. Many young people wish to be authors without having an impulse to write any particular book, or wish to be painters without having an impulse to create any particular picture. But a little experience will usually show the difference between a genuine and a spurious impulse; and there is less harm in indulging the spurious impulse for a time than in thwarting the impulse which is genuine. Nevertheless, the plain man almost always has a tendency to thwart the genuine impulse, because it seems anarchic and unreasonable, and is seldom able to give a good account of itself in advance.

What is markedly true of some notable personalities is true, in a lesser degree, of almost every individual who has much vigor or force of life; there is an impulse towards activity of some kind, as a rule not very definite in youth, but growing gradually more sharply outlined under the influence of education and opportunity. The direct impulse toward a kind of activity for its own sake must be distinguished from the desire for the expected effects of the activity. A young man may desire the rewards of great achievement without having any spontaneous impulse toward the activities which lead to achievement. But those who actually achieve much, although they may desire the rewards, have also something in their nature which inclines them to choose a certain kind of work as the road which they must travel if their ambition is to be satisfied. This artist's impulse, as it may be called, is a thing of infinite value to the individual, and often to the world; to respect it in oneself and in others makes up nine tenths of the good life. In most human beings it is rather frail, rather easily destroyed or disturbed; parents and teachers are too often hostile to it, and our economic system crushes out its last remnants in young men and young women. The result is that human beings cease to be individual, or to retain the native pride that is their birthright; they become machine-made, tame, convenient for the bureaucrat and the drill-sergeant, capable of being tabulated in statistics without anything being omitted. This is the fundamental evil resulting from lack of liberty; and it is an evil which is being continually intensified as population grows more dense and the machinery of organization grows more efficient.

The things that men desire are many and various: admiration, affection, power, security, ease, outlets for energy, are among the commonest of motives. But such abstractions do not touch what makes the difference between one man and another. Whenever I go to the zoölogical gardens, I am struck by the fact that all the movements of a stork have some common quality, differing from the movements of a parrot or an ostrich. It is impossible to put in words what the common quality is, and yet we feel that each thing an animal does is the sort of thing we might expect that animal to do. This indefinable quality constitutes the individuality of the animal, and gives rise to the pleasure we feel in watching the animal's actions. In a human being, provided he has not been crushed by an economic or governmental machine, there is the same kind of individuality, a something distinctive without which no man or woman can achieve much of importance, or retain the full dignity which is native to human beings. It is this distinctive individuality that is loved by the artist, whether painter or writer. The artist himself, and the man who is creative in no matter what direction, has more of it than the average man. Any society which crushes this quality, whether intentionally or by accident, must soon become utterly lifeless and traditional, without hope of progress and without any purpose in its being. To preserve and strengthen the impulse that makes individuality should be the foremost object of all political institutions.

## IV

We now arrive at certain general principles in regard to individual liberty and public control.

The greater part of human impulses may be divided into two classes, those which are possessive and those which are constructive or creative. Social institutions are the garments or embodiments of impulses, and may be classified roughly according to the impulses which they embody. Property is the direct expression of possessiveness; science and art are among the most direct expressions of creativeness. Possessiveness is either defensive or aggressive; it seeks either to retain against a robber, or to acquire from a present holder. In either case an attitude of hostility toward others is of its essence. It would be a mistake to suppose that defensive possessiveness is always justifiable, while the aggressive kind is always blameworthy; where there is great injustice in the *status quo*, the exact opposite may be the case, and ordinarily neither is justifiable.

State interference with the actions of individuals is necessitated by possessiveness. Some goods can be acquired or retained by force, while others cannot. A wife can be acquired by force, as the Romans acquired the Sabine women; but a wife's affection cannot be acquired in this way. There is no record that the Romans desired the affection of the Sabine women; and those in whom possessive impulses are strong tend to care chiefly for the goods that force can secure. All material goods belong to this class. Liberty in regard to such goods, if it were unrestricted, would make the strong rich and the weak poor. In a capitalistic society, owing to the partial restraints imposed by law, it makes cunning men rich and honest men poor, because the force of the state is put at men's disposal, not according to any just or rational principle, but according to a set of traditional maxims of which the explanation is purely historical.

In all that concerns possession and the use of force, unrestrained liberty involves anarchy and injustice. Freedom to kill, freedom to rob, freedom to defraud, no longer belong to individuals, though they still belong to great states, and are exercised by them in the name of patriotism. Neither individuals nor states ought to be free to exert force on their own initiative, except in such sudden emergencies as will subsequently be admitted in justification by a court of law. The reason for this is that the exertion of force by one individual against another is always an evil on both sides, and can only be tolerated when it is compensated by some overwhelming resultant good. In order to minimize the amount of force actually exerted in the world, it is necessary that there should be a public authority, a repository of practically irresistible force, whose function should be primarily to repress the private use of force. A use of force is *private* when it is exerted by one of the interested parties, or by his friends or accomplices, not by a public neutral authority according to some rule which is intended to be in the public interest.

The régime of private property under which we live does much too little to restrain the private use of force. When a man owns a piece of land, for example, he may use force against trespassers, though they must not use force against him. It is clear that some restriction of the liberty of trespass is necessary for the cultivation of the land. But if such powers are to be given to an individual, the state ought to satisfy itself that he occupies no more land than he is warranted in occupying in the public interest, and that the share of the produce of the land that comes to him is no more than a just reward for his labors. Probably the only way in which such ends can be achieved is by state ownership of land. The possessors of land and capital are able at present, by economic pressure, to use force against those who have no possessions. This force is sanctioned by law, while force exercised by the poor against the rich is illegal. Such a state of things is unjust, and does not diminish the use of private force as much as it might be diminished.

The whole realm of the possessive impulses, and of the use of force to which they give rise, stands in need of control by a public neutral authority, in the interests of liberty no less than of justice. Within a nation, this public authority will naturally be the state; in relations between nations, if the present anarchy is to cease, it will have to be some international parliament.

But the motive underlying the public control of men's possessive impulses should always be the increase of liberty, both by the prevention of private tyranny and by the liberation of creative impulses. If public control is not to do more harm than good, it must be so exercised as to leave the utmost freedom of private initiative in all those ways that do not involve the private use of force. In this respect all governments have always failed egregiously, and there is no evidence that they are improving.

The creative impulses, unlike those that are possessive, are directed to ends in which one man's gain is not another man's loss. The man who makes a scientific discovery or writes a poem is enriching others at the same time as himself. Any increase in knowledge or good-will is a gain to all who are affected by it, not only to the actual possessor. Those who feel the joy of life are a happiness to others as well as to themselves. Force cannot create such things, though it can destroy them; no principle of distributive justice applies to them, since the gain of each is the gain of all. For these reasons, the creative part of a man's activity ought to be as free as possible from all public control, in order that it may remain spontaneous and full of vigor. The only function of the state in regard to this part of the individual life should be to do everything possible toward providing outlets and opportunities.

In every life a part is governed by the community, and a part by private initiative. The part governed by private initiative is greatest in the most important individuals, such as men of genius and creative thinkers. This part ought only to be restricted when it is predatory; otherwise, everything ought to be done to make it as great and as vigorous as possible. The object of education ought not to be to make all men think alike, but to make each think in the way which is the fullest expression of his own personality. In the choice of a means of livelihood all young men and young women ought, as far as possible, to be able to choose what is attractive to them; if no money-making occupation is attractive, they ought to be free to do little work for little pay, and spend their leisure as they choose. Any kind of censure on freedom of thought or on the dissemination of knowledge is, of course, to be condemned utterly.

Huge organizations, both political and economic, are one of the distinguishing characteristics of the modern world. These organizations have immense power, and often use their power to discourage originality in thought and action. They ought, on the contrary, to give the freest scope that is possible without producing anarchy or violent conflict. They ought not to take cognizance of any part of a man's life except what is concerned with the legitimate objects of public control, namely, possessions and the use of force. And they ought, by devolution, to leave as large a share of control as possible in the hands of individuals and small groups. If this is not done, the men at the head of these vast organizations will infallibly become tyrannous through the habit of excessive power, and will in time interfere in ways that crush out individual initiative.

The problem which faces the modern world is the combination of individual initiative with the increase in the scope and size of organizations. Unless it is solved, individuals will grow less and less full of life and vigor, and more and more passively submissive to conditions imposed upon them. A society composed of such individuals cannot be progressive or add much to the world's stock of mental and spiritual possessions. Only personal liberty and the encouragement of initiative can secure these things. Those who resist authority when it encroaches upon the legitimate sphere of the individual are performing a service to society, however little society may value it. In regard to the past, this is universally acknowledged; but it is no less true in regard to the present and the future.

# CHAPTER V

## National Independence and Internationalism

In the relations between states, as in the relations of groups within a single state, what is to be desired is independence for each as regards internal affairs, and law rather than private force as regards external affairs. But as regards groups within a state, it is internal independence that must be emphasized, since that is what is lacking; subjection to law has been secured, on the whole, since the end of the Middle Ages. In the relations between states, on the contrary, it is law and a central government that are lacking, since independence exists for external as for internal affairs. The stage we have reached in the affairs of Europe corresponds to the stage reached in our internal affairs during the Wars of the Roses, when turbulent barons frustrated the attempt to make them keep the king's peace. Thus, although the goal is the same in the two cases, the steps to be taken in order to achieve it are quite different.

There can be no good international system until the boundaries of states coincide as nearly as possible with the boundaries of nations.

But it is not easy to say what we mean by a nation. Are the Irish a nation? Home Rulers say yes, Unionists say no. Are the Ulstermen a nation? Unionists say yes, Home Rulers say no. In all such cases it is a party question whether we are to call a group a nation or not. A German will tell you that the Russian Poles are a nation, but as for the Prussian Poles, they, of course, are part of Prussia. Professors can always be hired to prove, by arguments of race or language or history, that a group about which there is a dispute is, or is not, a nation, as may be desired by those whom the professors serve. If we are to avoid all these controversies, we must first of all endeavor to find some definition of a nation.

A nation is not to be defined by affinities of language or a common historical origin, though these things often help to produce a nation. Switzerland is a nation, despite diversities of race, religion, and language. England and Scotland now form one nation, though they did not do so at the time of the Civil War. This is shown by Cromwell's saying, in the height of the conflict, that he would rather be subject to the domain of the royalists than to that of the Scotch. Great Britain was one state before it was one nation; on the other hand, Germany was one nation before it was one state.

What constitutes a nation is a sentiment and an instinct, a sentiment of similarity and an instinct of belonging to the same group or herd. The instinct is an extension of the instinct which constitutes a flock of sheep, or any other group of gregarious animals. The sentiment which goes with this is like a milder and more extended form of family feeling. When we return to England after being on the Continent, we feel something friendly in the familiar ways, and it is easy to believe that Englishmen on the whole are virtuous, while many foreigners are full of designing wickedness.

Such feelings make it easy to organize a nation into a state. It is not difficult, as a rule, to acquiesce in the orders of a national government. We feel that it is our government, and that its decrees are more or less the same as those which we should have given if we ourselves had been the governors. There is an instinctive and usually unconscious sense of a common purpose animating the members of a nation. This becomes especially vivid when there is war or a danger of war. Any one who, at such a time, stands out against the orders of his government feels an inner conflict quite different from any that he would feel in standing out against the orders of a foreign government in whose power he might happen to find himself. If he stands out, he does so with some more or less conscious hope that his government may in time come to think as he does; whereas, in standing out against a foreign government, no such hope is necessary. This group instinct, however it may have arisen, is what constitutes a nation, and what makes it important that the boundaries of nations should also be the boundaries of states.

National sentiment is a fact, and should be taken account of by institutions. When it is ignored, it is intensified and becomes a source of strife. It can only be rendered harmless by being given free play, so long as it is not predatory. But it is not, in itself, a good or admirable feeling. There is nothing rational and nothing desirable in a limitation of sympathy which confines it to a fragment of the human race. Diversities of manners and customs and traditions are, on the whole, a good thing, since they enable different nations to produce different types of excellence. But in national feeling there is always latent or explicit an element of hostility to foreigners. National feeling, as we know it, could not exist in a nation which was wholly free from external pressure of a hostile kind.

And group feeling produces a limited and often harmful kind of morality. Men come to identify the good with what serves the interests of their own group, and the bad with what works against those interests, even if it should happen to be in the interests of mankind as a whole. This group morality is very much in evidence during war, and is taken for granted in men's ordinary thought. Although almost all Englishmen consider the defeat of Germany desirable for the good of the world, yet nevertheless most of them honor a German for fighting for his country, because it has not occurred to them that his actions ought to be guided by a morality higher than that of the group.

A man does right, as a rule, to have his thoughts more occupied with the interests of his own nation than with those of others, because his actions are more likely to

411

affect his own nation. But in time of war, and in all matters which are of equal concern to other nations and to his own, a man ought to take account of the universal welfare, and not allow his survey to be limited by the interest, or supposed interest, of his own group or nation.

So long as national feeling exists, it is very important that each nation should be self-governing as regards its internal affairs. Government can only be carried on by force and tyranny if its subjects view it with hostile eyes, and they will so view it if they feel that it belongs to an alien nation. This principle meets with difficulties in cases where men of different nations live side by side in the same area, as happens in some parts of the Balkans. There are also difficulties in regard to places which, for some geographical reason, are of great international importance, such as the Suez Canal and the Panama Canal. In such cases the purely local desires of the inhabitants may have to give way before larger interests. But in general, at any rate as applied to civilized communities, the principle that the boundaries of nations ought to coincide with the boundaries of states has very few exceptions.

This principle, however, does not decide how the relations between states are to be regulated, or how a conflict of interests between rival states is to be decided. At present, every great state claims absolute sovereignty, not only in regard to its internal affairs but also in regard to its external actions. This claim to absolute sovereignty leads it into conflict with similar claims on the part of other great states. Such conflicts at present can only be decided by war or diplomacy, and diplomacy is in essence nothing but the threat of war. There is no more justification for the claim to absolute sovereignty on the part of a state than there would be for a similar claim on the part of an individual. The claim to absolute sovereignty is, in effect, a claim that all external affairs are to be regulated purely by force, and that when two nations or groups of nations are interested in a question, the decision shall depend solely upon which of them is, or is believed to be, the stronger. This is nothing but primitive anarchy, "the war of all against all," which Hobbes asserted to be the original state of mankind.

There cannot be secure peace in the world, or any decision of international questions according to international law, until states are willing to part with their absolute sovereignty as regards their external relations, and to leave the decision in such matters to some international instrument of government.[5] An international government will have to be legislative as well as judicial. It is not enough that there should be a Hague tribunal, deciding matters according to some already existing system of international law; it is necessary also that there should be a body capable of enacting international law, and this body will have to have the power of transferring territory from one state to another, when it is persuaded that adequate grounds exist

---

[5] For detailed scheme of international government see *International Government,* by L. Woolf. Allen & Unwin.

for such a transference. Friends of peace will make a mistake if they unduly glorify the *status quo*. Some nations grow, while others dwindle; the population of an area may change its character by emigration and immigration. There is no good reason why states should resent changes in their boundaries under such conditions, and if no international authority has power to make changes of this kind, the temptations to war will sometimes become irresistible.

The international authority ought to possess an army and navy, and these ought to be the only army and navy in existence. The only legitimate use of force is to diminish the total amount of force exercised in the world. So long as men are free to indulge their predatory instincts, some men or groups of men will take advantage of this freedom for oppression and robbery. Just as the police are necessary to prevent the use of force by private citizens, so an international police will be necessary to prevent the lawless use of force by separate states.

But I think it is reasonable to hope that if ever an international government, possessed of the only army and navy in the world, came into existence, the need of force to enact obedience to its decisions would be very temporary. In a short time the benefits resulting from the substitution of law for anarchy would become so obvious that the international government would acquire an unquestioned authority, and no state would dream of rebelling against its decisions. As soon as this stage had been reached, the international army and navy would become unnecessary.

We have still a very long road to travel before we arrive at the establishment of an international authority, but it is not very difficult to foresee the steps by which this result will be gradually reached. There is likely to be a continual increase in the practice of submitting disputes to arbitration, and in the realization that the supposed conflicts of interest between different states are mainly illusory. Even where there is a real conflict of interest, it must in time become obvious that neither of the states concerned would suffer as much by giving way as by fighting. With the progress of inventions, war, when it does occur, is bound to become increasingly destructive. The civilized races of the world are faced with the alternative of coöperation or mutual destruction. The present war is making this alternative daily more evident. And it is difficult to believe that, when the enmities which it has generated have had time to cool, civilized men will deliberately choose to destroy civilization, rather than acquiesce in the abolition of war.

The matters in which the interests of nations are supposed to clash are mainly three: tariffs, which are a delusion; the exploitation of inferior races, which is a crime; pride of power and dominion, which is a schoolboy folly.

The economic argument against tariffs is familiar, and I shall not repeat it. The only reason why it fails to carry conviction is the enmity between nations. Nobody proposes to set up a tariff between England and Scotland, or between Lancashire and Yorkshire. Yet the arguments by which tariffs between nations are supported might be used just as well to defend tariffs between counties. Universal free trade would indubitably be of economic benefit to mankind, and would be adopted to-morrow if it were not for the hatred and suspicion which nations feel one toward another. From the point of view of preserving the peace of the world, free trade between the different civilized states is not so important as the open door in their dependencies. The desire for exclusive markets is one of the most potent causes of war.

Exploiting what are called "inferior races" has become one of the main objects of European statecraft. It is not only, or primarily, trade that is desired, but opportunities for investment; finance is more concerned in the matter than industry. Rival diplomatists are very often the servants, conscious or unconscious, of rival groups of financiers. The financiers, though themselves of no particular nation, understand the art of appealing to national prejudice, and of inducing the taxpayer to incur expenditure of which they reap the benefit. The evils which they produce at home, and the devastation that they spread among the races whom they exploit, are part of the price which the world has to pay for its acquiescence in the capitalist régime.

But neither tariffs nor financiers would be able to cause serious trouble, if it were not for the sentiment of national pride. National pride might be on the whole beneficent, if it took the direction of emulation in the things that are important to civilization. If we prided ourselves upon our poets, our men of science, or the justice and humanity of our social system, we might find in national pride a stimulus to useful endeavors. But such matters play a very small part. National pride, as it exists now, is almost exclusively concerned with power and dominion, with the extent of territory that a nation owns, and with its capacity for enforcing its will against the opposition of other nations. In this it is reinforced by group morality. To nine citizens out of ten it seems self-evident, whenever the will of their own nation clashes with that of another, that their own nation must be in the right. Even if it were not in the right on the particular issue, yet it stands in general for so much nobler ideals than those represented by the other nation to the dispute, that any increase in its power is bound to be for the good of mankind. Since all nations equally believe this of themselves, all are equally ready to insist upon the victory of their own side in any dispute in which they believe that they have a good hope of victory. While this temper persists, the hope of international coöperation must remain dim.

If men could divest themselves of the sentiment of rivalry and hostility between different nations, they would perceive that the matters in which the interests of different nations coincide immeasurably outweigh those in which they clash; they would perceive, to begin with, that trade is not to be compared to warfare; that the man who sells you goods is not doing you an injury. No one considers that the butcher and the baker are his enemies because they drain him of money. Yet as soon as goods come from a foreign country, we are asked to believe that we suffer a terrible injury in purchasing them. No one remembers that it is by means of goods exported that we purchase them. But in the country to which we export, it is the goods we send which are thought dangerous, and the goods we buy are forgotten. The whole conception of trade, which has been forced upon us by manufacturers who dreaded foreign competition, by trusts which desired to secure monopolies, and by economists poisoned by the virus of nationalism, is totally and absolutely false. Trade results simply from division of labor. A man cannot himself make all the goods of which he has need, and therefore he must exchange his produce with that of other people. What applies to the individual, applies in exactly the same way to the nation. There is no reason to desire that a nation should itself produce all the goods of which it has need; it is better that it should specialize upon those goods which it can produce to most advantage, and should exchange its surplus with the surplus of other goods produced by other countries. There is no use in sending goods out of the country except in order to get other goods in return. A butcher who is always willing to part with his meat but not willing to take bread from the baker, or boots from the bootmaker, or clothes from the tailor, would soon find himself in a sorry plight. Yet he would be no more foolish than the protectionist who desires that we should send goods abroad without receiving payment in the shape of goods imported from abroad.

The wage system has made people believe that what a man needs is work. This, of course, is absurd. What he needs is the goods produced by work, and the less work involved in making a given amount of goods, the better. But owing to our economic system, every economy in methods of production enables employers to dismiss some of their employees, and to cause destitution, where a better system would produce only an increase of wages or a diminution in the hours of work without any corresponding diminution of wages.

Our economic system is topsyturvy. It makes the interest of the individual conflict with the interest of the community in a thousand ways in which no such conflict ought to exist. Under a better system the benefits of free trade and the evils of tariffs would be obvious to all.

Apart from trade, the interests of nations coincide in all that makes what we call civilization. Inventions and discoveries bring benefit to all. The progress of science is a matter of equal concern to the whole civilized world. Whether a man of science is an Englishman, a Frenchman, or a German is a matter of no real importance. His discoveries are open to all, and nothing but intelligence is required in order to profit by them. The whole world of art and literature and learning is international; what is done in one country is not done for that country, but for mankind. If we ask ourselves what are the things that raise mankind above the brutes, what are the things that make us think the human race more valuable than any species of animals, we shall find that none of them are things in which any one nation can have exclusive property, but all are things in which the whole world can share. Those who have any care for these things, those who wish to see mankind fruitful in the work which men alone can do, will take little account of national boundaries, and have little care to what state a man happens to owe allegiance.

The importance of international coöperation outside the sphere of politics has been brought home to me by my own experience. Until lately I was engaged in teaching a new science which few men in the world were able to teach. My own work in this science was based chiefly upon the work of a German and an Italian. My pupils came from all over the civilized world: France, Germany, Austria, Russia, Greece, Japan, China, India, and America. None of us was conscious of any sense of national divisions. We felt ourselves an outpost of civilization, building a new road into the virgin forest of the unknown. All coöperated in the common task, and in the interest of such a work the political enmities of nations seemed trivial, temporary, and futile.

But it is not only in the somewhat rarefied atmosphere of abstruse science that international coöperation is vital to the progress of civilization. All our economic problems, all the questions of securing the rights of labor, all the hopes of freedom at home and humanity abroad, rest upon the creation of international good-will.

So long as hatred, suspicion, and fear dominate the feelings of men toward each other, so long we cannot hope to escape from the tyranny of violence and brute force. Men must learn to be conscious of the common interests of mankind in which all are at one, rather than of those supposed interests in which the nations are divided. It is not necessary, or even desirable, to obliterate the differences of manners and custom and tradition between different nations. These differences enable each nation to make its own distinctive contribution to the sum total of the world's civilization.

What is to be desired is not cosmopolitanism, not the absence of all national characteristics that one associates with couriers, *wagon-lit* attendants, and others, who have had everything distinctive obliterated by multiple and trivial contacts with men of every civilized country. Such cosmopolitanism is the result of loss, not gain. The international spirit which we should wish to see produced will be something added to love of country, not something taken away. Just as patriotism does not prevent a man from feeling family affection, so the international spirit ought not to prevent a man from feeling affection for his own country. But it will somewhat alter the character of that affection. The things which he will desire for his own country will no longer be things which can only be acquired at the expense of others, but rather those things in which the excellence of any one country is to the advantage of all the world. He will wish his own country to be great in the arts of peace, to be eminent in thought and science, to be magnanimous and just and generous. He will wish it to help mankind on the way toward that better world of liberty and international concord which must be realized if any happiness is to be left to man. He will not desire for his country the passing triumphs of a narrow possessiveness, but rather the enduring triumph of having helped to embody in human affairs something of that spirit of brotherhood which Christ taught and which the Christian churches have forgotten. He will see that this spirit embodies not only the highest morality, but also the truest wisdom, and the only road by which the nations, torn and bleeding with the wounds which scientific madness has inflicted, can emerge into a life where growth is possible and joy is not banished at the frenzied call of unreal and fictitious duties. Deeds inspired by hate are not duties, whatever pain and self-sacrifice they may involve. Life and hope for the world are to be found only in the deeds of love.